SOMETHING ABOUT THE AUTHOR®

Something about
the Author *was named
an "Outstanding
Reference Source,"
the highest honor given
by the American
Library Association
Reference and Adult
Services Division.*

ISSN 0276-816X

K

SOMETHING ABOUT THE AUTHOR®

**Facts and Pictures about Authors
and Illustrators of Books for Young People**

VOLUME 114

GALE GROUP

Detroit
New York
San Francisco
London
Boston
Woodbridge, CT

Riverside Community College
Library
4800 Magnolia Avenue
Riverside, CA 92506

Library of Congress Catalog Card Number 72-27107

ISBN 0-7876-4032-8
ISSN 0276-816X

Printed in the United States of America

10 9 8 7 6 5 4 3 2 1

Contents

Authors in Forthcoming Volumes

Below are some of the authors and illustrators that will be featured in upcoming volumes of *SATA*. These include new entries on the swiftly rising stars of the field, as well as completely revised and updated entries (indicated with *) on some of the most notable and best-loved creators of books for children.

Allen Appel: Appel sweeps readers off on adventurous journeys to historical places in his ìPastmasterî series. In *Time after Time*, the first book of the series, historian-hero Alex Balfour wakes to find himself in Russia during the 1917 Revolution.

*Arthur C. Clarke: Recipient of the Grand Master Award by the Science Fiction Writers of America, Clarke is a celebrated author whose writings, both fiction and nonfiction, have opened the eyes of generations of readers to the possibilities that exist in outer space. Clarke, whose writing career has spanned half a century, has received scores of awards for his works and was recently nominated for the Nobel peace prize.

Charles de Lint: Canadian author de Lint is widely recognized as a pioneer of modern fantasy because his works, unlike many others in the genre, incorporate an element of realism. *Someplace to Be Flying*, a recent novel by de Lint, has received acclaim for its winning combination of magic, myth, and realism.

Gloria Fuertes: Popular with both adults and children, Spanish poet Fuertes regularly incorporates social and autobiographical elements into her writing. Her work commonly features themes of God, love, and death and contains literary devices such as personification and the use of slang.

*S. E. Hinton: Best known for her young adult work *The Outsiders*, her classic novel that was later made into a movie, Hinton has recently delved into the realm of childrenís literature. *Big David, Little David* and *The Puppy Sister* are picture books that address the subjects of identity and sibling rivalry.

Ainslie Kertland Manson: *Just Like New*, Canadian author Mansonís tale of a young English girlís gift during the Second World War, was shortlisted for the Mr. Christie award in 1994.

*Keiko Narahashi: Born in Japan and raised in the United States, Narahashi is an author and illustrator of childrenís books that typically feature warm relationships of friends and family members. Her interest in Japanese and Chinese art is often expressed in her watercolor illustrations, which depict joyful characters in both bright and muted primary colors.

*Joan Lowery Nixon: The author of over a hundred works, Nixon has proven that she is the master of mystery novels for young readers. She has garnered the coveted Edgar Allan Poe Award for four of her juvenile mysteries and a host of other accolades for her work during a career that has spanned nearly forty years.

*Dav Pilkey: Though author-illustrator Pilkey is perhaps best known for his series of humorous books aimed at middle-graders, such as the ìCaptain Underpantsî series and the ìDumb Bunniesî collection, he is also the creator of sensitive and thought-provoking works. *The Paperboy*, one of the more serious works, was named a Caldecott Honor book in 1997.

Rhondi Vilott Salsitz: A prolific author who has written under a host of pseudonyms, Salsitz specializes in exciting and fast-paced fantasy novels. Salsitzís recent efforts include *Retribution* and *Whirlwind*, which were published under the name Elizabeth Forrest.

Roland Smith: Zookeeper-turned-childrenís writer Roland is the author of both adventurous fiction books as well as accessible and detailed nonfiction works. *Sasquatch*, a thriller about a father and sonís search for the title creature, was received with much critical praise upon its release in 1998.

Gloria Jean Watkins: Watkins, often called one of the foremost black intellectuals in America today, has published many books on social and cultural issues under the pseudonym bell hooks.

Introduction

Something about the Author (*SATA*) is an ongoing reference series that examines the lives and works of authors and illustrators of books for children. *SATA* includes not only well-known writers and artists but also less prominent individuals whose works are just coming to be recognized. This series is often the only readily available information source on emerging authors and illustrators. Youíll find *SATA* informative and entertaining, whether you are a student, a librarian, an English teacher, a parent, or simply an adult who enjoys childrenís literature.

What's Inside SATA

SATA provides detailed information about authors and illustrators who span the full time range of childrenís literature, from early figures like John Newbery and L. Frank Baum to contemporary figures like Judy Blume and Richard Peck. Authors in the series represent primarily English-speaking countries, particularly the United States, Canada, and the United Kingdom. Also included, however, are authors from around the world whose works are available in English translation. The writings represented in *SATA* include those created intentionally for children and young adults as well as those written for a general audience and known to interest younger readers. These writings cover the entire spectrum of childrenís literature, including picture books, humor, folk and fairy tales, animal stories, mystery and adventure, science fiction and fantasy, historical fiction, poetry and nonsense verse, drama, biography, and nonfiction.

Obituaries are also included in *SATA* and are intended not only as death notices but also as concise overviews of peopleís lives and work. Additionally, each edition features newly revised and updated entries for a selection of *SATA* listees who remain of interest to todayís readers and who have been active enough to require extensive revisions of their earlier biographies.

New Autobiography Feature

Beginning with Volume 103, *SATA* features three or more specially commissioned autobiographical essays in each volume. These unique essays, averaging about ten thousand words in length and illustrated with an abundance of personal photos, present an entertaining and informative first-person perspective on the lives and careers of prominent authors and illustrators profiled in *SATA*.

Two Convenient Indexes

In response to suggestions from librarians, *SATA* indexes no longer appear in every volume but are included in alternate (odd-numbered) volumes of the series, beginning with Volume 57.

SATA continues to include two indexes that cumulate with each alternate volume: the Illustrations Index, arranged by the name of the illustrator, gives the number of the volume and page where the illustratorís work appears in the current volume as well as all preceding volumes in the series; the Author Index gives the number of the volume in which a personís biographical sketch, autobiographical essay, or obituary appears in the current volume as well as all preceding volumes in the series.

These indexes also include references to authors and illustrators who appear in Galeís *Yesterday's Authors of Books for Children, Children's Literature Review,* and *Something about the Author Autobiography Series.*

Easy-to-Use Entry Format

Whether youíre already familiar with the *SATA* series or just getting acquainted, you will want to be aware of the kind of information that an entry provides. In every *SATA* entry the editors attempt to give as complete a picture of the personís life and work as possible. A typical entry in *SATA* includes the following clearly labeled information sections:

- *PERSONAL:* date and place of birth and death, parentsí names and occupations, name of spouse, date of marriage, names of children, educational institutions attended, degrees received, religious and political affiliations, hobbies and other interests.

- *ADDRESSES:* complete home, office, electronic mail, and agent addresses, whenever available.

- ï *CAREER:* name of employer, position, and dates for each career post; art exhibitions; military service; memberships and offices held in professional and civic organizations.

- ï *AWARDS, HONORS:* literary and professional awards received.

- ï *WRITINGS:* title-by-title chronological bibliography of books written and/or illustrated, listed by genre when known; lists of other notable publications, such as plays, screenplays, and periodical contributions.

- ï *ADAPTATIONS:* a list of films, television programs, plays, CD-ROMs, recordings, and other media presentations that have been adapted from the authorís work.

- ï *WORK IN PROGRESS:* description of projects in progress.

- ï *SIDELIGHTS:* a biographical portrait of the author or illustratorís development, either directly from the biographeeóand often written specifically for the *SATA* entryóor gathered from diaries, letters, interviews, or other published sources.

- ï *FOR MORE INFORMATION SEE:* references for further reading.

- ï *EXTENSIVE ILLUSTRATIONS:* photographs, movie stills, book illustrations, and other interesting visual materials supplement the text.

How a SATA Entry Is Compiled

A *SATA* entry progresses through a series of steps. If the biographee is living, the *SATA* editors try to secure information directly from him or her through a questionnaire. From the information that the biographee supplies, the editors prepare an entry, filling in any essential missing details with research and/or telephone interviews. If possible, the author or illustrator is sent a copy of the entry to check for accuracy and completeness.

If the biographee is deceased or cannot be reached by questionnaire, the *SATA* editors examine a wide variety of published sources to gather information for an entry. Biographical and bibliographic sources are consulted, as are book reviews, feature articles, published interviews, and material sometimes obtained from the biographeeís family, publishers, agent, or other associates.

Entries that have not been verified by the biographees or their representatives are marked with an asterisk (*).

Contact the Editor

We encourage our readers to examine the entire *SATA* series. Please write and tell us if we can make *SATA* even more helpful to you. Give your comments and suggestions to the editor:

BY MAIL: Editor, *Something about the Author,* The Gale Group, 27500 Drake Rd., Farmington Hills, MI 48331-3535.

BY TELEPHONE: (800) 877-GALE

BY FAX: (248) 699-8054

Acknowledgments

Grateful acknowledgment is made to the following publishers, authors, and artists whose works appear in the volume.

ALMOND, DAVID. Vojnar, Kamil, illustrator. From a dust jacket from *Skellig,* by David Almond. Delacorte Press, 1999. Jacket illustration copyright © 1999 by Kamil Vojnar. Reproduced by permission of Dell Books, a division of Random House, Inc. / Almond, David, photograph. Reproduced by permission of David Almond.

BERGIN, MARK. Bergin, Mark, illustrator. From an illustration in *A Greek Temple,* by Fiona Macdonald. Peter Bedrick Books, 1999. Copyright © 1992 by The Salariya Book Co Ltd. Reproduced by permission. / Bergin, Mark and John James, illustrators. From an illustration in *An Egyptian Pyramid,* by Jacqueline Morley. Peter Bedrick, 1991. Copyright © 1991 by The Salariya Book Co Ltd. Reproduced by permission. / Bergin, Mark, illustrator. From a cover of *A Frontier Fort on the Oregon Trail,* by Scott Steedman. Peter Bedrick, 1994. Copyright © 1993 by The Salariya Book Co Ltd. Reproduced by permission. / Bergin, Mark, photograph. Reproduced by permission of Mark Bergin.

BERNSTEIN, MARGERY. Handelman, Dorothy, photographer. From a cover of *My Brother, the Pest,* by Margery Bernstein. The Millbrook Press, 1999. Copyright © 1999 by The Millbrook Press, Inc. / Handelman, Dorothy, photographer. From a cover of *Stop That Noise!,* by Margery Bernstein. The Millbrook Press, 1999. Copyright © 1999 by The Millbrook Press, Inc. Reproduced by permission.

BETHKE, BRUCE. Galant, Dennis and Sandra Lewis, illustrators. From a cover of *Headcrash*, by Bruce Bethke. Warner Books, 1995. Copyright © 1995 by Bruce Bethke. Reproduced by permission.

BOSTOCK, MIKE. Bostock, Mike illustrator. From an illustration in *Gentle Giant Octopus,* by Karen Wallace. Walker Books, 1998. Reproduced by permission of Mike Bostock.

BROWN, TRICIA. Corral, Roy, photographer. From cover of *Children of the Midnight Sun: Young Native Voices of Alaska,* by Tricia Brown. Alaska Northwest Books, 1998. Reproduced by permission of Tricia Brown. / Brown, Tricia, photograph by Roy Corral. Reproduced by permission.

BURSZTYNSKI, SUE. From a dust jacket of *Starwalkers: Explorers of the Unknown,* by Sue Bursztynski. Omnibus Books, 1998. Reproduced by permission. / Bursztynski, Sue, photograph. Reproduced by permission of Sue Bursztynski.

CARRYL, CHARLES E. LaMarche, Jim, illustrator. From an illustration in *A Capital Ship; or The Walloping Window-blind* by Charles E. Carryl. Lothrop, Lee & Shepard Books, 1994. Illustration copyright © 1994 by Jim LaMarche. Reproduced by permission of HarperCollins Publishers.

CARTER, DAVID A. Carter, David A., illustrator. From an illustration in his *How Many Bugs in a Box?*. Little Simon, 1988. Copyright © 1988 by Intervisual Books, Inc. Reproduced by permission of Little Simon, an imprint of Simon & Schuster Macmillan. In the United States by North South Books. / Carter, David A., illustrator. From a cover of his *More Bugs in Boxes*. Little Simon, 1990. Copyright © 1990 by David A. Carter. Reproduced by permission of Little Simon, an imprint of Simon & Schuster Macmillan. In the United States by North South Books.

CATALANOTTO, PETER. Catalanotto, Peter, illustrator. From an illustration in his *Dad & Me.* DK Publishing, 1999. Copyright © 1999 by Peter Catalanotto. Reproduced by permission. / Catalanotto, Peter, illustrator. From an illustration in *Letter to the Lake,* by Susan Marie Swanson. DK Publishing, Inc., 1998. Illustration copyright © 1998 by Peter Catalanotto. Reproduced by permission. / Catalanotto, Peter, illustrator. From an illustration in his *The Painter.* Orchard Paperbacks, 1999. Copyright © 1995 by Peter Catalanotto. Reproduced by permission of the publisher, Orchard Books, New York. / Catalanotto, Peter, photograph. Reproduced by permission of Peter Catalanotto.

CATO, SHEILA. Cato, Sheila, photograph. Reproduced by permission of Sheila Cato.

COLMAN, PENNY. Colman, Penny. From a cover of her *Corpses, Coffins, and Crypts: A History of Burial* Henry Holt and Company, 1997. Cover photograph copyright © 1997 by Penny Colman. Reproduced by permission of Henry Holt and Company, LLC. / From a cover of *Rosie the Riveter: Women Working on the Home Front in World War II,* by Penny Colman. Crown Publishers, 1995. Copyright © 1995 by Penny Colman. Reproduced by permission of Crown Publishers, a division of Random House, Inc. / From a cover of *Strike!: The Bitter Struggle of American Workers from Colonial Times to the Present,* by Penny Colman. Cover photograph by Brown Brothers. Millbrook Press, 1995. Copyright © 1995 by Penny Colman. Reproduced by permission.

DALY, NIKI. Daly, Niki, illustrator. From an illustration in his *The Boy on the Beach.* Margaret K. McElderry Books, 1999. Copyright © 1999 by Niki Daly. Reproduced by permission of Simon & Schuster Macmillan. In the rest of the world by Bloomsbury Press and Human & Rousseau (pty) Ltd. / Daly, Niki, illustrator. From an illustration in his *Bravo Zan Angelo!.* Farrar, Straus & Giroux, 1998. Copyright © 1998 by Niki Daly. Reproduced by permission of Farrar, Straus & Giroux, a

Macdonald. Harcourt Brace & Company, 1997. Cover illustration copyright © 1997 by Michael Hussar. Reproduced by permission of Harcourt, Inc. / Romas, illustrator. From a cover of **The Price of the Stars,** by Debra Doyle and James D. Macdonald. A Tom Doherty Associates Book, 1992. Copyright © 1992 by Debra Doyle and James Macdonald. Reproduced by permission.

MARCHESI, STEPHEN. Marchesi, Stephen, illustrator. From an illustration in **Humpback Goes North,** by Darice Bailer. Copyright © 1998 by Trudy Corporation and The Smithsonian Institution. Reproduced by permission. / Marchesi, Stephen, illustrator. From an illustration in **The Mysterious Rays of Dr. Roentgen,** by Beverly Gherman. Atheneum, 1994. Illustration copyright © 1994, by Stephen Marchesi. Reproduced by permission of Atheneum, an imprint of Simon & Schuster Macmillan.

MARINO, JAN. Tylden-Wright, Jenny, illustrator. From a cover from **Searching for Atticus,** by Jan Marino. Simon & Schuster Books for Young Readers, 1997. Cover illustration copyright © 1997 by Jenny Tylden-Wright. Reproduced by permission of Simon & Schuster Books for Young Readers, an imprint of Simon & Schuster Macmilan. In the United States by Arena. / Marino, Jan, photograph. Reproduced by permission of Jan Marino.

MARK, JAN. Parkins, David, illustrator. From a cover of **God's Story: How God Made Mankind,** by Jan Mark. Candlewick Press Inc., 1997. Text copyright © 1997 by Jan Mark. Cover illustration copyright © 1997 by David Parkins. Reproduced by permission of Walker Books Ltd, London. / Wijngaard, Juan, illustrator. From the cover of **The Midas Touch,** by Jan Mark. Candlewick Press Inc., 1999. Text copyright © 1999 by Jan Mark. Cover illustration copyright © 1999 by Juan Wijngaard. Reproduced by permission of Walker Books Ltd, London. / Merriman, Rachel, illustrator. From a cover of **The Tale of Tobias,** by Jan Mark. Candlewick Press Inc., 1995. Tex copyright © 1995 by Jan Mark. Cover illustration copyright © 1995 by Rachel Merriman. Reproduced by permission of Walker Books Ltd, London. / Mark, Jan, photograph by Isobel Rose. Reproduced by permission of Jan Mark.

MCKAY, LAWRENCE. McKay, Lawrence, Jr., photograph by Charles B. Backus. Reproduced by permission.

MILLEN, C. M. Azarian, Mary, illustrator. From an illustration in **A Symphony for the Sheep,** by C. M. Millen. Houghton Mifflin Company, 1996. Illustration copyright © 1996 by Mary Azarian. Reproduced by permission of the Houghton Mifflin Company.

MONTGOMERY, SY. Bishop, Nic, illustrator. From a cover from **The Snake Scientist,** by Sy Montgomery. Houghton Mifflin, 1999. Cover photographs copyright © 1999 by Nic Bishop. Reproduced by permission of the Houghton Mifflin Company. / Montgomery, Sy, photograph by Phebe Lewan. Reproduced by permission of Sy Montgomery.

MORGAN, MARY. Morgan, Mary, illustrator. From an illustration in **Buba Leah and Her Paper Children,** by Lillian Hammer Ross. The Jewish Publication Society, 1991. Copyright © 1991 by Lillian Hammer Ross. Reproduced by permission. / Morgan, Mary, illustrator. From an illustration in her **Gentle Rosie.** Hyperion Books for Children, 1999. Copyright © 1999 by Mary Morgan Van Royen. Reproduced by permission. / Morgan, Mary, illustrator. From an illustration in **Hannah and Jack,** by Mary Nethery. Atheneum Books for Young Readers, 1996. Illustration copyright © 1996 by Mary Morgan. Reproduced by permission of Atheneum Books for Young Reader, an imprint of Simon & Schuster Macmillan. / Morgan, Mary, illustrator. From an illustraion in **I'm the Boss!,** by Elizabeth Winthrop. Holiday House, 1994. Illustration copyright © 1994 by Mary Morgan. Reproduced by permission of Holiday House, Inc.

OBERMAN, SHELDON. All personal photographs reproduced with permission from the author.

OLDER, EFFIN. Older, Effin, photograph. Reproduced by permission of Effin Older.

OLDER, JULES. Older, Jules, photograph. Reproduced by permission of Effin Older.

PINKWATER, DANIEL. Pinkwater, Jill, illustrator. From a dust jacket of **The Education of Robert Nifkin,** by Daniel Pinkwater. Farrar, Straus & Giroux, 1998. Copyright © 1998 by Daniel Pinkwater. Reproduced by permission of Farrar, Straus and Giroux, LLC. / Pinkwater, Jill, illustrator. From a cover of **Superpuppy: How to Choose, Raise, and Train the Best Possible Dog for You,** by Jill and D. Manus Pinkwater. Clarion, 1977. Copyright © 1977 by Jill and D. Manus Pinkwater. Cover illustration copyright © 1977 by Jill Pinkwater. Reproduced by permission of Houghton Mifflin Company. / Pinkwater, Daniel Manus, photograph by Kathy McLaughlin /John Raugalis Photography. Reproduced by permission.

REESE, DELLA. Reese, Della, photograph. Archive Photos. Reproduced by permission.

RIDDELL, CHRIS. Riddell, Chris, illustrator. From an illustration in **A Little Bit of Winter,** postcard by Paul Stewart. Anderson Press, 1988. Copyright © 1988 by Chris Riddell. Reproduced by permission. / Riddell, Chris, photograph. Reproduced by permission of Chris Riddell.

RINGGOLD, FAITH. Ringgold, Faith, illustrator. From an illustration in her **Aunt Harriet's Underground Railroad in the Sky.** Crown Publisher, Inc., 1992. Copyright © 1992 by Faith Ringgold. Reproduced by permission of Crown Childrenís Books, a division of Random House, Inc. / Ringgold, Faith, illustrator. From an illustration in her **Dinner at Aunt Connie's House.** Hyperion Paperbacks for Children, 1996. Text and illustrations copyright © 1993 by Faith Ringgold. Reproduced by permission. / From an illustration titled ìThe Letter: Bitter Nest Part, 1988î in **Faith Ringgold: A 25 Year Survey**, by Faith Ringgold. FAMLI, 1990. © Copyright 1988 Faith Ringgold. Reproduced by permission of Faith Ringgold. / Ringgold, Faith, photograph by C. Love. © 1986 Faith Ringgold, Inc. Reproduced by permission.

SOMETHING ABOUT THE AUTHOR

ADAMS, Nicholas
See MACDONALD, James D.

*   *   *

ALDRICH, Thomas (Bailey) 1836-1907

Personal

Born November 11, 1836, in Portsmouth, NH; died of a sudden illness, March 19, 1907, in Boston, MA; buried in Mount Auburn Cemetery, Cambridge, MA; son of Elias Taft (a merchant) and Sara Abba (Bailey) Aldrich; married Lilian Woodman, November 28, 1865; children: Charles and Talbot (twin sons). *Education:* Attended Samuel De Merritt's Academy, Portsmouth, NH; Yale University, M.A., 1881; Harvard University, M.A., 1896. *Religion:* Protestant. *Hobbies and other interests:* Travel.

Career

New York Commission office, clerk, 1852-55; *Evening Mirror,* junior literary critic, 1855; *Home Journal,* assistant editor, 1856; *Saturday Press,* associate editor, 1858; *New York Tribune,* war correspondent, 1861; *Illustrated News,* managing editor, 1862-65; *Every Saturday,* editor, 1865-74; *Atlantic Monthly,* editor, 1881-90. Freelance author and poet.

Awards, Honors

LL.D. from University of Pennsylvania, 1906.

Writings

The Bells: A Collection of Chimes, J. C. Derby (Boston)/ Phillips, Sampson (Cincinnati), 1855.
Daisy's Necklace and What Came of It: A Literary Episode, Derby & Jackson (New York)/H. W. Derby (Cincinnati), 1857.
The Course of True Love Never Did Run Smooth, Rudd & Carleton (New York), 1858.
The Ballad of Babie Bell, and Other Poems, Rudd & Carleton, 1859.
Pampinea, and Other Poems, Rudd & Carleton, 1861.
Out of His Head: A Romance, Carleton, 1862.
Poems, Carleton, 1863.
Songs of War, Munsell, 1863.
The Poems of Thomas Bailey Aldrich, Ticknor & Fields, 1865.
The Story of a Bad Boy (for children), Ticknor & Fields (Boston), 1865, published as *Tom Bailey's Adventures,* Osgood, 1877.
Pere Antoine's Date Palm, Welch, Bigelow, 1866.
Pansy's Wish: A Christmas Fantasy with a Moral, Marion, 1870.
Marjorie Daw and Other People, J. R. Osgood (Boston), 1873.
Cloth of Gold and other Poems, J. R. Osgood, 1874.
Prudence Palfrey, J. R. Osgood, 1874.
Flower and Thorn, Later Poems, J. R. Osgood, 1877.
A Midnight Fantasy [and] *The Little Violinist,* J. R. Osgood, 1877.
Miss Mehetabel's Son, J. R. Osgood, 1877.
The Queen of Sheba, J. R. Osgood, 1877.
A Rivermouth Romance, J. R. Osgood, 1877.
The Stillwater Tragedy, Houghton Mifflin (Boston), 1880.

The Poems of Thomas Bailey Aldrich, Houghton Mifflin, 1882.

From Ponkapog to Pesth, Houghton Mifflin, 1883.

Mercedes, and Later Poems, Houghton Mifflin, 1884.

The Household Edition of the Poems of Thomas Bailey Aldrich, Houghton Mifflin, 1885.

The Second Son, Houghton Mifflin, 1888.

Wyndham Towers, Houghton Mifflin, 1890.

The Sisters' Tragedy, with Other Poems, Lyric and Dramatic, Houghton Mifflin, 1891.

An Old Town by the Sea, Houghton Mifflin, 1893.

Two Bites at a Cherry, with Other Tales, Houghton Mifflin, 1894.

Unguarded Gates, and Other Poems, Houghton Mifflin, 1895.

Judith and Holofernes, Houghton Mifflin, 1896.

A Sea Turn and Other Matters, Houghton Mifflin, 1902.

Ponkapog Papers, Houghton Mifflin, 1903.

Pauline Pavlovna: A Drama in One Act, Houghton Mifflin, 1907.

Adaptations

Judith and Holofernes was adapted into the play *Judith of Bethulia,* which was produced in Boston, MA, at the Tremont Theater, October 13, 1904; *Judith of Bethulia* was adapted into a film by Biograph, 1913, and into the film *Her Condoned Sin* by Biograph, 1917; *Marjorie Daw and Other People* was adapted into a one-act musical, produced in New York City at the Library and Museum of the Performing Arts, February 2, 1970.

Sidelights

An astonishingly prolific writing career—primarily in poetry and adolescent prose—is only part of the literary legacy of Thomas Aldrich. His editorial career in the literary publications of his day, particularly his influential editorship of the *Atlantic Monthly,* placed him in the heart of the Eastern (particularly Bostonian) literary establishment of the late nineteenth century. Ferris Greenslet, writing in his biography *The Life of Thomas Bailey Aldrich,* maintained that "Under [Aldrich's] conduct the *Atlantic* attained a notable unity of tone and distinction of style." Kenneth M. Price suggested in his essay for the *Dictionary of Literary Biography* that "Aldrich, perhaps more than any other writer, represented for the Gilded Age all that was delightful, polished, cultured, and accomplished."

Aldrich began writing as a poet, publishing his first youthful efforts in the *Portsmouth Journal* by the age of sixteen. Though he had prepared to attend Harvard, family finances made that impossible, so Aldrich moved to New York to take a job clerking for his uncle, and wrote poetry in his spare time. In 1855, at the age of nineteen, he published his first collection of poetry, *The Bells: A Collection of Chimes,* and soon after devoted himself to a purely literary career. He went first to the *Evening Mirror,* serving as junior literary critic, but soon moved on to the *Home Journal,* taking on the position of subeditor. There he learned the ins and outs of publishing and wrote articles about New York society; but more importantly, he made the acquaintance of many of the leading writers of the day. One of those writers, Henry Clapp, founded the *Saturday Press* in 1858 and invited Aldrich to join the masthead as assistant editor, with the further assignment to write satirical articles poking fun at the American ideal of respectability. For a time, his editorial and authorial duties diverted his energies from poetry, but when the *Press* folded in 1860, he returned to his first literary love with vigor.

Aldrich achieved great success in that same year when he sold his first poetry to the *Atlantic Monthly,* then America's pre-eminent literary publication, which boasted such venerable contributors as Longfellow, Emerson, and Harriet Beecher Stowe. His career was interrupted by the outbreak of the Civil War, during which he served as a war correspondent for the *New York Tribune,* but returned to his hometown of Portsmouth in 1862. His return to the literary life meant both a return to writing (poetry and short stories) and to publishing: he took the post of managing editor of the *Illustrated News.* There followed a series of further editorial postings, during which time he continued to write.

After his marriage to Lilian Woodman in 1865, Aldrich moved to Boston, but he never severed his ties to Portsmouth, the city of his birth and in which many of his stories are set. In 1868, just before the birth of his twin sons, Aldrich published the work for which he remains best known, a serialized tale called "The Story of a Bad Boy" that was published by the children's magazine *Our Young Folks.* With this tale (later published as a book), he helped to change the face of the genre of adolescent fiction. Like his friend and contemporary, Mark Twain, Aldrich adopted a style of writing that had little in common with the moralizing stories of the time, but focused instead on realism in depicting the exploits of an adventurous boyhood. Described by critics as the first work in which an American boy is treated realistically, it remains of all his writings his greatest contribution to American letters.

The Story of a Bad Boy plays a very significant role in children's literature, for varying reasons. It explores many facets of life, tying in the pain and the joys that are experienced by people in their early and later years. The narrator of this pleasant, comical story, Tom, looks back on several years of his life and focuses on many of his childhood experiences, including some painful memories. The reader delights in Aldrich's not-so-fictional account of nostalgia, love, pain, loss, and happiness. Virginia L. Wolf declared in the *Dictionary of Literary Biography* that "it is to be valued for its vivid details and for its place in the history of realistic novels for children.... Without *The Story of a Bad Boy,* there would probably have been no *Adventures of Huckleberry Finn....* [It] clearly evolved from the tradition Aldrich fathered."

Aldrich continued to publish poetry, novels, and other prose pieces, but when, in 1891, he took on the position of editor of the *Atlantic Monthly,* his duties left him precious little time for creative work. In his new position, he published the work of many of the finest writers of the day, from Longfellow to Thomas Hardy and Oliver Wendell Holmes to Henry James. He brought the already well-respected periodical to an unprecedented level of international renown. Nonetheless, in 1890 he was pleased to step down from his role as editor, devoting his time fully to travel and writing. In 1901, his beloved son Charles, then age thirty-three, was diagnosed with tuberculosis, from which he died three years later. Aldrich was stricken terribly by this loss, writing no new works.

Aldrich's name may not roll off people's tongues as easily as that of Mark Twain's, but he certainly paved the way for other authors to follow. His role was pivotal in the development of the genre of realism.

Works Cited

Greenslet, Ferris, *The Life of Thomas Bailey Aldrich,* Houghton Mifflin, 1908.

Price, Kenneth M., *Dictionary of Literary Biography,* "Thomas Bailey Aldrich," Volume 71: *American Literary Critics and Scholars, 1880-1900,* Gale, 1988.

Wolf, Virginia L., *Dictionary of Literary Biography,* "Thomas Bailey Aldrich," Volume 42: *American Writers for Children Before 1900,* Gale, 1985.

For More Information See

BOOKS

Dictionary of Literary Biography, Gale, Volume 74: *American Short-Story Writers Before 1880,* 1988; Volume 79: *American Magazine Journalists, 1850-1900,* 1989.

Samuels, Charles E., *Thomas Bailey Aldrich,* Twayne, 1965.*

*   *   *

ALMOND, David 1951-

Personal

Born May 15, 1951, in Newcastle upon Tyne, England; son of James Arthur and Catherine (Barber) Almond; married Sara Jane Palmer; children: Freya Grace Almond-Palmer. *Education:* University of East Anglia, B.A. (honors).

Addresses

Home—15 Westwood Ave., Heaton, Newcastle NE6 5QT, England. *E-mail*—dalmond@lineone.net

Career

Teacher in primary, adult, and special education in England; creative writing tutor for the Arvon Foundation since 1987 and the Open college of the Arts, 1995-99; Huntington School, York, visiting writer, 1996-98; Hartlepool Schools, writer-in-residence, spring, 1999; visiting speaker and course leader.

Awards, Honors

Hawthornden Fellowship, 1997; Junior Literary Guild Selection, Children's Book of the Year, Whitbread Award, and Carnegie Medal, Library Association, all 1998, all for *Skellig;* Arts Council Award for outstanding literature for young people, 1998, and Smarties Silver Award, 1999, both for *Kit's Wilderness.*

Writings

FOR CHILDREN

Skellig, Hodder Children's (London, England), 1998, Delacorte Press (New York, NY), 1999.

Kit's Wilderness, Hodder Children's, 1999, Delacorte Press, 2000.

Heaven Eyes, Hodder Children's, 2000; Delacorte Press, in press.

OTHER

Sleepless Nights (short stories), Iron Press, 1985.

A Kind of Heaven (short stories), Iron Press, 1997.

Counting Stars (short stories), Hodder Children's Books, 2000.

Contributor to *London* and *Critical Quarterly; Panurge* (fiction magazine), editor, 1987-93; *Kit's Wilderness* and *Skellig* have been translated and published in several other languages.

David Almond

Michael and his friend Mina care for a mysterious creature, discovering the fragility of life and the healing power of love in Almond's lyrical first novel for young adults. (Cover illustration by Kamil Vojnar.)

Work in Progress

Writing *Secret Heart,* a fourth novel for young adults; a radio dramatization of *Skellig;* a play for children.

Sidelights

British writer David Almond wrote for adults for a number of years before he achieved what amounted to overnight success with his first novel for young adults, *Skellig.* This 1998 tale of a young boy's discovery of a possibly supernatural creature in his own backyard was unanimously praised by reviewers, sold out its first printing in four days, and went on to win Britain's prestigious Whitbread Children's Book of the Year Award and the Carnegie Medal.

Like the hero in *Skellig,* Almond grew up on the fringes of a Northern English city, a landscape that offered great imaginative possibilities for him as a youth. As Almond, who was born in 1951, told *SATA:* "Maybe ink was always in my blood. I don't remember it, of course, but as a baby in my mother's arms I used to visit my uncle's printing works on the narrow high street of our town. I

used to point and grin and gurgle as the pages of the local newspaper rolled off the machines. It was a small steep town with wild heather hills at the crest and the River Tyne flowing far below. From out windows, we looked out towards the city that packed the opposite bank, towards the distant sea, and even on clear days toward the hazy Cheviots an eternity away. It was a place that had everything necessary for the imagination.

"I grew up in a big extended Catholic family. I listened to the stories and songs at family parties. I listened to the gossip that filled Dragone's coffee shop. I ran with my friends through the open spaces and the narrow lanes. We scared each other with ghost stories told in fragile tents on dark nights. We promised never-ending friendship and whispered of the amazing journeys we'd take together. I sat with my grandfather in his allotment, held tiny Easter chicks in my hands while he smoked his pipe and the factory sirens wailed and larks yelled high above. I trembled at the images presented to us in church, at the awful threats and glorious promises made by black-clad priests with Irish voices. I scribbled stories and stitched them into little books. I disliked school and loved the library, a little square building in which I dreamed that books with my name on them would stand one day on the shelves. I loved Arthurian legends, Hemingway, John Wyndham, the tales of the fake Tibetan monk, Lobsang Rampa."

After earning a degree from the University of East Anglia, Almond became a teacher. In 1982, he quit a full-time job, sold his house, and moved to a commune in order to devote himself to writing. The result was a collection of stories, *Sleepless Nights,* published by a small press in 1985. As Almond told *SATA,* "I began to write properly after university, after five years of teaching. Short stories appeared in little magazines. A couple were broadcast on Radio 4. A small press collection, *Sleepless Nights,* appeared to a tiny amount of acclaim and a vast amount of silence. I ran a fiction magazine, *Panurge,* that excited and exhausted me for six years. I wrote The Great English Novel that took five years, went to 33 publishers and was rejected by them all. I went on writing. More stories, more publications, a few small prizes. Another novel, never finished. Another story collection was published, *A Kind of Heaven,* twelve years after the first. Then at last I started writing about growing up in our small steep town: a whole sequence of stories, half-real, half-imaginary, that I called *Stories from the Middle of the World.* They took a year to write."

It was the act of finishing the Newcastle stories that inexplicably led Almond to the opening lines of *Skellig:* "I found him in the garage on Sunday afternoon," recalls the book's narrator, ten-year-old Michael—an opening line that, Almond said, simply came to him as he was walking down the street. As he explained in an interview with *Publishers Weekly,* "When I wrote the last of these stories, I stuck them into an envelope, and as soon as I'd posted away the book to my agent, the story of *Skellig* just flew into my head, as if it had just been waiting there." On the Sunday in question on which *Skellig* begins, Michael and his family have just taken possession of an old, run-down house; also new to them is a newborn infant sister for Michael, who initially arrives home from the hospital but soon must return for heart surgery.

In the garage, behind a great deal of clutter, Michael discovers a man covered in dust and insects. At first he believes it is an old homeless man, but he finds that Skellig, who communicates with Michael but does not reveal much by way of explanation, has odd wing-like appendages. It seems Skellig has come there to die. As he begins his new school, while his mother is away with his sister at the hospital and his father is understandably preoccupied, Michael begins to bring Skellig food and medicine. He also befriends his new neighbor, a girl name Mina who is an intelligent, independent thinker. Mina explains to Michael a few of her interests, such as ornithology and the poetry of early nineteenth century Romantic writer William Blake. She also shows him a nest of rare owls, which may have something to do with Skellig's presence.

But as Perri Klass notes, writing about *Skellig* in the *New York Times Book Review,* the book's charm lies in its author's courage for allowing some things to remain a mystery. "[I]n its simple but poetic language, its tender refusal to package its mysteries neatly or offer explanations for what happens in either world, it goes beyond adventure story or family-with-a-problem story to become a story about worlds enlarging and the hope of scattering death." As the story progresses, Michael shares the secret of Skellig with Mina, and as they both tend to him in the garage, his health improves considerably. As a result, however, the mysterious occupant becomes even more secretive and mystical before he vanishes.

Michael feels his baby sister's heart beating one day, and realizes that love can achieve miracles that science cannot. Klass, in her *New York Times Book Review* critique, praised Almond's talent for weaving in the more prosaic details of life such as soccer practice and the daily school-bus ride with larger questions involving the metaphysical world. "Its strength as a novel is in its subtlety, its sideways angles," observed Klass. "It is a book about the business of everyday life proceeding on a canvas suddenly widened to include mystery and tragedy, although not everyone has eyes to see."

Other reviews were similarly positive. Cathryn M. Mercier, writing in *Five Owls,* called Skellig a "novel of faith and hope," and "a book of rare spirituality for young adults." *Reading Time* reviewer Howard George described it as "a haunting story" whose impact lies in "the deep emotions evoked by the family crisis and the love given out to Skellig."

Almond had already completed his second young-adult novel, *Kit's Wilderness,* before *Skellig* was nominated for or won several literary prizes in Britain, including the Whitbread and the Carnegie Medal. The focus of this second book is a game of pretend death that its characters play. "In my primary school—a spooky turreted place down by the river where the ancient coal mines had been—a bunch of kids used to play a fainting game in the long grass beyond the school yard wall," wrote Almond in *Carousel.* The story is far less insular than the secretive plot of *Skellig,* and Almond has noted that as a work of fiction it took him far longer to develop coherently.

Almond also admitted that, "at times I was scared stiff by what was happening in the tale," he wrote in *Carousel.* "Scared that it might all end dreadfully, scared that the darkness would gain the upper hand." But *Kit's Wilderness* was published in Britain to laudatory reviews, and, like *Skellig,* was slated for publication in not just North America but in several translations as well. His third novel for teens, *Heaven Eyes,* was published in the U.K. in January, 2000. Like Almond's other books, its plot blends everyday adventure with a dalliance in the netherworld; its characters are escapees of a juvenile home who flee on a raft to an old printing plant on the River Tyne. "These books are suffused with the landscape and spirit of my own childhood," Almond told *SATA.* "By looking back into the past, by re-imagining it and blending it with what I see around me now, I found a way to move forward and to become something that I am intensely happy to be: a writer for children."

Works Cited

Almond, David, "Writing for Boys," *Carousel,* summer, 1999, p. 29.

Devereaux, Elizabeth, "Flying Starts," *Publishers Weekly,* June 28, 1999, p. 25.

George, Howard, review of *Skellig, Reading Time,* May, 1999, p. 25.

Klass, Perry, review of *Skellig, New York Times Book Review,* June 6, 1999, p. 49.

Mercier, Cathryn M., review of *Skellig, Five Owls,* May-June, 1999, p. 110.

For More Information See

PERIODICALS

Publishers Weekly, May 10, 1999, p. 34.

*   *   *

APPLETON, Victor
See MACDONALD, James D.

*   *   *

AVERY, Lorraine
See OLDER, Effin

*   *   *

AVERY, Lorraine
See OLDER, Jules

B

BERGIN, Mark 1961-

Personal

Born April 4, 1961, in Hastings, England; son of Willy (an antique dealer) and Audrey Bergin; married, September 2, 1989, wife's name, Gillian; children: Hannah, Isabelle and Edward (twins). *Education:* Attended Bexhill College, 1976-78; earned diploma from Eastbourne College of Art, 1983. *Religion:* Church of England.

Addresses

Home and office—5 Larkhill, Bexhill-on-Sea, East Sussex TN40 1QZ, England.

Career

Illustrator of children's books, 1983—. *Member:* Chartered Society of Designers (diploma member).

Awards, Honors

Times Educational Supplement Award, 1991, for book illustration in the senior age group.

Writings

AUTHOR AND ILLUSTRATOR

Space Shuttle, Macdonald Young (Hove, England), 1998, Franklin Watts (New York, NY), 1999.
Wonders of the World, created and designed by David Salariya, Macdonald Young, 1998, Franklin Watts (New York, NY), 1999.
Castle, Franklin Watts (Danbury, CT), 1999.

ILLUSTRATOR

Leonard Matthews, *The Journeys of St. Paul,* Rourke Enterprises (Vero Beach, FL), 1984.
Matthews, *Jesus's Wonderful Miracles,* Rourke Enterprises, 1984.
Edwina Conner, *A Child in Victorian England,* Wayland (Hove, England), 1986.

Robin May, *A Colonial American Merchant,* Wayland, 1986, Rourke Enterprises, 1987.
May, *A Plains Indian Warrior,* Wayland, 1986, Rourke Enterprises, 1988.
May, *A Plantation Slave,* Wayland, 1986.
Marion Morrison, *An Inca Farmer,* Rourke Enterprises, 1986, Wayland, 1986.
(With John James) Miriam Moss, *A Slave in Ancient Greece,* Wayland, 1986.
Stewart Ross, *A Crusading Knight,* Wayland, 1986, Rourke Enterprises, 1987.
Lucilla Watson, *Boudicca and the Ancient Britons,* Wayland, 1986.
Fiona Somerset Fry, *A Soldier in Wellington's Army,* Wayland, 1987.
Miriam Moss, *A Norman Baron,* Wayland, 1987.
Moss, *A Teenager in the Sixties,* Wayland, 1987.
Ross, *The Ancient Britons,* Wayland, 1987.
Michael Gibson, *A Sailor with Captain Cook,* Wayland, 1987.
Nigel Hunter, *An Australian Pioneer,* Wayland, 1987.
May, *An American Pioneer Family,* Rourke Enterprises, 1987.
Fiona Macdonald, *A Medieval Castle,* Peter Bedrick Books (New York, NY), 1990, Simon & Schuster (London, England), 1990.
Jacqueline Morley, *A Roman Villa,* Peter Bedrick Books, 1990.
Richard Humble, *A World War II Submarine,* P. Bedrick Books, 1991, Simon & Schuster (New York, NY), 1991.
(With James) Morley, *An Egyptian Pyramid,* P. Bedrick Books, 1991, Simon & Schuster (New York, NY), 1991.
Eryl Davies, *Transport on Land, Road and Rail,* Watts (London, England), 1992.
(With Carolyn Scrace) David Lambert, *Seas and Oceans,* Watts, 1992, Raintree Steck-Vaughn (Austin, TX), 1994.
Macdonald, *A Greek Temple,* P. Bedrick Books, 1992, Simon & Schuster Young Books (Hemel Hempstead, England), 1992.
Peter Turvey, *Inventions,* Watts, 1992.

Mark Bergin

Fiona Clarke, *Columbus and the New World,* Simon & Schuster Young Books, 1993.

(With James) Clarke, *Greece in the Time of Pericles,* Simon & Schuster Young Books, 1993.

Clarke, *Rome in the Time of Augustus,* Simon & Schuster (London, England), 1993.

Humble, *A 16th Century Galleon,* Simon & Schuster Young Books, 1993, P. Bedrick Books, 1995.

Lizzy Pearl, *The Story of Flight,* Eagle Books, 1993, Troll Associates (Mahwah, NJ), 1994.

Scott Steedman, *A Frontier Fort on the Oregon Trail,* Peter Bedrick Books, 1993, also published as *A 19th Century Frontier Fort,* Simon & Schuster Young Books, 1994.

Macdonald, *A 16th-Century Mosque,* Peter Bedrick Books, 1994, Simon & Schuster Young Books, 1994.

Francesca Baines, *Castles,* Franklin Watts (New York, NY), 1995, Watts, 1995.

Macdonald, *How Would You Survive as an Aztec?,* created and designed by Salariya, Watts, 1994, Franklin Watts (New York, NY), 1995.

Macdonald, *How Would You Survive as an Ancient Greek?,* created and designed by Salariya, Franklin Watts (New York, NY), 1995, Watts, 1995.

Macdonald, *A Viking Town,* P. Bedrick Books, 1995, Macdonald Young, 1995.

Morley, *How Would You Survive as a Viking?,* created and designed by Salariya, Franklin Watts (New York, NY), 1995.

Steedman, *How Would You Survive As an American Indian?,* Franklin Watts (New York, NY), 1995.

Brian Williams, *The Spanish Armada,* Hamlyn (London, England), 1995.

Daisy Kerr, *Ancient Greeks,* Franklin Watts (London, England), 1996, Franklin Watts (New York, NY), 1997.

Peter Lafferty, *A History of Flight: From Balloons to Boeings,* created and designed by Salariya, Macdonald Young, 1996.

Andrew Langley, *Elizabeth I,* Heinemann (London, England), 1996.

Macdonald, *First Facts About the American Frontier,* Peter Bedrick Books, 1996.

Macdonald, *The Roman Colosseum,* Peter Bedrick Books, 1996, Macdonald Young, 1996.

(With James) Morley, *The Ancient Egyptians Facts of Life,* created and designed by Salariya, Macdonald Young, 1996, published as *First Facts About the Ancient Egyptians,* Peter Bedrick Books, 1996.

Morley, *First Facts About the Vikings,* Peter Bedrick Books, 1996.

Kerr, *Knights and Armor,* Franklin Watts (New York, NY), 1997.

Langley, *Food and Farming,* Heinemann Library (Oxford, England), 1997.

(With Field) Langley, *Tudor Palaces and Other Great Houses,* Heinemann Library, 1997.

Macdonald, *First Facts about the Ancient Greeks,* NTC/Contemporary Publishing, 1997.

(With James and Gerald Wood) Macdonald, *First Facts about the Middle Ages,* NTC/Contemporary Publishing, 1997.

Macdonald, *Marco Polo: A Journey Through China,* created and designed by Salariya, Watts, 1997, Franklin Watts (New York, NY), 1998.

Macdonald, *Castle Siege,* Reader's Digest Children's Publishing, 1997.

(With James Field and James) Jane Shuter, *Clothes and Costume,* Heinemann Library, 1997.

(With Field), Shuter, *Tudor Family Life,* Heinemann Library, 1997.

(With Nicholas Hewetson and John James) Giovanni Caselli, *Wonders of the World,* DK Pub. (New York, NY), 1998, Dorling Kindersley (London, England), 1998.

Jen Green, *Race to the Moon: The Story of Apollo 11,* created and designed by Salariya, Franklin Watts (New York, NY), 1998, Watts, 1998.

(With Field and James) Langley, *Trade and Transport,* Heinemann Library, 1998.

Macdonald, *Inca Town,* created and designed by Salariya, Watts (New York, NY and London, England), 1998.

Macdonald, *Magellan: A Voyage Around the World,* Franklin Watts (New York, NY), 1998.

Hazel Martell, *Roman Town,* Franklin Watts (Danbury, CT), 1998.

(With Field and James) Brenda Williams, *Houses and Homes,* Heinemann Library, 1998.

Terry Whalin, *Joshua and the Jericho Project,* Broadman and Holman, 1998.

Whalin, *Moses and the Great Escape,* Broadman and Holman, 1998.

Whalin, *Daniel and the Babylon Adventure,* Broadman and Holman, 1998.

Whalin, *Jesus and His Miracles,* Broadman and Holman, 1998.

Moira Butterfield, *Aircraft,* Watts, 1999.

(With Jeremy Pike and Mike Taylor) Langley, *Spanish Galleon,* Reader's Digest Children's Publishing, 1999.

Christopher Maynard, *Racing Cars,* Watts, 1999.

Morley, *Viking Town,* Franklin Watts (New York, NY), 1999.

Sidelights

Mark Bergin has illustrated a vast array of books for young readers since finishing art college in England in 1983. A resident of Bexhill-on-Sea in East Sussex—where he grew up—Bergin creates long-lost worlds for factual history books for elementary-age readers. Some of the first titles he illustrated belonged to the "How They Lived" series in the late 1980s. Books such as *A Plains Indian Warrior, An Inca Farmer,* and *A Colonial American Merchant* concentrated on a particular segment of a society and their daily life. Bergin's illustrations help provide further details to the text about food, housing, and dress.

Bergin told *SATA:* "I like to illustrate things so the viewer can get the most information from looking at the

images. Hopefully they will interest and entertain at the same time. For historical references and artifacts on recreation work, I use museums and consultants. I also try and get a new angle on the subjects when I can, i.e., eye levels or three-dimensional perspectives."

Bergin won especial praise for his detailed view of *A World War II Submarine* by Richard Humble in 1991. The book chronicles the origins of the submersible from the American Revolutionary War era to modern times, but concentrates on the submarines used in the Atlantic and Pacific oceans during the 1940s. Bergin's drawings, by use of cutaways, depict how a crew goes about its job on a daily basis to keep their vessel both up to speed and out of harm's way.

Bergin's skills as an illustrator have broadened to include a series on architectural styles throughout history. These include Fiona Macdonald's *A Medieval Castle,* published in 1990. The illustrations, which dominate the page, begin with a castle's design stage and construction, and then expose how its residents lived. Bergin's images capture the full range of life inside a castle—not just how its nobles and knights lived, but giving a glimpse into the meals, customs, and other aspects of daily life for its servants and laborers as well.

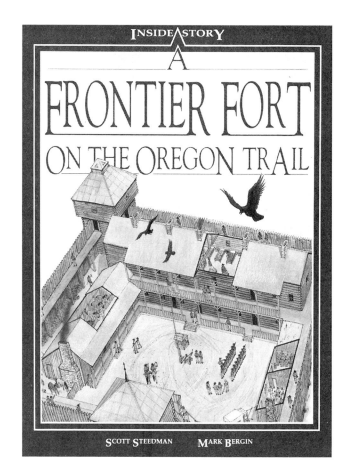

Bergin's detailed drawings accompany Scott Steedman's description of a pioneer fort. (Cover illustration by Bergin.)

Bergin illustrated this festive scene in **An Egyptian Pyramid** *by Jacqueline Morley.*

Another collaboration in the series between Bergin and Fiona Macdonald came with the 1992 book *A Greek Temple.* Bergin's full-color illustrations, which are once more lavish in scope, tell much of the story. *A Greek Temple* concentrates on the most famous Greek temple of all, the Parthenon. Reviewing this work with a similar title that Bergin also illustrated, Jacqueline Morley's *A Roman Villa, School Library Journal*'s Rosie Peasley called them "two attractive books that present an interesting array of information in short, easily digestible bites."

Bergin has also created images for Morley's *An Egyptian Pyramid* (1991), a work aimed at readers in grades four through six. Here, watercolor illustrations reveal how the massive structures were constructed by ingenious methods of ancient engineering, but also depict how the people who built them lived during the time. Reviewing *An Egyptian Pyramid* for *School Library Journal,* Cathryn A. Camper observed that the "well-executed" drawings from Bergin "expand the text."

Bergin's drawings for *A Frontier Fort on the Oregon Trail,* a 1993 title written by Scott Steedman, show how a typical fort's soldiers and their wives lived. Specific sections demonstrate to young readers the purpose of the fort and how the day's work was divided amongst its inhabitants. Illustrations that depict the construction and

maintenance of the defense structure, how a buffalo was killed and quartered for its meat and hide, and the importance of the railroad to the community provide a wealth of visual details. George Gleason, reviewing *A Frontier Fort* for *School Library Journal,* called it "a treasure on the topic."

Other cultures and eras into which Bergin has delved include ancient Britain, Viking society, and medieval Europe's age of exploration. Two titles that belong in this last category were also authored by Fiona Macdonald: *Marco Polo: A Journey Through China* and *Magellan: A Voyage Around the World,* both of which were published in the United States in 1998. Bergin has illustrated several titles in the "Metropolis" series from Franklin Watts that present a specific place in time to help readers understand history on a more intimate level. Inca culture and how it impacted daily life is sketched in Macdonald's *An Inca Town,* a 1998 title that reveals life in Cuzco, a famous city in Peru in the fifteenth century. *Roman Town,* written by Hazel Martell, is another title from this series also published in 1998.

Works Cited

Camper, Cathryn A., review of *An Egyptian Pyramid, School Library Journal,* December, 1991, p. 125.

A statue of Athena towers over visitors to the Parthenon. (From A Greek Temple, *written by Fiona Macdonald and illustrated by Bergin.)*

Gleason, George, review of *A Frontier Fort on the Oregon Trail, School Library Journal,* September, 1994, p. 236.

Peasley, Rosie, review of *A Greek Temple* and *A Roman Villa, School Library Journal,* January, 1993, p. 116.

For More Information See

PERIODICALS

Publishers Weekly, November 30, 1990, p, 71; January, 1999, p. 144.

School Library Journal, October, 1987, p. 122; June, 1989, p. 120; January, 1992, p. 127; July, 1997, p. 84; October, 1997, p. 148; July, 1998, p. 109.

Times Educational Supplement, March, 1999, p. 24.

*   *   *

BERNSTEIN, Margery 1933-

Personal

Born April 18, 1933, in Brooklyn, NY; daughter of Henry (a salesman) and Sylvia (a homemaker; maiden name, Bernstein) Weiss; married Edgar Bernstein, 1955 (divorced); children: Amy Beth, Hal Barnard. *Education:* University of California, Los Angeles, B.A., 1955; graduate course work at University of Chicago School of Education. *Hobbies and other interests:* Theatre, Archeology.

Addresses

Home—11119 Rte. 22, Austerlitz, NY 12017. *E-mail*—bern/passin@taconic.net.

Career

University of Chicago Lab School, Chicago, senior teacher, 1963-81; Mastery Education Corp., Watertown, MA, writer, 1980-86; freelance writer, editor, and researcher, 1980—; also worked as a reading consultant and program evaluator. Stage Manager for various theatre groups in greater Chicago area.

Writings

(With Janet Kobrin) *Earth Namer: A California Indian Myth,* illustrated by Ed Hefernan, Scribner's, 1974.

(With J. Kobrin) *Coyote Goes Hunting for Fire: A California Indian Myth,* illustrated by E. Hefernan, Scribner's, 1974.

(With Kobrin) *How the Sun Made a Promise and Kept It: A Canadian Indian Myth,* illustrated by Hefernan, Scribner's, 1975.

(With Kobrin) *The First Morning,* Scribner's, 1976.

(With Kobrin) *The Summer Maker: An Ojibway Indian Myth,* illustrated by Anne Burgess, Scribner's, 1977.

Raven Brings the Light, Scholastic, Inc., 1994.

(Contributor) *Read-Alouds,* Macmillan, 1997.

That's Hard, That's Easy, illustrated by Dorothy Handelman, Millbrook Press, 1998.

That Cat!, illustrated by D. Handelman, Millbrook Press, 1998.

My Brother, the Pest, Millbrook Press, 1999.

Stop That Noise!, Millbrook Press, 1999.

Work in Progress

A biography of Fanny Kemble for young readers; "If I Were Going," a notebook/guide to Greece for young travelers.

Sidelights

Margery Bernstein worked as a teacher and curriculum developer for many years before turning her talents to writing for young people. Featuring engaging prose designed to appeal to the beginning reading set, books such as *How the Sun Made a Promise and Kept It, The Summer Maker,* and *My Brother, the Pest* showcase Bernstein's lively approach to writing for children, and demonstrate her insights into the learning-to-read process.

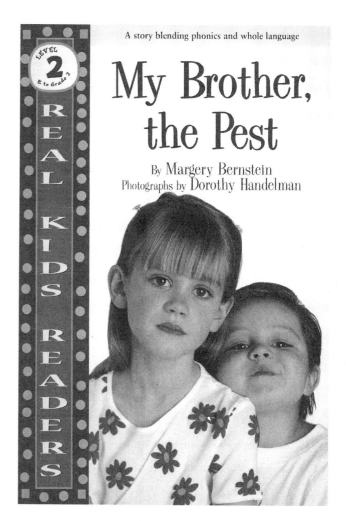

Margery Bernstein's realistic storyline explores a big sister/little brother relationship from a young reader's perspective.

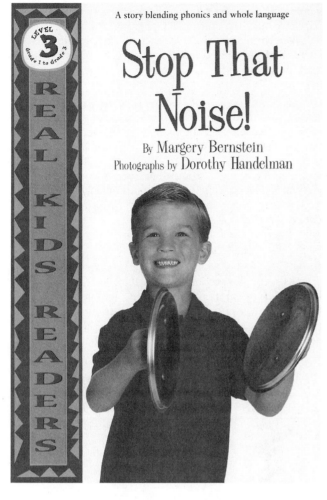

A story blending phonics and whole language

LEVEL 3
Grade 1 to Grade 3

REAL KIDS READERS

Stop That
Noise!

By Margery Bernstein
Photographs by Dorothy Handelman

*Three kids who can't stop making noise are formed into
a band for their school open house.*

Several of Bernstein's early works were retellings of
Native American stories, and were co-authored with
Janet Kobrin. *Coyote Goes Hunting for Fire* and *Earth
Namer* are each based on legends from tribes living in
California. The first recounts the humorous efforts of a
coyote to aid his fellow animals in their effort to steal
fire from a tribe of Wind people, while the second is a
myth that attempts to explain the origins of life on earth.
Calling the works "ingenuous and lively," a *Booklist*
reviewer went on to praise Bernstein's books for their
"modern, literal, and often comical qualities." *Library
Journal* contributor Barbara Mundall noted that, in
particular, *Earth Namer* "faithfully retains the spirit of
the [original Indian] legend."

Bernstein and Kobrin followed their initial success with
more adaptations of myths, this time turning to the
continent of Africa with *The First Morning.* Featuring
characters common to many tales from that vast
continent, *The First Morning* tells how light on Earth
was given as a reward for the efforts of Lion, Spider,
Mouse, and Fly to complete a series of tasks put to them
by the wily Sky King. Despite the efforts of the Sky
King to steal the light from them after they have earned
it, the animals ultimately invoke the rising sun, hasten-

ing the growth of all life on earth. Calling *The First
Morning* an "involving tale," a *Booklist* reviewer added
that the authors' "plain but not stark" retelling "keeps
pace with an action-filled plot." In *Bulletin of the Center
for Children's Books* a contributor commented that with
its "simple, direct style," the picture book "has the
appeals of small creatures triumphing over large ones."

Continuing their efforts to introduce youngsters to time-
honored tales from many cultures, Bernstein and Kobrin
released *The Summer Maker,* a picture book based on an
Ojibway Indian story. Reflecting the tribe's love of
warmer weather, the story finds a fisherman in search of
summer, which seems to have all but vanished from
earth. With help from friends Beaver, Lynx, Otter, and
Wolverine, as well as from a strange spirit called a
manitou, the fisherman discovers the way into a
summery world. From here he releases a group of birds
that rise into the air on warm winds, melting the snow
and ushering forth a warmer season. Praising the story's
pen-and-ink illustrations, Sara Miller commented in
School Library Journal upon the "pleasant" quality of
the authors' retelling.

In a change of pace from her successful refashioning of
traditional tales, Bernstein embarked on an enjoyable
adventure in creating a wholly original story in writing
the children's book *My Brother, the Pest.* She got the
idea for her beginning-reader-in-rhyme from a list of
"likes" and "dislikes" her granddaughter had made about
her own sister. "While it is apparent to all that the older
child genuinely adores her little sister, protects and cares
for her, glows with love when the little one hugs her, is
proud of her and so forth, it is equally apparent that
sometimes in an instant this can change and she will hate
her sister and her 'curly headed little self,'" Bernstein
explained to *SATA* in discussing the conflicting emotions
of many older children when dealing with younger
siblings. Writing *My Brother, the Pest* "really opened
my eyes to the not-so-subtle nuances of behavior
between siblings," added the author. A similar book,
Bernstein's *Stop That Noise!,* reflects some children's
desire to make loud and continuous music, and how one
teacher found a way to channel this behavior into a
creative activity in a book that *School Library Journal*
contributor Susan Hepler dubbed "earnest" and "moderately successful."

Works Cited

Review of *Coyote Goes Hunting for Fire, Booklist,*
    September 1, 1974, p. 38.
Review of *The First Morning, Booklist,* March 15, 1976, p.
    1052.
Review of *The First Morning, Bulletin of the Center for
    Children's Books,* June, 1976, p. 153.
Hepler, Susan, review of *Stop That Noise!, School Library
    Journal,* August, 1999, pp. 124-25.
Miller, Sara, review of *The Summer Maker, School Library
    Journal,* September, 1977, p. 102.
Mundall, Barbara, review of *Earth Namer, Library Jour-
    nal,* September 15, 1974, p. 2240.

For More Information See

PERIODICALS

Instructor, May, 1991, p. 35.
Publishers Weekly, October 19, 1998, p. 83.

*   *   *

BETHKE, Bruce Raymond 1955-

Personal

Born in 1955, in Milwaukee, WI.

Addresses

Home—P.O. Box 28094, Oakdale, MN 55128. *E-mail*—brbethke@ddb.com.

Career

Software developer in MN; has worked at various jobs including rock musician, teacher, and sausage maker.

Awards, Honors

Philip K. Dick Award, 1995, for *Headcrash.*

Writings

Maverick, Ace (New York City), 1990.
Headcrash, Warner Books (New York City), 1995.
Rebel Moon, Pocket Books (New York City), 1996.
(Contributor) *Lamps on the Brow,* edited by James Cahill,
    James Cahill Publishing (Aliso Viejo, CA), 1998.
Wild, Wild West, Warner Books, 1999.

Sidelights

Science fiction writer Bruce Bethke attracted significant notice with the publication of his first short story, "Cyberpunk," in 1983. The story circulated in manuscript before it was published in *Amazing Stories* in 1983 and is credited as the work that led editor Gardner Dozois to use the term "cyberpunk" to designate a new science-fiction subgenre. Cyberpunk fiction had its roots as far back as the 1940s and 1950s, in the work of Samuel B. Delany, Bruce Sterling, and others but became chiefly associated with the fiction of William Gibson, whose 1984 novel *Neuromancer* is considered the definitive cyberpunk novel.

Bethke did not invent the subgenre, but he did coin its name, which is an amalgam from the words "cybernetics," the science of replacing human body parts with computerized ones, and "punk," which refers to the aggressive and defiant music and sensibility of the 1980s counterculture. Bethke has explained that his invention of the term was prompted mostly by practicalities. "I was actively *trying* to invent a new term that grokked the juxtaposition of punk attitudes and high technology," he commented on a *Users.zetnet* website. "[But] my reasons ... were purely selfish and market-driven: I wanted to give my story a snappy, one-word title that editors would remember." "Cyberpunk" was considered an apt term to describe fiction that explored themes of social and personal alienation in a dehumanized, high-tech future world.

Bethke brings significant technological experience to his fiction. He describes himself as "an ex-surfer, ex-rock musician, ex-teacher, and ex-sausage maker" who works in software development for a large multinational company. He has written more than two hundred instruction manuals, articles, and books about computer software. His stories have been published in science fiction magazines such as *Amazing, Aboriginal, Hitchcock's Mystery,* and *Easyriders.*

In his first novel, *Maverick,* Book 5 in Isaac Asimov's RobotCity: Robots and Aliens series, basic cyberpunk themes are again prominent. In the novel, robots have built cities on uninhabited planets, looking for human beings to serve. Frustrated without any human masters, the machines accept a wolf-like race, the Kin, as human equivalents. A more complex type of robot, a "learning

Everyone is online and can get into your home over the Internet in Bruce Raymond Bethke's comic 1995 cyberpunk novel. (Cover photo by Dennis Galant and Sandra Lewis.)

machine," has already imprinted on the Kin and caused them to accept it as a sort of Messiah symbol before abandoning them; many of the Kin are obsessed now by the possibility of the learning machine's "Return," an event that they believe will be religiously redemptive. The novel's human characters, who include the scientist who developed the learning machine and her family, are threatened by the slave-taking Dr. Aranimas; and the book's title character, a Kin no longer, becomes involved with both romance and the tension between the Kin who believe in a Return and those who do not.

Edith Tyson, in *Voice of Youth Advocates,* found that much of the novel's effect is achieved through Bethke's shifts in viewpoint from humans to robots to Kin. "Bethke does a fair job with the humans and a better one with the robots, [but] he is masterful in the portrayal of the Kin; ... they are super-wolves all the way, yet we identify with them." Tyson added, however, that the book is very much a middle volume in a series (Asimov has allowed writers to add their own new books in a series with characters he created about a robot universe) and pointed out that readers unfamiliar with the series might find it difficult to keep the characters straight. *Kliatt* reviewer Amos C. Patterson, however, did not find this a drawback, having observed that *Maverick* "is an easy read and the excitement level is high."

Bethke has also written the novel *Headcrash,* in which his cyberpunk hero exploits the Internet to avenge himself after being fired from his computer programming job. The book received the 1995 Philip K. Dick award. Bethke's additional works include the 1996 book *Rebel Moon,* based on a computer game of the same name in which lunar colonists unite behind Dalton Starkiller in a seemingly doomed rebellion, and *Lamps on the Brow,* an anthology. Despite the outlandish characters and situations Bethke creates, according to information about Bethke published on a Warner Books website, he lives "a life of quiet bourgeois complacency in suburban Minnesota."

Works Cited

Bethke, Bruce, remarks on website, http://www.users.zetnet.co.uk/iplus/stories/cpunk.htm, March 13, 1999.

Patterson, Amos C., review of *Maverick, Kliatt,* September, 1991, p. 20.

Tyson, Edith, review of *Maverick, Voice of Youth Advocates,* December, 1990, pp. 293-294.

Warnerbooks.com website, http://www.twbookmark.com/authors/79/574/index.html.

For More Information See

BOOKS

Clute, John and Nicholls, Peter, editors, *The Encyclopedia of Science Fiction,* St. Martin's Press (New York City), 1993.

Science Fiction and Fantasy Literature, 1975-1991, Gale (Detroit, MI), 1992.

ON-LINE

Fashionmall.com, http://non.com/books/Bethke_Bruce/cc.html. March 13, 1999.*

* * *

BOSTOCK, Mike 1962-

Personal

Born August 29, 1962, in Bristol, England; son of Eric (a R.A.F. pilot and sales manager) and Barbara (Beavis) Bostock; partner: Helen Read (a designer). *Education:* Bath Academy of Art, Corsham, Wiltshire, England, B.A. (Honors in Illustration), 1984; University of Bristol, 1997-99. *Religion:* Church of England.

Addresses

Home and office—16 Ladas Rd., London, SE27 OUW, England.

Career

Freelance illustrator, London, England, 1984—.

Awards, Honors

Earthworm Award, Friends of the Earth, Junior Information Book Award, *Times Educational Supplement,* Kurt Maschler Award, and Parents' Choice Award, all 1993, all for *Think of an Eel;* runner-up, Mother Goose Award, 1994.

Illustrator

Karen Wallace, *Think of an Eel,* Walker Books, 1993.
Kathryn Lasky, *Pond Year,* Walker Books, 1995.
Karen Wallace, *Imagine You Are a Crocodile,* Hodder, 1996.
Judy Hindley, *A Song of Colours,* Walker Books, 1998.
Karen Wallace, *Imagine You Are a Dolphin,* Hodder, 1998.
Karen Wallace, *Gentle Giant Octopus,* Walker Books, 1998.

Work in Progress

"Continuing to develop picture book ideas on a variety of subjects."

Sidelights

Mike Bostock is the illustrator of the award-winning children's book *Think of an Eel,* as well as other critically acclaimed books for young people, including *Imagine You Are a Crocodile* and *Gentle Giant Octopus.*

Published in 1993, *Think of an Eel* was Bostock's first opportunity to illustrate a children's picture book. With text by Karen Wallace, the book traces the life cycle and habits of the eel from its birth in the Sargasso Sea, through its years in the ocean and its trip to freshwater, until it returns to the sea for spawning. *Horn Book* critic

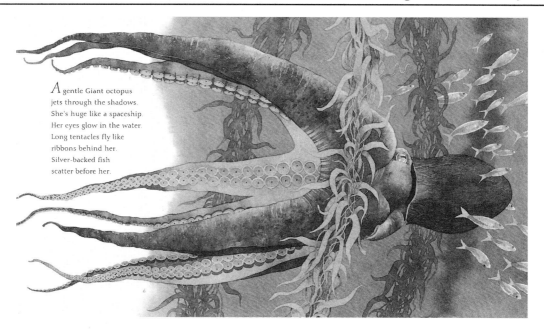

A mother octopus eyes her babies in Mike Bostock's iridescent watercolor paintings. (From Gentle Giant Octopus, *written by Karen Wallace.)*

Elizabeth S. Watson described Bostock's illustrations in *Think of an Eel* as "graceful, slithery watercolors, perfectly suited to the eel's underwater world."

Bostock collaborated with Wallace on several more books, including *Imagine You Are a Crocodile* and *Gentle Giant Octopus,* both of which follow the educational format of *Think of an Eel. Booklist* reviewer Carolyn Phelan noted the "well-conceived words and pictures" of *Think of an Eel,* then praised the similar success of *Imagine You Are a Crocodile,* claiming the book does "an exceptional job of suggesting how the world appears through crocodilian eyes and explaining why these ancient reptiles do the things they do." She later called Bostock's illustrations "beautiful" and "wonderfully effective."

Gentle Giant Octopus was also favorably received. A *Publishers Weekly* contributor found Bostock's illustrations to be "thoughtfully composed" and "tactile, accurate, and extremely attractive." Susan P. Bloom wrote in *Horn Book* that the author and illustrator "create ocean magic ... with simple elegance and beauty."

Commenting on his career as an illustrator, Bostock told *SATA:* "Since leaving art college in 1984 with a B.A. (Honors) in illustration I have enjoyed working full-time as an illustrator on a wide variety of jobs from editorial to advertising, book jackets to picture books. This range of experience has enabled me to continue learning about the combination of image and text and develop the sensitivity to apply this in differing situations. The sense of possibility on receiving a new text or layout with it's blank area marked up and awaiting my drawing is always a wonderfully exciting feeling.

"In 1992, I was commissioned to illustrate the children's picture book *Think of an Eel.* This first opportunity to work with narrative and create a sequence of images which combine with text across a thirty-two-page format made a big impact on me. It changed my direction to the extent that since that first commission I now work almost exclusively on children's picture books.

"This is because it is an area which I find uniquely challenging and stimulating. From background research, through initial rough layouts, to final finished artwork, every stage in the creation of every illustration for a picture book is a chance to learn something new, see a subject from a new angle, or apply a fresh idea. Hopefully that approach communicates an interest and a freshness to the images I create. The thought that these images may prompt the reader to feel those emotions too is fundamentally motivating and the most rewarding part of illustrating for children."

Works Cited

Bloom, Susan P., review of *Gentle Giant Octopus, Horn Book,* November-December, 1998, p. 757-58.

A review of *Gentle Giant Octopus, Publishers Weekly,* November 30, 1998, p. 70.

Phelan, Carolyn, review of *Imagine You Are a Crocodile, Booklist,* May 1, 1997, p. 1497.

Watson, Elizabeth S., review of *Think of an Eel, Horn Book,* July-August 1993, p. 478.

For More Information See

PERIODICALS

Booklist, May 15, 1993, p. 1695; May 15, 1995, p. 1652; November 15, 1998, p. 594.

Publishers Weekly, May 29, 1995, p. 84; March 2, 1998, p. 68

School Library Journal, December, 1993, p. 110; September, 1995, p. 181; July, 1997, p. 78; May, 1998, p. 133.

* * *

BRODY, Wendy
See STAUB, Wendy Corsi

* * *

BROWN, Tricia 1954-

Personal

Born August 14, 1954, in Rantoul, IL; daughter of Lawrence W., Sr. (a realtor) and Phyllis M. (a seamstress; maiden name, Larrigan; later surname, Walsh) Stinson; married Kenneth E. Olsen, December 2, 1973 (divorced, August, 1980); married Perry L. Brown (a geologist), June 7, 1986; children: (first marriage) Jennifer E. Olsen, Kristen E. Olsen. *Education:* University of Alaska, Fairbanks, B.A., 1983; University of Alaska, Anchorage, M.F.A., 1996. *Politics:* Independent. *Religion:* Baptist. *Hobbies and other interests:* Gardening, quilting, travel, Alaska history.

Addresses

Home—10155 NW St. Helens Rd., Portland, OR 97231. *Office*—P.O. Box 10306, Portland, OR 97296-0306. *E-mail*—triciabrown49@hotmail.com.

Career

University of Alaska, Fairbanks, graphic artist for Alaska Sea Grant Program, 1980-82; *Fairbanks Daily News-Miner,* Fairbanks, features editor, 1983-86; *Alaska,* Anchorage, AK, regional editor, 1987-89; *Anchorage Daily News,* Anchorage, feature writer, between 1989 and 1993; *Alaska,* editor, 1994-96; freelance writer and editor, 1996-99; Graphic Arts Center Publishing Co., Portland, OR, acquisitions editor, Alaska Northwest Books and WestWinds Press, 1999—. Alaska Center for the Book, member of board of directors; Writing Rendezvous (state writing conference), coordinator, 1993, 1995, 1999. *Member:* Alaska Center for the Book.

Awards, Honors

Writing awards from Alaska Press Club and Sigma Delta Xi, between 1983 and 1990; "Best of show" award, Rarified Light state photographic exhibition, 1992; Bronze Award, regional magazine of the year, City and Regional Magazine Association, 1996, and Gold Award, best travel issue, International Regional Magazine Association, 1997, both for *Alaska;* Reading Magic Award, *Parenting,* 1998, Independent Publishers Award, young adult/children nonfiction category, Independent Publishers Association, 1999, and Benjamin Franklin Award for Juvenile Nonfiction, Publishers Marketing Association, 1999, all for *Children of the Midnight Sun.*

Writings

(Editor) Lew Freedman, *Iditarod Silver: Twenty-Five Years of the Iditarod Trail Sled Dog Race,* illustrated by Jon Van Zyle, photographs by Jeff Schultz, Epicenter Press (Seattle, WA), 1997.

(Editor) *The Alaska Almanac,* Alaska Northwest Books, 1997, 1998, 1999.

Iditarod Country: Exploring the Route of the Last Great Race, photographs by Schultz, Epicenter Press, 1998.

Children of the Midnight Sun: Young Native Voices of Alaska (juvenile), illustrated by Roy Corral, Alaska Northwest Books (Seattle, WA), 1998.

(Editor) Otis Hahn and Alice Vollmar, *Pay Dirt: Fortunes and Misfortunes of an Alaskan Gold Miner,* Epicenter Press, 1998.

(Editor) Freedman, *Fishing for a Laugh: Reel Humor from Alaska,* illustrated by Sandy Jamieson, Epicenter Press, 1998.

(Editor) Ray Hudson, *Moments Rightly Placed: An Aleutian Memoir,* illustrated by Debra Dubac, Epicenter Press, 1998.

Lessons My Sled Dog Taught Me: Humor and Heartwarming Tails from Alaska's Mushers, illustrated by Amanda Brannon, Epicenter Press, 1999.

Tricia Brown

Brown profiles the lives of eight Native Alaskan children in her first book for children.

(With Nancy Lange Simmerman) *Wild Alaska,* Mountaineers Books (Seattle, WA), 1999.

(Editor) *Alaskan Wilderness,* Discovery Communications (Bethesda, MD), 1999.

(Editor) Freedman, *Father of the Iditarod: The Joe Redington Story,* Epicenter Press, 1999.

(Editor) Brian Patrick O'Donoghue, *Honest Dogs: A Story of Triumph and Regret from the World's Toughest Sled Dog Race,* Epicenter Press, 1999.

Fairbanks: Alaska's Heart of Gold, photographs by Roy Corral, Alaska Northwest Books, 2000.

Contributor to periodicals, including *Where* and *Alaska and the Yukon.*

Work in Progress

The Alaska Highway, a travel guide, to be published by Fulcrum Books; *Groucho's Eyebrows,* juvenile fiction, to be published by Alaska Northwest Books.

Sidelights

Tricia Brown told *SATA:* "For most of my career, I've written for adults, mostly in newspaper and magazine features. In the last few years, however, I've directed my attention toward books, both as a writer and as a freelance editor. I've edited a dozen books for various publishers—Alaska travel guidebooks, autobiography, history, memoir, an annual fact book about Alaska. All of it has been for adults. My single book for children, *Children of the Midnight Sun: Young Native Voices of Alaska,* has attracted more critical attention than any of my other work. Now people are calling me a children's book author! Mostly I think of myself simply as a writer, and children are one special audience out of many. I have really enjoyed hearing from the kids who have read *Children of the Midnight Sun,* and I have another children's book in the works.

"I was raised in Kankakee County, Illinois, where the land is flat and small towns are surrounded by fields of corn and soybeans. My entry into 'publishing' came at age eighteen in 1973, when I was hired as an ad-taker at the *Waukegan News-Sun.*

"In July, 1978, our little family (with my then-husband and our two preschoolers) drove up the Alaska Highway in a Chevy Blazer. We pulled a snowmobile trailer that was overloaded with our belongings, all crammed into a large plywood box on the little frame. It had terrible structural problems and its tires were so small compared to the truck tires that they did not just go flat, they exploded! On that four-thousand-mile journey to a new life in Alaska, we suffered twelve flat tires, along with a broken tongue and a broken axle on the trailer. The beauty outweighed the misery, though. I had never seen such incredible landscapes. At age twenty-four, I entered the University of Alaska journalism program, believing that I would study advertising, but one semester of news-writing class sold me on writing. With my degree, I was hired as features editor for the *Fairbanks Daily News-Miner.* There I had the privilege of founding their Sunday news magazine, *Heartland.* After eight years in Fairbanks, I moved to Anchorage, where I worked variously for the *Anchorage Daily News* and *Alaska* magazine. While my daughters were in high school, I worked for a nonprofit youth ministry called Anchorage Youth for Christ. I also completed a master of fine arts degree at the University of Alaska, Anchorage.

"For the last few years, I have been a board member for the Alaska Center for the Book, a nonprofit group that promotes literacy statewide. I have enjoyed helping to organize our annual statewide writing conference, the Writing Rendezvous. As for my own work, in November 1999, I left Alaska after twenty-one years to join the staff of Graphic Arts Center Publishing in Portland, Oregon. My two girls are grown now, and I am a grandmother. Gardening and quilting are my other favorite things. It's hard to believe I was in Alaska that long and, truthfully, I did complain about the cold more than I should have. But the tradeoffs were worth it. Despite the distance from major publishing markets in the 'Lower 48,' Alaskan writers find plenty of publishing outlets through excellent regional houses, as well as attention from national publishers who come to see this beautiful state for themselves. It's a great place for creative people to live."

For More Information See

PERIODICALS

Booklist, July, 1998, p. 1874.

Horn Book, July-August, 1998, p. 507.

Kirkus Reviews, June 1, 1998, p. 809.
Publishers Weekly, May 18, 1998, pp. 80-81.
School Library Journal, July, 1998, p. 103; September, 1998, p. 214.

*   *   *

BUCKLEY, James, Jr. 1963-

Personal

Born January 25, 1963, in Washington, DC; son of James F. and Alice Buckley; married Patricia Kelley (a graphic designer), 1992; children: Conor. *Education:* University of California, Berkeley, B.A. (English), 1985; Radcliffe Publishing Course, 1985. *Religion:* Catholic.

Addresses

Home—125 Santa Rosa Pl., Santa Barbara, CA 93109. *E-mail*—jbuckley@earthlink.net.

Career

East West Network, New York, senior editor, 1988-89; *Sports Illustrated,* New York, editorial project manager, 1989-93; *Santa Barbara Independent,* Santa Barbara, CA, columnist, 1993-94; NFL Publishing, Los Angeles, associate editor, 1994—; Shoreline Publishing Group, editorial director, 1999—. Member of board of directors of Santa Barbara Foresters Baseball Club.

Awards, Honors

Sports Story of the Year, California Newspaper Publishers Association, 1994; Top 10 Sports Books for Children, *Booklist,* 1998, for *America's Greatest Game.*

Writings

The Lost Cowboy Ghost, Scholastic, 1996.
America's Greatest Game, Hyperion, 1998.
NFL Rules!, Hyperion, 1998.
Football (DK "Eyewitness" series), Dorling Kindersley, 1999.
Baseball (DK "Eyewitness" series), Dorling Kindersley, 2000.

Also author of *GI Joe at Iwo Jima,* Scholastic, 1997; *GI Joe at D-Day,* Scholastic, 1998; and *Pokemon Puzzles,* Troll, 1999.

Work in Progress

Super Bowl, another book in the "Eyewitness" series, for Dorling Kindersley; a visual dictionary of baseball.

Sidelights

James Buckley, Jr., told *SATA:* "For as long as I can remember, sports have been central to my life, whether as a player, a fan, or a coach. Since high school, I've known that I wanted to be a writer, and I've been able to combine my loves for sports and writing.

"I sort of fell into writing for children, and enjoyed it immensely from the start. And through a variety of adventures in the publishing trade on both coasts, I have arrived at a point where I seem to be doing nothing but writing about sports for kids.

"But shouldn't I be writing about something more serious for kids, something that will help them develop as members of 21st-century society? Is sports something kids should read about when there are more important things out there? To people who think that, I say 'Lighten up.' When presented in the right way (and I hope readers and parents agree that our books are done in that 'right way'), sports can teach as many lessons as a lecture from a teacher. History, character, perseverance, style, physical fitness, goal-setting and goal-achieving—all these are part of the story of sports in the books I've been lucky enough to write or help create.

"Are there things wrong with sports? Sure, but why focus on the bad things and ignore the good things? My books focus on the good things. Let kids learn the bad stuff later. When they read the books I've written about sports, they're having fun. Do we teach them some things, too? Well, sure.

"But don't tell them that."

Buckley has written several books about football, including *America's Greatest Game* and *Football.* Critic Richard Luzer wrote in a *School Library Journal* review of *America's Greatest Game:* "This book consists mainly of outstanding full-color photographs of players at various levels of proficiency from peewee to pro." Luzer added that the book was "[c]ertain to be a popular browsing item for young football fans."

Works Cited

Luzer, Richard, review of *America's Greatest Game: The Real Story of Football and the NFL, School Library Journal,* February 1999, p. 114.

For More Information See

PERIODICALS

Booklist, November 15, 1998, p. 582.

*   *   *

BURKE, Patrick 1958-

Personal

Born January 20, 1958, in Athens, Greece; son of Donald Burke (a journalist) and Helena Malinowska-Wayne (a journalist). *Education:* University of Bristol, B.A. (honors); University of London, M.A. (German).

Addresses

Home—11 Holland St., Brighton, BN2 2WB, England. *E-mail*—BurkeP@wmin.ac.uk.

Career

Journal of European Nuclear Disarmament, London, England, sub-editor, then business manager, 1983-87; Oxford Research Group, Oxford, England, researcher, 1987-88; freelance author, editor, and translator, 1988-94.

Writings

(Editor) *The Nuclear Weapons World: Who, How, and Where,* Greenwood Press (Westport, CT), 1988.
Who's Who in Nuclear Weapons, Greenwood Press, 1989.
Germany, Thomson (New York City), 1995.
Revolution in Europe, 1989, Thomson, 1995.
Eastern Europe: Bulgaria, Czech Republic, Hungary, Poland, Romania, Slovakia, Raintree Steck-Vaughn (Austin, TX), 1997.

Work in Progress

Academic research at the Centre for the Study of Democracy, University of Westminster, London, on the topic of the peace movement and Eastern Europe in the 1980s.

Sidelights

Reflecting his interest in twentieth-century history, Patrick Burke has written several nonfiction books for young adults and adults. In *The Nuclear Weapons World,* Burke examined the involvement of the United States, the then-Soviet Union, the United Kingdom, France, and the People's Republic of China in the race to build nuclear arsenals. Basing his study on copious research, he explains how decisions about the development and/or acquisition of nuclear weapons are made by each nation. The book includes biographies of more than 750 individuals from around the world who were involved with nuclear weapons development, including nuclear scientists. Burke also details the hierarchies existing within various governments that developed in response to concerns over accountability for nuclear-related decision making. Reviewing the work for *Booklist,* a reviewer concluded: "*The Nuclear Weapons World* provides a useful unbiased overview of this topic for public and academic libraries."

In *Revolution in Europe,* Burke turned to a historic moment in twentieth-century history: the collapse of communism in the Union of Soviet Socialist Republics beginning in 1989. In a "well-written and very interesting" narrative, according to Vee Holliday in *Books for Keeps,* Burke outlines the reasons why the communist regime failed in the Soviet Union, and how Soviet head of state Mikhail Gorbachev's glasnost reform policies both accelerated the demise of communism in his country and set the stage for fundamental changes in the political culture of Eastern Europe. In his book, *Eastern Europe,* Burke focuses on the six countries formerly part of the Soviet Union that are commonly referred to as "Eastern Europe." Using a format that encourages comparisons between the countries—Poland, Hungary, Romania, Bulgaria, Slovakia, and the Czech Republic—Burke provides readers with an overview of life in each nation, including climate, geography, population, major types of industry, and a glimpse of daily life. "This [format] shows us that the countries have fewer differences than things in common and provides a well-illustrated look at the post-independence scenario," explained Ted Percy in *Books for Keeps.* The "strength" of *Eastern Europe,* remarked Elizabeth Talbot in *School Library Journal,* lies in its "emphasis on geography and . . . attractive format for quick overviews."

Works Cited

Holliday, Vee, review of *Revolution in Europe, Books for Keeps,* January, 1996, p. 17.
Review of *The Nuclear Weapons World, Booklist,* September 15, 1989, pp. 207, 209.
Percy, Ted, review of *Eastern Europe, Books for Keeps,* September, 1997, p. 28.
Talbot, Elizabeth, review of *Eastern Europe, School Library Journal,* August, 1997, p. 164.*

* * *

BURSZTYNSKI, Sue 1953-

Personal

Born in 1953; daughter of Ben (a textile engineer) and Mila (Altbaum) Bursztynski. *Education:* Monash University, B.A. (English literature; with honors); Diploma of Education; Royal Melbourne Institute of Technology, Graduate Diploma of Librarianship; additional studies at Inner Melbourne Institute of Technical and Further Education. *Hobbies and other interests:* Reading science fiction, popular science, early music, folk music, Renaissance dance, belly-dancing, handcrafting.

Addresses

E-mail—greatraven@netspace.net.au.

Career

Teacher-librarian in the Victoria, Australia, school system; Sunshine Secondary College, Melbourne, currently teacher and librarian; freelance writer. *Member:* Australian Society of Authors, Victorian Fellowship of Australian Writers, Australian Library and Information Association, Australian Education Union.

Awards, Honors

Mary Grant Bruce Short Story Award for Children's Literature, 1983, 1987; quarter-finalist, Writers of the Future Competition, for science fiction, 1991; runner-up, *Family Circle* writing competition, 1991; Notable Australian Children's Book, Australian Children's Book Council, 1996, for *Potions to Pulsars: Women Doing Science.*

Writings

Monsters and Creatures of the Night, Allen & Unwin (London), 1994.

Potions to Pulsars: Women Doing Science, Allen & Unwin, 1995, Independent Publishers Group, 1996.

Starwalkers: Explorers of the Unknown, Omnibus, 1998.

Contributor of short stories and articles to *N.S.W. School Magazine, Family Circle, Eye of Newt, Centero, Front Row Magazine,* the anthology *Inter Alia,* and the "Spinouts" series of children's science fiction.

Work in Progress

A young adult novel set in modern Melbourne, a young adult fantasy novel, and a book on archeologists to be published by Nelson.

Sidelights

Australian teacher and author Sue Bursztynski's books for children and young adults emphasize the fantastic in the realm of reality. In her first book, *Monsters and Creatures of the Night,* the author investigates numerous legends about frightening creatures such as Dracula, Frankenstein, the Loch Ness monster, Big Foot, were-wolves, dragons, and other mysterious beings such as fairies, ghosts, and goblins. Often times, noted a reviewer in *Junior Bookshelf,* Bursztynski's research reveals a hoax at the source of the legend. "The result is a fascinating collection of material," the features of which will appeal equally to children frightened by and attracted to scary phenomena, according to the reviewer.

Bursztynski's second book, *Potions to Pulsars,* features the life stories of seventeen women scientists ranging from the fourth century B.C. to the twentieth century A.D. and focusing on the difficulties each woman overcame in establishing herself in the male-dominated professions of science. In *Starwalkers,* Bursztynski's focus shifts to the science of conquering outer space. In this book, the author tells the story of astronauts and the space programs in several countries, providing "an excellent starting point for any upper primary student or lower secondary student with a project on, or an interest in, astronauts and space exploration," averred Jennifer R. Poulter in *Magpies.*

As Bursztynski told *SATA:* "I tell stories. I always have, since my Grade Two teacher put me up in front of the class to ad-lib. Currently, though I have a novel doing

Sue Bursztynski and nephew, Max Joel.

Readers share the fascinating true experiences of space travelers such as Yuri Gagarin, the first man in space.

the rounds and two more being written, I'm telling stories through non-fiction of the 'docu-drama' variety. Children, especially boys, enjoy *true* stories. You could use all my books to complete school assignments, I suppose, but that's not what they're for.

"I know it's unlikely a child will say: 'Oh, wow, a book about women scientists!' (though mine has generated a fan phone-call!), but *Potions to Pulsars: Women Doing Science* was a story that needed telling. When I told it to a children's club, they were fascinated by my heroines, even the boys. I chose my scientists carefully, women who had led exciting or bizarre lives, and opened each chapter with a hook to draw in my readers. (How about "'Kill her!" shouted the churchman.'?) I hoped that the young researcher would go on reading because this was good stuff. Many school libraries actually put my books in the fiction section to make them easier to find by browsers.

"I learn something new from each bout of research. *Monsters and Creatures of the Night,* my first book, was the only one for which I already had extensive background knowledge, and even that needed research. To write *Potions to Pulsars,* I had to bone up on my biology, astronomy, physics, and chemistry, so I could explain what my heroines had achieved.

"My third book, *Starwalkers: Explorers of the Unknown,* was the most pleasure to research and write. There was all that space science to study, of course—rockets and spacesuits and fuels and all those things children *will* ask you when you talk in public, such as: 'How do you go to the toilet in space?' (I get asked this every time and adore answering!)

"I also used the NASA web site and books and articles written by the astronauts themselves, because I wanted to tell a human story, not just an exciting one. So there were Shannon Lucid's letters from MIR space station, about corrupting poor cosmonauts with Jell-O and finishing an exciting novel only to find it was a series and the nearest bookshop was down on Earth. There was Andy Thomas's sense of wonder at the flakes of ice flying from the space shuttle and Yuri Gagarin's joyousness at a parachute ride down to earth and Ed White's at floating around outside his ship like Buck Rogers, and Michael Collins worrying about having to leave his companions behind if the moonwalk ended in disaster, even as he reveled in the quiet of space in the *Columbia.*

"My fiction is mostly fantasy, with a little SF; for years, my only published work was short fantasy fiction, in small-press publications, as well as a few articles and book reviews. I only discovered I was a children's writer when I won the Mary Grant Bruce Short Story Award, sharing it with Robin Klein, who was one of Australia's top children's writers at the time. That encouraged me to keep going in that genre, which I had always loved reading.

"I have a day job because in Australia very few writers have the luxury of writing full-time—our population is too small—but I'm lucky enough to be working with my public, as a teacher-librarian, so I doubt I'd give it up entirely even if I suddenly found myself able to write full-time.

"You can't write for human beings if you spend all day every day by yourself, can you?"

Works Cited

Review of *Monsters and Creatures of the Night, Junior Bookshelf,* October, 1995, p. 182.

Neale, Mary J., review of *Potions to Pulsars, School Librarian,* August, 1997, pp. 162-63.

Poulter, Jennifer R., review of *Starwalkers, Magpies,* May, 1998, pp. 43-44.

C

CARRYL, Charles E(dward) 1841-1920

Personal

Born December 30, 1841, in New York; died July 3, 1920; son of Nathan Taylor Carryl; married Mary Wetmore in 1869; children: Guy Wetmore Carryl and Constance Carryl.

Career

Worked in business for railroad companies, 1857-72; stock broker, 1874-1908; children's book writer, 1884-1920.

Writings

The Stock Exchange Primer, Sears & Cole (New York City), 1882.
Davy and The Goblin; or, What Followed Reading "Alice's Adventures in Wonderland," Ticknor (Boston, MA), 1885.
The Admiral's Caravan, Century (New York City), 1892.
Stories of the Sea, Scribners (New York City), 1893.
The River Syndicate and Other Stories, Harper (New York City), 1899.
Charades by an Idle Man, Little, Brown (Boston, MA), 1911.
A Capital Ship; or The Walloping Window-blind, Whittlesey House (New York City), 1963.

Sidelights

Charles E. Carryl is best known for his unashamedly silly children's books, which relate the kinds of fantastical adventures found in the work of Lewis Carroll. Carryl wrote his stories for his own children (one of whom would grow to be a writer), but when he published his stories they delighted children throughout the States. "Though forgotten by the young of today," explained Douglas Street in the *Dictionary of Literary Biography,* "Carryl, at the end of the last century, was hailed as the American Lewis Carroll, his nonsense classic *Davy and the Goblin* (1885), the *Alice in Wonderland* of America.... *The Goblin* expanded the realm of possibility in American fantasy for children."

Carryl was born on December 30, 1841, in New York. His father, Nathan Taylor Carryl, was a well-to-do businessman, wealthy enough to send his child to private schools. However, by sixteen, Charles had begun his primary career as a businessman. He worked for railroad companies until 1872, and he became a stockbroker two years later—this was to be his profession until 1908. While working as an officer of the railroad companies, however, he began the other important work of his life; he married Mary Wetmore in 1869 and together they raised a family of two, Guy and Constance.

Carryl raised his children through storytelling. The "nonsense fantasy world," as Street called Carryl's milieu, was developed for his children's amusement, but Carryl began in 1884 to amuse other children as well, by publishing the stories in a journal, *St. Nicholas.* Those stories were serialized and then published as *Davy and the Goblin* (1885). In his first book, Carryl relates the story of a little boy's "believing voyage"—a series of adventures on which he is led by a goblin. Carryl's work is openly reminiscent of Carroll's, and even begins with his hero, Davy, reading *Alice in Wonderland* on a snowy Christmas eve. As Street explained, "It is undeniable that his creations were influenced by the nonsense stories of Lewis Carroll, yet Carryl was not merely an imitator. *Davy and the Goblin* and *The Admiral's Caravan* (1892) employ a technique of blending nonsense and reality that in modern terms might be considered cinematic." By following this world's logic in a bizarre fantasy land, moreover, the silliness of both were emphasized. Moreover, Carryl always brought his sources vividly to the reader's attention; in some parts of Davy's journey, the boy met old literary favorites such as Sinbad the Sailor, Jack (from Jack and the Beanstalk), Robin Hood and Robinson Crusoe. In this way, Carryl was able to encourage his younger readers to love

The captain sat in a commodore's hat
And dined in a royal way
On toasted pigs and pickles and figs
And gummery bread each day.

A crew of high-spirited children sail an extraordinary ship in Charles E. Carryl's nonsensical **A Capital Ship; or The Walloping Window-blind,** *adapted and illustrated by Jim LaMarche.*

reading, and to find those books Davy seemed to know so well.

Carryl's second novel, *The Admiral's Caravan,* was put before the public much as *Davy* was: it first ran as a serial in *St. Nicholas,* and was then published in book form in 1892. The stories in it were not composed in the same way as *Davy and the Goblin,* however: by the time Carryl wrote his second book, his stories were no longer spun for his children's pleasure, but rather because it pleased Carryl. *The Admiral's Caravan* chronicles the adventures of a little girl named Dorothy, who follows some living statues on a journey into a nonsensical world. In *The Admiral's Caravan,* nonsense played an even larger role than it did in *Davy and the Goblin,* for Carryl at times allowed the narrative to become carried away with verbal tomfoolery, puns and quibbles. "There are instances in this story," Street commented, "in which nonsense and wordplay seem to serve the author's whim, having little impact on the plot itself." The book was less

successful than *Davy,* perhaps because of this deeper appreciation for sophisticated language games.

Carryl's next books, *Stories of the Sea* (1893), *The River Syndicate and Other Stories* (1899), and *Charades by an Idle Man* (1911), each followed in the path of the first two books: they blended nonsense with logic in order to produce the weirdest and most amusing adventures. Carryl continued to write such stories until his death in 1920, and some of the final nonsense lyrics were collected and published in 1963. That last collection, *A Capital Ship; or The Walloping Window-blind* (1963), was received warmly, suggesting that Carryl's nutty writing continues to allure children. *Christian Science Monitor* contributor Guernsey La Pelley wrote of the volume: "A buoyant book with the kind of silly charm which usually appeals to beginning readers, and will also make older readers smile nostalgically."

Works Cited

La Pelley, Guernsey, review of *A Capital Ship; or The Walloping Window-blind, Christian Science Monitor,* November 14, 1963, p. 2B.

Street, Douglas, essay in *Dictionary of Literary Biography,* Volume 42: *American Writers for Children before 1900,* Gale (Detroit, MI), 1985.

For More Information See

BOOKS

Attebery, Brian, *The Fantasy Tradition in American Literature,* Indiana University Press (Bloomington), 1980.

Jordan, Alice M., *From Rollo to Tom Sawyer and Other Papers,* Horn Book (Boston), 1948.

Science Fiction and Fantasy Literature, Gale, 1979.

PERIODICALS

Saturday Review of Literature, May 4, 1940, pp. 7-14.*

* * *

CARTER, David A. 1957-

Personal

Born March 4, 1957, in Salt Lake City, UT; son of H. Craig (a draftsperson) and Lavon (a homemaker; maiden name, Gill) Carter; married Noelle Lokvig (an illustrator and author), August 10, 1985; children: Molly, Emma. *Education:* Attended Utah State University. *Hobbies and other interests:* Skiing, travel, gardening, tennis.

Addresses

Home and office—110 Sylvan Vista Dr., Auburn, CA 95603. *E-mail*—PopArt123@aol.com

Career

Graphic designer and advertising illustrator, late 1970s; Intervisual communications, Inc., California, artist, paper engineer, and book designer until 1987; freelance author and illustrator of children's books since 1987.

Writings

AUTHOR AND ILLUSTRATOR

How Many Bugs in a Box?, Simon & Schuster (New York, NY), 1988.
What's in My Pocket?, Putnam (New York, NY), 1989.
More Bugs in Boxes, Simon & Schuster Books for Young Readers (New York, NY), 1990.
Surprise Party, Grosset & Dunlap (New York, NY), 1990.
Playful Pandas, National Geographic Society (Washington), 1991.
In a Dark, Dark Wood, Simon & Schuster, 1991.
George Santayana, Chelsea House (New York, NY), 1992.
Jingle Bugs, Simon & Schuster, 1992.
Opposites, Simon & Schuster, 1993.
Colors, Simon & Schuster, 1993.

Counting, Simon & Schuster, 1993.
I'm Shy, Simon & Schuster Books for Young Readers, 1993.
Says Who?, Simon & Schuster Books for Young Readers, 1993.
Alpha Bugs, Little Simon (New York, NY), 1994.
Love Bugs, Little Simon, 1995.
Feely Bugs, Little Simon, 1995.
Salvador Dali, Chelsea House, 1995.
Bugs in Space, Simon & Schuster, 1997.
Finger Bugs Love Bug, Simon & Schuster Children's (New York, NY), 1997.
Bugs at Play, Little Simon, 1997.
Busy Bugs, Lazy Bugs, Little Simon, 1997.
Stinky Bugs, Little Simon, 1998.

ILLUSTRATOR

Peter Seymour, *What's in the Jungle?,* Holt (New York, NY), 1988.
Seymour, *If Pigs Could Fly,* Child's Play, 1988.
Seymour, *What's in the Prehistoric Forest?,* Holt, 1990.
Seymour, *What's in the Deep Blue Sea?,* Holt, 1990.
Noelle Carter, *I'm a Little Mouse,* Holt, 1990.
Noelle Carter, *Merry Christmas, Little Mouse,* Holt, 1993.
Noelle Carter, *Peek-A-Boo Little Mouse,* Holt, 1993.
Seymour, *What's in the Cave?,* Holt, 1995.
Grace Maccarone, *Cars, Cars, Cars,* Scholastic (New York, NY), 1995.
Seymour, *What's at the Beach?,* Holt, 1995.
Sarah Weeks, *Noodles: A Pop-Up Book,* HarperCollins Children's Books (New York, NY), 1996.
Mary Serfozo, *There's a Square: A Book About Shapes,* Scholastic, 1996.
Alan Benjamin, *Curious Critters: A Pop-Up Menagerie,* Little Simon, 1998.

Carter is also the author or illustrator of several other pop-up books for children.

Work in Progress

The Nutcracker, a pop-up book.

Sidelights

David A. Carter is the author or illustrator for several dozen pop-up books for young children, several of them written with his wife, Noelle Carter. His works have won praise for their clever tactile surfaces and appealing shapes and colors. As Carter told *SATA:* "I am often asked by children where I get my ideas for books. I have spent many hours contemplating this question and I still do not have the answer.

"In the beginning of my career as an author, illustrator, and paper engineer, I honestly did not give much thought to why I created my books. They just happened, they were a compilation of many influences. I have always been an artist. I have always been very stimulated by visual images. To this day the first thing I do when I pick up any book, including a novel, is look for pictures.

The colorful, comical bugs in David A. Carter's self-illustrated counting book teach young children the numbers from one to ten. *(Cover illustration by Carter.)*

"A few years ago I received an e-mail from a student of children's literature. She asked a couple of questions about my work, and one in particular got me to thinking. She asked me to describe an average day in the life of an eight-year-old David Carter. My answer was simple. I would play outside all day spending hours on end in the fields around my home, lifting up rocks and boards in search of bugs. It was always very exciting to lift up the rocks because I never knew what I would find. I actually started to chuckle at this answer. Lifting something to find a bug was one of my greatest thrills as a child and that is exactly what I had created, unconsciously, in *How Many Bugs in a Box?*"

How Many Bugs in a Box? would be the first of many titles from Carter that used insects as a theme to enchant preschoolers. This debut was published in 1987, the same year that Carter left his job with a publisher to become a freelance writer, illustrator, and paper engineer. *How Many Bugs in a Box?* is a counting lesson,

with successive page spreads depicting a different type and number of insects, such as "seven space bugs." A *Publishers Weekly* reviewer found it rich in "startlingly bright illustrations" that might easily entice young readers.

After working or collaborating on several other books, Carter returned to the insect world with the 1990 title *More Bugs in Boxes.* Here, he created a series of questions to lead the young reader into guessing the contents of each box. The bugs revealed were, like the pages themselves, drawn in vivid colors and also boasted interesting textures—spitfire flies are silvery, for instance, while basketball bugs possess a rubbery texture. Anne Connor, reviewing it for *School Library Journal,* called *More Bugs in Boxes* an "engineering feat" with "sometimes amazing effects."

Carter has also won praise for other works that play upon children's fascination with the animal kingdom.

His 1989 book for preschoolers, *What's in My Pocket?*, employs a series of five animals whose heads pop up as the pages are turned. Carter's text poses questions that lead the reader to open another flap on each page, a pocket for the creature that, when lifted, shows what the animal's favorite food is—the rabbit has a carrot, the mouse hides cheese, and so forth. A reviewer for *Junior Bookshelf* found that "the animals have distinctive characters," and "altogether, there are many things to notice and plenty of movement" in *What's in My Pocket?* Reviewing it in *Bulletin of the Center for Children's Books,* Zena Sutherland admired Carter's talent for "nice composition and bright color in pictures with no clutter."

With his wife, author and illustrator Noelle Carter, Carter has also created such titles as *I'm a Little Mouse.* This story centers on a young mouse who has become lost; he then goes about introducing himself to other animals by explaining that he has fuzzy gray fur and a long tail. In response, the other creatures describe their unique characteristics to him, such as "slippery shiny skin" or "long shaggy hair." Carter created unusual simulations of such surfaces for young readers that reinforce the text. "Preschoolers will want to touch the mouse and his perky pals again and again," wrote a reviewer for *Publishers Weekly.*

Carter has also collaborated with several other authors of books for beginning readers, such as Mary Serfozo in their 1996 creation *There's a Square,* and Peter Seymour, with whom Carter has worked for several years. One of their joint efforts, *What's in the Deep Blue Sea?,* offered an unusual strategy: a young tiger stalks through the jungle on his way to the water, where he looks down to see a pair of whiskers, much like his own, appraising him. Some of Carter's animals here hide behind lift-up flaps, and like many books in the pop-up genre, a grand finale is designed to electrify young children. In a review of this particular title, a *Publishers Weekly* reviewer called Carter's images "luxuriant" and commended "the use of dark, saturant color and dry over dry painting to create stunning spreads."

As Carter told *SATA:* "I still cannot explain the creative process that goes on in my mind, but discovering that link between my childhood curiosities and thrills and my books has something to do with where my ideas come from.

More of Carter's fun bugs teach children their colors. (Cover illustration by Carter.)

"My goal in creating a book is to engage this natural curiosity, to entertain with surprise and silliness and whenever possible to educate, because for me the end result of curiosity is learning.

"In recent years the term interactive has become popular in reference to computer software. Pop-up books are also interactive; of course to a big kid like myself the term interactive is nothing more than a big word for play. I believe children learn by playing. One of the things that I like most about pop-up books is that a child who may not be reading yet can interact, or play, with the book. My hope is that this will draw the young reader into the book and hopefully into reading in general.

"If my books can entertain and excite a child who is not a reader, and draw him or her into books and reading, then I have accomplished my goal.

"Have fun."

Works Cited

Connor, Anne, review of *More Bugs in a Box, School Library Journal,* August, 1990, p. 126.
Review of *How Many Bugs in a Box?, Publishers Weekly,* December 11, 1987, p. 62.
Review of *I'm a Little Mouse, Publishers Weekly,* January 11, 1991, p. 100.
Sutherland, Zena, review of *What's in My Pocket?, Bulletin of the Center for Children's Books,* October, 1989, p. 30.
Review of *What's in the Deep Blue Sea?, Publishers Weekly,* October 12, 1990, p. 62.
Review of *What's in My Pocket?, Junior Bookshelf,* February, 1990, p. 23.

For More Information See

PERIODICALS

Booklist, January 15, 1995, p. 937.
Bulletin of the Center for Children's Books, January, 1992, p. 120.
Publishers Weekly, October 12, 1990, p. 62; January 15, 1996, p. 461; May 25, 1998, p. 92.
School Library Journal, February, 1991, p. 74; December, 1995, p. 85.*

*   *   *

CATALANOTTO, Peter 1959-

Personal

Surname is pronounced "KA-ta-la-NOT-to"; born March 21, 1959, in Brooklyn, NY; son of Anthony (a printer) and Ella Virginia (a homemaker; maiden name, Lawrence) Catalanotto; married Jo-Ann Carrie Maynard (a photographer), August 8, 1989; children: Chelsea. *Education:* Pratt Institute, B.F.A., 1981. *Hobbies and other interests:* Basketball, reading.

Addresses

Home—4331 Wismer Rd., Doylestown, PA 18901.

Career

Freelance illustrator, New York City, 1982-87; freelance writer and illustrator of children's books, New York City, 1987—. *Exhibitions:* Catalanotto's work is displayed with the Mazza Collection in Findlay, OH, and at Keene State Gallery in New Hampshire, and has been with the permanent collection at the Elizabeth Stone Gallery in Birmingham, MI, since 1991.

Awards, Honors

"Most Promising New Artist," *Publishers Weekly,* 1989; "Best Book for Teens" designation, American Library Association, 1990, for *Soda Jerk;* "Keystone Book," Pennsylvania, 1991, for *Cecil's Story;* "Best Book of 1992" designation, *Publishers Weekly,* for *Who Came Down the Road?;* Carolyn Field Award, 1993, for *Dreamplace;* "Best Book of 1998" designation, *Booklist,* for *Letter to the Lake;* "Best Books of 1999" designation, *Booklinks,* for *Dad & Me* and *Book; All I See* and *Dylan's Day Out* both received Junior Literary Guild citations.

Writings

SELF-ILLUSTRATED

Dylan's Day Out, Orchard Books, 1989.
Mr. Mumble, Orchard Books, 1990.

Peter Catalanotto

Christmas Always ..., Orchard Books, 1991.
The Painter, Orchard Books, 1995.
Dad & Me, DK Publishing, 1999.

ILLUSTRATOR

Cynthia Rylant, *All I See,* Orchard Books, 1988.
Cynthia Rylant, *Soda Jerk* (poems), Orchard Books, 1990.
George Ella Lyon, *Cecil's Story,* Orchard Books, 1991.
Cynthia Rylant, *An Angel for Solomon Singer,* Orchard Books, 1992.
George Ella Lyon, *Who Came Down the Road?,* Orchard Books, 1992.
George Ella Lyon, *Dreamplace,* Orchard Books, 1993.
SuAnn Kiser, *The Catspring Somersault Flying One-Handed Flip-Flop,* Orchard Books, 1993.
Susan Patron, *Dark Cloud Strong Breeze,* Orchard Books, 1994.
George Ella Lyon, *Mama Is a Miner,* Orchard Books, 1994.
George Ella Lyon, *A Day at Damp Camp,* Orchard Books, 1996.
Megan McDonald, *My House Has Stars,* Orchard Books, 1996.
Angela Johnson, *The Rolling Store,* Orchard Books, 1997.
Susan Marie Swanson, *Getting Used to the Dark,* DK Publishing, 1997.
Susi G. Fowler, *Circle of Thanks,* Scholastic, 1998.
Marie Bradby, *The Longest Wait,* Orchard Books, 1998.
Susan Marie Swanson, *Letter to the Lake,* DK Publishing, 1998.
Gilda Berger, *Celebrate!,* Scholastic, 1998.
George Ella Lyon, *Book,* DK Publishing, 1999.

Also illustrator of numerous young adult book jackets, including Judy Blume's *Just as Long as We're Together.*

Work in Progress

Illustrating *We Wanted You,* by Liz Rosenberg, for DK Publishing, expected 2001.

Sidelights

Peter Catalanotto is an author and illustrator of children's books whose work one *Kirkus Reviews* critic called "explosively joyful and expressive." In both his self-illustrated titles and the books he has illustrated for other authors, Catalanotto has created an impressive and distinctive body of award-winning work, teaming up with authors such as Cynthia Rylant and George Ella Lyon and working with editor Richard Jackson of Orchard Books. As noted in *Children's Books and Their Creators,* "The imagery throughout Catalanotto's evanescent watercolors encases emotions and reflects ruminations while enhancing the texts and adding new dimensions to the stories." It is this enhancement of text with pictures for which Catalanotto is especially known. As he stated in an essay for the *Something about the Author Autobiography Series* (SAAS), "I think the most successful picture books are when the words and pictures are wed to create something bigger and better than when separate."

Tommy is eager to share the first space walk with his father when he gets home from work. (From Dad & Me, *written and illustrated by Catalanotto.)*

Catalanotto once told *SATA,* "I grew up in a household in East Northport, Long Island, where four of the five children went to art schools in New York City. I remember when I started school I was amazed to learn everybody didn't draw like my family. I was a shy child. Although I had a lot of friends, I most enjoyed solitude, reading, doing jigsaw puzzles, or spending endless hours drawing. Comic book characters were my favorite things to draw, especially 'Spider-Man.'

"Throughout elementary school and high school I found art classes frustrating, because they were taught at a level to accommodate all students. It wasn't until college that I found my abilities challenged. At Pratt Institute I studied illustration, drawing, and painting. It was at Pratt that I developed the watercolor technique I still use today. I think it's important for an artist to find a medium that suits his/her personality. Watercolor allows me to stop and start without a lot of preparation. I can be loose or tight with my style with washes and rendering."

After graduation from Pratt in 1981, Catalanotto started freelance illustrating, working initially for newspapers, where he did most of his painting in black and white. From the newspaper work, he started getting assignments from magazines such as *Reader's Digest, Family Circle, Woman's Day,* and *Redbook.* Then in 1984 he started painting the covers of young adult book jackets. It was this illustration work that led him to his association with Richard Jackson at Orchard Books in 1987. "I did a couple of jackets for Orchard Books,"

Catalanotto told *SATA*, "including Judy Blume's *Just as Long as We're Together*. The editor, Richard Jackson, offered me a picture-book manuscript, *All I See*, written by Cynthia Rylant. I became enamored with the process of creating paintings for an entire story. The research included spending time on a lake, since this was the setting for the story. I spent thirteen hours in a rowboat, sketching and photographing the lake at all angles and times of the day. Seasick and sunburned, I started my sketches. As the months on this project passed, Jackson and I became friends and had many discussions on writing and illustrating books for children."

This eventually led to Catalanotto's self-illustrated picture book, *Dylan's Day Out,* done in black and white and detailing the adventures of a Dalmatian with a serious case of cabin fever. The book was well received and inspired Catalanotto to pursue further solo efforts in addition to the illustration work he was doing for other writers. In 1989 came his second solo title, *Mr. Mumble.* Catalanotto explained to *SATA:* "My own shyness as a child inspired this off-beat tale of one being misunderstood—a feeling I think most people, especially children, can relate to. I tried to create a character I felt everybody knew, so when I'm approached and told 'Mr.

Mumble is exactly like my grandfather,' I feel like I succeeded." A third picture book followed, *Christmas Always . . . ,* a story of a girl who gets more visitors than she expects on Christmas Eve. "When my parents would have parties on Christmas Eve," Catalanotto recalled, "I was always sent to bed long before the party ended. This story is simply what I wished happened to me, instead of being in that bedroom all by myself."

By this time, book illustration had become Catalanotto's creative focus. "I think writing and illustrating picture books suits my personality much more than simply illustrating book jackets and magazine articles," Catalanotto told *SATA*. "I can be quiet and subtle with my work while trying to catch someone's eye. A book jacket yells at you to take it off the shelf. An entire picture book slowly unfolds before you, almost inviting you to stay."

Meanwhile, Catalanotto was also doing illustration work for other authors. "In 1989, I did the paintings for *Soda Jerk,* a collection of poems by Cynthia Rylant," Catalanotto recalled for *SATA*. "Spending days in a soda shop/pharmacy (it took me weeks to find one), I sketched and photographed the people of Hudson, Ohio, as they

One rock is as smooth as a candle. The speckles on it remind me of dragonflies darting after bugs.

Catlanotto's striking paintings depict Rosie's memories of summer at the lake. (*From* Letter to the Lake, *written by Susan Marie Swanson.*)

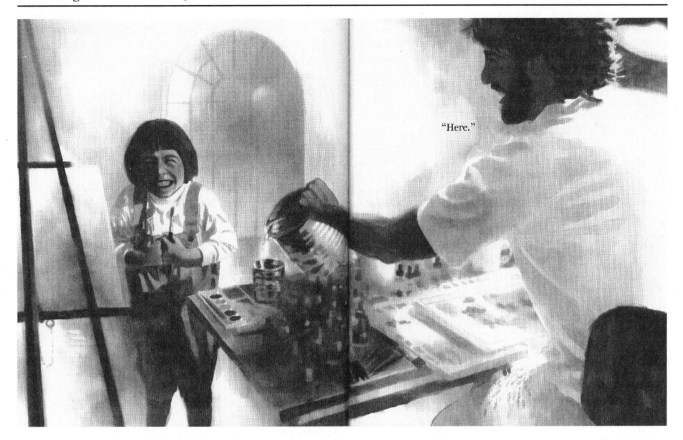

"Here."

A work-at-home artist finds time to spend with his daughter. (From The Painter, *written and illustrated by Catalanotto.*)

entered looking for cold drinks and cold remedies. It was at this soda fountain that I first met Cynthia Rylant. This surprises many since we previously did *All I See* together. Usually the author and illustrator are kept apart (unless, of course, they collaborated initially before presenting the book to a publishing house). I agree with the tactic of keeping them separate. This way the illustrator's approach is different from the author's. I believe the illustrations for a text have to be more than just beautiful paintings. They should add new dimensions to the text, not merely repeat in pictures what the writer has said in words." Catalanotto went on to a third collaborative effort with Rylant, *An Angel for Solomon Singer.*

The illustrations for *Cecil's Story* began a long cooperative effort between Catalanotto and George Ella Lyon. Lyon's powerful, yet simple poem about a boy whose father goes off to fight in the Civil War speaks of the boy's hopes and fears, leaving the imagery up to Catalanotto to create. "The images her words evoked in my mind were endless," Catalanotto told *SATA,* "and I spent many nights editing and altering to create what I felt were the right ones." Further collaborative efforts with Lyon followed. *Who Came Down the Road?* tells of a curious boy and his mother who discover a pathway through the woods. Though the mother and son are contemporary, the people who have used the road before—whom the mother speculates about as they walk along—come from epochs as distant as the Civil War and the age of the mastodon. For the illustrations of the

1993 Lyon book *Dreamplace,* Catalanotto traveled to Colorado to see Mesa Verde and the Anasazi Indian cliff dwellings. As Catalanotto explained in *SAAS,* he prefers on-location research to library work. "I much prefer experiencing what I'm going to recreate for a book. The spirit of the Anasazi people ... haunted me as I painted their stories. I walked in the same place as my characters." A *Publishers Weekly* critic noted that "Lyon and Catalanotto here offer an atmospheric, shimmering glance backwards.... Catalanotto's extraordinary watercolors clarify this journey through time."

Lyon is one of Catalanotto's favorite writers to illustrate for because, as he stated in *SAAS,* "I love how much room she leaves between her words for me to fill in with pictures. Her writing is based on emotions and thoughts, not descriptions. How the characters look is left up to me. I don't have to keep referring back to the text to find out the color of eyes or coats." Several other books attest to the mutual respect Lyon and Catalanotto have for each other: *Mama Is a Miner, A Day at Damp Camp,* and *Book.* Lyon's short poem about books in the last-named title is full of metaphors: "A BOOK is a HOUSE / that is all windows and doors." Many of the words from the poem are actually incorporated into Catalanotto's artwork.

Catalanotto has gone on to illustrate the works of several other authors. Reviewing his work for SuAnn Kiser's *The Catspring Somersault Flying One-Handed Flip-Flop,* a reviewer for *Publishers Weekly* noted Catalanotto's "sun-drenched watercolors, as lush and complex as ever." Writing in *Horn Book* about his artwork for Susan Patron's *Dark Cloud Strong Breeze,* Nancy Vasilakis commented on the artist's use of "an unusual three-dimensional effect" and concluded that Catalanotto's illustrations "really capture attention." Portraying children of many different cultures in Megan McDonald's *My House Has Stars,* Catalanotto produced "watercolor paintings in soft, misty colors" that "reflect the awesome quality of the universe as viewed by youngsters throughout the world," according to Sally R. Dow in *School Library Journal.* Reviewing Susan Marie Swanson's *Letter to the Lake,* a *Publishers Weekly* reviewer enjoyed Catalanotto's "exquisite paintings," while *Booklist*'s Shelle Rosenfeld called the same work a "fine and visually astonishing book about the power of dreaming and memories."

A mystical tale of the tundra informs Susi Fowler's *Circle of Thanks,* in which the rescuing of an otter sets off ever-increasing acts of benevolence among Arctic animals. Rosenfeld applauded Catalanotto's "[b]eautiful watercolor illustrations" that "dramatically portray the ever-changing landscape of the Far North," while Pam Gosner noted in *School Library Journal* that the "artist uses unusual points of view to increase the drama ... and beautifully captures ... the love shared by the boy and his mother." *The Longest Wait,* by Marie Bradby, details the effects of a blizzard on an African American family somewhere in rural, pre-industrial America. Thomas's father determines to deliver the mail, blizzard or no, and the family waits in anticipation for him to return, and then also waits for the father's resultant fever to break before Thomas can go outside and enjoy the winter landscape. A *Publishers Weekly* reviewer commented that the artist's "dreamlike drawings" portray both the "family's anxiety" and suggest "both past and future events."

Catalanotto's self-illustrated titles have also continued to win critical acclaim. *The Painter* tells the story of a little girl whose father is a busy painter. She is forbidden to enter his studio, and outside of the studio he is usually too busy to give her his full attention. Finally, however, the pair works out a solution, and the girl is rewarded for her patience after dinner with entrance to the studio where she paints her own family portrait. The book was in part inspired by Catalanotto's own child, Chelsea, for whom, as a very young child, his studio was off limits because of all the possibly dangerous implements lying around. A *Publishers Weekly* critic remarked that the "book subtly attests to the joy inherent in the creation of both life and art." A *Kirkus Reviews* contributor noted that "Catalanotto creates sparkling watercolors.... The loose fluid style focuses on important details.... The entire work is simply and beautifully done." Cassie Whetstone concluded in *The Five Owls,* "Peter Catalanotto draws a circle with a line of love that connects the mother, father, daughter, and dog and unites them into a unit that we know as a family."

Another busy, distracted dad is at the heart of *Dad & Me.* Tommy is looking forward to sharing the good news of Gemini Four—the first U.S. space walk—with his father. Rushing home from school, the boy dons a colander as space helmet. Returning from the office, dad is far from amused when he sees his son. Reprimanded for wearing the colander at dinner, Tommy is sent to his room. Finally, Tommy makes his father re-connect with a child's world by giving him a newspaper photo of the astronaut with a photograph of his own face inserted in it. A *Kirkus Reviews* critic commented that "Catalanotto's watercolors deftly capture both Tommy's disappointment and his longing for adventure," while a *Publishers Weekly* contributor called Catalanotto's watercolors "breathtaking."

"I feel very lucky that my job is something I love to do," Catalanotto concluded in *SAAS.* "My work is a constant challenge, and I grow as a writer and artist with every book. The most important thing I want children to know when I visit their school is this: if you love to write and draw, you can do it for life!"

Works Cited

Catalanotto, Peter, essay for *Something about the Author Autobiography Series,* Volume 25, Gale, 1998, pp. 37-52.

Review of *The Catspring Somersault Flying One-Handed Flip-Flop, Publishers Weekly,* July 26, 1993, p. 70.

Review of *Dad & Me, Kirkus Reviews,* July 15, 1999, p. 1131.

Review of *Dad & Me, Publishers Weekly,* August 19, 1999, p. 351.

Dow, Sally R., review of *My House Has Stars, School Library Journal,* October, 1996, pp. 102-03.

Review of *Dreamplace, Publishers Weekly,* January 25, 1993, p. 86.

Gosner, Pam, review of *Circle of Thanks, School Library Journal,* December, 1998, p. 82.

Review of *Letter to the Lake, Publishers Weekly,* April 20, 1998, p. 65.

Review of *The Longest Wait, Publishers Weekly,* September 21, 1998, p. 83.

Lyon, George Ella, *Book,* DK Publishing, 1999.

Review of *The Painter, Kirkus Reviews,* August 15, 1995, p. 1186.

Review of *The Painter, Publishers Weekly,* August 21, 1995, p. 64.

Rosenfeld, Shelle, review of *Letter to the Lake, Booklist,* April 15, 1998, p. 1454.

Rosenfeld, Shelle, review of *Circle of Thanks, Booklist,* September 15, 1998, p. 236.

Silvey, Anita, editor *Children's Books and Their Creators,* Houghton, 1995, p. 125.

Vasilakis, Nancy, review of *Dark Cloud Strong Breeze, Horn Book,* May-June, 1994, p. 318.

Whetstone, Cassie, review of *The Painter, The Five Owls,* September-October, 1995, p. 10.

For More Information See

PERIODICALS

Booklist, September 1, 1988, p. 83; October 1, 1989, p. 346; November 1, 1996, p. 508; December 1, 1998, pp. 669-70.
New York Times Book Review, June 3, 1990, p. 24.
Publishers Weekly, September 29, 1989, p. 65; July 13, 1990, p. 53; August 26, 1996, p. 97; October 19, 1998, p. 79.
School Library Journal, September, 1990, p. 196; May, 1998, p. 126; December, 1998, p. 81; June, 1999, p. 119.*

—*Sketch by J. Sydney Jones*

*   *   *

CATO, Sheila

Personal

Born in Tring, Hertfordshire, England; children: Wayne, Kim, Gavin. *Education:* Attended Wellington Teachers College, Wellington, New Zealand.

Addresses

Home—Derbyshire, England. *E-mail*—sheilacato@hot mail.com.

Career

Schoolteacher and writer.

Writings

Measuring, illustrated by Sami Sweeten, Carolrhoda (Minneapolis, MN), 1999.
Counting and Numbers, illustrated by Sweeten, Carolrhoda, 1999.
Addition, illustrated by Sweeten, Carolrhoda, 1999.
Counting, illustrated by Sweeten, Carolrhoda, 1999.
Division, illustrated by Sweeten, Carolrhoda, 1999.
Multiplication, illustrated by Sweeten, Carolrhoda, 1999.
Subtraction, illustrated by Sweeten, Carolrhoda, 1999.

Sidelights

Sheila Cato told *SATA:* "After residing in New Zealand for nearly forty years, I returned to my homeland in 1996 and finally settled in Derbyshire, where I continue to write.

"For the past twenty-five years I have been a schoolteacher with a particular interest in mathematics. It has always concerned me that children develop a negative attitude to this subject from a very early age. With this in mind, I have written several picture book series to make math more child-friendly by combining various genres with a fun approach.

Sheila Cato

"The series 'Question of Math' for five-to-eight-year-olds has recently been published in the United States. The books cover the four basic operations and counting and measuring. I am currently writing a further series for an older age group. The contents will include fractions, decimals, and percentages. Each book deals with one subject and is written in question-and-answer format. I have used questions that are most frequently asked by students and which cause the most confusion. Each double page is a cameo-story based on everyday problems to which children can relate.

"Another series, for three-to-five-year-olds and written in story form, incorporates an unusual animal character. The text is set around the spatial concepts which are the beginning of math for young children; for example, 'above,' 'below,' 'between,' 'beside,' and 'behind.' The emphasis is on learning new concepts in a fun and easy way.

"All of the material I write is suitable for use in the classroom, library, or home. I am convinced that a fresh approach to math will enable many children to achieve greater success in this area."

COLMAN, Penny (Morgan) 1944-

Personal

Born September 2, 1944, in Denver, CO; daughter of Norman Charles Morgan (a psychiatrist) and Maritza (an artist; maiden name, Leskovar) Morgan; married Robert Archer Colman, separated January, 1992; children: Jonathan, David, and Stephen. *Education:* University of Michigan, A.B. (with distinction), 1966; Johns Hopkins University, M.A.T., 1967; University of Oklahoma, postgraduate work, 1977; New York University, book publishing program certificate, 1980. *Hobbies and other interests:* "Exploring cemeteries to find graves of historic people I write about; adventure sports; going to every type of bookstore, especially used books; driving on long trips; jogging and bicycling; doing puzzles and playing Scrabble; thinking and talking about ideas."

Addresses

Home and office—146 Cambridge Ave., Englewood, NJ 07631.

Career

Free-lance writer and editor, 1975—; seminar leader and speaker, 1975—; United Presbyterian Church, New York City, program developer, 1977-81; Granger Galleries, New York City, founder and president, 1981-85; Center for Food Action, Englewood, NJ, executive director, 1986-87. Appointed to New Jersey Commission on Hunger, 1986, and New Jersey State Women Infant Children Advisory Council, 1987. Has appeared on radio and television programs. *Member:* Authors Guild, American Society of Journalists and Authors, Society of Children's Book Writers and Illustrators.

Awards, Honors

Silver Award, Lidman Prize Competition, 1990, for "Stamps!"; Paul A. Witty Short Story Award nomination, International Reading Association, 1990, for "But Not Ms. Anderson!"

Writings

FOR CHILDREN; NONFICTION

Breaking the Chains: The Crusade of Dorothea Lynde Dix, Shoe Tree (White Hall, VA), 1992.
Spies!: Women in the Civil War, Betterway (Cincinnati, OH), 1992.
Fannie Lou Hamer and the Fight for the Vote, Millbrook (Brookfield, CT), 1993.
A Woman Unafraid: The Achievements of Frances Perkins, Atheneum, 1993.
101 Ways to Do Better in School, Troll (Mahwah, NJ), 1994.
Madame C. J. Walker: Building a Business Empire, Millbrook, 1994.
Mother Jones and the March of the Mill Children, Millbrook, 1994.

Toilets, Bathtubs, Sinks, and Sewers: A History of the Bathroom, Atheneum, 1994.
Women in Society, Cavendish, 1994.
Rosie the Riveter: Women Working on the Home Front in World War II, Crown, 1995.
Mary McLeod Bethune and the Power of Education, Millbrook, 1995.
Strike!: The Bitter Struggle of American Workers from Colonial Times to the Present, Millbrook, 1995.
Corpses, Coffins, and Crypts: A History of Burial, Holt, 1997.
Girls!: A History of Growing Up Female in America, Scholastic, 2000.

FOR CHILDREN; FICTION

I Never Do Anything Bad, Paulist, 1988.
Dark Closets and Noises in the Night, Paulist, 1991.

FOR ADULTS; NONFICTION

(Editor) *Spiritual Disciplines for Everyday Living,* Character Research, 1982.
Grand Canyon Magic, PMC Books, 1987.
This is Bergen County Where People Make a Difference, League of Women Voters, 1989.
(With Stella Chess and Alexander Thomas) *Fifty Years Together: Researchers, Psychiatrists, Professors, and Parents,* self-published, 1993.
Equal Rights Amendment: A Curriculum Guide, National Education Association, 1993.

OTHER

Also author of *Dare to Seek* (one-act play), Granger, 1976. Author and editor of human resource manuals, including *Knowing Me and You,* Granger, 1976; and *Use and Power of Language,* National Council of Churches, 1981. Editor of newsletters, including *ACCESS* and *Sharing.* Author of script for videotape, *Education is the Key,* Broad Street Productions, 1988. Contributor to *Sports Illustrated for Kids, Cricket,* and *U.S. Kids.* Contributing editor, *The American Way,* Viking, 1976. Consulting editor, *The Cheyenne Way,* National Endowment for the Humanities, 1978. Contributor to *Teens: A Fresh Look,* John Muir, 1991.

Sidelights

Penny Colman is the author of a number of popular nonfiction books, including biographies of famous and not-so-famous women of history. She also writes kid-winning social histories such as *Toilets, Bathtubs, Sinks, and Sewers: A History of the Bathroom* and *Corpses, Coffins, and Crypts: A History of Burial.* Reviewing the latter title, *Booklist*'s Stephanie Zvirin asserted that "Colman's approach to her subject is worlds away from dry textbook tradition." Indeed, Colman is noted for her page-turning nonfiction style. "I write in the tradition of creative nonfiction," wrote Colman in her essay, "Nonfiction Is Literature Too," which appeared in the *New Advocate.*

Colman once told *SATA:* "I grew up in a noisy family. Very noisy. My three brothers and I were close in age, and we were always into something—backyard baseball

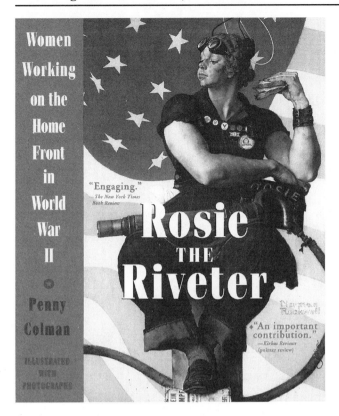

Penny Colman portrays women's role in the World War II workplace in her award-winning book.

games; canoeing, swimming, and fishing in the creek that ran behind our house; and fighting with each other about this and that. There was also always music. We had a family orchestra—my dad played the piano, my mom and brother Vin played the cello, my brother Kip and I played the violin, and my brother Jon played the clarinet. We kids weren't very good, but we played anyhow. For several years, my parents also owned a farm with a huge barn and a swimming hole. We had three horses, six sheep, a goat who jumped on the hood of moving cars, and a flock of exotic-looking chickens that my dad and I ordered from a catalog. When all the noise and activity got to be too much, I would go for long bike rides. I loved to ride with 'no hands' on the handle bar, and I got to be so good that I could read a book and ride my bike at the same time!

"After I grew up, I had three children who were *really* close in age. Jonathan was one year old when his identical twin brothers David and Stephen were born! They were noisy, too! And always into something—backyard basketball and break dancing. They sang all the time and even performed at a nightclub in New York City. One summer when Jonathan was twelve and David and Stephen were eleven, we drove across the United States in a red van called the 'Road Radish.' All the activities and adventures and noises of my life have given me lots to write about."

Generally, however, Colman keeps noise in the background of her well-researched books, focusing tightly on her subjects and keeping the reader glued to the page

right along with her. Her first nonfiction work, *Breaking the Chains: The Crusade of Dorothea Lynde Dix,* set the tenor of other books to come. Dix, an important figure in social reform for the treatment of the mentally ill, is painted in a three-dimensional portrait by Colman who "does an excellent job of citing primary sources, with many of the passages from her subject's own writing," as Kathleen L. Atwood pointed out in a *School Library Journal* review. Atwood concluded that "Colman's is a must purchase in the field of women's studies." Zena Sutherland, writing in *Bulletin of the Center for Children's Books* remarked that "Colman lets Dorothea Dix's achievements speak for themselves."

Colman has become adept at applying literary techniques to nonfiction. As she noted in her article for *The New Advocate,* she follows the five R's of creative nonfiction, as developed by the editor Lee Gutkind: "real life, reflection, research, reading, and 'riting." Colman went on to explain that the "initial task I undertake is discovering the structure, which is to nonfiction what plot is to fiction. Just as good fiction has a plot and subplots, good nonfiction has structure and substructures, or macro- and microstructures.... As I shape the structure, I also search for the essence of the story, the emotional insight, the cognitive concept that I want to illuminate." Colman's are not solely informational books, she is quick to point out, but factual accounts that draw the reader in by the use of frequent realistic examples and details.

The labor activist, Mother Jones, is the subject of another of Colman's well-received biographies, *Mother Jones and the March of the Mill Children.* A primer on the fledgling U.S. labor movement and on child labor in the United States, Colman's biography also details the twenty-day child labor protest march led by Mother Jones. Though the march failed to gain Jones an interview with President Theodore Roosevelt as planned, it did attract widespread press coverage and began to educate Americans about unfair labor practices. *Booklist*'s Mary Harris Veeder praised Colman's use of real materials, including "[p]hotographs of working children and of the march, along with clippings and editorial cartoons that appeared at the time."

Colman further examines labor in the United States with her *Rosie the Riveter: Women Working on the Home Front in World War II* and *Strike!: The Bitter Struggle of American Workers from Colonial Times to the Present.* Elizabeth Bush, reviewing the former title in *Bulletin of the Center for Children's Books,* commented, "Tightly focused and smoothly written, this account of women's participation in World War II home-front industry captures the range of motives that drew women into the labor force." Such motives were, in part, instilled in women through the propaganda of the Office of War Information, which did its best to make work outside the home seem not only patriotic, but also glamorous. Female workers became synonymous with the muscular, red-haired working woman of the Norman Rockwell painting, "Rosie the Riveter." Bush concluded that "Colman never launches a diatribe against government manipulation, but offers an even-handed discussion of wartime measures meeting wartime needs." *Booklist*'s Zvirin asserted that Colman provides readers with "a solid overview of the role women played in the wartime workplace."

In *Strike!*, Colman creates a succinct overview of two hundred years of labor struggles, all condensed to a mere eighty pages. A sequential litany of labor protests are addressed, including the 1834 mill worker strike in Lowell, Massachusetts; the brutal Haymarket Square protest, and the Pullman strike of 1894. Shirley Wilton, writing in *School Library Journal,* appreciated the "poignant detail" with which these and other events were described. "Colman's book is surprisingly readable," wrote Wilton, "and accomplishes its purpose of providing a general overview of labor history with style and accuracy." Julie Yates Walton remarked in *Booklist* that Colman's "comprehensive story of the 'bitter' struggle between American workers and their employers is a clear-eyed reminder of how ugly and violent the struggle actually was."

Two of Colman's most critically acclaimed books are social-anthropological histories. Rites of cleanliness are given a full history in *Toilets, Bathtubs, Sinks, and Sewers,* and burial customs are examined in *Corpses, Coffins, and Crypts.* These works are far from dry

Colman extensively researched and compassionately documented the burial rituals of different cultures in this compelling history. (Cover photo by Penny Colman.)

recitations of fact; they are filled with the human element—personal examples as well as historical anecdotes. Young readers will find it more than interesting to know that Queen Isabella of Spain, for example, had bragging rights to having taken only two baths in her lifetime. Reviewing *Toilets, Bathtubs, Sinks, and Sewers* in *Booklist,* Ilene Cooper commented that "while Colman stays within the bounds of good taste, she offers plenty of anecdotes that will have kids happily yelling, 'Gross!'" Cooper concluded, "Get two copies—one for the serious students of the sanitary arts, the other for captivated browsers." Kate Hegarty Bouman, reviewing the same title in *School Library Journal,* called it a "well-written book that provides interesting tidbits about the history of personal cleanliness and hygiene."

Colman's *Corpses, Coffins, and Crypts* was in part inspired by her own hobby of exploring cemeteries to locate the graves of the subjects about whom she writes. As Colman notes in the introduction to her book, such places are "brimming with art, architecture, history, horticulture, and stories—lots of stories." *Booklist*'s Zvirin noted that Colman uses "heartfelt personal experience and comments from people she interviewed to moderate the visceral impact of the information." "A sensitive, solid book," concluded Zvirin, "with answers to questions people often need and want to know but are

Colman takes another look at labor in the United States.

too reluctant to ask." Shirley Wilton observed in *School Library Journal* that death "has been underreported and mostly avoided in writing for young people," and went on to note that Colman's book "answers many questions and introduces fascinating facts."

Writing meaningfully of her craft in her article for the *New Advocate,* Colman stated: "Creating a high quality nonfiction book is not for the faint-hearted because it is a challenging, complex, time-consuming, and intense experience. Many of us do extensive research, including finding illustrative material that has to be carefully coordinated with the text. We spend countless hours thinking about structure and discovering the narrative. We glue ourselves to our chairs for endless days as we craft our writing in a way the will keep readers turning the page."

Works Cited

Atwood, Kathleen L., review of *Breaking the Chains, School Library Journal,* July, 1992, p. 92.

Bouman, Kate Hegarty, review of *Toilets, Bathtubs, Sinks, and Sewers, School Library Journal,* March, 1995, p. 209.

Bush, Elizabeth, review of *Rosie the Riveter, Bulletin of the Center for Children's Books,* July-August, 1995, p. 380.

Colman, Penny, *Corpses, Coffins, and Crypts,* Holt, 1997.

Colman, Penny, "Nonfiction is Literature, Too," *The New Advocate,* summer, 1999, pp. 215-223.

Cooper, Ilene, review of *Toilets, Bathtubs, Sinks, and Sewers, Booklist,* January 1, 1995, p. 818.

Sutherland, Zena, review of *Breaking the Chains, Bulletin of the Center for Children's Books,* July-August, 1992, p. 291.

Veeder, Mary Harris, review of *Mother Jones and the March of the Mill Children, Booklist,* May 1, 1994, p. 1596.

Walton, Julie Yates, review of *Strike!, Booklist,* November 15, 1995, p. 550.

Wilton, Shirley, review of *Corpses, Coffins, and Crypts, School Library Journal,* December, 1997, p. 134.

Wilton, Shirley, review of *Strike!, School Library Journal,* January, 1996, p. 132.

Zvirin, Stephanie, review of *Corpses, Coffins, and Crypts, Booklist,* November 1, 1997, p. 466.

Zvirin, Stephanie, review of *Rosie the Riveter, Booklist,* April 15, 1996, p. 1490.

For More Information See

BOOKS

Contemporary Authors, Volume 145, Gale, 1995.

PERIODICALS

Bulletin of the Center for Children's Books, February, 1998, p. 197.

Horn Book, March-April, 1995, p. 213; September-October, 1995, p. 617; January-February, 1998, p. 91.

New York Times Book Review, November 14, 1993, p. 40; September 10, 1995, p. 35.

Publishers Weekly, May 8, 1995, p. 297; November 3, 1997, p. 86; February 9, 1998, p. 98.

School Library Journal, April, 1993, p. 144; October, 1993, p. 138; November, 1993, p. 114; September, 1994, p. 226.

Voice of Youth Advocates, June, 1996, p. 86; August, 1996, p. 149.

Wilson Library Bulletin, June, 1994, p. 127.*

—Sketch by J. Sydney Jones

*   *   *

COOPER, Melrose
See KROLL, Virginia L(ouise)

D

DALY, Nicholas 1946-
(Niki Daly)

Personal

Born June 13, 1946, in Cape Town, South Africa; son of George (a carpenter) and Sarah (maiden name, Mathusen) Daly; married Judith Mary Kenny (an artist), July 7, 1973; children: Joseph, Leo. *Education:* Cape Town Technikon, diploma, 1970.

Addresses

Home and office—36 Strubens Rd., Cape Town, South Africa. *Agent*—Laura Cecil, 17 Alwyne Villas, London N1 2HG, England.

Career

CBS Record Company, London, England, singer and songwriter, 1971-73; Advertising Agency, Cape Town, South Africa and London, junior art director, 1973-75; freelance illustrator, London, 1975-79; East Ham Technical College, London, graphics teacher, 1976-79; Stellenbosch University, head of graphic design, 1983-89; David Philip Publishers, head of Songololo Books, 1989-1992; The Inkman Company, facilitator of children's picture books, 1993—; author and illustrator. *Exhibitions:* The artwork from *Why the Sun and Moon Live in the Sky* was exhibited at the Original Art Show of the Society of Illustrators, New York, 1995.

Awards, Honors

Award for Illustration, British Arts Council and Provincial Booksellers, 1978 for *The Little Girl Who Lived down the Road; Horn Book* Honor List, 1987, Parents' Choice Book Award for Literature, Parents' Choice Foundation, 1988, and Katrine Harries Award (South Africa) for illustration, 1988, all for *Not So Fast, Songololo; New York Times* Ten Best Illustrated Books list, 1995, and Anne Izard Story Teller's Choice Award, 1996, both for *Why the Sun and Moon Live in the Sky;*

IBBY Honors Award for illustration, for *All the Magic in the World* and *One Round Moon and a Star for Me;* Parents' Choice Award, 1999, for *Bravo, Zan Angelo!*

Writings

FICTION FOR CHILDREN; SELF-ILLUSTRATED UNDER NAME NIKI DALY

The Little Girl Who Lived down the Road, Collins (London, England), 1978.
Vim the Rag Mouse, Atheneum, 1979.
Joseph's Other Red Sock, Atheneum, 1982.
Leo's Christmas Surprise, Gollancz (London, England), 1983.

Nicholas Daly

Ben's Gingerbread Man, Walker (London, England), 1985, Viking, 1985.

Teddy's Ear, Walker, 1985, Viking, 1985.

Monsters Are Like That, Walker, 1985, Viking Kestrel, 1985.

Not So Fast, Songololo, Gollancz, 1985, Atheneum, 1986.

Just Like Archie, Walker, 1986, Viking Kestrel, 1986.

Look at Me!, Walker, 1986, Viking Kestrel, 1986.

Thank You Henrietta, Walker, 1986, Viking Kestrel, 1986.

Mama, Papa, and Baby Joe, Viking, 1991.

Papa Lucky's Shadow, McElderry, 1992.

(With Ingrid Mennen), *Somewhere in Africa,* illustrated by Nicolaas Maritz, Dutton, 1992.

Mary Malloy and the Baby Who Wouldn't Sleep, Golden, 1993.

Why the Sun and Moon Live in the Sky, Lothrop, Lee and Shepard, 1994.

My Dad, McElderry, 1995.

(With Wendy Hartmann) *The Dinosaurs Are Back and It's Your Fault Edward!,* McElderry, 1997.

Bravo, Zan Angelo!, Farrar, Straus and Giroux, 1996.

(With Nola Turkington), *The Dancer,* Human and Rousseau, 1996

The Boy on the Beach, McElderry, 1999.

Jamela's Dress, Frances Lincoln (London, England), 1999, Farrar, Straus and Giroux, 1999.

ILLUSTRATOR; UNDER NAME NIKI DALY

Kathleen Hersom, *Maybe It's a Tiger,* Macmillan (London), 1981.

Christopher Gregorowski, reteller, *Fly, Eagle Fly!,* Tafleberg, 1982, revised edition, McElderry, 2000.

Louis Baum, *I Want to See the Moon,* Bodley Head, 1984, Overlook, 1989.

Ruth Craft, *The Day of the Rainbow,* Heinemann, 1988, Viking Kestrel, 1989.

Reviva Schermbrucker, *Charlie's House,* Viking, 1991.

Wendy Hartmann, *All the Magic in the World,* Dutton, 1993.

Ingrid Mennen, *One Round Moon and a Star for Me,* Orchard, 1994.

Cari Best, *Red Light, Green Light, Mama and Me,* Orchard, 1995.

Adaptations

With Weston Woods, produced a video presentation of *Not So Fast, Songololo,* 1990.

Work in Progress

Picture book, *Pa's Perfect Pizza,* and further titles about Pa Bombelly for Transworld Books.

Sidelights

Niki Daly is a South African author-illustrator whose picture books celebrate the imaginative powers of children and their magnificent everyday lives. Notable about his style are his abilities to view the world from a child's perspective and to see the world in a rainbow of shades, reflective of multicultural modern South Africa. Indeed, many of Daly's solo efforts, as well as his

illustrations for other authors represent strongly African themes. In books such as *Not So Fast, Songololo, Somewhere in Africa, One Round Moon and a Star for Me, Charlie's House, All the Magic in the World, Why the Sun and Moon Live in the Sky, The Boy on the Beach,* and *Jamela's Dress,* Daly looks at the day-to-day interactions of the myths that shape black South African reality. As a writer, editor, and provider of art workshops, Daly has furthered the creation of a body of South African children's literature inclusive of all races and ethnic groups.

Nicholas Daly first became involved in drawing by using pencil stubs handed down from an uncle who painted watercolor pictures. Born in South Africa, Daly traveled to London at the age of twenty-four in order to pursue a career in singing and songwriting. However, economic difficulties ended his music career after two years, and Daly found work as a commercial artist, which eventually led to illustration for children's books.

Daly once commented to *SATA:* "My interest in illustrating for children started after I settled in London. My first book, *The Little Girl Who Lived down the Road,* was written by myself simply as an excuse to draw the pictures, after realizing that a completed product was more useful to a publisher than trying an unknown illustrator on the work of an established writer. I was very encouraged by the favorable reviews I received concerning the writing of *The Little Girl Who Lived down the Road*—which spurred me on to further books."

Partly inspired by the work of Maurice Sendak, *The Little Girl Who Lived Down the Road* is the story of a day at the sea that "has the inevitability of the folk tale," according to a reviewer for *Junior Bookshelf.* This story "is ideal material for the oral story-teller," concluded the reviewer. Carolyn O'Grady wrote in the *Times Educational Supplement* that Daly creates "endearing creatures which make the most of a child's love of animals." Winner of the British Arts Council Illustration Award, this debut effort encouraged Daly to believe he could actually make a living writing and illustrating children's books.

Inspired by a collection of ornaments and toys arranged on the windowsill of his London studio, Daly next wrote and illustrated *Vim the Rag Mouse* about a toy mouse who lives on a similar windowsill and longs for adventures. A *Publishers Weekly* critic called this book "a welcome fantasy," while a writer for *School Library Journal* commented that the "story has lots of action and a satisfyingly resolved plot." *Joseph's Other Red Sock,* another one of Daly's early works, is a read-aloud story for young children. In the story, the hunt for a missing sock, from one room to another, turns into imaginative play. The clutter in Joseph's closet—partly inspired by that of Daly's own son—becomes a monster who has the sock perched on his ear. "Cheerful pastel watercolors highlight the nonchalant pictures, which have a messy, real-kid feel to them," remarked a reviewer for *Booklist.*

One big wave is enough for a small boy, who finds adventure in an abandoned boat in Daly's self-illustrated **The Boy on the Beach.**

In 1980, Daly and his family returned to South Africa after ten years living abroad. During his first years back in South Africa, Daly produced several traditional books for the very young. In *Leo's Christmas Surprise* Daly explores the relationship between a young boy and a grandparent, a theme he used later in *Papa Lucky's Shadow* and *Not So Fast, Songololo. Leo's Christmas Surprise* follows Leo and his family through their Christmas festivities. They blow up balloons, decorate the tree, and ice the cake while Grandpa Bob is making Leo a surprise gift in the shed. *Growing Point*'s Margery Fisher lauded the book as a "good idea expressed in a spirited, individual manner." G. Bott noted in *Junior Bookshelf* that *Leo's Christmas Surprise* "has all the signs of qualifying as a Christmas favorite." Daly's other books for the very young include the six small books in the "Walker Storytime" series: *Ben's Gingerbread Man, Teddy's Ear, Monsters Are Like That, Just Like Archie, Look at Me!,* and *Thank You Henrietta.* Lucy Ellmann, writing in the *Times Literary Supplement,* commented that "Daly's Storytime books offer ... down-to-earth instruction on child psychology."

"My work is based on drawing rather than painting," Daly explained to *SATA*. "Because I love change I might like to discover a way in which I could illustrate work in a more painterly way. I find that there are two needs to fulfill as an illustrator: one is to develop as an artist and one is to always serve the needs of the text you're illustrating. As a writer/illustrator, I'm interested in themes that evolve around young children (one to six years) as they play around the home and on little excursions outside their home, the usual way children observe and interpret things which hold no charm to the adult eye—bath plugs which become telephones when held to the ear, or steering wheels when held firmly between fingers. I'm fascinated by the dual reality children have when playing games. On one level they know the bath plug is 'just a plug,' but on another they can transform it into other things by their belief. As my children grow up, I return to my own childhood and discover a pool of fantasy waiting to be resurrected."

When Daly and his family returned to South Africa, the country was experiencing great unrest as a result of apartheid. Daly told *SATA*: "I wrote and illustrated a number of books which reflected the lives of the children on the other side of the racial divide. In retrospect, I see these books (*Not so Fast Songololo, Charlie's House, Papa Lucky's Shadow,* and *All the Magic in the World*) as half-way bridges between white and black children who live[d] separate and unequal lives determined by the appalling apartheid system. In order to do these books I ignored the myth propagated through apartheid and some political activists who said that there are differences between people."

The award-winning *Not So Fast, Songololo* explores South African themes from a South African viewpoint. Young Songololo guides his grandmother on and off the bus as the pair goes to town to buy the boy some new shoes. A *Kirkus Reviews* critic called the book an "evocative depiction of a young black boy in South Africa and his warm relationship with his grandmother." Karla Kuskin noted in the *New York Times Book Review* that there "is a sweet spirit in this simple, neatly constructed story." Kuskin went on to remark that Daly's "easy watercolors over loose pencil sketching pick up bright patterns and make sensitive studies of individual black faces."

In *Papa Lucky's Shadow,* Papa Lucky dusts off his dancing shoes and shows why he was a dancing champion in his younger days—much to the delight of his granddaughter, Sugar. "The peppy bebop quality of Sugar's narrative might inspire some impromptu toe-tapping," noted a reviewer for *Publishers Weekly.* Ilene Cooper commented in *Booklist* that the "exuberant artwork" adds "spice to a story that might otherwise have been too sweet." Sian Griffiths observed in a review in *Times Educational Supplement* that "Daly is at the forefront of a wave of South African writers and illustrators ... who have made their mark abroad."

In the late 1980s, Daly established a children's book imprint for David Philip Publishers in South Africa, calling it Songololo Books. As an editor he attempted to promote children's literature for all the children of South Africa, and to this end tried to cultivate not only stories *about* black South Africans, but *by* them as well. He illustrated several books by other authors—Reviva Schermbrucker's *Charlie's House* and Wendy Hartmann's *All the Magic in the World* among them. In the former title, a small boy watches his elders build a makeshift hut of corrugated iron in his shanty town and then attempts to do the same with his own materials. Writing in *School Librarian,* Nansi Taylor concluded: "This book will be invaluable for younger children, who will compare their lives with others or will simply enjoy the story and appreciate Charlie's ingenuity; and also for

Angelo takes part in a **commedia dell'arte** *performance on Carnival day in Renaissance Venice, and saves the day for his famous grandfather's failing troupe. (From* Bravo, Zan Angelo!, *written and illustrated by Daly.)*

older children who will perceive its social message." Set in the wheat lands of the Cape, *All the Magic in the World* tells of the games of a group of farm laborers' children.

After the establishment of a free South Africa, Daly and millions others voted for the first time as equal South Africans in 1994. This was about the time he was working on his *Why the Sun and Moon Live in the Sky,* a Nigerian mythic tale, as well as his very realistic story, *My Dad,* which harkened back to the difficulties Daly felt as a youth with an alcoholic father. Of the former award-winning title, a *Publishers Weekly* contributor noted that Daly's "witty illustrations" invest the tale with "offbeat charm." The reviewer applauded the book's "wonderful balance of high energy and refined aesthetics." Nancy B. Cardozo commented on the wide appeal of the book in the *New York Times Book Review,* concluding that the youngest children "are likely to be hooked by the lovely pictures; the older ones will

respond to the characters and themes; parents may end up having the most fun of all as they watch their children fill the wild and hopeful spaces in this fine book with their own wild hope."

A departure from South African scenes and themes is Daly's *Bravo, Zan Angelo!,* set in eighteenth-century Venice. A little boy wants to join his rather grumpy grandfather's commedia dell'arte street theater group. Grandfather, a once-famous clown, reluctantly gives in, allowing Angelo to play a small part as a rooster. Mary Simons, writing in the *New York Times Book Review* observed that "here the illustrations, exquisitely drawn and illuminated with Venetian light, carry the story farther than the words." *Booklist* critic Michael Cart wrote: "Daly's good-natured story about an unusual subject ... is greatly enhanced by his beautiful illustrations."

The story and vibrant pictures of Daly's **Jamela's Dress** *were inspired by the fabrics of his native South Africa.*

Daly returned to books with South African motifs in *Jamela's Dress* and *The Boy on the Beach.* Fun-loving playful Jamela adores the fabric her mother has bought to make herself a dress for a friend's wedding. Jamela wraps herself in the soft colorful material and parades through town like royalty, luxuriating in the chants of "Kwela Jamela African Queen!" Unfortunately, Jamela doesn't notice that her royal garb has suffered the indignities of bicycle grease and chicken pecking; the fabric is stained and torn. Everyone is angry with her until a photographer, who has caught Jamela's royal exploits on film, wins a prize for his photograph and shares the award money with his photo's royal subject. Jamela is then able to replace the damaged fabric and even get a little extra for a dress of her own. Joan Zaleski commented in *School Library Journal* that the "story is filled with the musical language of South Africa. Daly's illustrations are vibrant and colorful and impart a child's eye view of the world." Zaleski concluded that *Jamela's Dress* was a "delightful read-aloud that will be enjoyed by a wide audience." A *Publishers Weekly* writer remarked, "Daly splashes luminous watercolors across the pages of this warmly evocative picture book, set in his native South Africa.... A sympathetic and light-hearted slice of life."

A young boy on a South African beach, reminding Daly of what it was like to be a young child again himself, provided the inspiration for *The Boy on the Beach.* According to a reviewer for *Publishers Weekly,* the book "summons the sights and sounds of a summertime outing through sun-drenched watercolors and keenly tuned language." When the boy on the beach becomes separated from his parents, a lifeguard takes him to Lost and Found where he is reunited with them. "Daly maintains a rigorous visual pace by varying broad vistas of busy seashore activity with close-ups," commented the *Publishers Weekly* reviewer. Kate McClelland observed in *School Library Journal* that "Daly's watercolor illustrations are cheerfully energetic in depicting the vibrant colors of the busy beach, the sprightliness of little Joe ... and his parents' carefree enjoyment of the day."

Daly's themes and motifs continue to surprise. His picture books range from the sublime to the silly, and in between they poke and prod at one's social conscience without ever being didactic. Daly summed up his achievement in an essay he wrote for *Something about the Author Autobiography Series* (*SAAS*): "My motivation—a love for drawing pictures and a wish to be famous for something I do well—has remained with me since I was a kid.... What has emerged though, after ... years of illustrating and writing children's books, is my position on the ideological battleground. I've discovered that I'm a banner-carrying subversive. Emblazoned on my banner is the message 'STRUT YOUR STUFF!'"

Works Cited

Bott, G. review of *Leo's Christmas Surprise, Junior Bookshelf,* December, 1983, p. 234.

Review of *The Boy on the Beach, Publishers Weekly,* May 10, 1999, pp. 66-67.

Cardozo, Nancy B., review of *Why the Sun and Moon Live in the Sky, New York Times Book Review,* November 5, 1995, p. 31.

Cart, Michael, review of *Bravo, Zan Angelo!, Booklist,* August, 1998, p. 2014.

Cooper, Ilene, review of *Papa Lucky's Shadow, Booklist,* September 15, 1992, p. 145.

Daly, Niki, essay in *Something about the Author Autobiography Series,* Volume 21, Gale, 1996, pp. 75-102.

Ellmann, Lucy, "Childhood's Image," *Times Literary Supplement,* October 25, 1985, p. 1218.

Fisher, Margery, review of *Leo's Christmas Surprise, Growing Point,* November, 1983, p. 4168.

Griffiths, Sian, "Mum and Dad and Gran," *Times Educational Supplement,* July 2, 1993, p. 10.

Review of *Jamela's Dress, Publishers Weekly,* May 10, 1999, p. 67.

Review of *Joseph's Other Red Sock, Booklist,* July, 1982, p. 1442.

Kuskin, Karla, review of *Not So Fast, Songololo, New York Times Book Review,* June 1, 1986, p. 48.

Review of *The Little Girl Who Lived Down the Road, Junior Bookshelf,* June, 1978, p. 134.

McClelland, Kate, review of *The Boy on the Beach, School Library Journal,* June, 1999, p. 42.

Review of *Not So Fast, Songololo, Kirkus Reviews,* March 15, 1986, pp. 468-69.

O'Grady, Carolyn, "Paradise Lost and Found," *Times Educational Supplement,* June 23, 1978, p. 21.

Review of *Papa Lucky's Shadow, Publishers Weekly,* June 29, 1992, pp. 62-63.

Simons, Mary, review of *Bravo, Zan Angelo!, New York Times Book Review,* December 6, 1998, p. 78.

Taylor, Nansi, review of *Charlie's House, School Librarian,* February, 1992, pp. 17-18.

Review of *Vim the Rag Mouse, Publishers Weekly,* July 29, 1979, p. 105.

Review of *Vim the Rag Mouse, School Library Journal,* December, 1979, pp. 72, 74.

Review of *Why the Sun and Moon Live in the Sky, Publishers Weekly,* May 15, 1995, p. 72.

Zaleski, Joan, review of *Jamela's Dress, School Library Journal,* August, 1999, p. 132.

For More Information See

BOOKS

Children's Literature Review, Volume 41, Gale, 1997.

Sixth Book of Junior Authors and Illustrators, edited by Sally Holmes Holtze, H. W. Wilson, 1989.

St. James Guide to Children's Writers, 5th edition, edited by Sara Pendergast and Tom Pendergast, St. James, 1999.

PERIODICALS

Booklist, February 15, 1994, p. 1093; May 1, 1995, p. 1579; September 1, 1995, p. 82; June 1, 1997, p. 1717; March 15, 1999, p. 1333.

Bulletin of the Center for Children's Books, June, 1995, p. 341.

Horn Book, March-April, 1992, p. 193; November-December, 1993, p. 732.

New York Times Book Review, July 17, 1994, p. 18; June 18, 1995, p. 25.

Publishers Weekly, April 3, 1995, p. 62; April 14, 1997, p. 74.

School Library Journal, December, 1993, p. 88; September, 1994, p. 190; June, 1995, p. 79; June, 1997, p. 90; September, 1998, p. 165.*

—Sketch by J. Sydney Jones

*   *   *

DALY, Niki
See DALY, Nicholas

*   *   *

DAVIS, H(arold) L(enoir) 1894-1960

Personal

Born October 18, 1894, in Rone's Mill, OR; died October 31, 1960, in San Antonio, TX; married Marion Lay, 1928 (divorced, 1943); married Elizabeth Tonkin Martin del Campo, 1953.

Career

Author, translator, and literary critic. Worked briefly in various jobs, including deputy county assessor, General Land Office survey crewman, bank clerk, and railroad track layer. *Military service:* U.S. Army, 1918.

Awards, Honors

Guggenheim fellowship, 1932; Harper Prize Novel, 1935, and Pulitzer Prize, 1936, both for *Honey in the Horn.*

Writings

(With James Stevens) *Status Rerum: A Manifesto upon the Present Condition of Northwestern Literature Containing Several Near-Libelous Utterances upon Persons in the Public Eye,* privately printed, 1927.

Honey in the Horn, Harper (New York), 1935.

Proud Riders and Other Poems, Harper, 1942.

Harp of a Thousand Strings, Morrow (New York), 1947.

Beulah Land, Morrow, 1949.

Winds of Morning, Morrow, 1952.

Team Bells Woke Me and Other Stories, Morrow, 1953.

The Distant Music, Morrow, 1957.

Kettle of Fire, Morrow, 1959.

The Selected Poems of H. L. Davis, Ahsahta Press (Boise, ID), 1978.

Contributed fiction to *American Mercury, Colliers, Saturday Evening Post,* and *Adventure.* Contributed poems to *Poetry,* and essays to *Holiday.*

H. L. Davis

Sidelights

H. L. Davis is best remembered for his fiction, which was mostly set in the late nineteenth/early-twentieth-century American West, and which addressed large, mythic themes such as journeys of initiation, alienation from society, and redemption through community and love. Although during his lifetime critics often viewed his work as run-of-the-mill Western romance and adventure, posterity has recognized him as an important writer with insight into the travails of the human soul. In addition to five novels and many short stories, Davis also wrote poetry, essays, and literary criticism, and he won a Pulitzer for *Honey in the Horn* in 1936.

Davis was born on October 18, 1894, in Rone's Mill, Oregon. His rural upbringing strongly influenced the tone and color of his writings as an adult. Davis graduated from high school in 1912 in The Dalles, Oregon. In 1918, he was drafted into the army. In the service he worked as a clerk at Fort McDowell, California, and it was here that he first began to write poetry. His early poems contained vibrant descriptions of Oregon's natural landscape. They first appeared in *Poetry* magazine in 1919, and they drew praises from the likes of Carl Sandburg and Robinson Jeffers.

Davis was discharged from the army in December of 1918, and he returned to The Dalles, where he continued to write poetry as he worked various odd jobs. He also began making the acquaintance of other writers, such as James Stevens—with whom he co-wrote a pamphlet that attacked the pomposity and pretension of university

English professors and other ivory tower literary elites—and H. L. Mencken, who advised him to try his hand at writing fiction. In 1926, Davis's short stories began to appear in *American Mercury,* which was published by Mencken. In 1928, Davis married Marion Lay, and they moved from Oregon to Winslow, Washington. Davis continued to write sketches and short stories which appeared in *American Mercury,* the *Saturday Evening Post,* and *Colliers.* He published his first novel, *Honey in the Horn,* in 1935.

Honey in the Horn is the odyssey of a teenage orphan, Clay Calvert, who roams the Oregon countryside searching vaguely for work, love, and belonging, and finding all of them in one fashion or another. Critic Fanny Butcher wrote in the *Chicago Daily Tribune,* "Mr. Davis has told his story with gusto and color and humor. *Honey in the Horn* is a literary long drink and a heady one. Those who like it will pass it around with all the pride of one of Mr. Davis' heroes." On the other hand, *New Republic* critic Robert Cantwell saw it this way: "*Honey in the Horn* is full of quaint characters and bustling activity, but never gets anywhere. It might have been a great novel if it had succeeded in being a novel at all." Another *New Republic* reviewer, Malcolm Cowley, opined that "the fact remains that the plot is inadequate, that the general conception is lacking in drama, that the two principal characters are unappealing and unrevealed in action." In spite of these dissenters, *Honey in the Horn* won the Pulitzer Prize for fiction in 1936, and the Harper Prize in 1935.

Davis' next book was a volume of poetry, *Proud Riders and Other Poems,* published in 1942. Again, the critical reception, though largely positive, was somewhat mixed. "Rather heavy-footed the lines, but interesting," wrote Pearl Strachan for the *Christian Science Monitor,* while *Saturday Review of Literature* critic S. H. Hay called it "a distinguished collection. It is distinguished not only because of the authority of material and concept, because it presents a locale, the far west of the United States, in singularly fresh and vivid terms; but because it has a peculiarly intense quality of emphasis on a personal landscape."

After the success of *Honey in the Horn,* the Davises moved to Napa, California, but their marriage failed and they divorced in 1943. During this time, Davis was also embroiled in a dispute with his publisher, Harper and Brothers, concerning the contract terms for his second novel. In 1947, Davis switched to another publisher, William Morrow of New York. His second novel, *Harp of a Thousand Strings,* appeared that year. *Harp* is a complex, interweaving, allegorical story of the travels of three American seamen and one Frenchmen during the time of the French Revolution. *New York Herald Tribune* critic James Hilton deemed it "not an easy novel to read. Characters are introduced abruptly [and] there are random divagations that seem to have little to do with the main narrative." At the same time, Mary McGrory declared in the *New York Times* that "Mr. Davis' virtuoso style, biblical in its cadences, is a continuous joy."

Davis' third novel, *Beulah Land,* published in 1949, was the story of a young half-Indian girl and an Indian foundling white boy, and their journeys together up and down the Mississippi River and across the West. Once again, Davis received mixed reviews. *Saturday Review of Literature* reviewer D. L. Morgan called *Beulah Land* a "fascinating story, filled with a sense of the richness and vastness of America as it existed a century ago." But Ann Schakne, writing for the *New York Times,* declared "[I]t is not a good novel; it lacks vitality and animation."

Davis's fourth novel, 1952's *Winds of Morning,* is widely considered his best novel. "A western in a sense and a mystery in a sense, *Winds of Morning* is much more than either or both of these." wrote A. B. Guthrie for the *New York Times. Winds* is another story of life on the Northwestern frontier, concerning a young deputy sheriff and an old settler who travel through the Oregon countryside. One character discovers love; the other comes to terms with his troubled past.

Davis remarried in June of 1953 and published a collection of short stories and sketches, *Team Bells Woke Me,* that same year. His final novel, *The Distant Music,* a family chronicle set in southeastern Oregon, came out in 1957. It was often seen as a step down from the triumphant *Winds of Morning. Christian Science Monitor* critic Horace Reynolds wrote that it was "a disappointing, inconclusive book." And a *Kirkus Reviews* writer called it "An erratic book, ... but with an authoritative power that has characterized H. L. Davis since his unforgettable *Honey in the Horn.*"

In 1959, shortly before Davis' death in 1960, a collection of his essays and one short story were published in a volume entitled *Kettle of Fire.* The reviews were generally laudatory. *Christian Science Monitor* contributor Harlan Trott called *Kettle of Fire* "a collection of reflective adventures packed with fine descriptive writing, history flavored with folklore." William Hogan wrote in the *San Francisco Chronicle,* "While we might welcome a sound H. L. Davis novel at this time more than a collection of relatively minor pieces by a major writer, *Kettle of Fire* is better than no Davis at all."

H. L. Davis is appreciated today for his vivid depictions of landscape and his precise and realistic characters. He was also one of the first writers to discern and to illustrate the relationship between challenges posed by a wilderness environment without, and the struggles of the human spirit within.

Works Cited

Butcher, Fanny, review of *Honey in the Horn, Chicago Daily Tribune,* August 24, 1935.

Cantwell, Robert, review of *Honey in the Horn, New Republic,* September 4, 1935.

Cowley, Malcolm, review of *Honey in the Horn, New Republic,* December 11, 1935.

Review of *The Distant Music, Kirkus Review,* November 1, 1956.

Guthrie, A. B., review of *Winds of Morning, New York Times,* January 6, 1952.

Hay, S. H., review of *Proud Riders and Other Poems, Saturday Review of Literature,* August 15, 1942.

Hilton, James, review of *Harp of a Thousand Strings, New York Herald Tribune,* November 2, 1947.

Hogan, William P., review of *Kettle of Fire, San Francisco Chronicle,* November 13, 1959.

McGrory, Mary, review of *Harp of a Thousand Strings, New York Times,* November 16, 1947.

Morgan, D. L., review of *Beulah Land, Saturday Review of Literature,* June 11, 1949.

Reynolds, Horace, review of *The Distant Music, Christian Science Monitor,* January 31, 1957.

Schakne, Ann, review of *Beulah Land, New York Times,* June 5, 1949.

Strachan, Pearl, review of *Proud Riders and Other Poems, Christian Science Monitor,* April 18, 1942.

Trott, Harlan, review of *Kettle of Fire, Christian Science Monitor,* October 15, 1959.

For More Information See

BOOKS

Bain, Robert, *H. L. Davis,* Boise State University Press, 1974.

Bryant, Paul T., *H. L. Davis,* Twayne, 1978.

Contemporary Literary Criticism, Volume 49, Gale (Detroit, MI), 1988.

Dictionary of Literary Biography, Volume 9: *American Novelists, 1910-1945,* Gale, 1981.*

*   *   *

DELRIO, Martin
See MACDONALD, James D.

E

ELLISON, Emily

Personal

Female.

Addresses

Home—Atlanta, GA. *Agent*—c/o Longstreet Press, 2140 Newmarket Parkway, Suite 118, Marietta, GA 30067.

Career

Writer, 1979—.

Writings

Alabaster Chambers, St. Martin's Press (New York City), 1979.
First Light, Morrow (New York City), 1985.
(Editor with Jane B. Hill) *Our Mutual Room: Modern Literary Portraits of the Opposite Sex,* Peachtree Publishers (Atlanta, GA), 1987.
The Picture Makers, Morrow, 1990.

FOR CHILDREN

My Reading List: A Child's Personal Reading Record, Longstreet Press (Atlanta, GA), 1995.
A Keepsake Journal of Books Read to Me, Longstreet Press, 1995.
Rocky Bobocky the Pizza Man, illustrated by Vickey Bollinger, Longstreet Press, 1996.

Sidelights

Editor, novelist, and children's book writer, Emily Ellison is a commentator on Southern life. Her novel *First Light* tells the story of a dutiful daughter, who returns to Georgia to take care of her cancer-suffering mother, deal with other relatives, and contemplate her own life. "This isn't a novel of obvious plot, but one of surprise and unfolding with wonderful, singular moments along the way," asserted Holly Prado in the *Los*

Emily Ellison's Pizza Man loves to entertain his customers but needs help from some math wizards to save his business. (Cover illustration by Vickey Bolling.)

Angeles Times Book Review. The world where Ellison's characters exist, "isn't dull for a moment, and the powerful final scene provides the joyful glow that gives the book its title," she concluded.

With Jane B. Hill, Ellison edited a collection of short stories that are intended to represent the best in cross-genre writing, that is, works written by imagining the interior life of characters who are the opposite sex of the writer. Ellison compiled *Our Mutual Room: Modern Literary Portraits of the Opposite Sex* to refute the contention of Reynolds Price that fewer contemporary writers are daring to write about characters of the opposite gender. The collection includes fifteen novel excerpts and two short stories by such authors as Alison Lurie, Gail Godwin, Louise Erdrich, Anne Tyler, Raymond Carver, John Irving, and John Updike. "The book is intellectually exciting and worthwhile," praised Jacqueline Eis in a review for *Prairie Schooner.* "Its message is that times *have* changed. The sheer abundance of materials gathered here is convincing evidence that the cross-gender novel should no longer be considered a rare exception." "The stories in *Our Mutual Room* spotlight changes in sex roles today more effectively than many nonfiction pop sociology texts," determined Alex Raksin for the *Los Angeles Times Book Review.*

The Picture Makers is about just that, people for whom making pictures is a primary life activity: artists, photographers, indeed, all creators of art. It is told through monologues by seven main characters and fluctuates in time between 1963 and 1988. The work elicited mixed reviews. Writing in *Library Journal,* Thomas L. Kilpatrick called Ellison a "talented young writer" who is a "fine example of Southern regional literature." W. L. Taitte in the *New York Times Book Review* praised Ellison's talent in bestowing to "each of her characters an inner voice that her readers cannot quite tell from their own, to make each one a picture of a human being capable of—worthy of—being identified with and being loved. I wonder if anyone has ever written another novel in which it is such a pleasure to dwell in so many narrators' consciousness, to have access to the deepest part of so many sympathetically imagined lives."

Among Ellison's works for children include the picture book *Rocky Bobocky, The Pizza Man,* about a pizza maker who needs business sense and a math-whiz mother who needs a cook for her six children. A *Publishers Weekly* reviewer found the mood upbeat and the tone enthusiastic, and concluded the book to be "an enjoyable outing."

Works Cited

Eis, Jacqueline, review of *Our Mutual Room: Modern Literary Portraits of the Opposite Sex,. Prairie Schooner,* winter, 1989, pp. 119-122.

Kilpatrick, Thomas L., review of *The Picture Makers, Library Journal,* June 1, 1990.

Prado, Holly, review of *First Light, Los Angeles Times Book Review,* September 1, 1985 p. 114.

Raskin, Alex, review of *Our Mutual Room: Modern Literary Portraits of the Opposite Sex, Los Angeles Times Book Review,* September 6, 1987, p. 14.

Review of *Rocky Bobocky the Pizza Man, Publishers Weekly,* April 22, 1996, p. 72.

Taitte, W. L., "Heart Like a Car," *New York Times Book Review,* October 14, 1990, p. 16.

PERIODICALS

Booklist, June 15, 1990, p. 1956.

Kirkus Reviews, May 15, 1985, p. 436.

Library Journal, October 15, 1991, p. 152.

New York Times Book Review, April 26, 1992, p. 32;

Publishers Weekly, May 24, 1985, pp. 62-63; March 23, 1992, p. 68.

School Library Journal, April, 1986, p. 71; October, 1997, p. 126; November, 1998, p. 105.

Southern Living, August, 1986, p. 81; March, 1991, p. 118.*

Autobiography Feature

Judith Ross Enderle

1941-

In the Beginning

Books and my childhood go together like peanut butter goes with jelly. In my family, books and the love of reading were handed down. So I owned my mother's childhood books, inscribed "To Ellenore on her fourth birthday"—a set of Mother McGrew stories with

visible morals, like the donkey having long ears because he listened at keyholes.

Before I could read, my mother read to me. I heard all the nursery rhymes and memorized them. The wolf would never have fooled me, I was certain, when I heard "Red

Judith Ross Enderle

Riding Hood." And I felt sorry for the baby bear when Goldilocks broke his chair and ate all his porridge. "Little Black Sambo" was a child who outsmarted a tiger. If ever a tiger chased me up a tree, I would know just what to do. When we visited my grandmother or she visited us, I was treated to Uncle Wiggly stories, one each night at bedtime. My father told me stories, too—stories about a mouse and his many adventures. My parents were and still are avid readers.

When I learned to print my name, I made sure that the books I loved were marked as mine. Inside *The Shy Little Kitten, The Lively Rabbit,* and my very favorite *The Poky Little Puppy* by Janette Sebring Lowrey, my name was inscribed—Judith Ross with a backward J. I loved *The Poky Little Puppy* best because of the sounds of the words "roly-poly, pell-mell, tumble-bumble" and the idea of a puppy exploring the world and coming home to eat dessert even though he was in trouble. This book influences me even now; in my writing, the sound of words is important, I still love dessert, and I'm always up for an adventure in the "wide, wide world."

From the beginning, books were important, and the beginning began in November, 1941. Until my sister arrived almost three years later, I was the center of my parents' universe and the first grandchild on my mother's side. I didn't grow up surrounded by a large, extended family. My closest bond was with my maternal grandparents, especially my grandmother. I barely knew my paternal grandparents or most of my aunts, uncles, or cousins. Both

of my parents had left their home states for college in Michigan, my mother moving from Ohio and my father from Massachusetts. They met at a dance, married after graduation, and stayed in Detroit. My sister and I have followed this tradition of leaving our home states; my sister lives on the east coast and I live on the west coast.

My earliest memory is of a Detroit winter when my mother spread newspaper on the floor and scraped snow off the windowsill into a cup so I could play in the snow. This must have been when I was about two. I vaguely remember wanting to play with the children in my neighborhood, but whether this is a true memory or one acquired because of a photo from my childhood where I am the last in a line of kids on the block, I can't say. My most vivid memories start around this time, however.

Each summer for the first five years of my life, we packed up and crossed the river to Canada where my grandmother owned a cottage. After we had driven through the tunnel under the Detroit River and passed the customs booths, we traveled for what seemed forever to me. Getting close meant the stench of the pea-canning plant; nearer was signalled by rumbling across the metal bridge; I knew we were almost there when the car passed the tiny store where a cooler stood on the wooden porch, the store that sold my favorite summer ice cream cones. At last we bumped over the railroad tracks. Queen Anne's lace and tiger lilies grew wild in front of fat cattails all along the railroad tracks. We drove down the gravel road past other lakefront homes and turned by the painted rock into a narrow drive lined with trees. We'd always wait to see if the grounds were flooded, for some years the lake waters rose to fill the yard. If the lake had moved up, my parents waded to the house. If not, we'd walk past the pole where the scarlet trumpet vine grew, past the grape arbor that would yield grapes for jam later in the summer, under the rose trellis, then across a yard dotted with weeping willows and apple trees, until we reached the house. Both the front and back of the house sported screened porches, boarded for the winter.

The best thing about the back porch was the big painted table where we ate our meals and its porch light that resembled a small red house. The bulb made it look as if someone lived inside, and I liked to pretend it was home for the elves and fairies I so firmly believed in. I've never seen another like it. Though there was a doorway, table settings and food were passed through the window that opened between the porch and the kitchen. If you could go through the window, why use the door? The adult joke always seemed to be "While you're up . . ." with a contest to see who would be the first to rise from the table and take orders for seconds. I was always willing to be first so I could climb through the window, but I was never big enough to be a contestant.

But I've got us eating family meals and we were just arriving at the cottage. Settling in involved a fire lit in the fireplace to chase the dampness out, a check for dead critters who may have moved in during the winter, water line inspection to be sure they hadn't been damaged by a freeze, and finally boxes unpacked.

The dark oak sideboard in the living room contained treasures galore: dominoes, playing cards, pick-up-sticks, tiny china dolls, marbles, board games, and books, always books. There was something to do, rain or shine, at the cottage in Canada.

My father came to the cottage during his vacation and on the weekends. My grandfather was an occasional visitor, as were my aunt and some of her friends.

This must have been a truly happy time in my childhood for, though the cottage was sold when I was five, I can still draw the floor plan, see the mounds of bluebells that lined the walk to the beach, picture the birdbath surrounded by hen and chick plants, the rock garden that rose up to the sand, smell the mustiness of the leather furniture and the sweetness of the honeysuckle. I can hear the rhythmic creak of the porch swing and can sing snatches of the songs played on the wind-up Victrola, songs like "Mis-sis-sippi," "Don't Bring Lulu," and "Ka-Ka-Ka-Katy."

I can still recount the events that impressed me at the Canadian cottage:

On the beach, I met a nursemaid who had come with the renters next door to watch their children. She was cooling her feet in the water, and I rubbed her toe to see why the dark color had not washed off in the lake. When I asked her about it, she laughed and said, "That's the way God made me." But she didn't know why the palms of her hands and bottoms of her feet were lighter. "Maybe that color wore off from all my hard work," she told me.

There was the Fourth of July, when the weather was so hot my mother and grandmother were certain that the fireworks my dad bought would blow up inside the house before the night arrived. I recall chairs lining the sand on the beach and Roman candles soaring over the water to explode in a shower of color, sparklers that I held straight out in front of me, spinning pinwheels that shot stars into the night for a grand finale.

My grandmother and I made frequent visits to the neighbor, Coreen, who had a cookie jar on top of her icebox, always filled with sugar cookies just for me. It was my job to announce our approach as we squeezed between the snowball bushes that separated our properties. "Yoo-hoo, Coreen, I'm here," I'd call. That family had a woody wagon that I wanted to ride in, though I'm not sure that I ever did.

The lake bottom was squishy and I hated the feeling between my toes. My father taught me to dog paddle and let me help row the wooden boat.

There were tea parties with my aunt, my mother's sister, with real tea and fruitcake. I'm the only one I know besides my aunt and my mother who really likes fruitcake.

I recall the nights when my father packed rakes with newspaper and lit them like torches to set fire to the webs of tent caterpillars that were devouring my grandmother's plum trees.

My memory is filled with the buying of flats of zinnias, marigolds, gallardias, and petunias to plant in the gardens (even today I love going to a nursery and choosing plants), putting coffee grounds on the roses (my job), beach bonfires, the wooden lawn swing with facing seats, the vegetable man who came in his truck, the ice man who brought the huge frozen blocks to keep the icebox cold, saving watermelon rinds to make pickles, the smell of bubbling grape jam poured into small jars and sealed with wax, homemade apple pie, the sawdust on the floor at the butcher shop, going to the hotel dining room to eat frog legs and a chocolate malt, rainbow cookies and rolled cinnamon bread from the bakery, a toaster that folded out

on both sides, vanilla ice cream cones, a weasel that tried to get into the attic, the Shawnee Gun Club where premeal appetizers were cottage cheese and pickled beets and where stuffed animal heads lined the walls, a hammock made from barrel staves where I occasionally napped, mock french fries made from the bread crusts I absolutely refused to eat but which tasted wonderful in their new disguise, my painted iron bed that rocked when the train passed down on the railroad tracks.

Then there was my grandmother's terrier, Skippy, chasing mice in the cupboard, the clay man figurine who grew hair when you sprinkled him with grass seed, cut flowers that fit into the little holes in a glass flower arranger, pouring salt on the weeds in the gravel drive, trapping wasps in the windows, hundreds of fish flies clinging to the sides of the house during their brief life cycle, threading needles for my grandmother who made me dresses to wear when I started kindergarten, maple sugar candy, and all the freedom and lack of cares that should be a part of childhood.

My love of flowers and gardening, my lack of fear and respect for insects, my enjoyment of the outdoors were born in me at this cottage from my childhood.

I don't recall my sister Mariellen being born or me having any resentment over her arrival, though I know we did have our share of childhood arguments and even today we debate whether Mom likes her best. Our family moved after her birth from our small house on the east side of Detroit into a larger home on Oakfield Avenue on the west side. Out front was a huge maple that provided tons of leaves and twirly seeds. In back a giant oak created shade. Wide concrete steps led up to a front porch where we sat on many summer nights until the mosquitoes drove us inside. Here, I first shared a room with my sister then later had my own private room. This is the house where I suffered the chicken pox, measles, and earaches. This is the house where I grew up and lived until I was married in 1962. Our neighborhood was full of children, and I made new friends, Lana and Mary Ann.

My mother was a teacher when newly married and again when my sister and I were old enough to come home from school and be alone. She taught third and fourth grades, then high school. My dad was an engineer for the Goodyear Tire and Rubber Company and later for Detroit Edison where he worked in the nuclear power division.

Summers that used to be spent at the cottage in Canada were now spent traveling. By the time I was in high school, I'd visited many of the states. My parents poured over maps and brochures in their planning. When my sister and I were young, my mother used to make surprise bags for our trips. If we were good, we could choose one gift from the bag. It might be a coloring book, or a magic slate, a storybook, or a deck of cards. Whatever it was, the gift kept us occupied during the long drive. My father believed in following a schedule, so we never got to see the two-headed buffalo or the snake farm or stop at the town carnival. We left early in the morning, went to the places on the schedule, and stopped just before sundown at the motel where he'd made reservations. When we got older, I read my way through our vacations. First the Bobbsey twins and then Nancy Drew went along. I don't think I ever appreciated the trips as a child. To me they were taking me away from my friends at home. When I've revisited some of the same places as an adult, I don't have strong memories of having been there, the way I remember the cottage in Canada. But I see now why my parents enjoyed seeing the United States.

Perhaps my Canadian memories have something to do with my grandmother. I remember that she went on a trip with my mother and my sister and me to Florida one winter. We took the train and I shared a bunk with her in the small compartment. We stayed at a motel in Daytona Beach and explored the sand for shells, jumped in the shallow waves, met some other kids who were staying there, and my sister got bit by a stray cat.

One summer I visited my grandmother at her apartment in Cleveland for a couple of weeks. I slept in the Murphy bed, a bed that folded out of the closet in the wall on her sun porch. When I was small, I always worried that the bed would fold up with me in it, but it never did. We listened to *Stella Dallas* and *One Life to Live* and her other radio soaps. She took me to see *Gone with the Wind,* and shopping for a coat, and then to the cafeteria where I could choose whatever I wanted to eat. We shared a pineapple sundae. And I got to visit with her friends while she played bridge.

My grandmother was a great card player. She loved gin rummy, bridge, poker, and pinochle. I taught her to play canasta; she taught me to play solitaire and gin. Whenever she came to visit, we always played cards. She attended my high school graduation and my wedding, but she never saw any of my children. She died of a heart attack at the age of seventy-one. I still miss her.

And So to School

But back to my early childhood. In school I was a good student. I started out in an educational training kindergarten connected to Marygrove College, my mother's alma mater. From there I went on to St. Scholastica Elementary School, Our Lady of Mercy High School, and the University of Detroit. Until college, as long as the weather wasn't horrendous, I walked to school. On the way home, my friends and I would often stop at Dengle's corner store to buy candy—Powerhouse bars, chocolate babies, paper dots, or wax lips.

My favorite part of kindergarten was marching band. I always wanted to play the triangle or the tambourine, but usually got stuck with the sticks or the sandpaper blocks. I learned how to play "Farmer in the Dell" and "Bluebird." My first friends were Nancy and Mary, and I got in trouble for hanging upside down on the climbing bars and letting my underwear show. Since this was a teaching school, it wasn't unusual to be subjected to tests where you put together puzzles and tried to put the right peg in the right hole. To me, it was all fun. The teacher read to us, but we didn't learn how to read on our own.

Preparation for first grade was almost as exciting as first grade itself. Every child needed a cigar box which was obtained at the drugstore. Inside was kept a square of oil cloth to spread on the desk so it wouldn't get covered with paste, a box of crayons, pencils, kid's scissors, and an eraser. The challenge was to paste on your worksheets without making lumps. I think I'm still trying to avoid making lumps; sometimes I'm not any more successful than I was in first grade, but sometimes I manage one really smooth worksheet. What more can anyone ask in life?

All during elementary school I wanted a lunch box with a thermos; I wasn't allowed a thermos because it could get dropped and broken. In my family, breaking, losing, and spilling were all major offenses. I realize now that this was probably a result of my parents experiencing the Depression and the sacrifices of the war years, thus putting great value on what they were able to afford at last. But I remember crying all the way home if I'd lost a sweater or a book at school, knowing I'd be scolded for not being more responsible and keeping track of my things.

My new friends in first grade were Mary Ann Mack, who lived on the next street, and Karen Paul, who had long braids and sat near me in class. Karen and I went all the way through high school together.

The miracle of reading happened in first grade. My grade school was taught by Dominican nuns. Using the phonics that we learned from large charts, I made an easy transition to sounding out the words in *Dick and Jane,* then moved on to series like "Streets and Roads" and "More Streets and Roads." I took to reading as if I'd always known how—and perhaps I had. I can still remember being called on to read from *Dick and Jane* and the feeling of accomplishment when I knew the words on the page. Each year I looked forward to finding out what stories we'd find in our reading books.

Second grade brought First Communion time, and this was the year I thought I'd be a nun when I grew up. First Confession was a serious experience. I found it difficult to figure out which sins I had committed, so picked out those I thought would probably make good confessions whether I'd done them or not. The priest told me I probably had not committed adultery. I almost missed First Communion because I fell off our porch (hanging upside down off the rail) and sprained my wrist. My mother thought I'd broken it, but I was fine and even looked angelic as I walked down the aisle at church. This was also the year I almost knocked out my brand new two front teeth by falling off my bike, and the year I got in trouble for sliding down the fender of my grandmother's old car. I don't recall if I confessed either one.

In third grade I made more friends: Kay Cornell and Carolyn Schultz, friends with whom I'm still in touch. Sister Patrick Mary was my teacher and she helped me with my math, learning how to borrow. It seemed so hard, and this was the first time I really didn't understand how to do something in school.

One of the highlights of third grade was going to see movies in the church hall. We got to see *Francis, the Talking Mule* and *So Dear To My Heart* among others. At our neighborhood theater, kids could go to the matinees for nine cents. I didn't get to go when I was in third grade, but when I was older my friends and I loved going to the show.

In fourth grade I realized how much I liked to write. We had two assignments where I could put my imagination to work. The first was using our spelling words to create a story. I thrived on the challenge of the assignment. The other writing opportunity came from a lesson in the back of our English books—"Take the Wheel." This exercise gave the beginning of a story and the student was to complete it. I would have willingly skipped math (like borrowing, times tables and long division were a complete mystery to me), but I never had to be convinced to do my English or spelling homework. Thanks to the nuns and teachers at St. Scholastica School, I learned to read, to write, to diagram sentences, to punctuate—and even how to borrow, divide, and do my times tables. They were all good preparation for the writer I was to become.

Of course books continued to be important, both in and out of school. We had a small school library, but our neighborhood had no public library, and so my first experience with borrowing books came from the bookmobile that visited our block in the evenings. Whether this was my first visit, I don't know, but a winter evening stands out in my mind. The streetlight on the corner spotlighted fat snowflakes sifting down to coat the lawns and the roofs. My breath made fat puffs of steam in the night air. Snow crunched under my boots with the clamp-on buckles, and my dad held my hand as I climbed the steps of the bookmobile. The lady inside the bookmobile showed me the shelves, and right behind the driver's seat I found the children's books. On the bottom shelf were the colored fairy-tale books (red, green, blue, etc.). I wanted to read them all. I'm not sure how long after that the library was built and the bookmobile no longer came, but it was a while. Getting my own library card made me feel very important, and I always took out as many books as I was allowed, sometimes begging for a few extra. I'd read them fast and then return for a new stack. My goal was to read my way through the children's section in alphabetical order. Alas I got as far as E when I discovered Eleanor Estes and Elizabeth Enright and was immediately hooked on the Moffats and the Saturdays and all their family adventures. How appealing large families seemed to me! This, too, is the time I realized that people wrote books. I'd never met an author; no authors visited our school; and I'd never thought about where the books came from until I noticed that the books I loved had an author's name right under the title, and that these same authors had written more than one book. Because of the E's in the library, I began to read by author. I've often thought it an interesting coincidence that my married name begins with E and that I am now on the E shelf in the library.

Though it may seem I was the epitome of a bookworm, that wasn't the case. There was more, much more. My childhood included ballet lessons, starting when I was five and ending when I was eleven. I danced in our parish church minstrel shows which were fundraisers. I loved dancing and wanted to take tap dancing, too. My mother discouraged me, saying that tap shoes made too much noise. She did relent one year, however, and I got to take tap for a summer. Recently a friend and I took tap lessons. It's much harder as an adult, I found, but still fun.

Our neighborhood was full of interesting people by whom we could tell the time of day or the time of year, especially summer. There was the vegetable man with his cart, the bakery man in his truck with the big bell, the Twin Pines Dairy milkman who brought cottage cheese in aluminum tumblers and other fancy containers, the scissors grinder, the photographer with his pony, and best of all the Good Humor man who sent all the neighborhood children scurrying to their front doors to get a dime to buy ice

With her parents, Theodore and Ellenore Ross, about 1943.

cream. What a decision it was! Toasted Almond Bar, Fudgesicle, or Creamsicle?

We played hopscotch, jump rope, spun yo-yos, played ball until the streetlights came on, made bead bracelets, roller-skated on skates that needed a key to clamp them to your shoes, rode bicycles, played house and cowboys, and had summer shows in the garage where, after days of rehearsal, the singing and dancing and acting talents of every kid were on display to the younger kids and parents who paid a penny to see the show. One summer, we married my little sister in a full wedding to the little boy across the street. Hours were spent playing school with desks made from cardboard boxes, creating secret clubs with secret codes and secret passwords, playing tag, hide-and-seek, and statues. I climbed trees and jumped off a garage roof without killing myself. My sister and I belonged to the Brownies and Girl Scouts and went to day camp. My mother created treasure hunts and craft days for the whole neighborhood. The old barrel hammock that had hung between the willow trees at the Canadian cottage now hung between our garage and the old oak in our backyard, and I spent many hours lying in that hammock, reading. Then television arrived on our block.

The first TV belonged to a boy named Bobby Eubanks, who lived down the street. The kids would line up on his porch, hoping to be invited inside to watch *Howdy Doody,* or *Kukla, Fran, and Ollie.* Then at last, one by one, the rest of our families got a television. This was better than the drive-in movies, where my parents often took us in the summer. TV evenings were a family affair. I desperately wanted to watch *Lights Out* and get scared, but wasn't allowed. Later, watching *The Mickey Mouse Club,* I was certain that if I lived in California I would be discovered and become a Mouseketeer.

Winter time meant getting out sleds and skates. We built snowmen and forts and had snowball fights. One year we had an igloo in the backyard. Most of all winter meant Christmas. All holidays were important at our house: we made valentines, dyed Easter eggs and hunted for baskets of candy, trick or treated at Halloween, had huge Thanksgiving dinners, but there was nothing like Christmas (except maybe birthdays).

Santa was always generous to our family, and our living room overflowed with gifts. Even today I can recall the anticipation of Christmas morning, of finding out what Santa brought, of looking in my stocking that hung by the fireplace. We always had the tallest tree that would fit in our living room and lots of ornaments. The creche below the tree was handpainted by my mother, and the stable had been made by my grandfather from an old crate. There was the year of the new bike, the stilts, the pogo stick. There were always games and puzzles and dolls and, of course, books. Only one year stands out as a major disappointment. I was in seventh or eighth grade and desperately wanted a phonograph. My sister got the phonograph.

Christmas had the best music, the solemnity of midnight Mass, the anticipation of opening presents. Later, until it was time to go back to school, there was visiting with the other kids on the block to show and to share.

I still enjoy Christmas and birthdays. I love the giving of gifts; choosing just the right thing for each family member, for each friend, is important to me.

When I was in fifth grade, I wrote an autobiography in which I described myself as arriving with the Thanksgiving turkey (my birthday, November 26, often coincides with Thanksgiving). I got an A. That year I also wrote about a caterpillar named Powderpuff and created a booklet on transportation for social studies. Sister Ann Martin read one chapter of *Lassie Come Home* to the class each week.

I also learned about Dominican Camp from my teacher, who was going to work at the camp that summer. More than anything I wanted to go to Dominican Camp, a girls' camp on Kelley's Island in Ohio. My parents checked it out and agreed I could go. So did the parents of several other girls in my class. Parents worried about summer polio epidemics and so they were glad to have us out of the city for part of the summer.

At camp, I wasn't in a dorm with any of the girls I knew, but I bunked with a girl who lived on the east side of Detroit and we became good friends. Her name was Marilyn Mauser, and once again we live across town from each other, this time in California. In a way, it's because of Marilyn that I moved away from Michigan.

Her family invited me to travel to California with them one summer. This was one state I'd never visited with my parents (though I did a couple of years later). I returned with the smell of orange blossoms in my blood and tales of all the tourist sights. Once I'd had a taste of the Golden State, I wanted to return. Sadly the scent of orange blossoms is now gone from Los Angeles; the orange groves have been replaced by homes.

Camp was a wonderful experience for me. I learned to shoot a bow and arrow, to swim, to crochet, and I spent hours with other campers picking cherries that we later pitted so the nuns could make cherry pies for the whole camp. There were field trips to the Glacial Grooves and Crystal Caves as well as Cedar Point, an amusement park. The summers spent at camp were special.

Sixth grade brought with it the discovery of boys. Oh, I'd had a crush on Hopalong Cassidy, but he was a cowboy. Now I liked real boys. I won my first boyfriend by racing another girl in a bike race. His name was Gerald, and I don't think he even knew he was the prize. Sixth grade makes me think of skating parties, both roller-skating and ice-skating, being in the choir, and riding my bike everywhere. In sixth grade I started reading my parents' books—*A Tree Grows in Brooklyn, Rebecca,* and others.

Seventh and eighth grades were occupied with more boys and the latest fads, like wearing dog collars around your ankle and turning the collar of your blouse up. Pony tails or duck tails were the hair styles for the girls, and the important colors were pink and black for both boys and girls, though at school we didn't have to worry about that because we all wore blue-and-white uniforms. Our school had expanded, so the "older" kids were now in a new building with new lockers. We danced at the church hall on Friday nights and in front of the television while watching *American Bandstand.* At parties we played kissing games. Schoolwork was harder and so was concentrating on it, but there were high school entrance tests to take so we couldn't

While spending the summer at her maternal grandmother's cottage in Canada, with baby sister, Mariellen, 1945.

slack off in our studies. The girls at St. Scholastica School went on to either Our Lady of Mercy High School or Immaculata High School, both all-girl schools. No more distractions in the classroom, but that didn't keep us from thinking about or from meeting boys.

I passed all my tests, graduated from eighth grade, and entered Our Lady of Mercy High School. Our uniforms were maroon jumpers over beige, long-sleeved blouses with Peter Pan collars, and maroon-and-white saddle shoes that had to be polished. There was no talking in the school halls or in study hall. We were there to learn and to go on to college. We formed girls' clubs with Greek names, belonged to goal-oriented groups like Future Teachers and Future Nurses, and entered essay contests. My friends were the same girls I'd known since elementary school and some new girls. There was Carolyn, Kay, June, Leonore, Donna, Angela, Ginny, Helen, Karen, and others. We were a group growing up together, playing, partying, and planning for the future.

Tenth grade was memorable because I was first published in a national high school poetry anthology, and I met my first serious boyfriend at driver's training, an afterschool program where I was one of two girls enrolled. His name was Larry and we dated all through high school. We partied, hung out at the drive-in restaurant, went to lots of movies, and all the proms. The first young adult novel I wrote, *Cheer Me On,* starts out with a girl meeting her boyfriend in driver's training. She almost runs over him, not the way I met Larry, but authors do tend to embroider on their own experiences.

In high school I excelled in English, managed three years of math, struggled through Latin, liked French, found history full of too many dates, suffered through gym, was dismal at chemistry, and barely squeaked through typing (I made up for this later). I was in the choir and was a French doll in the school production, *Babes in Toyland.* Graduation ceremonies were conducted with the girls wearing long white dresses and carrying red roses. My group of friends celebrated with a trip to Houghton Lake, where we walked through town singing and skinny-dipped in the lake after dark. Most of us were going on to college.

A lot changes after high school. Larry and I parted ways when I went off to college at the University of Detroit. He went into the service when he graduated.

At college I thought I'd follow in my mother's footsteps and become a teacher, but one afternoon, when on a dare I was walking around the student union wearing army boots that belonged to one of the guys, I met my husband-to-be, Dennis. Dennis is a quiet guy, always thinking, not talking much. We are as opposite as the old cliche—night and day.

The year after we met I transferred into a two-year business course and we graduated in June, 1962. I had three years of college and a certificate in business; he had a degree in accounting. Both of us held jobs during school; I worked as a sales clerk at the J. L. Hudson Company and as a typist for an insurance company, where I later learned how to rate policies. The August following graduation, we were married at St. Scholastica's Church. We've been married almost thirty-five years.

My wedding day is hazy in my mind. My sister was my maid of honor, my bridesmaids were my friends from elementary school: Kay and Carolyn plus Dennis's sister, Suzanne. His little sister Maryann was my flower girl. I remember that the altar society didn't get the money we'd given the priest, and so there were no fresh flowers on the altar. Funny how you remember what went wrong, not all the things that went right.

We honeymooned in the Poconos, then married life started in a one-bedroom flat on Turner Avenue in Detroit. I worked first for the insurance company where I'd been employed while in college, then for the Department of Health, then finally for the Ford Motor Company at Wixom. I was bored by the repetition and routine of the work. Still, the experience in business has stood me in good stead because writing is also a business. Besides, I'm still a fast typist, me who almost flunked typing in high school.

We saved our money and bought our first home on Utley Road in Woodcreek Farms, a small village in the Farmington area. On February 10, 1965, I became a mom; we celebrated the birth of Kevin. Eighteen months later, on September 19, 1966, we celebrated once more when Brian was born. With two small boys, I was a stay-at-home mom.

I love being a mom. My kids are terrific, just ask me. I loved watching my children grow and learn. I enjoyed playing, pretending, rediscovering the world through their eyes. Because of my children my thoughts first turned to writing. I had pulled out all my favorite childhood books to share with the boys and thought that I'd like to write stories. My efforts were brief. I had no idea how hard writing would be. Kevin was three; Brian was two. I was frustrated trying to be a wife, a mother, and a writer, so I put the writing away.

About this time Dennis was looking for a new job, and winter was taking its toll on us. Potty-training two little boys in snowsuits can get the best of any mom. I remembered how much I loved California and described the state my husband had never seen in terms the tourist industry would envy. Dennis was convinced, and it wasn't long before he was hired by Teledyne in Los Angeles, we sold our home, and we were headed west.

Our first California home was on Excelente Road in Woodland Hills in the San Fernando Valley. The price of California real estate was a shock. The home we could afford was on a small lot and the house was smaller than the one we'd left. But I loved the house with its gingerbread trim and crisscrossed window panes. The boys could play outside on the patio, I could grow flowers year round, what could go wrong. Well . . . .

We felt like true pioneers that first winter when we didn't have snow but had rain that was making houses slide down the mountains and our backyard as soggy as my childhood Canadian cottage yard.

But the sun does come out again in California. We settled in to stay. I got a library card. Then in 1969 we were blessed with the birth of our daughter, Monica, our California baby, and we moved to a larger house in Tarzana, named after the character made famous by his creator Edgar Rice Burroughs. Our family of three was now complete, and we added a Dalmation named Patches. At this house, the children learned to swim in our backyard pool. Here, we experienced our first major earthquake, one

Judith in front of the house on Oakfield in Detroit, about 1950.

that turned the pool water into a mini tidal wave and shattered our large picture windows.

Before I knew it my boys were into preschool, then kindergarten. Since my husband and I were both educated at parochial schools, we wanted our children to get their start the same way. For first grade, we enrolled our oldest, Kevin, at Our Lady of Malibu school. This meant a long drive each morning from the valley to the beach. It wasn't a year before we were looking at houses and property in Malibu. We found the perfect lot, a good builder who would start a house we could finish ourselves, and once more we were off.

We rented a very tiny house (smaller than our Woodland Hills home), a one-bedroom place just around the corner from our lot. Dennis and I slept in the living room and all three kids were in the bedroom. After reams of preliminary paperwork, construction got underway on our home at last. Building a home is an adventure and a challenge. I'd do it again, but I know many friends who wouldn't even begin to tackle this kind of project. I was contractor because I was the one home, and this took a lot of scheduling and a lot of supervision. When all of the outside had been completed and the drywall was up on the inside, my husband and I took over. We put up molding, stained, painted, and landscaped. The kids still talk about all the bricks they laid for our patios and our drive. Everyone helped.

Friends back in the midwest had threatened to leave us out of their address books because we had moved so much since arriving in California. But Malibu has been our home for close to twenty-five years.

Building couldn't have been a bad experience for our family, for we also built a cottage at Lake Naciemento and bought a ski boat. Until the boys were in high school, we spent holidays and summer vacations at the lake. This wasn't the cottage of my childhood, but it was a place to get away, a place to be family, a place to write. Yes, write!

When my daughter, Monica, was in third grade, I took my writing out again. Just as my mother had returned to teaching when my sister and I were old enough to manage alone, now I was going to try to establish a career I'd postponed until my children could get their own snacks and go outside to play on their own. I decided to give myself a year to get something published. Prior to this, I'd satisfied my creative urges with papier-mache, oil painting, and needlework. And all along I'd continued to read.

I set up office in my living room with a portable typewriter. I wrote story after story and my kids listened patiently as I read to them. At first I sent my work out and got only rejections back. Then, when nine months had passed, following the guidelines for a magazine called *Highlights For Children,* I wrote a story called "Mr. Purple's Christmas Stocking." That story finally brought that long awaited "We'd like to publish your story" letter from Kent Brown Jr. at *Highlights.* I was walking on air. Even today, I can remember the total delight of selling that first story.

I'd done it once and now I wanted to do it again and again. But the second sale didn't come right away. It was another two years before I made a second sale to a religious magazine. Still I wanted to write a book and see it published.

I'd read all the "how-to write" books that were on the Malibu Library shelf, immersed myself in hundreds of children's books, and was still looking for the secret that would unlock the door to becoming a truly successful children's book writer. I needed to know more. And my needs were answered. The University of California at Los Angeles was offering a course in Writing the Picture Book. I enrolled and my teacher was Sue Alexander.

Sue opened the world of the picture book; she was a tough, honest, excellent teacher. She generously critiqued her students' writing and I deluged her with my efforts. I was on the right track but needed to do more showing, less telling. I needed to know what I was trying to say in my story. I needed a story that children would care about. I protested some of her comments; she patiently explained her reasoning. I rewrote. I soaked up every word she and her guest speakers said. I asked her how many of her students had been published, and the answer was a small number. They gave up too easily, I decided. Sue showed her students that the secret was no secret. Hard work, determination, and education—those were the keys to getting published. Those are the keys to any kind of success. And she told the class about a wonderful support network dedicated just to children's authors and illustrators, the Society of Children's Book Writers (now known as the Society of Children's Book Writers and Illustrators). I joined immediately.

At home, I applied what I'd learned and continued to read the shelves of children's books at the library—this time I didn't stop at the E's. I studied the *Horn Book, The Writer, Publishers Weekly, Writer's Digest, School Library Journal,* anything and everything that mentioned children's literature. I continued to subject my children to more of Mom's stories. To their credit they listened with little complaining, sometimes to the same story more than once, and often gave me valuable feedback. "That doesn't sound like something a kid would say," my daughter would tell me. I wrote and I wrote and I wrote some more. I collected lots and lots of rejection slips and an occasional encouraging word. Sometimes it was just a "Try us again." But it meant so much.

Then, in the *Bulletin,* the newsletter published by the SCBW, I learned of a small press looking for picture book manuscripts. I sent my latest manuscript off, one based on my younger son, Brian. Brian was a collector. On his way home from school he gathered nuts, bolts, and other odds and ends. I'd find them in his pockets or on the porch, and he always had a use for them (or at least a plan). One of the strangest things I ever found in his pocket was a pat of butter. Anyway, using the idea of a child who collected things, just like Brian, I wrote *Good Junk.*

It was only about six weeks later that I got the letter that meant at last my dream had come true! My first picture-book sale was made to Dandelion Press. *Good Junk* would be a book and it was to be illustrated by another newcomer to the field, Gail Gibbons. I was giddy for weeks.

But a contract signed does not immediately a published book make. Dandelion Press struggled but didn't make it. They sold their list to Elsevier-Dutton, and this was the company that eventually published my first picture book.

In the meantime family life flowed as family life does. My children progressed through school. There were glasses, swimming lessons, soccer, flute lessons, sprains, scrapes, the miseries of math (sound familiar?), and more. My husband changed jobs. My boys got taller than their mom.

But my other life, my writing life, inched ahead. More determined than ever to be successful as a children's book writer, I signed up for the next class offered in writing for children, a class taught by Eve Bunting—Writing the Contemporary Novel for Young People. This would prove to be a true test of my dedication because that was 1979, the year that, after heavy rains, a giant boulder fell onto the Pacific Coast Highway, the main road in and out of Malibu. To get to school, I had to drive over the canyon to the San Fernando Valley, then back over the mountains again to reach Los Angeles and the university. Drive I did and it was meant to be, for in Eve's class I met a number of soon-to-be-successful children's authors as well as my future writing partner, Stephanie Gordon Tessler.

Friendships and Partnerships

The first day of class, Eve asked us to introduce ourselves and tell a little about our writing. When I heard that Stephanie was from Malibu and she heard that I was from Malibu, we interrupted the whole class exchanging phone numbers. Both of us had that long drive because of the rock. Now we could carpool.

It was during those drives to class that Stephanie and I got to know each other. We've often said that it's quite amazing that we became friends and have stayed friends for almost eighteen years now. Stephanie and I are alike in many ways: we are both oldest of two, we both had mad crushes on Hopalong Cassidy when we were children, our wedding dresses were almost identical and so were our bridesmaids' dresses, our children are almost the same ages and same birth pattern—two boys and a girl, our husbands had similar careers when we first met, we have the same writing goals, and our writing strengths and weaknesses balance perfectly.

But we are also polar opposites: Stephanie grew up in California and I grew up in Michigan, she grew up Jewish and I grew up Catholic, I'm an optimist and she's a pessimist, I'm calm and she's not, she likes popcorn and I like chocolate, and when we met we were on opposing sides of a school closure battle in Malibu. During our drives back and forth to class, we laughed a lot, we talked a lot, and I invited her to join a writing group that had just begun in Malibu—a group to which we both belonged for several years—and we planned another writing group to be formed from the members of Eve Bunting's class.

Eve was an encouraging teacher. She also took our work home. She read it aloud in the class so you could hear what you'd put on paper. Eve made you feel as if you could succeed if you just tried hard enough. For me, she made it clear what point of view meant and how to stay inside a character's head. She explained how to know if you have a whole story or just a slight idea. She shared her "bathtub" secrets for getting your story moving again. The members

Sisters Judith (left) and Mariellen, dressed for the Alumni Ball, 1959.

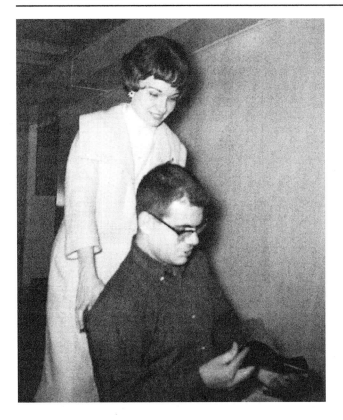

The author and her husband, Dennis Enderle, at a surprise party, 1964.

in that class were determined in the same way that I was determined to succeed in publishing.

From Eve's class came that second writing group. We would meet every month to critique our manuscripts, trying to figure out what worked, what didn't, and why. If we were stuck with a plot, we'd brainstorm together. We shared market information, celebrated sales, bemoaned rejections. All the members of our critique group formed from Eve Bunting's class are published authors now. Many of those same authors also studied with Sue Alexander.

Like the other members of that critique group, I have been published. One of the first breaks in my career came about because Connie McAllister, an editor at *Highlights For Children,* contacted me. She had enjoyed "Mr. Purple's Christmas Stocking" and wondered if I'd try writing some rebus stories to submit to the magazine. Imagine! An editor called and *asked* for my writing! I certainly didn't hesitate. After studying some samples she sent me, I went to work on rebuses. I've lost track of how many sales I've made to *Highlights* since, but it must be close to a hundred, many of them rebus stories.

With a number of magazine credits and a picture book published, I signed on to teach an extension class in Writing For Children at the Santa Monica Community College. Based on my writing experience, I applied for a life credential to teach Writing For Children in the California Community Colleges. Teaching, following at last in my mother's footsteps, made my own writing improve along with that of my students.

At home time passed with birthdays celebrated. We sold the cottage. We had to put our Dalmation to sleep (and it was left to me to make the trip; one of the most difficult

things I've ever had to do). My daughter got a horse—much more work than a dog. Horses get colic! The boys moved from their skateboards through their motorbike phases and into driver's training. My daughter went from childhood to womanhood. I watched and worried, kept the lines of communication as wide open as I could, and continued to write. I was selling to magazines, but my picture book manuscripts came back, often with encouraging letters, but no contracts.

Suddenly the young-adult romance genre blossomed. Again, SCBW played a part in my publishing career. Kathy O'Hehir, an editor at Berkley Publishing, sent a request to members to submit proposals for a new line of young-adult paperback books. Why not? I thought. I can try. But my experience so far had been in writing picture books and magazine stories. Still, I had taken a class on how to write the contemporary novel. So I headed for the store and bought some of the teen romances already on the shelf. I analyzed them: what happened in the first chapter, how were the characters introduced, how much was description, how much dialogue, how did the chapters end, how long was each chapter. When I had an idea of how a teen romance was structured, I sifted through my teen years, developed an idea, worked on a chapter and an outline, and mailed it off.

We were having a California rainstorm the day I came home from teaching my writing class to hear the phone ringing. I dropped everything inside the front door and ran to answer. "Hello, this is Kathy O'Hehir from Berkley Publishing. I love your proposal for *Cheer Me On.* I'd like to send you a contract," said the person on the other end of the phone. My first thought was, I can't write that many words. But what I said, was "Terrific. Thank you." This turned out to be the first of seventeen young-adult paperback romances that I'd write for Berkley, Scholastic, Silhouette, and New American Library. One, *S.W.A.K., Sealed With A Kiss,* got a terrible review and made the best-seller list. Teenagers were devouring these books and teenagers write letters. They wanted to know where I got the ideas, were the characters real, could they meet the girls or the boys on the cover of the book? Some readers recognized themselves or their friends in the stories. "This could have happened in my town," one girl wrote. When an author hears from her readers, it makes you realize the responsibility you have to make your stories the best that you can. A book can make a difference to a reader. Through your words you can touch someone.

My children were still subjected to "listening." They were teenagers and had the vocabulary and the insight that helped me make the stories contemporary.

But I wasn't the only one to land teen romance contracts. My friend, Stephanie, also received a contract to write for Berkley Publishing as did two other members of our Malibu critique group. Stephanie and I talked on the phone while we were writing. We compared notes. We cheered each other on.

Just like the plot in a novel, life moves up and down, like a series of mountains. We, the climbers, continue to scale one after the other. I had the second of two major surgeries in my life and survived. My family also survived the fires and floods that make Malibu almost as famous as the movie stars who live in one small nook in our community. By this time I was getting contracts for three young adult romances at a time, met frequently with my writing groups, and kept bouncing ideas back and forth with my friend Stephanie.

As it does throughout the year, the UCLA Extension Catalog arrived in the mail. As always, I scanned the writing classes offered. I called my friend and found Stephanie was also thinking that she would like to take another writing class. We signed up for a class in Writing the Genre Novel. This was about writing for the adult paperback market, so we needed something new to take to class. Putting our heads together, we created a murder mystery. We plotted, we planned, we scared ourselves, we scared our classmates, we never got the story published because we didn't finish it or submit it to anyone. But we realized that we enjoyed the process of team writing. "Let's try writing a children's book together," I said (or she said). That first story, written together, was called "Grandma G and Me in the Sidecar." Today it's called "Lizzy All Alone" and is still making the rounds. Someday we'll sell the very first book that we wrote together.

We returned to writing young-adult novels and created a proposal for the "Bayshore Medical Center" series. This was a young-adult series about nurses-in-training at a California medical center. It wasn't long before we got a call from our newly acquired agent to say she'd sold four of the six books proposed, with an option for the other two. Though we'd both graduated from portable standard typewriters to portable electric typewriters, it was time for us to get even more serious about working, so we bought our first computers—IBMs with all of 64K memory—and learned to use them by each writing two of the books for the series, exchanging manuscripts and disks, rewriting

Enderle with her three children: Kevin, Brian, and Monica, 1972.

each other's work, trading back again, until we were satisfied. Our styles blended. We were a writing team.

Writing Is a Business

For awhile we continued to write separately as well as together, but gradually more and more of our projects were joint projects. It seemed like a good idea for a team to write at the same place. Our first office together was at Stephanie's house because her son was the first to leave for an out-of-state college. We commandeered his bedroom and worked on one computer.

We also volunteered to become the regional advisors for the Southern California chapter of the Society of Children's Book Writers and planned our first conference on their behalf. This was the beginning of our chapter's growth, and it has now topped two-thousand members.

In our writing life, our agent sold several more young-adult romances. It was my pleasure to be able to call Stephanie while she was traveling in Japan just to tell her that we'd sold another book, *The Journal of Emily Ross.* She said her husband was so surprised that the phone call was for her.

When Scholastic started a series of historical novels called "Sunfire," we proposed a story set in New York. Ann Reit called and asked if we'd write a story set in Chicago during the Depression. Since I was the one who talked to her, I said, "Yes." Then I realized that I hadn't even asked Stephanie. We knew nothing about the Depression and neither of us had ever been to Chicago. I guessed she'd either hug me or hate me. Well, she didn't hate me. We went to the library and began our research (Stephanie loves research, it turns out). Our parents' friends and other acquaintances who'd grown up during the Depression in Chicago shared incidents from their lives. We got maps and figured out where our heroine lived. We drew floor plans of her home, then her flat. When our manuscript was finished, we turned it in and then came the phone call. "The cover has been planned to have a certain amount of space for the picture and a certain amount for the title. There won't be room for two authors' names. Do you want to drop one name?" The answer was a resounding "No." We'd worked too hard and too long to drop a name. But what we did do was combine our names into one. And so from Judy and Stephie came Jeffie. Ross was my maiden name. Gordon was Stephanie's maiden name. Thus, Jeffie Ross Gordon was born and her name fit perfectly on the cover of *Jacquelyn.*

Jeffie followed the Great Depression novel with the San Francisco earthquake of 1906 novel called *Nora.* While researching this book, we came across the story of Francis, a terrier that was found in the basement of the St. Francis Hotel during quake renewal. We wrote a small dog into our story, but upon final editing we were told that the manuscript was too long and we had to delete the dog. Sid Fleischman, another generous children's book writer, once said in a speech, that if you couldn't use something you loved in a book, to put it in a doggie bag and use it later. So, Francis went into a doggie bag to be resurrected several years later in a picture book called *Francis the Earthquake Dog* with both our names on the cover. When we started writing picture books, our publisher told us that bookstores were getting confused. They expected a guy named Jeff to show up to sign books and two ladies showed up. Would we mind going back to using both names? We had no problem. We still use Jeffie Ross Gordon for magazine stories, but as long as there's room on the cover, we'll be putting both names on our books.

I'd had magazine stories published, novels published, a picture book published. I was attaining the success I'd dreamed of. So was Stephanie.

One of the nicest things about writing for children is the generosity of the people in this publishing field. We have a legacy given to us by our teachers to share the wisdom. How could we share what we knew besides teaching and our activities through SCBW? In what other way could we use what we knew about writing?

We decided to create a business called Malibu Writers Ink (later changed to just Writers Ink). Through this business we critique manuscripts through the mail, specializing in children's fiction only. For a reasonable fee, we serve as a fresh eye to aspiring authors and give them detailed comments about what works, what doesn't work, and suggestions on how the manuscript might be improved and tightened. If the work is ready to submit to a publisher, we'll suggest possible markets. Though we can't promise a sale, we do promise that the writing will be improved if the author follows our suggestions. So we were writing, teaching, working with SCBW, and critiquing manuscripts through Writers Ink. And all the while, we were still wives and mothers.

They say that time flies when you are having fun. It also flies when you have growing children. Before I knew it we'd transitioned from parent/child to parent/friend, though our children never cease to be our children when it comes to worrying and we were always friends. My husband was still putting in his days at the office. I was still putting mine into writing.

Then Stephanie and her husband decided to move into the city, closer to her husband's work place. We had to make a decision: could we continue to write together and, if so, how?

Generously, Stephanie's husband offered us an office in the front part of a building where he was storing automobiles and office supplies. We jumped at the chance. So for the first time, since I'd left Ford Motor Company, I was now traveling a distance to work every day—this time to write. That office led to another office where Stephanie could bring her dogs to work and yet a third office where we work now. When we visit schools, the first overhead that we show is a picture of the office dogs, who still come to work with Stephanie.

When we moved to our second office, the boom in young adult romances was waning. Time to shift gears again. This time we went back to picture books. How can two people write a picture book? The same way we write longer books: we brainstorm the idea, one of us writes the first draft, then we pass the story back and forth. When writing novels we each choose chapters and pass those back and forth. Whichever we write, our styles blend when we are finished. One of our secrets is reading aloud. Whether we are working on picture books like *Six Sandy Sheep* or *Nell Nugget and the Cow Caper* or middle grade chapter books like *What's the Matter, Kelly Beans?,* we read the text aloud to hear the rhythm of the words. This gives us a feeling for the pacing of the story and helps us

Stephanie Gordon Tessler, illustrator Chris L. Demarest, and Judith Ross Enderle at a Highlights conference, New York, July, 1992.

know if there are parts that are too slow, parts that don't add to the plot, parts that need more development. When we were working on Nell Nugget, our office was down the hall from an accounting office. One afternoon a few months after we'd sent our manuscript off to our agent, there was a knock on our door. An accountant poked his head inside the office. "What ever happened to Moo, moo, moo. Woo, woo, woo?" he asked. "We liked hearing that story." Sometimes you never know where you'll find your audience.

One of the best things about being a writing partner with Stephanie is that she is also up for an adventure in the "wide, wide world." Opportunities come our way and we always say yes.

For example, we learned through a friend that the Fox Children's Network was going to create a children's magazine. Were we interested in editing? We said, "Yes." After making an appointment to talk with the executives at Fox Broadcasting, we sat down and went over everything we knew about magazine publishing. We were confident that we knew enough to put together an entire publication. After a couple of meetings, we became the Final Word Guys for the *Totally Fox Kids Magazine.* The magazine challenged us to look at the world in a zany way. We honed our nonfiction skills, learning to "punch up" ordinary text to give it the "Fox edge." Today we serve as consultants and final look editors and have seen this publication grow from its original few pages to a regular magazine format.

We've also been readers and freelance editors for Boyds Mills Press. When we were attending the ABA conference, Kent Brown Jr. invited us to dinner and announced that he was starting a book publishing company, Boyds Mills Press. He said he'd like to take a rebus we'd written and have us develop it into a book. That was *Six Sleepy Sheep,* the first of several sheep books that have been well received. A couple of months later, we talked to

Kent about becoming readers. He was pleased with our comments and, since we'd had experience both with our critique service and teaching, Kent asked us to do some freelance editing for his new venture. I'm pleased to have worked with Vashanti Rahaman, Isaac Olaleye, and Don Reed. Vashanti makes me especially proud because I was also her instructor during the years I taught for the Institute of Children's Literature. She was one of the students I knew would succeed if she stuck with it.

Then there was our foray into children's television. Because Stephanie and I had been working on the *Totally Fox Kids Magazine,* we had the opportunity to interact with some of the people who put together the children's television programs. One afternoon the phone rang and one of those executives asked if we knew anything about writing for film. Since we had continued taking classes, Stephanie and I had completed several film writing courses and dabbled with creating both movie and television scripts. We'd even had one of our afterschool special treatments optioned. Well, we were told that a new children's program was in development and they needed story editors who knew how young children thought, how they talked, how they reacted. Several people had tried but hadn't achieved the right voice. The characters in the show would be animals, portrayed by rug people—actors wearing plush costumes—with voice-overs recorded offstage. These

The Enderle family at daughter Monica's wedding: (from left) Brian, Dennis, the bride, Judith, and Kevin.

"My writing partner, Stephanie (right), and I with two sleepy sheep," Medina, Ohio, 1993.

animals represented a group of children who lived on an island with a kindly adult named Rimba. We were asked to revise a sample script over the weekend—a story editor takes scripts written by a number of writers and makes sure the voices and mannerisms of the characters are consistent throughout, and that the show works well within the time frame. First we read everything about the program. Then, using a large marker board, we mapped out the characters by name and characteristic, noting the age each child represented. Then we sat side-by-side at the computer and went to work. By the end of the weekend, we had a revised script. Now we waited. The following week we were invited to another meeting, this time with the producer of the program. "Which animal would work best as the adult?" they asked. They had thought the elephant, but the elephant couldn't hold anything in its hands. Perhaps the giraffe or the gorilla. It was decided that the gorilla had the most flexibility. We were to work at the production offices, not out of our own office, and we had to learn how to use Microsoft Word. (We'd been using an ancient program called Easy Writer.) Could we do it? "Yes," we said. We always say, "yes."

Contracts were negotiated; we headed to our new office. There were twenty-six scripts in all and a variety of writers, including us. We had to approve story lines, guide other writers, revise all the scripts, get approvals from the producer, the psychologist, the NEA, and get the scripts to the music department, the props department, and the production department. A show that normally takes six months or more to develop had to be done in three. Not since our children were babies had we put in such unending days. We were still at the office when the cleaning crew arrived each night and sometimes into the early morning hours. When the scripts were finally done and approved, we went to the set to listen to the actors read and time the scripts. Last minute cuts and revisions were made. It was fun to see the characters we'd created brought to life by the

actors and their voice-over counterparts. We were pleased with the results.

We learned a lot working on "Rimba's Island," enough to be invited to write a script called "The Circus" for a series based on Don Freeman's Corduroy the bear. Writing for television was a challenge, but we weren't giving up our first love, writing children's books.

Is it any wonder that one of our favorite book themes is: "Be careful what you wish for, you just might get it"?

We work five days a week at our office. Each day has a lot of parts. Part of our time is spent writing, part working for the Society of Children's Book Writers and Illustrators, part critiquing manuscripts through Writers Ink, part freelance editing and reading, part working on *Totally Fox Kids Magazine.* We still work on computers, more powerful than those first IBMs. We've graduated to Microsoft Word for Windows, an easy transition after our television work. Our computers are networked together, so we don't have to trade manuscripts pages; we can just tune into each other's computers. I can work on Stephanie's pages; she can work on my pages. But we still print and read out loud.

Our local critique group is small; we read with our first teacher, Sue Alexander. We also have two long distance critique groups; we exchange manuscripts with our friends Cheryl Byrd Zach and Laurie Lazzaro Knowlton. Additionally, there's our Shop Talk group, a group of six published writers who meet to discuss contracts, promotion, and the other business of writing.

Sometimes our adventures in the "wide, wide world" take us to speak at schools or writing conferences, to share our love of language, our love of books, our knowledge about writing. Getting in touch with our audience is often a joy and sometimes a surprise. Little ones like telling you stories. A child will tell you who snores in his family after hearing *Six Sleepy Sheep.* Whole classes will expand on *Two Badd Babies,* one of our favorite books because the idea came to us when we were traveling. This book also has been one of the favorites with our readers. We've had classes recite it for us, act it out, and create pages with pictures about The Further Adventures of.... It's been gratifying to see that not only elementary school children respond to picture books, but high schoolers can be captured with the rhythm of the words, the fabulous art (thanks to all of our wonderful illustrators), the idea of writing a whole story in just three pages. And adults— sometimes adults are the best audience of all. Teachers and parents will laugh and nod as Littlest Pig gathers his family to "find out what the cows are doing" when we share *A Pile of Pigs.* We've also found this is a wonderful book for teaching the craft of story development. Sometimes we surprise ourselves with the many threads that can be unwound from our stories, making them useful in the classrooms. Had we meant for them to be so complex? Maybe yes and then again—we like surprises, too.

As my career has developed, I've been fortunate to have a supportive family. My children are still sounding boards for some of my manuscripts. "I really like that one," my daughter might say, as I corner her to listen one more time. She's doing the same thing to me these days as she explores her own writing voice. "It's good, Mom," my sons tell me—Brian, the mechanic, and Kevin, the entrepreneur. And my husband, Dennis, still a quiet guy, brags to co-workers as well as strangers about his wife, the children's book writer. When my writing first gave me the opportunity to travel to conferences or schools to speak, to bookstores to sign, he learned how to make omelets and hamburgers and to make the bed himself. Though I'm still in charge of laundry, he's a man of the millennium; he can iron.

In seventeen years, Stephanie and I have written more than twenty-five books together and almost as many individually, so that our combined books tally over fifty. We are still married to the same husbands. We've celebrated birthdays, anniversaries, numerous holidays, and successes. Our children are grown. Two of mine are married—Kevin and Monica. And there will be more weddings, more holidays, more celebrations and, we hope, more successes in the future.

I've turned fifty-five. Inside, I'm still the kid who spent her summers at the cottage in Canada, who grew up on the west side of Detroit, who spread her wings all the way to California. Life has been "roly-poly, pell-mell, tumble-bumble" sometimes. More often it's been an adventure in "the wide, wide world."

Writings

FOR CHILDREN; FICTION

Good Junk, illustrated by Gail Gibbons, Elsevier-Dutton (New York City), 1981.
Cheer Me On!, Tempo Books, 1982.
Someone for Sara, Tempo Books, 1982.
Adrienne and the Blob (fantasy), Silhouette, 1986.

WITH STEPHANIE GORDON TESSLER

(Under joint pseudonym Jeffie Ross Gordon) *Rutabaga Ruby* (poetry), Curriculum Associates, 1989.
(Under joint pseudonym Jeffie Ross Gordon) *Hide and Shriek* (riddle book), Lerner Publications (Minneapolis), 1991.
(Under joint pseudonym Jeffie Ross Gordon) *Six Sleepy Sheep,* illustrated by John O'Brien, Boyds Mills Press (Honesdale, PA), 1991.
Six Creepy Sheep, illustrated by John O'Brien, Boyds Mills Press, 1992.
(Under joint pseudonym Jeffie Ross Gordon) *Two Badd Babies,* illustrated by Chris L. Demarest, Boyds Mills Press, 1992.
(Under joint pseudonym Jeffie Ross Gordon) *Muriel and Ruth,* Boyds Mills Press, 1992.
A Pile of Pigs, illustrated by Charles Jordan, Boyds Mills Press, 1993.
The Good-for-Something Dragon, illustrated by Les Gray, Boyds Mills Press, 1993.
(Under joint pseudonym Jeffie Ross Gordon) *Rebus Treasury II,* Boyds Mills Press, 1993.
Six Snowy Sheep, illustrated by John O'Brien, Boyds Mills Press, 1994.
What Would Mama Do?, illustrated by Chris L. Demarest, Boyds Mills Press, 1995.
Nell Nugget and the Cow Caper, illustrated by Paul Yalowitz, Simon and Schuster, 1995.

Francis, the Earthquake Dog, illustrated by Brooke Scudder, Chronicle Books (San Francisco), 1996.
What's the Matter, Kelly Beans?, Candlewick Press, 1996.
Here's Bobby's World: How a TV Cartoon is Made, Celebration Press (Don Mills, ON, Canada), 1996.
Dear Timothy Tibbitts, illustrated by Carolyn Ewing, Marshall Cavendish (New York City), 1997.
Six Sandy Sheep, illustrated by John O'Brien, Boyds Mills Press, 1997.
Where Are You Little Zack?, illustrated by Brian Floca, Houghton Mifflin, 1997.
Upstairs, Boyds Mills Press, 1998.
(With Stephanie Jacob Gordon) *Something's Happening on Calabash Street,* Boyds Mills Press, 2000.

FOR YOUNG ADULTS; ROMANCE FICTION

S.W.A.K., Sealed with a Kiss, Tempo Books, 1983.
Programmed for Love, Tempo Books, 1983.
When Wishes Come True, Tempo Books, 1983.
With Love, Lark, Dutton, 1983.
Sing a Song of Love, Tempo Books, 1984.
Will I See You Next Summer?, Tempo Books, 1984.
T.L.C., Tender Loving Care, Tempo Books, 1984.
Secrets, Silhouette, 1984.
Sixteen Sure Ways to Succeed with Sean, New American Library (New York City), 1984.
Ready, Set, Love, Tempo Books, 1985.
Kisses for Sale, Scholastic, Inc. (New York City), 1985.
Meet Super Duper Rick Martin, New American Library, 1985.
Love and Kisses, Tempo Books, 1986.

"BAYSHORE MEDICAL CENTER" SERIES (WITH STEPHANIE GORDON TESSLER)

Andrea Whitman: Pediatrics, Walker & Co. (New York City), 1983.
Monica Ross: Maternity, Walker & Co., 1983.
Elizabeth Jones: Emergency, Walker & Co., 1984.
Gabriella Ortiz: Hot Line/Crisis Center, Walker & Co., 1984.

WITH TESSLER; UNDER PSEUDONYM JEFFIE ROSS GORDON

Jacquelyn, Scholastic, Inc. (New York City), 1985.
A Touch of Genius, Silhouette, 1986.
The Journal of Emily Ross, Silhouette, 1986.
A Touch of Magic, Silhouette, 1987.
Nobody Knows Me, Silhouette, 1987.
Nora, Scholastic, Inc., 1987.
Gimme a Z, Silhouette, 1988.

OTHER

Also author of *Let's Be Friends Again,* Dandelion Press, and (with Tessler) the "Read-a-Picture" series, Modern Publishing, 1989. Contributor to *Writer's Digest Handbook of Short-Story Writing,* 1986, and *Writing for Children and Teenagers,* by Lee Wyndham and Arnold Madison. Contributor to periodicals, including *Highlights for Children* and *Writer's Digest.* Story writer and editor (with Tessler) for the first season of FOX TV's *Rimba's Island* series, and writer (with Tessler) for Viacom's *Corduroy* Animation Specials. Enderle's books have been translated into French, Italian, Spanish, German, Danish, Finnish, and Dutch.

F

FERGUS, Charles

Personal

Married, wife's name Nancy; children: William.

Addresses

Home—RD 2, 340 Mountain Rd., Port Matilda, PA 16870.

Career

Naturalist and writer, c. 1984—.

Writings

The Wingless Crow, Pennsylvania Game Commission, 1984, Lyons & Burford (New York City), 1993.
Rabbit Hunting, Allegheny Press (Elgin, PA), 1985.
Shadow Catcher, Soho (New York City), 1991.
A Rough-Shooting Dog: The First Season of a Hunting Spaniel, illustrated by Joe Fornelli, Lyons & Burford, 1991.
Gun Dog Breeds, Lyons & Burford, 1992.
The Upland Equation: A Modern Bird Hunters Code, Lyons & Burford, 1995.
Swamp Screamers: At Large with the Florida Panther, Farrar, Straus (New York City), 1996.
Summer at Little Lava: A Season at the Edge of the World, Farrar, Straus, 1998.

Sidelights

Naturalist Charles Fergus has written on a variety of topics: the joys of hunting, hunting companions, the endangered Florida panther, and seeing the ordinary and wondrous in the natural world. He also penned a memoir of his sojourn in Iceland, *Summer at Little Lava,* and a historical novel, *Shadow Catcher,* which deals with Native Americans in the West during the early twentieth century.

In 1985 the Pensylvania Game Commission compiled and published thirty-three essays that had first appeared in the *Pennsylvania Game News* as *The Wingless Crow.* With these short essays, Fergus told readers about the lives of starlings, lightning, hats, heating with wood, and hunting, among other topics. It is, to quote Charles Solomon of the *Los Angeles Times Book Review,* like "an informal chat with a knowledgeable friend." James Kaufman of the *Christian Science Monitor* noted that while Fergus easily draws readers into the essays, he "does not end as well as he begins. Sometimes the essays end in midair, arbitrarily, and other times he tries a little too hard for a compelling image, but these are minor matters. For the most part, you will simply be sorry the piece had to end." Fergus, Kaufmann added, "possesses a child's sense of wonder, an adult's ability to assemble matters into perspective, and a craftsmanlike prose that has rendered it all into a very fine book."

Fergus is also a hunter and has written about this sport in *Rabbit Hunting, A Rough-Shooting Dog, Gun Dog Breeds,* and *The Upland Equation. A Rough-Shooting Dog* is a memoir of how Fergus trained Jenny, a springer spaniel puppy, to hunt game birds. As a *Kirkus Reviews* critic noted, the book provides "pleasant reading" for the general reader as well as the more specialized information for the nature love or hunter. Phoebe-Lou Adams, writing in *Atlantic Monthly,* remarked on the "almost lyrical appreciation" with which Fergus described nature and hunting alike. On the same subject is Fergus's collection of essays entitled *Upland Equation,* an "instructive, impassioned look" at bird hunting and bird dogs, to quote Denise Perry Donavin of *Booklist.* In *Sports Afield,* Stephen Bodio declared *Upland Equation* to be a "very short and very good book."

For his look at the endangered Florida panther, *Swamp Screamers,* Fergus interviewed wildlife biologists, Seminole Indians, and landowners and other local people, as well as observing the panther for himself. In nontechnical language, he described the problems the panthers and those who want to ensure their survival face. According to a *Publishers Weekly* critic, Fergus makes a "compelling case" for further conservation efforts in *Swamp Screamers.*

Shadow Catcher diverged from Fergus's usual work. It is a historical novel in which the action revolves around the third "Rodman Wanamaker Expedition to the North American Indian" that took place in 1913. During this expedition, which was really a publicity stunt, an unofficial photographer took photos of the real lives—not the staged one of official photographs—of the Native Americans. *Shadow Catcher* caught the attention of reviewers. Although Mason Buck, writing in the *New York Times Book Review,* found the premise "intriguing" and Fergus's depiction of the West "skillful," he faulted what he considered to be flat characters and an "unsatisfying" denouement. Likewise, Schuyler Ingle of the *Los Angeles Times Book Review* commented on Fergus's depiction of the American West: "The book offers a pleasant excursion through one of many possible American Wests, the considerable skills of Charles Fergus making palpable life in a Navajo hogan or Plains Indian reservation shack." Ingle countinued: "In *Shadow Catcher,* Charles Fergus gives the reader new and old ways of witnessing the West. He touches on both what was regrettably true as well as what may hopefully come to pass. In the end, the West remains as elusive as ever, a shadow open to anyone's interpretation." Despite the author's "often graceful" writing style, a *Publishers Weekly* critic found the work to be lacking in subtlety.

While Fergus was planning a family vacation to Iceland, his mother was tragically murdered during a robbery. Despite the difficult circumstances, Fergus and his wife and son spent the summer season at a stone cottage without running water or electricity on the west coast of Iceland. While there, Fergus kept a journal, which was later published as *Summer at Little Lava.* Fergus catalogued the flora and fauna, and described the otherworldly landscape of volcanoes that had previously inspired such writers as Jules Verne and W. H. Auden. Fergus told of the country's folklore and hospitable people. And he grieved, but only as a subtext in his journal. *Summer at Little Lava* is a "compelling mix of adventure, travel, natural history, and emotional recovery," to quote a *Kirkus Reviews* commentator. In *Library Journal* Tim J. Markus called the work "fascinating" and in *Booklist* Alice Joyce declared the journal "compelling." Angeline Goreau, writing in the *New York Times Book Review,* found "many pleasures to be had in Fergus's late-twentieth-century restaging of *Walden,* but the passionate imaginative life of the place seems oddly absent."

Works Cited

Adams, Phoebe-Lou, a review of *A Rough-Shooting Dog, Atlantic Monthly,* March, 1992, p. 125.
Bodio, Stephen, review of *The Upland Equation, Sports Afield,* winter, 1995, p. 62.
Buck, Mason, review of *Shadow Catcher, New York Times Book Review,* November 10, 1991.

Donavin, Denise Perry, review of *The Upland Equation: A Modern Bird Hunters Code, Booklist,* July, 1995, p. 1853.
Goreau, Angeline, "Turning Nature Upside Down," *New York Times Book Review,* August 30, 1998, p. 11.
Ingle, Schuyler, "A Curious Slice of American History," *Los Angeles Times Book Review,* November 10, 1991, p. 8.
Joyce, Alice, review of *Summer at Little Lava, Booklist,* July 19, 1998.
Kaufman, James, "Essays of a naturalist full of wonder, perspective," *Christian Science Monitor,* April 16, 1985, p. 24.
Markus, Tim J., review of *Summer at Little Lava, Library Journal,* June 15, 1998, p. 102-103.
Review of *A Rough-Shooting Dog, Kirkus Reviews,* July 1, 1991, p. 837.
Review of *Shadow Catcher, Publishers Weekly,* July 5, 1991, p. 57.
Solomon, Charles, review of *The Wingless Crow, Los Angeles Times Book Review,* June 20, 1993, p. 9.
Review of *Summer at Little Lava, Kirkus Reviews,* June 1, 1998, p. 790.
Review of *Swamp Screamers: At Large With the Florida Panther, Publishers Weekly,* December 4, 1995, p. 51.

For More Information See

PERIODICALS

American Forests, June, 1985, p. 57.
Booklist, August, 1991, p. 2085; October 1, 1991, pp. 240, 310; February 1, 1996, pp. 906, 922.
Christian Science Monitor, November 21, 1991, p. 10.
Library Journal, August, 1991, pp. 106, 144; January, 1996, p. 134.
Los Angeles Times Book Review, November 19, 1995, p. 11.
Publishers Weekly, July 5, 1991, p. 57; July 19, 1991, p. 40; May 11, 1998, p. 56.
School Library Journal, March, 1992, p. 266.
Washington Post Book World, February 22, 1998, p. 12.*

*   *   *

FOX, Louisa
See KROLL, Virginia L(ouise)

*   *   *

FRISCHMUTH, Barbara 1941-

Personal

Born July 5, 1941, in Alt-Aussee, Styria, Austria. *Education:* Attended University of Graz; Oriental studies at University of Vienna, 1964-67.

Career

Children's writer, novelist, and short story author.

Awards, Honors

Austrian Prize, 1972, for children's books; Literary Prize of Styria, 1973; Anton Wildgans Prize, 1974; Prize of the City of Vienna, 1975 and 1979; Award of the Cultural Circle of German Industry, 1975; Honor Roll, Hans Christian Andersen Prize, 1975; Sandoz Prize for literature, 1977; Gedok Prize for literature, 1983; Ida Dehmel Prize, 1983.

Writings

IN TRANSLATION

The Convent School, translated by Gerald Chapple and James B. Lawson, Adriadne Press (Riverside, CA), 1996 (originally published as *Die Klosterschule,* Suhrkamp, 1968).

The Shadow Disappears in the Sun, translated by Nicholas J. Meyerhofer, Ariadne Press, 1998 (originally published as *Das Verschwinden des Schattens in der Sonne: Roman,* Suhrkamp, 1973).

Chasing After the Wind: Four Stories, translated by Gerald Chapple and James B. Lawson, Ariadne Press, 1996 (originally published as *Haschen nach Wind: Erzaehlungen,* Residenz, 1974).

UNTRANSLATED WORKS

Amoralische Kinderklapper, Suhrkamp (Frankfurt am Main), 1969.

Geschichten fuer Stanek, Literarisches Colloquium (Berlin), 1969.

Der Pluderich, Insel (Frankfurt am Main), 1969.

Philomena Mueckenschnabel, Insel (Frankfurt am Main), 1970.

Polsterer, Insel (Frankfurt am Main), 1970.

Tage und Jahre: Saetze zur Situation, Residenz (Salzburg), 1971.

Ida—und ob!, Jugend und Volk (Munich and Vienna), 1972.

Die Prinzessin in der Zwirnspule und andere Puppenspiele fuer Kinder, Ellermann (Munich), 1972.

Ruekkehr zum vorlaeufigen Ausgangspunkt: Erzaehlungen, Residenz (Salzburg), 1973.

Grizzly Dickbauch und Frau Nuffl, Pfaffenweiler Presse (Pfaffenweiler), 1975.

Die Mystifikationen der Sophie Silber: Roman, Residenz (Salzburg), 1976.

Amy oder Die Metamorphose: Roman, Residenz (Salzburg), 1978.

Kai und die Liebe zu den Modellen: Roman, Residenz (Salzburg and Vienna), 1979.

Entzug—ein Menetekel der zaertlichsten Art, Pfaffenweiler Presse (Pfaffenweiler), 1979.

Bindungen: Erzaehlung, Residenz (Salzburg), 1980.

Die Ferienfamilie: Roman, Residenz (Salzburg and Vienna), 1981.

Landschaft fuer Engel, Molden (Vienna and New York), 1981.

Vom Leben des Pierrot: Erzaehlungen, Pfaffenweiler Presse (Pfaffenweiler), 1982.

Die Frau im Mond: Roman, Residenz (Salzburg), 1982.

Traumgrenze: Erzaehlungen, Residenz (Salzburg), 1983.

Kopftaenzer: Roman, Residenz (Salzburg), 1984.

Herrin der Tiere: Erzaehlung, Residenz (Salzburg), 1986.

Ueber die Verhaeltnisse: Roman, Residenz (Salzburg), 1987.

TRANSLATOR

(With Robert Stauffer) *Sandor Weoeres, Der von Ungarn: Gedichte und fuenf Zeichnungen,* Suhrkamp (Frankfurt am Main), 1969.

Edward Lear, Die Jumblies, Insel (Frankfurt am Main), 1970.

(With Vera Thies and Ita Szent-Ivanyi) *Das elfte Gebot: Moderne ungarische Dramen,* Reclam (Leipzig), 1977.

Sidelights

Barbara Frischmuth is one of Austria's best known women writers. While her creative talent transcends genre, she is most noted as an author of children's books, novels, and short stories. Much of Frischmuth's work reflects the influence of philosopher Ludwig Wittgenstein, who is credited with introducing a language philosophy into literature. Her work has also been influenced by the feminist movement. Frischmuth's writing often reflects her concerns about the ongoing struggle of women to seek the perfect balance between work and home, a balancing act that Frischmuth herself was unable to successfully carry off. Married and divorced at an early age, Frischmuth's personal struggles are evident in much of her writing. It is this honesty and compassion for her fellow women that make her writing strong, as well as popular.

Frischmuth was born in July of 1941 in Austria. She spent her early years immersed in her education. A passionate student, Frischmuth's thirst for knowledge was placated at the University of Graz, as well as the University of Vienna where she collectively studied the Turkish and Hungarian languages, as well as Oriental studies.

Frischmuth first made her mark on the literary scene in 1968 with *Die Klosterschule* (published in English translation as *The Convent School*). A depiction of life at a Catholic girls' boarding school, the story uses Frischmuth's own childhood experiences at a similar school as fodder for the novel. In the story, she addresses the manipulative control that strict religious schools can inflict upon young women. *The Convent School* was written in part as a response to Ludwig Wittgenstein's work of the 1950s. Wittgenstein, an Austrian-British philosopher, was influenced greatly by math and science. In the 1920s, he had taken this interest in the sciences, combined it with his fascination with words, and came up with a philosophy that would shape literature not only in Austria, but throughout the world. His early philosophy was based on the notion that the world was composed of complex facts that could be analyzed into much simpler facts until arriving at one, atomic fact. He believed that the nature of language required these elementary facts, in conjunction with elementary propositions, to create meaning. His theory boiled down to this: the only true propositions that can be reduced to simple facts were of a scientific nature.

Thus, science, he believed, was the only philosophy that possessed any meaning. In the 1950s, however, Wittgenstein re-vamped his entire philosophy. He now claimed that philosophy was a battle against the bewitchment of human intelligence by means of language. Under this new theory, words, Wittgenstein hypothesized, were tools that served different manipulative functions.

The Convent School reflects a belief in Wittgenstein's later theory. In the novel, Frischmuth discusses the influence of Catholic schools upon young women. She believes that these schools present limited options to young women about their future. In short, Frischmuth claims that while it is difficult enough for young women to establish their independence, it is even more challenging when they are constantly presented with the roles of wife and mother as their only available options in adult life. In her opinion, the Catholic church relies on manipulative language to coerce young women into early marriage and motherhood, a fate Frischmuth herself did not escape.

After *The Convent School,* Frischmuth's next literary efforts were geared towards children. In the late 1960s, and early 1970s, she primarily wrote children's books, including *Der Pluderich* (1969), *Philomena Mueckenschnabel* (1970), *Polsterer* (1970), *Die Prinzessin in der Zwirnspule* (1972), *Ida—und ob!* (1972), and *Grizzly Dickbauch und Frau Nuffl* (1975). These works illustrate Frischmuth's creative diversity, as well as her humor and ability to connect with children on their own level.

During the early 1970s, along with her books for kids, Frischmuth continued writing semi-autobiographical and philosophical literature for adults. Once again utilizing the ideals of Wittgenstein, she wrote a collection of short stories titled *Tage und Jahre: Saetze zur Situation* ("Days and Years: Sentences on the Situation"). These stories appear to have little relation to one another. However, they represent Frischmuth's attempt at non-manipulative storytelling. Her goal was for readers to put the pieces together on their own, drawing their own conclusions.

In the 1970s, Frischmuth also began addressing issues close to her heart: mainly, the plight of women struggling for independence. The first of these novels, *Haschen nach Wind* (published in English translation as *Chasing After the Wind*), was published in 1974; it dealt with the struggles women encounter when trying to balance work and family. According to *Dictionary of Literary Biography* essayist Donald G. Daviau, of the four stories presented in *Haschen nach Wind,* none end happily, nor does Frischmuth provide solutions to the problems she addresses. Daviau stated, "They are stories with dead ends: things cannot continue this way any longer, think the women, who no longer know which way to turn. But things do continue this way .... These stories are for reliving, for recalling, for self-recognition. They do not help us out of problems, they help us into them."

Frischmuth's next novel was the first in a trilogy of female-driven novels. *Die Mystifikationen der Sophie Silber* ("The Mystification of Sophie Silber") was published in 1976. In this story, the spirit world is threatened by the human exploitation of natural resources. Thus, spirits congregate in Austria to talk about their fate. The title character, Sophie Silber, is invited to the spiritual conference and sees a vision of her future. This vision brings about a change in Sophie, and she returns to her life determined to change the course of her destiny through increased confidence and self-awareness. When Sophie reconnects with a son she has not seen in eighteen years, the spirits decide to take human form in an effort to save other humans like they saved Sophie. Daviau pointed out that Sophie's adventure "presents a feminist program for the future: the humanized female spirits will not become political activists but will simply live well-integrated, happy, successful lives as independent career women and thus serve as role models for other women." Throughout Frischmuth's work, it is clear that she believes in presenting women with healthy role models, as well as lifelong opportunities other than that of wife and mother.

Frischmuth's second work in the trilogy is 1978's *Amy oder Die Metamorphose* ("Amy; or, The Metamorphosis"). This story centers on Amaryllis, one of the spirits-turned-human, as she embodies Amy Stern, a young medical student inflicted with both physical and emotional problems. In the course of the novel, Amaryllis transforms Amy into a vivacious, healthy young woman. While she experiences the ups and downs of life, Amy eventually chooses independence over being taken care of, as well as pursuing her own career interests rather than the ones presented her with ease. By the end of the novel, Amy's transformation represents a strong woman that will act as a great role model for other women.

The third in Frischmuth's trilogy is *Kai und die Liebe zu den Modellen* ("Kai and the Love of Possibilities"), published in 1979. In this final installment, Amy is raising her five-year-old son Kai in a unique fashion. Wanting him to understand that girls are equal to boys, she often dresses him up in girls' clothing. With this novel, Frischmuth addresses the issues of putting children first over temporary love relationships. The story illustrates Amy's devotion to her son by choosing not to let the father, Klemens, move in with them. While Amy cares for Klemens, she senses that he is caught up in his career and is not sincerely interested in raising a child.

Frischmuth continued writing throughout the 1980s, publishing in a variety of literary forms. While some stories mirrored themes used in much of her earlier work, others were a departure from it. *Entzug—ein Menetekel der zaertlichsten Art* ("Withdrawal—a Most Tender Warning"), strays the most. The two stories presented in this work deal with erotic imagery and sexual longing. In the first tale, a woman longs for her absent lover. In the second, a young teacher fantasizes about the perfect lover.

"Frischmuth's writings offer a model study of the development of contemporary Austrian literature from an aesthetic preoccupation with language to a concern for social issues . . . ," concluded Daviau. "Frischmuth's characters, even the supernatural ones, stand out vividly; the only apparent weakness is a lack of roundedness and depth, especially in the male characters."

Works Cited

Daviau, Donald, G., article in *Dictionary of Literary Biography,* Volume 85: *Austrian Fiction Writers after 1914,* Gale, 1989.*

G

GARDEN, Nancy 1938-

Personal

Born May 15, 1938, in Boston, MA; daughter of Peter (an executive and fund raiser) and Elisabeth (a psychologist and social worker; maiden name, Yens) Garden. *Education:* Columbia University, B.F.A. from School of Dramatic Arts, 1961, M.A. from Teacher's College, 1962. *Hobbies and other interests:* Reading, First Amendment issues, gardening, weaving, hiking, running, traveling.

Addresses

Home—Carlisle, MA, and West Tremont, ME.

Career

Scholastic Magazines, New York City, began as assistant editor, became associate editor, 1966-70; Houghton Mifflin Co., Boston, MA, editor, 1971-76; writing teacher, freelance writer, and book reviewer, 1976—. Has also worked in theater as an actress and lighting designer, taught at various levels, and done freelance editorial work for various publishers. Gives talks at schools and libraries to children on writing and speaks at writers', librarians', and teachers' conferences for adults. *Member:* Society of Children's Book Writers and Illustrators.

Awards, Honors

Editor's Choice, *Booklist,* 1982, Best Books, American Library Association (ALA), 1982, Best of the Best 1970-1983, ALA, and Best Books for Young Adults 1969-1994, ALA, all for *Annie on My Mind;* Books for the Teen Age, New York Public Library, 1995, for *Dove and Sword;* Lambda Book Award, 1996, Notable Children's Trade Book in the Field of Social Studies, National Council for the Social Studies and Children's Book Council, and Books for the Teen Age, New York Public Library, both 1997, all for *Good Moon Rising.*

Writings

FICTION

What Happened in Marston, illustrated by Richard Cuffari, Four Winds, 1971.
The Loners, Viking, 1972.
Maria's Mountain, illustrated by Barbara Brascove, Houghton, 1981.
Annie on My Mind, Farrar, Straus, 1982.
(Adaptor) *Favorite Tales from Grimm,* illustrated by Mercer Mayer, Four Winds, 1982.
Prisoner of Vampires, illustrated by Michele Chessare, Farrar, Straus, 1984.
Peace, O River, Farrar, Straus, 1986.
Lark in the Morning, Farrar, Straus, 1991.
My Sister, the Vampire, Knopf, 1992.
Prisoner of Vampires, Farrar, Straus, 1993.
My Brother, the Werewolf, Bullseye Books, 1994.
Dove and Sword, Farrar, Straus, 1995.
Good Moon Rising, Farrar, Straus, 1996.
The Year They Burned the Books, Farrar, Straus, 1999.
Holly's Secret, Farrar, Straus, 2000.

"FOURS CROSSING" SEQUENCE

Fours Crossing, Farrar, Straus, 1981.
Watersmeet, Farrar, Straus, 1983.
The Door Between, Farrar, Straus, 1987.

"MONSTER HUNTERS" SERIES

Mystery of the Night Raiders, Farrar, Straus, 1987.
Mystery of the Midnight Menace, Farrar, Straus, 1988.
Mystery of the Secret Marks, Farrar, Straus, 1989.
Mystery of the Kidnapped Kidnapper, Minstrel, 1994.
Mystery of the Watchful Witches, Minstrel, 1994.

NONFICTION

Berlin: City Split in Two, Putnam, 1971.
Vampires, Lippincott, 1973.
Werewolves, Lippincott, 1973.
Witches, Lippincott, 1975.
Devils and Demons, Lippincott, 1976.
Fun with Forecasting Weather, Houghton, 1977.
The Kids' Code and Cipher Book, Linnet, 1981.

Nancy Garden

OTHER

Also author of a serial novel, *The Secret of Smith's Hill,* syndicated by Breakfast Serials, published in newspapers across the nation, 1999-2000.

Work in Progress

A middle-grade novel, a young adult novel, an adult novel, and a picture book.

Adaptations

What Happened in Marston was adapted for television and broadcast by the American Broadcasting Company (ABC) as an "ABC After School Special" under the title *The Color of Friendship; Annie on My Mind* was adapted for radio and first broadcast by the British Broadcasting Corporation (BBC) in 1992, and was adapted for the stage and performed in 1994.

Sidelights

Nancy Garden's books for young people vary between the realistic and the fantastic. *What Happened in Marston* tells of racial problems in a small town in the 1960s in New York. *Annie on My Mind* is a love story in which two girls realize they are gay. The "Fours Crossing" sequence is a several-part fantasy. Other volumes, including the "Monster Hunters" series, look at supernatural creatures like vampires, werewolves, and witches. "I write for young people because I like them," Garden once commented, "and because I think they are

important. Children's books can be mind-stretchers and imagination-ticklers and builders of good taste in a way that adult books cannot, because young people usually come to books with more open minds. It's exciting to be able to contribute to that in a small way."

"I suppose the fact that I was an only child played a big part in my becoming a writer," Nancy Garden declared in an autobiographical essay in *Something about the Author Autobiography Series* (*SAAS*). Garden was born in Boston, Massachusetts, in 1938, to a Red Cross executive of Sicilian ancestry, and his wife, a trained social worker with parents of German descent. Both of her parents strongly influenced Garden's thinking. "When I was growing up," Garden related in *SAAS,* "Dad used to tell me that a girl could do anything a boy could do, but that in order to get recognized, she had to do it twice as well. I could do anything I wanted, he'd say, if I worked hard enough at it. Mum was a strong woman, both physically and emotionally. She was my best friend while I was growing up, my confidante, and my rock. I could talk about almost anything with her, and she always encouraged me to think for myself." Almost as influential was Garden's great-aunt Anna, called "Tanna" by the family. "She had been born in Germany ... [and] had no children of her own, but she brought up my mother and her brother and sister," Garden explained. "She understood children and dogs as did few adults, and had unending patience with both."

"We moved a lot when I was a child," Garden continued in *SAAS,* "partly because of my father's job with the American Red Cross and partly because of the housing shortage that followed World War II." Although she was born in Boston, Garden's family moved to New York City, then to Cambridge and Concord, Massachusetts. Garden spent her early school years in Scarsdale, New York. Her family soon moved to nearby White Plains and then to Crestwood before finally settling in North Providence, Rhode Island, in 1947. A few years later they moved again, this time to Providence. Her uprooted early life meant that she had to make new friends often. Like many authors, Garden spent a lot of time reading. She recalls first encountering A. A. Milne's adventures of Christopher Robin and Winnie-the-Pooh, and Robert Lawson's *Rabbit Hill* while living in Scarsdale.

"I was sick a lot, too, and that meant I often had to amuse myself," Garden commented in *SAAS.* "Since I loved to read and had always been read to by my parents, this wasn't hard, nor was it much of a step from reading to acting out what I read and making up stories based on my favorite characters." The same summer that she moved to White Plains, New York, the author continued, she came down with scarlet fever. "I spent most of our time in White Plains being sick, recovering, and then being sick again," Garden stated, "for I ran around too much when I was finally allowed out, and had a relapse." She spent the time reading Anna Sewell's *Black Beauty* and reenacting scenes from Rudyard Kipling's *The Jungle Books.* Garden also declared in *SAAS* that she "discovered another wonderful author—Hugh Lofting—and his lovable character, Dr. Doolittle."

Garden recalled other influences on her writing, including stories from World War II and the fears of the emerging Cold War. "I can still see the *Life* magazine photos of mass graves in the concentration camps," Garden related in *SAAS,* "and I know that like many other World War II children, I lived in terror of the atom bomb. The world could end at any moment; life could end, and there was nothing anyone—even grown-ups—could do about it. People have asked me why so many of my books deal with death in some way; perhaps this is why." *Berlin: City Split in Two,* Garden's first nonfiction book, tells about one of the consequences of the war: the division of Germany's capital city between the occupying forces of the Soviet Union and the Western Allies—the U.S., France, and Great Britain.

When she entered Lincoln School, a private institution run by the Society of Friends (the Quakers) in the early

Gabrielle follows her friend Joan of Arc onto the battlefield in Garden's gritty work of historical fiction. (Cover illustration by Brian Leister.)

1950s, Garden found a new interest. "At Lincoln I discovered theater, and realized that I wanted to be an actress," Garden explained. "It was an obsession with me, akin to what I imagine a religious vocation is like for a girl of the same age." While she attended Lincoln School, Garden met her best friend and future companion Sandra Scott, and began a career doing backstage work and performing in professional summer stock theater in Peterborough, New Hampshire. Her experiences there showed up in some of her fiction: *Good Moon Rising*'s theater setting came out of Garden's theater background, and *Mystery of the Secret Marks* is partly based on some strange fires that occurred while she was working at Hilltop, a summer stock theater outside Baltimore, Maryland. "Was it arson? We never really knew, but one member of the acting company was let go, as was a young odd-jobs man, and the fires stopped," Garden recalled.

Her love for theater led to Garden's decision to enroll in the Columbia (University) School of Dramatic Arts in New York City, where she studied acting, directing, and lighting design. She did "pretty well as an actress, both in college and in stock," Garden stated in *SAAS,* "and I loved acting dearly, but I felt directing was more creative. Also, I was a character actress, and since many character parts are of older people, and there are plenty of older people around to play them, there's a lot of unbeatable competition around for a young character actor or actress in the professional theater. After a while, though, it became clear that I was going to have trouble supporting myself in theater," she continued, "and so ... I decided to go to Columbia Teachers College and major in speech." She received her Master's degree in 1962.

After completing her studies Garden settled in Brooklyn Heights and began teaching at Hunter College. However, her Hunter job was only part-time; and she had to work first for an accountant and then in an insurance office to make ends meet. The insurance company failed, Garden related in *SAAS,* but while she was there she made two new friends, Barbara Seuling and Winnette Glasgow. "While we were all at the insurance company," she stated, "Barb and I discovered we were both 'interested' in children's books, she as an illustrator and me as a writer. We collaborated on a book called *Aloysius P. Bookworm,* in which we made, I think, every mistake a young writer and illustrator can possibly make." The book was never published. "We learned an enormous amount from those mistakes," Garden concluded, "and we've both gone on to have pretty successful careers, Barb as a writer, illustrator, and teacher, and me as a writer and teacher." In the 1960s, Garden began working as an editor for an editorial service that masqueraded as a literary agency. "We had a good time," she wrote, "but we also tried to do our best for our poor clients, and we did manage to learn, from our work and from each other, a fair amount about writing and editing."

After a few years as an editor Garden took an extended trip to Europe with a friend, Renee Cafiero. "It was largely through visiting Wales and Scotland and reading about both that I began to learn about Celtic lore," Garden stated in *SAAS*, "which led directly to my books about the made-up village of Fours Crossing, New Hampshire." *Fours Crossing,* according to *Horn Book* reviewer Paul Heins, concerns the "strange happenings caused by a religious rift in the community at the time of its settlement in the seventeenth century." The protagonist, Melissa Dunn, travels to Fours Crossing to live with her grandmother after the death of her mother. The townspeople preserve many of the traditional Celtic customs of their ancestors, including welcoming the spring season by carrying an evergreen tree around the village. The year that Melissa arrives, however, winter lingers on and spring refuses to come. In company with her friend Jed, Melissa discovers that an old hermit is preventing the onset of springtime through magic spells. "He is convinced," wrote *School Library Journal* contributor Virginia Golodetz, "that the people must be punished for growing lax in following the Old Ways." The hermit captures Jed and Melissa and holds them prisoner in his root cellar. Finally Melissa manages to break the hermit's hold on the seasons and releases spring to the town.

The sequel to *Fours Crossing,* titled *Watersmeet,* continues Melissa's adventures. Although the hermit's power has been broken, the release of spring has caused the flooding of the village. A newcomer, named Rhiannon, also brings dissent to the community. Many of the villagers—including, for a time, Jed—believe that she is allied with the hermit. Melissa is one of the few that believe in Rhiannon's innate goodness and the positive effects of her power. "A succession of events," noted *Horn Book* reviewer Mary M. Burns, "provides a battleground for conflict between the old ways and the new as the hermit manipulates ancient rituals and contemporary fears into an attack on stable community institutions."

Garden continues the story of Fours Crossing in *The Door Between.* Melissa has discovered that she is the descendant of the true Keepers of the Old Ways—the job that the mad hermit has hitherto claimed. With the aid of Jed, his dog Ulfin, and her sparrowhawk Llyr, Melissa travels to the world of the dead to defeat the hermit and merge the Old Ways with the new. "Melissa wins the hermit over with a new-found compassion and maturity," declared a *Publishers Weekly* reviewer. Despite some reservations—reviewers noted that it was difficult for readers unfamiliar with the earlier volumes to follow the story line—critics generally praised Garden's "Fours Crossing" sequence. "Melissa is a resourceful character," declared a *Booklist* writer, "and readers of the first two books won't want to miss the third saga in this projected quartet." The fourth "Fours Crossing" book, *The Joining,* which completes the story, has yet to be published.

Some time after the "Fours Crossing" novels, Garden launched the "Monster Hunters" series. Like Melissa's adventures, the stories of the "Monster Hunters" tell about preteens—Brian, Numbles, and Darcy—who vow to rid the world of monsters. In the first volume, *Mystery of the Night Raiders,* Brian launches an investigation of a series of mysterious cattle deaths on his grandparents' Vermont farm. Brian, a mystery fan; Numbles, a budding scientist; and Darcy, an athlete, are unprepared "for the possibility that something supernatural is behind the deaths of the cows," according to a *Publishers Weekly* reviewer, "until it looks as if Brian has become the next dish on a vampire's menu." The second volume in the series, *Mystery of the Midnight Menace,* looks at the possibility that one of Brian's classmates is in fact the werewolf that has been terrifying Central Park. "This is a creepy, moody piece for lovers of the genre," declared JoEllen Broome in *Voice of Youth Advocates,* "and big chuckles for the more skeptical among us."

Garden has also explored the problem of the undead in several non-series titles, including *Prisoner of Vampires* and *My Sister, the Vampire.* In *Prisoner of Vampires,* preteen Alexander Darlington has an enthusiasm for vampires—until he actually meets one in the person of Radu. Radu, "a red-lipped specter of a man who has a taste for rare roast-beef sandwiches," according to a *Booklist* contributor, haunts the basement of a small library where Alexander is doing research for his project on the undead. Radu gains power over Alexander and uses him to victimize Alexander's older sister Peggy. "Thanks to Alexander's brave friend Mike and a wise old neighbor, Mrs. Potter," wrote a *Publishers Weekly* critic, "the villain is done in and the prisoners are saved." "It's a chilling, gorey and absurdly funny story with perfectly suited black-and-white illustrations," declared Trev Jones in *School Library Journal.* "Horror fans will love it."

My Sister, the Vampire tells the story of three siblings—Tim, Sarah, and Jenny—who are left alone at their family's summer home in Maine. Strange events haunt their time, dampening their pleasure at being on their own. "Hundreds of bats invade the house," explained Lyle Blake Smythers in *School Library Journal;* "the girl in the neighboring cabin is wasting away, haunted by disturbing dreams; and Sarah seems to be developing the same symptoms." Eventually the children, together with the neighbor girl's brother John, confront the mysterious new owners of nearby Spool Island and bring the matter to a close. "Sure to be popular with those who like to be scared but not terrified," concluded Sally Estes in *Booklist.*

Because of its subject matter, *Annie on My Mind,* published in 1982, became the subject of a federal court case in 1995. In 1993, a gay group called Project 21, whose purpose is to encourage schools to include accurate materials about homosexuality in their libraries and curricula, donated copies of *Annie on My Mind* and of Frank Mosca's *All American Boys* to forty-two schools in and around Kansas City. A fundamentalist minister burned a copy of *Annie* outside the building housing the Kansas City School Board, and several school boards voted to remove the book after they discovered it was on their district's shelves. The school board of the Olathe, Kansas, district was among those that voted to ban *Annie on My Mind*—even though no students or parents had complained about the book during the decade it had been on library shelves. The controversy came to a head in Olathe, whose school board, dominated by members who believed that homosexuality is wrong, directed the library to remove the book from circulation, despite the protests of both librarians and students. In response, some students, their parents, and a science teacher who was also a parent, filed suit in federal district court, claiming that the school board had violated their constitutional rights of free speech and due process. The American Civil Liberties Union and the American Library Association supported the suit. According to a *Kansas City Star* reporter, "School officials replied that they were exercising their right to choose material for students and their right not to succumb to the agenda of a special interest group."

Garden testified at the trial, as did Olathe media specialists and members of the Olathe school board. In November, 1995, United States District Court Judge Thomas Van Bebber ruled that "the book was unconstitutionally removed from the shelves," and the Olathe school board decided not to appeal the decision, though they did announce plans to revise their book selection process. *Annie on My Mind* has since been returned to school library shelves. In a *Voice of Youth Advocates* article titled "*Annie* on Trial: How It Feels To Be the Author of a Challenged Book," Garden stated, "I believe any challenge to any book endangers the First Amendment. Still, I entered this battle with equal measures of fear, rage, and eagerness—and sometimes a desire for it all to go away so I could work on my next book." She added that "we must stand firmly together in our resolve to protect the amendment that protects us and that allows people in this country free access to all ideas. *Annie* won, but there are other battles still to fight."

"Garden's *Annie on My Mind*," declared Roger D. Sutton in the *Bulletin of the Center for Children's Books,* "was a groundbreaker in its romantic treatment of a gay theme." *Lark in the Morning,* the critic continued, "is notable in that it presents a gay relationship as just one (and a subordinate one, at that) story element." *Lark in the Morning* tells of Gillian Harrison, seventeen years old and in a committed relationship with her best friend, Suzanne. Gillian arrives at her parents' summer home in Pookatasset, Rhode Island only to find that the place has been burglarized and a number of items—including her diary, which spells out the details of her relationship with Suzanne—have been taken. Gillian sets out to recover her lost property and soon uncovers the culprits: two young runaways from an abusive home, Jackie and Lark, who are hiding in an old hut nearby. Gillian coaxes Lark out of her suicidal depression, and supports Lark's plan to take Jackie to their aunt's home in New Hampshire—even though, to do that, Gillian has to lie to her family, her friend Brad, and the authorities. "By interweaving the issues of child abuse, suicide, runaways, and homosexuality with ethical questions regarding helping 'outlaws' and lying ... in order to protect others," asserted *School Library Journal* contributor Dona Weisman, "Garden offers readers much food for

thought." "Garden, author of the remarkable *Annie on My Mind*," declared Rebecca Sue Taylor in *Voice of Youth Advocates,* "again creates an honest and realistic look at love, truth, and responsibility."

Peace, O River echoes the themes that Garden examined back in *What Happened in Marston.* In it, stated *New York Times Book Review* contributor Merri Rosenberg, "Nancy Garden uses the contemporary issue of nuclear waste to propel what is essentially a thinly veiled tale about class and social status." It tells the story of sixteen-year-old Kate Kincaid, who has returned to her childhood home of River View, Massachusetts, after her father's heart attack. River View, which is an affluent neighborhood, has a long-standing feud with its companion town of Hastings Bay, a blue-collar area. Recently the rumor of a nuclear waste dump to be located in the area has made the feud worse. Kate and her new friend from Hastings Bay, Pippa Brown, try to end the bad feelings. However, the anger spills over into the local high school. Kate's brother is attacked and beaten; Pippa is nearly raped, and Kate's old friend Jon drowns in the river. Jon's death finally ends the feud. "The novel's main interest," stated a *Booklist* reviewer, "lies in the conflicts about ideas—is it 'heartless' to care more for the general good than for family and friends? Is it 'bossy' to try to change things? Does total pacifism always make sense, locally and globally?" The book, declared a *Horn Book* critic, "is a valiant attempt to help teenagers understand the tremendous difficulties faced by those who would seek to solve difficult problems through direct nonviolent intervention."

In *Dove and Sword,* a historical novel set in fifteenth-century France, Garden looks at the pros and cons of war. The book tells the story of Joan of Arc through the eyes of a fictional friend, Gabrielle, who is taken with Joan's inspirational voices and violent death. Gabrielle provides a modern perspective on the events leading up to Joan's martyrdom. "This is a fascinating and well-written historical novel," enthused Ann W. Moore in *School Library Journal,* "filled with rich details, evocative descriptions, and interesting characters." Garden's "strategically plotted novel," declared a *Publishers Weekly* critic, "achieves the highest goals of historical fiction—it vivifies the past, robustly and respectfully, then uses its example to steer the audience toward a more courageous future."

Garden's experiences with the *Annie* trial and her ongoing concern about censorship issues prompted her to write *The Year They Burned the Books.* "This is a novel driven by issues," wrote *Booklist*'s Michael Cart. "Garden's treatment of her themes is courageous, believable, and fair-minded.... This is an important book that deserves a wide readership."

In the novel Jamie Crawford, editor of her high school's newspaper, has written an editorial about her school's new sex education curriculum and the importance of condom availability for students. Lisa Buel, a conservative who is running for a position on the school board, is vehemently opposed to the new curriculum, especially its acceptance of homosexuality. She founds a group called Families for Traditional Values (FTV), and speaks out against the stand the high school paper, and later an underground paper founded by Jamie and her staff, continues to take. A heated debate involving the entire community ensues. In the end, Jamie, who has meanwhile come to terms with her own sexuality, realizes that "maybe the truth is a lot more elusive that I thought. FTV believes it's arguing for the truth, and I believe I am, and we each believe our facts are right . . . . I'm pretty sure of one thing: that people, no matter what they believe or what their differences are, have to be able to live together without hurting each other." "Garden has written a book to make a point about important contemporary issues," wrote Pat Scales in *School Library Journal.* "Students will come away from it with enough insight to at least think before they make judgments about people, their lifestyles, and their first-amendment rights." Garden told *SATA:* "It is my hope that *The Year They Burned the Books* will spark discussions, especially in classrooms—for it is only by sharing ideas and information that we are ever going to resolve these and other difficult issues."

Garden maintained in *SAAS* that she regards writing as a wonderful occupation. "What nicer requirements could there be for a career? Think of it: when you curl up with a book on a rainy day; when you visit a new place or meet a new person; when you feel sorrow or joy, you're not just being lazy or having fun or living life as anyone might live it—you're also, even if you're not aware of it, *working.* What joy!"

Works Cited

"Board Tells Reason for Banning Book," *Kansas City Star,* October 5, 1955, p. C4.

Broome, JoEllen, review of *Mystery of the Midnight Menace, Voice of Youth Advocates,* February, 1989, p. 284.

Burns, Mary M., review of *Watersmeet, Horn Book,* October, 1983, pp. 580-81.

Cart, Michael, review of *The Year They Burned the Books, Booklist,* August, 1999.

Review of *The Door Between, Publishers Weekly,* July 24, 1987, p. 187.

Review of *The Door Between, Booklist,* November 1, 1987, p. 476.

Review of *Dove and Sword, Publishers Weekly,* October 16, 1995, p. 62.

Estes, Sally, review of *My Sister, the Vampire, Booklist,* July, 1992, p. 1931.

Garden, Nancy, essay in *Something about the Author Autobiography Series,* Volume 8, Gale, 1989.

Garden, Nancy, "*Annie* on Trial: How It Feels To Be the Author of a Challenged Book," *Voice of Youth Advocates,* June, 1996.

Garden, Nancy, *The Year They Burned the Books,* Farrar, Straus, 1999.

Golodetz, Virginia, review of *The Door Between, School Library Journal,* December, 1987, pp. 99-100.

Heins, Paul, review of *Fours Crossing, Horn Book,* August, 1981, pp. 431-32.

Jones, Trev, review of *Prisoner of Vampires, School Library Journal,* February, 1985, pp. 73-74.

Moore, Ann W., review of *Dove and Sword, School Library Journal,* November, 1995, p. 119.

Review of *Mystery of the Night Raiders, Publishers Weekly,* November 13, 1987, p. 71.

Review of *Peace, O River, Horn Book,* January-February, 1986, pp. 91-92.

Review of *Peace, O River, Booklist,* March 1, 1986, p. 973.

Review of *Prisoner of Vampires, Publishers Weekly,* January 25, 1985, p. 94.

Review of *Prisoner of Vampires, Booklist,* April 1, 1985, p. 1119.

Rosenberg, Merri, review of *Peace, O River, New York Times Book Review,* March 2, 1986, p. 29.

Scales, Pat, review of *The Year They Burned the Books, School Library Journal,* August 16, 1999.

Smythers, Lyle Blake, review of *My Sister, the Vampire, School Library Journal,* September, 1992, p. 252.

Sutton, Roger D., review of *Annie on My Mind, School Library Journal,* August, 1982, p. 125.

Sutton, Roger D., review of *Lark in the Morning, Bulletin of the Center for Children's Books,* June, 1991, p. 236.

Weisman, Dona, review of *Lark in the Morning, School Library Journal,* June, 1991, pp. 124-25.

For More Information See

BOOKS

Gallo, Donald R., editor and compiler, *Speaking for Ourselves, Too,* National Council of Teachers of English, 1993.

Twentieth-Century Young Adult Writers, St. James Press, 1994, pp. 233-34.

PERIODICALS

Bulletin of the Center for Children's Books, October, 1987, p. 27.

Publishers Weekly, June 7, 1991, p. 676; July 6, 1992, p. 56.

School Library Journal, November, 1987, pp. 104-05; December, 1988, p. 103.

Voice of Youth Advocates, June, 1986, p. 78.

*   *   *

GARLAND, Sherry 1948-
(Lynn Lawrence)

Personal

Born July 24, 1948, in McAllen, TX; daughter of Joseph (a farmer and carpenter) and Desla (a homemaker) Allison; married Clyde L. Garland, July 4, 1971. *Education:* University of Texas at Arlington, B.A. (with honors), 1970, graduate studies, 1970-71. *Politics:* Independent.

Addresses

Home—Houston, TX. *Office*—c/o Harcourt, Brace, Jovanovich, 1250 Sixth Ave., San Diego, CA 92101.

Career

Texas A & M University, College Station, TX, librarian in oceanography/meteorology department, 1972-75; secretarial work for various homebuilders in Houston, TX, 1976-89; lecturer and writer. *Member:* Society of Children's Book Writers and Illustrators, Romance Writers of America, Manuscriptor's Guild, Golden Triangle Writers' Guild, Houston Novel Writers Club.

Awards, Honors

Guilded Quill Award in juvenile fiction, and Society of Children's Book Writers works-in-progress grant, both 1990, both for *Song of the Buffalo Boy.*

Writings

FOR ADULTS

(Under pseudonym Lynn Lawrence) *The Familiar Touch,* Berkley, 1982.
(Under pseudonym Lynn Lawrence) *Deep in the Heart,* Berkley, 1983.
Writing for Young Adults, Writer's Digest Books, 1998.

FOR CHILDREN

Vietnam: Rebuilding a Nation (nonfiction), Dillon/Macmillan, 1990.
Where the Cherry Trees Bloom (novel), [Germany], 1991.
Best Horse on the Force (novel), Holt, 1991.
Song of the Buffalo Boy (novel), Harcourt (San Diego, CA), 1992.
The Lotus Seed (picture book), illustrated by Tatsuro Kiuchi, Harcourt, 1993.
Why Ducks Sleep on One Leg (picture book), illustrated by Jean and Mou-sien Tseng, Scholastic, Inc., 1993.
The Silent Storm (novel), Harcourt, 1993.
Shadow of the Dragon (novel), Harcourt, 1993
I Never Knew Your Name (picture book), illustrated by Sheldon Greenberg, Houghton, 1994.
Summer Sands, illustrated by Robert J. Lee, Harcourt, 1995.
Indio, Harcourt, 1995.
Cabin 102, Harcourt, 1995.
Letters from the Mountain, Harcourt, 1996.
The Last Rainmaker, Harcourt, 1997.
A Line in the Sand: The Alamo Diary of Lucinda Lawrence, Scholastic, 1998.
My Father's Boat (picture book), illustrated by Ted Rand, Scholastic, 1998.
Goodnight, Cowboy, Scholastic, 1999.
Voices of the Alamo, Scholastic, 2000.

Sidelights

Sherry Garland has combined her interest in many cultures and her love of storytelling into a successful career as an author of books for young readers. With several picture books to her credit, Garland has also authored novels for both beginning readers and teens, including *Shadow of the Dragon, Indio,* and *A Line in the Sand.*

Born in Texas's Rio Grande Valley into a large family, Garland's parents were tenant farmers. "Living on farms and in small towns influenced me greatly," she once told *SATA.* "I was an outdoor child who preferred playing with animals and climbing trees to the company of other children. Many long summer days and nights were spent making up complicated stories in my head. Everything in our back yard or the nearby woods had a role to play—the roof was a palace, the porch columns were handsome guards, the swing was a chariot, the trees had names, and I danced with the rosebushes. While we lived on top of a cedar-covered mountain, I spent many hours tracking down wild birds' nests or rabbit holes."

Although her parents constantly struggled to make ends meet, they encouraged each of their nine children to do what they themselves were never given the opportunity to do: complete school and work hard enough to get into college. Garland took their advice, and excelled at English, where she studied with the same teacher and students for most of her high school years. "I credit [my teacher] Mrs. Mary Galvan with inspiring me to become a writer," Garland later stated. "She made us see the beauty and power of the written word. Because of her enthusiasm, I developed an insatiable taste for the classics, from Greek plays to Shakespeare to Mark

A Vietnamese girl keeps a lotus seed in memory of the emperor and country she leaves behind in Sherry Garland's picture book. (From The Lotus Seed, *illustrated by Tatsuro Kiuchi.*)

Twain and William Faulkner. I wrote poetry secretly, hiding it between mattresses or tucked away in drawers, never showing it to anyone."

An essay submitted to a local writing contest when she was seventeen won, and Garland used the prize money to cover a semester's tuition at a local college. "I was even on television and the essay appeared in the newspapers," she later recalled. "All the glory made me realize that I would like to be a writer."

Even with this start to her writing career, it would be another fifteen years before Garland seriously pursued writing as a career. Although she continued to write poetry and short stories, she devoted most of her time to completing college, marrying, raising her children, and doing her share to support her family through work. Finally, her need to write made itself known: "One morning in 1979 I awoke from a dream so vivid that I felt as if it had really happened. The place (sixteenth-century France) and the characters' names came clearly in the dream. I wrote what had happened, embellished the story, and after one year had a 250,000-word historical novel. It hasn't sold yet, but it did signify the beginning of my writing career in earnest. From that day forth, I concentrated on becoming a writer, attending writers' conferences, joining writers' clubs, and submitting my work to publishers."

Garland's first two published books were the adult romance novels *The Familiar Touch* and *Deep in the Heart.* While she achieved a measure of positive critical recognition for her work, she felt constrained by the romance genre's formula, and soon grew discouraged about making writing her career. In addition to her full-time job as a secretary, Garland funneled her energy into helping families of Vietnamese immigrants become established in her area. These efforts would ultimately re-fuel her writing career.

"I had been working with Vietnamese families since 1982 as a friend, advisor, and 'big sister,'" Garland once explained to *SATA.* "I learned a lot about the Vietnamese culture—food, customs, history, festivals, weddings, etc. In 1988 I saw an ad in a writer's magazine seeking someone to write a nonfiction social studies book about Vietnam. I mailed in a proposal and was excited to learn that I had been chosen to do the project. For my book, *Vietnam: Rebuilding a Nation,* I researched Vietnamese history, conducted interviews, and provided photographs—a process that took about a year and a half. It was very hard work, but well worth it. I developed an even deeper appreciation for the Vietnamese people, and made many more friends."

By the time *Vietnam: Rebuilding a Nation* was published in 1990, Garland knew that writing children's books was what she wanted to do. "So I turned to my favorite topic—horses," she recalled. "One day I met a . . . mounted policeman and his horse at a city park. After hearing him explain how special these horses are and how they are trained to tolerate crowds and loud noises, and after learning that at one time teenagers did

volunteer work at the stables, I knew I had the ingredients for a unique story." Garland's *Best Horse on the Force,* published in 1991, proved to be one of her most popular books and generated a great deal of fan mail.

The Vietnam War was a subject of great interest to Garland, and it became the subject for her next book, *Song of the Buffalo Boy.* While she realized she could not write convincingly about the battlefields as they were outside her personal experience, she could write about the many men, women, and children who had been affected by the war through their relationships. "One day I saw a photograph of a beautiful Amerasian—her father had been an American GI in Vietnam. As I read about the plight of these forgotten and abandoned victims of war, I knew I had to tell their story. *Song of the Buffalo Boy* took about two years of intensive research and writing, but the hard work paid off." Indeed, Garland would receive two awards for her efforts on this young adult novel.

Garland continued to draw on her personal experiences in *The Silent Storm,* published in 1993. Recalling 1983,

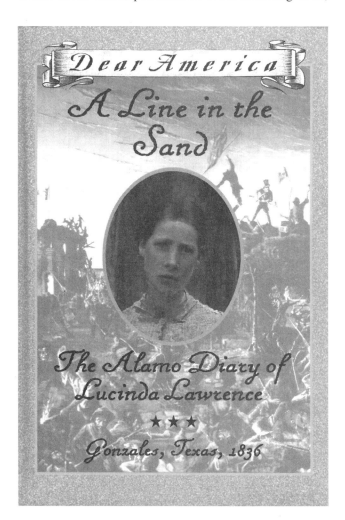

Garland describes events leading to the historic battle of the Alamo through the diary of a thirteen-year-old in this fictional account.

*A Vietnamese-American boy learns the fishing tra-
ditions of his ancestors in Garland's* **My Father's Boat,**
illustrated by Ted Rand.

the year Hurricane Alicia hit Texas with its fury, she was
inspired to write a story showing the fury of a hurricane.
"I just *had* to name the character Alyssa, in honor of that
storm," Garland remarked. The author combined the
storm with a stable of sturdy ponies and a heroine unable
to speak due to the trauma of witnessing her parents
killed at sea, and created a complex, challenging novel.
From her extensive research in preparation for writing
The Silent Storm, Garland learned a great deal about
hurricanes, the life of a shrimper, and the history of
Galveston Island.

Other books combining Garland's interest in history, her
curiosity, and her insight into human nature include
Indio, a young adult novel about Southwestern Indians
and Spanish conquistadors, and *A Line in the Sand: The
Alamo Diary of Lucinda Lawrence.* Featuring a thirteen-
year-old protagonist who witnesses the events leading up
to the Battle of the Alamo in 1836, *A Line in the Sand*
was hailed by *School Library Journal* critic Phyllis
Graves as "carefully researched and historically accurate," the critic adding that Garland's attention to detail
adds "interest and give[s] a clear picture of the many
hardships and simple joys of early Texas farm life."

Garland had never considered writing picture books,
realizing that they require a great deal of planning.
Using the outline of another novel, she composed *The
Lotus Seed,* a capsule version of an immigrant woman's
life: her childhood, marriage, World War II, moving to
the United States, and having grandchildren who are far
more American than Japanese. Japanese artist Tatsuro
Kiuchi created the illustrations accompanying the text.

An editor at a 1990 writer's conference mentioned to
Garland she was looking for Asian folk tales, and
Garland's response was to create *Why Ducks Sleep on*

One Leg. A light-hearted collection of stories, the book
contains a great deal of insight into Vietnamese culture
and traditions. Vietnamese culture also figures in the
plot of her 1998 picture book *My Father's Boat,* which
focuses on Vietnamese-American shrimpers working
along the Gulf Coast. Dubbed a "thoughtful and loving
family story" by *School Library Journal* contributor
Carol Schene, *My Father's Boat* finds a boy and his
father working aboard their boat while the father tells
tales of fishing in the South China Sea, and vows that
the two will one day experience that together. Garland
"welds telling details of the sea, sky, and fishing life into
a powerful narrative," according to a *Publishers Weekly*
reviewer, while Schene praised a prose style that "flows
effortlessly."

Works Cited

Graves, Phyllis, review of *A Line in the Sand, School
   Library Journal,* January, 1999, p. 127.
Review of *My Father's Boat, Publishers Weekly,* June 1,
   1998, p. 48.
Schene, Carol, review of *My Father's Boat, School Library
   Journal,* July, 1998, p. 74.

For More Information See

PERIODICALS

Booklist, April 1, 1992, p. 1438; November 15, 1993, p.
   621; June 1, 1997, p. 1675.
Bulletin of the Center for Children's Books, July, 1992, p.
   294; April, 1995, p. 274; September, 1998, 13.
Horn Book, fall, 1993, p. 298; fall, 1998, p. 292.
Kirkus Reviews, March 1, 1990, p. 341; March 15, 1992, p.
   393; May 15, 1998, p. 737.
Publishers Weekly, February 17, 1992, p. 64; June 1, 1998,
   p. 61.
School Library Journal, July, 1993, p. 60; December, 1995,
   p. 104; June, 1997, p. 117.
Voice of Youth Advocates, October, 1992, p. 223; December, 1993, p. 290; December, 1995, p. 300; August,
   1997, p. 183.*

*   *   *

GEORGE, Twig C. 1950-

Personal

Born September 18, 1950, in Ann Arbor, MI; daughter
of Dr. John L. (a wildlife professor) and Jean C. (an
author) George; married David M. Pittenger (an aquarium director), 1982; children: Rebecca and Anna ("Caity"). *Education:* Bennington College, B.S., 1973; Bank
Street College of Education, M.S., 1977.

Addresses

Home—Baltimore, MD. *E-mail*—twiggertwo@aol.com.
Agent—Ginger Knowlton, Curtis Brown LTD., 10 Astor
Pl., New York, NY 10003.

Twig C. George

Career

Writer. Worked for many years in education and marine conservation.

Awards, Honors

Junior Literary Guild selection, 1996, for *A Dolphin Named Bob.*

Writings

A Dolphin Named Bob, illustrated by Christine Herman Merrill, HarperCollins, 1996.
Swimming With Sharks, illustrated by Yong Chen, HarperCollins, 1999.

Work in Progress

Jellies, a picture book about jelly fish, for Millbrook Press, due in 2000; researching a third chapter book.

Sidelights

Twig C. George is the author of chapter books about the lives and habits of various marine animals, such as dolphins and sharks. She told *SATA:* "I grew up in a family of scientists and artists. My mother, Jean Craighead George, is the author of over 85 children's books. My father, now retired, was a wildlife biologist with a gift for teaching. During my childhood we raised over 173 wild animals in our home. The animals became the subjects of research for my father and books for my mother. Over the years I have maintained an interest in the natural world. My husband, David Pittenger, is director of the National Aquarium in Baltimore. My two daughters, Rebecca and Caity, each began visiting the Aquarium when they were two days old, and have made thousands of trips since! When a particularly spunky little dolphin was born at the Aquarium in 1992, I began to see the possibilities of a book which, while telling a story, could teach the children about these amazing creatures. In 1996 *A Dolphin Named Bob* was published.

"As *Bob* was being published I began working on *Swimming With Sharks.* After a long period of research and observation of sharks at the Aquarium, I went to visit Dr. Samuel H. Gruber at the Bimini Biological Field Station in the Bahamas. Two hours after I landed on the little island of Bimini he had me in an open boat heading for a reef where he promised I would see sharks. Not only see them, but swim with them. I spent one week with Dr. Gruber, came home and wrote the book *Swimming With Sharks* in two weeks (first draft, that is).

"Next? Jelly fish!"

For More Information See

PERIODICALS

Booklist, February 1, 1996, p. 938; July, 1999, p. 1946.
Kirkus Reviews, December 1, 1995, p. 1702.
School Library Journal, May, 1996, p. 112; July, 1999, p. 96.

*   *   *

GOODE, Diane (Capuozzo) 1949-

Personal

Born September 14, 1949, in Brooklyn, NY; daughter of Armand R. (a dentist) and Paule (maiden name, Guerrini) Capuozzo; married Dr. David A. Goode (an author and professor), May 26, 1973; children: Peter. *Education:* Attended the Ecole des Beaux Arts, Aix-en-Provence, France, 1971-72; Queens College of the City University of New York, B.F.A., 1972.

Addresses

Home and office—33 Prospect Ave., Watchung, NJ 07060-5029.

Career

Children's book illustrator and writer, 1975—. Substitute teacher at New York City public schools, 1972-73; teacher of a studio workshop on children's book illustration, University of California, Los Angeles, 1976-79. *Exhibitions:* Exhibitor at museums, colleges, and libraries including the Metropolitan Museum of Art, 1982, Denver Public Library, 1985, Krasl Art Center,

1987, Mount Holyoke College Art Museum, 1991-92, and Cedar Rapids Museum of Art, 1998-2001.

Awards, Honors

Southern California Council on Literature for Children and Young People award for illustration, 1976, for *The Selchie's Seed* and *Little Pieces of the West Wind,* and 1979, for *Dream Eater;* Caldecott honor book award, American Library Association, 1983, for *When I Was Young in the Mountains;* Parents' Choice Award, 1985, for *Watch the Stars Come Out,* and 1986, for *I Go with My Family to Grandma's; Redbook* Top Ten Children's Picture Books, Reading Rainbow Feature Selection, both 1985 for *Watch the Stars Come Out;* Best Children's Books of the Year, Child Study Children's Book Committee, 1987, for *I Go with My Family to Grandma's,* and 1989, for *I Hear a Noise;* Picks of the List, *American Bookseller,* for *Where's Our Mama?, Diane Goode's American Christmas, The Diane Goode Book of American Folk Tales and Songs, Watch the Stars Come Out,* and *I Go with My Family to Grandma's;* Notable Children's Trade Books in the Field of Social Studies, National Council of Social Studies-Children's Book Council, for *The Diane Goode Book of American Folk Tales & Songs, Watch the Stars Come Out, I Go with My Family to Grandma's,* and *When I Was Young in the Mountains;* Notable Book, American Library Association, for *Tattercoats: An Old English Tale, Watch the Stars Come Out,* and *When I Was Young in the Mountains;* Teachers' Choice award, National Council of Teachers of English, for *Watch the Stars Come Out* and *When I Was Young in the Mountains;* Library of Congress Children's Book of the Year, for *When I Was Young in the Mountains;* Children's Choice citation, International Reading Association-Children's Book Council, for *The Unicorn and the Plow.* Storytelling World Awards, 1998, for *Diane Goode's Book of Giants and Little People.*

Writings

SELF-ILLUSTRATED

I Hear a Noise, Dutton, 1988.
The Diane Goode Book of American Folk Tales and Songs, compiled by Ann Durell, Dutton, 1989.
Diane Goode's American Christmas, Dutton, 1990.
Where's Our Mama?, Dutton, 1991.
Diane Goode's Book of Silly Stories and Songs, Dutton, 1992.
Diane Goode's Christmas Magic: Poems and Carols, Random House, 1992.
The Little Books of Nursery Animals (contains *The Little Book of Cats, The Little Book of Farm Friends, The Little Book of Mice,* and *The Little Book of Pigs*), Dutton, 1993.
Diane Goode's Book of Scary Stories and Songs, Dutton, 1994.
Mama's Perfect Present, Dutton, 1996.
Diane Goode's Book of Giants and Little People, Dutton, 1997.
The Dinosaur's New Clothes, Blue Sky, 1999.

Cinderella, the Dog, and Her Little Glass Slipper, Blue Sky, 2000.

ILLUSTRATOR

Christian Garrison, *Little Pieces of the West Wind,* Bradbury, 1975.
Shulamith Levey Oppenheim, *The Selchie's Seed,* Bradbury, 1975, revised edition Harcourt Brace, 1996.
Christian Garrison, *Flim and Flam and the Big Cheese,* Bradbury, 1976.
Flora Annie Steele, *Tattercoats: An Old English Tale,* Bradbury, 1976.
(And translator) Madame de Beaumont, *Beauty and the Beast,* Bradbury, 1978.
Garrison, *The Dream Eater,* Bradbury, 1978.
Emoeke de Papp Severo, translator, *The Good-Hearted Youngest Brother* (translation of the Hungarian folktale, "A joszivu legenyke"), Bradbury, 1981.
Louise Moeri, *The Unicorn and the Plow,* Dutton, 1982.
Cynthia Rylant, *When I Was Young in the Mountains,* Dutton, 1982.
Diane Goode's Little Library of Christmas Classics (contains *The Nutcracker, Christmas Carols, The Fir Tree,* and *The Night before Christmas*), Random House, 1983.
J. M. Barrie, *Peter Pan,* edited by Josette Frank, Random House, 1983.
Carlo Collodi, *The Adventures of Pinocchio,* Random House, 1983.
Amy Ehrlich, adapter, *The Random House Book of Fairy Tales,* Random House, 1985.
Riki Levinson, *Watch the Stars Come Out,* Dutton, 1985.
Deborah Hautzig, *The Story of the Nutcracker Ballet,* Random House, 1986.
Riki Levinson, *I Go with My Family to Grandma's,* Dutton, 1986.
(Reteller) Julian Hawthorne, *Rumpty-Dudget's Tower,* Knopf, 1987.
(And translator) Charles Perrault, *Cinderella,* Knopf, 1988.
Noel Streatfeild, *Ballet Shoes,* Random House, 1991.
Noel Streatfeild, *Theater Shoes,* Random House, 1994.
Lloyd Alexander, *The House Gobbaleen,* Dutton, 1995.
Robert Louis Stevenson, *A Child's Garden of Verses,* Morrow, 1998.

Also illustrator of record album covers. *Watch the Stars Come Out* was translated into Spanish as *Mira como salen las estrellas,* Dutton, 1992.

Sidelights

Diane Goode is an award-winning author-illustrator of children's books best known for her anthologies of folktales and songs, including *The Diane Goode Book of American Folk Tales and Songs, Diane Goode's Book of Scary Stories and Songs, Diane Goode's Christmas Magic: Poems and Carols,* and *Diane Goode's Book of Giants and Little People.* Two of Goode's other popular books are *Where's Our Mama?* and *Mama's Perfect Present,* both featuring two adorable children, searching the streets of Paris with a single purpose, and stumbling upon unexpected exploits. The versatile Goode has also paired her illustrations with the writings of other authors

Diane Goode's self-illustrated collection contains both classics and new selections from around the world.
(From Diane Goode's Book of Scary Stories & Songs.*)*

to create works including the Caldecott honor book, *When I Was Young in the Mountains* and many beautiful renditions of classics such as *Peter Pan, Beauty and the Beast, The Night Before Christmas,* and *A Child's Garden of Verses.*

"When I was a child I loved books and art," Goode told *SATA.* "Reading allowed me to escape into the reality of others, and drawing let me create my own. My father was of Italian descent, and my mother was French. My brother and I enjoyed the richness of both cultures. We traveled to Europe every summer from the time we were infants, visiting family and the great cathedrals and museums of the world. These early impressions helped shape my appreciation for life and art. I was bedazzled by Michelangelo's 'Descent from the Cross.' Could marble be warm and luminous? Could monumental forms be at once tender and powerful? Man's creative ability seemed staggering. I saw the works of Da Vinci, Rembrandt, Botticelli, Lautrec, Monet, Manet, Cezanne, and all the great artists. I was awestruck. I was in love with art!

"I have been drawing ever since I can remember, but my formal education began at Queens College in art history. I soon switched to fine arts, where I tried my hand at everything: drawing, painting, sculpture, etching, and

color theory. I took a year off to study at Les Beaux Arts in Aix-en-Provence. It was an artist's dream.

"After graduating, I taught high school for a year, putting together a portfolio at night. In my blissful ignorance of publishing, I had decided to illustrate children's books. It was just as well that I was so naive, or else I would have been too afraid to try. As luck would have it, I was contracted to illustrate my first picture book in 1973. I was twenty-four then and knew nothing at all about commercial art. Since I was living in California, my New York publisher taught me color separation over the phone!"

An early award-winner for Goode was *The Selchie's Seed,* by Shulamith Oppenheim. The work's success acted as an encouragement to Goode in her craft and an entry to future illustrating for other authors and publishers. With the 1983 boxed set *Diane Goode's Little Library of Christmas Classics,* Goode lent her artist's vision to some of the most popular Christmas tales: *The Fir Tree, The Night before Christmas, The Nutcracker,* and even a collection of well-known Christmas carols. "This small, gaily decorated slipcase holds four books that Goode has illustrated in extremely pretty, full-color, animated holiday scenes," noted a reviewer for *Publishers Weekly.* George A. Woods observed in the *New York Times* that the "star of this package ... is Diane Goode, whose illustrations lend just the right accompanying note to each book."

Goode delights in retelling and illustrating oft-told tales and verses, and many critics delight in her resulting efforts. Her adaptation of Julian Hawthorne's *Rumpty Dudget's Tower* brought praise from Jeanne Marie Clancy in *School Library Journal:* "Goode's colorful cross-hatched illustrations for her adaptation enhance the story and capture the spirit of the characters, especially the mischievous Rumpty-Dudget." A *Booklist* reviewer commented that the "beauty and wit of Goode's well-composed artwork will draw readers into the rather old-fashioned tale." *Horn Book* critic Margaret A. Bush concluded that Goode's "fine execution of both text and illustration breathes new life into the old story, making it freshly accessible as an old-fashioned fairy tale, eminently suited for reading aloud." Goode's illustrations have also been credited with attractively interpreting Robert Louis Stevenson's collection *A Child's Garden of Verses. School Library Journal* critic Robin L. Gibson asserted that the artist "applies her characteristically charming illustrations to Stevenson's poems with appealing results." Gibson went on to observe that Goode "captures the exuberance of childhood in many pictures."

"All of my work is done on opaline parchment," Goode told *SATA.* "I sketch lightly in pencil and use watercolors applied with very fine sable brushes. Sometimes I use color pencil with the paint to soften the atmosphere. I always begin with several rough dummies and then work on the individual pages, sketching very loosely and fast to establish movement and composition. I do these dozens of times, repositioning, enlarging, reducing, adding, and omitting. There are always hundreds of sketches for each book. It sounds tedious, but it is the most exciting part of creating the book."

Goode began creating her own self-illustrated books in 1988 with the publication of *I Hear a Noise,* and has gone on to write and illustrate a dozen more titles since that time. A reviewer for *Junior Bookshelf* deemed the debut "a joyously funny book." The "whiff of Sendak's Wild Things" noted by the critic in some of Goode's monsters did not seem to detract from his enjoyment. On the whole, he summarized: "In its high spirits, its high humour, the book is entirely original." Goode tells the story without narrative, employing only dialogue and artwork to address the familiar fear of bedtime fiends. Like many little boys, the hero, lying in bed, complains that he hears a noise. While his mother tries to comfort him, a green dragon swoops in, snatches them, and flies off with both in tow. Back at its castle, the monster's siblings argue over these human trophies. Until, that is, their mother steps in, insisting that the captives be returned to their home. "Goode ... puts an amusing new twist on the well-worn subject of monsters at bedtime," declared a *Kirkus Reviews* critic. A reviewer for *Booklist* called Goode's first book a "gloriously

Goode illustrated a 1998 edition of Robert Louis Stevenson's classic **A Child's Garden of Verses.**

spine-tingling thriller.""Goode's engagingly expressive creatures ...," concluded the critic, "will leave young-sters clamoring for yet one more read of this soft-edged, bedtime chiller."

After launching her writing career, Goode began focus-ing much of her creative energy on anthologies. She wrote and illustrated volumes of folktales and silly stories, and with *Diane Goode's Book of Scary Stories and Songs* she tackled tales featuring ghosts and goblins from around the world. *Horn Book*'s Nancy Vasilakis dubbed the book a "welcome addition to the Halloween or storytelling shelves." A *Publishers Weekly* reviewer, noting that the funny stories "are rather tame," assured readers that the book "will be appreciated more for its rich multicultural flavor than for its fright value." With *Diane Goode's Book of Giants and Little People,* the author-illustrator dealt with the theme of the "triumph of a small but clever hero over a gigantic adversary," according to *Booklist* reviewer Julie Corsaro. Working once again with tall tales and folktales from around the world, Goode put together a smorgasbord of stories. Corsaro went on to note that "Goode's elegant watercol-ors bring it all together, her appealing cartoon-style art displaying a penchant for the compelling contrast between big and small." A *Publishers Weekly* critic felt that her stories of giants and little people added to Goode's "stable of stellar collections." "With this blithely spirited book," concluded the reviewer, "Goode has done it again ... and that's no exaggeration."

Goode's French heritage and travels proved essential to the creation of two further books, *Where's Our Mama* and *Mama's Perfect Present.* In the first title, two children have become separated from their mother at the Gare d'Orsay train station in Paris. Aided by a kindly French *gendarme,* the brother and sister set out to find their beautiful mother, treking from one place to the next. The reader all the while sees the mother in one corner of a crowded page, and finally the children see her, as well. Set earlier in the century, *Where's Our Mama* was written in tribute to Goode's own mother. A writer for *Kirkus Reviews* observed that the book is reminiscent of a Russian folktale and called it "a charming transformation of a story that deftly dramatizes the child's-eye view of a most important person." *Horn Book*'s Mary M. Burns concluded her enthusiastic review by stating that "the book is as gallic as a shrug, as logical as Pascal, and as winning as a song by Maurice Chevalier. A witty, wonderful production. *C'est magni-fique!*"

"Mayhem? Mais Oui! The rosy-cheeked children who searched Paris high and low in *Where's Our Mama?* are back," celebrated a *Publishers Weekly* review of *Mama's Perfect Present.* Now accompanied by their dachshund, Zaza, who leaves destruction in its wake, the siblings are searching for the perfect birthday gift for their beloved mother. Not surprisingly, each place they visit is also visited with chaos as a result of their rambunctious dog. A *Publishers Weekly* critic promised that this sequel "will leave young readers chuckling at Zaza's exploits and everyone else chuckling an apprecia-

And so the Emperor marched in his procession, and all who saw him cried out, "Look at the Emperor's beautiful new clothes. What a magnificent train! What a cloak!"

They all pretended to see the garments that were not there, for they did not dare to appear stupid. None of the Emperor's clothes had ever been so successful.

In the lavishly detailed **The Dinosaur's New Clothes,** *Goode retells and illustrates Hans Christian Andersen's folktale from an amusingly different perspective.*

tive ooh-la-la." Mary M. Burns asserted in *Horn Book:* "This is a true picture story, with the understated text serving as a straight-faced, innocent commentary on the action, which is visualized through careful manipulation of line, deft shading, and delicate hatching." In a *Booklist* starred review, Ilene Cooper commented that "the story is clever and full of fun, but it is really the pictures that make this come alive."

With *The Dinosaur's New Clothes,* Goode wryly gave a Hans Christian Andersen classic "a prehistoric make-over," according to a *Publishers Weekly* critic. Goode parodies the original royals with a gaggle of pompadoured dinosaurs holding court at Versailles. In this palace, a Tyrannosaurus rex—*king* of all dinosaurs—stars as the clothes-horse emperor of Andersen's original. "It's all good silly fun," concluded the critic, "a light parody of Andersen's send-up of gullibility and greed."

Goode's often humorous work is grounded in a private life that provides the author with the necessary stability and lightness. "I've been married since 1973," Goode told *SATA.* "Our son Peter was born in 1978 and is a fine artist already. I often rely on him to read manuscripts for an opinion and critique of my work. He has helped me see the world through a child's eyes.

"We have lived in four states and have had many small pets along the way: parrots, love birds, hamsters, cats, and mice. We've settled in Watchung, New Jersey, and each day we are visited by wild deer, raccoons, rabbits, hedgehogs, a pheasant, and an owl. We now have a Welsh Corgi named Katie and a big yellow Lab named Jack. We love to travel in France, and we love to cook. I still read as much as I can. I listen to books on tape as I paint.

"Working in the field of children's literature has been a great joy. How lucky to be able to do the work I love and also contribute in some small way to the lives of our children. How lucky to find in my work the two things I've cherished since childhood: art and books."

Works Cited

Burns, Mary M., review of *Mama's Perfect Present, Horn Book,* November-December, 1996, pp. 723-24.

Burns, Mary M., review of *Where's Our Mama?, Horn Book,* November-December, 1991, pp. 727-28.

Bush, Margaret A., review of *Rumpty Dudget's Tower, Horn Book,* March-April, 1988, pp. 199-200.

Clancy, Jeanne Marie, review of *Rumpty Dudget's Tower, School Library Journal,* January, 1988, p. 66.

Cooper, Ilene, review of *Mama's Perfect Present, Booklist,* July, 1996, p. 1824.

Corsaro, Julie, review of *Diane Goode's Book of Giants and Little People, Booklist,* September 15, 1997, p. 237.

Review of *Diane Goode's Book of Giants and Little People, Publishers Weekly,* July 28, 1997, p. 73.

Review of *Diane Goode's Book of Scary Stories and Songs, Publishers Weekly,* July 4, 1994, p. 60.

Review of *Diane Goode's Little Library of Christmas Classics, Publishers Weekly,* September 2, 1983, p. 80.

Review of *The Dinosaur's New Clothes, Publishers Weekly,* June 28, 1999, p. 78.

Gibson, Robin L., review of *A Child's Garden of Verses, School Library Journal,* January, 1999, p. 121.

Review of *I Hear a Noise, Booklist,* December 1, 1988, pp. 647-48.

Review of *I Hear a Noise, Junior Bookshelf,* April, 1989, p. 61.

Review of *I Hear a Noise, Kirkus Reviews,* July 1, 1988, p. 973.

Review of *Mama's Perfect Present, Publishers Weekly,* September 2, 1996, p. 129.

Review of *Rumpty Dudget's Tower, Booklist,* January 15, 1988, p. 862.

Vasilakis, Nancy, review of *Diane Goode's Book of Scary Stories and Songs, Horn Book,* January-February, 1995, p. 75.

Review of *Where's Our Mama?, Kirkus Reviews,* August 1, 1991, p. 1010.

Woods, George A., review of *Diane Goode's Little Library of Christmas Classics, New York Times,* December 4, 1983, pp. 77-79.

For More Information See

BOOKS

Children's Book Illustration and Design, edited by Julie Cummins, PBC International, 1992.

Fifth Book of Junior Authors and Illustrators, edited by Sally Holmes Holtze, H. W. Wilson, 1983.

PERIODICALS

Booklist, October 1, 1994, p. 321

Bulletin of the Center for Children's Books, September, 1991, p. 10; December, 1996, p. 136.

Five Owls, September-October, 1991, p. 9.

Horn Book, September, 1988, p. 615; September, 1992, p. 592.

Junior Bookshelf, June, 1992, p. 102.

New York Times Book Review, April 19, 1992, p. 16; January 19, 1997, p. 24.

Publishers Weekly, July 29, 1988, p. 230; June 29, 1992, p. 61; September 7, 1992, p. 67.

School Library Journal, February, 1989, p. 69; September, 1992, p. 215; September, 1994, p. 207; September, 1996, p. 178; November, 1997, p. 107.

Washington Post Book World, February 9, 1992, p. 11.*

—Sketch by J. Sydney Jones

H

HEYMAN, Ken(neth) 1930-

Personal

Born October 6, 1930, in New York, NY; son of David M. and Ruth (Stein) Heyman; married Wendy Drew, September 11, 1960 (divorced); married Brenda Redmond, 1983; children: Jennifer C., Timothy E., Christopher D., Jason D., Armanda K. *Education:* Columbia University, B.A., 1953.

Addresses

Home—3 East 76th St., New York, NY 10021.

Career

Author and photojournalist. Has held positions of photographer for *Life* magazine, 1956-62; Alliance for Progress projects in Latin America, U.S. Information Agency, 1962-63; Meridian Photographers, New York City, president; director of Photo-200. *Exhibitions:* Has exhibited work at the Smithsonian Institution, 1965, Hallmark Gallery, New York City, 1966, and International Center of Photography, New York City. *Military service:* U.S. Army, 1952-54.

Awards, Honors

World Understanding Award, Pictures of the Year Photo Competition and Exhibition, 1976.

Writings

AND ILLUSTRATOR

(With Margaret Mead) *Family,* Macmillan, 1965.
City Duck (for children), L. W. Singer, 1969.
The World's Family, Putnam, 1983.
(With John Durniak) *The Right Picture,* Amphoto, 1986.
Hipshot: One-handed, Auto-focus Photographs by a Master Photographer, Aperture, 1988.

Contributor of articles and photographs to periodicals, including *Popular Photography* and *U.S. Camera.*

PHOTOGRAPHIC ILLUSTRATOR; FOR CHILDREN

Michael Mason, *Clyde of Africa,* Macmillan, 1963.
M. Mason, *Willie,* Ridge Press, 1963.
Robert Cohen, *The Color of Man,* Random House, 1968, revised edition, 1973.
Ann Morris, *Hats, Hats, Hats,* Lothrop, 1989.
A. Morris, *Bread, Bread, Bread,* Lothrop, 1989.
Morris, *Loving,* Lothrop, 1990.
Morris, *On the Go,* Lothrop, 1990.
Morris, *On Their Toes: A Russian Ballet School,* Atheneum, 1991.
Morris, *Tools,* Lothrop, 1992.
Morris, *Houses and Homes,* Lothrop, 1992.
Morris, *Puddle Jumper: How a Toy Is Made,* Lothrop, 1993.
Morris, *Just One Seed,* Hampton-Brown, 1993.
Morris, *Seven Hundred Kids on Grandpa's Farm,* Dutton, 1994.
Morris, *How Teddy Bears Are Made: A Visit to the Vermont Teddy Bear Factory,* Scholastic, 1994.
Morris, *Machines,* Addison-Wesley, 1995.
Morris, *The Animal Book,* Silver Press, 1996.
Morris, *The Mommy Book,* Silver Press, 1996.
Morris, *The Baby Book,* Silver Press, 1996.
Morris, *The Daddy Book,* Silver Press, 1996.
Morris, *Play,* Lothrop, 1998.
Morris, *Work,* Lothrop, 1998.
Morris, *The Grandpa Book,* Silver Press, 1999.
Morris, *The Grandma Book,* Silver Press, 1999.

PHOTOGRAPHIC ILLUSTRATOR; FOR ADULTS

John Rublowsky, *Pop Art,* Basic Books, 1965, published as *Pop Art: Images of the American Dream,* T. Nelson (London), 1965.
Lyndon B. Johnson, *This America,* Random House, 1966.
John Gruen, *The Private World of Leonard Bernstein,* Viking, 1968.
Bob Rowland, *Listen Christian,* Pflaum-Standard, 1968.
Edmund Carpenter, *They Became What They Beheld,* Outerbridge & Dienstfrey, 1970.

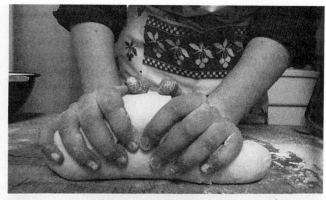

Making bread, shaping bread,

Ken Heyman's color photographs capture the many types of bread and those who eat it in **Bread, Bread, Bread,** *written by* **Ann Morris.**

Margaret Mead, *World Enough: Rethinking the Future,* Little, Brown, 1975.

Also photographic illustrator of *Where There's a Woman,* 1967.

Adaptations

Several books illustrated by Heyman have been adapted for use in English-as-a-Second Language programs.

Sidelights

Ken Heyman's photographic portraits of people from many countries and all walks of life have enriched the pages of books for both adults and children. Beginning his career as a protege of noted anthropologist Margaret Mead, Heyman has gone on to highlight both the differences and the similarities in men, women, and children from all walks of life, attempting to promote acceptance of cultural and racial differences. In photographic essays such as *The World's Family,* as well as in the many books for children he has illustrated for author Ann Morris, Heyman "has made some superb photographs of people the world over," in the opinion of *Booklist* contributor Gretchen Garner—"touching, sympathetic, and honest." Since beginning his career as a

photojournalist, Heyman has taken pictures in more than sixty countries. His photographs have found their way into several major exhibits, two books co-authored by Mead, and a number of titles for both children and adults.

Born in New York City in 1930, Heyman became interested in photography during his high school years. Later, while a student at Columbia University—between a two-year stint in the U.S. Army—his expertise as a photographer expanded, although he continued to consider picture-taking a hobby. However, two events in college would direct Heyman toward his eventual career in photography. First, when he sent selections of his work to two national photographic annuals, both publications asked to print his photographs. Second and more important, as a student of anthropologist Mead, Heyman fulfilled a term paper requirement by submitting a photographic essay. His photographs so interested Mead that they sparked a friendship and collaboration between student and teacher that continued for over two decades, until Mead's death in 1979.

Heyman and Mead's first collaborative effort began in 1953, shortly after Heyman's graduation from Columbia, when Mead invited him to accompany her as a photographer on a trip to Bali. Other field trips followed, including excursions to Mexico and Sicily with Mead, and several solo trips to destinations around the world. Many of these pictures were included among the 350 black-and-white photographs published in *The World's Family,* a book that echoes noted photographer Edward Steichen's classic *Family of Man* exhibit of the mid-1950s. Linked by poetry and excerpts from noted writers, Heyman presents what a *Publishers Weekly* contributor characterized as "a forceful portrait of a world beset by war, poverty, disease, and fools in high places, but also blessed with nature's beauty, laughter, music, and ... love."

Many of Heyman's published books have been geared toward young readers, and most have been collaborations with writer Ann Morris. Promoting the understanding and appreciation of cultural differences has been the focus of many of these books, including *On Their Toes: A Russian Ballet School.* Published in the wake of the more open cultural exchange that began between the United States and Russia in the early 1990s, *On Their Toes* follows a group of Russian students as they train for a demanding career as a dancer with the world-famous Kirov Ballet. Praising Heyman's full-colored

photographic images as "dynamic" and "vivid," a *Publishers Weekly* reviewer added that among the pictures are several that "reflect the graceful beauty and endless hopes" of these Eastern European committed students.

In addition to differences among people of different nationalities, Heyman's photographs also reflect the choices individuals make and the manner in which they live their life. Different types of jobs are the focus of books like *Puddle Jumper: How a Toy Is Made* and *Seven Hundred Kids on Grandfather's Farm.* Both fictional stories penned by Morris, each book shows men, women, and children engaged in vastly different vocational pursuits. In *Puddle Jumper,* a girl named Sarah works with her father to design, market, and manufacture wooden toys, while the life of a goat farmer is depicted in *Seven Hundred Kids.* Among the many photographs in each of these books are several that "reinforc[e] ... the connection between joyful work and play," in the opinion of *Booklist* contributor Hazel Rochman. Calling Heyman's photographs "crisp and interesting," Illene Cooper added in her *Booklist* appraisal of *Seven Hundred Kids* that the work "should intrigue both browsers and the youngest report writers."

Heyman and Morris collaborated on *Tools,* a look at the basic implements used by people around the world to assist them in the day-to-day tasks necessary for survival: "cutting, pounding, digging, cooking, eating, cleaning, writing and counting, and drawing and painting," related *School Library Journal* reviewer Eunice Weech. Encompassing fifteen different countries, Heyman's photographic illustrations "take listeners literally on a trip around the world," explained Kay Weisman in her *Booklist* appraisal of *Tools.* Accompanying *Tools* is *Houses and Homes,* another book that combines a photographic survey with a straightforward text in a book that "will attract armchair travellers of all ages," in the opinion of *Booklist* reviewer Julie Corsaro. Other similar books by Morris and Heyman include *Hats, Hats, Hats* and *Bread, Bread, Bread,* each one surveying a single aspect of life from an international perspective. The scope of such books has made them useful teaching aids in classes introducing the English language to non-English-speaking students of many ages.

Works Cited

Cooper, Illene, review of *Seven Hundred Kids on Grandpa's Farm, Booklist,* March 1, 1994, p. 1265.

Corsaro, Julie, review of *Houses and Homes, Booklist,* October 1, 1992, p. 22.

Garner, Gretchen, review of *The World's Family, Booklist,* January 15, 1984, p. 709.

Review of *On Their Toes: A Russian Ballet School, Publishers Weekly,* November 8, 1991, p. 66.

Rochman, Hazel, review of *Puddle Jumper, Booklist,* May 15, 1993, p. 1694.

Weech, Eunice, review of *Tools, School Library Journal,* October, 1992, p. 107.

Weisman, Kay, review of *Tools, Booklist,* December 1, 1992, pp. 672-73.

Photographs by Heyman and text by Ann Morris point out some of the devices that people around the world use to make their lives easier. (From Tools.*)*

Review of *The World's Family, Publishers Weekly,* September 9, 1983, p. 53.

For More Information See

BOOKS

Contemporary Authors, Vol. 112, Gale, 1985.
Freeman, Lucy, editor, *Celebrities on the Couch,* Price, Stern, 1970.

PERIODICALS

New Yorker, June 14, 1976.
New York Times Book Review, October 14, 1984, p. 44.
School Library Journal, February, 1992, pp. 103-04; October, 1992, p. 106; May, 1993, p. 100; April, 1994, p. 121; October, 1994, p. 112; May, 1996, p. 95; March, 1998, p. 199.

*   *   *

HOLM, Sharon Lane 1955-

Personal

Born December 31, 1955, in Newark, NJ; daughter of James (employed by Bell Systems) and Bridget (a homemaker; maiden name, Favero) Lane; married Gregory W. Holm (employed by Pepsi Co. International), November 21, 1981; children: Michael James. *Education:* Fort Lauderdale Art Institute, 1979. *Politics:* "Undecided." *Religion:* Catholic.

Addresses

Home and office—6 North Forty Dr., New Fairfield, CT 06812. *Agent*—Cornell and McCarthy, 2-D Cross Highway, Westport, CT.

Career

Illustrator. Has worked as an art director at a number of agencies and studios in Boca Raton and Fort Lauderdale, FL, and in Danbury, CT. Freelance children's book designer, illustrator, and consultant. *Member:* M.E.O.W./Help for Pets and other animal welfare organizations, Society of Children's Book Writers and Illustrators.

Awards, Honors

Twelve Addys (regional advertising award); Outstanding Achievement Award, Fort Lauderdale Art Institute, 1979; five public service awards for advertising/design; three Scholastic Art Awards; Pick of the Lists award, American Library Association, 1995, for *Every Day Is Earth Day: A Craft Book.*

Illustrator

Martin J. Gutnik, *Experiments That Explore the Greenhouse Effect,* Millbrook Press, 1991.
Gutnik, *Experiments That Explore Oil Spills,* Millbrook Press, 1991.
Gutnik, *Experiments That Explore Recycling,* Millbrook Press, 1992.
Robert Gardner, *Celebrating Earth Day: A Sourcebook of Activities and Experiments,* Millbrook Press, 1992.
Gutnik, *Experiments That Explore Acid Rain,* Millbrook Press, 1992.
Gutnik and Natalie Brown Gutnik, *Experiments That Explore Energy,* Millbrook Press, 1993.
Kathy Ross, *Crafts for Halloween,* Millbrook Press, 1993.
The Mind at Work, Millbrook Press, 1993.
The United States Navy, Millbrook Press, 1993.
The United States Air Force, Millbrook Press, 1993.
The Marines, Millbrook Press, 1993.
The Coast Guard, Millbrook Press, 1993.
The United States Army, Millbrook Press, 1993.
Ross, *Crafts for Kwanzaa,* Millbrook Press, 1994.
Julie Orr, *Alphabet Fun,* School Zone Publishing, 1994.
Orr, *Animal Fun,* School Zone Publishing, 1994.
Ross, *Crafts for Valentine's Day,* Millbrook Press, 1995.
Ross, *Every Day Is Earth Day: A Craft Book,* Millbrook Press, 1995.
Joan Hoffman, *Thinking Skills,* School Zone Publishing, 1995.
Susan Lang, *Nature in Your Backyard: Simple Activities for Children,* Millbrook Press, 1995.
Ross, *Crafts for Thanksgiving,* Millbrook Press, 1995.
Ross, *Crafts for Christmas,* Millbrook Press, 1995.
Ross, *Crafts for Easter,* Millbrook Press, 1995.
Ross, *Crafts for Hanukkah,* Millbrook Press, 1996.
Ross, *A Year of Crafts for Kids,* Millbrook Press, 1996.
Cindy Chang, *Trucks All Around,* Dutton, 1996.
Arlene Erlback, *Sidewalk Games around the World,* Millbrook Press, 1997.
Ross, *The Best Holiday Crafts Ever!,* Millbrook Press, 1997.
Ross, *Crafts for Kids Who Are Wild about Outer Space,* Millbrook Press, 1997.
Ross, *Crafts for Kids Who Are Wild about Dinosaurs,* Millbrook Press, 1997.
Ross, *Crafts for Kids Who Are Wild about Insects,* Millbrook Press, 1997.
Ross, *Crafts for Kids Who Are Wild about Rainforests,* Millbrook Press, 1997.
Erlback, *Happy Birthday, Everywhere!,* Millbrook Press, 1997.
Linda Glaser, *Beautiful Bats,* Millbrook Press, 1997.
Ross, *Crafts for Kids Who Are Wild about Oceans,* Millbrook Press, 1998.
Ross, *Crafts for Kids Who Are Wild about Reptiles,* Millbrook Press, 1998.
Lang, *More Nature in Your Backyard,* Millbrook Press, 1998.
Ross, *Christmas Ornaments Kids Can Make,* Millbrook Press, 1998.
Ross, *Crafts for Kids Who Are Wild about Deserts,* Millbrook Press, 1998.
Ross, *Crafts for Kids Who Are Wild about Polar Life,* Millbrook Press, 1998.
Ross, *Crafts for Kids Who Are Wild about the Wild,* Millbrook Press, 1998.
Milton Meltzer, *Food: How We Hunt and Gather It; How We Grow and Eat It,* Millbrook Press, 1998.
Barkan, *Splish! Splash!,* Random House, 1998.

Sharon Lane Holm provided step-by-step illustrations for twenty simple crafts in this informational book by Kathy Ross. (Cover illustration by Holm.)

Barkan, *Scrub a Dub-Dub!,* Random House, 1998.

Ross, *Crafts for St. Patrick's Day,* Millbrook Press, 1998.

Ross, *The Best Birthday Parties Ever,* Millbrook Press, 1999.

Ross, *Christmas Decorations Kids Can Make,* Millbrook Press, 1999.

Nayer, *Arts and Crafts Projects for Preschoolers,* McClanahan Book Co., 1999.

Ross, *More Christmas Decorations Kids Can Make,* Millbrook Press, 2000.

Ross, *Crafts from Your Favorite Bible Stories,* Millbrook Press, 2000.

Ross, *Happy New Year Everywhere!,* Millbrook Press, 2000.

Also illustrator of educational workbooks for Houghton Mifflin; Macmillan/McGraw Hill; Harcourt, Brace, Jovanovich; and Proctor and Gamble.

Sidelights

Sharon Lane Holm worked as an art director for over a decade—and achieved a great deal of success in her field—before switching her talents to illustrating books for children. Focusing on nonfiction and how-to books for the most part, Holm counts among her published works *Celebrating Earth Day: A Sourcebook of Activities and Experiments* by Robert Gardner and *Trucks All Around,* by Cindy Chang, as well as a number of craft books by author Kathy Ross. "I love my job," the illustrator once enthused. "Each project is new and

exciting and I feel my art must reflect that enthusiasm. The children of today are so much more visually attuned because of video games and television."

"I decided that I had always wanted to be an illustrator, specifically a children's book illustrator," Holm once explained to *SATA.* When the chance came to make her dream a reality and become a full-time illustrator, Holm had already tested the waters by providing publishers with artwork for several books on a freelance basis. Determined to be a success at her new career, Holm worked hard to promote her work, and soon began an affiliation with Millbrook Press, providing illustrations and book design for several of the Connecticut-based publisher's popular series books.

Many of the books enhanced by Holm's artwork are included in the "Crafts" series authored by writer Kathy Ross. An installment in this series, *Crafts for Halloween,* instructions for noise-makers, candy sacks, and table decorations are provided, along with Holm's color illustrations of the materials necessary. Dot Minzer concluded in *School Library Journal* that the work was "an attractive offering," while *Booklist* contributor Mary Harris Veeder noted that the illustrations for the twenty craft projects included "are plentiful as well as gaily colored." In a related series by Ross, books such as *Crafts for Kids Who Are Wild about Polar Life* and

Holm used pen-and-ink and watercolor wash illustrations for Susan S. Lang's nature guide. (Cover illustration by Holm.)

Crafts for Kids Who Are Wild about Oceans also feature artwork by Holm. Praising the books' tone as "light-hearted and cheerful," *School Library Journal* reviewer Marcia W. Posner cited as well their "clear instructions," "full-color illustrations," and "easy-to-find materials."

Using pen-and-ink and watercolor wash, *Nature in Your Backyard* and *More Nature in Your Backyard* provided Holm the opportunity to illustrate the step-by-step activities devised for young people by nature-buff Sharon Lane. Containing twenty activities apiece, each volume encourages youngsters to observe and explore the out-of-doors, in part through the appealing and detailed pictures Holm provides. Other nature-related books contributed to by Holm include Milton Meltzer's *Food: How We Hunt and Gather It; How We Grow and Eat It,* a volume *School Library Journal* reviewer Marilyn Fairbanks called an "entertaining" overview of eating habits throughout history that is decorated with Holm's pen-and-ink drawings.

Holm has credited her experience as an art director with making her aware of the importance of providing illustrations in a variety of styles, a skill that has enabled her to illustrate science-based books as well as craft books and reading workbooks. "I'd love to educate," she added, "but with a touch of humor and whimsy. I think that best describes my style of illustrating."

Works Cited

Fairbanks, Marilyn, review of *Food: How We Hunt and Gather It; How We Grow and Eat It, School Library Journal,* January, 1999, p. 147.

Minzer, Dot, review of *Crafts for Halloween, School Library Journal,* January, 1995, p. 105.

Posner, Marcia W., review of *Crafts for Kids Who Are Wild about Polar Life, School Library Journal,* April, 1999, p. 122.

Veeder, Mary Harris, review of *Crafts for Halloween, Booklist,* October 15, 1994, p. 433.

For More Information See

PERIODICALS

Booklist, March 1, 1996, p. 1186.

Publishers Weekly, September 18, 1995, p. 40.

School Library Journal, May, 1992, p. 143; June, 1994, p. 138; May, 1997, p. 118; May, 1998, p. 136; August, 1998, p. 152.

K–L

KROLL, Virginia L(ouise) 1948-
(Melrose Cooper, Louisa Fox)

Personal

Born April 28, 1948, in Buffalo, NY; daughter of Lester H. (a United States immigration inspector) and Helen (a registered nurse and model; maiden name, Szewczyk) Kroll; married David Haeick (in construction); children: Sara, Seth, Joshua, Hannah, Katya, Noah. *Education:* Attended State University of New York at Buffalo and Canisius College. *Religion:* Roman Catholic. *Hobbies and other interests:* Reading, crafts, friends, pets.

Addresses

Home—214 Maple Avenue, Hamburg, NY 14075-4810.

Career

Fifth grade teacher in the Buffalo, NY area, 1968-69 and 1980-81; Hamburg Memorial Youth Center, Hamburg, NY, recreation assistant, 1978-80. Medaille College, Buffalo, college instructor for Writing for Children course, 1993; Institute of Children's Literature, instructor, 1999—.

Writings

PICTURE BOOKS

Helen the Fish, illustrated by Teri Weidner, Whitman, 1992.

My Sister, Then and Now, illustrated by Mary Worcester, Carolrhoda, 1992.

Masai and I, illustrated by Nancy Carpenter, Four Winds Press/Macmillan, 1992.

Naomi Knows It's Springtime, illustrated by Jill Kastner, Boyds Mills Press, 1993.

Woodhoopoe Willie, illustrated by Katherine Roundtree, Charlesbridge, 1993.

Africa Brothers and Sisters, illustrated by Vanessa French, Four Winds Press/Macmillan, 1993.

A Carp for Kimiko, illustrated by Katherine Roundtree, Charlesbridge, 1993.

When Will We Be Sisters?, Scholastic, 1993.

I Wanted to Know All about God, illustrated by Debra Reid-Jenkins, Eerdmans, 1994.

Beginnings: How Families Come to Be, illustrated by Stacey Schuett, Whitman, 1994.

Pink Paper Swans, illustrated by Nancy Clouse, Eerdmans, 1994.

Sweet Magnolia, illustrated by Laura Jakes, Charlesbridge, 1994.

Jaha and Jamil Went down the Hill: An African Mother Goose, illustrated by Roundtree, Charlesbridge, 1994.

The Seasons and Someone, illustrated by Tatsuro Kiuchi, Harcourt Brace, 1994.

New Friends, True Friends, Stuck-Like-Glue Friends, illustrated by Rose Rosely, Eerdmans, 1994.

Fireflies, Peach Pies, and Lullabies, illustrated by Nancy Cote, Simon & Schuster, 1995.

Hats off to Hair!, illustrated by Kay Life, Charlesbridge, 1995.

Shelter Folks, illustrated by Jan N. Jones, Eerdmans, 1995.

(Under pseudonym Louisa Fox) *Every Monday in the Mailbox,* illustrated by Jan Naimo Jones, Eerdmans, 1995.

Can You Dance, Dalila?, illustrated by Nancy Carpenter, Simon & Schuster, 1996.

Christmas Cow, Players Press, 1996.

Butterfly Boy, illustrated by Gerardo Suzan, Boyds Mills Press, 1997.

Hands!, illustrated by Cathryn Falwell, Boyds Mills Press, 1997.

The Making of Angels, illustrated by Victoria Lisi, Spindle Press, 1997.

With Love, to Earth's Endangered Peoples, illustrated by Roberta Collier-Morales, Dawn, 1998.

Motherlove, illustrated by Lucia Washburn, Dawn, 1998.

Faraway Drums, illustrated by Floyd Cooper, Little, Brown, 1998.

When God Made the Tree, illustrated by Roberta Collier-Morales, Dawn, 1999.

Cat!, illustrated by K. Dyble Thompson, Dawn, 1999.

She Is Born: A Celebration of Daughters, Beyond Words, 2000.

Contributor of more than sixteen hundred articles to periodicals.

UNDER PSEUDONYM MELROSE COOPER

I Got a Family, illustrated by Dale Gottlieb, Henry Holt, 1993.
Life Riddles (chapter book), Henry Holt, 1994.
I Got Community, illustrated by Dale Gottlieb, Henry Holt, 1995.
Life Magic (chapter book), Henry Holt, 1996.
Pets!, illustrated by Yumi Heo, Henry Holt, 1998.
Gettin' Through Thursday, illustrated by Nneka Bennett, Lee and Low, 1998.

Sidelights

Virginia L. Kroll is the author of almost forty picture books for young readers and more than sixteen hundred magazine pieces, a versatile and prolific writer who only began publishing her works in 1992. So plentiful is Kroll's imagination and output that she writes under two pseudonyms as well to confound critics who worry about over-productivity. Her subject matter ranges from domestic tales of sisters, to multiracial and multicultural topics, to the environment and religion. Unafraid to take chances in her work, Kroll writes from the point of view of young African Americans in *Masai and I, Woodhoopoe Willie, Pink Paper Swans,* and *Faraway Drums;* from the point of view of a blind girl in *Naomi Knows It's Springtime;* as a Japanese girl in *A Carp for Kimiko;* and a Hispanic youth in *Butterfly Boy.* Writing under the pseudonym Melrose Cooper, Kroll has also penned inspirational stories of family life and overcoming the effects of illness.

Kroll once told *SATA:* "All I ever wanted to be is an author. And now that I am one, all I ever want to be is an author. In between the desire and the realized dream, I became a mother. Good thing. My six children and one grandchild give me stories every day. So do the children I visit in schools. There is a story in everyone I meet, everything I encounter, because they induce wonder."

Kroll has written several books dealing with the African-American experience. "*Masai and I* began as a discussion with my former fifth graders about each other's heritage," Kroll explained to *SATA.* In the book, a young African-American girl learns about the Masai culture in school. Each day she goes home and compares herself to the East African child she is studying. She wonders where a Masai girl would sleep, what she would do in her free time, and what she would wear and eat. Readers learn that while the everyday lives of Americans are

Virginia Kroll

Kimiko learns to accept tradition on a Japanese holiday in Kroll's charming picture book. (*From* A Carp for Kimiko, *illustrated by Katherine Roundtree.*)

different than the everyday lives of the Masai, children are still children, no matter where they live. In a *School Library Journal* review, Martha Topol called *Masai and I* "an interesting, richly blended book that connects two different worlds ... pointing out similarities and differences."

Woodhoopoe Willie again deals with African heritage, this time looking at the music of that continent. Willie, a young African-American boy who simply cannot sit still, shows a great but undeveloped talent for playing the drums. His continual percussive music making brings to mind the drums of Africa that his grandfather experienced on a trip to his ancestral homeland. Willie finally gets a chance to play these native handmade instruments during a Kwanzaa festival. A *Publishers Weekly* reviewer concluded that "Kroll's melodic tale conveys the warmth among Willie's loving family as well as the musical legacy of several African peoples," while a *Kirkus Reviews* critic noted that Kroll's story

presented an "effective interweaving of wholesome family dynamics and African heritage in the context of observance of Kwanzaa."

Kroll might be considered an inspiration for many writers since most of her books were accepted from the "slush pile." Despite the positive response from editors, Kroll has had several negative responses which bothered her. One has been a prejudice some editors have against a white author writing about other cultures. Kroll feels it's foolish to believe a white person is not capable of writing "black material," another's term, not hers. She doesn't want to write about a suburban middle-class white woman's world. So she writes whatever she has a desire to write.

In *Africa Brothers and Sisters,* an only child complains to his father about not having any brothers or sisters, and his dad responds that he has hundreds of them in Africa. The father and son go on to talk about all these "relatives," providing something of a primer of African cultures. Writing in a featured *Booklist* review for Black History Month, Quraysh Ali noted that it was "refreshing" to have the often absent black father very present in this title. "This book might unlock the door for many children in search of African heritage and identity, African American or not." Though noticing that some of "the information about the tribes is sometimes sketchy and obtrusive," Roger Sutton, writing in *Bulletin of the Center for Children's Books,* found the work to be "a cozy slice-of-life."

Further books dealing with African Americans and presenting a multicultural message are *Pink Paper Swans* and *Faraway Drums.* In the former title, Janetta, a young black girl, is fascinated by the origami that her neighbor, Mrs. Tsujimoto, makes to sell in shops. When the neighbor gets arthritis and her livelihood is endangered, Janetta becomes the fingers that create new origami. Sutton wrote in the *Bulletin of the Center for Children's Books* that though the text was somewhat long, "kids will enjoy the conversations of these coworkers, an ebullient girl and a gentle elderly woman, as well as the fanciful products of their cooperative occupation." A *Publishers Weekly* reviewer also praised the story, describing it as "gentle and affecting." In *Faraway Drums,* Kroll writes about Jamila Jefferson and

her younger sister Zakiya as they stay home alone for the first time. Noises abound in their urban landscape, frightening the girls, until Jamila remembers a game played by her great-grandmother. She turns the scary sounds of the city and apartment house into those of the friendly drums and handmade musical instruments of Africa. Dawn Amsberry noted in *School Library Journal* that "[i]mages of Africa are subtly woven into the realistic backdrop of the girls' apartment," and recommended the title to parents "in search of picture books about moving to a new home."

More multicultural fare is served up in *A Carp for Kimiko* and *Butterfly Boy.* Kimiko wants a carp kite to fly on Children's Day just like her brother's, but Japanese tradition says that only boys can have colorful kites. Kimiko's parents are understanding, however, and the day after the festival Kimiko awakes to find a real carp swimming in the fish tank in her room. Janice Del Negro commented in *Booklist* that Kroll's story "succeeds" in "relaying its information with a minimum of didacticism and more than a little charm." Susan Middleton, writing in *School Library Journal,* called the book a "straightforward story that focuses on a Japanese holiday," while a *Kirkus Reviews* contributor dubbed it "a gentle story distinguished by unusual warmth and subtlety." *Butterfly Boy* looks at an extremely sympa-

I wondered how tall God makes his people, and the girl next to me looked up and smiled.

Children wonder about God and his creation in Kroll's Christian-oriented I Wanted to Know All about God, *illustrated by Debra Reid Jenkins.*

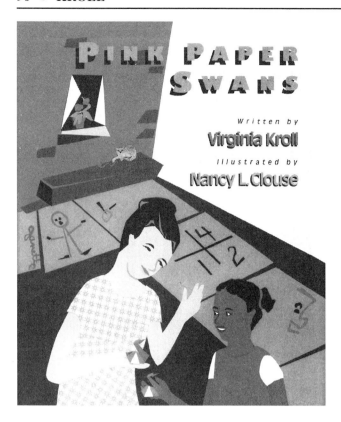

Eight-year-old Janetta learns the art of origami from her neighbor, Mrs. Tsujimoto, and becomes her friend and business partner. (Cover illustration by Nancy L. Clouse.)

thetic and caring Hispanic boy. Emilio takes care of his wheelchair-bound grandfather and reads to him about butterflies, even though others in the family feel the old man can no longer understand. Del Negro observed in the *Bulletin of the Center for Children's Books* that "Kroll's text is touching but crisp as she skillfully balances on the line between sweet and saccharine." Lisa S. Murphy, writing in *School Library Journal,* called the book a "tender story about a loving Hispanic family," concluding that the "close relationship between grandfather and grandson shines through brightly."

A potpourri of families is presented in *Beginnings: How Families Come to Be,* with various tales of how six children began their life on Earth. There is a single parent, a Korean family, and an adopted child from South America. "Each vignette features a conversation between children and parents that has a realistic feel," noted *Booklist*'s Ilene Cooper. According to Cooper, "[t]he multicultural families represented here show that love has no borders." Kroll has also delved into inspirational tales from a Christian standpoint. *I Wanted to Know All about God* emphasizes "nature and human relationships," according to Julie Corsaro in *Booklist.* A multiracial cast plays together on snowy hills and at the beach, finding the answers to their questions about God in nature. A contributor to *Publishers Weekly* complained that the book was "somewhat treacly," but suggested that it "may appeal to those looking for short, inspirational bedtime reading."

After discovering that some reviewers felt she was writing too many books too fast, Kroll began writing under a pseudonym, choosing one which neither reveals her sex nor hints at her race. The first time she submitted a manuscript under the new name, it was immediately accepted. Publishing as Melrose Cooper, Kroll has written several groups of companion books, including *I Got a Family* and *I Got Community,* as well as *Life Riddles* and *Life Magic.* The latter two books, novels for middle grade readers, feature members of the same family, focusing on different characters in each title. In *Life Riddles,* twelve-year-old Janelle wants to be a writer, but family poverty and an absent father prove obstacles to such a goal. In *Voice of Youth Advocates,* reviewer Civia Tuteur called the book a "light, easy to read up-beat novel full of hope, support, and encouragement." Janelle's younger sister, Crystal, takes stage center in *Life Magic,* dealing with the death of her beloved Uncle Joe from AIDS.

Lighter in tone is the rhyming text to the picture book, *Pets!,* in which a young child searches for a pet at the circus. A critic in *Publishers Weekly* dubbed the work a "whimsical paean to pets." A writer for *Kirkus Reviews* called the author's text "joyful" and noted that "there is even a bit of a mystery here: What animal will the top-shaped boy take home from the show?"

Coming to writing late, Kroll is reverent of the gift of being a published writer and works hard at her craft. When people tell her how wonderful it is that she has a gift that she can get paid for, her usual comment is, "This is true, but talent needs work. A gift can sit there and look beautiful, but it is worth nothing at all until it is unwrapped and used properly."

Works Cited

Ali, Quraysh, review of *Africa Brothers and Sisters, Booklist,* February 15, 1993, p. 1068.

Amsberry, Dawn, review of *Faraway Drums, School Library Journal,* May, 1998, p. 119.

Review of *A Carp for Kimiko, Kirkus Reviews,* August 1, 1993, p. 1004.

Cooper, Ilene, review of *Beginnings, Booklist,* March 15, 1994, p. 1374.

Corsaro, Julie, review of *I Wanted to Know All about God, Booklist,* February 15, 1994, p. 1086.

Del Negro, Janice, review of *A Carp for Kimiko, Booklist,* December 1, 1993, pp. 698-99.

Del Negro, Janice, review of *Butterfly Boy, Bulletin of the Center for Children's Books,* September, 1997, p. 16.

Review of *I Wanted to Know All about God, Publishers Weekly,* January 3, 1994, p. 81.

Middleton, Susan, review of *A Carp for Kimiko, School Library Journal,* March, 1994, p. 202.

Murphy, Lisa S., review of *Butterfly Boy, School Library Journal,* June, 1997, pp. 95-96.

Review of *Pets!, Kirkus Reviews,* February 15, 1998, p. 265.

Review of *Pets!, Publishers Weekly,* January 19, 1998, p. 377.

Review of *Pink Paper Swans, Publishers Weekly,* June 13, 1994, p. 63.

Sutton, Roger, review of *Africa Brothers and Sisters, Bulletin of the Center for Children's Books,* April, 1993, p. 255.

Sutton, Roger, review of *Pink Paper Swans, Bulletin of the Center for Children's Books,* October, 1994, pp. 52-53.

Topol, Martha, review of *Masai and I, School Library Journal,* October, 1992, p. 91.

Tuteur, Civia, review of *Life Riddles, Voice of Youth Advocates,* August, 1994, p. 144.

Review of *Woodhoopoe Willie, Kirkus Reviews,* February 1, 1993, p. 149.

Review of *Woodhoopoe Willie, Publishers Weekly,* February 15, 1993, p. 236.

For More Information See

PERIODICALS

Booklist, May 15, 1993, p. 1691; November 1, 1997, p. 483.

Bulletin of the Center for Children's Books, April, 1994, p. 254; May, 1995, p. 302.

Children's Book Review Service, spring, 1992, p. 135.

Kirkus Reviews, September 1, 1992, p. 1131; May 15, 1993, p. 664; March 1, 1994, p. 306; August 15, 1996, pp. 1233-34; October 1, 1998, p. 1455.

New York Times Book Review, September 5, 1993, p. 17.

Publishers Weekly, June 29, 1992, p. 62; December 28, 1992, p. 26; March 30, 1998, p. 81.

School Library Journal, June 6, 1992, p. 96; November, 1992, p. 94; July, 1993, p. 58; September, 1993, p. 210; June, 1994, p. 107; July, 1995, p. 55; February, 1997, p. 100; April, 1998, p. 97.

—Sketch by J. Sydney Jones

*   *   *

LaFONTAINE, Bruce 1948-

Personal

Born August 23, 1948, in Rochester, NY; children: Matthew Eric. *Education:* Rochester Institute of Technology, A.A.S. (communication design), 1979; State University of New York, Empire State College, B.F.A. (illustration), 1981.

Addresses

Home—284 Crittenden Way, No. 6, Rochester, NY 14623. *Office*—P.O. Box 301, West Henrietta, NY 14586.

Career

Illustrator and writer. Xerox Corporation, Webster, NY, art director and technical illustrator, 1976-93; freelance illustrator and writer, 1983—. Monroe County Community Education, Fairport, NY, drawing instructor, 1996-98. *Military service:* U.S. Air Force, 1971-74; served as staff sergeant. *Member:* Society of Illustrators, National

Bruce LaFontaine

Writers Union, American Society of Aviation Artists, National Association of Art Educators, Air Force Art Collection Association, Guild of Natural Science Illustrators, Society of Technical Communications, National Cartoonists Association, Illustrators Forum of Rochester.

Awards, Honors

MVP Award, American Motorcyclist Association, 1995, for *Motorcycles.*

Writings

NONFICTION; SELF-ILLUSTRATED

Our Solar System, World of Science/Safari, 1989.

History of Space Exploration, Dover Publications, 1990.

Bridges of the World, Dover Publications, 1994.

Motorcycles, Dover Publications, 1995.

History of Trucks, Dover Publications, 1996.

Famous Buildings of Frank Lloyd Wright, Dover Publications, 1997.

History of Great Inventions, Dover Publications, 1998.

Exploring the Solar System, Dover Publications, 1998.

History of the Sword, Dover Publications, 1998.

The Great Steamships, Dover Publications, 1999.

History of Classic Sports Cars, Dover Publications, 1999.

Charles Lindbergh and the Spirit of St. Louis, Dover Publications, 1999.

Submarines and Underwater Exploration, Dover Publications, 2000.

X-Planes: Experimental Aircraft 1940-1990, Dover Publications, 2000.

Story of the Wright Brothers, Dover Publications, 2000.

Tanks and Armored Vehicles, Dover Publications, in press.

Story of Women Aviators, Dover Publications, in press.

Historic Houses of American Presidents, Dover Publications, forthcoming.

Skyscrapers of the World, Dover Publications, forthcoming.

History of Locomotives, Dover Publications, forthcoming.

History of Lighter-than-Air Flight, Dover Publications, forthcoming.

ILLUSTRATOR

Biker Theme Rub-on Tattoos for Kids, Dover Publications, 1995.

Chinese Dragon Rub-on Tattoos for Kids, Dover Publications, 1996.

Classic Sports Cars Sticker Book, Dover Publications, 1998.

Solar System Sticker Book, Dover Publications, 1998.

Trains Sticker Book, Dover Publications, 1998.

Classic Motorcycles Sticker Book, Dover Publications, 1999.

Spacecraft Sticker Book, Dover Publications, 1999.

Historic Aircraft Sticker Book, Dover Publications, 2000.

Racing Cars Sticker Book, Dover Publications, 2000.

The Planets Little Activity Sticker Book, Dover Publications, 2000.

Heavy Construction Vehicles Sticker Book, Dover Publications, forthcoming.

Streamlined Locomotives Stained Glass Coloring Book, Dover Publications, forthcoming.

Also designer and illustrator of posters.

Work in Progress

Writing and illustrating *Exploring the Moon in Fact and Fantasy.*

Sidelights

Bruce LaFontaine has been illustrating and writing nonfiction for children since the late 1980s. Coming from a high-pressure job as a corporate art director, LaFontaine was encouraged by a college professor to develop his writing skills to augment his talents as an artist; more than twenty books with LaFontaine as author/illustrator have been the result. Among the titles written and illustrated by LaFontaine are *Bridges of the World, Charles Lindbergh and the Spirit of St. Louis,* and *Submarines and Underwater Exploration,* each of which reflect the author's personal interest in science and technology.

"I specialize in creating books about the history of science, technology, transportation, space and aviation, and architecture," LaFontaine explained to *SATA.* "These are all areas that were of great interest to me as a child but seemed unrealistic to pursue because of my poor math skills (having a right-brain orientation, which of course was not understood when I was growing up in the 1950s and 1960s)." LaFontaine structures his texts to middle-grade (ages 8-12) readers, and makes an effort to introduce young people to new terms in the area of their interest. "My intention is to imply the meaning of a word through the context in which it's used," LaFontaine explained, "motivating a child to either ask an adult what the word means or else look it up themselves.

"The main goal in my book work is to educate, entertain, and hopefully, inspire kids about the amazing world that they are part of," the author/illustrator noted. For this reason, one of the characteristics of LaFontaine's many books is that the subject under examination is presented as it developed throughout history, from its earliest conception, through advances in technology to its most current incarnation, whether it be a motorcycle, a stone bridge, or a sword. *Motorcycles,* for instance, spans the history of the motorized bicycle from the first three-wheeled powered cycle made by Gottlieb Diamler in 1895 to a 1913 V-twin engine Excelsior Auto Cycle to the modern motocross "dirt bike," while *History of the Sword* extends its scope over five thousand years, covering a broad range of cultures. "I hope to give kids a sense of connection to this [development] process and its relation to the world of today. By using examples of historical events and personalities, I hope to inspire kids to believe that they are also capable of making important contributions, perhaps even great achievements, that could become part of the historical perspective."

LaFontaine considers himself fortunate to work with few creative constraints from his publisher, Dover Publications. "This fact, in combination with being able to work in subject areas that I have a special interest in, gives me a lot of satisfaction from my work," he explained. "I am also gratified by the opportunity to reach kids with idealism and hopefulness that may turn them in a direction that will be important and meaningful to their own lives."

Born in 1948, LaFontaine was influenced by many things on his path to becoming an author/illustrator. "I fondly remember books by Beverly Cleary and Robert Lawson, with their wonderful black-and-white ink and pencil illustrations," he recalled to *SATA.* "As a pre-teen and teenager, I was an avid fan of *MAD* magazine, comic books, and science fiction. Although I was born in Rochester, New York, and have lived here for many years, I spent most of my childhood and adolescence growing up in suburban Los Angeles (Conga Park). There, I was influenced by both the culture of the West (cowboys) and Hollywood (films and T.V.)."

Many of the techniques of cartoon drawing—variations in line thickness, methods of shading, simplified backgrounds—have been adopted by LaFontaine in the detailed pen-and-ink drawings used in many of his books, most of which have been designed to be colored in by relatively sophisticated coloring-book users.

A prolific author/illustrator, LaFontaine often has several projects going at once. As he explained: "I usually work on the art for one book while doing the writing for another. All of my illustration work is created using traditional drawing and painting methods and medium including pencil, pen and ink, watercolor dyes, and colored pencil."

LAIRD, Elizabeth (Mary Risk) 1943-

Personal

Born October 21, 1943, in Wellington, New Zealand; daughter of John MacLelland (a general secretary) and Florence Marion (a homemaker; maiden name, Thomson) Laird; married David Buchanan McDowall (a writer), April 19, 1975; children: Angus John, William Alistair Somerled. *Education:* University of Bristol, B.A. (with honors), 1966; London University, Certificate of Education, 1967; Edinburgh University, M.Litt., 1971. *Religion:* Church of England. *Hobbies and other interests:* Chamber music, gardening.

Addresses

Home—31 Cambrian Rd., Richmond, Surrey TW10 6JQ, England.

Career

Writer, 1980—. Bede Mariam School, Addis Ababa, Ethiopia, teacher, 1967-69; Pathway Further Education Centre, Southall, London, England, lecturer, 1972-77. *Member:* Society of Authors and Illustrators, Anglo-Ethiopian Society.

Awards, Honors

Carnegie Award runner-up, 1988, for *Red Sky in the Morning;* Children's Book Award, Federation of Children's Book Groups, 1992, Sheffield Children's Book Award, 1992, and Glazen Globe prize, Royal Dutch Geographical Society, 1993, all for *Kiss the Dust;* Smarties Young Judges Award, 1994, for *Hiding Out;* Carnegie Medal Shortlist, British Library Association, 1996, for *Secret Friends;* Lancashire Book Award, 1997, for *Jay.*

Writings

Anna and the Fighter, illustrated by Gay Galsworthy, Heinemann Educational, 1977.
The House on the Hill, illustrated by Galsworthy, Heinemann Educational, 1978.
The Garden, illustrated by Peter Dennis, Heinemann Educational, 1979.
The Big Green Star, illustrated by Leslie Smith, Collins, 1982.
The Blanket House, illustrated by Smith, Collins, 1982.
The Doctor's Bag, illustrated by Smith, Collins, 1982.
Jumper, illustrated by Smith, Collins, 1982.
(With Abba Aregawi Wolde Gabriel) *The Miracle Child: A Story from Ethiopia,* Holt, 1985.
The Dark Forest, illustrated by John Richardson, Collins, 1986.
The Long House in Danger, illustrated by Richardson, Collins, 1986.
Henry and the Birthday Surprise, illustrated by Mike Hibbert, photographs by Robert Hill, British Broadcasting Corporation, 1986.

The Road to Bethlehem: An Ethiopian Nativity, foreword by Terry Waite, Holt, 1987.
Prayers for Children, illustrated by Margaret Tempest, Collins, 1987.
Wet and Dry, Pan Books, 1987.
Hot and Cold, Pan Books, 1987.
Light and Dark, Pan Books, 1987.
Heavy and Light, Pan Books, 1987.
Busy Day, illustrated by Carolyn Scrace, Children's Press Choice, 1987.
Happy Birthday! A Book of Birthday Celebrations, illustrated by Satomi Ichikawa, Collins, 1987.
Hymns for Children, illustrated by Tempest, Collins, 1988.
Sid and Sadie, illustrated by Alan Marks, Collins, 1988.
(With Olivia Madden) *The Inside Outing,* illustrated by Deborah Ward, Barron, 1988.
Red Sky in the Morning, Heinemann, 1988, published as *Loving Ben,* Delacorte, 1989.
Graces for Children, Collins, 1989.
Crackers, Heinemann, 1989.
Fireman Sam and the Missing Key, Heinemann, 1990.
Rosy's Garden: A Child's Keepsake of Flowers, illustrated by Ichikawa, Philomel, 1990.
Kiss the Dust, Dutton, 1991.
The Pink Ghost of Lamont, Heinemann, 1991.
Pandemonium, Little Mammoth, 1992.

Elizabeth Laird

Dolly Rockers, Little Mammoth, 1992.
Hiding Out, Heinemann, 1993.
(With Susan Hellard) *Stinker Muggles and the Dazzle Bug,* Collins, 1995.
Secret Friends, Hodder and Stoughton, 1996, Putnam, 1999.
Jay, Heinemann, 1997.
Forbidden Ground, Hamish Hamilton, 1997.
Rosy's Winter: A Child's Fireside Book, illustrated by Ichikawa, Heinemann, 1997.
The Listener, illustrated by Pauline Hazelwood, A. and C. Black, 1997.
A Funny Sort of Dog, illustrated by Russell Ayto, Heinemann, 1997.
On the Run, illustrated by Carrie Herries, Mammoth, 1997.
(Editor) *Me and My Electric,* illustrated by Polly Dunbar, Mammoth, 1998.
Gabriel's Feather: The Story of the Nativity, illustrated by Bettina Patterson, Scholastic, 1998.
King of the Supermarket, illustrated by Ailie Busby, Little Hippo, 1999.
A Book of Promises, illustrated by Michael K. Frith, Dorling Kindersley, 2000.

"CUBBY BEARS" SERIES

The Cubby Bears' Birthday Party, illustrated by Scrace, Collins, 1985.
The Cubby Bears Go Camping, illustrated by Scrace, Collins, 1985.
The Cubby Bears Go on the River, illustrated by Scrace, Collins, 1985.
The Cubby Bears Go Shopping, illustrated by Scrace, Collins, 1985.

"LITTLE RED TRACTOR" SERIES

The Day The Ducks Went Skating, illustrated by Colin Reeder, Tambourine Books, 1991.
The Day Veronica Was Nosy, illustrated by Reeder, Tambourine Books, 1991.
The Day Sidney Ran Off, illustrated by Reeder, Tambourine Books, 1991.
The Day Patch Stood Guard, illustrated by Reeder, Tambourine Books, 1991.

"TOUCAN 'TECS" SERIES

The Grand Ostrich Ball, illustrated by Peter Lawson, Heinemann, 1989.
Arctic Blues, illustrated by Lawson, Heinemann, 1989.
Gopher Gold, illustrated by Lawson, Heinemann, 1989.
High Flyers, illustrated by Lawson, Heinemann, 1989.
Going Cuckoo, illustrated by Lawson, Heinemann, 1989.
Fine Feathered Friends, illustrated by Lawson, Heinemann, 1989.
Kookaburra Cackles, illustrated by Lawson, Heinemann, 1989.
Peacock Palace Scoop, illustrated by Lawson, Heinemann, 1989.
Highland Fling, illustrated by County Studio, Buzz Books, 1991.
The Big Drip, illustrated by County Studio, Buzz Books, 1991.
Desert Island Ducks, illustrated by County Studio, Buzz Books, 1991.

The Snail's Tale, illustrated by County Studio, Buzz Books, 1991.

"WILD THINGS" SERIES

Leopard Trail, Macmillan, 1999.
Baboon Rock, Macmillan, 1999.
Elephant Thunder, Macmillan, 1999.
Rhino Fire, Macmillan, 1999.
Red Wolf, Macmillan, 1999.
Zebra Storm, Macmillan, 1999.
Turtle Reef, Macmillan, 2000.
Parrot Rescue, Macmillan, 2000.
Chimp Escape, Macmillan, 2000.
Lion Pride, Macmillan, 2000.

FOR ADULTS

English in Education, Oxford University Press, 1977.
Arcadia, Macmillan, 1990.

Also author of school readers, including *Anita's Big Day, Australia, Dead Man's River, The Storm, Simon the Spy, Karen and the Artist, Americans on the Move, The Earthquake, Clara, Ask Me Again, Sugar and Candy, Americans at Home, Faces of the U.S.A.,* and *Faces of Britian* for Longman and Penguin.

Work in Progress

When the World Began, a collection of Ethiopian traditional tales.

Sidelights

Elizabeth Laird is a well-respected and award-winning author of children's picture books and easy readers, but is best known for her novels for young adults. Her *Loving Ben,* published in England as *Red Sky in the Morning,* about a young girl caring for her hydrocephalic baby brother, was a critical success upon publication in 1989, and has continued to be a favorite in classrooms around the world. Laird has paired a love of travel with a love for books in a long list of novels about Muslim countries, the Middle East, and East Africa. Her *Kiss the Dust* deals with the realties of a Kurdish rebellion in Iraq; *Forbidden Ground* is set in a nameless North African country and deals with a young girl coming to grips with moral issues; the "Wild Things" series is set in Kenya and Ethiopia and feature a core cast of characters who deal with wildlife issues in each volume.

Born in New Zealand to Scottish parents, Laird now makes her home in England. She has been inspired by her experiences as a traveler and teacher, and was particularly motivated to adapt Ethiopian Christian folklore for a European audience after spending two years in Ethiopia. "I always had a burning desire to travel," Laird once told *Something about the Author* (*SATA*), "and as soon as I possibly could, at the age of eighteen, I took off from home (with my parents' blessing!) and went to Malaysia where I spent a year as a teacher's aide in a boarding school for Malay girls. That experience only gave me a taste for more, so after I had graduated in French (which involved a wonderful spell as a student in Paris) I headed off to Ethiopia, and worked for two years in a school in Addis Ababa. In those days the country was at peace, and it was possible to travel to the remotest parts by bus and on horseback."

That experience provided the background for a series of easy readers for teaching purposes, as well as for *The Miracle Child: A Story from Ethiopia,* which was written in collaboration with Abba Aregawi Wolde Gabriel. The book recounts the life of Takla Haymanot, a thirteenth-century Ethiopian saint revered for the miracles of healing the sick and raising the dead. The text is accompanied by reproductions of eighteenth-century paintings by Ethiopian Monks. Vincent Crapanzano, contributor to the *New York Times Book Review,* asserted that the reproductions are "informative and explain many of the artistic conventions of Ethiopian painting in a manner so simple as to be understandable to a child, yet interesting to an adult."

Laird's second adaptation of Ethiopian religious folklore followed the same format. *The Road to Bethlehem: An Ethiopian Nativity* is an Ethiopian account of the events surrounding the birth of Jesus. The tale presents a more earthly account of the nativity than the standard Christian version and credits Mary with an active role as a healer and saint. "Mary is no ordinary woman in these stories, and not just because she is the mother of Jesus," observed Rosemary L. Bray in the *New York Times Book Review.* "As the Holy Family flees Herod into Egypt, Mary embarks on a ministry of healing: 'The dumb spoke, the lame ran, the deaf heard, and the blind could see.'" A reviewer from the *Bulletin of the Center for Children's Books* concluded that *The Road to Bethlehem* combines familiar themes of the New Testament "with popular legends and miracles into a cohesive narrative."

Laird's first novel for young adults was inspired by the birth and death of a younger brother. *Red Sky in the Morning* (released as *Loving Ben* in the United States) tells the story of Anna, the twelve-year-old narrator, whose brother, Ben, is born brain damaged. Through Anna, Laird recreates the family struggle of raising a handicapped child and the confusing feelings of pain and release experienced when the child dies. "Anna's voice rings true throughout as she moves from awkwardness and judgmental statements to a more mature empathy," wrote Barbara Chatton in a *School Library Journal* review. Critics also praised the author's rendering of the adult characters outside Anna's family. The adults who help Anna understand new aspects of human nature "are sufficiently real, and the story homely and natural enough for the wisdom of the moral lessons conveyed to be palatable," wrote a *Junior Bookshelf* reviewer. A critic in *Horn Book Guide* concluded that the story, told in Anna's "wise and witty voice tugs at the heart."

Laird's interest in foreign places inspired another novel, *Kiss the Dust.* Set in Iraq, the novel tells the story of Tara Khan, a twelve-year-old Kurdish girl, whose family is forced to relocate when the Iraqi government attempts to suppress the Kurds. Tara's family escapes first to Iran, where she is forced to adopt a highly conservative

Muslim lifestyle, and finally to England, where she must confront the shock of an entirely new, secular culture. Critics have commented on the graphic depiction of violence in the story, and although some find the detail unnecessary, others find it appropriate to, and accurate for, the wartime situations in which Tara is embroiled and fleeing. "*Kiss the Dust* is filled with wonderfully researched ethnographic details about both Kurdish and refugee culture, and opens a door to a foreign world," wrote Elizabeth Cohen, a *New York Times Book Review* contributor. This is particularly the case, observed Cohen, when Tara makes comparisons between her journey's beginning in urban Sulaimaniya and its end in a working-class neighborhood in London. A critic for *Kirkus Reviews* felt that Laird "builds a sympathetic portrait of the embattled Kurds and a compelling portrait of Tara," and concluded that the book was an "important contribution to the growing number of refugee stories."

Laird has also written for younger children. Her book *Rosy's Garden: A Child's Keepsake of Flowers,* is a collection of flower lore and legend dispensed within the framework of Rosy's visits to her garden-loving grandmother's house. In addition to the story-telling, Rosy's grandmother teaches her to make such garden trifles as rose water, potpourri, and herb sandwiches. *Rosy's Garden* is an "unusual treasury of flower lore" according to Carolyn Phelan's review in *Booklist.* Laird has also written the text for several picture books, including the "Cubby Bears" and "Little Red Tractor" series. In the latter, a tractor and its driver, Stan, come to the rescue of farmers and livestock in need of assistance. While Duncan, the tractor, is never given human thoughts or actions, it still becomes something of a character in the gentle stories. According to *School Library Journal* contributor Nancy Seiner "child appeal is assured by the winning personalities of the animals and the major role played by the tractor." Writing in *Magpies,* Lyn Linning commented that both series "are appealing pictures books for preschoolers." Linning went on to comment about Laird's writing for very young readers in general, claiming "Elizabeth Laird knows how to entertain middle primary readers while extending their facility with books and language."

Though Laird does write the occasional picture book as well as books for middle primary readers, she has concentrated mostly on juvenile novels with her later work. *Secret Friends* does not borrow an exotic locale, though it does look at a newly immigrated family in England. Rafaella feels an outsider at school, except for the one girl, Lucy, who befriends her. But Lucy does not want to risk being a social outcast herself and has even given her secret friend the pejorative nickname "Earwig" because of Rafaella's large ears. Taunted and teased on the playground for this physical anomaly, Rafaella finally undergoes corrective surgery, but dies of heart failure during the operation. Lucy is haunted with guilt as a result. "The power of the story," noted *Booklist*'s Hazel Rochman, "is the honesty of Lucy's first-person narrative, her uneasiness as a bystander to the bullying, torn between shame and pity." Rochman added that what gives "unexpected depth to the outsider theme" is

Lucy's envy of Rafaella's happy home life, a stark contrast to her own.

With *Forbidden Ground,* Laird moved back to more exotic locales with a novel of a love that challenges conventions set in an unnamed North African country. Hannah has just moved to the city from the conservative country and is finding difficulty in adjusting to the more cosmopolitan moral values she encounters there. These internal conflicts are only increased when she meets Simi, who may or may not be sincere in his love for her. George Hunt noted in *Books for Keeps* that the book "is a romantic, but realistic and unsentimental story; its cultural and geographic settings are vividly evoked, but the universality of the emotional dilemmas it describes gives the story a very wide relevance and appeal." Sarah Mears concluded in *School Librarian* that Laird's was a "readable story which provides a view of life in a modern Islamic community."

Another unnamed foreign country is the backdrop for *On the Run,* a "feel-good" novel about a resourceful but lonely child, according to Chris Stephenson in *School Librarian.* Hania is left behind with her grandfather when her parents flee the country to avoid being conscripted to the Nationalist cause in a civil war. Hania finds consolation feeding the chickens until a wounded freedom fighter comes her way and she nurses him back to health in the barn, unknown to the gruff grandfather. Finally she discovers that her grandfather too supports the freedom movement and has been looking for the wounded soldier. Stephenson concluded that the novel was "somewhat far-fetched, but ultimately a heart-warming moral tale."

An ongoing project for Laird are the books of the "Wild Things" series, with a cast of three main recurring characters: an English boy, a Kenyan boy, and an Ethiopian-American girl. Set in East Africa, the short novels all deal with trouble the three encounter each time they find a different wild species at risk. In the first of the series, *Leopard Trail,* Tom, Joseph, and Afra discover the difficulty of re-locating leopards. *Baboon Rock* confronts Afra with the knowledge that adopting an injured baby baboon might not be the smartest thing to do. Tom intercedes between humans and pachyderms in *Elephant Thunder,* while Joseph confronts a band of illegal hunters in *Rhino Fire.* Deadly rabies is at the heart of *Red Wolf,* and a drought parches the plains in *Zebra Storm.* All the while, the trio of characters must also deal with the usual childhood dilemmas of growing up.

Commenting on her varied work to *SATA,* Laird wrote: "I feel immensely privileged to be able to earn my living as a writer. I cherish the freedom. I enjoy working on my own thing in my own time. I also love the unexpectedness. I never know where the inspiration will strike next, or into what exciting byways it will lead me."

Works Cited

Bray, Rosemary L., review of *The Road to Bethlehem, New York Times Book Review,* December 6, 1987, p. 80.

Chatton, Barbara, review of *Loving Ben, School Library Journal,* September, 1989, p. 252.

Cohen, Elizabeth, review of *Kiss the Dust, New York Times Book Review,* October 4, 1992, p. 22.

Crapanzano, Vincent, "Takla the Wonderworker," *New York Times Book Review,* November 10, 1985, p. 38.

Hunt, George, review of *Forbidden Ground, Books for Keeps,* January, 1998, pp. 19-20.

Review of *Kiss the Dust, Kirkus Reviews,* April 15, 1992, p. 539.

Linning, Lyn, "Know the Author: Elizabeth Laird," *Magpies,* July, 1999, pp. 14-15.

Review of *Loving Ben, Horn Book Guide,* July, 1989, p. 77.

Mears, Sarah, review of *Forbidden Ground, School Librarian,* November, 1997, p. 21.

Phelan, Carolyn, review of *Rosy's Garden, Booklist,* March 15, 1990, p. 1446.

Review of *Red Sky in the Morning, Junior Bookshelf,* August, 1988, p. 197.

Review of *The Road to Bethlehem, Bulletin of the Center for Children's Books,* January, 1988.

Rochman, Hazel, review of *Secret Friends, Booklist,* January 1, 1999, p. 878.

Seiner, Nancy, review of *The Day Patch Stood Guard* and *The Day Sidney Ran Off, School Library Journal,* September, 1991, p. 236.

Stephenson, Chris, review of *On the Run, School Librarian,* spring, 1997, p. 34.

For More Information See

PERIODICALS

Booklist, June 1, 1991, p. 1879; January 15, 1995, p. 946.

Books for Keeps, September, 1998, p. 22.

Bulletin of the Center for Children's Books, October, 1989, p. 36.

Kirkus Reviews, October 1, 1989, p. 1476; March 1, 1990, p. 349.

Publishers Weekly, October 27, 1989, p. 70; April 27, 1992, p. 269.

School Library Journal, July, 1990, p. 61; July, 1992, p. 90; March, 1999, p. 210.

—*Sketch by J. Sydney Jones*

*   *   *

LAWRENCE, Lynn
See GARLAND, Sherry

*   *   *

LENNON, John (Ono) 1940-1980

Personal

Born John Winston Lennon, October 9, 1940, in Liverpool, Lancashire, England; name legally changed April 22, 1969; died of gunshot wounds, December 8, 1980, in New York, NY; son of Alfred (a porter) and Julia (Stanley) Lennon; married Cynthia Powell, August 23, 1962 (divorced November 8, 1968); married Yoko Ono (an artist, vocalist, songwriter, and author), March 20, 1969; children: (first marriage) John Julian; (second marriage) Kyoko (stepdaughter), Sean Taro Ono. *Education:* Attended Liverpool College of Art.

Career

Composer, lyricist, performer (vocals, guitar, piano, organ, harmonica), writer. Member of the Nurk Twins, 1957; co-founder and member of the Quarrymen musical group, 1958; member of the Moondogs trio, 1959; member of the Silver Beatles, 1960; premiered with the Beatles in Liverpool, England, 1960; performed with the Beatles at clubs in Hamburg, West Germany, and Liverpool during early 1960s, in Sweden, 1963, with Royal Variety Show at Prince of Wales Theatre in London, England, 1963, in Paris, France, Denmark, Hong Kong, Australia, New Zealand, and the United States, 1964, in France, Spain, Italy, and the United States, 1965, in Japan, Greece, Canada, and the Far East during late 1960s; co-owner of Apple Boutique, London, 1967-68; Apple Corp., Ltd., London, partner, 1968-80. Founder and member of the Plastic Ono Band, beginning in 1969. Guest on numerous television shows, including: *Juke Box Jury,* British Broadcasting Corp. (BBC), December 7, 1963; *The Ed Sullivan Show,* Columbia Broadcasting System (CBS), February 9, 1964, and February 23, 1964; *Magical Mystery Tour,* BBC, 1967; *Not Only—But Also,* BBC, c. 1967; *Rock and Roll Circus,* 1968. Actor in motion pictures, including: *A Hard Day's Night,* United Artists, 1964; *Help!,* United Artists, 1965; *How I Won the War,* United Artists, 1967;

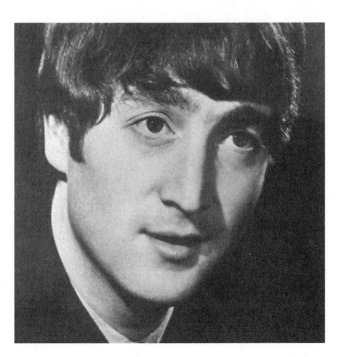

John Lennon

Let It Be, United Artists, 1970; *Dynamite Chicken,* EYP Programs, 1972. Creator and director of film *Apotheosis,* shown at Cannes Filmmaker Fortnight Festival, 1971; creator of short films *Erection, Cold Turkey,* and *The Ballad of John and Yoko,* all shown with *Apotheosis* at Whitney Museum of American Art, New York City, 1971. Held one-artist exhibits of lithographs at London Arts Gallery and at Lee Nordness Galleries in New York City, 1970.

Awards, Honors

Foyles Literary Prize, 1964, for *In His Own Write;* winner, with the Beatles, of Grammy Awards from National Academy of Recording Artists: for best new artists, 1964, for album of the year, best album cover, best contemporary rock and roll recording, and best engineered recording, all for *Sgt. Pepper's Lonely Hearts Club Band,* all 1967, for best engineered recording for *Abbey Road,* 1969, and for best original score for movie or television for *Let It Be,* 1970; member of Order of the British Empire, 1965; Ivor Novello Award, 1970, for "Get Back" and "Ob-La-Di, Ob-La-Da"; platinum album awards for *Abbey Road, Meet the Beatles, Hey Jude, Let It Be, Sgt. Pepper's Lonely Hearts Club Band, Rubber Soul, A Hard Day's Night, The White Album, Magical Mystery Tour, Revolver,* and *Help;* gold album awards for *Imagine* and *John Lennon/The Plastic Ono Band.*

Writings

In His Own Write (humor), self-illustrated, Simon & Schuster, 1964.
A Spaniard in the Works (humor), self-illustrated, Simon & Schuster, 1965.
The Penguin John Lennon (contains *In His Own Write* and *A Spaniard in the Works*), Penguin, 1966, published as *In His Own Write [and] A Spaniard in the Works,* New American Library, 1967.
(With Adrienne Kennedy and Victor Spinetti) *The Lennon Play* (one-act; adapted from *In His Own Write* and *A Spaniard in the Works;* first produced in London at the National Theatre, June 27, 1968), J. Cape, 1968, Simon & Schuster, 1969.
Bag One: A Suite of Lithographs (exhibit guide), [New York], 1971.
My Mummy's Dead, Mini-Books, 1971.
(With Jann Wenner) *Lennon Remembers,* Straight Arrow Books, 1971.
(As illustrator) Stanley Kapepa, *A Canoe for Uncle Kila,* Polynesian Voyaging Society, [Honolulu], 1976.
John Lennon in His Own Words, compiled by Barry Miles, designed by Pearce Marchbank, Quick Fox, 1981.
The Lennon Tapes: John Lennon and Yoko Ono in Conversation with Andy Peebles, 6 December, 1980, British Broadcasting Corporation (London, England), 1981.
The Playboy Interviews with John Lennon and Yoko Ono: Conducted by David Sheff, edited by G. Barry Golson, Playboy Press, 1981.

Skywriting by Word of Mouth, and Other Writings, Including the Ballad of John and Yoko, Harper & Row, 1986.

(With Yoko Ono) *Ai: Japan through John Lennon's Eyes,* Shogakkan (Tokoyo, Japan), 1990, Cadence Books (San Francisco, CA), 1992.

John Lennon: Drawings, Performances, Films, edited by Dorothee Hansen and Wulf Herzogenrath, Cantz (Ostfildern), 1995.

The Lost Lennon Interviews, by Geoffrey Giuliano and Brenda Giuliano, Adams Media Corp (Holbrook, MA), 1996.

Real Love: The Drawings for Sean, Random House, 1999.

SONGBOOKS

(With Paul McCartney) *Eine Kleine Beatlemusik,* Northern Songs Ltd., 1965.

(With McCartney and George Harrison) *The Golden Beatles,* Northern Songs Ltd., 1966.

(With McCartney) *The Music of Lennon and McCartney,* Hansen, 1969.

(With McCartney) *Great Songs of Lennon and McCartney,* edited by Milton Okun, Dan Fox, and Victoria Heller, Quadrangle, 1973.

(With McCartney and Harrison) *The Beatles Lyrics,* Futura, 1975, reprinted as *The Beatles Lyrics Illustrated,* Dell, 1975.

(With McCartney) *Yesterday,* Roja Music Publications, 1981.

(With McCartney) *Yellow Submarine,* Hal Leonard Corp., 1987.

(With McCartney) *Easy Beatle Hits,* Hal Leonard Corp., 1988.

Imagine, Carol Publishing Group, 1990.

Grow Old With Me, Hal Leonard Corp., 2000.

(With Ono) *The John Lennon Family Album,* Chronicle Books, 2000.

Author with wife, Yoko Ono, of television documentary film, "Rape," 1969.

Contributor of poems and stories to periodicals. Recordings with the Beatles: *Please Please Me,* Parlophone, 1963; *Introducing the Beatles,* Parlophone, 1963; *Meet the Beatles!,* Capitol, 1964; (with Tony Sheridan and others) *The Beatles With Tony Sheridan and Their Guests,* MGM, 1964; (with Frank Ilfield) *Jolly What! The Beatles With Frank Ilfield on Stage,* Vee Jay, 1964, reissued, 1967; *The Beatles' Second Album,* Capitol, 1964; (with George Martin and Orchestra) *A Hard Day's Night,* United Artists, 1964; *Something New,* Capitol, 1964; (with the Four Seasons) *The Beatles Versus the Four Seasons,* Vee Jay, 1964; (with Sheridan and the Swallows) *Ain't She Sweet?,* Atxo, 1964; (with the Four Seasons) *Songs, Pictures, and Stories of the Fabulous Beatles,* Vee Jay, 1964; *The Beatles' Story,* Capitol, 1964; *Beatles '65,* Capitol, 1964; *The Early Beatles,* Capitol, 1965; *Beatles VI,* Capitol, 1965; *Help!,* Capitol, 1965; *Rubber Soul,* Capitol, 1965; *A Collection of Beatle Oldies,* Parlophone, 1966; *Yesterday ... and Today,* Capitol, 1966; *Revolver,* Capitol, 1966; (with Sheridan and others) *This Is Where It Started,* Metro, 1966; (with the Swallows) *The Amazing Beatles,* Clarion, 1966; *Sgt.*

Pepper's Lonely Hearts Club Band, Capitol, 1967; *Magical Mystery Tour,* Capitol, 1967; *The Beatles* (two-record set; also known as *The White Album*), Apple, 1968; *Yellow Submarine,* Apple, 1969; *Abbey Road,* Apple, 1969; *Hey Jude,* Apple, 1970; *Let It Be,* Apple, 1970; *The Beatles/1962-66,* Apple, 1973; *The Beatles/1967-70,* Apple, 1973; *Rock 'n' Roll Music,* Capitol, 1976; and *Love Songs,* Capitol, 1979. Other recordings: (With Y. Ono) *Unfinished Music No. 1—Two Virgins,* Apple, 1968; (with Y. Ono) *Unfinished Music No. 2—Music With the Lions,* Apple, 1969; (with Y. Ono) *Wedding Album,* Apple, 1969; (with the Plastic Ono Band) *The Plastic Ono Band: Live Peace in Toronto,* Apple, 1970; (with the Plastic Ono Band) *John Lennon/Plastic Ono Band,* Apple, 1970; (with the Plastic Ono Band and the Flux Fiddlers) *Imagine,* Apple, 1971; (with Y. Ono, the Plastic Ono Band, Elephant's Memory, and the Invisible Strings) *Sometime in New York City* (two-record set), Apple, 1972; (with the Plastic U.F. Ono Band) *Mind Games,* Apple, 1973; (with the Plastic Ono Nuclear Band) *Walls and Bridges,* Apple, 1974; *Rock 'n' Roll,* Apple, 1975; *Shaved Fish,* Apple, 1975; and (with Y. Ono) *Double Fantasy,* Geffen, 1980. Lyricist and composer of songs, including: "Woman Is the Nigger of the World," "Sisters O Sisters," "Attica State," "Born in a Prison," "New York City," "Sunday Bloody Sunday," "The Luck of the Irish," "John Sinclair," "We're All Water," "Bring on the Lucie (Freda People)," "Nutopian National Anthem," "Mind Games," "Meat City," "Going Down on Love," "Whatever Gets You Through the Night," "Number Nine Dream," "Give Peace a Chance/Cold Turkey," "Instant Karma (We All Shine On)," "Remember Love," "Who Has Seen the Wind?," "Power to the People," "Beef Jerky," "Move Over Ms. L.," "Working Class Hero," "No Bed for Beatle John," "Oh Yoko!," "Starting Over," and "Woman." Lyricist and/or composer of songs with Paul McCartney, including: "I Saw Her Standing There," "Please Please Me," "Love Me Do," "Baby, It's You," "Do You Want to Know a Secret?," "A Taste of Honey," "There's a Place," "Twist and Shout," "P.S. I Love You," "It Won't Be Long," "All I've Got to Do," "Don't Bother Me," "All My Loving," "Little Child," "I Wanna Be Your Man," "I Want to Hold Your Hand," "This Boy," "Not a Second Time," "From Me to You," "Ask Me Why," "Thank You Girl," "I Call Your Name," "She Loves You," "A Hard Day's Night," "I'll Cry Instead," "I'm Happy Just to Dance With You," "I Should Have Known Better," "If I Fell," "And I Love Her," "Can't Buy Me Love," "Things We Said Today," "Anytime at All," "When I Get Home," "Slow Down," "Matchbox," "No Reply," "I'm a Loser," "Baby's in Black," "I'll Follow the Sun," "Mr. Moonlight," "I'll Be Back," "Everybody's Trying to Be My Baby," "She's a Woman," "I Feel Fine," "Eight Days a Week," "You Like Me Too Much," "I Don't Want to Spoil the Party," "The Word," "What You Doing?," "Dizzy Miss Lizzie," "Tell Me What You See," "Every Little Thing," "I've Just Seen a Face," "Norwegian Wood," "You Won't See Me," "Michelle," "It's Only Love," "Girl," "I'm Looking Through You," "In My Life," "The Night Before," "Wait," "Run for Your Life," "Help!," "You've Got to Hide Your Love Away," "I Need You," "Another Girl,"

"Ticket to Ride," "You're Gonna Lose That Girl," "We Can Work It Out," "Yellow Submarine," "Bad Boy," "Day Tripper," "Paperback Writer," "Eleanor Rigby," "Drive My Car," "I'm Only Sleeping," "Nowhere Man," "And Your Bird Can Sing," "What Goes On," "She Said She Said," "Good Day Sunshine," "For No One," "Got to Get You Into My Life," "Tomorrow Never Knows," "Magical Mystery Tour," "The Fool on the Hill," "Your Mother Should Know," "I Am the Walrus," "Hello Goodbye," "Strawberry Fields Forever," "Penny Lane," "Baby, You're a Rich Man," "All You Need Is Love," "Come Together," "Oh! Darling," "I Want You (She's So Heavy)," "Because," "You Never Give Me Your Money," "Sun King," "Mean Mr. Mustard," "Polythene Pam," "She Came in Through the Bathroom Window," "Golden Slumbers," "Carry That Weight," "The End," "Her Majesty," "Lady Madonna," "Hey Jude," "Rocky Raccoon," "Two of Us," "I Dig a Pony," "Across the Universe," "Dig It," "Let It Be," "Maggie Mae," "I've Got a Feeling," "One After 909," "The Long and Winding Road," "For You Blue," "Get Back," "Back in the U.S.S.R.," "Dear Prudence," "Glass Onion," "Ob-La-Di, Ob-La-Da," "Wild Honey Pie," "The Continuing Story of Bungalow Bill," "Happiness Is a Warm Gun," "Martha My Dear," "I'm So Tired," "Blackbird," "Why Don't We Do It in the Road," "Julia," "I Will," "Birthday," "Yer Blues," "Mother Nature's Son," "Everybody's Got Something to Hide Except Me and My Monkey," "Sexy Sady," "Helter Skelter," "Revolution," "Honey Pie," "Cry Baby Cry," "Revolution No. 9," "Good Night," "Sgt. Pepper's Lonely Hearts Club Band," "With a Little Help From My Friends," "Lucy in the Sky With Diamonds," "Getting Better," "Fixing a Hole," "She's Leaving Home," "Being for the Benefit of Mr. Kite," "When I'm Sixty-Four," "Lovely Rita," "Good Morning Good Morning," and "A Day in the Life." Lyricist and composer, with McCartney, of original soundtrack for film, *All This and World War II,* Twentieth-Century Records, 1976.

Sidelights

"The Beatles will be remembered not only for their considerable contribution as songwriters and recording artists," predicted Nicholas Schaffner in *Beatles Forever,* "but also as the most remarkable cultural and sociological phenomenon of their time. During the 1960s they seemed to transform, however unwittingly, the look, sound, and style of at least one generation." For example, Schaffner continued, "they were among the first major public figures of our time to break down the barriers dividing the sexes, with their long hair and vivid attire; champion the use of 'mind-expanding' drugs and the innovations in sound, language, design, and attitude these substances inspired; and, in general, show the way to a life style that defied so many of the conventions taken for granted in 1963."

The John Lennon/Paul McCartney partnership began in 1956, shortly after the two met at a Liverpool rock concert where they were both performing. Together they first performed as the Nurk Twins. Against some resistance from Lennon, McCartney introduced his

schoolmate George Harrison into the group in 1958, and the three guitarists soon joined drummer Pete Best to form the Quarrymen. Slowly building a local following in Liverpool cellar clubs, the group evolved through several name changes—the Moondogs, the Moonshiners, the Silver Beatles—before settling on the Beatles in 1960. For a while the four were joined by guitarist Stuart Sutcliff, a friend of Lennon's from the Liverpool College of Art.

In 1959, the group took a tramp steamer to Hamburg, West Germany, where they got their first lucrative nightclub bookings. It was there they met Ringo Starr, who replaced Pete Best as the group's drummer. "The quick-witted, witheringly cynical Lennon was by all accounts the driving spirit behind the Beatles in those days," Schaffner commented. In Hamburg's Kaiserkeller Club, where the crowd consisted largely of gangsters, prostitutes, and transvestites, the band was often expected to play for eight-hour stretches. But, in Schaffner's opinion, the hard work greatly improved their music: "Their act grew livelier. The Beatles were encouraged to Mak Schau [put on a show] at all costs; so the sweating, leather-clad musicians learned to writhe, vamp, and mug for hours on end, punctuating their repertoire with obscene insults, food, and beer tossed at each other and at the audience. Lennon would often taunt the Germans with his impressions of Hitler, and was wont to appear on stage wearing nothing but a toilet seat and a pair of shorts." Schaffner also pointed out that "these stories, of course, did not come to light until long after the Beatles' later incarnation as cherubic moptops had won the hearts of millions." Stuart Sutcliff decided to stay in Germany when Lennon, McCartney, Harrison, and Starr returned to Liverpool.

It was on their return to England that the Beatles were discovered by Brian Epstein, who became their manager. Epstein was impressed with what he saw: "I sensed that something was happening, something terribly exciting," he said. "There was this amazing communication with the audience and this absolutely marvelous humor." Epstein persuaded the four to stop their onstage swearing and food-fighting, to exchange their scruffy leather jackets for collarless Pierre Cardin suits, and to trim their shaggy hair. He also arranged prestigious engagements and a contract with Electrical and Musical Industries Ltd. (EMI). Schaffner reported that "Lennon [had] said he felt a few qualms about 'selling out' when the Beatles began to launder their once-raunchy image, but McCartney was always there to make sure his tie was straight."

The Beatles' first EMI recording in 1962 was the Lennon-McCartney composition "Love Me Do," which sold one hundred thousand copies. That record and the group's first British television appearance marked the beginning of a spectacular career. In the following years the group played a command performance for the British royal family and held sell-out concerts in other European countries as well as in the United States, Australia, New Zealand, Canada, and Japan.

Beatlemania became an international phenomenon. Hysterical fans filled auditoriums and sports stadiums to see their idols, even though the music was often drowned out by the din of screaming teens. Beatle boots, books, posters, and bubblegum cards sold as fast as they could be made. The sheets and towels the group used at one hotel were cut into one-inch squares and sold as souvenirs.

Beatlemania continued, but the group members grew weary of having their clothes ripped and their hair pulled and clipped by hysterical admirers. Ringo told of a night when the band had been forced to climb a twenty-five story drain pipe to escape fans and the press. Exhausted, the Beatles decided that their 1966 concert at San Francisco's Candlestick Park would be their last live performance together. Ringo stated: "If it had gone on, I personally would have gone insane."

It was at this time that the group also began to tire of much of the music they had been putting out. Lennon complained: "I can't stand listening to most of our early stuff ... songs like 'Eight Days a Week' and 'She Loves You' sound like big drags to me now. I turn the radio off if they're ever on." The Beatles began experimenting with compositions more sophisticated than their early four-four beat music had been. Lennon and Harrison had also been taking hallucinogenic drugs for several years by this time, and their new music reflected these experiences.

The release of the *Revolver* album in 1966 marked the Beatles' emergence as a studio band. "This almost flawless album," observed Roy Carr and Tony Tyler in *The Beatles: An Illustrated Record*, "can be seen as the peak of the Beatles' creative career.... And it could probably have only been made at this particular juncture in the Beatles' career. Touring was, for them, a bar to music ... the final assembly of all their influences in one place at one time, plus the growing infatuation with drug based ideology (and the drugs themselves) ... all combined to create a pool of assets [that] was joyfully put to use in almost staggering fashion." Subsequent albums, most notably *Sgt. Pepper's Lonely Hearts Club Band, The White Album,* and *Abbey Road,* illustrated the Beatles' maturation of musical style and achieved critical and commercial success.

As the music of the group developed, so did the individual styles and interests of each member. In 1967, Lennon made his solo acting debut in the motion picture "How I Won the War," and soon afterward the other Beatles followed in pursuing their separate ventures. Harrison parted for India to study transcendental meditation with Maharishi Mahesh Yogi; McCartney began work on a movie soundtrack; and Starr appeared in the film *Candy.* The founding of Apple Records in 1968 helped keep the Beatles together for a few more recordings, but the bonds that once held the group together had begun to disintegrate.

A number of events contributed to the Beatles disbandment. Lennon traced the beginning of the split to the

Lennon expresses his love for and joy in his son Sean with funny drawings and captions in **Real Love: The Drawings for Sean.** *(Adapted by Al Naclerio from drawings by Lennon.)*

death of manager Epstein in 1967: "After Brian died, we collapsed." Lennon's 1969 marriage to artist Yoko Ono created further turmoil within the group. "I presumed that I would just carry on, and bring Yoko into our life," Lennon recalled. "But it seemed I had to either be married to them or to Yoko, and I chose Yoko, and I was right." Tension among the members of the group was evident again when the movie *Let It Be* was released in 1970. "I felt sad, you know," Lennon said. "I felt ... that the film was set up by Paul for Paul. That is one of the main reasons the Beatles ended." One year after the release of *Let It Be,* the Beatles officially announced their breakup.

By the time of the Beatles' separation, Lennon had already proven himself as a literary talent and a successful solo recording artist. His collections of satirical poems and stories, *In His Own Write* and *A Spaniard in the Works,* were compared with works of Lewis Carroll, James Joyce, and James Thurber. A *Virginia Quarterly Review* critic stated: "One shouldn't have been surprised at the wit and the intelligence of the leader of the Beatles considering the cleverness evident in their success, but the skill (one even toys with the word 'genius') which Lennon shows in this collection of comic poems and prose pieces places him in the great comic tradition of Twain, Perelman, the Marx brothers, and the best of the new seriously comic novelists of this country."

After forming the Plastic Ono Band in 1969, Lennon achieved his first commercial success outside the Beatles. The group's second release was the gold-album-winning *John Lennon/Plastic Ono Band.* Throughout the early 1970s Lennon remained in the popular-music spotlight with such single recordings as "Instant Karma," "Imagine," "Power to the People," and "Mind Games." After the 1975 release of his album *Shaved Fish,* however, Lennon withdrew from public life.

Lennon used the break to reassess himself as a person and as an artist. Lennon attributed some of his newly found peace to the solitude that had allowed him "to re-establish me for myself." He recalled that his "actual moment of awareness" occurred while he was on a tour around the world, a trip he had made, at Ono's suggestion, by himself. "I wandered around Hong Kong at dawn, alone, and it was a thrill," reflected Lennon. "I thought—aha! This is the feeling that makes you write or paint . . . . It was with me all my life! And that's why I'm free of the Beatles—because I took the time to discover that I was John Lennon before the Beatles and will be after the Beatles and so be it."

Beginning in 1975, Lennon lived quietly at home raising his son Sean. "My life revolves around Sean," he told interviewers in 1980. "Now I have more reason to stay healthy and bright . . . . And I want to be with my best friend. My best friend's my wife. If I couldn't have worked with her, I wouldn't have bothered." Just before Lennon's fortieth birthday, he and Ono released a new album, *Double Fantasy.* Lennon's contributions to the record, "simple, direct, and melodic, were celebrations of love and domesticity that asked for, and required, no apology," said *Time*'s Jay Cocks.

While returning home after a December 8, 1980, recording session, Lennon was shot and killed outside his New York City apartment. News of his death brought thousands of mourners to gather outside his home, and radio stations throughout the world played his music in tribute. For many, Lennon's death marked the end of an era. But before his death, Lennon had spoken optimistically about his music and his personal life— "Starting Over" was the title of his latest single. "We had planned so much together," reflected Ono. "We had talked about living until we were eighty. We even drew up lists of all the things we could do for all those years. Then, it was all over. But that doesn't mean the message should be over. The music will live on."

In 1999, Yoko Ono released *Real Love: The Drawings for Sean,* a collection of cartoons that Lennon created for his son Sean when he was between the ages of two and five. According to Ono, interviewed by John Zinsser in *Publishers Weekly,* John bonded with Sean this way. "John kept trying to connect with him every day. Of course, his way of doing this was drawing. He would draw something and say, 'Sean, look, what's this?' And Sean would say, 'That's an elephant.' It was touching," Ono said.

The resultant sketchbook is comprised of Lennon's puns and nonsensical sayings illustrated by wry drawings that have been enhanced with computer manipulated patterns and multicolored lines. An illustration with the caption "Collieflower" shows a budding plant with the face of a dog. A "hippotato" is a cross between a root vegetable and an animal. "The camel dances and having danced moves on" shows a humped camel leaving a purple pyramid and a palm tree behind under a sunny sky. A reviewer for *Publishers Weekly* called the pairings of image and brief text "lyrical, and the pleasure evident in sound and line makes this a winsome little volume, a sort of a verbal and visual version of a musical riff." Steven Stolder, in his review of the book on *Amazon.com,* called Lennon a "witty punster" and stated that "*Real Love* is the kind of book that will capture the attention of Beatles collectors, but it should also spark the imaginations of its intended audience—little Lennonists in the making."

Works Cited

Carr, Roy, and Tony Tyler, *The Beatles: An Illustrated Record,* Harmony Books, 1975.
Cocks, Jay, *Time,* December 22, 1980.
Review of *In His Own Write, Virginia Quarterly Review,* summer, 1964.
Review of *Real Love, Publishers Weekly,* May 3, 1999, p. 74.
Schaffner, Nicholas, *Beatles Forever,* Cameron House, 1977.
Review of *A Spaniard in the Works, Virginia Quarterly Review,* autumn, 1965.
Stolder, Steven, review of *Real Love, Amazon.com,* July 8, 1999.
Zinsser, John, "John Lennon's Drawings for His Son Sean," *Publishers Weekly,* May 3, 1999, pp. 26-27.

For More Information See

BOOKS

Contemporary Literary Criticism, Volume 12, Gale, 1980.
Davies, Hunter, *The Beatles: The Authorized Biography,* McGraw, 1968.
Fast, Julius, *Beatles: The Real Story,* Putnam, 1968.
Fawcett, Anthony, *John Lennon: One Day at a Time,* Grove, 1976.
Lennon, Cynthia, *A Twist of Lennon,* Avon, 1978.
Mellers, Wilfred, *Twilight of the Gods: The Beatles in Retrospect,* Faber, 1973.
Schaumburg, Ron, *Growing Up With the Beatles,* Harcourt, 1976.
Tremlett, George, *The John Lennon Story,* Futura, 1976.

Obituaries

PERIODICALS

Chicago Tribune, December 9, 1980.
Current Biography, February, 1981.
Detroit Free Press, December 9, 1980; December 10, 1980.
London Times, December 10, 1980.
Newsweek, December 22, 1980.
New York Times, December 9, 1980.
Washington Post, December 9, 1980.*

LINGARD, Joan (Amelia) 1932-

Personal

Born April 8, 1932, in Edinburgh, Scotland; daughter of Henry James (Chief Yeoman of Signals in the Royal Navy) and Elizabeth (a homemaker; maiden name, Beattie) Lingard; married first husband, c. 1954 (divorced, 1970); married second husband, Martin Birichaws (an architect and lecturer), c. 1972; children: (first marriage) Kersten, Bridget, Jenny. *Education:* Attended Bloomfield Collegiate School, Belfast; Moray House Training College of Education, Edinburgh, General Certificate of Education, c. 1954. *Religion:* Raised Christian Scientist. *Hobbies and other interests:* Being a grandmother, reading, walking, travel.

Addresses

Home—72 Great King St., Edinburgh EH3 6QU, Scotland. *Agent*—c/o David Higham Assoc., 5/8 Lower John St., London W1R 4HA, England.

Career

Author, scriptwriter, and educator. Teacher in Belfast, Ireland, c. 1948, and Midloathian district, Edinburgh, Scotland, 1953-61; freelance writer, 1963—. Scriptwriter for the Scottish Television network and the British Broadcasting Corporation (BBC). Has also worked in a bank in Belfast and as a library assistant in Edinburgh. *Member:* International PEN, Society of Authors.

Awards, Honors

Scottish Arts Council bursary, 1969; Junior Literary Guild selection, 1983, for *Strangers in the House;* Buxtehude Bulle Prize for Children's Literature (West Germany), 1986, for *Across the Barricades;* Federation of Children's Book Group Award, Sheffield Book Award, and Carnegie Medal shortlisting, 1989, and Lancashire Children's Book Club Book of the Year Award runner-up, 1990, all for *Tug of War;* Scottish Arts Council Award, 1994, for *After Colette;* Scottish Arts Council Award, 1999, for *Tom and the Tree House.* Lingard was made a member of the Civil Division of the Most Excellent Order of the British Empire (MBE), 1998.

Writings

FOR CHILDREN AND YOUNG PEOPLE; FICTION AND PICTURE BOOKS

Frying as Usual, illustrated by Priscilla Clive, Hamish Hamilton (London), 1973, illustrated by Kate Rogers, Puffin (Harmondsworth), 1986.

Snake among the Sunflowers, Thomas Nelson (Nashville), 1977.

The Gooseberry, Hamish Hamilton, 1978, published in the United States as *Odd Girl Out,* Elsevier/Nelson Books (New York), 1979, illustrated by Dyfed Rowlands, Gomer (Llandysul, Wales), 1990.

Joan Lingard

The File on Fraulein Berg, Elsevier/Nelson Books (New York), 1980, Julia MacRae (London), 1980.

Strangers in the House, Hamish Hamilton, 1981, Dutton (New York), 1983.

The Winter Visitor, Hamish Hamilton, 1983.

The Freedom Machine, Hamish Hamilton, 1986.

The Guilty Party, Hamish Hamilton, 1987, illustrated by John Rowlands, Gomer (Wales), 1988.

Rags and Riches, Hamish Hamilton, 1988.

Tug of War, Hamish Hamilton, 1989, Dutton Lodestar, 1990.

Glad Rags, Hamish Hamilton, 1990.

Between Two Worlds, Hamish Hamilton, 1990, Dutton, 1991.

Can You Find Sammy the Hamster?, illustrated by Jan Lewis, Walker (London), 1990.

Morag and the Lamb, illustrated by Patricia Casey, Walker, 1991.

Hands Off Our School! illustrated by Mairi Hedderwick, Hamish Hamilton, 1992.

Night Fires, Hamish Hamilton, 1993.

Lizzie's Leaving, Hamish Hamilton, 1995.

Dark Shadows, Hamish Hamilton, 1998.

A Secret Place, Hodder & Stoughton (London), 1998.
Tom and the Tree House, illustrated by Paul Howard, Hodder & Stoughton, 1998.
The Egg Thieves, Hodder & Stoughton, 1999.

"KEVIN AND SADIE" SERIES; YOUNG ADULT FICTION

The Twelfth Day of July, Hamish Hamilton, 1970, Thomas Nelson (Nashville), 1972, illustrated by Kenny McKendry, Puffin (London), 1996.
Across the Barricades, Hamish Hamilton, 1972, Thomas Nelson, 1973.
Into Exile, Thomas Nelson, 1973.
A Proper Place, Thomas Nelson, 1975.
Hostages to Fortune, Hamish Hamilton, 1976, Thomas Nelson, 1977.

"MAGGIE" SERIES; YOUNG ADULT FICTION

The Clearance, Hamish Hamilton, 1973, Thomas Nelson, 1974.
The Resettling, Thomas Nelson, 1975.
The Pilgrimage, Thomas Nelson, 1976.
The Reunion, Hamish Hamilton, 1977, Thomas Nelson, 1978.

"FLIPPERS" SERIES; PICTURE BOOKS; ILLUSTRATED BY JACQUI THOMAS; PUBLISHED BY MACMILLAN (LONDON)

Secrets and Surprises, 1991.
Clever Clive and Loopy Lucy, 1993.
Slow Flo and Boomerang Bill, 1994.
Sulky Suzy and Jittery Jack, 1995.

FOR ADULTS; FICTION

Liam's Daughter, Hodder & Stoughton (London), 1963.
The Prevailing Wind, Hodder & Stoughton, 1964.
The Tide Comes In, Hodder & Stoughton, 1966.
The Headmaster, Hodder & Stoughton, 1967.
A Sort of Freedom, Hodder & Stoughton, 1968.
The Lord on Our Side, Hodder & Stoughton, 1970.
The Second Flowering of Emily Mountjoy, Paul Harris (Edinburgh), 1979, St. Martin's, 1980.
Greenyards (historical fiction), Putnam (New York), 1981.
Sisters by Rite, St. Martin's, 1984, Hamish Hamilton, 1984.
Reasonable Doubts, Hamish Hamilton, 1986, Trafalgar Square, 1987.
The Women's House, St. Martin's, 1989.
After Colette, Sinclair-Stevenson (London), 1993, Trafalgar Square, 1995.
Dreams of Love and Modest Glory, Sinclair-Stevenson, 1995.

OTHER

Also author of television scripts for the British Broadcasting Corporation (Scotland), including "Maggie," an eighteen-part serial based on her novels that was broadcast in 1981 and 1982; author of scripts for the Scottish Television network, including those for the soap opera "High Living." Author of television plays "The Sandyford Place Mystery" and "A Kiss, A Fond Embrace," both adapted from the novel *Square Mile of Murder* by Jack House, 1980, and "Her Mother's House," 1982. Some of Lingard's books have been translated into Danish, Finnish, French, German, Japanese, Norwegian, Polish, Slovak, Swedish, and Welsh.

Adaptations

Across the Barricades was adapted as a play script by David Ian Neville and published by Oxford University Press, 1990.

Work in Progress

"A novel for children set in present-day Scotland and in Russia during the 1917-18 Revolution."

Sidelights

Considered one of Scotland's most accomplished contemporary writers for children and young adults, Joan Lingard is regularly praised for creating works that are characterized by challenging themes, authentic portrayals of current and historical events, and perceptive depictions of people and relationships. The author of picture books for preschoolers, stories for primary and middle graders, novels for young adults, and fiction for adults, she is regarded as an exceptional storyteller whose books are candid and thought-provoking, interesting and accessible. Lingard is often recognized for the objective, impartial stance that she takes toward the difficult issues that she presents in her works. For example, her "Kevin and Sadie" series of young adult novels, which are some of the author's best-known books, features a Catholic boy and Protestant girl who try to maintain their love against the background of "the Troubles," Northern Ireland's violent religious war. The author, who spent her formative years in Belfast, is credited with presenting her subject realistically and without judgment. In her other works, Lingard addresses such issues as the implications of producing nuclear weapons; displacement, both physical and emotional; adjustment to a new homeland; balancing personal desire and family responsibility; and dealing with the remarriage of a parent.

Lingard is often commended for her skill in depicting place and period; in addition to Northern Ireland, she has set her books in Scotland, France, Latvia, and Canada. The author is also recognized for making specific experiences universal and relevant; for her characterizations, especially of vibrant young women; for her understanding of her audience; and for presenting sober issues with restraint, humor, and optimism. In addition, several of the author's works are considered important books that discuss problems not often considered in titles for their respective age groups. Lingard is generally recognized as an author whose unique perspective, literary talents, and appreciation for young readers has given her a strong critical and popular reputation. Writing in *Twentieth-Century Children's Writers,* Gillian Klein stated, "Joan Lingard is tough and uncompromising, also lively, humorous, and unfailingly accessible. It is partly her honesty that evokes, within a few opening pages of each novel, a sharply realised world peopled by real, flawed humans. No one better expresses prejudice without falling into the all-too-common trap of merely expressing it." Writing in the *St. James Guide to Young Adult Writers*, Eileen Dunlop and Judson Knight added that Lingard has "a natural empathy with adolescent readers, understanding their hopes, aspirations, and emotional uncertainties, yet paying her readers the compliment of engaging them on an intellectual level as adults. . . . She creates a world which young readers instantly recognize as their own, and they compliment her in return: she is one of the few quality writers whose books teenagers, notoriously unbookish, eagerly buy for themselves."

Lingard told Jennie Renton of *Capital Letter,* "The stories I have created have mostly come out of the backgrounds of my life or of people close to me." Born in Edinburgh, Scotland, Lingard arrived in the world in a taxi cab traveling down the city's Royal Mile. In her essay in the *Something about the Author Autobiography Series* (*SAAS*), she wrote, "I've always been pleased about the circumstances of my birth. . . . I like the idea of the taxi, for it suggests mobility, and of the Royal Mile, for it is redolent with memories of the past, being the ancient High Street of Edinburgh which dates back to the sixteenth century." When she was two, Lingard moved to Belfast, Northern Ireland, where her father, Henry, a Londoner who joined the Royal Navy Volunteer Reserve after nearly thirty years of service to the Royal Navy, was sent to be in charge of communications on a trading ship. Joan lived in Belfast until she was eighteen. She wrote in the *Fifth Book of Junior Authors and Illustrators* (*FBJAI*), "[A]ll my formative years were spent in that city. This is reflected in my writing. I would say, in fact, that it is reflected in my life also, for the experiences, sights, sounds, and smells of childhood are so intense that they stay with one forever afterwards." While living in Belfast, Lingard's mother, Elizabeth—"Edinburgh born and bred," according to her daughter in *SAAS*—learned from friends in the next street about Christian Science, a religion that teaches that there is no sin, disease, or death and that the mind can control matter. Lingard wrote in *SAAS* that she "was a fervent believer right through my teens." Since Henry Lingard was often away from home and was recalled to active service in the Royal Navy in 1939, Elizabeth Lingard often played the role of single parent to Joan and her older sister, Doris; when Doris, who was eleven years Joan's senior, left to work in London at seventeen, Joan, as she noted "led the life of an only child."

Lingard wrote in her autobiographical essay, "I was crazy about books as a child. I read and read and read—school stories, adventure novels, *Grimms' Fairy Tales, The Wind in the Willows, Alice in Wonderland, Little Women, Anne of Green Gables,* anything I could get my hands on. I borrowed them from friends or from the library. For birthdays and Christmas, I always asked for books. . . ." She added in *FBJAI,* "My own life seemed too limited; I wanted to cross frontiers, live in the country, at the sea, in the city, climb the Himalayas, track down smugglers, go up the Amazon in pursuit of Colonel Fawcett. One way to do it was through books. When I read, I inhabited different worlds, lived inside

different skins." Lingard told *Something about the Author* (*SATA,*) "I started to write because I loved reading so much and could never get enough to read, so when my mother suggested I write a book of my own I thought, 'Why not?' So I got lined, foolscap paper, filled my fountain pen with green ink—since that, I thought, would be suitable for an author—and began. The books that I wrote were of the improbable adventure type, much in the mode of British children's author Enid Blyton. I didn't write anything set in Belfast. Later, I came to realize that I would write more convincingly if I wrote about people and places I knew and understood." After completing her first book at the age of eleven, Lingard wrote in *FBJAI* that she "had only one ambition, as regards a career anyway."

As a teenager, Lingard continued to write her own books, works set in places such as Brazil, the Yorkshire moors, and the northwest of Scotland. She once wrote, "[O]ne reason why I am sure I read so much and then began to write was that I wanted to push out the boundaries of my life. I could not accept that it was enough to live in this one body, inhabit this one house in this one city." However, as she matured Lingard realized that she would write more convincingly "[i]f I knew my backgrounds at first-hand and understood the kind of people who inhabited them. And so it proved." During World War II, Lingard lived both in Belfast and on her paternal grandmother's farm twenty-five miles outside of London. She wrote in *SAAS,* "We were encouraged to hate Germans, all Germans. . . . And so, when I went to secondary school, which was a small school for girls only, and a new teacher arrived to teach us German, and she turned out to be German herself, we were flabbergasted. We were convinced, of course, that she must be a spy. What else?" Joan and two of her classmates spied on their teacher, copying down every detail that they could find, "which," Lingard wrote "was not a lot. . . . We must have been truly horrible and she must have known that we were following her. . . . When the war ended we learned something which turned our ideas about her upside down and made us feel ashamed." This incident later inspired *The File on Fraulein Berg,* a young adult novel about three girls who believe that their German teacher is a Nazi spy. Autobiographical material also comprises a great part of one of Lingard's novels for adults, *Sisters by Rite,* which describes the friendships of three girls—a Protestant, a Catholic, and a Christian Scientist—from 1943 to 1970. The war, Lingard wrote, "had dominated my childhood, coloured it, and is inextricably entwined with my recollections of it."

As an adolescent, Lingard read the works of such authors as Dickens, Tolstoy, Flaubert, Hemingway, Grahame Greene, and Jane Austen. She also had an active social life, forming a close-knit group called "the Gang" with seven other girls from her school. Despite these happy times, Lingard's adolescence, as she wrote in *SAAS,* "was troubled with anxiety and, subsequently, grief." When she was fourteen, her mother was diagnosed with breast cancer and died eighteen months later. Lingard wrote, "This was the most traumatic event of my life. I was devastated and so was my father." The summer after the death of her mother, Lingard traveled from place to place, staying with her sister or her father; the author noted, "I felt completely disorientated." After returning to Belfast, she got a job at sixteen as a primary school teacher in a poor area of the city: "Totally untrained," she recalled "I stood before a class of fifty-four six-year-olds." The conditions at the school were deplorable, and some of the children had tuberculosis. The author noted, "It was like something out of a novel by Charles Dickens." Although she enjoyed her pupils, Lingard left her position after a year and went to work in the head office of the Ulster Bank. Shortly thereafter, she left Belfast to return to her birthplace, Edinburgh, where her father was living. Lingard said that this move "marked very definitely the end of the first part of my life."

For six months after moving to Edinburgh, Lingard worked as an assistant in the public library and lived in a boarding house; there, she became friends with the landlady's two daughters, who were Christian Scientists. Although she went to church and joined the youth club, Lingard's views were changing. She decided at eighteen that there she could no longer accept the Christian Scientist tenet that there is no sin, disease, or death; consequently, Lingard stopped going to church. "That was," she wrote in *SAAS,* "the next big traumatic event in my life for it meant more than just not going to church; it meant giving up a way of life, and friends." The author added, "I felt like the sinner who has fallen. I felt as if I had gone out into the wilderness." Lingard entered the Moray House Training College of Education in Edinburgh. She once wrote that "the three years that I spent there turned out to be the three most stultifyingly boring years of my life."

After graduation, Lingard got a job teaching in a primary school in the city. At the end of that year, she married and went to live in a cottage in Temple, a small village twelve miles outside of Edinburgh. While working as a teacher in the Midloathian district of Edinburgh, Lingard began writing. Her first book was an eighty thousand word novel about a teacher's training college with a fictitious name. She mused in *SAAS,* "It was thinly disguised . . . and had the book ever been published I might well have been brought up on libel charges." The fledgling author ended up burning what she called her "hymn of hate." In 1961, Lingard's first child, her daughter Kersten, was born. When Kersten was five or six weeks old, Lingard received notice that her adult novel *Liam's Daughter* had been accepted for publication. "I did feel lucky," Lingard wrote. "I had a child, and I was to be a published writer. My only sadness was that my mother was not alive to share the happiness." In 1963, Lingard had her second daughter, Bridget; the next year, her daughter Jenny was born. Lingard noted, "When I look back on those years I wonder how I did manage to produce the work that I did. I published another four novels in the sixties, all for adults, and that marked the end of the first phase of my published writing career."

In 1967, Lingard and her family moved from the Edinburgh countryside back to the city; three years later, her marriage broke up. Short of money, she decided to try writing for a more lucrative market: television. Lingard became part of the team that wrote the soap opera "High Living" for the Scottish Television network. She noted in *SAAS,* "It was all good experience and it stood me in very good stead when I came to write original plays of my own and to adapt my 'Maggie' books into eighteen parts for BBC television." In 1970, Lingard published *The Lord on Our Side,* an adult novel about the religious and political divisions in Ulster from the 1940s to the 1960s. She noted, "What had started as a civil rights movement for Catholics in 1968 had swollen into something approaching civil war." A friend of Lingard's, Honor Arundel, herself a respected author of children's literature, had read *The Lord on Our Side* and made the suggestion that she write a book for young people about what was happening in the province. Lingard recalled "I thought about it and realised that I had a book almost waiting in my head, as it were, to come out." That book, *The Twelfth Day of July,* was the first of Lingard's series of "Kevin and Sadie" books.

Set at the beginning of "the Troubles," *The Twelfth Day of July* describes how two Catholic children, fourteen-year-old Kevin McCoy and his younger sister, Brede, and two Protestant children, thirteen-year-old Sadie Jackson and her younger brother, Tommy, become embroiled in the prejudice and tension that surrounds preparations for the day referred to in the book's title. On that day in 1690, King William of Orange, a Protestant, defeated the Catholic army in the Battle of the Boyne, and since then Orange supporters have celebrated the victory. When Kevin and his friend Brian vandalize the picture of William on a wall in the Protestant section of Belfast, Sadie and her friends change the slogan "God Bless the Pope" to "God Bless King Billy" on a poster in the Catholic section of town. The Jackson house is burned down, and arson by Catholics is suspected. On the eleventh of July, a bonfire night for Orange supporters, Sadie and Tommy and their friends go to the stretch of ground that separates the Protestant and Catholic sides. Kevin, Brian, and their friends take positions across the divide. Stones are thrown, and a battle takes place; Brede, Kevin's sister, is struck on the head and severely wounded. Meeting in the middle of the road, Kevin, Sadie, and Tommy take Brede to the hospital. Later, the children spend the next day at the seaside. A reviewer for the *Times Literary Supplement* called *The Twelfth Day of July* "a good and important book. . . . [I]t is no tract but a fully realized and moving work of fiction. . . . Lingard sees that the only real hope of peace is in getting the two sides together, and this she manages with a naturalness that is itself a cause for hope. . . . This book should be compulsory reading in the Six Counties and, for its wider implications, far beyond." Writing in the *Bulletin of the Center for Children's Books,* Zena Sutherland added that, for American readers, the book "may clarify to some extent the bitterness rampant in Northern Ireland today."

Across the Barricades takes place three years after the conclusion of *The Twelfth Day of July*. Although they have not kept in touch during this time, Kevin and Sadie bump into each other and become friends again. They fall in love, but the stones and paint pots of the first book have given way to guns, and the animosity between Catholics and Protestants has escalated. Sadie defies her parents and friends to go out with Kevin, who is beaten by former schoolmates for dating a Protestant. Sadie's former teacher Mr. Blake offers the girl a job as his housekeeper and allows the young couple to meet in his home. When his house is bombed, Mr. Blake is killed for his kindness. At the end of the novel, Kevin and Sadie leave Belfast for Liverpool. Several critics have noted that *Across the Barricades* is the finest novel of the series. *Twentieth-Century Children's Writers* contributor Gillian Klein called it "arguably the best in the series," while Eileen Dunlop and Judson Knight stated in the *St. James Guide to Young Adult Writers* that *Across the Barricades* is "[p]robably the best and most powerful of these novels," adding that the development of the protagonists's love "against a bitter background of family disapproval and civil disintegration is a moving variation on a classic theme of young love under a comfortless star." Writing in *Library Journal,* Carole L. Stanke concluded that the book "will bring alive the current situation in Ireland."

In the third novel of the series, *Into Exile,* Kevin and Sadie are married, living in London, and, in the words of a critic in *Times Literary Supplement,* "trying to make a home for themselves in one room and to keep their marriage alive in poverty and stress." When his father is killed by a bomb in Belfast, Kevin is called back home, where he finds that his mother is still hostile toward his marriage. Sadie, who is feeling insecure in her relationship, is almost led astray by some friends. Finally, the two realize that they must go off on their own if their union is to withstand the pressure. The reviewer for the *Times Literary Supplement* continued, "There is a simplicity and sadness about the way *Into Exile* is written that reflects the limitations and background of all the characters," while Stanke called *Into Exile* "a timely novel that will appeal to teenagers because of its exploration of the problems of young marriage and the current conflict in Northern Ireland."

In the fourth volume of the series, *A Proper Place,* Kevin has returned from Ireland, and he, Sadie, and their new son, Brendan, have moved to a cramped flat in Liverpool. Their marriage is tested when Sadie's bigoted mother comes to visit and when Gerald, Kevin's problematic younger brother, comes to stay. Finally, Kevin finds work as a farmhand on an estate in Cheshire, a situation that brings with it a house to live in and an easing of some of the tension. Lesley Croome wrote in the *Times Literary Supplement* that Lingard's books "reflect the complexities of the inflammable situation in Northern Ireland with a rare accuracy. . . . Joan Lingard has a gift for conveying the authentic sense of the places she is describing, though this would count for little were she not so well attuned to the changing emotional states of her characters." Croome added, "Her latest novel is quieter in tone than the earlier ones but it is still not lacking in dramatic conflict."

Hostages to Fortune is the fifth volume of the "Sadie and Kevin" series. In this work, the couple and Brendan have moved to their cottage on a Cheshire farm; however, when Kevin's employer dies, they are forced to relocate once again. They go to a village in Wales to fill in for a pubkeeper who is ill and decide to settle there. However, the couple faces a number of domestic crises, including the presence of Kevin's runaway sister Clodagh, whom Cecilia Gordon described in the *Times Literary Supplement* as "unforgivably perverse," and Sadie's biased mother. The couple's marriage is further tested when Sadie has a stillborn daughter. However, by the end of the novel Kevin and Sadie have weathered their trials and have begun to communicate more openly. Gordon noted, "Those who help and support Kevin and Sadie are all older people, even elderly. Typically, Joan Lingard underlines differences and then shows how barriers can be crossed. Many children will recognize such bridging of the generation gap and will appreciate the picture of loving mothers who are much less help than outsiders." Writing in the *Bulletin of the Center for Children's Books,* Zena Sutherland stated, "Lingard has created well-defined, sympathetic characters in this series, she writes about them with practiced ease and consistent candor, and she touches on problems that are discussed in few books for young readers." *Junior Bookshelf* contributor M. Hobbs called the events of the novel "laudably absorbing and relevant to today, for those who have followed the McCoys' adventures so far. The style is so naturally Belfast in grammar and idiom that one can hear the accents."

Lingard once told *SATA* that she wrote *The Twelfth Day of July* "basically as an appeal for tolerance, to try to show children that they need not accept their parents' prejudices, because I believe that the only hope for peace must come through changing the attitudes of children first. Indoctrination and prejudice begin so young; this is seen very clearly in the Ulster situation. It is pathetic how young some of the children who have been involved are." She added in *SAAS,* "It seems to me that the only way a situation such as the Ulster one will ever change will be when the young rebel against its continuing and decide to reject the prejudices of their parents and grandparents and great-grandparents. And if I have been successful in writing it in an unbiased way then I believe it is due to my upbringing as a Christian Scientist and also because I have left Belfast and can look back more objectively than if I were caught up in the middle of the trouble itself." Lingard did not intend to write any more about Kevin and Sadie after she finished her first novel about them. However, as she wrote in *SAAS,* "they turned out to be the kind of characters who won't lie down in one's head. I kept wondering what would have happened to them afterwards so I just had to go on and find out."

In addition to her series about Sadie and Kevin, Lingard is the creator of another popular series of young adult novels about Maggie McKinley, an independent, enterprising, and high-spirited adolescent from working-class Glasgow who wants to attend college and be a social anthropologist. Begun as a respite from writing about Ulster and its problems, the series—which includes four novels, *The Clearance, The Resettling, The Pilgrimage,* and *The Reunion*—is lighter and more humorous than the works about Kevin and Sadie; however, Lingard is generally credited with exploring themes such as class distinction, family responsibility, and early marriage with her usual insightfulness. A critic noted in a *Times Literary Supplement* review of the first novel in the series, *The Clearance,* "Joan Lingard has always revealed a sure touch in describing the tensions and crosscurrents of family relationships. Now she also shows a sympathetic understanding of the varied roles a girl is forced to play vis-a-vis her family, her school and her boy friends." In another issue of the same periodical, Gillian Cross called the third volume of the series, *The Pilgrimage,* "a very skillful piece of work. . . . It is extremely entertaining, and its humour and unpretentiousness should not blind one to the author's skill in describing unstereotyped relationships, nor to the depth of her discussion of marriage at an early age."

Assessing the final volume in the series, *The Reunion,* D. A. Young mused in the *Junior Bookshelf,* "I cannot help feeling that a resourceful girl like Maggie will find a way of getting into print again." Writing about the series in the *St. James Guide to Young Adult Writers,* Eileen Dunlop and Judson Knight noted, "Nowhere does Lingard display her talent for seeing the world through young eyes more amusingly than she does in these books." Lingard wrote in *SAAS* that the theme of the quartet of stories about Maggie "is that of being displaced—or cleared—from one's environment against one's will and having to resettle. I am interested in characters caught at a point of social or historical change." Lingard wrote the scripts for the eighteen-part television adaptation of the "Maggie" books that was shown on the Scottish Television network in 1981 and 1982; she also bought a cottage in Inverness, Scotland, that figures prominently in the series to use as a summer home.

In the early 1970s, Lingard married her second husband, Martin Birichaws, a Latvian-born Canadian architect and lecturer. Twenty years later, she used his childhood experiences as the background for two stories, *Tug of War* and *Between Two Worlds,* that are directed at young adults. These books describe how the Peterson family, forced to flee their home in Latvia during the Soviet Invasion of 1944, survive displacement to reunite in Canada, where their struggle continues. Lingard shows the difficulties faced by strangers in a foreign country— such as hostility, fear, distrust, and grueling work— while depicting a close, resilient family. At the end of the second novel, the Petersons are able to buy a plot of land on which to build a house and have begun to make friends in their new homeland. Zena Sutherland of the *Bulletin of the Center for Children's Books* called *Tug of War* "a narrative of fear and courage," while Marcus Crouch of *Junior Bookshelf* dubbed *Between Two Worlds* "a remarkable piece of historical writing."

Lingard is also the author of another well-received book for young people that is set in Eastern Europe, *Night Fires.* Set in the 1980s in an unnamed country, the story portrays two children caught up in a revolution to overthrow the harsh regime that has ruled their country since the 1930s. The youngsters, Laura and Nik, are among the eldest wards of a state-run orphanage. Left on their own, they go into the city and become committed to an underground movement. The children put themselves in danger, but find friends and comrades in their search for freedom. *Books for Keeps* critic David Bennett called *Night Fires* "[o]ne of the most approachable political novels of recent years," while John Murray noted in *Magpies* that the book "conveys something of the fear and distrust of living under a totalitarian regime."

Lingard told *SATA,* "I have recently published three books, all in a short space of time, on different themes, in different settings, and for different ages. *Tom and the Tree House* (for seven-to-nine year olds) is about a boy who is adopted trying to come to terms with his adoptive parents producing a child of their own whom he classes as their 'real' child while he is the 'unreal' one. In *A Secret Place* (for readers nine to twelve), a Spanish father, frustrated because his former wife is blocking his access to his children, snatches them from their school gate in Scotland and takes them to a white village high in the mountains of Spain. And in *Dark Shadows* (for ten-to-fourteen year olds), I returned to Belfast to tell the tale of Jess and Laurie, two cousins of different religions who meet for the first time when they are fifteen years old. Their families had fallen out twenty years previously and the girls decide to try to bring about a reconciliation, which does not prove to be easy. The divisions between the two families are deep, just as they are in Northern Ireland itself." Lingard concluded, "I like variety in my writing, just as I do in my reading. I have published more than thirty books now for young people and thirteen adult novels. But I enjoy writing especially for young people. They are so much more responsive and appreciative than their elders. They don't hesitate to tell you that they thought your book was fantastic. Any author enjoys hearing that!"

Works Cited

Bennett, David, review of *Night Fires, Books for Keeps,* January, 1996, p. 12.

Review of *The Clearance, Times Literary Supplement,* July 5, 1974, p. 721.

Croome, Lesley, "Progression from Childhood," *Times Literary Supplement,* July 11, 1975, p. 766.

Cross, Gillian, "Past Presences," *Times Literary Supplement,* July 16, 1976, p. 885.

Crouch, Marcus, review of *Between Two Worlds, Junior Bookshelf,* February, 1992. p. 56.

Dunlop, Eileen, and Judson Knight, entry in *St. James Guide to Young Adult Writers,* edited by Tom Pendergast and Sara Pendergast, 2nd edition, St. James, 1999, pp. 517-19.

Gordon, Cecilia, review of *Hostages to Fortune, Times Literary Supplement,* December 10, 1976, p. 1548.

Hobbs, M., review of *Hostages to Fortune, Junior Book-shelf,* April, 1977, p. 117.

Review of *Into Exile, Times Literary Supplement,* September 28, 1973, p. 1118.

Klein, Gillian, entry in *Twentieth-Century Children's Writers,* edited by Tracy Chevalier, 3rd edition, St. James, 1989, pp. 591-92.

Lingard, Joan, essay in *Fifth Book of Junior Authors and Illustrators,* edited by Sally Holmes Holtze, Wilson, 1983, pp. 195-96.

Lingard, Joan, essay in *Something about the Author Autobiography Series,* Volume 5, Gale, 1988, pp. 223-36.

Lingard, Joan, interview with Jennie Renton in *Capital Letters,* quoted on *James Thin Home Page,* http://www.jamesthin.co.ud/lingard.htm.

Murray, John, review of *Night Fires, Magpies,* November, 1994, p. 33.

Stanke, Carol L., review of *Across the Barricades, Library Journal,* July, 1973, p. 2202.

Stanke, Carol L., review of *Into Exile, School Library Journal,* February, 1974, p. 71.

Sutherland, Zena, review of *Hostages to Fortune, Bulletin of the Center for Children's Books,* July-August, 1977, pp. 176-77.

Sutherland, Zena, review of *Tug of War, Bulletin of the Center for Children's Books,* September, 1990, pp. 11-12.

Sutherland, Zena, review of *The Twelfth Day of July, Bulletin of the Center for Children's Books,* April, 1973, p. 128.

Review of *The Twelfth Day of July, Times Literary Supplement,* December 11, 1970, p. 1457.

Young, D. A., review of *The Reunion, Junior Bookshelf,* June, 1978, p. 156.

For More Information See

BOOKS

Major Authors and Illustrators for Children and Young Adults, Gale, 1993, pp. 1477-79.

PERIODICALS

Lion & the Unicorn, September, 1997.
School Librarian, summer, 1999, p. 89.
Scottish Book Collector, Volume 5, number 4, 1996, p. 30.
Times Educational Supplement, July 3, 1998, p. 19.

ON-LINE

Additional Literature: Joan Lingard: http://www.englisch.schule.de/cal.addition.html.
Puffin Author I.D. Card: Joan Lingard: http://www.puffin.co.uk/living/aut_30.html.

—*Sketch by Gerard J. Senick*

LOBATO, Jose Bento Monteiro 1882-1948

Personal

Born in 1882, in Sao Paulo, Brazil. *Education:* Sao Paulo Law School, 1904.

Career

Fiction writer and essayist. District attorney, Areias, Paraiba Valley, Brazil; worked variously as a publisher, commercial attache, and petroleum entrepreneur.

Writings

FOR CHILDREN

Narizinho arrebitado (title means "Little Turned-Up Nose"), 1921.
O saci, 1921.
Fabulas, 1922.
O marques Rabico, 1922.
A cacada da onca, 1924.
Novas reinacoes de Narizinho, 1933.
Historia do mundo para criancas, 1933.
Aritmetica de Emilia, 1935.
Geografia de Dona Benta, 1935.
Sitio do pica-pau amarelo (title means "Yellow Woodpecker Farm"), 1939.
Os doze trabalhos de Hercules, 1944.

FOR ADULTS

Cidades mortas (title means "Dead Cities"), 1919.
Ideias de Jeca Tatu, 1919.
Negrinha (title means "Little Black Girl"), 1920.
A onda verde, 1921.
Mundo da lua, 1923.
O macaco que se fez homem, 1923.
Brazilian Short Stories, Haldeman-Julius (Girard, KS), 1925.
Mr. Slang e o Brasil (title means "Mr. Slang and Brazil"), 1929.
Ferro (title means "Iron"), 1931.
America, 1932.
Na antevespera, 1933.
O escandalo do petroleo (title means "The Petroleum Scandal"), 1936.
(With Geofredo Rangel) *A barca de Gleyre* (correspondence; title means "The Gleyre Boat"), 1944.
Obra infantil completa, Editoria Brasiliense (Sao Paulo), 1981.

Also author of *Urupes* and *O presidente negro ou o choque das racas* (novel; title means "The Black President or Race Shock").

Sidelights

Jose Bento Monteiro Lobato, a native of Brazil, was a writer of both fiction and nonfiction. Schooled as a lawyer, Lobato graduated from Sao Paulo Law School in 1904 and then worked as a district attorney in the

Paraiba Valley. Eventually Lobato moved on to manage his family's estate, Buquira, from 1911 to 1917. After the estate was sold, Lobato returned to Sao Paulo and dove into the world of publishing.

Lobato acquired a publishing company and founded two others. One of the publishing houses failed in 1925, and from 1927 to 1931 Lobato worked in New York City as a commercial attache for Brazil. Inspired by the creativity of U.S. businesses, he later established his own petroleum company in Brazil. After a quarrel with the oppressive government of dictator Getulio Vargas over the rights to iron and petroleum, Lobato was sent to prison in 1941, then suffered a period of exile in Buenos Aires.

Lobato was a writer who never lacked an opinion. Possessing naturalist tendencies, he enjoyed writing about rural themes in the pre-modern fashion. Lobato felt that writing should be a direct expression of one's thoughts. Although Lobato did not always follow his own instructions, the literary world is, according to Severino Joao Albuquerque in *Dictionary of Brazilian Literature,* "indebted to him for . . . Lobato's theory of style: essentially, a forceful call for Brazilian writers to shun obscure allusions, outdated constructions, and infatuation with literature and to adopt, instead, a colloquial, genuinely Brazilian vocabulary and syntax, as well as a new, more familiar, visually dynamic imagery."

Lobato was a controversial, outspoken intellectual whose fiction works took a back seat to his nonfiction. According to Isaac Goldberg in *Dictionary of Brazilian Literature,* Lobato was "not a teller of stories but a critic of men." In fact, Lobato did write stories, but the stories usually took a back seat to the messages contained within them. In the 1914 essays "Velha praga" ("Old Plague") and "Urupes" (a kind of mushroom), Brazilian culture comes under fire as Lobato criticizes the farming techniques being used and chastises Brazilians for being apathetic and backwards. The essays sparked interest in Lobato's viewpoints and Lobato responded with fictional stories about Brazilian farmers. In *Urupes* and *Cidades mortas,* two collections of short stories, he uses sarcasm, cynicism, and empathy to tell the stories of indifferent, alienated men.

Negrinha ("Little Black Girl") is Lobato's third collection of short stories. The writing in the book resembles journalistic writing; it was this style that best served Lobato and his insatiable desire to instruct and critique. Lobato uses the books *Mr. Slang e o Brasil* ("Mr. Slang and Brazil") and *America* to make arguments for advancing technology, production awareness, and practicality in society. In the 1930s, Lobato saw a bright economic future for Brazil through iron and oil production, and he argues for such endeavors in *Ferro* ("Iron") and *O escandalo do petroleo* ("The Petroleum Scandal").

Lobato also enjoyed writing stories for children, and he authored numerous such works. His creation of colorful characters in books such as *Narizinho arrebitado* ("Little Turned-up Nose") and *Sitio do pica-pau amarelo* ("Yellow Woodpecker Farm") endeared him to many and seemed to compensate him for the resistance that met his adult work. The Brazilian theater community turned several of Lobato's children's stories into operas for young people, and Lobato is regarded by many as the founder of children's literature in Brazil.

Lobato was never really fully appreciated during his lifetime. Some time after the public arguments with the defenders of Anita Malfatti subsided, Oswald de Andrade, one of Lobato's harshest critics, conceded that Lobato was important to Brazilian literature. Alberto Conte writes in *Monteiro Lobato: O homem e a obra* that Lobato had "a very singular way of seeing things; in a word, he had a *philosophy.*"

Works Cited

Albuquerque, Severino Joao, *Dictionary of Brazilian Literature,* Greenwood Press (New York City), 1988.
Conte, Alberto, *Monteiro Lobato: O homen e a obra,* Editora Brasiliense (Sao Paulo), 1948.
Goldberg, Isaac, *Dictionary of Brazilian Literature,* Greenwood Press (New York City), 1988.

For More Information See

BOOKS

Modern Latin American Literature, Ungar (New York City), 1975.*

M

MACDONALD, James D. 1954-
(Robyn Tallis, Nicholas Adams, Victor Appleton, Martin Delrio, joint pseudonyms)

Personal

Born in 1954, in White Plains, NY; son of a chemical engineer and an artist; married Debra A. Doyle (a writer and teacher); children: four. *Education:* University of Rochester, received degree (medieval studies). *Hobbies and other interests:* Science fiction, cats, computers.

Addresses

Home—Colebrook, NH. *Agent*—Avon Books, 1230 Avenue of the Americas, New York, NY 10019. *E-mail*—doylemacdonald@sff.net.

Career

Journalist and science fiction/fantasy author. *Military service:* United States Navy, served fifteen year tour of duty as both an enlisted man and as an officer.

Awards, Honors

Mythopoetic Fantasy Award for children's literature, 1992, New York Public Library Books for the Teen Age list, 1993, both for *Knight's Wyrd;* Best Young Adult Science Fiction Award, *Science Fiction Chronicle,* 1997, for *Groogleman.*

Writings

NOVELS; "CIRCLE OF MAGIC" SERIES, WITH WIFE, DEBRA A. DOYLE

School of Wizardry, Troll Books (Mahway, NH), 1990.
Tournament and Tower, Troll Books, 1990.
City by the Sea, Troll Books, 1990.
The Prince's Players, Troll Books, 1990.
The Prisoners of Bell Castle, Troll Books, 1990.

The High King's Daughter, Troll Books, 1990.

NOVELS; "MAGEWORLDS" SERIES, WITH DOYLE

The Price of the Stars, Tor (New York City), 1992.
Starpilot's Grave, Tor, 1993.
By Honor Betray'd, Tor, 1994.
The Gathering Flame, Tor, 1995.
The Long Hunt, Tor, 1996.

NOVELS; "BAD BLOOD" SERIES, WITH DOYLE

Bad Blood, Berkley (New York City), 1993.
Hunter's Moon, Berkley, 1994.
Judgement Night, Berkley, 1995.

OTHER NOVELS; WITH DOYLE

Timecrime, Inc. (Robert Silverberg's "Time Tours" no. 3), Harper (New York City), 1991.
Night of the Living Rat (Daniel Pinkwater's "Melvinge of the Megaverse" no. 2), Ace (New York City), 1992.
Knight's Wyrd, Harcourt (New York City), 1992.
Groogleman, Harcourt, 1996.

NOVELS UNDER JOINT PSEUDONYM ROBYN TALLIS; WITH DOYLE

Night of Ghosts and Lightning, ("Planet Builders" series, no. 2), Ivy (New York City), 1989.
Zero-Sum Games ("Planet Builders" series, no. 5), Ivy, 1989.

NOVELS UNDER JOINT PSEUDONYM NICHOLAS ADAMS; WITH DOYLE

Pep Rally ("Horror High" series, no. 7), Harper, 1991.

NOVELS UNDER JOINT PSEUDONYM VICTOR APPLETON; WITH DOYLE

Monster Machine ("Tom Swift" series, no. 5), Pocket Books (New York City), 1991.
Aquatech Warriors ("Tom Swift" series, no. 6), Pocket Books, 1991.

NOVELS UNDER JOINT PSEUDONYM MARTIN DELRIO

Mortal Kombat (movie novelizations: adult and young adult versions), Tor, 1995.

THERE'S NO SHIP IN THE GALAXY LIKE IT, AND IT'S YOURS.
ALL YOU HAVE TO DO IS FIND YOUR MOTHER'S ASSASSIN.

THE PRICE OF THE STARS

BOOK ONE OF MAGEWORLDS
DEBRA DOYLE AND JAMES D. MACDONALD

Spacecraft pilot Beka arranges her own death and takes on a new identity to bring her mother's assassins to justice in James D. Macdonald and Debra Doyle's first Mageworld book. (Cover illustration by Romas.)

Spider-Man Super-Thriller: Midnight Justice, Byron Press Multimedia/Pocket Books (New York City), 1996.
Spider-Man Super-Thriller: Global War, Byron Press Multimedia/Pocket Books, 1996.
Prince Valiant (movie novelization), Avon (New York City), 1997.

OTHER

Contributor, with Doyle, of short stories to anthologies, including "Bad Blood," in *Werewolves,* edited by Jane Yolen and Martin Greenberg, Harper Junior Books, 1988; "Nobody Has to Know," in *Vampires,* edited by Jane Yolen and Martin Greenberg, HarperCollins, 1991; "The Last Real New Yorker in the World," in *Newer York,* edited by Lawrence Watt-Evans, Roc, 1991; "Now and in the Hour of Our Death," in *Alternate Kennedys,* edited by Mike Resnick and Martin Greenberg, Tor, 1992; "Uncle Joshua and the Groogleman," in *Bruce Coville's Book of Monsters,* edited by Bruce Coville, Scholastic, Inc., 1993; "Why They Call It That," in

Swashbuckling Editor Stories, edited by John Betancourt, Wildside Press, 1993; "The Queen's Mirror," in *A Wizard's Dozen,* edited by Michael Stearns, Harcourt, 1995; "Crossover," in *A Starfarer's Dozen,* edited by Michael Stearns, Harcourt, 1995; "Witch Garden," in *Witch Fantastic,* edited by Mike Resnick and Martin Greenberg, DAW, 1995; "Holly and Ivy," in *Camelot,* edited by Jane Yolen, Philomel, 1995; "Please to See the King" in *The Book of Kings,* edited by Richard Gilliam and Martin Greenberg, Roc, 1995; "Stealing God," in *Tales of the Knights Templar,* edited by Katherine Kurtz, Warner, 1995; "Ecdysis," in *Otherwere,* edited by Laura Ann Gilman and Keith R. A. DeCandido, Berkley/Ace, 1996; "Up the Airy Mountain," in *A Nightmare's Dozen,* edited by Michael Stearns, Harcourt, 1996; and "Jenny Nettles," in *Bruce Coville's Book of Spine Tinglers,* edited by Bruce Coville, Scholastic, Inc., 1996.

Contributor of short stories to anthologies, including (with Alan Rodgers) "Rosemary—Scrambled Eggs on a Blue Plate" and "Souvenirs," in *Alternate Kennedys,* edited by Mike Resnick and Martin Greenberg, Tor, 1992; "A True Story," in *Bruce Coville's Book of Ghosts,* edited by Bruce Coville, Scholastic, Inc., 1994.

Sidelights

In close collaboration with his wife, Debra A. Doyle, James D. Macdonald writes science fiction and fantasy for children, young adults, and adults. In an interview with *Amazon.com,* Macdonald related that he writes the first drafts of the stories and novels and that his wife works on the revisions. Macdonald said, "I have final say on the plot and characters, she has final say on the words and descriptions." He commented that the books of J. R. R. Tolkein have had an impact on his writing and said that he also enjoys reading the work of Robert Heinlein and Alexandre Dumas. Together, Macdonald and Doyle have written over twenty novels and innumerable short stories, primarily fantasy and science fiction for young adults.

Doyle and Macdonald's first series, "Circle of Magic" (1990) intended for an elementary and junior high audience, consists of six novels chronicling the story of Randal and his adventures in fulfilling his destiny to become a wizard. *School of Wizardry* introduces twelve-year-old Randal, who is determined to become a wizard after a wayfaring wizard visits his home. Initially delighted to be admitted as an apprentice into the famous Schola Sorceriae (School of Wizardry), he soon realizes that he must conquer many enemies before becoming a master wizard, among them Lord Fess, who plans to destroy the school and gain supreme power through his evil spells.

Tournament and Tower, the second installment in the "Circle of Magic" series, opens with Randal being granted permission to graduate from the School of Wizardry with the provision that he refrain from using his magic until Balpesh, the master wizard, exonerates him for breaking his pledge not to use a weapon. In the meantime, Randal becomes a squire to his cousin

Walter. In a tournament, Walter sustains serious injuries, but Randal, lacking his magical powers, cannot rescue Walter. Balpesh, who can rescue him, is himself in great peril. It is up to Randal to free the wizard, who can then save Walter and restore to Randal his magical powers.

In *City by the Sea,* Randal, now a fifteen-year-old journeyman wizard, embarks on one of his most hazardous undertakings when he accepts a statue from a dying stranger and promises to fulfill the man's deathbed wish that the statue be brought to Dagon, a soldier of fortune. Randal soon learns that the statue has magical powers of its own, and that Dagon is not the only person seeking the statue.

The series continues with *The Prince's Players,* which places Randal and his friend Lys on their way to visit Prince Vespian's palace. Here, Randal learns tricks of illusion from the court's master wizard, Petrucio. He thinks his new talent is to be used in royal stage productions; instead, he discovers that Petrucio has more diabolical plans for his new skills. A dangerous adver-sary seeks to conquer Prince Vespian's kingdom, drawing Randal and Lys into political intrigue.

In *The Prisoners of Bell Castle,* Randal confronts Lord Fess, his old enemy, when he and his friends agree to guard a boatload of gold needed as wages for Baron Ector's armies, who have put Fess's ancestral home, Bell Castle, under siege. When the gold disappears, Randal is implicated in the theft and must triumph over Lord Fess in order to prove his innocence and recover the gold. The final novel in the *Circle of Magic* series, *The High King's Daughter,* follows Randal, Walter, and Lys as they journey into Elfland to rescue Diamante, the High King's daughter, and restore her to her rightful throne. In order to do so, they must enter a magical realm and confront Lord Hugo de la Corre, who has proclaimed himself High King in Diamante's absence.

Doyle and Macdonald's fantasy novel, *Knight's Wyrd,* won the Mythopoetic Fantasy Award for Children's Literature in 1992 and was placed on the acclaimed New York Public Library Books for the Teen Age list in 1993. *Knight's Wyrd* combines a realistic story of knighthood with fantasy elements such as magic, drag-ons, and wizards. Just as young Will Odosson is about to be knighted, the castle wizard predicts his wyrd (fate): Will is not destined to inherit his father's title and lands and will soon meet death. Although the wizard's prophecy comes to pass, it does not occur in the manner Will expects. A young man of strong character, Will becomes a knight despite his wyrd and leaves home seeking adventure. In the course of the novel, Will rescues Isobel, his betrothed, is double-crossed by his Duke, and becomes entangled in high magic. Indeed, he does meet death, but it is in the form of Lord Death, who observes Randal slay the ogre who cannot be killed. A *Kirkus Reviews* critic praised *Knight's Wyrd*'s "strong sense of time, place, and code of honor." A *Horn Book* reviewer called it "a lively story," and a *School Library Journal* critic recommended it as "suspenseful" with a lively tempo.

In their next series, the spine-tingling "Bad Blood" series, Macdonald and Doyle explore the kind of horror stories told around campfires after dark. *Bad Blood,* which takes its name from the series, begins with hair-raising tales shared around a campfire in the woods. Valerie Sherwood and her friends never expected any of the stories to come true, since their friend Jay's strange tale of moonlight and werewolves is just make believe. That night, however, they hear the beast prowling around the camp and they remember Jay's words: "By morning, you'll all be dead."

In *Hunter's Moon,* the sequel to *Bad Blood,* Valerie, now a werewolf, uses her power to protect her commu-nity from a group of vampires while trying to live a "normal" suburban life. But soon she suspects that werewolves are powerless against vampires and she must find a new way to save her loved ones. In *Judgement Night,* the final installment, Valerie is haunted by her own nightmares and by the Wendigo, an

Thirteen-year-old Dan volunteers to try to rescue the village healer from the creepy Groogleman in Macdonald and Doyle's fast-paced, suspenseful fantasy. (Cover illustration by Cliff Nielsen.)

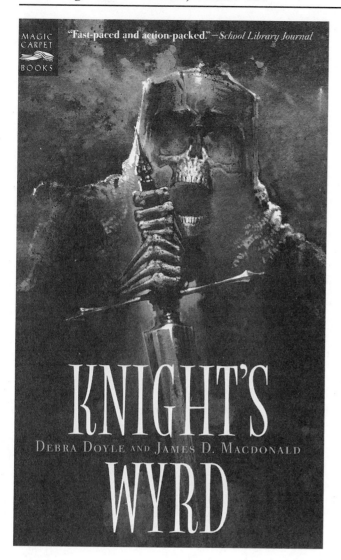

Will meets horrible creatures and an evil unlike anything he has ever known in Macdonald and Doyle's award-winning fantasy. (Cover illustration by Michael Hussar.)

ancient force that calls to her from the mountains and thrives on her fear.

The popular "Mageworlds" series, begun in 1992, focuses on the centuries-long conflict between the human Republic and the mysterious Mageworlds. In *The Price of the Stars,* the first in the series, Beka Rosselin-Metadi is tired of constantly hearing about her parents' heroic roles in the human galaxy's history. When her mother is murdered on the Senate floor, however, she finds new pride in her heritage and vows to bring the assassin to justice. Her father offers her *Warhammer,* his cherished ship, for her use in capturing the murderer. As the plot develops, Beka plans her own demise so that she can, with a different identity, conquer the dangerous enemies of the galaxy.

In *Starpilot's Grave,* Beka continues the search for the man who arranged her mother's assassination, but soon it is revealed that the Magelords have breached the

Republic's stronghold. Beka, in searching for her mother's killer, infiltrates the Magezone and learns that the Republic is far more vulnerable than she ever imagined. The Magelords have triumphed over the Republic in the third book of the series, *By Honor Betray'd.* Confronted with betrayal and surrounded by enemies, Beka strives to reclaim what she can from the wreckage of the Republic.

The Gathering Flame, fourth in the "Mageworlds" series, describes Beka's parents' contributions to the Republic's struggle against the Magelords. The novel chronicles attempts by the Magelords to ravage the galaxy, planet by planet. However, the Magelords must take on several individuals to succeed in their plans: Perada Rosselin, Domina of Entibor, Jos Metadi, a notorious privateer who prefers to battle Mage ships one-on-one, and Errec Ransome, who is acquainted with the customs of the Magelords but has confidences he will not reveal. When the Magelords attack Entibor, the three must work together.

In *The Long Hunt,* set in the era following the Second Magewar, Entibor again faces attack by the Magelords. Meanwhile, on the planet Khesat, a crisis unfolds and all depends on Jens Metadi-Jessan D'Rosselin, unwilling heir to the throne. Warring factions and criminal guilds know that control of the heir means control of Khesat and the galaxy. But young Jens, eager for adventure, sets off with his cousin Faral to see the galaxy. However, in their travels they encounter more action than anticipated. Writing in *Locus,* Carolyn Cushman called the "Mageworlds" series "a space opera with unusual depth, and some wonderful characters I'm eager to see in further adventures."

A critic for *Science Fiction Chronicle* declared *Groogleman* "the best young adult science fiction" of 1996. In this fantasy novel, the plot centers around thirteen-year-old Dan Henchard, a student healer who must save his teacher, Leezie, a natural healer, from her abductor. Dan, believing the kidnapper is the Groogleman, travels to the Dead Lands in search of Leezie, knowing that failure means certain death for him. Along the way he receives help from a hunter named Joshua and in the process learns much more about himself. Selections from "historical documents" introduce each chapter and provide clues to the secret purpose of the Groogleman. A reviewer for *Realms of Fantasy* magazine wrote that *Groogleman* is "filled with adventure and action—a must read," and a *Science Fiction Chronicle* writer praised it as "an old fashioned post collapse adventure."

In an interview with *Amazon.com,* Macdonald explained that he attempts to write every day but said that "can be an hour or it can be ten hours, depending on how things are going." Reflecting that he served fifteen years in the U.S. Navy as both an enlisted man and an officer before becoming a full-time writer, he advised would-be writers to "go out and have a life to write about, then write and keep writing."

Works Cited

Review of *Groogleman, Realms of Fantasy*, April, 1997.

Review of *Groogleman, Science Fiction Chronicle*, April-May, 1997.

Review of *Knight's Wyrd, Horn Book*, January-February, 1993, pp. 89-90.

Review of *Knight's Wyrd, Kirkus Reviews*, October 1, 1992.

Review of *Knight's Wyrd, School Library Journal*, December, 1996, pp. 120-121.

Macdonald, James D., interview on *Amazon.com* website, http://www.amazon.com.

Macdonald, James D., and Debra Doyle, *Bad Blood*, Berkley (New York City), 1993.

PERIODICALS

Bulletin of the Center for Children's Books, December, 1996, p. 132.

Horn Book, March-April, 1996, p. 202.

Kirkus Reviews, October 1, 1992.

Locus, August, 1995.

ON-LINE

Author's website, *Doyle and Macdonald—About our Books*, at http://www.sff.net/people/doylemacdonald (December 11, 1998).*

*   *   *

MARCHESI, Stephen 1951-
(Steve Marchesi)

Personal

Born December 30, 1951, in Astoria, NY; son of Ennio (a factory worker) and Rose (an office clerk; maiden name, Lucchi) Marchesi; married Christine Kettner (a book designer), April 30, 1988; children: Alexander. *Education:* Received B.F.A. from Pratt Institute. *Politics:* Independent. *Religion:* Roman Catholic.

Addresses

Agent—Publishers Graphics, 251 Greenwood Ave., Bethel, CT 06801.

Career

Children's book illustrator. *Member:* Society of Children's Book Writers and Illustrators.

Illustrator

Phyllis R. Fenner, compiler, *The Endless Dark: Stories of Underground Adventure*, Morrow (New York, NY), 1977.

Alfred Hitchcock's Witches Brew, Random House (New York, NY), 1977.

Jean Thompson, *Brother of the Wolves*, Morrow (New York, NY), 1978.

Jon Jameson, *Monsters of the Mountains*, Watts (New York, NY), 1980.

Patricia Giff Reilly, *Suspect*, Dutton (New York, NY), 1982.

Milton Meltzer, *Betty Friedan: A Voice for Women's Rights*, Viking Kestrel (New York, NY), 1985.

Thompson, *Ghost Horse of the Palisades*, Morrow (New York, NY), 1986.

Milton Meltzer, *Winnie Mandela: The Soul of South Africa*, Viking Kestrel (New York, NY), 1986.

Meltzer, *Mary McLeod Bethune: Voice of Black Hope*, Viking Children's Books (New York, NY), 1987.

Clint Hatchett, *The Glow-in-the-Dark Night Sky Book*, Random House Books for Young Readers (New York, NY), 1988.

Gloria Whelan, *Silver*, Random House Books for Young Readers (New York, NY), 1988.

Patricia Beatty, *Sarah and Me and the Lady from the Sea*, Morrow (New York, NY), 1989.

Barbara Cary, *Meet Abraham Lincoln*, Random House Books for Young Readers (New York, NY), 1989.

Margaret Davidson, *The Story of Alexander Graham Bell, Inventor of the Telephone*, Bantam Doubleday Dell Books for Young Readers, 1989.

Joan Heilbroner, *Meet George Washington*, Random House Books for Young Readers (New York, NY), 1989.

Joyce Milton, *Greg Louganis*, Random House (New York, NY), 1989.

Ken Follett, *The Mystery Hideout*, Morrow (New York, NY), 1990.

Annabel Johnson and Edgar Johnson, *Gamebuster*, Dutton Children's Books (New York, NY), 1990.

Howard Tomb, *Living Monsters: The World's Most Dangerous Animals*, Simon & Schuster Children's Books (New York, NY), 1990.

Daniel Cohen, *Railway Ghosts and Highway Horrors*, Dutton Children's Books (New York, NY), 1991.

Liz Damrell, *With the Wind*, Orchard Books (New York, NY), 1991.

O'Connor, Jim, *The Story of Roberto Clemente, All-Star Hero*, Dell (New York, NY), 1991.

Lee B. Hopkins, *Mama*, Simon & Schuster Children's Books (New York, NY), 1992.

Margaret B. Stevens, adapter, *Don Quixote & Sancho Panza*, Simon & Schuster Children's Books (New York, NY), 1992.

Katharine Ross, *The Glow-in-the-Dark Zodiac Storybook*, Random House Books for Young Readers (New York, NY), 1993.

Joan Davenport Carris, *Stolen Bones*, Little, Brown (Boston, MA), 1993.

Hopkins, *Mama & Her Boys*, Simon & Schuster Children's Books (New York, NY), 1993.

Beverly Gherman, *The Mysterious Rays of Dr. Roentgen*, Simon & Schuster Children's Books (New York, NY), 1994.

Dorothy Hoobler, *South American Portraits*, Raintree Steck-Vaughn (Austin, TX), 1994.

(With Jan Skrobisz) Clement C. Moore, *The Night Before Christmas: Told in Signed English*, Kendall Green Publications (Washington, DC), 1994.

Etta Wilson, *The Miracles of Jesus*, Publications International (Lincolnwood, IL), 1994.

Michael Card, *Close Your Eyes So You Can See*, Harvest House Publishers (Eugene, OR), 1996.

Little Whale makes the hazardous journey from the Caribbean to the waters of Maine for the first time. (From Humpback Goes North, *written by Darice Bailer and illustrated by Marchesi.)*

Baron Johnson, *History Takes a Wild Ride,* Raintree Steck-Vaughn (Austin, TX), 1996.

Patricia Leitch, *Pony Club Rider,* HarperCollins Children's Books (New York, NY), 1996.

Leitch, *Cross-Country Gallop,* HarperCollins Children's Books (New York, NY), 1996.

Leitch, *The Perfect Horse,* HarperCollins Children's Books (New York, NY), 1996.

Florence M. White, *The Story of Junipero Serra, Brave Adventurer,* Gareth Stevens (Milwaukee, WI), 1996.

Mary O. Osborne, *The Story of Christopher Columbus, Admiral of the Open Sea,* Gareth Stevens (Milwaukee, WI), 1997.

Dana Del Prado, *Terror Below! True Shark Stories,* Putnam (New York, NY), 1997.

Leitch, *Mystery Horse,* HarperCollins Children's Books (New York, NY), 1997.

Darice Bailer, *Humpback Goes North,* Soundprints (Norwalk, CT), 1998.

Patricia Demuth, *Mars: The Red Planet,* Putnam (New York, NY), 1998.

Linda Lingemann, *Hammerhead Shark: Nomad of the Sea,* Soundprints (Norwalk, CT), 1999.

Lingemann, *Survival in the Sea,* Soundprints (Norwalk, CT), 1999.

Work in Progress

Snakebite, a picture book to be published in 2000, and illustrations for *Box Turtle at Silver Pond Lake* by Susan Korman, also to be published in 2000; working on another book on western lore titled *Shootin' Stars.*

Sidelights

Stephen Marchesi has illustrated dozens of books for children since receiving a fine arts degree from New York City's Pratt Institute. Many of his early titles were biographies, such as Milton Meltzer's 1986 examination of *Winnie Mandela: The Soul of South Africa.* Written during the era of apartheid, when Mandela's husband Nelson was imprisoned for his part in fighting the human-rights abuses of South Africa's white government, the biography presents her life and explains the politics of the time; Marchesi created black and white drawings that depict Mandela and her life. A *Publishers Weekly* reviewer termed them "appealing, soft, even quiet drawings [that] call out in hopeful counterpoint."

Another biography illustrated by Marchesi is Florence M. White's *Story of Junipero Serra, Brave Adventurer,*

Stephen Marchesi illustrated the story of the discovery of X rays in Beverly Gherman's **The Mysterious Rays of Dr. Roentgen.**

aimed at readers in grades three through six. His illustrations show the Roman Catholic priest and his life in what would later become California, where he established several missions in the 1700s. Marchesi also created images for Margaret Hodges's adaptation of the famed work of Spanish literature, *Don Quixote and Sancho Panza.* This retelling introduces late elementary-grade readers to the adventures of the noble and his inimitable servant, and a *Publishers Weekly* reviewer praised "Marchesi's vigorous illustrations—particularly his lively, expressive figures."

Beverly Gherman's 1994 book *The Mysterious Rays of Dr. Roentgen* presented a unique arena for Marchesi's skills as an illustrator, for its aim was to explain how x-ray technology was invented in the 1890s by the German scientist Wilhelm Roentgen. Here he used oil drawings that *School Library Journal*'s Christine A. Moesch described as "textured, informative," and "add to the volume's appeal."

Marchesi has also won accolades for his illustrations in more fictional works for young readers. These include Jean Thompson's 1978 book *Brother of the Wolves* and

Ghost Horse of the Palisades, published eight years later. In this latter work, Molly is an eleven-year-old who lives on a ranch in a world of her own daydreams. The mysterious "ghost horse" steals one of her family's mares, but her father manages to take the culprit, which is actually one of the wild horses that Molly loves. Marchesi also sketched another young heroine's personal difficulties in Patricia Beatty's 1989 novel *Sarah and Me and the Lady from the Sea,* set a hundred years in the past. Its title character spends the summer in rural Oregon, worrying about her family's possible bankruptcy.

In creating the images for a 1990 novel, *The Mystery Hideout* by Ken Follett, Marchesi needed to imagine what an abandoned movie studio in England might look like in this juvenile sleuth tale by an acclaimed author of several adult books. Two London boys, Mick and Izzie, like to roam about the building and are apprehensive about talk of its demolition. They find a real-life gang of bank robbers hiding out, and in the end manage to save the studio. Marchesi's drawings, noted a *Publishers Weekly* reviewer, "capably highlight the most exciting moments of the boys' adventures."

Marchesi's illustrations for Joan Davenport Carris's 1993 novel, *Stolen Bones,* helped chronicle the summer of Alec, who is spending his eleventh summer on an archeological dig with his grandfather. Alec's grandfather is a famed scientist, and seems to take little interest in Alec and his eagerness to learn. Marchesi has also illustrated several nonfiction titles about underwater creatures, such as Darice Bailer's *Humpback Goes North* and *Terror Below! True Shark Stories* by Dana Del Prado.

Works Cited

Review of *Don Quixote and Sancho Panza, Publishers Weekly,* September 28, 1992, p. 81.
Moesch, Christine A., review of *The Mysterious Rays of Dr. Roentgen, School Library Journal,* September, 1994, p. 228.
Review of *The Mystery Hideout, Publishers Weekly,* April 13, 1990, p. 66.
Review of *Winnie Mandela, Publishers Weekly,* October 31, 1986, p. 74.

For More Information See

PERIODICALS

Booklist, May 1, 1993, p. 1588; December 4, 1994, p. 671.
Horn Book, March/April, 1993, p. 227.
School Library Journal, September, 1986, p. 140; December, 1986, p. 106; March, 1988, pp. 211-212; October, 1988, p. 153; November, 1989, p. 102; May, 1990, p. 106; April, 1993, p. 117; October, 1997, p. 117.*

*   *   *

MARCHESI, Steve
See MARCHESI, Stephen

MARINO, Jan 1936-

Personal

Born in Boston, MA; daughter of Ernest D. and Helen (Brown) Rejo; married Leonard Marino (an artist and illustrator); children: Leonard E., Christopher J., Betsy E. *Education:* Attended Katherine Gibbs School, 1950s; attended Nassau Community College, Hofstra University, New School for Social Research.

Addresses

Home—P.O. Box 201771, Denver, CO 80220.

Career

Client coordinator at an investment counseling firm, 1972-85; author and lecturer, 1985—. Instructor in writing, Long Island University, C. W. Post College, and Southampton College. Participant in writing workshops at Bread Loaf Writer's Conference, Bennington College, and Long Island University. Workshop leader for Society of Children's Book Writers and Illustrators, Writer's Voice at Silver Bay, Hofstra Writer's Conference, Barbara Bush Literacy Council, among many others. *Member:* Society of Children's Book Writers and Illustrators, Author's Guild, Poets & Writers, Rocky Mountain Women's Institute.

Awards, Honors

"Book for the Teen Age," New York Public Library, Editor's Choice, *Booklist,* Best Book, *School Library Journal,* and Alabama Reading Incentive Award, all 1992, all for *The Day That Elvis Came to Town;* "Book for the Teen Age," New York Public Library, 1993, for *Like Some Kind of Hero.*

Writings

Eighty-Eight Steps to September, Little, Brown (Boston, MA), 1989.
The Day That Elvis Came to Town, Little, Brown (Boston, MA), 1991.
Like Some Kind of Hero, Little, Brown (Boston, MA), 1992.
For the Love of Pete, Little, Brown (Boston, MA), 1993.
The Mona Lisa of Salem Street, Little, Brown (Boston, MA), 1995.
Searching for Atticus, Simon & Schuster Books for Young Readers (New York), 1997.
Write Me a Happy Ending, Simon & Schuster Books for Young Readers (New York), 2001.

Contributor to the *New York Times* and *Boston Globe;* Marino's young-adult novels have been translated and published in England, France and Italy.

Work in Progress

The Rainbow Connection, a young-adult novel to be published by Simon & Schuster; *Driving,* an adult novel.

Sidelights

Young-adult novelist Jan Marino has won accolades for her sensitive portrayals of adolescents experiencing rather tough, often family-centered crises. Peopled with adults who in some cases could be described as eccentric, Marino's novels usually end on a positive note and affirm a teen's ability to solve dilemmas and grow from them. All of Marino's novels, including *Eighty-Eight Steps to September* and *Searching for Atticus,* have garnered positive reviews and a devoted readership. Marino is a Colorado resident who also leads workshops that encourage teens to develop crisis-management skills through creative writing.

Marino was born in 1936 in Boston. As she told *SATA:* "In the house were I grew up there was a leather-bound set of the Harvard Classics. At the age of eight or so, I decided to read all fifty volumes—always known to have one foot in fantasyland. The first five titles rather intimidated me and so I went on to number six, *Poems and Songs* by Robert Burns. Since I loved to sing and imagined myself a poet, this volume appeared to be the perfect beginning. But when I asked my mother over and over to explain what the poet meant by, 'Ha! Whaur ye

Jan Marino

gaun, ye crowlin ferlie?' and 'Sal-alkali o'midge-tail clippings' my mother gently suggested I move on.

"I did. To Volume 29, Charles Darwin's *Voyage of the Beagle*. But when I learned on page one that the *Beagle* wasn't the four-legged variety, but a 'ten-gun brig in her Majesty's Navy,' and page two described 'singular encrustations, atmospheric dust with infusoria, and the causes of a discoloured sea,' my interest vanished.

"Discouraged, but not defeated, I followed my mother's not-so-gentle suggestion to move on to Volume 17: *Aesop, the Brothers Grimm, and Hans Christian Andersen's Folklore and Fable*. I loved it from the start, even though it caused me considerable concern. I worried about Hansel and Grethel, Little Red Cap and all the rest. How could a father lead his children into the forest and leave them? How could a mother let a little girl go off alone to visit her ailing grandmother? And what about Snow White? What was she thinking of when she neglected to invite the dwarves to her wedding? I was bitterly disappointed, so I wrote my own endings. Hansel and Grethel's father sent the stepmother off into the forest. Little Red Cap took a taxi to Grandma's and she and Grandma ate sweet cakes and had a happy visit. And, at her wedding Snow White danced the night away with the dwarves. I was good at making up endings that pleased me. I could do that for any story. Except one.

"When I was nine, my brother Robbie died. It was a terrible time. I remember the sadness and silence that filled the house. Nobody spoke of him. Determined never to forget him, I wrote stories and poems about him, but it wasn't until *Eighty-Eight Steps to September* that I truly came to accept the loss of him."

It was nearly forty years later that Marino explored this painful time in her life in novel form. After graduating from the Katherine Gibbs School in Boston, she married an artist, with whom she had three children. The family lived on Long Island, and she worked for a number of years as a client coordinator at an investment counseling firm. But when her youngest child entered junior high, Marino began taking college courses, where she was encouraged by teachers to develop her writing talents further. Marino attended both Long Island's Hofstra University as well as the New School for Social Research in New York City, and won scholarship grants to the Bread Loaf Writer's Conference at Bennington College and other workshops. She eventually quit her job in 1985, wrote for Long Island newspapers, and began work on *Eighty-Eight Steps*, which was published four years later.

The novel is set in 1948 and at first, depicts the contentious sibling rivalry between eleven-year-old Amy and her brother Robbie. They fight constantly, and Amy, who recounts these memories in the novel, reveals herself as stubborn. When Robbie goes into the hospital, her obstinacy initially helps her deny the situation, believing that her brother is eventually going to come home. But one morning her father tells her that her brother has died. The family's grief-stricken days, and

Amy's emergence as a less obdurate young person, carry the work to its conclusion. "Few authors, fledgling or established, can create a consistently believable first-person child narrator; with Amy Marino accomplishes this feat poignantly," declared an essay on the author in *Children's Books and Their Creators*.

"So many scenes in *Eighty-Eight Steps* are just the way they happened back then," Marino told *SATA*, "especially the scene where Amy's father tells her that Robbie is dead. 'He's gone, Amy,' he says. 'Robbie's gone. Goddamnit. He didn't make it.' My father never swore, and I never saw him cry, but he did both that morning.

"And when Amy's teacher, Miss Farrell, calls her into the cloakroom to ask about Robbie, Amy is determined not to cry, just as I was. Instead she concentrates on Miss Farrell's nose. 'I looked up and kept my eyes on her nostrils, trying to count the little hairs I saw. I bit my lip and said nothing. I prayed I wouldn't cry, because all the kids were in the classroom waiting for the three o'clock bell to ring.'"

Marino's family history also helped her create the characters and setting for her next young-adult story, *The Day That Elvis Came to Town*. This 1991 novel follows some hardships experienced by Wanda, whose family runs a boarding house. Her father drinks, which brings periodic crises to the household, but when a bi-racial jazz singer named Mercedes Washington becomes a boarder, Wanda is enchanted by the glamorous life Mercedes apparently leads. Soon she comes to realize that Mercedes' status in the South in 1963 is a difficult and even dangerous one. "Not a writer of mere problem novels, Marino offers Wanda no quick fixes or easy outs," observed *Children's Books and Their Creators* about this work.

As Marino told *SATA:* "While not all of my books are autobiographical, each one of them has a little bit of my past in them. *The Day That Elvis Came to Town* is set in a boarding house in Georgia. I never lived in the South, nor did I ever live in a boarding house, but my aunt owned a boarding house in Cambridge, Massachusetts. Since Harvard was close by, my aunt had a wonderful assortment of boarders. One was a professor at Harvard who prefaced every conversation with a quote. He also found his way into *Elvis,* as did my aunt. The setting for *Like Some Kind of Hero* is really Oyster Bay, the town where my children grew up. Ted, the 'hero,' is a composite of my two sons."

Like Some Kind of Hero was Marino's third novel published by Boston's Little, Brown, and appeared in 1992. Its protagonist, Ted, is a talented classical guitarist, but craves acceptance for more "normal" teen traits. He decides to become a lifeguard, and finds he can indeed excel in this as well, but in the end conflicts force him to choose between artistic talent and social acceptance. Marino's next novel, *For the Love of Pete,* was published in 1993. Set in Georgia in the 1970s, it recounts the difficulties experienced by Phoebe, whose mother died in childbirth, and whose father was never told that the infant survived. Phoebe lives with her well-to-do grandmother, whose household staff includes the English butler, Bishopp, an African-American cook and his brother, and the eccentric chauffeur.

When Phoebe's grandmother becomes ill, she must enter a nursing home, and the family fortune dwindles. Fearing for her future, her grandmother decides that she must be sent to her next of kin—the father who did not know she even existed. The staff is enlisted with the task of taking Phoebe from Georgia to Maine in a vintage automobile. Bertie, the chauffeur, refuses to drive on the interstate highways, so they must take the back roads; along the way they meet interesting characters, but it is Phoebe's inner turmoil that forms the basis of the plot in *For the Love of Pete.* The servants are really the only family she has ever known, and she is devastated about having to leave them; moreover, she is apprehensive about her father, and wonders whether or not he will love her as they do. "The cast is vividly developed," opined Betsy Hearne in *Bulletin of the Center for Children's Books,* and "Phoebe's narration is consistent and believable." The novel won similar praise from other quarters as well. "There is humor when the story's strong personalities bicker and Phoebe's anguish about leaving all that is familiar is realistically conveyed," wrote Jacqueline Rose for *Voice of Youth Advocates.*

"The butler in *For the Love of Pete,* Bishopp, was a butler I once knew and loved," Marino told *SATA.* "And Pa in *The Mona Lisa of Salem Street* is the grandfather I always wanted but never had." Published in 1995, this fifth novel from Marino also chronicles an adolescent who is without a conventional family structure. Twelve-year-old Nettie DeAngelus and her shy, quiet little brother, John Peter, are orphans who have been shunted about to the homes of various family members. As a last resort, they are handed over to their grandfather in Boston.

Nettie is initially unhappy with this situation, and considers the grandfather "Pa," a retired undertaker, decidedly eccentric. He lives above his former funeral home and talks to his deceased wife, and Nettie is determined not to form a bond with him—partially because she has been forced to live with so many different relatives. But to her surprise, John Peter likes Pa from the start, and his stutter even abates. As they settle into their new life in this Italian-American neighborhood of Boston known as North End, Nettie and John Peter make friends with the children across the street, whose mother is the "Mona Lisa" of the title. Nettie envies the children for their "normal" life, though in reality their mother suffers from a phobia that makes it impossible for her to leave the house; instead she sits by the window and watches the action on the street, as if she is framed in a painting.

Nettie also envies her older aunt, who still has delusions of a career on the stage and promises Nettie extravagances that never materialize. *The Mona Lisa of Salem Street*'s crisis occurs when the grandfather decides to take a job in order to support them better. This panics

Fifteen-year-old Tessa accompanies her father, a Vietnam War veteran, on a search for happiness and love, but is distracted by a dangerous infatuation in Marino's timeless story. (Cover illustration by Jenny Tylden-Wright.)

Nettie; she is fearful that they will again be forced to move on to other relatives, and resolves to help in any way so that they might stay. She fixes dinner one afternoon, but sets the kitchen afire; traumatized, she runs away, but Pa finds her, offers forgiveness, and assures her that she and her brother will never have to leave again. "The story invokes great sympathy for Nettie and her brother and for the grandfather, too, who was lost and alone until his grandchildren arrive and gave him reason to live again," remarked Merlyn Miller in *Voice of Youth Advocates.* Miller also termed it a novel "filled with sadness, yet the reader is rewarded with a happy ending." Nettie's journey from a guarded, somewhat unfriendly adolescent "to someone who is able to come to terms with her parents' death and deal realistically with her own life makes a natural and affecting narrative," asserted Nancy Vasilakis in *Horn Book.*

Marino's first book for Simon & Schuster—where her longtime editor had been hired and then brought her along as an author—was the 1997 novel *Searching for*

Atticus. The author described this work to *SATA* as "the story of sixteen-year-old Tess's yearning to have a father like Atticus Finch from Harper Lee's *To Kill a Mockingbird,* my favorite book and fictional character." Instead, Tessa's father is a Milwaukee surgeon whose life changes irrevocably when he volunteers for a tour of duty as a field surgeon in the Vietnam War. He comes back to Wisconsin a far different man, traumatized by his experiences, and unable to practice medicine at all.

Tessa accompanies her father on a road trip down South so that he might look into a job opening, but he suffers a nervous breakdown and they instead spend the summer with an aunt in Taloosa. There, Tessa makes a new friend, Selina, and they begin working together at a day camp on the grounds of a Roman Catholic convent. Tessa also develops a crush on an older boy, Caleb, a handsome senior with a promising future. Caleb tries to seduce Tessa, who discovers that he has also had a relationship with a new entrant to the women's religious community. When the postulant became pregnant, he had arranged for an abortion. Caleb believes that Tessa will blackmail him with this secret and keep him from entering West Point in the fall. When Caleb pushes her from a ladder, her father is there to save her.

"Tessa is fully believable in her emotional confusion," remarked Janice M. Del Negro in *Bulletin of the Center for Children's Books,* who termed *Searching for Atticus* "a solid work of fiction with some admirably drawn characters who grow and change in realistic and satisfying ways." An assessment from Chris Crowe in *Voice of Youth Advocates* echoed that of many other reviewers of Marino's young-adult novels: "Marino has well-developed main characters and makes good use of dialogue and action to advance the plot and provide needed exposition," Crowe wrote.

Marino describes her next work, *Write Me a Happy Ending,* as "the story of sixteen-year-old Jake Haddam's acceptance of his gay father," she told *SATA* about this title scheduled for publication in 2001. The author further noted that the work "is set in the Florida Keys, a place I know well." Marino continues to draw upon her past to create her characters, though there is one family member who "has not found her way into my work—as yet," the author told *SATA* about her grandmother. "She found me terribly annoying as a child, always telling me how dramatic I was. How I daydreamed. How I never missed a trick. How I eavesdropped on adult conversations. How she hoped I would one day outgrow what she called 'character defects.' As yet, I haven't and hope I never will.

"I love to write. To read. I've gone through much of my father's set of the Harvard Classics, but none pleases me as much as Volume 17. I love to imagine. To create characters. Yes, there are days of frustration. Days when I stare at the lifeless computer screen. Days when my characters refuse to talk to me. But give up? Never. I cajole. I plead and beg until I hear their voices. And when my computer screen finally comes alive, I am beyond happy."

Works Cited

Essay in *Children's Books and Their Creators,* edited by Anita Silvey, Houghton Mifflin, 1995, p. 234.

Crowe, Chris, review of *Searching for Atticus, Voice of Youth Advocates,* December, 1997, p. 318.

Del Negro, Janice M., review of *Searching for Atticus, Bulletin of the Center for Children's Books,* December, 1997, p. 134.

Hearne, Betsy, review of *For the Love of Pete, Bulletin of the Center for Children's Books,* July-August, 1993, p. 362.

Miller, Merlyn, review of *The Mona Lisa of Salem Street, Voice of Youth Advocates,* August, 1995, pp. 161-162.

Rose, Jacqueline, review of *For the Love of Pete, Voice of Youth Advocates,* June, 1993, p. 91.

Vasilakis, Nancy, review of *The Mona Lisa of Salem Street, Horn Book,* July-August, 1995, p. 459.

For More Information See

PERIODICALS

Booklist, March 1, 1995, pp. 1242-1243.
Kirkus Reviews, May 15, 1993, p. 665.
Publishers Weekly, July 28, 1997, p. 75.*

*   *   *

MARK, Jan(et Marjorie) 1943-

Personal

Born June 22, 1943, in Welwyn, Hertfordshire, England; daughter of Colin and Marjorie Brisland; married Neil Mark (a computer operator), March 1, 1969 (divorced, 1989); children: Isobel, Alexander. *Education:* Canterbury College of Art, N.D.D., 1965. *Politics:* Labour. *Religion:* None.

Addresses

Home—98 Howard St., Oxford OX4 3BG, England. *Agent*—David Higham, 5/8 Lower John Street, Golden Square, London W1R 4HA, England.

Career

Southfields School, Gravesend, Kent, England, teacher of art and English, 1965-71; full-time writer, 1975—. Oxford Polytechnic, Arts Council Writer Fellow, 1982-84. University of Reading, Berkshire, England, lecturer in creative writing, 1999-2000.

Awards, Honors

Penguin/*Guardian* Award, 1975, Library Association Carnegie Medal, 1976, American Library Association Notable Book, all for *Thunder and Lightnings; The Ennead* was named a Notable Children's Trade Book in the field of social studies by the National Council for Social Studies and the Children's Book Council, 1978; runner-up for Library Association Carnegie Medal, 1981, for *Nothing to Be Afraid Of;* co-winner of Young

Jan Mark

Observer/Rank Teenage Fiction Prize, 1982, for *Aquarius;* Library Association Carnegie Medal, 1983, for *Handles;* Angel Literary Award for fiction, 1983, for *Feet,* and 1987, for *Zeno Was Here;* British nominee for International Hans Christian Andersen Medal, 1984; runner-up for *Guardian* Award for Children's Fiction, 1986, for *Trouble Half-Way;* Mother Goose Award, 1990, for *Strat and Chatto.*

Writings

NOVELS; FOR CHILDREN AND YOUNG ADULTS, EXCEPT WHERE INDICATED

Thunder and Lightnings, illustrated by Jim Russell, Kestrel, 1976, Crowell, 1979.
Under the Autumn Garden, illustrated by Colin Twinn, Kestrel, 1977, U.S. edition illustrated by Judith Gwyn Brown, Crowell, 1979.
The Ennead, Crowell, 1978.
Divide and Rule, Kestrel, 1979, Crowell, 1980.
The Short Voyage of the Albert Ross, illustrated by Gavin Rowe, Granada, 1980.
The Dead Letter Box, illustrated by Mary Rayner, Antelope Books, 1982.
Aquarius, Kestrel, 1982, Atheneum, 1984.
At the Sign of the Dog and Rocket, Longman, 1985.
Handles, illustrated by David Parkins, Kestrel, 1983, Antheneum, 1985.
Trouble Half-Way, illustrated by David Parkins, Viking Kestrel, 1985, Antheneum, 1986.
Dream House, illustrated by Jon Riley, Viking Kestrel, 1987.
Zeno Was Here (for adults), Cape, 1987, Farrar, Straus, 1988.
The Twig Thing, illustrated by Sally Holmes, Viking Children's, 1988.
Man in Motion, illustrated by Jeff Cummins, Viking Kestrel, 1989.
Finders, Losers, Orchard, 1990.

The Hillingdon Fox, Turton & Chambers, 1991.
Great Frog and Mighty Moose, Walker, 1992.
The Snow Maze, illustrated by Jan Omerod, Walker, 1992.
All the Kings and Queens, Heinemann, 1993.
Taking the Cat's Way Home, illustrated by Paul Howard, Walker, 1994.
They Do Things Differently There, Bodley Head, 1994.
Harriet's Turn, illustrated by Jane Cope, Longman, 1994.
A Worm's Eye View, illustrated by Bethan Matthews, Piccadilly, 1994.
A Fine Summer Knight, illustrated by Bob Harvey, Viking, 1995.
Under the Red Elephant, illustrated by Jeffrey Reid, HarperCollins, 1995.
My Frog and I, illustrated by Lesley Harker, Mammoth, 1997.
The Sighting, Viking, 1997.
The Coconut Quins, illustrated by Anna C. Leplar, Viking, 1997.
Worry Guts, illustrated by J. Reid, Longman, 1998.
The Eclipse of the Century, Scholastic, 1999.
Lady Long-Legs, illustrated by Paul Howard, Walker, 1999.

STORY COLLECTIONS; FOR CHILDREN AND YOUNG ADULTS EXCEPT WHERE INDICATED

Nothing to Be Afraid Of (includes "William's Version"), illustrated by David Parkins, Kestrel, 1980, Harper, 1981.
Hairs in the Palm of the Hand (contains "Time and the Hour" [also see below] and "Chutzpah"), illustrated by Jan Ormerod, Kestrel, 1981, published as *Bold as Brass,* Hutchinson, 1984.
Feet and Other Stories (includes "Posts and Telecommunications," "Enough Is Too Much Already" [also see below] and "A Little Misunderstanding"), illustrated by Bert Kitchen, Kestrel, 1983.
Two Stories (for adults; contains "Childermas" and "Mr. and Mrs. Johnson"), illustrated by Clive King, Inky Parrot Press (Oxford), 1984.
Frankie's Hat (includes "It Wasn't Me"), illustrated by Quentin Blake, Viking Kestrel, 1986.
Enough Is Too Much Already and Other Stories, Bodley Head, 1988.
(Editor) *School Stories,* Kingfisher, 1989.
A Can of Worms, Bodley Head, 1990.
Too Old To Rock and Roll: Short Stories, illustrated by Nicki Elson, retold by Diane Mowat, Oxford University Press, 1990.
In Black and White (ghost stories), Viking, 1991.
(Editor) *The Puffin Book of Song and Dance,* Viking, 1992.
(Editor) *Oxford Book of Short Stories,* Oxford University Press, 1993.
Do You Read Me?: Eight Stories, Heinemann, 1994.
God's Story, illustrated by David Parkins, Walker, 1997, Candlewick Press, 1998.

Contributor of stories to anthologies and periodicals.

OTHER; FOR CHILDREN AND YOUNG ADULTS, EXCEPT WHERE INDICATED

The Long Distance Poet (picture book), illustrated by Steve Smallman, Dinosaur, 1982.

Izzy (television screenplay), 1983, adapted as a three-act play, Longman, 1985.

Fur (picture book), illustrated by Charlotte Voake, Harper, 1986.

Out of the Oven (picture book), illustrated by Antony Maitland, Viking Kestrel, 1986.

Interference (television screenplay), 1986, adapted as a three-act play, Longman, 1987.

(With Stephen Cockett) *Captain Courage and the Rose Street Gang* (two-act play), Collins, 1987.

Fun (picture book), illustrated by Michael Foreman, Gollancz, 1987, Viking Kestrel, 1988.

Strat and Chatto (picture book), illustrated by David Hughes, Walker, 1989.

Time and the Hour (two plays), Longman, 1990.

Great Frog and Mighty Moose (travel), Walker, 1992.

This Bowl of Earth (picture book), illustrated by Gay Shephard, Walker, 1993.

Fun with Mrs. Thumb (picture book), illustrated by Nicola Bayley, Candlewick Press, 1993.

Carrot Tops and Cotton Tails (picture book), illustrated by Tony Ross, Andersen, 1993, published in the U.S. as *Silly Tails,* illustrated by Tony Ross, Atheneum, 1993.

Haddock (picture book), illustrated by Fiona Moodie, Simon and Schuster, 1994.

The One That Got Away (picture book), illustrated by Jan Lewis, Ginn, 1994.

The Tale of Tobias (picture book), illustrated by Rachel Merriman, Candlewick Press, 1996.

The Midas Touch (picture book), illustrated by Juan Wijngaard, Candlewick Press, 1999.

Mr. Dickens Hits Town (picture book), illustrated by Regolo Ricci, Tundra Books, 1999.

Author of television plays and radio dramas; contributor of articles for adults to magazines; contributor of essays to *The Cambridge Guide to Children's Books.*

Adaptations

The Dead Letter Box was adapted as an audiocassette, Puffin/Cover to Cover, 1987; *Frankie's Hat, Hairs in the Palm of the Hand,* and *Nothing to Be Afraid Of* were adapted as audiocassettes, Chivers Press, 1987, 1988, and 1989, respectively; *Handles* was adapted for television, 1989.

Sidelights

Two-time winner of the prestigious Carnegie Medal as well as one of Great Britain's most notable children's authors, Jan Mark "owns what must surely be one of the most extraordinary imaginations in children's literature," according to Nick Tucker writing in *Carousel.* Mark has written a variety of works, including picture books, plays, stories, and novels, all of which appeal to a wide audience, from young children to adults. Although most of her work attracts young readers, Mark once told *SATA* that "I do not write specifically for children, any more than I write for adults. I tend rather to write about children." With this approach, Mark has created some unusually sophisticated books for young readers, including *Thunder and Lightnings, Handles,* and *Trouble Half-*

Way, among other novels; such popular and humorous short story collections as *Nothing to Be Afraid Of, Frankie's Hat, Feet and Other Stories,* and *Hairs in the Palm of the Hand;* and beginning easy readers such as *The Snow Maze* and *Taking the Cat's Way Home.*

Critics praise Mark's unique characters, sharp wit, and clear prose, noting that she comments insightfully on the behavior, problems, and joys of young people. Unlike the majority of children's authors, she often provides a bleak and uncompromising view of the world. "Mark stretches the range of children's books," *New York Times Book Review* contributor Jane Langton declared. "She provides for young people the combination of fine prose and strong realism generally reserved for adults." This bleak view of the world is especially apparent in her science fiction novels for older readers, *The Ennead, Divide and Rule, Aquarius,* and *The Eclipse of the Century.*

Only a portion of Mark's beginning readers, novels for older readers, and short stories have been published in the United States, where she is perhaps best known for her picture books. Mark's works in this genre are noted for a trademark droll humor and concentrated use of language. Picture books such as *Fun, Silly Tails, Fun with Mrs. Thumb, The Tale of Tobias,* and *The Midas Touch* have all made Mark popular with the preschool set on both sides of the Atlantic.

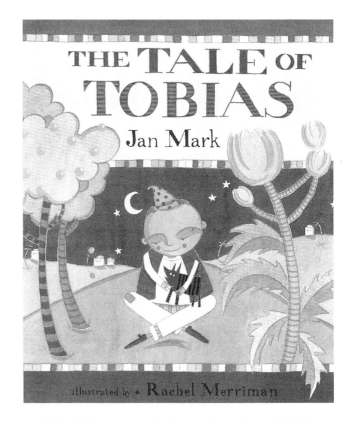

Tobias's dog narrates the journey he makes with Tobias and a magical stranger in Mark's retelling of the story from the biblical Apocrypha. (Cover illustration by Rachel Merriman.)

Mark brings to life stories from the Old Testament.
(Cover illustration by David Parkins.)

Born in Welwyn, England, Mark spent a great deal of time reading as a child. She once told *SATA:* "My educational career comprised fourteen glorious years of state-subsidized reading time. I cannot recall doing very much else, certainly not learning, since I reckoned, along with one of my fictional characters, that anything I wanted to know would stick." Mark learned to read at the age of three and was able to write by age four. The author was soon attracted to writing fiction, and she wrote stories, poems, and plays, hoping to become a published author before she even finished high school. Although this goal was not realized, Mark continued to write; in college, she composed fragments of a novel. After graduating from college, however, Mark found that her job teaching art and English kept her busy, leaving her little of the spare time or energy that writing required.

Mark was married with two children when a newspaper advertisement inspired her to finally pursue a career in writing. The London *Guardian* was sponsoring a writing contest in which an award would be given for the best

children's novel by an unpublished author. Mark wrote *Thunder and Lightnings* for the competition and won. Reflecting upon her somewhat late start in writing, Mark commented to *SATA:* "I did not begin writing seriously until I was in my thirties and am in retrospect glad of it, since I had by then developed a voice of my own." The author continued, "I started well by winning a competition for new fiction but this has imposed on me the challenge to produce always something at least as good as the first book. I dare not fall below that standard."

In addition to winning the *Guardian* contest, *Thunder and Lightnings* received a Carnegie Medal and set her literary career on a firm footing. The novel examines an unlikely friendship between two young boys—Andrew, a bright though naive middle-class youngster, and Victor, a working-class boy who is uninterested in school but who knows much about the ways of the world. Winifred Whitehead observed in *The Use of English* that "behind the apparent simplicity, [and] the everydayness of the story's events . . . lies a penetrating analysis of the two boys and their lives." Graham Hammond, writing in *Children's Literature in Education,* described *Thunder and Lightnings* as "a series of contrasts: between appearance and reality, official estimation and real worth, formal schooling and out-of-school learning, artificial projects and genuine interests, fear and love."

Thunder and Lightnings also addresses life's injustices. For instance, when Andrew tells his mother about an incident in which Victor was punished unfairly, his mother responds, "Nothing's fair. There's no such thing as fairness. It's a word made up to keep children quiet. When you discover it's a fraud, then you're starting to grow up." Though Mark's message may seem disheartening, it is softened, reviewers noted, by humor and gentle irony. Hammond observed that "for all her serious intent, [Mark] has a light touch, a flair for word play, and a warm sense of fun." Robbie March-Penney noted in *Children's Literature in Education* that Mark's first novel "sparkles with humour—sometimes gentle and sometimes irreverent, frequently at the expense of adults." Other reviewers pointed out Mark's finely nuanced relationship between Victor and Andrew. Valerie Alderson, writing in *Children's Book Review,* praised Mark's "unerring eye" in her "vivid account of the relationship between two boys who find a common enthusiasm for aeroplanes," concluding that it is Mark's understanding of the two boys and how they "are enriched by their friendship which makes the book such compulsive reading."

With *Thunder and Lightnings,* as with later novels such as *Under the Autumn Garden, The Dead Letter Box, Handles, Trouble Half-Way, The Snow Maze, Taking the Cat's Way Home,* and *The Eclipse of the Century,* Mark has been noted for her attention to detail, well-rounded characters, and realistic dialogue. Her novels for younger readers frequently lack plot development, focusing instead on characters and relationships in school or home settings, and Mark often gives a bittersweet look at childhood and adolescence. *Times Educational Sup-*

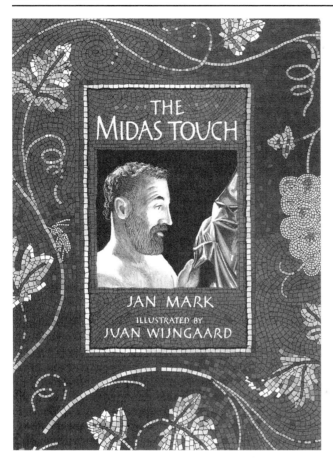

Mark brilliantly retells the classic story of the king with the golden touch. *(Cover illustration by Juan Wijngaard.)*

plement contributor Neil Philip remarked: "What is so refreshing about her writing both about and for children . . . is the accuracy with which she reflects the real concerns of childhood; an accuracy born of careful observation."

With *Under the Autumn Garden,* she puts ten-year-old Matthew in the spotlight, telling the tale "through his eyes with vivid economy and a wry assurance," according to Jonathan Croall in *Times Educational Supplement.* Set in a Norfolk village, the story tells of Matthew's efforts to finish a school history project. His efforts at digging up some of the medieval history of the town are in part thwarted by the motherless family of five who suddenly move in next door. "The novel's apparent simplicity and everdayness belies a richness of characterization, and a superb feel for the shape of a story," Croall concluded. Writing in *Bulletin of the Center for Children's Books,* Zena Sutherland called *Under the Autumn Garden* "a book that is rich in characterization, sensitive to relationships among children, lightened by the humor of the dialogue and colored by local idiom."

Mark's *The Dead Letter Box,* about friendship and the power of the written word, is a "satisfying story" about "the untaught lessons of literacy," according to Margery Meek in *The School Librarian.* Writing in *Books for Keeps,* Colin Mills declared, "This is one of those rare

books that not only engage seven to tens on the level of 'what happens next?', but holds within it some of the powerful ideas most of them are beginning to think about." *Growing Point*'s Margery Fisher concluded, "We need far more books of this kind—alert, individual yet wholly accessible for children to cut their teeth on."

With the 1983 *Handles,* Mark won her second Carnegie Medal, telling the story of thirteen-year-old Erica who, on vacation in rural Norfolk, misses the city and dreams of becoming a motorcycle mechanic. "This tale of a holiday that offers Erica pleasure and pain, growth and self-knowledge, is described with verbal wit, with affectionate perception, with pictorial precision and an unerring dramatic instinct," according to *Growing Point*'s Fisher. "It is a jewel of a book." John Rowe Townsend commented in *Times Educational Supplement,* "It's a graceful, witty book, a pleasure to read, and not as slight in theme as in action."

Trucking is at the heart of another Mark novel, *Trouble Half-Way,* a "British book with universal appeal," according to Sylvia S. Marantz in *School Library Journal.* Marantz went on to call the book an "enjoyable story with touches of humor that contains much wisdom about human nature," while *Kirkus Reviews* felt, "Anyone who enjoys the English countryside will enjoy this gentle story of a girl traveling through it on a journey of self-discovery."

Aimed at much older readers, Mark's 1999 novel *The Eclipse of the Century* "is like a cross between a Rider Haggard adventure story and a Kafka parable," according to Tucker in *Carousel.* Twenty-year-old Keith has a near death experience and as a result is summoned to a remote country in central Asia where he meets a mysterious tribe of people who are waiting for a sign to take them back to their origins. Soon others come to the lost city, and, as Dianna Wynne Jones described in a review for the *Sunday Telegraph,* "the novel quietly flips from dream to nightmare." In the same review Jones praised *The Eclipse of the Century* as "full of . . . astute observations, hilarious humor, sly references to other literatures, a strong sense of historical sense, and an even stronger sense of present-day forces. These make a triumphantly compulsive mixture." Like much of Mark's other fiction for older, more sophisticated readers, *The Eclipse of the Century* takes a dark and uncompromising view of the world. "It is a grim message, full of truth," wrote Jones, "but it makes gripping reading, too, because it is so magnificently done."

Mark's work is also noted for its conciseness—she is able to write in the easy reader format and still deliver depth. Reviewing Mark's *The Snow Maze* in *The Junior Bookshelf,* M. Crouch noted that though the book was "brief and undemanding," it "holds within its small compass some big ideas." Crouch went on, "It takes only 60 pages, largely pictures, for changes to take place, characters to develop, attitudes to change, all with no sense of contrivance." Joan Zahnleiter commented in *Magpies,* "Jan Mark has demonstrated her versatility here with a beautifully crafted story." A book about multiracial relationships with a touch of fantasy, *The Snow Maze* is a "rewarding read for young beginners," concluded Zahnleiter. Mark also turns trouble at school into a "very readable, clever and sensitive book" in *Taking the Cat's Way Home,* according to Gill Roberts in *Books for Keeps.* Crouch, in noting the same easy reader in *The Junior Bookshelf,* commented that the author is among those writers "who bring to the slightest of their books the same creativity and technical excellence as to their long and 'important' novels."

A trio of such "important" novels were produced between 1978 and 1984. Though her portrayal of life as difficult and unjust surfaces in many of her books, it is especially evident in *The Ennead, Divide and Rule,* and *Aquarius,* three novels written specifically for an older, young adult audience. These books stand apart from Mark's works for younger readers; requiring a more sophisticated audience, the novels have a bleaker tone, exploring such issues as manipulative relationships, the power of religion, and the fate of those who are unwilling to conform to the rules of society. Instead of being set in contemporary England like most of Mark's writings, these works are set in fictitious societies and have sometimes been labeled science fiction. The main characters in these books are, as Mark described in *SATA,* "likely to be . . . amoral or downright corrupt." Her protagonists are not victims; Mark explained that they are, rather, "authors of their own downfalls. . . . The forces of evil currently fashionable are not supernatural, but human ignorance and complacency."

Mark discussed these works for older children with Philip, commenting that "the idea of manipulation is what I'm working on in all three books. Not only why we do it, but why do we allow it? How much capital do you think you can make out of allowing yourselves to be used?" Mark also noted in *Books for Keeps* that in the three books "I'm setting up situations and inviting the reader to explore the situation along with the writer. They're for a sophisticated reader and they're deliberately written to discourage an unsophisticated reader. . . . I like to make the reader work hard."

Although some critics faulted Mark for the despairing message she presents in *The Ennead, Divide and Rule,* and *Aquarius,* Marcus Crouch asserted in the *Junior Bookshelf* that "it is some indication of the power of her writing that . . . Mark leaves us exhilarated rather than depressed." In *Painted Desert, Green Shade,* David Rees observed that "scarcely anyone writing today presents youth with a more somber picture of life than does Jan Mark. Sometimes the reader may feel that her novels go to an extreme beyond which it is not possible to venture in books for children and teenagers. This doesn't matter: the harsh truths of her vision of the world are infinitely preferable to the cozy pap that is sometimes served up for the young."

Mark's power of observation is also evident in her short fiction. Her story collections, which include *Nothing to Be Afraid Of, Hairs in the Palm of the Hand,* and *Feet,* are considered to be among the best examples of her work. In a *Horn Book* article, Mark described the differences between writing stories and novels: "I much prefer writing short stories. I have to explain this to schoolchildren. They think I like writing short stories because short stories are quickly done and therefore easy. . . . In fact, writing short stories is harder than writing novels. You can't get away with anything in a short story. . . . It is said that in a novel every chapter must count; in a short story every sentence must count." Also writing in *Horn Book,* Aidan Chambers noted that *Nothing to Be Afraid Of* "indicated just how appropriate the [short story] form is for [Mark's] talents. The collection is funny, uncomfortably accurate in its dialogue and in the persuasiveness of its narrative situations, and written throughout with the combination of an unflinchingly sharp eye for human foible and a detached sympathy for the underdog . . . that makes fiction . . . more potent than real life for the observing reader."

Reviewing the collection *Hairs in the Palm of the Hand,* Philip wrote in the *Times Educational Supplement,* "Jan Marks is living proof that the best writing for children can also be the most popular." Philip felt that there was nothing in these stories "to bore, to confuse or patronize the young. . . . They are hilariously funny, meticulously observed, shaped with mature skill in economical, precise prose." A much later anthology of stories, *God's Story,* all drawing on the Midrash Rabbah, tells tales from the Old Testament, including the story of Adam and Eve, Noah, Abraham, and Moses. "Mark's telling of these old stories is fresh, sometimes funny," noted *Booklist*'s Ilene Cooper in a starred review, "and she manages to give them an air of immediacy that brings them right into the life of modern-day readers." Patricia Pearl Dole, writing in *School Library Journal,* felt that even though the material was not new, "Mark has filled it with new vigor, insight, and even fun."

Mark is increasingly well known in the United States not for her gritty novels for older readers or her easy readers or short stories, but for picture books for preschoolers. In books such as *Fun, Silly Tails, Fun with Mrs. Thumb, The Tale of Tobias,* and *The Midas Touch,* Mark displays her penchant for detail and humor to the delight of both parents and kids. With *Fun,* she pokes some of the aforementioned at hyper parents who want their kids to have "fun" with a vengeance. Sally R. Dow noted in *School Library Journal,* "This is a consciousness raising book for parents . . . but one which may hit the mark with many children." Talking vegetables and pacifistic bunnies inform *Silly Tails,* an "offbeat treasure," according to *Kirkus Reviews.* Of that same title, *Publishers Weekly* noted, "Humor with a British accent distinguishes Mark's latest yarn, which drolly explains rabbits' predatory approach to carrots."

Mark tells a rhyming story from a cat's point of view in *Fun with Mrs. Thumb,* a "little gem," according to Linda Wicher in *School Library Journal. Booklist*'s Annie Ayres called it "a treasure in miniature." The Old Testament Apocrypha and Greek myth respectively provide inspiration for *The Tale of Tobias* and *The Midas Touch.* In the former, old Tobit is stricken with blindness and sends his son Tobias along with his dog and a companion to collect a family debt. The companion is the angel Raphael in disguise who helps Tobias battle a demon and marry the lovely Sarah as well as providing a cure to Tobit's blindness. Kathy Piehl in *School Library Journal* called the picture book "an intriguing interpretation of a little-known but exciting tale."

Whether writing picture books for the very young, novels and easy readers for beginning readers, or more mature tales for the YA audience, Jan Mark "punctuates her stories with plot twists and pungent comments on wide-ranging matters," according to Kathy Piehl writing in *Twentieth-Century Young Adult Writers.* "Her high levels of invention and productivity assure her a place of continuing importance in contemporary fiction for young adults."

Works Cited

Alderson, Valerie, review of *Thunder and Lightnings, Children's Book Review,* October, 1976, p. 39.

Ayres, Annie, review of *Fun with Mrs. Thumb, Booklist,* January 1, 1994, p. 833.

"Authorgraph No. 25: Jan Mark," *Books for Keeps,* March 1984, pp. 12-13.

Chambers, Aidan, "Letters from England: A Mark of Distinction," *Horn Book,* September-October, 1984, pp. 665-70.

Cooper, Ilene, review of *God's Story, Booklist,* October 1, 1997, p. 321.

Croall, Jonathan, "Coping with Adults," *Times Educational Supplement,* February 3, 1978, p. 36.

Crouch, M., review of *The Ennead, The Junior Bookshelf,* February, 1979, pp. 56-57.

Crouch, M., review of *The Snow Maze, The Junior Bookshelf,* February, 1993, p. 22.

Crouch, M., review of *Taking the Cat's Way Home, The Junior Bookshelf,* December, 1994, p. 217.

Dole, Patricia Pearl, review of *God's Story, School Library Journal,* January, 1998, p. 127.

Dow, Sally R., review of *Fun, School Library Journal,* January, 1989, p. 65.

Fisher, Margery, review of *The Dead Letter Box, Growing Point,* September, 1982, p. 3944.

Fisher, Margery, review of *Handles, Growing Point,* January, 1984, pp. 4186-87.

Hammond, Graham, review of *Thunder and Lightnings, Children's Literature in Education,* summer, 1982, pp. 58-59.

Langton, Jane, review of *Handles, New York Times Book Review,* July 28, 1985, p. 25.

Marantz, Sylvia S., review of *Trouble Half-Way, School Library Journal,* May, 1986, p. 95.

March-Penney, Robbie, "I Don't Want to Learn Things, I'd Rather Just Find Out: Jan Mark's *Thunder and Lightnings,*" *Children's Literature in Education,* spring, 1979, pp. 18-24.

Mark, Jan, *Thunder and Lightnings,* Crowell, 1979.

Mark, Jan, "The Short Story," *Horn Book,* January-February, 1988, pp. 42-45.

Meek, Margery, review of *The Dead Letter Box, The School Librarian,* September, 1982, p. 236.

Mills, Colin, review of *The Dead Letter Box, Books for Keeps,* November, 1983, p. 12.

Philip, Neil, "Don't Pander, Don't Patronize," *Times Educational Supplement,* August 7, 1981, p. 17.

Philip, Neil, "Read Mark, Learn," *Times Educational Supplement,* June 3, 1983, p. 37.

Piehl, Kathy, "Mark, Jan," *Twentieth-Century Young Adult Writers,* St. James Press, 1989, pp. 420-22.

Piehl, Kathy, review of *The Tale of Tobias, School Library Journal,* October, 1996, p. 115.

Rees, David, "No Such Thing as Fairness: Jan Mark," *Painted Desert, Green Shade: Essays on Contemporary Writers of Fiction for Children and Young Adults,* Horn Book, 1984, pp. 62-74.

Roberts, Gill, review of *Taking the Cat's Way Home, Books for Keeps,* July, 1995, pp. 10-11.

Review of *Silly Tails, Publishers Weekly,* April 5, 1993, p. 78.

Review of *Silly Tails, Kirkus Reviews,* May 1, 1993, p. 601.

Sutherland, Zena, review of *Under the Autumn Garden, Bulletin of the Center for Children's Books,* October, 1979, p. 32.

Townsend, John Rowe, "Nicknames," *Times Educational Supplement,* January 13, 1984, p. 38.

Review of *Trouble Half-Way, Kirkus Reviews,* February 1, 1986, p. 210.

Tucker, Nick, review of *The Eclipse of the Century, Carousel,* Summer, 1999, p. 27.

Whitehead, Winifred, "Jan Mark," *The Use of English,* spring, 1982, pp. 32-39.

Wicher, Linda, review of *Fun with Mrs. Thumb, School Library Journal,* March, 1994, pp. 204-05.

Zahnleiter, Joan, review of *The Snow Maze, Magpies,* July, 1993, p. 28.

For More Information See

BOOKS

Authors of Books for Young People, 3rd edition, edited by Martha E. Ward, Scarecrow Press, 1990.

Children's Literature Review, Volume 11, Gale, 1986.

Contemporary Authors, New Revision Series, Volume 17, Gale, 1986.

Fifth Book of Junior Authors and Illustrators, edited by Sally Holmes Holtze, H. W. Wilson, 1983.

St. James Guide to Young Adult Writers, 2nd edition, edited by Tom Pendergast and Sara Pendergast, St. James Press, 1999.

PERIODICALS

Bulletin of the Center for Children's Books, December, 1978; June, 1980; April, 1982; July-August, 1984; May, 1985; April, 1986; December, 1996, p. 142.

Children's Literature in Education, Winter, 1983.

Growing Point, July, 1982; May, 1988, p. 4982; July, 1990, p. 5365.

Horn Book, October, 1978; July-August, 1986; March-April, 1987; January-February, 1997, p. 77; January-February, 1998, pp. 92-93.

Kirkus Reviews, October 15, 1993, p. 1332.

New York Times Book Review, July 17, 1988.

Publishers Weekly, April 15, 1988; November 15, 1993, p. 81.
School Library Journal, September, 1993, p. 216.
Times Educational Supplement, October 23, 1992, p. 12; November 4, 1994, p. 16; December 5, 1997, p. 17; January 9, 1998, p. 17.

—*Sketch by J. Sydney Jones*

* * *

McBRIER, Michael
See OLDER, Effin

* * *

McBRIER, Michael
See OLDER, Jules

* * *

McKAY, Lawrence, Jr. 1948-

Personal

Born August 24, 1948, in Pittsburgh, PA; son of Lawrence (in business) and Elizabeth (Slocum) McKay; married Susan F. McKay (an executive coach), April 21, 1983; children: Elizabeth Teal, Galen James. *Education:* University of Denver, B.A.; American Film Institute, M.A. *Hobbies and other interests:* Cycling, soccer, music (have played the 5-string banjo for 35 years), cricket.

Addresses

Home and office—12108 Southwest 148th St., Vashon Island, WA 98070. *Agent*—Rosemary Stimola. *E-mail*—Fen@ix.netcom.com.

Career

Equities trader in Vashon, WA, 1985—; freelance writer. Certified soccer coach for boys, ages 4-13.

Writings

Caravan, illustrated by Darryl Ligasan, Lee & Low, 1995.
Journey Home, illustrated by Dom and Keunhee Lee, Lee & Low, 1998.

Work in Progress

A young adult novel titled *Frost Heave.*

Sidelights

Lawrence McKay, Jr.'s first book for children, *Caravan,* was hailed as an unusual rite-of-passage story. Set in the Hindu Kush mountains of Afghanistan, *Caravan* is the first-person narrative of ten-year-old Jura's first journey

Lawrence McKay, Jr.

down the mountainside with his father, leading camels laden with furs through narrow, snowy trails down into the city to trade for supplies. The story emphasizes Jura's pride in taking part in the journey, and his admiration for his father, whom he tries to emulate as they make their perilous but necessary journey. "The poetic writing skillfully describes a world far different from one containing automobiles, VCR's, and computers," remarked Susan Middleton in *School Library Journal.* Other reviewers similarly highlighted McKay's lyrical prose style, while Martha V. Parravano also commented in her *Horn Book* appraisal that *Caravan* "is full of fascinating details" revealed through both the author's words and the illustrator's brush. The resulting book "will give readers an armchair tour of a unique locale," observed a *Kirkus Reviews* critic.

McKay's second book, *Journey Home,* was also well received. Narrated by Mai, a ten-year-old Vietnamese American girl, *Journey Home* is the story of Mai and her mother's return to Vietnam to search for her mother's birth family, who disappeared after leaving Mai's mother at an orphanage in Saigon during the Vietnam War. Mai's mother was adopted by an American family and raised in the United States. Her only link to her heritage is a beautiful kite. As Mai and her mother search for the truth "the unfolding detective work ... makes a compelling story," according to author of a review for the Parents' Choice Foundation, published online at *Amazon.com.* A contributor to *Kirkus Reviews* called *Journey Home* "enormously touching," and Hazel Rochman wrote in *Booklist* that the book "will encourage readers to ask about their own family stories of the journey home."

McKay revealed to *SATA*: "I am constantly involved with not only my own children, ages 14 and 11, but others as well. As a 4-13 boys soccer coach I am extremely busy with kids, driving and teaching three times a week with a game every Saturday during the fall into December. The kids take it seriously and I do, too.

"I am also an equities trader, working out of my home. On one side of my office is a trading station with four monitors; on the other side is my writing desk. I slide between the two desks in my chair. It is a busy, but wonderful life.

"I also play the 5-string banjo, bluegrass or jazz. I have played professionally, although I am not doing so currently. I guess I should start another band."

Works Cited

Review of *Caravan, Kirkus Reviews,* October 15, 1995, p. 1496.
Review of *Journey Home, Kirkus Reviews,* May 1, 1998, p. 662.
Review of *Journey Home,* Parents' Choice Foundation, published online at *Amazon.com,* http://www.amazon.com. (February 9, 2000)
Middleton, Susan, review of *Caravan, School Library Journal,* December, 1995, pp. 85-86.
Parravano, Martha V., review of *Caravan, Horn Book,* July-December, 1995, pp. 37-38.
Rochman, Hazel, review of *Journey Home, Booklist,* May 1, 1998, p. 1518.

For More Information See

PERIODICALS

Publishers Weekly, May 25, 1998, p. 90.
School Library Journal, June, 1998, p. 114.

*   *   *

MILLEN, C(ynthia) M. 1955-

Personal

Born October 28, 1955; married James Roberts (a physician), March 29, 1980; children: Kerry, Meaghan and Katharine (twins), Pierce and Callan (twins). *Education:* Bowling Green State University, B.A. (geography), 1977; North Kentucky University, J.D., 1983; Trinity College (Dublin), M.Litt. (law), 1997. *Religion:* Roman Catholic.

Addresses

Home—2428 Edgehill Road, Toledo, OH 43615. *E-mail*—irish@toltbbs.com.

Career

University of Toledo College of Law, Toledo, OH, instructor, 1983-84; Juvenile Court, Toledo, guardian-ad-litem, 1984-85; Prosecutor's Office, Wood County, OH, attorney, 1985-86; St. Vincent Medical Center, Toledo, house counsel, 1986; full-time poet and writer, 1991—. Poet-in-residence, Sauder Farm, 1999. Volunteer work includes as Toledo-area coordinator of Project Children, 1989—; host family for children from Northern Ireland, 1989-96; founder and coordinator of Project Shakespeare (taking twelve children to London annually to see a Royal Shakespeare Company production), 1993—.

Awards, Honors

American Booksellers Pick of the List, and Parents' Choice Award for Best Picture book, both 1996, and *Scientific American* Best Children's Books designation, 1997, all for *A Symphony for the Sheep;* Northern Ireland Arts Council grant, 1997.

Writings

FOR CHILDREN

A Symphony for the Sheep, illustrated by Mary Azarian, Houghton Mifflin (Boston), 1996.
The Low Down Laundry Line Blues, Houghton Mifflin, 1999.

Author of *Ulster out Loud,* 1994, and *On the Street Where I Live,* illustrated by students of St. Vincent's Girls' School, Dublin, Ireland, 1997. Editor of *Between the Rhymes,* a collection of poems written by children in central Belfast, Dublin, and Toledo, OH, 1998. Poems have been published in Ireland and the United States.

OTHER

The Right to Privacy and Its Natural Law Foundations in the Constitutions of the United States and Ireland, Gaunt, 1998.

Former editor-in-chief, *Northern Kentucky Law Review,* c. 1982.

Sidelights

C. M. Millen is an attorney who maintains connections with Ireland and the British Isles through educationally oriented volunteer work. Millen's picture poetry book, *A Symphony for the Sheep,* celebrates the traditional arts associated with working with wool as still practiced in modern-day Ireland. *A Symphony for the Sheep* is a musical paean to the shearer, the spinner, the weaver, and the knitter that describes the work of each through rollicking rhymes that beg to be sung in the round, remarked *Booklist* reviewer Stephanie Zvirin. The critic explained that Millen's book "is best suited to group use" because of its multi-voiced narrative, and concluded that *A Symphony for the Sheep* "offers some wonderful opportunities for fun and learning" because of the broad good humor of its lyrics and the use of

After which the skeins are weighed
and hung aloft to set them straight.
And so it goes and so it comes—
there's always wool which must be spun.

C. M. Millen's first picture book, **A Symphony for the Sheep,** *celebrates the sheep of Ireland and the shearing and knitting of their wool. (Illustrated by Mary Azarian.)*

technical terms of the knitter's craft. A critic for *Kirkus Reviews* noted that Millen's lyrics and the volume's woodcut illustrations "are a perfect match, rich, earthy, and of good cheer."

Works Cited

Review of *A Symphony for the Sheep, Kirkus Reviews,* August 1, 1996, p. 1155.
Zvirin, Stephanie, review of *A Symphony for the Sheep, Booklist,* August, 1996, p. 1908.

*   *   *

MONTGOMERY, Sy 1958-

Personal

Born February 7, 1958, in Frankfurt, Germany; daughter of Austin James (a U. S. Army general) and Willa Zane (Brown) Montgomery; married Howard Mansfield (a writer), September, 1987. *Education:* Syracuse University, dual B.A.'s (French and psychology; magazine journalism), 1979. *Politics:* "Town meeting." *Religion:* Christian. *Hobbies and other interests:* "I have a ten-year-old, seven-hundred-fifty-pound pig."

Addresses

Agent—Sarah Jane Freymann, 59 West 71st St. #9B, New York, NY 10023.

Career

Freelance journalist. Has lectured on conservation topics at the Smithsonian Institution, American Museum of Natural History, California Academy of Sciences, and other schools, universities, and conservation organizations. *Member:* Society of Women Geographers, New England Environmental Educators.

Awards, Honors

Ray Bruner science writing fellow, American Public Health Association, 1982; Best New Nonfiction, New England Writers and Publishers Project, and finalist, *Los Angeles Times* science book award, both 1991, both for *Walking with the Great Apes;* Chris Award for Best

Sy Montgomery with Siberian tiger cub.

Science Documentary, Columbus Film Festival, 1998, for *Mother Bear Man.*

Writings

Walking with the Great Apes: Jane Goodall, Dian Fossey, Birute Galdikas, Houghton Mifflin, 1991.

Nature's Everyday Mysteries: A Field Guide to the World in Your Backyard (essays), foreword by Roger Tory Peterson, illustrated by Rodica Prato, Chapters (Shelburne, VT), 1993.

(Contributor) *The Nature of Nature: New Essays by America's Finest Writers on Nature,* Harcourt, 1994.

Spell of the Tiger: The Man-Eaters of Sundarbans, Houghton Mifflin, 1995.

Seasons of the Wild: A Year of Nature's Magic and Mysteries (essays), foreword by Elizabeth Marshall Thomas, illustrated by R. Prato, Chapters, 1995.

(Author of script) *Spell of the Tiger* (documentary), National Geographic, 1996.

(Author of script) *Mother Bear Man* (documentary), National Geographic, 1999.

The Snake Scientist (juvenile), illustrated by Nic Bishop, Houghton Mifflin, 1999.

Journey of the Pink Dolphins: An Amazon Quest, Simon & Schuster, 2000.

Contributor to journals, including *International Wildlife, Geo, Nature, Animals Magazine, Orion, Boston Globe Sunday Magazine,* and *Ranger Rick's Nature Magazine,* and to *Encyclopedia Britannica.* Author of monthly column for the *Boston Globe,* of radio commentaries on nature for National Public Radio's *Living on Earth* program, and of scripts for "National Geographic Explorer" television programs.

Work in Progress

The Man-eating Tigers, for Houghton Mifflin, expected in 2001; and *Search for the Golden Moon Bear,* for adults, expected in 2003.

Sidelights

Sy Montgomery's writings about the natural world extend from the ordinary to the exotic, from the common firefly of many North American backyards to the elusive man-eating tigers of Borneo. In her first book, *Walking with the Great Apes,* the author profiles three famous women primatologists, Englishwoman Jane Goodall, American Dian Fossey, and Canadian Birute Galdikas, each of whom has been fundamentally transformed by her years of research and living among apes, Montgomery argues. "This is an exciting book," attested Sally Estes in *Booklist,* who was attracted to the author's characterization of her subjects' pursuit of the apes as a kind of vision quest not easily articulated in scientific language. Genevieve Stuttaford in *Publishers Weekly* referred to this aspect of Montgomery's book as "the intriguing view of these scientists as pioneers of a particularly female way of scientific knowing." Estes dubbed *Walking with the Great Apes* "a splendid, well-written account ... that will draw in readers unfamiliar with the research projects [of Goodall, Fossey, and Galdikas] as well as those who have been following them through the years."

In *Nature's Everyday Mysteries,* a collection of Montgomery's columns from the *Boston Globe,* the author provides many little-known facts about the natural world all around us. "For readers who know little about the natural world, [Montgomery's] writing will entertain and inform in equal proportions," averred Jon Kartman in *Booklist.* For her third book, *Spell of the Tiger,* however, Montgomery returned to the realm of the exotic. For this work, the author traveled to the Bay of Bengal, home to the world's largest mangrove swamp, and to the only population of tigers that seeks out human beings as prey rather than shying away from mankind as most tigers do. The people of the Sundarbans worship the tiger as a god even as hundreds of them are hunted and killed by the animals they call Daksin Ray every year. "Montgomery writes lyrically of an alien land where outlines blur, tree roots reach for the sky, cyclones claim whole villages, and chanted mantras keep tigers from becoming angry," observed a critic for *Kirkus Reviews.* Other reviewers, like a critic writing in *Publishers Weekly,* similarly focused on the author's "vivid picture of the coastal forest and its people." *Booklist* reviewer Donna Seaman noted that Montgomery appeared to "absorb the unique and surprisingly cosmic dynamic of the delta" as her pursuit of her elusive subject continued, and concluded: "After all, there can be no revelation more humbling than the recognition that we, like other animals, are meat."

While Montgomery's first books were written for the general reader, her *The Snake Scientist* was specifically written for a younger audience. The strength of this

Montgomery shares a close-up view of Dr. Robert Mason's field study of the world's largest concentration of snakes in Manitoba, Canada. (Cover photo by Nic Bishop.)

work, according to Ruth S. Vose in her appraisal for *School Library Journal,* is that it exhibits "the excitement of science in action." Montgomery's text centers on a zoologist who studies the red-sided garter snake in Canada, while the book's sidebars include information about aspects of the species that continue to mystify scientists and how to visit snake dens. Montgomery's "lively text" makes this an "outstanding" science book for young people, Vose averred.

Montgomery told *SATA:* "I write for both adults and children in order to help us remember our duty to the earth. Children are a particularly important audience for they have an intuitive connection with plants and animals I hope to help honor and foster in my work. If our kind is to avert the poisonings and extinctions now in progress, today's children will do it.

"To research my books and articles, I have been chased by an angry silverback gorilla in Zaire and bitten by a vampire bat in Costa Rica. I have spent a week working in a pit with 18,000 snakes in Manitoba. I have been deftly undressed by an orangutan in Borneo, hunted by a tiger in India, and—for my upcoming book, *At the Meeting of the Waters*—swum with piranhas, eels, and dolphins in the Amazon.

"*Journey of the Pink Dolphins: An Amazon Quest* is the true story of my quest to follow an enigmatic, little-studied species of freshwater dolphin into the heart of the Amazon. My research required four separate expeditions, each a journey not only into some of the world's greatest jungles, but also a trip back into time, and a foray into a mythical, enchanted world where people say the dolphins can turn into people and seduce both men and women to live with them in a beautiful city beneath the water.

"For my third book, *Spell of the Tiger,* I avoided being eaten by my study subjects while living in a mud hut among the most deadly man-eaters in the world. My work with the tigers and people was the subject of a National Geographic "Explorer" TV documentary filmed in West Bengal. The film, whose script I also wrote and narrated, first aired in 1996 to a worldwide audience.

"I also developed and scripted the Chris Award-winning documentary *Mother Bear Man* for National Geographic that aired [in April 1999]. The film profiles the lives of three orphaned bear cubs and their unlikely mother—Ben Kilham, a friend of mine who raised these babies like a mother bear would: by spending nine hours a day roaming the woods with them. The film chronicles Ben's extraordinarily intimate observations of these normally shy animals as they grow into some of the largest carnivores in North America."

Works Cited

Estes, Sally, review of *Walking with the Great Apes, Booklist,* March 15, 1991, p. 1441.

Kartman, Jon, review of *Nature's Everyday Mysteries, Booklist,* April 1, 1993, p. 1395.

Seaman, Donna, review of *Spell of the Tiger, Booklist,* January 15, 1995, p. 878.

Review of *Spell of the Tiger, Kirkus Reviews,* December 1, 1994, p. 1596.

Review of *Spell of the Tiger, Publishers Weekly,* January 9, 1995, p. 53.

Stuttaford, Genevieve, review of *Walking with the Great Apes, Publishers Weekly,* January 11, 1991, p. 85.

Vose, Ruth S., review of *The Snake Scientist, School Library Journal,* May, 1999, pp. 140-41.

*   *   *

MOON, Sheila (Elizabeth) 1910-1991

OBITUARY NOTICE—See index for *SATA* sketch: Born December 25, 1910, in Denver, CO; died of complications of Alzheimer's disease, August 25, 1991, in San Francisco, CA. Psychology professor, analyst, and poet. Sheila Moon maintained a private practice as a psychotherapist in Los Angeles and San Francisco from 1945 on. Her first book was *And a Time to Die* (1969), which was followed by the first in the Maris young adult science fiction series, *Keep-Deep in Thunder* (1967), *A Magic Dwells: A Poetic and Psychological Study of the Navaho* (1984), *Collected Poems, 1972-1985* (1985), and her last book, *Deepest Roots* (1986). She also contributed her poetry to various of the literary journals.

OBITUARIES AND OTHER SOURCES:

BOOKS

The Seeded Furrow: Papers Presented to Sheila Moon on the Occasion of Her 65th Birthday, December 25, 1975, Guild for Psychology Studies Publishing House, 1977.

PERIODICALS

San Francisco Chronicle, August 29, 1991, p. A16.

MORGAN, Mary 1957-
(Mary Morgan-Vanroyen)

Personal

Born December 14, 1957, in Chicago, IL; daughter of Jere and Delores Wilson; children: Dylan. *Education:* Attended San Miguel de Allende.

Addresses

Home—7115 Walnut, Kansas City, MO.

Career

Writer and illustrator.

Writings

SELF-ILLUSTRATED

The Pudgy Merry Christmas Book, Grosset and Dunlap, 1989.

Four Seasons, Grosset and Dunlap, 1989.

Guess Who I Love?: A Pudgy Book, Grosset and Dunlap, 1992.

Benjamin's Bugs, Bradbury Press, 1994.

(As Mary Morgan-Vanroyen) *Night Ride,* Atheneum, 1997.

Wild Rosie, Hyperion, 1999.

Gentle Rosie, Hyperion, 1999.

Patient Rosie, Hyperion, 2000.

Curious Rosie, Hyperion, 2000.

ILLUSTRATOR

Cecil Frances Alexander, *All Things Bright and Beautiful,* Platt & Munk, 1987.

Jane Fine, *Surprise!,* Viking Kestrel, 1988.

Teddy Slater, *Molly's Monsters,* Grosset & Dunlap, 1988.

Harriet Ziefert, *Let's Trade,* Viking Kestrel, 1989, Puffin, 1996.

Dorothy Hinshaw Patent, *Singing Birds and Flashing Fireflies,* F. Watts, 1989.

Barbara G. Hennesey, *Jake Baked the Cake,* Viking Penguin, 1990.

Anne Baird, *The Guppies of Hilly Dale House,* Simon & Schuster, 1990.

Sleepy Time, Random House, 1990.

Lillian Hammer Ross, *Buba Leah and Her Paper Children,* Jewish Publication Society, 1991.

Kathleen V. Kudlinski, *Animal Tracks and Traces,* F. Watts, 1991.

Bobbi Katz, selector, *Puddle Wonderful: Poems to Welcome Spring,* Random House, 1992.

Lauren Ariev, *What Can Baby Do?,* Golden Books, 1992.

Ariev, *Who Are Baby's Friends?,* Golden Books, 1992.

Elizabeth Winthrop, *Asleep in a Heap,* Holiday House, 1993.

Rhoda Blumberg, *Bloomers!,* Bradbury Press, 1993.

Alice McLerran, *Hugs,* Scholastic, 1993.

McLerran, *Kisses,* Scholastic, 1993.

Wendy Cheyette Lewison, *Christmas Cookies,* Grosset and Dunlap, 1993.

Lewison, *Happy Thanksgiving!,* Grosset and Dunlap, 1993.

Lewison (compiler), *Baby's First Mother Goose,* Western
Publishers, 1993.

Winthrop, *I'm the Boss!,* Holiday House, 1994.

Mary Nethery, *Hannah and Jack,* Bradbury Press, 1995.

Lewison, *I Wear My Tutu Everywhere!,* Grosset and
Dunlap, 1996.

Dian Curtis Regan, *Daddies,* Scholastic, 1996.

Regan, *Mommies,* Scholastic, 1996.

(As Mary Morgan-Vanroyen) Barbara Shook Hazen,
Where Do Bears Sleep?, HarperCollins, 1998.

Carolyn Otto, *Our Puppies Are Growing,* HarperCollins,
1998.

Little Miss Muffet, Publications International, 1998.

Patricia Lauber, *The Tiger Has a Toothache,* National
Geographic Society, 1999.

Also illustrator of *Bike Ride.*

Sidelights

Mary Morgan is an illustrator of children's books with a
small but well-received number of books of her own to
her credit in addition to the almost thirty titles she has
illustrated for other authors. Working in warm pastels
and cheerful watercolors, she creates lively visions of
the past, as in Rhoda Blumberg's *Bloomers!,* cozy takes
on holidays as in Wendy Lewison's *Christmas Cookies*
and *Happy Thanksgiving!,* and cheery animal stories as
in her own *Benjamin's Bugs* and the "Rosie" books. In
her self-illustrated works, Morgan lets the pictures carry
the story, keeping text to a minimum, with books
targeted largely to the pre-school and early primary
audience.

Born in Chicago in 1957, Morgan's first children's
publication came in 1987 with illustrations for Cecil
Frances Alexander's *All Things Bright and Beautiful.*
Soon she had developed a distinctively warm style, as
can be witnessed in the 1990 picture book *Jake Baked
the Cake,* by Barbara G. Hennesey. A town is getting
ready for a wedding, and Jake the baker is putting the
finishing touches on a beautiful cake. A *Publishers
Weekly* critic felt that "Morgan's detailed, pastel drawings" along with text by Hennesey "convey the buoyant
spirit of this old-fashioned wedding, with just the right
amounts of humor and warmth." Joan McGrath, writing
in *School Library Journal,* praises Morgan's depiction
of the characters—"Hummel look-alikes—round, rosy,
and childlike." McGrath concluded that this "charming
book absolutely insists upon being read aloud." *Horn
Book*'s Elizabeth S. Watson commented that "Morgan's
pictures are full of homey scenes, humor, . . . and
present a delightful picture of the Victorian village
wedding complete with storks on the church chimney."

Morgan helped to give line and color to the Jewish
immigrant experience in her illustrations for Lillian
Hammer Ross's *Buba Leah and Her Paper Children.*
Polish Buba Leah hears news from her children in
America via letters, her "paper children" as she calls
them, and one day receives a ticket in the mail to join
them. A *Publishers Weekly* critic observed that "Morgan's earthy illustrations render village life and the

*Mary Morgan's tender illustrations reveal the
bittersweet fulfillment of Buba Leah's longing to see
her children in America. (From* Buba Leah and Her
Paper Children, *written by Lillian Hammer Ross.)*

special bonds between family members in an affectionate light," while Susan Kaminow noted in *School
Library Journal* that "full-color realistic illustrations of
the characters and village life add dimension." *Booklist*
reviewer Ellen Mandel drew special attention to Morgan's "tenderly drawn illustrations" which "reflect the
realities of shtetl life and the warmth of intergenerational
love."

Morgan's cozy illustrative style has also appeared in
small-format books, such as *Hugs* and *Kisses* by Alice
McLerran, and *Mommies* and *Daddies* by Dian Curtis
Regan. Sharing emotional closeness is the topic of the
first two, told in verse. Linda Wicher commented in
School Library Journal that Morgan's illustrations for
both *Hugs* and for *Kisses* depict "happy scenes of
children, pets, families, and friends in homes and
suburban neighborhoods." Wicher went on to note that
though the figures of "rosy-cheeked children and adults
are idealized, they represent a variety of ethnic groups."
Reviewing *Mommies,* a *Publishers Weekly* contributor
observed that the illustrations, "soft and clean as a
baby's layette, reinforce the tender tones."

Much more ambitious are Morgan's illustrations for
Blumberg's *Bloomers!,* a picture book telling the story
of the early days of the women's rights movement and

Morgan depicts middle sister Julia's authority complex in Elizabeth Winthrop's amusing picture book. (From I'm the Boss!)

of the clothing that eventually symbolized that movement. Tracing the history of the bloomer, a trouser-like bottom worn under a skirt in the mid-nineteenth century, the book deals with such luminaries as Elizabeth Cady Stanton and Susan B. Anthony, as well as the editor Amelia Bloomer after whom the new fashion trend was named. "Morgan's bright, cheerful, watercolor paintings convey a sense of time and place while they carry the narrative along," commented Linda Greengrass in *School Library Journal*. *Horn Book*'s Margaret A. Bush noted that "Pretty, muted tones soften the ambiance and the demeanor of women who were speaking out for the interest of women."

Morgan teamed up with Elizabeth Winthrop for several picture books, including *Asleep in a Heap* and *I'm the Boss!*, which feature a young child who gets very tired of being told what to do. In *Asleep in a Heap*, Julia outlasts the rest of her family in getting ready for bed, putting her dolls to sleep first and taking a bubble bath while the rest of her family slowly drops off to sleep. Judy Constantinides observed in *School Library Journal* that "this joyful book has a gently humorous text and vibrant illustrations that are full of fun. Morgan's red-headed Julia is a charmer." *Booklist* critic Deborah Abbott concluded that "Morgan's deft watercolor illustrations capture the bathroom scenes with bubbles galore, apt facial expressions, and a comfortable gentleness." Julia makes an encore appearance in *I'm the Boss!*, in which she attempts to boss her older and younger sisters by dressing up in her mother's clothes. "Morgan's uncluttered watercolor illustrations depict Julia and her family in rosy hues," remarked Kathleen Odean in *School Library Journal*, "but clearly and humorously convey the cross looks, pouts, and self-

satisfied smiles on the children's faces." *Booklist*'s Stephanie Zvirin remarked that "Morgan's crisp, lively, colorful illustrations capture the goings-on with charm and good humor."

Animals are at the center of three further Morgan-illustrated titles, *Hannah and Jack*, *Where Do Bears Sleep?*, and *Our Puppies Are Growing*. In the first title, written by Mary Nethery, Hannah cannot be separated from her beloved cat, Jack. But when Hannah's family goes to visit grandma, she must leave Jack behind and becomes heartbroken. Encouraged by her grandmother, Hannah includes Jack in the vacation by sending him postcards and buying him a present before returning home and giving him a party. Hanna B. Zeiger concluded in *Horn Book* that readers "will enjoy both the sweet watercolor and gouache illustrations of a child and loved pet and the fact that Hanna is able to solve her problems independently," while Kathy Mitchell, writing in *School Library Journal*, complimented the "vivid watercolor and gouache illustrations" which "are appealing and match the story line quite nicely."

Barbara Shook Hazen's *Where Do Bear's Sleep?* is a newly illustrated version of her popular 1970 title, a bedtime tale told in rhyme. Martha Topol, writing in *School Library Journal*, felt that the "illustrations add

Hannah misses her cat, Jack, when she stays with Grandma but finds a way to keep in touch. (From Hannah and Jack, *written by Mary Nethery and illustrated by Morgan.*)

Rosie likes to cuddle with Mama in Morgan's self-illustrated **Gentle Rosie.**

considerably to the success" of the new edition. "Each focused watercolor emanates serenity and warmth. They bring the poem full circle." *Our Puppies Are Growing,* written by Carolyn Otto, is part of the "Lets-Read-and-Find-Out" science series from HarperCollins, part story, part fact. The information on dogs is presented through a preschooler whose dog gives birth to seven puppies and now must learn how to care for each new addition. Hazel Rochman noted in *Booklist* that the "physicalness of the words is echoed in the bright line-and-watercolor pictures that show the child and her family taking care of the puppies." *School Library Journal* contributor Jane Claes remarked that "[b]right, pleasant illustrations accompany the text, giving the book a happy, cozy look."

This "happy, cozy look" is something Morgan carries over into her self-illustrated books as well. In the course of a handful of solo efforts, Morgan has established a unique and distinct appearance for her work, employing primarily watercolors along with minimal text. Her cameo-like presentations generally have a calmness to them, as well as a reassuring warmth and gentleness.

One of Morgan's most popular titles, *Benjamin's Bugs,* deals with a couple of cuddly porcupines, Benjamin and his mother, Mama Porcupine, as they share a day in the meadow. Benjamin's adventures are domestic: he tastes a dandelion, talks to an ant, and pays close attention to crickets and worms. Eventually when he makes his way up a tree, Mama is there to help him get back down. Close upon this, he falls into a pond, and once again

Mama is there to rescue him. At the end of the day, Benjamin and his mother go home where he takes a bath, has a snack, and climbs into bed with a nighttime story from Mama. Calling this book a "reassuring story," *School Library Journal* critic Nancy Seiner noted that the "[i]llustrations appear in attractive cameos of predominantly blue and green watercolors" and even the endpapers "are designed for enjoyment." A *Publishers Weekly* reviewer observed that "Morgan takes the sort of small-scale activities that define a preschooler's day and weaves them into a gently reassuring story, rounded out by winsome watercolors of the chubby, fetching porcupine cub and his mother."

Morgan has also created a winning mouse character, Rosie, in a series of paper-over-board books. The toddler mouse, who was dubbed "Charming" by a *Publishers Weekly* critic, displays various sides of her personality in matching books. In *Gentle Rosie* she tickles a caterpillar and gives her baby brother a smooch. But when her wild side kicks in, Rosie can be a terror, finger painting all over the place and splashing the bath water. Playing with her food is another naughty habit. "Each book provides six or seven examples of Rosie's behavior," explained the *Publishers Weekly* reviewer, "with sunny-bright artwork and pastel polka-dot or gingham borders against a white background." Morgan shows other sides of Rosie in *Patient Rosie* and *Curious Rosie,* and has also created a set of finger puppets to accompany the books. "Morgan creates an affable heroine who has a healthy measure of spunk," concluded the *Publishers Weekly* contributor.

From bloomer-wearing feminists to plucky adolescent mice, Morgan has employed her warm and cheerful palette to enriching the world of picture books. Known for her humor and soft appealing line, she has rapidly become a popular illustrator as well as an author-illustrator of note.

Works Cited

Abbott, Deborah, review of *Asleep in a Heap, Booklist,* November 15, 1993, p. 634.

Review of *Benjamin's Bugs, Publishers Weekly,* February 14, 1994, p. 87.

Review of *Buba Leah and Her Paper Children, Publishers Weekly,* July 25, 1991, p. 53.

Bush, Margaret A., review of *Bloomers!, Horn Book,* September-October, 1993, pp. 616-17.

Claes, Jane, review of *Our Puppies Are Growing, School Library Journal,* July, 1999, p. 88.

Constantinides, Judy, review of *Asleep in a Heap, School Library Journal,* January, 1994, pp. 101-02.

Review of *Gentle Rosie* and *Wild Rosie, Publishers Weekly,* June 28, 1999, p. 77.

Greengrass, Linda, review of *Bloomers!, School Library Journal,* September, 1993, p. 222.

Review of *Jake Baked the Cake, Publishers Weekly,* February 23, 1990, p. 216.

Kaminow, Susan, review of *Buba Leah and Her Paper Children, School Library Journal,* January, 1992, p. 97.

Mandel, Ellen, review of *Buba Leah and Her Paper Children, Booklist,* January 1, 1992, p. 835.

McGrath, Joan, review of *Jake Baked the Cake, School Library Journal,* April, 1990, p. 91.

Mitchell, Kathy, review of *Hannah and Jack, School Library Journal,* March, 1996, p. 179.

Review of *Mommies, Publishers Weekly,* May 6, 1996, p. 79.

Odean, Kathleen, review of *I'm the Boss!, School Library Journal,* July, 1994, p. 92.

Rochman, Hazel, review of *Our Puppies Are Growing, Booklist,* November 1, 1999, p. 88.

Seiner, Nancy, review of *Benjamin's Bugs, School Library Journal,* June, 1994, p. 111.

Topol, Martha, review of *Where Do Bears Sleep?, School Library Journal,* June, 1998, pp. 108-09.

Watson, Elizabeth, review of *Jake Baked the Cake, Horn Book,* May-June, 1990, p. 324.

Wicher, Linda, review of *Hugs* and *Kisses, School Library Journal,* January, 1993, p. 82.

Zeiger, Hanna B., review of *Hannah and Jack, Horn Book,* July-August, 1996, p. 453.

Zvirin, Stephanie, review of *I'm the Boss!, Booklist,* May 1, 1994, p. 1610.

For More Information See

PERIODICALS

Booklist, August, 1993, p. 2064; May 1, 1996, pp. 1512-13; June 1 & 15, 1996, p. 1736.

Publishers Weekly, December 14, 1992, p. 55; July 12, 1993, p. 80; September 20, 1993, p. 31.

School Library Journal, July, 1996, p. 70; August, 1999, p. 140.*

—Sketch by J. Sydney Jones

MORGAN, Wendy
See STAUB, Wendy Corsi

*   *   *

MORGAN-VANROYEN, Mary
See MORGAN, Mary

*   *   *

MORNINGSTAR, Mildred (Whaley) 1912-1997

OBITUARY NOTICE—See index for *SATA* sketch: Born June 18, 1912, in Chicago, IL; died February 23, 1997, in Fort Collins, CO. Freelance writer and editor. Mildred Morningstar was a freelance writer and editor for most of her life, although she was also employed variously as a public schoolteacher, as a writer for the Conservative Baptist Foreign Mission Society in Wheaton, as an editor for Baptist Publications, and as a writer and editor for Accent Books in Lakewood, Colorado. Her first book was *Reaching Children* (1944), followed by nearly two dozen additional titles written mostly for the children's market, including *Christian Nursery Rhymes* (1947), *Billy Listens* (1954), and *The Bible Says* (1960). Her last book was *Danger at the Sheep Ranch* (1983). She was also the editor of various church school materials for Baptist Publications, and the author of a monthly column for women in *Good News Broadcaster,* in addition to numerous articles contributed to such periodicals as *Baby Talk, His, Success, My Counselor, Hi-Time,* and *Pastors' Manual,* among others. She also organized and trained teachers and directed summer programs for children.

—Obituary by Robert Reginald and Mary A. Burgess

O

Autobiography Feature

Sheldon Oberman

1949-

WANDERING AND WONDERING

The creative spirit loves to wander and wonder. Yet it also has a goal: to create something wonderful. That's how it is with the creative people I have known: writers, actors, artists, designers, architects, directors. That's how it's been with me, writing books, plays, and songs, directing theater and film, and performing as a storyteller. I feel most alive when my imagination is at play or at work, when I can experience something in a new way or I can create something new and interesting.

I feel lucky to be able to do this. I've known many people with great talent and determination, but for one reason or another, things didn't work out.

Luck is peculiar, and sometimes you don't know when you are lucky or unlucky. When I was young, I would not have thought there was anything fortunate about being poor or being in a minority group or being alone so much of the time. Yet those very things that seemed to be disadvantages turned out to be great assets; they helped to shape me as a writer.

I was born in 1949 in Winnipeg, Canada, where my parents had a small clothing store in the city's immigrant North End. We lived above the store overlooking Main Street. The building was old and shabby with a cranky coal furnace and not enough hot water for a bath on Saturday night. My parents had to take in a boarder, Bert, a fifty-year-old bus driver, to help pay the rent. Bert and I shared one small bedroom with bunk beds. I got the top one. My parents didn't have a car—I travelled by bus or by sitting on my dad's handlebars as he rode me on his bike. There were no vacations or summer camp or fancy birthday parties. Those things took spare time and spare money; my parents had neither.

No one around us was any better off, so by comparison, my life felt normal. In fact, the neighbours considered us well off since we "owned" a business. What my parents actually owned was a pile of debts which they worked sixty hours a week to keep from getting worse.

Still, we had decent clothes and decent food. Friday night we would eat at the Good Earth Chinese Restaurant across the street, and on Saturday after they shut the store, we'd go to the movies. Best of all, we had a good time together, so it didn't matter that some people whom we had never even met had much more money than we did.

Of course, my parents wanted me to have a better life, but that didn't mean being rich—it meant getting a good education so I could find work that was fulfilling and useful in the world.

As I grew older and compared myself to others beyond our neighbourhood, I realized how poor we actually were. Yet even then I understood that our poverty was not the "destructive" kind; it was not inescapable or demeaning. I was growing up in the fifties and sixties, a time of increasing opportunities. I could look beyond the present to a promising future; it would just take work.

That was no problem—I had learned how to work. When I was an infant my mother kept me in a bassinet beside the cash register—I was already part of the business. I grew up helping out in the store, and later when we had a coffee shop, I worked there, too. Much of our family time was spent working together, though I must admit that my favourite chore was done in solitude—I'd peel potatoes for an hour or more each day, mulling and musing and making French fries for the coffee shop. Some people distance themselves from their work and concentrate on other parts of their life. For me, work has always been an essential part

Sheldon Oberman

of who I am, and fortunately, my work generally has been rewarding.

I grew up alone as an only child with no other children nearby, but I wasn't lonely in the way some people get when they are separated from others. I was used to being alone and learned to enjoy my own company and my own thoughts. I'd take pleasure looking out my parents' store window with its faded mannequins, watching the people passing by on Main Street. I'd hang about the other stores or wander the back lanes meeting the odd characters of the neighbourhood. I'd sit on the narrow stairs that led up to our apartment and I'd daydream, travelling even further through my imagination.

My World of Books

Soon, books offered me even better fantasies than my own; after all, they were created by professional dreamers with much more experience. The public library introduced me to Mark Twain, Jules Verne, Alexandre Dumas, Robert Service, Lewis Carroll, Robert Louis Stevenson, and Enid Blyton, great storytellers one and all. The drugstore teamed me up with Superman and Batman. The supermarket

supplied the first books I ever owned, *The Golden Book Encyclopedia*. I bought one volume each week with my allowance. They were a wonderful hodgepodge of exotic facts and colorful pictures—the perfect material for daydreams. I was alone, but I had myself and I had books.

Of course, I didn't actually share much in common with the heroes of my books. Most of them were rich and upper-class with many noble companions. If they were poor, they were British, French, or American poor. They weren't Canadian and they certainly weren't Jewish.

I felt different from my classmates, too. Occasionally someone made me feel badly about being "a Jew," though it seldom happened openly. I learned about the Holocaust and about earlier persecutions such as the ones in Russia that killed my great grandparents and others in our family. Even the stories of the Bible ended with the destruction of ancient Israel and the Jewish people expelled. The more I learned the history of my people, the more vulnerable I felt. I had wanted to be a hero, but my Jewishness seemed to be telling me that I was fated to be a victim.

I didn't like the many rules of Judaism, either, like keeping kosher and going to synagogue. I was glad my parents weren't observant; in fact they used the excuse of our gentile boarder to have a Christmas tree. I suppose Christmas was a good reason for us to celebrate; it was a big event in the store—the Christmas shoppers paid our bills.

I accepted being poor and being alone, but it was harder to accept being Jewish. The only attraction I felt for it was through my grandfather, a gentle, loving man who seldom spoke yet had great wisdom. He became the spirit of my heritage, and after he died I felt him offering that heritage to me in the form of an heirloom. I put his gift aside and forgot about it for many years. But more of that later.

Many things that might seem like disadvantages turned out to be a great help in making me a writer. Being alone taught me how to use my imagination and it made me a friend who will be with me as long as I live: my own true self. What I learned from being poor is worth more than money can buy. And when I did accept my heritage, I realized the greatness of my own people, not only of the famous like King Solomon, Elijah, and the wonder-working Ba'al Shem Tov, but also the greatness of ordinary people with extraordinary hearts and spirits, an inspiration for endless stories.

My Father, the Champ

My parents had their own extraordinary qualities. They displayed their creativity most evenings at the supper table through some surprising insight or a well-told tale. My mother was the sharp observer. My father was the storyteller. She'd describe fascinating things about the people she met each day, things that even they might not have realized. He could turn a simple event into a hilarious story.

My dad had been a boxing instructor in the army and a weight-lifting champ as well, though he was a gentle, peace-loving man like his father. Yet it was impossible for either him or his father to find any peace in their family. Dad's brothers and sisters were an extraordinary group: some were bootleggers and gamblers, others were eccentric artists, one was a religious visionary; all of them were intense and loud.

Dad helped out in the family business, Obie's Steam Bath, where the locals came to strip, sweat, and play poker. He'd stay up late into the night as the regulars joked, bragged, and consumed surprising amounts of herring, corned beef, and rye whisky. He'd clean up, then catch some sleep and hurry to his day job loading trucks and carrying huge crates up flights of stairs.

My mom was an impulsive young woman from small-town Saskatchewan. She had won a beauty contest but also earned the highest marks in the high school provincial exams. Her parents decided that it wasn't proper for her to go to university; she should stay home and help in the store. Instead, she ran off to the big city. She met Dad, and six weeks later they were married. The day after their honeymoon, they opened Dobie's Style Shoppe on Main Street.

I wrote about that street in *This Business with Elijah,* a literary book of connected short stories centered on a ten-year-old boy, Danny Stein. His world is based on mine, and his stories intertwine with those of the street's many colorful characters.

I modelled two characters on my father, though they became quite different as they developed. One is the muscled storekeeper who is a total loss trying to sell women certain "delicate" items of clothing. The other runs a coffee shop.

My dad's actual coffee shop was a sixties-style diner, a hangout for tough kids who played the pinball and jukebox. Not a high-class crowd, their idea of a hot meal was French fries with gravy. A sophisticated drink to them was a Mickey of lemon gin they'd keep hidden in the men's toilet tank.

Still, they had remarkable talents, especially with their hands. My job was to wash dishes and to watch them so no one skipped out on a bill or stole anything on the way out. But quick hands can also be open hands, and they were always ready to help their own. Every so often some couple's relationship shocked everyone by a sudden swerve into lawful wedlock. But it was no shock to see some grinning bride and groom still in tuxedo and long, lacy gown stop off for burgers between their wedding and reception. One time the gang welcomed a wedding couple with stunning gifts of silverware and crystal. For one half hour, my dad's café looked more like Ben Moss Jewellers (the unfortunate store where they did their shoplifting).

My book looks closer and harder at one of those teenagers. Pop, the coffee shop owner, is trying to reach a kid who is both troubled and in trouble, a kid who needs to be tough to survive but also needs someone to care about him. Pop is so entangled by his own needs and problems that he fumbles his chance to help. Everything he's done turns sour, and they become bitter enemies. Pop is so upset that he abandons the coffee shop, feeling as trapped and hopeless as the boy he tried to rescue. It's a sad story, like the lives of many real people whom I knew all too well.

My Mother, the Psychic

I used my mother as a model for Danny's mother. However, I left out one part that eventually took my real mother out of the store and into a very different world.

Mom was and still is very psychic. She'd wake up with some dream or another. "A man means number two," she'd say. "A desk means four." She'd rush off to bingo to play the lucky numbers. Often enough, she'd bring back a new radio or toaster.

Her special ability wasn't something she discussed. Mom grew up in Kamsack, Saskatchewan, which was much like an uprooted Eastern European village. Few townsfolk scoffed at psychic phenomena, many accepted it completely. As witchcraft.

Her parents suspected she had the "gift." So when my mother, at ten years old, woke up late at night crying that the boarding house across town was burning, her parents listened. They knocked at the dark and silent building. A moment later they heard shouts of "Smoke! Fire!" Sure enough, someone who had drunk too much had fallen asleep with a burning cigarette. The boarding house was saved, but Mom's reward was a stern lecture. She had to promise to block out those disturbing thoughts.

She tried to keep such thoughts at a distance for many years until she finally found someone who understood her. That was Tamarra—a huge, boisterous, irrepressible woman who had learned the craft of the seer in Russia a half century before. We never had a family doctor, but we always had Tamarra, our family fortune teller. She taught

"My dad, Allan Oberman, lifting a 220-pound army friend."

Mom how to manage her powers, and when Tamarra died, she gave Mom a blessing. It was not the sort of blessing that could be recorded in words; instead, it registered in psychic voltage. Mom's apprenticeship was over.

She set up business in her home, letting in immigrants, judges, prostitutes, social workers, stockbrokers, healers and dealers, cops and robbers. They all sat side by side on her living room couch, waiting to get to her kitchen table where their futures would be unfolded in her comforting hands.

Murderers, too. And potential murderers, wanting to know: "Can I get away with it?" "Yes," she told one, "until they do the autopsy." Or the tearful wife: "My husband's terribly sick. How much longer has he got to live?" "He'll get better," Mom answered. "He'll last another ten years. Maybe twelve." The woman stood up with a scowl, threw down her money, and stomped out. You can't please them all.

Mom has finally had to slow down. When the manager of the Marlborough, a grand old hotel, asked her to find their resident ghost, she refused. "Too many stairs to climb," she said. She might have liked to train one of us to take over, but psychic reading hasn't become a family business. Whatever "visions" I receive all turn to images for my stories, though certainly some of my tales have mystical elements. My older son, Adam, who has the strongest "gift," became a mathematician. Go figure.

Of all my mother's psychic accomplishments, our favourite is the reading she gave a woman some twelve years ago. Mom saw an "S" in her cup and accurately described the character of the man the woman was soon destined to meet. But Mom couldn't see his face or any details of his life. Four weeks later, the woman met the man whose name began with "S." She didn't mention the reading; he didn't tell her about his mother, the psychic reader. It eventually came out, well before the two of them, Lisa Dveris and I, were married. It's what we call Our Psychic Connection.

An Ancient Guide

There is one other major character to acknowledge from that book, though he had no single model. Mr. Werner is the caretaker whom Danny discovers in the building's basement workshop. Mr. Werner is an old Jewish immigrant who can tell the ancient mystical tales of their people and his own thrilling stories of his life in the Old Country and in this New Country.

The old man and the boy form a special friendship that serves them both. Danny is hungry to learn about heroes and the ways of the world, tales to prepare him for his future. Old Werner needs to tell his stories so he can gather the precious moments of his past and make some final sense of his long life:

I'd visit Mr. Werner often, stirring about his worktable as he drifted through his memories. Perhaps my visits changed him, woke him up, because his stories grew more lively. He did, too, as if he'd brushed himself off and got back to the work of living once again.

He guided me through my family's Passover seder, he taught me how to work with my hands and with my head.

He started me dreaming of another world, woven by his memories and folktales, a world greater than any in my comic books. I'd tell him things, as well, chattering about my family and school; neither of us needing the other to listen very carefully.

One time I found that I'd planed the end of a two-by-four into a paper-thin wedge. I'd been daydreaming, had lost the wood and then lost the daydream. Another time, I shuffled down the stairs, aching from an insult. Werner was working on a padlock. I grabbed a scrap of lumber and hammered it with larger and larger nails until I split the wood. I tossed the broken pieces, then hunched over a coffee tin of loose nuts and bolts to sort and match. All this time not a word was spoken, not a look exchanged. As I threaded pairs of nuts and bolts, I barked out my story.

I'd been watching two pigeons on a branch outside my classroom window. Their throats were glazed with purple, their heads were bobbing in a mystery of need as they jostled one another toward the end of the branch which bowed to their weight and tapped against the glass. It was golden in the sun, just like Elijah's magic branch. Mr. Werner had told me how the spirit of the Prophet Elijah gave the Ba'al Shem Tov a branch from a wonder tree on Mount Carmel. The Ba'al Shem Tov carved it into a walking stick to call down miracles. When the Ba'al Shem's great deeds were all completed, Elijah took it back, returning it to the wonder tree to become a living branch again. So I watched in awe as a golden branch tapped against the classroom window, offering itself to me.

Until the laughter of my classmates blew my fantasy apart. My name was shouted. Thirty faces cooed, hooted, and above them all was Mrs. Maitland commanding me to copy out a lesson all through recess.

"It wasn't fair," I complained to Mr. Werner. "I knew what she was teaching. She was picking on me."

"Did you explain about the branch?" he asked.

"Huh! What does she care? She's got no time for stories."

"Yah," he said. "Grownups got no time. But you got time for branches. And for comic books. And even to build and break with nails."

I felt my throat tighten. I lowered my head to the hurt that was rooting in my chest.

"And me, I'm just the same," Mr. Werner said. "I got time to free a lock that doesn't even have a key—a lock to shut a workshop that's got nothing anyone would want to steal." His hand, rough as bark, rubbed across my cheek and came to rest upon my shoulder. "It's not so bad," he assured me. "We can't be standing at attention all day long. A boy has got to build his hopes and dreams. And old men have lots of memories that need putting into place."

For a long moment we said nothing, we thought nothing and felt no differences between us. Though we worked and told our stories each for different ends, this dreamy silence

Author's mother, Dorothy Stein Oberman, at work in her kitchen, 1985.

from which all our stories seemed to come, made the two of us one and the same.

(from *This Business with Elijah*, p. 174)

A Great Teacher

One of my greatest teachers was not a teacher at all, at least not a schoolteacher. And I was probably the only student he ever had.

Mr. Freedman was a butcher at Omnitsky's Kosher Meats, down the street from our store. He was a short, stout, and homely man. He had a bad lisp and glasses as thick as Coke bottles. Yet he could walk confidently into a room, face an audience, and hold their attention with a convincing and entertaining speech.

My mother decided that if Mr. Freedman could overcome his obvious handicaps, he could certainly teach me how to overcome mine. I was merely awkward, self-conscious, and lacking basic social skills, typical afflictions of a thirteen-year-old, especially a "loner."

Mr. Freedman had me write and memorize a five-minute speech and present it to him in his living room. He was tremendously impressed. He then showed me how to speak, how to pause, and how to use my hands. The next week I returned with a better speech and a better presentation. Again, he was tremendously impressed and taught me with even more techniques. I did about fifteen speeches before he judged me ready for the next level. He

took me downtown to the Toastmasters Club, his public speaking group. He had me speak before a group of professionals and business people. All of them were tremendously unimpressed. After all, I was just a kid. Mr. Freedman kept training me until even those grouchy Toastmasters accepted me with their grudging applause.

My parents taught me a love of creativity. Books inspired me with exciting stories and ideas. Mr. Freedman gave me my voice.

Fast Talk

Once I learned how to get a group's attention, I did it every chance I got. I became a major headache to my teachers. Detentions didn't stop me; in fact I set a school record—forty-five detentions from my geography teacher alone. My classmates saw me as a useful mouthpiece and elected me class president—it was my job to talk the teachers out of as much work as I could.

Being a good talker also got me my first well-paid summer job. At fifteen, I became a door-to-door salesman selling Watkins products—spices, vitamins, cosmetics, ointments, cleansers, and a catalogue full of high-quality household items "which you (sir or madam) and your family simply won't want to do without especially after allowing me to present you with these free samples of Watkins shampoo and conditioner while I show you some particularly fine products which, by the way, are presently on sale—half price!" And so I talked, grinned, and gestured on countless doorsteps, turning empty talk into solid money—more dollars an hour than either of my parents was making. It was pretty heady stuff for a kid off Main Street.

I kept talking after work as well, making friends and acquaintances as I hung around the pool hall or outside the local café, telling stories and cracking jokes. All I did was speak my magic words, and a whole new world opened up. Around midnight, I'd join the crowd gathering in the parking lot behind the café. My pals and I would trade wisecracks while others, less verbal, traded blows. It was puberty with a punch or punch line. I can't imagine anything I'd rather have been doing.

By the second summer, the power of the gab was losing its appeal. I was still making a ridiculous amount of money and even getting awards from the company for selling so much. My family was still impressed, telling everybody how I was so successful. People said I should become a businessman or lawyer, but something felt wrong.

I felt I was misusing what I'd been taught by Mr. Freedman. Selling door to door was different from making speeches. It wasn't presenting an insightful opinion or a clever story. It was fast talk. I was conning people, getting them to buy overpriced goods that they often didn't need or couldn't afford. The more "successful" I got at it, the worse I felt.

It all came to a head in one bizarre incident when I was demonstrating an air freshener to a man and I accidently sprayed it in his eyes. As he stumbled about, his eyes stinging, I grabbed a tin of Watkins Medicated Ointment and tried to sell it to him. It still took me half a day to realize what a self-centered, predatory jerk I had become. I quit. I'd had enough of fast talk.

A Different Track

The next summer I took a job, for a third of the pay, as a pantryman on the CPR Transcontinental, washing dishes in a steaming kitchen sixteen hours a day as the train rattled and rolled between Winnipeg and Vancouver. It was exhausting work, but I was glad to be a "worker" doing hard honest labour with my hands instead of my mouth. Even if I tried to talk, I couldn't—the kitchen was too noisy and too busy. Of course, the downside was that I felt like an insignificant cog in a hot, greasy, and relentless machine.

Feeling insignificant was an appropriate preparation for the last years of high school. I had always been an ambitious student, but St. Johns, my big high school, seemed like an anonymous storage center for adolescents who were too young for the work force and too old to be left with their parents. We were packed forty to a room and kept busy by teachers who were, except for the memorable few, too burned out to make any special effort. So I didn't either. I got lazy and moody, shifting between being a passive goof-off and an irritating goof.

My only creative effort was in pulling pranks. Once during a hideously boring school operetta, *Die Fledermaus,* I crashed a scene in a gorilla costume (a rather crude form of theatrical criticism). The chorus of girls in courtly gowns scattered with an off-key scream, their fans aflutter. I climbed a table, beat my chest, and howled, sounding like a cross between an adolescent ape and an apelike adolescent. My two accomplices then chased me through the audience yelling, "Tonka has escaped!" I was only saved from expulsion by the school president, who brought me onstage at the end of the play, pulled off my gorilla head, and had me bow to the audience. I received such a huge ovation that our purple-faced principal couldn't punish me. The best part was that my teachers had unwittingly paid the rental of my costume. I had collected the money from them for a "special presentation" on closing night.

Being a wise guy was better than being a zombie, but it didn't help me pass my courses. I failed math and French and almost the whole year. After summer school I had an even greater shock, one that pushed me completely out of my adolescence.

I was working as a second cook in the day-coach diner. The train was snaking up a mountain pass in the Canadian Rockies. At 7 a.m. I made my way through the day coaches calling out that breakfast was being served. Most people were awake waiting for the call, and as I returned to the kitchen they crowded into the diner and began to order. Suddenly the whole train jolted. We just managed to steady the tall urn of hot coffee before it spilled over us. A couple more jolts and the train ground to a halt. The chef and I figured the engine had hit a moose, but it was far worse.

A six-ton boulder had rolled off the mountain. It hit the train, derailing six of the train cars. A day coach took the hardest blow—it was unrecognizable, a gaping wreck of metal and glass with half the seats torn away. When the boulder hit, the engineer had sped up and manoeuvered so the cars derailed against the mountain wall. Otherwise they would have fallen over the edge into the river six hundred feet below and would have pulled the entire train down with them.

"Dad and I outside the store."

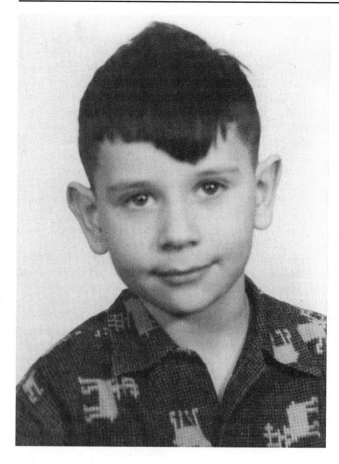

Sheldon at nine.

We rushed about getting first-aid supplies for the injured. Luckily most people had left the day coach when I made the call for breakfast, except for a university student who had stayed behind to sleep a little longer. They found her body far down the tracks. I had walked through that coach only minutes before the boulder hit. As my shock wore off, I realized how close I had been to death.

Helicopters came for the injured, and the passengers were evacuated by a relief train. As we waited our turn, I sat at a counter in the diner writing to a friend, describing the events and my feelings as fully as I could. It was my first truly serious writing. I had written letters to amuse some friends and assignments to please my teachers, but this was different. I was writing to express what I could not say aloud, feelings and thoughts that grew and deepened as I set them on the page. I never mailed it, and to this day I have never felt the need to read it. The important thing was that I had found the heart to write it.

Hippie Days

I could no longer be a wise guy or a goof-off. I entered university with a serious purpose—to learn what was true and important. I read the great writers and philosophers. I studied the best minds of the ages. I loved university and the people I met there. Many of them, like myself, wanted more than just a degree that would lead to a job. They wanted knowledge, and that meant a full awareness of themselves and their world. I learned as much

from them as from my books and my professors, and I am still grateful for their friendships.

We were the Baby Boomers, born after World War Two ended when our parents could finally settle down, have children, and get to work. The country became so prosperous that by the time we graduated high school, universities were affordable and easy to enter. We didn't have to work much—summer paid enough for the rest of the year, including tuition. So there was no rush to get into a career or to get a degree, no rush to grow up at all. We were the Hippies.

We were, however, in a rush to experience the world. That summer after first year university I bought a backpack at Army Surplus and told my mother that I was heading to Toronto, thirteen hundred miles east. Maybe I'd find a job there. Or something. She told my father, and he pretended not to know because he had no idea what to say or do about it. I was so eager to get going that I slipped out of the apartment at 6 a.m. and hurried across Main Street to hitchhike out of town. It was far too early; the street was completely deserted. Finally I spotted my first car and stuck out my thumb. It was a police cruiser.

The officer stopped and asked, "Where are you headed, son?"

"Toronto," I answered.

"That's an awful long way," he said. "Where you coming from?"

"Across the street." I pointed to the apartment over our store.

"You haven't got very far, have you?" he laughed. He shook his head as he drove off.

But I did get far. I slept in a couple of pretty rough places on the way, and I met my share of strange characters, but I made it to Toronto. That was the summer of Woodstock.

Suddenly I was twenty, living on my own, making my own rules. So was everyone else I met. There were so many people my age that we seemed to have our own separate world. We went to coffeehouses to hear old folk songs and new songs of protest. We talked late into the night in communal houses lit by candles and musty with incense.

We discovered books like *Catcher in the Rye, On the Road, Catch-22,* and *One Flew over the Cuckoo's Nest,* and music by the Beatles and the Rolling Stones, Joni Mitchell, Bob Dylan, and Leonard Cohen. We saw strange movies like *Harold and Maude, Easy Rider, Alice's Restaurant, 2001, Man from La Mancha*—all telling us to Dream the Impossible Dream and sometimes to Live Impossibly Bizarre Dreams. A new attitude was forming. Be free and don't trust anyone to tell you how to think or act, especially no one in authority.

It was then that I began to write a journal, not a diary of events as much as a record of my thoughts and feelings. I wrote it in a black notebook that I carried in my back pocket. I still keep it these thirty years later, though now I type it into a notebook computer that I carry in my satchel.

Travels Abroad

I needed to experience more of the world, so in 1970 after second year university I went travelling for a year. I had always imagined travelling through Europe in a storybook sort of way. Suddenly I was heading there with a few friends whom I'd talked into coming as if it was a party or a camping trip. When we landed in London we found the streets crowded with other young travellers. It was as if the same message had relayed through all our minds at the same time—DROP EVERYTHING. BUY A PLANE TICKET. HEAD TO EUROPE. It helped that a flight to Europe was only one hundred dollars one way—about a week's wages.

We were totally unprepared. We had hiking boots, army ponchos, water canteens, and Swiss Army knives as if we were exploring the Canadian woodlands, not the London subway system and the British Museum.

Soon we all went our own ways, following separate fantasies. Mine took me hitchhiking through the British Isles, up to Holland, and then through Belgium, France, and into Spain. By early winter I was in Morocco heading further south on the Marrakesh Express.

I knew almost nothing about Morocco. I was drawn there by a handful of beads. I'd seen them one night by firelight while I was camping on a beach in Belgium next to an old German bunker. An Irish fellow dressed in motorcycle leathers asked if he could bed down beside my fire. He was returning from North Africa, and he opened a leather case to show me a treasure he'd found there—"pierres du Mauritania" he called them. Legend had it that they were made by God in the Sahara Desert. Actually they came to Morocco by camel caravan from Mauritania where they had been crafted by some secret process for over two thousand years. Those mysterious and lovely beads fired my imagination. I headed for Morocco.

Marrakesh is an exotic and ancient walled city. No more hiking boots and army ponchos, I switched to sandals and a jloba—the hooded robe used for protection from the harsh sun. I made friends with young merchants in the marketplace and taught them English. They taught me Arabic and showed me a Morocco most foreigners never saw.

My adventures had far harsher edges and harder landings than in my childhood storybooks. The shock of a different culture left me disoriented. I lost the little common sense I had and became quite reckless. I ended up living in a mud hut village, and while exploring some old ruin in the desert I was attacked by a pack of dogs. I fought them off, but one bite drew blood and I had to get shots for rabies. A UNICEF post gave me the long needles, thicker than pencil leads, which were injected into my liver for the next sixteen days. It was a gruelling time, and the serum affected my mind as if I really was touched by animal madness.

I moved in with a pack of hippies by the sea and spent those days and nights in tormented dreams. All the ugliness and beauty of Morocco swirled in my thoughts: the beggars and thieves; the rats and filth; the haunting chime of camel bells and wail of the muezzin praying from his minaret; the strange faces of the natives who didn't share your language, your beliefs, or even understand how you think or act; the Blue Men of the Sahara stained by dye; the women of Agadir so covered in white sheets and veils that they seemed like clouds drifting in the streets; the fire-eaters, snake charmers, acrobats, and African dancers of the marketplace; the disfigured waiter who served me sweet tea in glasses filled with fresh mint leaves and hovering bees; the Arab preacher who stopped me in a narrow street, stern

as Moses with one hand pointing up to heaven and the other stretched out for money. And my lovely beads, the "pierres du Mauritania" that I had finally found; I gripped them as tightly as I could through those long days and nights of illness.

On the day of my last injections I heard that two Austrians with a Volkswagen bus were leaving for Spain. I jumped in and told them that I was leaving with them, whether they wanted me or not. I had followed my fantasies so far and so naively that I stumbled into danger and into the dark side of the imagination. Others were even less fortunate. I saw some have serious breakdowns or waste away or die through some foolish accident. Some simply disappeared, no one knew where.

I smartened up, but I still wasn't very smart. I got stuck in a blizzard for three days in the mountains of Yugoslavia wearing my jloba because I had given away my coat. When the blinding storm cleared, we found our van in the snow where we had given up pushing it. We had unknowingly pushed it off the mountain road to the very brink of a deadly drop. Another time I landed in Cypress having mixed it up with Crete, where I had hoped to swim and sun on some exotic beach. Instead I spent the next few days with UN soldiers who were grimly guarding it from civil war.

Eventually I got to Israel and volunteered on a farm kibbutz. It was all orange groves and laughter, a time of healing, strengthening, making friends and exploring the land of the Bible. For all the political trouble in that country, I was never in a place where I felt so welcome. I was not a stranger in that land.

Settling Back

When I returned home, ten months and twenty countries later, so much had changed. In me. My parents'

"At twelve with my dog, Spotty, and Bert, who boarded with us."

Hitchhiking through Turkey, 1971.

A Creative Return

I did have some regret about becoming so responsible so abruptly. When I was a child I would think about how I would someday have to give up my childhood and turn into one of those large, moody creatures called adults and how I would forget what it was like to be a child. So I promised myself that somehow I would make myself remember, I would make everybody remember. Of course, I got caught up in my needs and obligations and stuck in many new roles: teacher, parent, husband, home owner, taxpayer, mortgagee. And I forgot.

To my surprise, I was led back to childhood by my own children. My son, Adam, and my daughter, Mira, would ask me to tell them stories, especially stories about me as a child. They loved that, of course. It put me on their level. Soon I began making up stories and songs at bedtime, and we were sharing the same childlike sense of delight at a good tale.

One of their favourites was a rhyming story about a boy who rode out late at night and was surprised by a fearful creature:

"I'm a witch, John R. W., a horrible witch!
Cackle and hackle and snaffley snitch!
Watch my face turn all green and my ugly nose
  twitch!
Cackle and hackle and snaffley snitch!
I can turn to a toad and make your skin itch!
Cackle and hackle and snaffley snitch!"
Said John Russell Watkins, "Why you don't scare me.
You're as little and silly and sad as can be.
And I've seen all those tricks while watching TV."
And rode off, clipidy clop, clop clop.

A ghost and troll have no better luck scaring John. Finally all three creatures burst into tears as they beg him:

"Please pretend to be scared. Please could you try?"
"No!" said John R. W., "That would be a lie!"
And he rode off, clipidy clop, clipidy clop
He rode off, clipidy clop, clipidy clop.

I gave a copy to my friend Fred Penner, whom I had met when we were both acting in plays. He was starting out as a children's entertainer, so I hoped he could give me tips about writing for children and a bit of encouragement. Instead he told me he was planning a children's album and asked if he could use my poem. What an encouragement! Fred Penner and I went on to create many poems and songs for his albums and then for his national TV show.

One of the narrative poems led to my first children's book, *Julie Gerond and the Polka Dot Pony,* about a girl who loves riding on a merry-go-round despite the nasty and peculiar woman who runs it. Julie discovers that her favourite wooden pony is actually a real pony who has been bewitched:

"I am caught in this circle. I am stuck on this pole.
And unless I touch earth, ever round I must go!"

home felt smaller; my family and friends seemed distant and bewildered by my stories and my manner. Home began to feel like a foreign place.

I completed my B.A. at the University of Winnipeg and returned to Israel in 1972 where I studied Conrad and Yeats at the University of Jerusalem. Israel had always been a center of civilization, connecting three continents and merging people from everywhere in the world. I thought it would be the perfect focus for culture and learning. But the country was too intense for me. Certainly, people of every country were coming together in Israel, but they didn't seem to harmonize very well.

I returned to Winnipeg, the place I knew best, and married Lee Anne Block, who was also returning after teaching in India. I wanted to find worthwhile work; I had had enough learning and experiencing, I needed to produce and to create. I trained as a teacher and in 1974 began teaching in a small town, the same year that we had Adam, our first child. The next year I taught English and drama in a Jewish high school in Winnipeg. We bought a gracious old duplex house with another couple and settled in.

Julie finds a way to rescue the pony, and they escape before the angry witch can catch them:

Julie Gerond and the polka dot pony
Ride away to a grey willow tree
They hear wind in the leaves and branches that sigh
On the edge of a shimmering sea.

I also began to write for adults. Something creative had been released; I no longer felt "bewitched" by the demands of adulthood. In fact, I could use my adult discipline and maturity to write. Without it I might keep on dreaming, but I'd produce little.

I took a year off teaching in 1978 and freelanced for Winnipeg's main paper. I wrote about whatever interested me: "The Pinball Prince of Portage Avenue," "Emergency Ward—the Fight for Life," "The Naked Zoo—Private Lives of Animals behind Bars," "Step Right Up—Working on the Midway." I was astonished by the power of being a reporter. I only had to say I was from the *Free Press* and suddenly I could enter almost anywhere and ask anybody almost anything. I'd then write up a story, get it published immediately, and be paid to boot.

One of my first books came through my training in journalism. *The Folk Festival Book* was written during six intense weeks as I interviewed hundreds of people from famous performers and folk festival staff to volunteers and members of the audience—all the folk who make up a folk festival. Most of my other books, even storybooks, take more than six years.

The other breakthrough of that year occurred on a trip to Toronto. I had a day and a half alone without distractions, only the Ontario wilderness outside my window and the comforting rattle and roll of the train. My mind drifted back to my childhood on Main Street, and I wrote my first significant short story. It took another twenty drafts, but it became a published work.

I returned to teaching and kept writing whenever I could. I loved writing, but I didn't know if I should dedicate myself to it. I needed to know if I had what it takes. The Banff School of Fine Arts in Alberta gave me the answer. I was accepted into its summer writing program, directed by W. O. Mitchell, a great Canadian writer. His method was perfect for my improvisational nature. For six weeks twenty of us put aside all previous writing. We began practising "Free Fall," a directed form of stream of consciousness writing to uncover fresh images, characters, settings—the raw material of our imagination. Formal writing was not accepted. No rewriting either. Free Fall was an exercise in discovery. Each morning, interesting work from the previous day was read aloud and discussed by the group without any negative criticism. The rest of the afternoon and evening was spent in writing.

Most of my earlier writing had imitated other writers. Here, I was going deeply into my own experiences and emerging with my own distinctive expression. I've been in many workshops, courses, and various writing groups. They all had particular skills to teach, but W. O. Mitchell showed me how to find my creative sources and how to believe in myself as a writer.

Vagabonding in the van with daughter Mira (left) and son Adam, 1982.

Experiments

I continued seeking out interesting experiences. I did a couple fire walks across a path of hot coals. I collected "found" objects to create collage art which I still do as my "hobby." I took workshops in everything from massage and I Ching readings to group therapy and neurolinguistic programming. I'd rent out my house each summer and travel through Canada and the States in an old Econoline van that I set up for sleeping, eating, and, of course, writing. It was a gypsy life that delighted my kids as much as me. Lee Anne and I were no longer married, but the children were with me half the time. My eccentric interests didn't bother my kids; in fact they tell me that our best times together were when I was the most "far out."

I became a member of a commune in southern Manitoba. I bought an old caboose, moved it onto the land, and converted it into a rustic retreat. I'd drive out whenever I had a break, with the kids or on my own, light some candles, toss logs into the stove, and set the water boiling for my coffee. I would jump into my writing with the same delight as jumping into the creek outside my door.

Sometimes, there would be a knock and one of the members would call in, "Sweat lodge tonight, Obie. When the moon comes up." We never knew when Herman, an Ojibway medicine man, would stop by to conduct a sweat lodge ceremony for us "crazy white people."

I'd follow the creek to where the woods opened onto a prairie field. There the sweat lodge stood, a low dome of four thick willow poles covered in canvas. Long ago, it would have been covered by buffalo skins, but otherwise it was the same lodge as in the distant past.

Eight or ten of us stripped and put on shorts. We placed ritual offerings of tobacco on a crescent-shaped mound that sheltered the fire and represented the moon. We crawled into the lodge and waited to welcome the seven large rocks as they were pulled from the outside fire. The rocks represented the Seven Grandfathers, guiding spirits of the Ojibway. The tent was sealed and became hotter than any sauna and utterly dark except for the glowing rocks. Then came drums and rattles, native chants and prayers. At certain moments the medicine man dashed the rocks with water so the steaming "breath" of the Grandfathers would make us groan and sing with more vigour. It was a place of endurance that woke up the body as well as the spirit, a place for healing, visions, guidance, and thanksgiving. Sometimes a second set of rocks was added, sometimes a third. When the ceremony was complete and the tent opened, we'd crawl out so heated up by the Grandfathers' "spirit" and so entranced by the chanting and drama of the ceremony that we'd fall into the creek or onto the dewy grass and watch the stars as if we'd never seen them before. When I got back at the caboose I'd dream the whole night through or stay up writing till the morning light surprised me at my desk.

I wasn't trying to become a full-time, old-time commune hippie or an Ojibway Indian, either, but I am grateful to that community and to the native sweat lodge ceremony. They raised my spirits and cleared my thoughts.

Creative Play

I continued to teach at the same high school, and I still teach there part-time, over twenty years later. Teaching keeps me sharp and lets me share the literature that I love and the energy of the young who are still questioning and learning.

My first years of teaching drama were especially exciting. I began directing students to create their own scenes and short plays through improvisation. I'd have them do physical warm-ups beforehand, and then they'd "warm up" their imaginations by pantomiming an experience as I was describing it. They'd enact fantasy journeys, exploring different places—some very ordinary, others strange and dreamlike. I didn't realize how powerful the exercises were until some students reported feeling and smelling the objects that they were creating through mime. The students were having sensory hallucinations. I was inadvertently hypnotising them.

I became more cautious in my drama direction but began studying hypnosis and guided imagery. After some courses and training, I offered help to people with creative blocks or who wanted to better manage their feelings and responses. I showed them how to enter a trance, and I gave them direction as they imagined ways of dealing with their problems. It worked pretty well, and it was very enjoyable work though I eventually moved on. It taught me a lot about communicating, especially how words and images affect us at a subconscious level—important information for a writer. I also became more receptive to my own subconscious. I still keep a dream diary—a record of that one third of one's life spent asleep and dreaming. It's as valuable to me as my writer's journal.

For a few years in the mid-eighties my creative work shifted to writing and directing independent films. Every day of filmmaking was new and unpredictable. I remember finding an abandoned train station that I could use as a setting for a scene. (Why is my life so involved with trains?) When I returned with my film crew to prepare the scene, we discovered that someone had bought the eighty-year-old station and moved it away. No one knew where.

We had to delay the film and rewrite the scene. Another time, after editing a film, I realized I needed one more shot of a certain character. When I called the actress, I discovered she had cut off her long hair. We had an awful time getting a wig that resembled her original look. I found filmmaking a thrilling, all-encompassing, and transformative experience. Thank heavens I quit before it got in my blood.

Soon after I became involved in a children's game. It began when Henry, my next-door neighbour, called to me from his front porch. Henry had time on his hands; he'd even walk my dog when I couldn't. He asked me to join him in a game he was making up. Players got cards with moral questions on them. They guessed how other players would answer. I smiled, saying, "Sorry, Henry, I've got to get to work." I thought I was being the productive one and he was wasting his time. I was wrong.

Six months later, I was surprised to see a news crew at Henry's. He was being interviewed about his game. More crews showed up over the next week, and soon every time I visited, he was on the phone with some reporter or radio host. His game, A Question of Scruples, was a huge success. It was even played a number of times by Johnny Carson on "The Tonight Show."

I didn't turn down his next invitation to play. I found it was a fascinating game that offered real insight into people's character and motivation. I suggested that he make a kids version.

"Kids don't have moral issues," he replied.

"Sure they do, Henry. They're always getting into new situations where they have to decide what's right and wrong."

"On tour," Baker Lake, Northwest Territories, April 1989.

Directing a film shot on location, 1987.

"Make up some questions," he said. "Let's see if it works."

The game needed 240 questions. After three fourteen-hour days I had two hundred.

"This could be a great game," said Henry.

"Terrific," I said. "I'll write another forty questions and we're done."

"Not so fast," he said. "So far you've only got fourteen really good ones."

I ended up writing 4500 questions that we rewrote and whittled down into 220 acceptable ones. We got the other twenty from kids. Hasbro bought the game for world distribution, and it was especially gratifying to see it produced in different languages.

I was occasionally invited to schools to talk about my work, but when the Junior Edition of A Question of Scruples came out, invitations increased and I developed presentations for different ages. At first I read my stories and poems, but soon I was performing them and discussing how they came to be. I involve the students so they can realize that they, too, can develop their creativity. Presenting at schools, festivals, and conferences has become a third career for me, blending my teaching and my writing in a way that keeps me improving both.

One of my first tours as a writer took me to the Northwest Territories in the spring of 1989. It wasn't spring there. It was fifty below as I debarked from the plane, and what I thought was the roar of the plane's engines turned out to be the howling north wind. Simon Tookoome, an Inuit artist and hunter, came for me in his dogsled. I was a bizarre sight, clutching two crates that held my Apple E2 computer while being "mushed" over the hardened snow. We stopped at a high snow drift that turned out to be completely covering his home. Everything felt strange to me: eating raw caribou meat, exploring a wilderness without trees or bush, and speaking only through translators. Yet when Simon began to tell me tales of his shaman uncle, his adventures with his pet wolf, and how he survived blizzards and famine, I felt at home, for they were stories told by one storyteller to another.

Simon Tookoome has since become a godparent to my younger son, whom Lisa and I named Jesse Paul Shoshan Tookoome Dveris-Oberman. Inuit tradition has it that since my son shares Tookoome's name, Simon, though sixty years old, is our spiritual son. I am completing a book with Simon about the adventures of his youth. It turns out that Simon is very much like me after all; he, too, wants to remember and recount the wonders of his childhood.

The Always Prayer Shawl

However much I may play with different creative forms, I always care most about a good story simply told. I wrote one of my most important stories as a gift to my son Adam. It is a story about a gift, one which was offered to me but which took years for me to accept.

My grandfather Zaida had died when I was twelve and was buried wearing his sabbath shawl. His high holiday shawl went to me. I loved my grandfather deeply, but when my father handed me that shawl I almost flinched. I would have been happy with Zaida's watch or his cuff links, his old leather wallet, almost anything but that shawl.

The prayer shawl seemed to represent religious demands and restrictions that repressed me as an individual: "Go to synagogue. Recite the prayers. Follow the laws. Don't grow. Don't change!" I put it away in a drawer and likewise I put it out of my mind. In fact, I never even had a Bar Mitzvah.

Years later I found myself preparing for my own son's Bar Mitzvah, and I came across that prayer shawl again still in that drawer, still waiting for me.

As I held it, I smelled a faint trace of Zaida's shaving soap. Soon came a rush of memories—his whiskery face, his gentle voice, the softness of his shawl against my cheek when I would lean against him, the way he wrapped the "tseetseet" around his fingers—those woollen strings tied to the garment that he would tie to himself—strings meant to awaken the memory of our history, of our covenant. More memories still—the way he would rise and rock back and forth in prayer and how the prayer shawl swayed with him, as if it might open and spread out like great white wings.

Had the shawl changed so much since I'd put it away? No, but I realized that I had. I was middle-aged, halfway between the child I used to be and the old man I may someday become. I had all the individuality I needed. What I was craving next was peace of mind, wisdom, a faith in something beyond myself—and the quiet strength that my grandfather had drawn from his beliefs. I wondered if I might find it by honouring what he honoured and by drawing upon its power. So I finally accepted my grandfather's gift, in my own way.

Soon afterwards, I wrote *The Always Prayer Shawl* for Adam so he might know my grandfather who had died so long ago. It was published as a children's book in 1994, received a number of awards, and produced as a play a year later. It is about a boy who left Russia during the revolution taking with him a single precious gift, his grandfather's prayer shawl. It describes the changes that happen to the boy and to the shawl until the time comes for him as an old man to pass the shawl on to his own grandchild.

*"**After the debut of my play** **The Always Prayer Shawl,** **with my son and my father.**"*

"The merged family: little Jesse, teenagers Mira, Adam, on one side, my wife Lisa beside me," 1996.

By 1994 my life had reached another stage. My first children, Adam and Mira, were teenagers; Lisa and I had married; we had merged as a family and had Jesse, now a two-year-old. My career as a writer was also reaching a new stage. Along with *The Always Prayer Shawl* I published two other books: *This Business with Elijah* and a children's picture book, *TV Sal and the Game Show from Outer Space*. TV Sal was a spoof teasingly directed at Mira, who had been deeply rooted into the couch and firmly attached to the TV remote control.

I began speaking at conferences and performing my works as well as telling traditional Jewish tales across Canada and the States. I developed workshops for teachers, writers, and communities on personal and family storytelling, even a website. One good story leads to another, and soon everyone in the workshops would be sharing stories. I also had my students record family stories and do video interviews of an elder relative. When Boyds Mills Press asked me for another book, I wanted to write one that had that intimate sense of personal and family stories. I recalled some of the stories that had moved me most.

One of my students shared the story of his grandfather Samuel, who had survived the Buchenwald concentration camp. Samuel was walking out of Germany, confused and in despair, when he stopped at a house to ask for water. There he saw a prayer shawl being used as a tablecloth. He managed to barter something for the shawl, and by rescuing

it, he was changed. He felt that somehow he had rescued himself and restored his identity.

Another person told of visiting a Spanish immigrant woman and discovering an old menorah, a Jewish ritual candleholder. It had been in the woman's family for centuries, but she had not known what it was or that her ancestors were possibly Marranos, secret Jews who had hidden their religion since the Spanish Inquisition's edict of expulsion of 1492. When the Spanish woman learned more about Jewish traditions, she made sense of her grandparents' odd rituals and secretive ways. More than that, she began to make sense of her past and how it had shaped her.

Another story was about a chaplain during World War Two. He had dedicated himself to rescuing pieces of stained glass from bombed-out churches. It was dangerous work, often near the front lines, and during one mission he was killed. A soldier kept up his work, and the glass later was assembled into a commemorative window in the chaplain's hometown church.

These stories were defining moments for the people who told them. At a personal level, they were like the great moments in history that shape a nation's identity. I began to think of the stories that the Jewish people recall on holidays such as Passover and Hanukkah. This all coalesced as I wrote *By the Hanukkah Light*. Rachel hears two tales from her grandfather: a tale of their people and a tale of their own family, both miraculous tales of the Hanukkah light.

The tale of Hanukkah recounts how the light of the Temple, the Jewish symbol of spirit and faith, was almost lost but then rescued and miraculously restored. The grandfather's second story is in some ways parallel to the ancient one. He recalls being a child in Europe and his family being afraid because they were Jews, how they could not celebrate Hanukkah openly and finally fled, leaving behind their hanukkiah, the lamp of Hanukkah. He told how he returned later as an Allied soldier and fought "like the old Maccabees." Miraculously, at the end of the war, he recovered his hanukkiah in the ruins of his house, the same hanukkiah that he and the grandchildren have just cleaned and lighted.

The two stories become equally moving and meaningful. Rachel promises her grandfather, "When I grow up and have children, I will tell them these stories, the story of our people and the story of our family as we gather by the Hanukkah light." For me, stories of our past are heirlooms to treasure and to pass on to the next generation.

The White Stone in the Castle Wall is an heirloom story of an entire city. It takes place at Casa Loma, Toronto's famous "castle," which was built in 1912 by Sir Henry Pellatt. I took a tour of the old castle and became fascinated by the tour guide's talk of Sir Henry, a sort of benevolent capitalist who didn't mind spreading a bit of his wealth. When he was building his outer wall, he offered the people of Toronto a dollar for each large field stone they brought him, a full day's wages at the time. The stone rush was on, and Sir Henry bought 250,000 stones.

As I looked at the grand stone walls I noticed a single brilliantly white quartz stone. I then realized that it was the only white stone in the entire wall. My writer's "spider sense" tingled. Why only one white stone? Who brought it and how?

I turned local history into historical fiction by writing a story of John Tommy Fiddich, a poor immigrant lad who had a garden "where he worked hard every day." His harvest would earn him a silver dollar, making him "the luckiest boy of all!"

Then the hail beat everything down
the insects ate everything up
and the wind blew the rest away
except for a dirty, grey stone.

John's luck hits bottom but shoots up again when Sir Henry Pellatt calls for stones. He heaves the stone into a cart, hauls it through Old Toronto during a heavy storm, and struggles up the hill to Casa Loma. But the rain washes the grey dirt from the stone, and the master of the wall has to reject it. Sir Henry asked for only dull-colored stones:

"Your stone is all bright white.
Sir Henry will not want it.
I cannot buy it from you for his wall."
John told him, "Sir Henry owns this great castle.
He owns all the lights in the streets of the city.
All that I own is this one white stone
and I hauled it up the hill for him."
The builders of the wall,
the drivers of the wagons,
the servants of the castle all said:
"John Tommy Fiddich,

your white stone is worthless.
You're the unluckiest boy of all."

In the spirit of the Horatio Alger fantasies that inspired our grandparents' generation, John's hard work and sincerity are rewarded. He fatefully meets and impresses Sir Henry, who buys the white stone for his wall and gives John a job working in his English flower garden. Is John once again the luckiest boy of all, as everybody says?

"I've been lucky and unlucky,"
answers John Tommy Fiddich,
"but I earned a silver dollar all the same.
And I brought Sir Henry Pellatt
a great white stone for Casa Loma,
a stone that's worth a lot to him and to me."

John has created something he feels good about. That's been my goal as well. I've looked at factors in my childhood: being poor, being alone, being from a minority, and I've seen how they shaped me as a person and a writer. I've looked at my adulthood, and I've made some sense of what I've achieved and what I haven't. I suppose I could have charted all my "ups and downs," deciding where and how I've been lucky or unlucky, but like most of us, I've learned that luck is not the point. Lucky and unlucky, we do what we can with what we've got.

I've been doing what I can, trying to stay true to the people that I love and to that creative impulse that has given me such joy.

Writings

FOR CHILDREN

Julie Gerond and the Polka Dot Pony, Hyperion, 1988.
The Lion in the Lake (alphabet book), Peguis, 1988.
TV Sal and the Game Show from Outer Space, illustrated by Craig Terlson, Red Deer, 1993.
The Always Prayer Shawl, illustrated by Ted Lewin, Boyds Mills, 1994.
The White Stone in the Castle Wall, illustrated by Les Tait, Tundra Books, 1995.
You Can Always Tell Cathy from Caitlin, W. Pye, 1997.
By the Hanukkah Light, Boyds Mills, 1997.
(Contributor) Simon Tookoome, *The Shaman's Nephew : A Life in the Far North,* Stoddart Kids, 2000.

FOR ADULTS

The Folk Festival Book, Turnstone, 1983. (Editor with Elaine Newton)
Mirror of a People: Canadian Jewish Experience in Poetry and Prose, Coteau, 1985.
This Business with Elijah, Turnstone, 1993.

Author of family play *The Always Prayer Shawl,* 1995. Songwriter for Fred Penner's children's albums; "Fred Penner's Place," CBC national television; and songs recorded by Eric Nagler and Ed Desjarlais. Author of questions for the Junior Edition of A Question of Scruples (game), Hasbro. Writer and director of films distributed by Winnipeg Film Group: "No Act of God," 1984; "The Amazing Creation of Al Simmons," 1985; and "House of the Wind," 1987.

OLDER, Effin 1942-
(Lorraine Avery, a joint pseudonym; Michael McBrier, a joint pseudonym)

Personal

Born December 18, 1942, in Brownington, VT; daughter of Carroll (a farmer) and Phyllis (Reid) Lawes; married Jules Older (a writer), 1965; children: Amber and Willow. *Education:* University of Vermont, B.A., 1964; City College of New York, M.S., 1970. *Hobbies:* Skiing, snowboarding, biking, gardening, hiking.

Addresses

Home and office—P.O. Box 163, Albany, VT 05820. *Agent*—Sally Brady, Heartland Four Corners, VT 05049.

Career

TVNZ, Dunedin, New Zealand, television scriptwriter, director, and presenter, 1980-84; McIndoe Publishing, Dunedin, New Zealand, editor, 1985-86; freelance writer and photographer, 1986—. *Member:* Society of Children's Book Writers and Illustrators, PEN, National Writers Union, League of Vermont Writers.

Awards, Honors

Best resort and travel production, and Grand Prize (co-winner), both from the International Ski Film Festival, and Vermont Travel and Tourism Recognition of Excellence, all 1995, all for *Tales from the Mountain: Mount Snow's First 40 Years.*

Writings

FOR CHILDREN

Donna's Diary: A Book About Obeying, illustrated by Pat Schories, Golden Books, 1986.

(With Jules Older) *Hot Henrietta and Nailbiters United,* illustrated by Lisa Kopper, Heinemann (London), 1987.

(With J. Older) *Little Smugglers,* Smugglers' Notch Ski Resort, 1987.

(With J. Older under joint pseudonym Michael McBrier) *Oliver's Barnyard Blues,* illustrated by Blanche Sims, Troll, 1987.

(With J. Older under joint pseudonym Lorraine Avery) *The Runaway Winner,* illustrated by Linda Thomas, Troll, 1990.

(With J. Older under joint pseudonym Lorraine Avery) *The Creepy Carousel,* illustrated by Linda Thomas, Troll, 1990.

(With J. Older) *Hank and Henrietta Take Off,* illustrated by Lisa Kopper, Heinemann, 1991.

Tree House Trio and the Pirates of Piccadilly, illustrated by Jan Smith, Orchard (London), 1991.

Trouble at the North Pole, illustrated by Russell Ayto, Heinemann, 1992.

You're Invited to Mary Kate and Ashley's Birthday Party, Scholastic, 1998.

Snowboarding, Stackpole Books, 1999.

My Two Grandmothers, illustrated by Nancy Hayashi, Harcourt Brace, in press.

"SILVER BLADES FIGURE EIGHTS" SERIES; ALL ILLUSTRATED BY MARCY RAMSEY

Ice Dreams, Skylark, 1996.

Star For a Day, Bantam Books, 1996.

The Best Ice Show Ever!, Skylark, 1996.

Bossy Anna, Skylark, 1996.

Special Delivery Mess, Bantam, 1997.

Randi's Missing Skates, Bantam, 1997.

Randi's Pet Surprise, Bantam, 1997.

Randi Goes for the Gold, Skylark, 1998.

Also co-author with Jules Older of the screenplay for the award-winning documentary film *Tales From the Mountain: Mount Snow's First 40 Years.*

Work in Progress

More children's books.

Effin Older

Sidelights

Effin Older is a freelance writer, photographer, and internationally published children's author. She has written nonfiction books about downhill skiing and snowboarding, the "Silver Blades Figure Eights" fiction series about young figure skaters, and a number of other works for children, including six books with her husband, author Jules Older.

*   *   *

OLDER, Jules 1940-
(Lorraine Avery, a joint pseudonym; Michael McBrier, a joint pseudonym)

Personal

Born May 1, 1940, in Baltimore, MD; son of Morris (a certified public accountant) and Ruth (a social worker) Older; married Effin (a writer), 1965; children: Amber and Willow. *Education:* University of Vermont, B.A., 1962; New York University, Ph.D., 1970. *Hobbies and other interests:* skiing, mountain biking, gardening.

Addresses

Home and office—P.O. Box 163, Albany, VT 05820. *Agent*—Sally Brady, Hartland Four Corners, VT 05049.

Career

Writer and editor-in-chief of *Ski Press* and *Adventure Press.* Worked variously as a ski instructor, disc jockey, medical educator, college counselor, psychology professor, and writing instructor. *Member:* PEN, National Writers Union, North American Snowsports Journalists, League of Vermont Writers.

Awards, Honors

Books of the Year, National Book Guild of Great Britain, 1985, for *Jane and the Pirates;* runner-up, Other Award, 1986, for *Hank Prank in Love;* Pick of the Lists, American Booksellers Association, 1997, and Best Books of 1997, Rathbone Children's Book Service, both for *Cow;* Kroepsch-Maurice Award for Excellence in Teaching, University of Vermont, 1997. Has received numerous awards and grants for his work in the field of psychology, including the Philip J. Zlatchin Award from the New York University Department of Psychology and the New Zealand Psychological Society Award. Best resort and travel production, and Grand Prize (co-winner), both from the International Ski Film Festival, and Vermont Travel and Tourism Recognition of Excellence, all 1995, all for *Tales From the Mountain: Mount Snow's First 40 Years.*

Jules Older

Writings

The Pakeha Papers, McIndoe (Dunedin, New Zealand), 1978.

Touching is Healing, Scarborough House, 1982.

Hank Prank and Hot Henrietta, illustrated by Lisa Kopper, Heinemann (London), 1984.

Jane and the Pirates, illustrated by Michael Bragg, Heinemann (London), 1984.

Hank Prank in Love, illustrated by Lisa Kopper, Heinemann (London), 1985, Scholastic, 1991.

Don't Panic!, illustrated by J. Ellen Dolce, Golden Books, 1986.

Who Hates Harold?, illustrated by Bruce Lemerise, Golden Books, 1986.

Don't Start!, illustrated by Carolyn Bracken, Golden Books, 1986.

(With Effin Older) *Hot Henrietta and Nailbiters United,* illustrated by Lisa Kopper, Heinemann (London), 1987.

(With E. Older) *Little Smugglers,* Smugglers' Notch Ski Resort, 1987.

(With E. Older under joint pseudonym Michael McBrier) *Oliver's Barnyard Blues,* illustrated by Blanche Sims, Troll, 1987.

(With E. Older under joint pseudonym Lorraine Avery) *The Runaway Winner,* illustrated by Linda Thomas, Troll, 1990.

(With E. Older under joint pseudonym Lorraine Avery) *The Creepy Carousel,* illustrated by Linda Thomas, Troll, 1990.

(With E. Older) *Hank and Henrietta Take Off,* illustrated by Lisa Kopper, Heinemann (London), 1991.

Shipwreck!, Octopus (New Zealand), 1991.

Ski Vermont!, Chelsea Green Press, 1991.

Ben & Jerry—The Real Scoop!, illustrated by Lyn Severance, Chapters Publishing, 1993.

Cow, illustrated by Lyn Severance, Charlesbridge, 1997.

Anita! The Woman Behind the Body Shop, illustrated by Lisa Kopper, Charlesbridge, 1998.

Cross-Country Skiing for Everyone, photography by Effin Older, Stackpole, 1998.

Telling Time, illustrated by Megan Halsey, Charlesbridge, 2000.

Ice Cream, Charlesbridge, in press.

Oinkers, Charlesbridge, in press.

Also co-author with Effin Older of the screenplay for the award-winning documentary film *Tales from the Mountain: Mount Snow's First 40 Years.* Contributor of articles to newspapers and magazines, including the *London Times, New York Times, Los Angeles Times, Washington Times, The Guardian, GEO, Hemispheres, New Choices, SKIING, Powder,* and *Cross Country Skier.*

Work in Progress

A children's book on hate crimes.

Sidelights

Jules Older is the author of more than fifteen children's books published in England, New Zealand, and the United States. His writings cover a variety of topics, ranging from the mischievous fictional adventures of young boys and girls in such popular titles as *Jane and the Pirates, Hank Prank in Love,* and *Who Hates Harold?,* to nonfiction picture books about cows, ice cream, and famous entrepreneurs. Several of his books, including *Hot Henrietta and Nailbiters United, Little Smugglers,* and *Hank and Henrietta Take Off,* have been written in collaboration with his wife, author Effin Older.

Older's first children's book, *Hank Prank and Hot Henrietta* chronicles the everyday adventures of young Hank and his sister Henrietta. A *Junior Bookshelf* critic considered the stories of "excellent length for bedtime reading" and complimented their "agreeable authenticity." Similarly, a *Books for Keeps* reviewer recommended the book for its "[s]uper dialogue" and "fresh and tangy" jokes.

In 1997's *Cow,* Older and illustrator Lyn Severance team up for an entertaining and educational look at dairy cows. Deborah Stevenson of the *Bulletin of the Center for Children's Books* commended the book's "cheerful simplified graphics and ebullient text" but found "too much deliberate wackiness to the tone and a bit too much jumping around." A *Publishers Weekly* contributor described *Cow* as a "trivial but amusing offering" that would pair well with a pint of ice cream.

Older told *SATA:* "I grew up in Baltimore in the shadow of Pimlico Racetrack, and I still consider the Chesapeake Bay Blue Point crab the finest food ever served at a table. My finest moment in an otherwise undistinguished high school career was to fly a 'Nixon Go Home!' flag from the school's tower. That was in 1957. (Even then he knew.)

"I went to the University of Vermont (UVM) because: a.) I wanted to see if I could survive in the Frozen North; and b.) they (then) accepted under-achievers.

"At UVM I learned to ski, a sport I've now turned into a profession as a ski writer, editor, and occasional ski instructor. As an undergraduate I participated in the historic picketing of Woolworths, one of the first attempts at ending racial segregation in the United States. I also helped lead one of the first of the sixties campus protests—in our case, against unwarranted intrusion into the private lives of students. The protest was peaceful, humorous, serious, and successful. In my senior year I was editor of the *Vermont Cynic,* the campus newspaper. And it was at UVM that I met my wife, a farmer's daughter from the hills of Vermont. The farmer's daughter is writer and photographer Effin Older.

"One college summer I worked as a ditch digger. At first I was a success, but that success created problems. The company hired another college boy, the owner's nephew, and we spent more time talking than we did digging. By week's end, we were both fired.

"Now unemployed, and with more than half a summer to go, I signed on as a child care worker at a hospital for disturbed kids. Despite bruised shins, a sore jaw, and some amazing new word combinations in my vocabulary, I got hooked on the helping racket and spent the next few months as a nurse's aide in the locked ward of a psychiatric hospital and as a trainee with disturbed preschoolers. By now I was thoroughly addicted and went on to study clinical psychology at New York University, which eventually gave me a Ph.D.

"During my years in New York I was: a.) arrested for allegedly assaulting the biggest policeman in New York while I was leading a civil rights picket line (I weighed 145 pounds at the time, the cop weighed at least 200, and I've never been *that* crazy!); b.) given the Philip J. Zlatchen Award for Courage in Serving Humanity; and c.) congratulated by all the local cops and most of my neighbors for hitting an armed junkie with a brick as he was robbing my neighbor's apartment. (Shortly after my adrenaline returned to normal, we left New York for New Zealand.)

"My 'real' job in New Zealand was Coordinator of the Behavioural Science Course at Otago Medical School, but I managed a few other things as well. Two stand out as the most fun. For three years I hosted "American Pie," a weekly radio show on a rock-and-roll station. A critic described it as 'one of the most original and individualistic programmes to be heard in New Zealand.' And, largely through having the right accent at the right time, I played the lead in a TV documentary about the last man to be hanged in New Zealand. I am one of the happy few who have been hung and are still walking.

"In New Zealand I was an organizer of a successful day of learning about Maori land rights and was a frequent visitor to the New Zealand Women's Prison. It was a proud moment when the inmates gave me the Good Guy of the Month Award.

"In 1986 the Older family left New Zealand *and* academia to become full-time writers in Vermont. We still are, but every Wednesday in the fall term I drive to UVM's Montpelier campus to teach 'Writing for Real' for the English Department. My daughters, Amber and Willow, took the course in 1990 and are now writers themselves. My students nominated me for UVM's teaching award, and I was granted the award in 1997.

"Besides children's stories, my writing subjects include skiing, travel, food, gardening, home office and adventure.

"Effin and I got married on a camping trip in the Virgin Islands and since then have camped through Europe, and across the United States and bits of New Zealand."

Works Cited

PERIODICALS

Review of *Cow, Publishers Weekly,* August 11, 1997, p. 400.
Review of *Hank Prank and Hot Henrietta, Books for Keeps,* November, 1987.
Review of *Hank Prank and Hot Henrietta, Junior Bookshelf,* April, 1985, pp. 83-84.
Stevenson, Deborah, review of *Cow, Bulletin of the Center for Children's Books,* February, 1998, p. 215.

For More Information See

PERIODICALS

Horn Book Guide, spring 1998, p. 142.
School Librarian, June, 1985, pp. 140-41.
Times Literary Supplement, November 30, 1984, p. 1377.

P

PATERSON, John (Barstow) 1932-

Personal

Born November 22, 1932, in Middletown, CT; son of Arthur Elliott (a minister) and Harriet (a teacher; maiden name, Barstow) Paterson; married Katherine Womeldorf (a writer), July 14, 1962; children: Elizabeth Polin Pierce, John Barstow, Jr., David Lord, Mary Katherine Nah-he-sah-pe-che-a. *Education:* Swarthmore College, B.A., 1953; Union Theological Seminary, New York City, M.Div., 1956; Princeton Theological Seminary, Th.M., 1964; Lancaster Theological Seminary, D.Min., 1981. *Politics:* Democrat.

Addresses

Agent—c/o Clarion Books, 215 Park Ave. S., New York, NY 10003.

Career

Associate pastor of Presbyterian church in East Aurora, NY, 1956-61; pastor of Presbyterian church in Tonawanda, NY, 1961-63; assistant pastor of Presbyterian church in Princeton, NJ, 1963-66; pastor of Presbyterian churches in Takoma Park, MD, 1966-79, and Norfolk, VA, 1979-86; First Presbyterian Church, Barre, VT, pastor, 1986-95. Filled interim pastorates in Danville, East Thetford, Randolph, Strafford, and Williamstown, VT. Member of board of directors, Central Vermont Habitat for Humanity, People's Health and Wellness Clinic, and Wood Art Gallery; member of development board, Vermont Center for the Book.

Writings

(With wife, Katherine Paterson) *Consider the Lilies: Plants of the Bible,* illustrated by Anne Ophelia Dowden, Crowell (New York City), 1986.

(With K. Paterson) *Images of God,* illustrated by Alexander Koshkin, Clarion Books (New York City), 1998.

Sidelights

John Paterson told *SATA:* "The title of my D.Min. thesis was 'Living the Christian Faith in Artistic Creations.' This theme embodies my conviction that, whatever is one's profession and/or hobby, one's calling is to exercise God-given talents and to aid and encourage others to do so, whether it be in listening, writing, speaking, crafting art objects, or being a steward of resources in some other fashion."

For More Information See

PERIODICALS

Booklist, May 1, 1998, p. 1515.
Bulletin of the Center for Children's Books, November, 1986, p. 55.
Horn Book, March, 1987, p. 224.
Kirkus Reviews, September 1, 1986, p. 1378.
New York Times Book Review, December 14, 1986, p. 29; May 17, 1998, p. 26.
Publishers Weekly, March 23, 1998, p. 95.
School Library Journal, October, 1986, p. 181; April, 1998, p. 152.
USA Today, December 5, 1986, p. 4D.
Voice of Youth Advocates, December, 1986, p. 248.

* * *

PINKWATER, Daniel Manus 1941- (Manus Pinkwater)

Personal

Born November 15, 1941, in Memphis, TN; son of Philip (a ragman and entrepreneur) and Fay (a chorus girl; maiden name, Hoffman) Pinkwater; married Jill Miriam Schutz (an author and illustrator), October 12, 1969. *Education:* Bard College, B.A., 1964. Studied sculpture privately with David Nyvall. Also studied at the Art Institute of Chicago, Harvard University, the University of Liverpool, and University College, Nairobi, Kenya. *Politics:* "Taoist." *Religion:* "Republican." *Hobbies and other interests:* "Various."

Addresses

Home—111 Crum Elbow Rd., Hyde Park, NY 12538.

Career

Author and illustrator of children's books, and radio commentator. *All Things Considered,* National Public Radio (NPR), regular commentator, 1987—. Host of *Chinwag Theater* and book reviewer on *Weekend Edition Saturday with Scott Simon* for NPR. *Member:* American Federation of Theater and Radio Artists.

Awards, Honors

American Library Association Notable Book designation, 1976, for *Lizard Music;* Junior Literary Guild selection, 1977, for *Fat Men from Space; New York Times* Outstanding Book designation, 1978, for *The Last Guru;* Children's Choice, International Reading Association and the Children's Book Council, 1981, for *The Wuggie Norple Story;* Parents' Choice Award (literature), 1982, for *Roger's Umbrella;* Emphasis on Reading Award (grades K-1), 1983-84, for *The Big Orange Splot;* Charles Flint Kellogg Medal, Bard College, 1999.

Writings

FOR CHILDREN; AS MANUS PINKWATER

The Terrible Roar, Knopf, 1970.

Daniel Manus Pinkwater

(Self-illustrated) *Bear's Picture,* Holt, 1972.
Fat Elliot and the Gorilla, Four Winds, 1974.
Three Big Hogs, Seabury, 1975.
(Self-illustrated) *Blue Moose* (also see below), Dodd, 1975.
(Self-illustrated) *Wingman,* Dodd, 1975.
Around Fred's Bed, illustrated by Robert Mertens, Prentice-Hall, 1976.

FOR CHILDREN; SELF-ILLUSTRATED; AS DANIEL MANUS PINKWATER

Wizard Crystal, Dodd, 1973.
Magic Camera, Dodd, 1974.
Lizard Music, Dodd, 1976.
The Blue Thing, Prentice-Hall, 1977.
The Big Orange Splot, Hastings House, 1977.
Fat Men from Space, Dodd, 1977.
The Hoboken Chicken Emergency, Prentice-Hall, 1977.
The Last Guru (also see below), Dodd, 1978.
Return of the Moose (also see below), Dodd, 1979.
Pickle Creature, Four Winds, 1979.
The Magic Moscow, Four Winds, 1980.
Tooth-Gnasher Superflash, Four Winds, 1981.
Attila the Pun: A Magic Moscow Book, Four Winds, 1981.
I Was a Second Grade Werewolf, Dutton, 1983.
Ducks!, Little, Brown, 1984.
Devil in the Drain, Dutton, 1984.
The Moosepire, Little, Brown, 1986.
The Muffin Fiend, Lothrop, 1986.
The Frankenbagel Monster, Dutton, 1986.
Aunt Lulu, Macmillan, 1988.
Guys from Space, Macmillan, 1989.
Uncle Melvin, Macmillan, 1989.
Doodle Flute, Macmillan, 1991.
Wempires, Macmillan, 1991.
The Phantom of the Lunch Wagon, Macmillan, 1992.
Author's Day, Macmillan, 1993.
Blue Moose and Return of the Moose, Bullseye Books, 1993.
Ned Feldman: Space Pirate, Macmillan, 1994.
Mush: A Dog from Space, Atheneum, 1995.

FOR CHILDREN; AS DANIEL MANUS PINKWATER

(With wife, Jill Pinkwater) *Superpuppy: How to Choose, Raise, and Train the Best Possible Dog for You* (nonfiction), illustrated by J. Pinkwater, Seabury (New York), 1977.
Alan Mendelsohn, the Boy from Mars (also see below), Dutton, 1979.
Yobgorgle: Mystery Monster of Lake Ontario, Clarion, 1979, revised edition, Bantam, 1981.
(With Luqman Keele) *Java Jack,* Crowell, 1980.
The Wuggie Norple Story, illustrated by Tomie dePaola, Four Winds, 1980.
The Worms of Kukumlima, Dutton, 1981.
Slaves of Spiegel: A Magic Moscow Story (also see below), Four Winds, 1982.
Young Adult Novel (also see below), Crowell, 1982.
Roger's Umbrella, illustrated by James Marshall, Dutton, 1982.
The Snarkout Boys and the Avocado of Death (also see below), Lothrop, 1982.
The Snarkout Boys and the Baconburg Horror, Lothrop, 1984.

Jolly Roger: A Dog of Hoboken, Lothrop, 1985.

Borgel, Macmillan, 1990.

Spaceburger: A Kevin Spoon and Mason Mintz Story, Macmillan, 1993.

Wallpaper from Space, illustrated by J. Pinkwater, Atheneum, 1996.

Goose Night, Random House, 1996.

Five Novels (includes *Alan Mendelsohn: The Boy from Mars, Slaves of Spiegel, The Snarkout Boys and the Avocado of Death, The Last Guru,* and *Young Adult Novel*), Farrar, Straus, 1997.

Magic Goose, Scholastic, 1997.

Second Grade Ape, illustrated by J. Pinkwater, Scholastic, 1997.

At the Hotel Larry, illustrated by J. Pinkwater, Marshall Cavendish, 1998.

Bongo Larry, illustrated by J. Pinkwater, Marshall Cavendish, 1998.

The Education of Robert Nifkin, Farrar, Straus, 1998.

Rainy Morning, illustrated by J. Pinkwater, Atheneum, 1998.

Wolf Christmas, illustrated by J. Pinkwater, Marshall Cavendish, 1998.

Big Bob and the Thanksgiving Potatoes, illustrated by J. Pinkwater, Scholastic, 1998.

Young Larry, illustrated by J. Pinkwater, Marshall Cavendish, 1998.

Ice Cream Larry, illustrated by J. Pinkwater, Marshall Cavendish, 1999.

Big Bob and the Winter Holiday Potato, illustrated by J. Pinkwater, Scholastic, 1999.

Big Bob and the Halloween Potatoes, illustrated by J. Pinkwater, Scholastic, 1999.

Big Bob and the Magic Valentine's Day Potato, illustrated by J. Pinkwater, Scholastic, 1999.

FOR ADULTS

Young Adults (fiction in three parts; first part based on *Young Adult Novel*), Tor, 1985.

Fish Whistle: Commentaries, Uncommentaries, and Vulgar Excesses (essays; also see below), Addison-Wesley, 1990.

Chicago Days, Hoboken Nights (autobiographical essays; also see below) Addison-Wesley, 1991.

The Afterlife Diet (novel), Random House, 1995.

Hoboken Fish and Chicago Whistle (combines *Fish Whistle* and *Chicago Days, Hoboken Nights*), Xlibris, 1999.

OTHER

Author· of *Comic Cosmic Novel* and *I Snarked with a Zombie* for Lothrop. Contributor of articles, reviews, and illustrations to periodicals, such as *Cricket, Gnomon, Island Review, Liberation, New York Times, Smithsonian Magazine, Washington Post,* and *Zen Notes.*

Adaptations

Wingman was made into a cassette by Listening Library, 1981; *Blue Moose* was produced as a videocassette by Positive Images, 1982; *The Hoboken Chicken Emergency* was adapted for television by the Public Broadcasting System (PBS), 1984; *I Was a Second Grade Werewolf* was made into a cassette by Live Oak Media, 1986. *Fish Whistle* was released as a sound recording by Bantam Audio, 1990. *Chicago Days/Hoboken Nights* was released as an audio book, narrated by Pinkwater, by Dove Audio, 1991. *Lizard Music* was adapted into a musical by Pinkwater and Christina Calrit with music by Douglas Wood and was produced by Lifeline Theatre, Chicago, 1992; it was revived in 1997.

Work in Progress

"Much."

Sidelights

Daniel Manus Pinkwater is a prolific and popular author and illustrator who is celebrated as a particularly original, imaginative, and versatile contributor to literature for children and young adults. Renowned as a humorist and satirist, Pinkwater creates unusual books that characteristically point out the absurdity of reality, especially as related to contemporary society, while presenting young readers with both solid morals and plenty of laughs. The author is well known for his irreverent—some say anarchic—sensibility as well as for the droll wit that he uses to skewer his targets. Directing his picture books and fiction to primary and middle graders, junior high school students, and young adults, Pinkwater is often praised for his clear recollections of childhood as well as for his understanding of children and of what appeals to them. Pinkwater depicts the entrance of the fantastic into the everyday while presenting the intrusion of the bizarre and ludicrous as a regular, and natural, occurrence. Often parodying genre fiction such as the detective story, the horror story, the adventure tale, and the science fiction and young adult novels, Pinkwater typically features ordinary characters—often boys from Rochester, New York and Hoboken, New Jersey—who are placed in incredible, improbable situations. In many of his books, Pinkwater makes his protagonists misfits and outsiders, though highly intelligent and aware. Their fantastic, often frenetic adventures lead these boys and girls to meet an array of odd creatures, both human and otherwise. As a result of their experiences, the young people learn to adjust to their own personal realities while discovering the joys of nonconformity and individuality.

As a writer, Pinkwater fills his works with puns, nonsense words, one-liners, vivid imagery, and allusions to other books (some of them his), food, and popular culture. The author favors a deadpan tone that belies the outlandishness and wild humor of his stories. Pinkwater, who often includes surprise twists at the end of his stories, is often noted for his playfulness and exuberance as well as for the color and vitality of his characterizations. As an artist, Pinkwater usually creates his illustrations in a deceptively simple, cartoonlike style—black and white drawings, often outlined with heavy lines and filled with bright colors—that is credited with complementing the energetic quality of his texts. In some of his later works, the artist uses colorful computer graphics. Thematically, Pinkwater underscores his books with a philosophy that encourages children to question the status quo while developing passionate interests and self-respect. Some reviewers fault the author for creating erratic, muddled books that are illogical, idiosyncratic, or just plain ridiculous. However, most critics consider Pinkwater a masterful humorist whose stories are both inspired nonsense and accurate assessments of modern life, making the author especially popular with young people. Called "one of the star authors in the junior high stable" by Susan B. Madden of *Voice of Youth Advocates,* he has been, according to Peter Andrews of the *New York Times Book Review,* "rightly praised as a children's author who does not treat his audience as if they are little darlings." Writing in *Twentieth-Century Children's Writers,* Janice M. Alberghene stated, "If Daniel Pinkwater were not so funny, so fond of wordplay, and so prolific, he would probably receive much greater recognition from adults as an important children's book author. Adults welcome humor as entertainment, but rarely give it serious consideration. Pinkwater's child readers, on the other hand, know a good book when they see it. . . . By turns satiric and serious, Pinkwater's imagination is utopian at heart." Christine Hepperman of *Children's Books and Their Creators* added, "When the stories are at their best, their jocularity carries them to ludicrous new heights. . . . Pinkwater's gang of offbeat characters and preposterous occurrences blend nicely with commonplace settings, forcing the reader to question reality—and then to laugh at it."

Pinkwater's books are filled with references to his own life. Born in Memphis, Tennessee, he moved to Chicago when he was two. His family stayed there until Pinkwater was eight; after moving to Los Angeles, he came back to Chicago as a teenager. Pinkwater told *Something about the Author (SATA),* "Upon my return I experienced a tremendous feeling of rising up, of getting back to a *real* place, and that excitement never wore off." Writing in his collection of autobiographical essays *Chicago Days, Hoboken Nights (CDHN),* he said, "I regarded Chicago, and that first large apartment, as home. I used to dream of living there, and frequently imagine it as the setting for works of fiction I write." In an interview with Deborah Kovacs and James Preller in *Meet the Authors and Illustrators, Vol. II (MTAAI),* he noted, "All of my stories are based in Chicago in one apartment." The author's father Philip, who has been characterized in his son's works, came to the United States from Poland, walking across Germany and France on the way to America. While still in Poland, Philip Pinkwater had been a hold-up man, hijacking things from other Jews; in New York City, he worked as a bootlegger, among other jobs. In Memphis, Philip got into the rag business, selling the rags used to wipe off dipsticks. Pinkwater's father found success when he bought a carload of worn-out army boots, which he refurbished and sold back to the army. As Philip Pinkwater developed his business, he traveled around the country. Pinkwater told *SATA* that his father was "like one of Isaac Babel's father characters—just the kind of father a boy wants to have. . . . I loved my father. He toughened me." Pinkwater's mother, a dancer, was the daughter of a rabbi. In an interview with Marilyn

Wann on the *Fat!So?* website, Pinkwater stated, "I come from a highly dysfunctional family. Fortunately, I had an elder half-brother and half-sister, whom my mother had at one time parked in an orphanage for a few years because that was convenient. They acquired human values there, and they raised me. But my actual biological parents were straight out of the Pleistocene."

In *CDHN,* Pinkwater recalled, "I used to be a jerk, a wimp, and a weenie. I was a sissy. And a big fat sissy to boot. I was so shy and uncomfortable that my very presence inflicted agony on everyone I met, adults especially." He found solace in watching television; listening to the radio; playing the flute; becoming a yo-yo expert; writing; and most of all, reading, especially comics like *Batman, Pogo, Krazy Kat,* and *Little Nemo,* and the books of Mark Twain. In his tongue-in-cheek essay in *Something about the Author Autobiography Series (SAAS),* Pinkwater noted, "Of my early life I remember many hardships and privations, the worst of which consisted of tripping over a root in Lincoln Park, in Chicago, and scraping my knee on a sharp rock. I remember my sister putting iodine and two Band-Aids on the wound. It hurt a lot. I believe that my resolve to become some sort of artist began during the period of recuperation from that injury. I decided that I wanted to work indoors." Pinkwater recalls receiving two pencils, a black one and a red one, at the age of two. He remembers writing one-page parodies in the fifth grade, enjoying grammar and logic exercises, and being inspired by *Mad* magazine; in grade school, Pinkwater used to write funny notes to pass around the classroom and get his friends to laugh out loud, thus getting them into trouble. When he won a short-story contest and was given a subscription to *National Geographic,* Pinkwater had a revelation: in his interview in *MTAAI,* he stated, "That's how I first learned that you could get things by writing." As a boy in Chicago, Pinkwater began the practice of what he calls "urban tourism," exploring out-of-the-way places to search for historical and/or unusual things. "What I was doing, it turned out" he wrote in *CDHN,* "was preparing for the trade I would follow later, and did not dream of then."

While living in Los Angeles, Pinkwater found a store that sold art supplies, which fascinated him. He wrote in *CDHN,* "It had the sort of appeal for me that a shop which sold model airplanes might have had. I liked the display of brushes and tools, and colors." After buying a drawing kit at the store that included crow quill pens and drawing paper, Pinkwater began drawing trees. He once described how "They got better and better. I experienced for the first time what an artist experiences. Then the other thing that artists experience happens. I wanted to show them to someone." Pinkwater's parents and his aunt, an artist, refused to believe that he had drawn the pictures; they felt that they were the work of a much older boy. Pinkwater realized that, as he noted "it would be a mistake to ever again let these adults I lived with know what I was doing. I never tried to draw again when I lived at home. . . . But my adventures in art were not over—only postponed."

Pinkwater told *SATA*, "It would be modest to the point of immodesty to claim that I wasn't brighter than the average kid, but when I was growing up, I used to pal around with other boys who were very much like me. We were like the 'Wild Dada Ducks' in my books and identified with each other. We had interests in common, and were able to form enough of a society so that we didn't feel especially alienated." After a stint in military school, Pinkwater moved back to Chicago at fourteen. After school, or instead of going to school, he would go to the Loop, Chicago's downtown business district. Pinkwater went to the library; to the lobby of the elegant Palmer House hotel, where he could do his homework and people-watch while enjoying a Havana cigar; and to the Department of Water and Sewers in City Hall, where a friend who worked there let him play with the traffic light control panel: "I like to think we never killed anyone," Pinkwater wrote in *CDHN*.

After graduating from high school, Pinkwater enrolled at Bard College in New York's Hudson River Valley, the area where he currently lives. Initially, Pinkwater majored in English, philosophy, history, drama, and religion. However, when his father threatened to take him out of school, Pinkwater switched his major to art. When he went to his sculpture teacher, the man told Pinkwater that he might as well start getting some experience; consequently, the new student was made to teach all three sections of Sculpture 101. "This began," Pinkwater wrote, "my formal education as an artist." In order to complete a research project, Pinkwater got a job as an intern in a sculpture foundry; Navin Diebold, a sculptor whom he met at the foundry, agreed to take him on as an apprentice. The author wrote, "I began as the pupil of Navin Diebold, the product of whose teaching I am, for better or worse, to this day." Pinkwater studied with Diebold—his pseudonym for David Nyvall—for three years. In his senior year at Bard, Pinkwater was given his own studio, where he worked on his senior project, a series of woodblock prints. After John F. Kennedy was assassinated, Pinkwater began questioning his artistic endeavors as empty exercises. "Gradually," he wrote, "I became convinced that the best way I could address the big evils of the big world would be to keep chipping away at something comparatively small." At the end of their sessions, David Nyvall told Pinkwater that he would never be a sculptor; instead, Nyvall told his student that he would be a writer.

After leaving Bard College, Pinkwater went to New York City to make his name as—despite his teacher's prediction—an artist. Before departing, he had three shows; the most successful one was in a saloon. In Chicago, Pinkwater had worked as a woodcarver, carving ornamental pieces out of wood. In New York in 1964 he visited art museums, museums of ethnology, and interesting stores, such as the House of Antiquities, a Manhattan shop that sold authentic ancient artifacts. He soon moved to Hoboken, New Jersey, a picturesque town across from New York City that was filled with colorful characters. Hoboken, which was to become Pinkwater's home for the next dozen years, also became, as he noted in *CDHN*, "my spiritual home for the rest of

my life." While working on his art, Pinkwater took extensive courses in art therapy, then worked as an art teacher in settlement houses and youth centers around New York City and New Jersey. He also traveled to Africa, joining an artists' cooperative in which he was the only member who was not from the Chagga tribe. In 1969, Pinkwater married Jill Schutz, a teacher, writer, and artist who, as Jill Pinkwater, has created works of her own and has illustrated several of her husband's books.

While trying to sell his sculptures and prints, Pinkwater became friends with a New York couple, the Silvers, whom he described in *CDHN* as "my only collectors." At a party given by the Silvers, Pinkwater met a children's book editor who was looking for pictures to go with a book of African folktales that she was editing. Learning that Pinkwater had recently returned from Africa, the editor suggested that he might like to try illustrating the story. After going to his studio, the editor told Pinkwater that he should try writing and illustrating

Pinkwater teamed up with his wife, Jill, for this thorough guide to puppy ownership. (Cover illustration by Jill Pinkwater.)

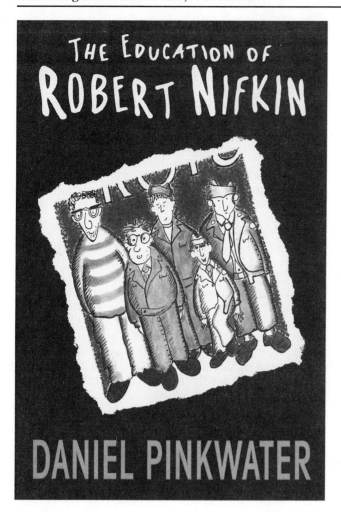

Robert Nifkin describes his outrageous high-school experiences in the form of a college application essay in Pinkwater's novel for children. (Cover illustration by Jill Pinkwater.)

his own book. The author told *SATA,* "I had to get a story first and, not wishing to deal with writers because I knew what *they* were like, I wrote one. Knopf published the book, and gave me money." He added in *SAAS,* "I knew at once that I had found my calling."

Pinkwater's first book, *The Terrible Roar,* was published in 1970 under the name Manus Pinkwater. A picture book about a little lion whose big roars make everything around him disappear, the story is, as described by *School Library Journal* critic Ann D. Schweibish, "simple and rhythmically repetitive." The critic went on to say that the book "is made by the exceedingly bright, flat-planed, simple and humorous color pictures which children will love." For the next few years, Pinkwater continued to create picture books and stories that were mostly well-received. For example, a critic in *Publishers Weekly* had this to say about *Wizard Crystal,* the story of an unhappy wizard who is changed into a happy frog after he finds a magic crystal: "For sheer fun, smashing pictures, and a socko ending, this book is hard to beat." In a review of *Magic Camera,* the story of a boy whose father brings him an unusual antique camera, a reviewer

in *Booklist* concluded that "a fanciful and warmly naive quality leaves no doubt that the magic of childhood has remained to grace this author-artist's work."

In 1975, Pinkwater published *Blue Moose,* the first of his three books about the title character, who changes the life of a lonely chef who runs a gourmet restaurant on the edge of the North Woods; the moose becomes the chef's maitre d', winning him popularity among the woodsmen. A reviewer in *Publishers Weekly* called *Blue Moose* "[a]nother star performance" and "a witty and touching fantasy," while a critic in *Kirkus Reviews* concluded, "[T]his author's 'yep' is worth more than another's whole thesaurus." In the second volume, *Return of the Moose,* the Blue Moose learns about the vagaries of the publishing world when he pens his memoirs. Discovering that his publishers have changed his book into a hot love story, the moose eats six thousand copies of his book in order to get rid of them. The third volume of the series, *The Moosepire,* describes how the Blue Moose tracks down Deadly Eric (or Eric the Dead), a vampire moose.

In 1976, Pinkwater produced *Lizard Music,* a fantasy that is considered among his best works. First, eleven-year-old Victor sees a movie on late-night television about pods invading the earth; then, he sees pod people on a talk show as well as a lizard band on television playing incredibly beautiful music. After this, he starts seeing lizards everywhere. Next, Victor meets the Chicken Man, an old black man with a performing chicken named Claudia. The Chicken Man takes Victor to an invisible island inhabited by friendly lizards; here, Claudia hatches the egg that, according to legend, will lead the lizards in conquering the pods. A critic in *Kirkus Reviews* stated that *Lizard Music* is "that rarity, a children's fantasy that is truly contemporary in sensibility as well as setting. It's funny, properly paranoid, shot through with bad puns and sweet absurdities. . . ." The critic concluded that the concept of the lizard legend "is certainly a more significant feat, . . . than are any of those traditionalist victories of light over darkness that are still being (over) sold as high fantasy." In *Introducing More Books: A Guide for the Middle Grades,* Diana L. Spirt commented that *Lizard Music* "has a theme that augments its value as an exciting story. Its abstract concerns with simplicity of life-style, genuineness of human beings, and awareness of the environment are woven into the fabric of the story by a masterful plotter. It speaks directly to children who will absorb and appreciate the deep underlying message."

From 1974 to 1976, Pinkwater and his wife operated a dog training school; in 1977, the couple produced *Superpuppy: How to Choose, Raise, and Train the Best Possible Dog for You.* Daniel's sole book of nonfiction for children, *Superpuppy* offers instruction on finding and caring for dogs while providing the Pinkwaters' opinions on such subjects as pet stores and people who buy canine junk food. A critic in *Kirkus Reviews* called the work a "super puppy book, refreshingly sensible and undogmatic. . . . [T]he Pinkwaters quietly and personably set forth a thorough, thoughtful, and sympathetic

Dr. Spock of puppy care." A critic in *Publishers Weekly* added that *Superpuppy* "should almost be required reading of anyone thinking about owning a pet."

With *Alan Mendelsohn, the Boy from Mars,* a book published in 1979, Pinkwater created one of his most highly regarded titles. When Leonard Neeble moves from the city to the suburbs and begins attending Bat Masterson Junior High, he is snubbed by the snobbish faculty and students. Leonard finds friendship with Alan Mendelsohn, a fellow classmate who claims that he is a Martian. Leonard and Alan discover the Bermuda Triangle Chili Parlor, where they meet Samuel Klugarsh, a used book dealer who has developed a cabalistic mind-control system, and Clarence Yojimbo, a Venusian who leads them to the existential plane of Waka-Waka. At the end of the novel, Alan returns to Mars and Leonard returns to school better able to make friends with other students who have been dismissed by the snobs. Ann S. Haskell of the *New York Times Book Review* called *Alan Mendelsohn* Pinkwater's "most ambitious book to date ... that is, in spots, reminiscent of E. Nesbit, and everywhere vintage Pinkwater." The critic added, "[F]or imaginative plot and decorative detail, Mr. Pinkwater's scores go off the charts. All his life he has been collecting funny odds and ends—names of people, places, products and mannerisms, for example—that give depth to his stories and which, taken together, sometimes add up to rather remarkable sociological commentary." *Kliatt* reviewer Fran Lantz called *Alan Mendelsohn* "Pinkwater's best book since *Lizard Music,*" while Zena Sutherland of *Bulletin of the Center for Children's Books* concluded, "If nothing succeeds like excess, the author has achieved a triumph of improbable folderol."

In 1982, Pinkwater created a send-up of young adult novels—called, appropriately enough, *Young Adult Novel*—that remains one of his most popular books. In the first four pages of this short novel, the author introduces Kevin Shapiro, a gay, alcoholic thirteen-year-old who supports himself by stealing and selling drugs. Kevin's mother is locked away in a madhouse, his father is severely mentally impaired, and his sister is a prostitute. Readers of *Young Adult Novel* learn that Kevin is the hero of a story by the Wild Dada Ducks, a group of five high-school friends who have modeled themselves on the Dada movement of twentieth-century artists and writers. When the Ducks find that there really is a Kevin Shapiro at their school, they turn the boy—an antisocial nerd—into president of the student body. Shapiro retaliates by forming an alternate group, the Fanatical Praetorians, who provide a comeuppance for the Wild Dada Ducks. Patty Campbell, writing in *Wilson Library Bulletin,* called *Young Adult Novel* "an absolutely exquisite putdown, a piece of delicious dada fluff," while Stephanie Zvirin of *Booklist* noted that Pinkwater makes the story work "in fewer than 60 pages and makes it entertaining as well." Although Peter Andrews, a contributor to the *New York Times Book Review,* felt that Pinkwater "smothers his young readers with a racy bonhomie that smacks too much of adults who think that they are getting close to young people by slam dancing

with them, an enterprise distressing to children and degrading to adults," Susan B. Madden, a *Voice of Youth Advocates* reviewer, concluded that of all Pinkwater's books, this "particular wonderfully titled piece of nonsense is the best of all. . . . As is typical with Pinkwater, the wit pinpoints some very real adolescent concerns and feelings."

Uncle Melvin, a picture book published in 1989, is considered by critics as one of Pinkwater's most touching works. Uncle Melvin is mentally ill, spending his days with little Charles and his family and his nights in what he calls the "Looney Bin." Melvin sends messages to flying saucers and thinks that the President of the United States is a lizard. When he claims that he can start the rain and make rainbows, Melvin tests his family's limits. However, when he makes good on his claim, Charles becomes, in the words of Susan Perren of *Quill & Quire,* "an apostle for life." Perren noted, "With a few deft squiggles of the pen, a generous rainbow palette of colour, and the right number of well-chosen words, Daniel Pinkwater's *Uncle Melvin* gives the young an amusing and intriguing portrait of a family's 'crazy' relative and, indirectly, that family's capacity to hold that relative within its boundaries." In a *Bulletin of the Center for Children's Books* review, Robert Strang stated, "It is very nice to have a picture book that shows the mentally ill as capable of love, work, and responsibility, but the fairytale aura confuses the issue." However, Anna Biagioni Hart concluded in a *School Library Journal* review, "The family's gentle acceptance of this extraordinary individual is an appealing part of this out-of-the-ordinary picture book, and it goes a long way toward calming an adult reader's unease with this *naif.*"

The Education of Robert Nifkin, a young adult novel published in 1998, is one of Pinkwater's most directly autobiographical works. Written by its title character as his college application essay, the book describes how Robert, a friendless, overweight boy in the Chicago of the late 1950s, learns to survive high school and begin to find himself. Robert attends Riverview High School, a place filled with strange, paranoid, and anti-Semitic teachers; consequently, the boy begins spending more time exploring the city of Chicago, where he meets a variety of interesting nonconformist friends. One of them tells Robert about the Wheaton School, a private school that, in the words of Ann A. Flowers of *Horn Book,* "makes the adjective *progressive* look inflexible." Since attending classes at Wheaton is voluntary, Robert spends much of his time attending lectures at the University of Chicago, playing chess in bookstores, and discussing philosophy at a luncheonette, among other stimulating activities. Through his self-education, Robert makes himself a candidate for college. Flowers commented, "If the book weren't so funny, it could almost be a prescription for an interesting education. . . . [T]his book will find its way to the hearts of individualists everywhere." Stephanie Zvirin of *Booklist* added that the novel "literally crackles and the comedy is occasionally laugh-out-loud funny. . . ." Writing in *Bulletin of the Center for Children's Books,* Deborah Stevenson called Pinkwater "Jean Shepherd edged with Damon Runyan" and noted that he "effectively conveys the bizarreness of—well—everybody. . . ." A critic in *Kirkus Reviews* concluded, "Falling somewhere between Candide and Holden Caulfield, Robert is an inexperienced but savvy teen, with an ability to land on his feet and capacity for sardonic observations that will have readers rocking with laughter."

In 1987, Pinkwater embarked on a new career as a radio commentator. Appearing on the National Public Radio programs *All Things Considered* and *Car Talk,* he has become a well-known figure among radio audiences. In addition, Pinkwater created and co-hosted *Chinwag Theater,* a program for young people, and reviewed books for *Weekend Edition Saturday with Scott Simon.* His radio commentaries were collected in two volumes, *Fish Whistle: Commentaries, Uncommentaries, and Vulgar Excesses,* a book published in 1990, and *Chicago Days, Hoboken Nights,* a collection of autobiographical essays published the following year. Although directed to adults, *Chicago Days, Hoboken Nights* is often enjoyed by young readers. The volume, which recounts Pinkwater's childhood through his becoming a writer, is described by *School Library Journal* contributor Judy McAloon as "great reading" by a "superb storyteller." McAloon concluded that Pinkwater's "deceptively simple and often funny stories will enchant YAs," before going on to describe the author as "talented, funny, and smart—a real mensch." Donna Seaman of *Booklist* stated, "Pouncing on the kernel of absurdity hidden in every situation, Pinkwater gently reminds us of what really counts." Pinkwater has also written two books of adult fiction, *Young Adults,* which incorporates part of *Young Adult Novel,* and *The Afterlife Diet.*

When asked by Marilyn Wann on the *Fat!So?* website about how he writes a book for children, Pinkwater responded, "I imagine a child. That child is me. I can reconstruct and vividly remember portions of my own childhood. I can see, taste, smell, feel, and hear them. Then what I do is, not write about that kid or about his world, but start to think of a book that would have pleased him." Pinkwater told *SATA,* "I'm not literary. I'm a streetfighter and a subversive artist. I feel I'm in a different world from the arbitrators of what's good, the self-congratulatory types who are involved in literature for the 'betterment of children.' It is my intention to blow these people sky high, and I've done my very best in that direction. The readers are clear about what's synthetic and what's genuine and I'm honored by their choices." He added, "The most gratifying type of letter from a kid says, 'I don't ordinarily like to read, but I've read five of your books and I'm looking for more.' That gladdens my heart, because I know I've caught another soul for the Master. I like making converts." Pinkwater concluded by saying, "I set store by courage, and I try to be as brave as I can afford. . . . I want my readers to feel encouraged and *snarky,* because basically they are kids taking on a hostile and/or indifferent world. My books are about finding favoring signs in the world, about discovering riches—things which are not dead. My stories are about people prevailing." He added in *SAAS,* "Beneath the glitter, I like to think that I am the same loveable paranoid who hurt his knee so many years ago. My advice to young writers and those who aspire to write is this: stay away from me, you bums."

Works Cited

Alberghene, Janice, essay in *Twentieth-Century Children's Writers,* 3rd edition, St. James Press, 1989, pp. 781-782.

Andrews, Peter, review of *Slaves of Spiegel* and others, *New York Times Book Review,* April 25, 1987, p. 51.

Review of *Blue Moose, Kirkus Reviews,* June 15, 1975, p. 661.

Review of *Blue Moose, Publishers Weekly,* June 9, 1975, p. 63.

Campbell, Patty, review of *Young Adult Novel, Wilson Library Bulletin,* March, 1982, p. 533.

Review of *The Education of Robert Nifkin, Kirkus Reviews,* April 15, 1998, p. 585.

Flowers, Ann A., review of *The Education of Robert Nifkin, Horn Book,* July/August, 1998, pp. 495-96.

Hart, Anna Biagioni, review of *Uncle Melvin, School Library Journal,* January, 1990, p. 88.

Haskell, Ann S., "The Fantastic Mr. Pinkwater," *New York Times Book Review,* April 29, 1979, pp. 32, 43.

Hepperman, Christine, entry in *Children's Books and Their Creators,* edited by Anita Silvey, Houghton Mifflin, 1995, p. 528.

Lantz, Fran, review of *Alan Mendelsohn, the Boy from Mars, Kliatt,* September, 1981, p. 14.

Review of *Lizard Music, Kirkus Reviews,* August 1, 1976, p. 846.

Review of *Lizard Music, Publishers Weekly,* October 18, 1976, p. 64.

Madden, Susan B., review of *Young Adult Novel, Voice of Youth Advocates,* June, 1982, p. 36.

Madden, Susan B., review of *The Snarkout Boys and the Baconburg Horror, Voice of Youth Advocates,* August, 1986, p. 144.

Review of *Magic Camera, Booklist,* April 1, 1974, p. 878.

McAloon, Judy, review of *Chicago Days, Hoboken Nights, School Library Journal,* April, 1992, p. 168.

Perren, Susan, review of *Uncle Melvin, Quill & Quire,* January, 1990, p. 18.

Pinkwater, Daniel Manus, interview in *Something about the Author,* Volume 46, Gale, 1987, pp. 178-191.

Pinkwater, Daniel Manus, essay in *Something about the Author Autobiography Series,* Volume 3, Gale, 1987, pp. 221-25.

Pinkwater, Daniel Manus, excerpts from *Chicago Days, Hoboken Nights,* Addison-Wesley, 1991, 168 pp.

Pinkwater, Daniel Manus, interview with Deborah Kovacs and James Preller, *Meet the Authors and Illustrators, Vol. II,* Scholastic, 1993.

Schweibish, Ann D., review of *The Terrible Roar, School Library Journal,* March, 1971, p. 123.

Seaman, Donna, review of *Chicago Days, Hoboken Nights, Booklist,* October 15, 1991, p. 399.

Spirt, Diana L., "Appreciating Books: 'Lizard Music,'" *Introducing More Books: A Guide for the Middle Grades,* Bowker, 1978, pp. 217-20.

Stevenson, Deborah, review of *The Education of Robert Nifkin, Bulletin of the Center for Children's Books,* July/August, 1998, p. 408.

Strang, Robert, review of *Uncle Melvin, Bulletin of the Center for Children's Books,* November, 1989, pp. 69-70.

Review of *Superpuppy: How to Choose, Raise, and Train the Best Possible Dog for You, Kirkus Reviews,* July 15, 1977, p. 731.

Review of *Superpuppy: How to Choose, Raise, and Train the Best Possible Dog for You, Publishers Weekly,* August 1, 1977, p. 115.

Sutherland, Zena, review of *Alan Mendelsohn, the Boy from Mars, Bulletin of the Center for Children's Books,* September, 1979, p. 54.

Wann, Marilyn, "Daniel Pinkwater and the Afterlife," *Fat!So?* website: http://www.fatso.com/interview.html.

Review of *Wizard Crystal, Publishers Weekly,* February 26, 1973, p. 123.

Zvirin, Stephanie, review of *Young Adult Novel, Booklist,* April 1, 1982, p. 1014.

Zvirin, Stephanie, review of *The Education of Robert Nifkin, Booklist,* June 1, 1998, p. 1749.

For More Information See

BOOKS

Authors & Artists for Young Adults, Volume 1, Gale, 1989, pp. 231-41.
Children's Literature Review, Volume 4, Gale, 1982.
Contemporary Literary Criticism, Volume 35, Gale, 1985, pp. 317-21.
Landsberg, Michele, *Reading for the Love of It,* Prentice-Hall, 1987.
St. James Guide to Young Adult Writers, St. James Press, 1999, pp. 693-95.

PERIODICALS

Book World, September 7, 1997, p. 11.
CM: Canadian Materials, February 27, 1998.
People, December 21, 1981.
Publishers Weekly, July 7, 1997, p. 70.

—*Sketch by Gerard J. Senick*

*   *   *

PINKWATER, Manus
See PINKWATER, Daniel Manus

*   *   *

PYRNELLE, Louise-Clarke 1850-1907

Personal

Born June 19, 1850, on Ittabena plantation, near Uniontown, AL; died August 26, 1907, in Birmingham, AL; daughter of Richard (a physician) and Elizabeth Carson (Bates) Clarke; married John R. Pyrnelle, 1880 (died, 1901). *Education:* Attended Hammer Hall, Montgomery, AL, and Mrs. Anna Randall Diehl's College of Education in Long Island, New York; graduated from Professor McKay's Delsarte Academy, New York City.

Career

Writer of books for children, 1882-1907. Governess in the American south, c. 1870. Teacher in public schools in Alabama, Georgia, Florida, and Texas.

Writings

Diddie, Dumps, and Tot; or, Plantation Childlife, Harper (New York City), 1882.
Miss Li'l' Tweetty, Harper, 1917.

Sidelights

"Louise-Clarke Pyrnelle's works, once moderately popular," declared *Dictionary of Literary Biography* contributor Susan E. Miller, "are now anachronistic. Both the author and her books are products of another era, a time far removed from the life experiences of today's children." Pyrnelle used material drawn from her own life in her two children's novels, *Diddie, Dumps, and Tot* and *Miss Li'l' Tweetty,* and they reflected the plantation society in which she was raised. The books demonstrate the often contradictory relationship between masters and slaves—a relationship that was based in some ways on mutual trust, and in others on nearly absolute power. "When the stories are viewed in relation to Pyrnelle's personal history," Miller explained, "it is possible to get a feeling for the confusion, pain, and frustration that the fall of the South must have brought her as an adolescent child who had the supports of life pulled out from under her."

Both *Diddie, Dumps, and Tot* and *Miss Li'l' Tweetty* depict plantation society very favorably. "Through the selective eyes and memory of childhood," wrote Miller, "the author recalls a life which was idyllic for both the aristocracy and the slaves. In this version of reality, free slaves and poor whites represent the lowest and most unfortunate members of society." The three heroines of *Diddie, Dumps, and Tot* (nine-year-old Madeleine, five-year-old Elinor, and three-year-old Eugenia) are the privileged children of a plantation owner. Although most of the book chronicles the girls' play and the stories told by the oldest slave, Daddy Jake, Pyrnelle depicts confrontations between the children and their protector, Mammy. The author also describes the three youngsters' visit to a slave-trader's camp and records self-deprecating stories told by the slaves about themselves. *Miss Li'l' Tweetty* features as its two protagonists Li'l' Tweety (Mary) and Popsy, her servant. Miller noted, "the class distinctions are still evident" in the later story, although "the derogations are less obvious and a sense of personal loss no longer haunts the story."

Diddie, Dumps, and Tot in particular reflects Pyrnelle's profound sense of loss in the post-Civil War South. The story, Miller explained, concluded with a summary of the effect the war had on the family and their former slaves. Both Diddie's husband and her father are killed in the war, and the plantation is destroyed. Diddie turns her attention to raising her only son. The children's mother loses her sanity, and Dumps, who never married, devotes the rest of her life to caring for her. "The reader," Miller stated, "is told that only Tot escaped the trauma of the war, dying instead as a blameless child before the world she knew fell to ruins." The former young slave Jim was the only one to profit from the war, becoming a member of the state legislature and, wrote Miller, quoting Pyrnelle, "making long and exciting speeches to the loyal leaguers against the Southern white, all unmindful of his happy childhood, and of the kind and generous master who strove in every way to render his bondage (for which that master was in no way to blame) a light and happy one."

Works Cited

Miller, Susan E., *Dictionary of Literary Biography,* Volume 42: *American Writers for Children before 1900,* Gale, 1985.*

R

REESE, Della 1931(?)-

Personal

Born Deloreese Patricia Early, July 6, 1931 (some sources say 1932), in Detroit, MI; daughter of Richard (a steelworker) and Nellie (a cook) Early; married Vermont Adolphus Bon Taliaferro (a factory worker; divorced); married Leroy Basil Gray (an accountant), 1962 (marriage invalidated); married Franklin Thomas Lett Jr. (a concert and television producer and businessman), c. 1982; children: Deloreese Daniels, James Barger, Dominique, Franklin Lett III. *Education:* Attended Wayne State University, 1949-50.

Addresses

Agent—William Morris Agency, 151 El Camino, Beverly Hills, CA 90212.

Career

Singer, actress, and composer. Mahalia Jackson Troupe, performer, 1946-49; Meditation Singers (women's gospel group), founder, c. 1949; toured in revue *Some of My Best Friends Are the Blues,* created by husband Frank Lett, beginning 1992. Understanding Principles for Better Living, Los Angeles, founder and minister, 1983—. Worked variously as a hostess/singer in a bowling alley-nightclub and as a taxi cab driver, truck driver, barber, and switch-board operator.

Has performed on radio shows and in nightclubs across the United States, singing with the Clara Ward Singers, Roberta Martin Singers, Beatrice Brown's Inspirational Singers, and the Erskine Hawkins Orchestra. Recordings include: *I've Got My Love to Keep Me Warm,* Jubilee, c. 1955; *Time after Time,* Jubilee, c. 1955; *In the Still of the Night,* Jubilee, c. 1956; *One More Time,* ABC-Paramount, 1956; *And That Reminds Me,* Jubilee, 1957; *A Date with Della—at Mr. Kelly's,* Jubilee, 1958; *Della by Starlight,* RCA Victor, 1960; *Della, Della, Cha Cha Cha,* RCA Victor, 1960; *I Like It like Dat,* ABC-

Della Reese

Paramount, c. 1960; *Special Delivery, Della Reese,* RCA Victor, 1961; *Della on Stage,* RCA Victor, 1962; *The Classic Della,* RCA Victor, 1962; *Waltz with Me, Della,* RCA Victor, 1963; *Three Great Girls,* RCA Victor, 1963; *Della Reese at Basin Street East,* RCA Victor, 1964; *C'mon and Hear,* ABC-Paramount, 1965; *Moody, Della Reese,* RCA Victor, 1965; *On Strings of Blue,* ABC-Paramount, 1967; *The Best of Della Reese,* RCA Victor, 1972; *Let Me in Your Life,* Lee Magid, 1972; *Della Reese,* ABC-Paramount, 1976; *One of a Kind, Jazz a Language Arts Carte,* 1978; *Hush, Somebody's Callin' My Name,* CUT, 1979; *Sure Like Lovin' You,* Dell Reese (Applause), 1983; *Amen,* Jubilee, and *The*

Story of the Blues, Jubilee, c. 1983; *Della Reese and Brilliance,* AIR Co., 1987; *Black Is Beautiful,* AVCO-Embassy; *What Do You Know about Love?,* Jubilee; and *My Soul Feels Better Right Now,* Jubilee.

Actress in movies, including *Let's Rock,* 1958, *The Last Minstrel Show,* (stage play), 1978, *The Distinguished Gentleman,* and *Harlem Nights,* 1989. Actress in television productions, including (hostess) *Della Variety Show,* 1969-70, *The Royal Family,* CBS, 1991-92, and *Touched by an Angel,* CBS, 1994—. Has made guest appearances on various television shows, including *The Tonight Show, Merv Griffin Show, Ed Sullivan Show, Jackie Gleason Show, Joey Bishop Show, Perry Como Show, Hollywood Palace Show, Mike Douglas Show, Pat Boone Show, McCloud, Police Woman, Twice in a Lifetime, The Mod Squad, Chico & the Man, Petrocelli, Mike Douglas Show, The Love Boat, The Great American Gospel Show, Grand Ole Opry, The "A" Team, MacGyver, Night Court, Crazy like a Fox, Young Riders, Designing Women, L.A. Law, Pickett Fences,* and a variety of game shows and television specials.

Awards, Honors

Most Promising Girl Singer, 1957, *Billboard, Variety,* and *Cashbox;* Emmy nomination for best supporting actress, 1977, for *Nightmare in Badman County;* Grammy nomination for best female soloist—gospel, 1987; awarded a star on the Hollywood Walk of Fame, 1994; NAACP Image Award for best female actress in a dramatic series, 1996, 1997, 1998, 1999; Emmy nomination for best supporting actress, and Screen Actors Guild nomination for best supporting actress, both 1998, both for *Touched by an Angel;* numerous Gold Records.

Writings

Angels along the Way: My Life with Help from Above, Putnam (New York City), 1997.
God Inside of Me, Hyperion Books for Children (New York City), 1999.

Sidelights

Angels along the Way: My Life with Help from Above is a self-portrait of Della Reese, an ordained minister, a singer of gospel, pop, and blues, and an actress and television personality "well known for her clear, powerful voice, distinctive diction, and emotional delivery," according to *Contemporary Musicians* essayists Sandy J. Stiefer and Jeanne M. Lesinski. Reese was born Deloreese Patricia Early, but assumed the stage name of Pat Ferro, an adaptation of her first husband's name, during her first major engagements as a paid performer—eighteen weeks at Detroit's Flame Showbar. After divorcing her first husband, she changed her name to Della Reese. "Dividing her first name [in two]," explained Stiefer and Lesinski, "she created her professional name, one that would become synonymous with blues, jazz, and gospel music." "Della Reese," summarized Robert L. Johns in *Notable Black American Women, Book II,* "was one of the major black stars

leading the breakout of black women musicians into the mainstream of pop music in the late 1950s. Her popularity led to numerous appearance on television, where she was the first black woman to host a variety show. Through her championship of gospel music in clubs, she played a part in bringing about the recognition of gospel by the general public. After her early recording success declined to some degree, she continued to be popular in clubs and on television."

A *Jet* contributor summarizing Reese's 1997 autobiography reported that "the supportive wheedling by her husband [Lett] convinced her to [write *Angels along the Way,* which]... turned out to be a catharsis for her in some ways." While writing the book Reese discovered that anger resided beneath her seemingly "indifferent" feelings toward her abusive first husband. In addition, noted the *Jet* contributor, she realized that "she still hadn't fully let go of her mother's 'transition,'"—her death in 1949. "Hailing from a poor section of Detroit, Reese endured racism and humiliation as a performer and was nearly killed by an aneurysm in 1980," stated Peter Castro in *People Weekly.* "Reese ... credits the many miracles in her life ... to the many human angels who have helped her along the way"; among them, her husband, Franklin Lett, comedian Eddie Murphy, and her late mother." "Reese," concluded the writer for *Jet,* "wants the book to send an inspirational message to readers. 'I want to show people that if He would do this for me, He will do the same thing for you,' says Reese.'"

Angels are the central characters in one of Reese's most recent roles as an actress. She plays the character Tess in the CBS television series *Touched by an Angel."* The show, which *New Republic* essayist Ruth Shalit described as "featuring a dream team of ethnically balanced angles who rove around the country twiddling heartstrings and performing good works," was introduced to TV audiences in 1994 and has since become one of the top-rated dramatic series. "The program's popularity has taken everyone in the industry quite by surprise," remarked *America* contributor James Martin, explaining: "Here is a pleasant, unprepossessing television series that has clung consistently to its Top 10 ratings—with no car chases, sleazy sexual escapades, celebrity tell-all confessions or infantile humor.... And, wonder of wonders, it's about religion, or rather, 'spirituality.'"

Touched by an Angel was described by Martin as "a pleasant, family-values series about angels (a redoubtable Della Reese and a gentler Roma Downey) who appear to help out individuals at difficult moments in their lives.... To their credit, the scriptwriters have resisted the temptation to turn Ms. Reese and Ms. Downey into comforting angels who simply dispense heavenly favors.... Instead," added Martin, "these messengers ask for ethical behavior and an adult understanding of one's responsibility to God and humanity." Calling *Touched by an Angel* "unabashedly inspirational," Castro detailed: "As Tess, a seasoned seraph who takes Monica, a rookie angel (played by Roma

Downey), under her wing, the smoky-voiced Reese ... gets to dispatch faith, hope, and wisdom to people at a crossroads in their lives."

Works Cited

Review of *Angels along the Way, Jet,* November 24, 1997, pp. 38-39.

Castro, Peter, "Counting Her Blessings," *People Weekly,* February 24, 1997, p. 113.

Johns, Robert L., essay in *Notable Black American Women, Book II,* Gale Research, 1996.

Martin, James, review of "Touched by an Angel," *America,* May 31, 1997, p. 24.

Shalit, Ruth, "Quality Wings," *New Republic,* July 20, 1998, p. 24.

Stiefer, Sandy J. and Jeanne M. Lesinski, essay in *Contemporary Musicians,* Volume 13, Gale Research, 1995.

For More Information See

BOOKS

Contemporary Black Biography, Volume 6, Gale Research (Detroit, MI), 1994.

Dictionary of Twentieth-Century Culture, Volume 5: *African-American Culture,* Gale Research, 1996.

In Black and White, 3rd edition, Gale Research, 1980.

Murrells, Joseph, *Million Selling Records from the 1900s to the 1980s,* Arco (New York City), 1984.

PERIODICALS

Black Elegance, July, 1992.

Broadcasting & Cable, October 13, 1997.

Ebony, March, 1960; July, 1962; May, 1977; September, 1977; May, 1989.

Entertainment Weekly, November 4, 1994; June 13, 1997; October 17, 1997.

Good Housekeeping, April, 1997.

Jet, September 23, 1991; October 28, 1991; December 9, 1991; July 5, 1993; March 10, 1997; July 6, 1998.

Library Journal, November 1, 1997.

Los Angeles Times, July 16, 1992.

Melody Maker, August 29, 1987.

New Republic, July 20, 1998.

New York Sunday News, December 29, 1957.

People Weekly, May 19, 1980; February 26, 1996.

Saturday Evening Post, May-June, 1997.

Time, October 20, 1997.

Variety, November 18, 1981; May 7, 1986.

Village Voice, March 16, 1982.*

*   *   *

RIDDELL, Chris(topher Barry) 1962-

Personal

Born April 13, 1962, in Capetown, South Africa; son of Morris Stroyan (an Anglican priest) and Pamela Aileen (Moyle) Riddell; married Joanna Kathleen Burroughes (an artist), November 7, 1987; children: William, Katy, Jack. *Education:* Attended Epsom School of Art &

Design, 1980-81; Brighton Polytechnic, B.A. (first class; illustration), 1984.

Addresses

Office—c/o Anderson Press, 20 Vauxhall Bridge Rd., London SW1V 2SA, England.

Career

Illustrator and writer. Political cartoonist for London periodicals, including *Economist,* 1988-95, and *Observer,* 1995—.

Awards, Honors

Kate Greenaway Medal special commendation, 1995, and UNESCO Prize, 1997, both for *Something Else;* Ragazza Prize honorable mention, Bologna Book Fair, 1998, and Kurt Maschler Award shortlist, 1998, both for *The Swan's Stories.*

Writings

SELF-ILLUSTRATED

Ben and the Bear, Walker, 1985.

Mr. Underbed, Holt, 1986.

Bird's New Shoes, Holt, 1987.

The Fibbs, Walker, 1988.

The Trouble with Elephants, Walker, 1988.

When the Walrus Comes, Walker, 1989.

The Bear Dance, Simon & Schuster, 1990.

The Wish Factory, Walker, 1990.

The World of Zoom, Walker, 1993.

ILLUSTRATOR

Sarah Hayes, reteller, *Gruesome Giants,* Derrydale, 1985.

Mary Hoffman, *Beware, Princess!,* Heinemann, 1986.

Ted Hughes, *Ffangs the Vampire Bat and the Kiss of Truth,* Faber, 1986.

Kate Andrew, *Beyond the Rolling River,* Collins, 1988.

J. M. Barrie, *Peter Pan,* Magnet, 1988.

T. Hughes, *Moon-Whales,* revised edition, Faber, 1988.

M. Hoffman, *Dracula's Daughter,* Heinemann, 1988, Barron's, 1989.

Robert McCrum, *The Dream Boat Brontosaurus,* Methuen, 1989.

Andrew Gibson, *Ellis and the Hummick,* Faber, 1989.

A. Gibson, *The Abradizil,* Faber, 1990.

K. Andrew, *The Prism Tree,* Collins, 1990.

Kathryn Cave, *Henry Hobbs, Alien,* Viking, 1990.

K. Cave, *Jumble,* Blackie, 1991.

Helen Cresswell, *Lizzie Dripping and the Witch,* BBC Books, 1991.

A. Gibson, *Jemima, Grandma, and the Great Lost Zone,* Faber, 1991.

K. Cave, *Out for the Count: A Counting Adventure,* Barron's, 1991.

Freida Hughes, *The Thing in the Sink,* Simon & Schuster, 1992.

Catherine Baker, editor, *An Armful of Bears* (poetry), Methuen, 1993.

Chris Riddell

A. Gibson, *The Amazing Witherspoon's Amazing Circus Crew,* Faber, 1993.

K. Cave, *Something Else,* Viking, 1994.

F. Hughes, *Rent-a-Friend,* Simon & Schuster, 1994.

Miles Gibson, *Say Hello to the Buffalo,* Heinemann, 1994.

A. Gibson, *Chegwith Skillett Escapes,* Faber, 1995.

T. Hughes, *Collected Animal Poems,* Volume 1: *The Iron Wolf,* Faber, 1995.

Louise Howard, *Buddhism for Sheep,* St. Martin's Press, 1996.

Cave, *The Emperor's Gruckle Hound,* Hodder & Stoughton, 1996.

Alan Durant, *Angus Rides the Goods Train,* Viking, 1996.

Hans Christian Andersen, *The Swan's Stories,* selected and translated by Brian Aldersen, Walker, 1997.

R. McGough, *Until I Met Dudley: How Everyday Things Really Work,* Walker, 1997.

Philip Ridley, *Kasper in the Glitter,* Dutton, 1997.

L. Howard, *Feng Shui for Cats,* Ebury, 1997.

Howard, *Feng Shui for Dogs,* Ebury, 1997.

F. Hughes, *The Tall Story,* Macdonald, 1997.

Paul Stewart, *Beyond the Deep Woods,* Doubleday, 1998.

Cave, *Horatio Happened,* Hodder & Stoughton, 1998.

P. Stewart, *A Little Bit of Winter,* Andersen Press, 1998.

Cave, *William and the Wolves,* Hodder & Stoughton, 1999.

Richard Platt, *Castle Diary: The Journal of Tobias Burgess,* Walker, 1999.

Stewart, *Storm Chaser,* Doubleday, 1999.

Claire Nielson, *Buddhism for Bears,* St. Martin's Press, 1999.

Stewart, *The Birthday Presents,* Andersen Press, 1999.

Worked as a cover artist for London-based periodicals, including *Literary Review* and *New Statesman.*

Sidelights

Chris Riddell is an author and illustrator who specializes in creating lively, color-filled books for young readers. Among Riddell's self-authored works are *Ben and the Bear, The Wish Factory,* and *The Trouble with Elephants,* while his illustration projects include bringing to life texts by authors such as Kathryn Cave, Andrew Gibson, and Paul Stewart. Of Riddell's work on *The Swan's Stories,* a collection of tales by Hans Christian Andersen, *Horn Book* contributor Ann A. Flowers noted: "The illustrations are superb, a cross between [Arthur] Rackham and Shepard with a touch of Carl Larsson. . . . This is a beautiful book." When not engaged in adding a dose of whimsy to books for children, Riddell casts a quizzical eye on the games of adult politicians, contributing wry political cartoons to such noted British publications as the *New Statesman* and the London *Observer*.

Riddell was born in 1962 in Capetown, South Africa, but moved to London as a child and attended British schools. Graduated from Brighton Polytechnic in 1984, he earned a degree in visual communications and achieved first-class honors. His first published book, *Ben and the Bear,* appeared in 1985, the same year his illustrations began appearing in picture books by other authors.

The humorous *Ben and the Bear* was quickly followed by *Mr. Underbed.* Reflecting a fear that many children have of creatures hiding under their beds at nighttime, *Mr. Underbed* finds young Jim making countless introductions to the host of surprisingly congenial monsters that reside not only under his bed but in all sorts of spots in his bedroom. In fact, Mr. Underbed and his monster friends are so much fun to be with that by story's end Jim has opted to sleep under the bed with his new friends. *Books for Keeps* reviewer Jill Bennett deemed this work "an attractive read alone" and a successful

bedtime tale due to its simple text and appealing illustrations.

In 1987's *Bird's New Shoes,* Riddell pokes fun at the world of high fashion. Bird's latest fashion find, a pair of bright red shoes, causes Rat to covet a pair (or two) of his own. Of course, a new tie would look *fabulous* with the shoes, but when Rat parades around in his dashing new duds, Warthog simply must have not only the same shoes, but an equally snazzy tie as well. And so it goes in one-upmanship in a book that a *Publishers Weekly* contributor called "a fun picture book with a simple story line." Particular praise was lavished on Riddell's vibrantly colored illustrations: the *Publishers Weekly* critic dubbed them "bright, busy and cartoony," while in *School Library Journal* critic Lauralyn Persson added that "the animals are cleverly drawn, . . . [with] lots of innate comic personality."

Animals again figure prominently in *The Trouble with Elephants,* as a young girl clutching a much-loved stuffed elephant thinks up all manner of imaginary problems that living with real-live elephants might cause: pink rings in the bathtub, snoring at night, and terribly unfair games of see-saw and hide-and-go-seek.

Rabbit promises to save some winter for his hibernating friend Hedgehog in Paul Stewart's **A Little Bit of Winter,** *illustrated by Riddell.*

And never mind letting them ride on your bicycle, even once, or they'll squash it flat! Amid this litany of elephantine flaws scampers a herd of happy-go-lucky elephants, whose demeanor "are sure to elicit grins," according to *School Library Journal* contributor Lori A. Janick. Phillis Wilson agreed in her review of *The Trouble with Elephants* for *Booklist,* commenting that Riddell's "use of exaggeration is a delightful addition to the gently engaging narrative."

The Wish Factory again delves into a child's imagination; like *Mr. Underbed* it focuses on bedtime. Here, young Oliver is taken to a magical place in the clouds called the Wish Factory, where he is given a wish to be used the next time a bad dream threatens to disturb his sleep. Called "a beautifully illustrated ... picture book in night-time colors" by *School Librarian* contributor Margaret Banerjee, *The Wish Factory* also received praise from critic Liz Waterland, who noted in her review for *Books for Keeps* that readers "will find [Riddell's] story straightforward and reassuring, especially if they're afraid of the dark."

While Riddell makes his home in England, he continues to travel to Europe and spends many summers in Italy. In addition to drawing for his profession, Riddell enjoys spending his free time drawing and painting.

Works Cited

Banerjee, Margaret, review of *The Wish Factory, School Librarian,* February, 1991, p. 20.
Bennett, Jill, review of *Mr. Underbed, Books for Keeps,* March, 1988, p. 17.
Review of *Bird's New Shoes, Publishers Weekly,* February 27, 1987, p. 164.
Flowers, Ann A., review of *The Swan's Stories, Horn Book,* November-December, 1997, p. 689.
Janick, Lori A., review of *The Trouble with Elephants, School Library Journal,* March, 1989, pp. 168-69.
Persson, Lauralyn, review of *Bird's New Shoes, School Library Journal,* September, 1987, p. 169.
Waterland, Liz, review of *The Wish Factory, Books for Keeps,* November, 1992, p. 16.
Wilson, Phillis, review of *The Trouble with Elephants, Booklist,* October 15, 1988, p. 413.

For More Information See

PERIODICALS

Kirkus Reviews, September 1, 1988, p. 1327.
New York Times Book Review, November 16, 1997.
Publishers Weekly, July 19, 1999, p. 194.
Reading Time, May, 1999, p. 16.
School Library Journal, November, 1986, p. 82; March, 1991, p. 179; November, 1997, p. 110.

RINGGOLD, Faith 1930-

Personal

Born October 8, 1930, in New York, NY; daughter of Andrew Louis Jones, Sr. and Willi (maiden name, Posey) Jones; married Robert Earl Wallace, 1950 (divorced, 1956); married Burdette Ringgold, 1962; children: (first marriage) Barbara, Michele. *Education:* City College of the City University of New York, B.S., 1955, M.A., 1959.

Addresses

Home—La Jolla, CA and New York, NY. *Agent*—(literary) Marie Brown Associates, Room 902, 625 Broadway, New York, NY 10012.

Career

Painter, mixed media sculptor, performance artist, and writer. Art teacher in public schools, New York City, 1955-73. Professor of art, University of California, San Diego, 1984—. In 1960s, after trip to Europe, completed first political paintings and held first one-person show. In 1972, began making paintings framed in cloth (called tankas), soft sculptures, costumes, and masks. Later used these media in masked performances of the early and mid-1970s. In 1980, produced first painted quilt and in

Faith Ringgold

1983, created first story quilt. Performances include appearances at various colleges, universities, and museums, including Purdue University, 1977, University of Massachusetts, 1980, Rutgers University, 1981, Occidental College, 1984, Long Island University, 1986, Baltimore Museum of Art, 1988, De Pauw University, 1989, and Washington and Lee University, 1991. Visiting lecturer and artist at art centers, universities, and museums, including Mills College, 1987, Museum of Modern Art, 1988, University of West Florida, 1989, San Diego Museum, 1990, Museum of African American Art, 1991, and Atlantic Center for the Arts, 1992.

EXHIBITIONS: Artwork has been nationally exhibited in many museums and numerous galleries as well as in Europe, Asia, South America, and Africa. Artwork has been featured in many one person shows, including shows at the Spectrum Gallery, New York City, 1967, 1970; Bernice Steinbaum Gallery, 1987, 1989, 1992; Reina Sofia Museum, Madrid, 1994; and Cairo Biennial, 1994. Artwork is in many public and private collections, including Boston Museum of Fine Art, Chase Manhattan Bank Collection, Clark Museum, Guggenheim Museum, High Museum, Metropolitan Museum of Art, Museum of Modern Art, Newark Museum, Phillip Morris Collection, and Studio Museum in Harlem. Her work has also appeared in "Faith Ringgold: A 25 Year Survey," a nationally touring retrospective exhibition, curated by the Fine Arts Museum of Long Island, 1990-93.

Awards, Honors

Best Illustrated Book of 1991, *New York Times,* Parents' Choice Award for Picture Book, Parent's Choice Foundation, 1991, Coretta Scott King Illustrator Award, American Library Association (ALA), Caldecott Honor Book Award, ALA, and Children's Books of Distinction, Hungry Mind Review, all 1992, Ezra Jack Keats New Writer Award, New York Public Library, 1993, all for *Tar Beach;* Jane Addams Picture Book Award, Jane Addams Peace Association, 1993, for *Aunt Harriet's Underground Railroad in the Sky.* Artwork has received numerous awards, including Creative Artists Public Service Award, 1971; American Association of University Women Award for travel to Africa, 1976; National Endowment for the Arts Awards, 1978, for sculpture, 1989, for painting; John Simon Guggenheim Memorial Foundation fellowship, 1987, for painting; New York Foundation for the Arts Award, 1988, for painting; and Henry Clews Foundation Award, 1990, for painting in the south of France. Honorary Doctor of Fine Arts degrees from Moore College of Art, 1986, College of Wooster, 1987, Massachusetts College of Art, 1991, City College of the City University of New York, 1991, and Brockport State University, 1992.

Writings

FOR CHILDREN, SELF-ILLUSTRATED

Tar Beach, Crown, 1991.
Aunt Harriet's Underground Railroad in the Sky, Crown, 1992.
Dinner at Aunt Connie's House, Hyperion, 1993.

My Dream of Martin Luther King, Crown, 1995.
Bonjour, Lonnie, Hyperion, 1996.
The Invisible Princess, Crown, 1998.
If a Bus Could Talk: The Story of Rosa Parks, Simon & Schuster, 1999.

FOR ADULTS

(Contributor) Amiri Baraka and Amina Baraka, editors, *Confirmation: An Anthology of African American Women,* Morrow, 1983.
Faith Ringgold: A 25 Year Survey (catalog), Fine Arts Museum of Long Island, 1990.
We Flew Over the Bridge: The Memoirs of Faith Ringgold, Little, Brown, 1995.
Talking to Faith Ringgold, with Linda Freeman and Nancy Roucher, Crown, 1996.

Also contributor of articles, essays, and short stories to numerous periodicals, including *Artpaper, Heresies: A Feminist Publication on Art and Politics, Women's Art Journal, Women's Artists News, Feminist Art Journal, Arts Magazine,* and *Art Gallery Guide.*

Work represented in catalogs, including *Faith Ringgold Change: Painted Story Quilts,* Bernice Steinbaum Gallery, 1987, and *The French Collection,* B MOW Press, 1992.

Sidelights

Blending painting and quilt-making with a natural storyteller's sense of rhythm, Faith Ringgold, a widely respected and accomplished painter, mixed media sculptor, performance artist, and college professor, has created a half-dozen imaginative and sensitive picture books for children. Beginning with her first book, the Caldecott honor award-winning *Tar Beach,* Ringgold has combined a sense of African-American history and culture with a vibrant palette to celebrate dreams of freedom. Focusing on African American women in *Aunt Harriet's Underground Railroad in the Sky* and *Dinner at Aunt Connie's House,* Ringgold has also explored the life of celebrated civil rights leader Martin Luther King, Jr. in *My Dream of Martin Luther King.* Ringgold's 1998 *The Invisible Princess* expands her artistic horizons with a blend of fairy tale and American slave history.

Considered by many critics to be the leading black woman artist in America today, Ringgold is perhaps best known for her beautifully created and intricately designed story quilts that piece together Ringgold's past, present, and future. Several of these quilts have proved inspiration for her children's books. When asked to define her art, Ringgold told Eleanor Flomenhaft in *Faith Ringgold: A 25 Year Survey:* "I'm a painter who works in the quilt medium; and that I sew on my painting doesn't make it less of a painting; and that it's made into a quilt does not make it not a painting. It's still a painting."

Growing up in New York City during the Great Depression of the 1930s, Ringgold was the youngest of three children born to Andrew Louis Jones, Sr., a

Harriet Tubman guides Cassie along the Underground Railroad to be reunited with her younger brother in Ringgold's self-illustrated **Aunt Harriet's Underground Railroad in the Sky.**

sanitation department truck driver, and Willi Posey Jones, a housewife who became a dressmaker and fashion designer in the 1940s. Ringgold once described her childhood to *Something about the Author* (*SATA*): "Life for me was quite wonderful! While I had asthma and was home sick a lot, I got a chance to do a lot of things with my mother. When I was recuperating my mother would take me to see live performances of people like Duke Ellington and Jimmy Lunceford and Count Basie. Actually those people were my first stars—my first artists. Part of my being with my mother a lot was that I was the youngest in the family. So when the other kids were in school she would take me to the museums. Also because I would be home with asthma, she would teach me and give me crayons and paper so I could draw. My mother would also give me pieces of fabric since she was a dressmaker. Later on, my mother became a fashion designer but at the time she was just making clothes for my family. She learned the skill from her mother and her mother learned from her mother and so on, and I learned from my mother."

Except for her periodic bouts with asthma, Ringgold's childhood was very much like that of her friends and neighbors. She attended the local public elementary and high schools, played with her friends, listened to music, and lived the life of the average New York City child. Ringgold also learned to work with fabrics at her mother's side, and often visited the many great museums located in New York City. As she remembers: "I was

always the class artist. I drew and painted constantly. That was a natural thing to me—making pictures and pieces of art. I cannot remember a time I did not do that. Still, I had no idea that I would be an artist when I grew up. I did know, however, that I would go to college because we had been told all of our lives that we would go to college."

In 1948 after her graduation from high school, Ringgold enrolled at the City College of the City University of New York, declaring a major in art. She recalled: "When I was asked: 'What do you want to major in?' I said 'If I have to say one thing that I want my life's work to be then it's going to be art because I can't picture my life without it.' But I had no idea what it was to be an artist. I had no idea of the difficulties involved for an African American woman in the field of visual art."

Studying at City College, Ringgold learned a great deal about her chosen field of study and her talents as an artist began to develop and shine. While her instructors provided a very sound technical education, Ringgold searched for her own voice and hungered for more information and insight on African American art and artists. Looking back on her education, Ringgold explained to Flomenhaft in *Faith Ringgold: A 25 Year Study:* "When I went on to City College they taught art in a traditional way. We copied Greek busts; we copied Cezanne and Degas; we copied the European masters. It was generally thought that we weren't experienced

Ringgold's stunning artwork is especially suited to her **Dinner at Aunt Connie's House,** *in which Melody and Lonnie discover speaking portraits of famous African-American women painted by artist Aunt Connie.*

enough to be original; and if we were original we were sometimes up for ridicule."

With a desire to create work that reflected what she felt as an African American woman artist, Ringgold set out on her own to learn more about this area of art. "African art and African American artists are interests that I had to pursue on my own after I had my degrees," Ringgold recounted to *SATA*. "I researched African—my own art, the classical art form of Black people—on my own. I really taught myself because there were no courses being taught on African Art and artists. Even today there aren't very many courses taught on African Art. I had to get my education [and] then I had to get my reeducation which was what I gave myself."

Ringgold eloped with jazz musician Robert Earl Wallace in college, and the couple had two daughters during their first year of marriage. However, the relationship came to an early end as Wallace's problems with drug addiction put a strain on the marriage. By 1956, the two divorced. Out of college and a single mother, she taught for several years before deciding to work on her art full time. A trip to Europe, and finally seeing in person all of the artwork she had only seen previously in books, was a

seminal experience for her. Once back in the United States, she turned to her own career with renewed vigor, working tirelessly to arrange exhibits, sending her work across the country, and calling agents and galleries.

Ringgold's early pieces were paintings done in oil on stretch canvas. Many of these paintings were political though traditional in technique. By the end of the 1960s, Ringgold's work began to reflect her passion for African art and her desire to more accurately express her ethnicity. Both influenced by and involved in the growing civil rights movement during this period, Ringgold began to vigorously explore the burning political issues of the day—race, class, and gender. In time, her work started mirroring her rising social and political consciousness. In 1972, Ringgold's art underwent another major change in focus: from painting in oils on stretch canvas to creating paintings on canvas that were framed in fabric and quilted.

On a trip to Holland, Ringgold visited museums where she was introduced to Tibetan and Nepalese tankas—paintings framed in cloth—dating back to the fourteenth century. Ringgold remarked to *SATA:* "I was amazed that those works were not always framed under glass but had been framed in fabric in beautiful brocade. I decided I wanted to work that way because I could do my pictures, frame them in cloth, and then I could roll them up and transport them anywhere I wanted to. I thought that was a great idea because one of the problems that I had was getting an audience, having people see my work."

Consequently, desiring to bring her art to greater numbers of people, Ringgold began experimenting with the tanka form she had seen in Holland in her own work. She collaborated with her mother who used her sewing skills as a dressmaker to create the tankas. Ringgold turned her focus toward painting on canvas that her mother framed in cloth, thereby producing her own tankas. By the 1980s, this technique had led to her innovative story quilts for which she is well known.

"In 1983, I started writing what I call picture story quilts," Ringgold told *SATA*. "I had already done the tankas—many of which had words on them—a little story—so it was a natural progression. I really felt that writing was very important. It helped to develop the work in the minds of other people in a way that just a picture could not, that the words could go places that pictures could not go.... I had very specific things I wanted to say and I wanted to get those things published and I couldn't count on getting a publisher to do it for me. So I would write the words on the quilts and as the quilts were published, the words would be too."

After seeing one of Ringgold's story quilts from her "A Woman on a Bridge" series, Andrea Cascardi, an editor at Crown Publishers approached Ringgold about making "Tar Beach" into an illustrated book for children. At first, Ringgold could not envision this work, which depicts an eight-year-old girl lying on the tarpaper rooftop of a Harlem apartment dreaming of flying, as possible subject material for children's literature. Ringgold told *SATA:* "The editor saw that this was a children's book and I never saw it. I was just doing my work. I was doing [the] 'A Woman on a Bridge' series and I did 'Tar Beach' because it comes out of my childhood."

Eventually, Ringgold was persuaded and the result was her first book, *Tar Beach.* Elaborating on the idea from the original story quilt, the book tells the story of the hopes and dreams of the eight-year-old girl, Cassie, who dreams about traveling wherever she wants, whenever she wants. One night, while lying on the rooftop—otherwise known to the family as "Tar Beach"—Cassie is lifted up by the stars and soars above the clouds of her Harlem apartment building. As her family, neighbors, and friends play cards on the rooftop below, the young girl glides through the dark sky and is treated to a dazzling "world of living color" that gives her a tremendous sense of freedom and joy. "Anyone can fly," young Cassie proclaims in *Tar Beach.* "All you need is somewhere to go that you can't get to any other way. The next thing you know, you're flying among the stars."

"Few picture books are as visually dazzling or as poetically immediate as this story," Michele Landsberg stated in *Entertainment Weekly*. Ringgold's narrative of a child's self-affirmation and love of family is fresh, direct, and poignant. Her full-page paintings vibrate with ravishing colors." Landsberg concluded that Ringgold's first book is an "exhilarating celebration of a child's life in the city."

Corky Pollan remarked in *New York* magazine that "in *Tar Beach,* Faith Ringgold has woven black history with autobiography and fiction; but, more important, she has created a children's book that is magical and inspiring.... *Tar Beach* explodes with the artist's exuberant pictures." *Horn Book*'s Nancy Vasilakis noted that Ringgold managed to "produce a fascinating book, originally created as a story quilt, without compromising the integrity of either art form." Vasilakis went on to comment that this "allegorical tale sparkles with symbolic and historical references central to African American culture." *New York Times Book Review* critic Rosellen Brown wrote of *Tar Beach,* "It's hard to imagine a child who wouldn't willingly imagine something—a place, a tough spot, a hard life or a high ambition—worth flying out of or into. Fortunately [the story is] not exclusive: it's not only for African Americans, or girls, or even—I'll testify—for children."

Ringgold followed up this success with a second children's book, *Aunt Harriet's Underground Railroad in the Sky,* which again uses the motif of flying to freedom. Be Be, the baby brother from *Tar Beach,* is central to this fantasy story. Out flying with Cassie, Be Be jumps aboard a nineteenth-century train operated by abolitionist Harriet Tubman. Left behind, Cassie nonetheless is guided by Aunt Harriet to freedom in Canada following the underground railway. Reunited, Be Be confides to his sister that it is wonderful to be together again, but being free is most important of all. Kate McClelland, reviewing the title in *School Library Journal,* stated that "With gripping immediacy, Ringgold puts readers in the story on the side of the victims, insuring, through powerful words and images, 'that we will never forget the cost of freedom.'" Enola G. Aird declared in the *New York Times Book Review,* "I look forward to Cassie's next trip."

Ringgold's next trip into children's picture books was *Dinner at Aunt Connie's House,* another tale inspired by one of the artist's story quilts, introducing young Melody and her adopted male cousin Lonnie. In their attic, Melody and Lonnie discover twelve portraits of famous African American women, including one of Harriet Tubman. Each picture tells the children a different story and inspires them to follow their dreams to become what they want to be. Melody is determined to become president of the United States while Lonnie knows that opera is his calling. A *Publishers Weekly* contributor commented that the "heart of the book—the pages in which the women tell their stories—is at once a magical and a ringing affirmation of their achievements."

Part of Ringgold's "Bitter Nest Series," this 1988 work titled "The Letter" depicts a young man confronting the woman who raised him after he discovers a haunting letter from his biological mother. (From Faith Ringgold: A 25 Year Survey.)

Lonnie appears again in *Bonjour, Lonnie,* another fantasy which tells of the young boy's long trip to France to find his roots. He discovers that his grandfather went to France in the First World War and there married a French woman. He also learns about his parents, discovering that his father died in World War II and his Jewish mother had to give him up for adoption before the Nazis tracked her down. Back at Aunt Connie's house, Lonnie finds his real home.

In *My Dream of Martin Luther King,* Ringgold emphasizes the power of dreams, both literal and metaphorical. The young narrator dreams of King and the joys and pain of that leader's own youth. The girl also experiences King's famous "I have a dream" speech in Washington, as well as the events that led to his tragic death. In the end, she sees people replacing their prejudices with King's vision of a peaceful biracial world. A *Publishers Weekly* critic concluded in a review of the work that as the young narrator awakens, "we share with her a powerful message: EVERY GOOD THING STARTS WITH A DREAM."

A third story based on a story quilt, *The Invisible Princess,* is at once both fairy tale and history, "an evocative, if mystifying picture book," according to a *Publishers Weekly* reviewer. Mama and Papa Love, both slaves, fear that their unborn child will be sold by the plantation owner, Captain Pepper. When the beautiful daughter is born, they beg the Great Lady of Peace to save her from slavery. Their wish is granted, and just after birth the baby is taken away by the Prince of Night and made invisible to all but the blind daughter of the slave master. The Invisible Princess ultimately saves her parents and the other plantation slaves, helping them to find happiness in the invisible village of Peace, Freedom, and Love. *Booklist* contributor GraceAnne A. DeCandido called Ringgold's artwork in the book "gorgeous," while Rudine Sims Bishop, writing in *Horn Book,* called Ringgold's story a "serious ... literary fairy tale set in the days of slavery. The colors are strong, and the images are memorable." Bishop concluded that the book presented "Ringgold at her best as a picture book artist."

Ringgold maintains a busy schedule, dividing her time between her art, teaching, and writing both adult and children's books. As she noted in her memoir, *We Flew Over the Bridge:* "My books are ... about children having dreams, and instilling in them a belief that they can change things. [A]ll good things start with a dream."

Works Cited

Aird, Enola G., review of *Aunt Harriet's Underground Railroad in the Sky, New York Times Book Review,* February 21, 1993, p. 22.
Bishop, Rudine Sims, "Heaven Is Three African American Literary Folktales," *Horn Book,* March-April, 1999, pp. 180-81.
Brown, Rosellen, "Children's Books," *New York Times Book Review,* February 24, 1991, p. 30.
DeCandido, GraceAnne A., review of *The Invisible Princess, Booklist,* December 1, 1998, p. 672.
Review of *Dinner at Aunt Connie's House, Publishers Weekly,* August 16, 1993, p. 104.
Flomenhaft, Eleanor, "Interviewing Faith Ringgold/A Contemporary Heroine," *Faith Ringgold: A 25 Year Survey,* Fine Arts Museum of Long Island, 1990, pp. 7-15. Amended by Faith Ringgold.
Review of *Invisible Princess, Publishers Weekly,* November 23, 1998, p. 67.

Landsberg, Michele, "Up on the Roof and on to the 'Beach'," *Entertainment Weekly,* February 8, 1991, pp. 68-69.
McClelland, Kate, review of *Aunt Harriet's Underground Railroad in the Sky, School Library Journal,* December, 1992, pp. 88, 90.
Review of *My Dream of Martin Luther King, Publishers Weekly,* January 1, 1996, p. 70.
Pollan, Corky, "'Tar' Quality," *New York,* February 18, 1991, p. 56.
Ringgold, Faith, *Tar Beach,* Crown, 1991.
Ringgold, Faith, *We Flew Over the Bridge: The Memoirs of Faith Ringgold,* Little, Brown, 1995.
Vasilakis, Nancy, review of *Tar Beach, Horn Book,* May-June, 1991, p. 322.

For More Information See

BOOKS

Authors and Artists for Young Adults, Volume 19, Gale, 1997, pp. 201-09.
Chadwick, Whitney, *Women, Art, and Society,* Thames and Hudson, 1990.
Contemporary American Women Artists, Cedco, 1991.
Davis, Marianna W., *Contributions of Black Women to America: The Arts,* Kenday, 1982.
Miller, Lynn, and Sally S. Swenson, *Lives and Works: Talks with Women Artists,* Simon & Schuster, 1981.
Munro, Eleanor, *Originals: American Women Artists,* Simon & Schuster, 1979, pp. 409-416.
Sills, Leslie, *Inspirations: Stories of Women Artists for Children,* A. Whitman, 1988, pp. 40-51.
Slatkin, Wendy, *Women Artists in History: From Antiquity to the Twentieth Century,* 2nd edition, Prentice-Hall, 1990, pp. 190-92.
Witzling, Mara R., editor, *Writings in Voicing Our Visions: Writings by Women Artists,* Universe, 1991.

PERIODICALS

Booklist, March 15, 1992, p. 1367; October 1, 1996, p. 359.
Gallerie Women's Art, Volume 6, 1989, pp. 40-43.
Los Angeles Times Book Review, February 24, 1991, p. 8.
New York Times Book Review, February 11, 1996, p. 25; February 2, 1997, p. 18.
Publishers Weekly, February 15, 1991, pp. 61-62.
School Arts, May, 1989, pp. 23-26.
School Library Journal, July, 1996, p. 311; December, 1998, p. 89.

—*Sketch by J. Sydney Jones*

* * *

RIPKEN, Cal(vin Edward), Jr. 1960-

Personal

Born August 24, 1960, in Havre de Grace, MD; son of Cal Ripken Sr. (deceased; a former baseball player, manager, and coach); married, wife's name Kelly; children: Rachel, Ryan.

Addresses

Office—c/o Baltimore Orioles, Oriole Park at Camden Yards, 333 W. Camden St., Baltimore, MD 21202-2435.

Career

Baltimore Orioles, professional baseball player, 1978—; writer. Minor league player for Bluefield, Miami, Charlotte, and Rochester baseball teams, 1978-81.

Awards, Honors

Rookie of the Year, International League, 1981; Rookie of the Year, American League, Baseball Writers Association, 1982; American League Rookie of the Year, *Sporting News,* 1982; American League Player of the Year, *Sporting News,* 1983 and 1991; Major League Player of the Year, *Sporting News,* 1983; American League Most Valuable Player, 1983 and 1991; Silver Slugger awards, 1983-86, 1989, 1991, and 1993-94; Gold Glove award for shortstops, 1991-92; member of American League All-Star Team, 1983-99; Sportsman of the Year, *Sports Illustrated* and *Sporting News,* both 1995. Set major league records for most home runs by a shortstop, single-season fielding percentage (both 1990), most consecutive games played (1995), and most errorless games by a shortstop (1995).

Writings

Ripken: Cal on Cal (autobiography), edited by Mark Vancil, with photographs by Walter Iooss, Jr., Summit (Arlington, TX), 1995.
(With Greg Brown) *Count Me In* (children's autobiography), with illustrations by Doug Keith, Taylor (Dallas, TX), 1995.
(With Mike Bryan) *The Only Way I Know* (autobiography), Viking, 1997.
(With Mike Bryan) *Cal Ripken, Jr.: My Story* (children's autobiography), adapted by Dan Gutman, Millbrook Press (Brookfield, CT), 1999.
(With Mike Bryan) *Cal Ripken, Jr.: Play Ball!* (children's autobiography), adapted by Gail Herman, illustrated by Stan Silver, Dial, 1999.

Sidelights

Cal Ripken, Jr. became an American sports legend by quietly doing his job, day after day after day, and doing it exceptionally well. At a time when cynicism was rampant among sports fans, athletes, and journalists alike, his breaking of Lou Gehrig's longstanding record for consecutive games played seemed to signal a possible return to traditional values of hard work. For many years, the record had been considered one of the few "unbreakables" in sports. In the words of Richard Hoffer, in an article crowning Ripken as *Sports Illustrated*'s Sportsman of the Year for 1995, Ripken "almost single-handedly restored the once loyal fan's faith in baseball, single-handedly turned attention to a pioneer work ethic."

Cal Ripken, Jr.

The event, which had been widely anticipated for years (given the predictability of a season's 162-game schedule and the equal predictability of Ripken's attendance at the park), was "one of the great feel-good events in sports—ever," Hoffer avowed. "It released a pent-up emotion after two strike-shortened seasons, a missed World Series and a general surliness had destroyed a hundred-plus years' worth of fan loyalty."

Ripken himself is known as a stable, steady person who possesses superior self-discipline and who, in describing himself, declared: "The word *stubborn* does come to mind." His hair thinning and graying by the time of the consecutive-games record, he looked older than his thirty-five years, but played with the intensity and pleasure of a younger man. His physical conditioning, on- and off-season, is superb, as a result of his diligent exercise. Ripken is also fiercely devoted to spending time with his family, which includes his wife Kelly and his children, Rachel and Ryan. Ripken himself had grown up in a baseball family, the son of Baltimore Orioles player, Cal Ripken, Sr., who later became a noted hitting coach for that team.

The advantages of being surrounded by knowledgeable, talented people within the baseball community as a youngster were surely part of the development of Ripken, yet as a minor-league prospect he was not highly touted: in 1978, he was the ninth shortstop selected in the baseball draft. Hard work made Ripken a first-rate player, good enough to be selected Rookie of the Year in 1982 and Most Valuable Player in 1983 and 1991. Though not a flashy shortstop, he won Gold Gloves in 1991 and 1992 as the best at his position, achieving the highest fielding percentage in history and the longest errorless streak ever for a shortstop. The latter two records, bespeaking consistency and a search for perfection, seemed to embody the spirit of Ripken. This is not to say that there were no downturns in his career. In 1989 his batting average was only .257, and the following season, when his average sank below .220 in June, some argued that he should be benched. According to his own account, Ripken did consider taking a rest, but was convinced by a teammate, pitcher Rick Sutcliffe, that rest would not solve the problem. Ripken worked through the slump and went on to an outstanding season in 1991.

Shortly before the breaking of the Gehrig record in 1995, suggestions were made in public and in private, for commercial reasons and from motives of homage to Gehrig, that Ripken ought to purposely sit out a game before September 5 and then resume a new streak the day afterward. Typically, he shrugged off the advice and continued on his unswerving path: "I wasn't doing this for a record in the first place, so I wasn't going to not do it for the record either. It never entered my mind," he told Hoffer. The response to Ripken's breaking of the record was warmly emotional on the part of teammates, opponents, and fans alike; and it was somewhat emotionally overwhelming to Ripken, the star admitted, though it did not visibly affect his play. The event, Hoffer surmised, came at a time when "there's hardly anything to root for anymore.... No home teams, few reliable citizens, and ... not always a World Series.... a sad time when neither virtue nor achievement can be taken for granted." Indeed, even the feat of remaining with just one team throughout a long career, as Ripken had done, seemed unusual, and his habit of patiently remaining after games to sign autographs was sometimes looked upon by teammates as bizarre. Ripken's attachment to solid, old values, Hoffer suggested, might mark a subtle shift in the attitudes of an entire nation; hard work seemed to become fashionable again: "Ripken's example prompted a hurried search [in the media] for people with unusual work records." Whether or not the effect would continue in the world at large, there was no sign of any change in the work habits of Cal Ripken, Jr.

Ripken's own words on his life and career are available in three autobiographies: two, for adults, *Ripken: Cal on Cal,* and *The Only Way I Know;* and one for younger readers, *Count Me In. The Only Way I Know* was adapted twice for children: *Cal Ripken, Jr.: My Story,* for middle graders and young adults, and *Cal Ripken, Jr.: Play Ball!,* for primary graders. The latter effort, a chapter book describing the ups and downs of Ripken's baseball career as well as his personal experiences, was a hit with beginning readers. Wendy Lukehart, writing in *School Library Journal,* praised the work as "a pro in a genre glutted with farm leaguers."

Works Cited

Hoffer, Richard, "Hand It To Cal," *Sports Illustrated,* December 18, 1995, pp. 70-90.
Lukehart, Wendy, review of *Cal Ripken, Jr.: Play Ball!, School Library Journal,* June, 1999, p. 120.

For More Information See

BOOKS

Buck, Ray, *Cal Ripken, Jr., All-Star Shortstop,* Childrens Press, 1985.
Gibbons, Jack, editor, *Cal Touches Home: The Biggest Sports Story of 1995 in Baltimore,* Baltimore Sun, 1995.
Joseph, Paul, *Cal Ripken, Jr.,* Abdo & Daughters, 1997.
Macnow, Glen, *Sports Great Cal Ripken, Jr.,* Enslow, 1993.
Nicholson, Lois, *Cal Ripken Jr., Quiet Hero,* Tidewater, 1993.
Rambeck, Richard, *Cal Ripken, Jr.,* Child's World, 1993.
Rosenfeld, Harvey, *Iron Man: The Cal Ripken, Jr. Story,* St. Martin's, 1995.
Thornley, Stew, *Cal Ripken, Jr.: Oriole Ironman,* Lerner, 1992.

PERIODICALS

Booklist, March 15, 1997, p. 1203.
Kliatt, July, 1998, p. 27.
New York Times, March 28, 1997, p. B14.
People, December 25, 1995, p. 10.
Publishers Weekly, March 27, 1997, p. 64; March 22, 1999, p. 94.
Sport, June, 1997, p. 68.
Sporting News, December 18, 1995, p. 10.
Sports Illustrated, June 25, 1990, p. 70; June 8, 1992, p. 67; May 31, 1993, p. 78; September 11, 1995, p. 56.
Time, September 7, 1992, p. 23.*

*   *   *

ROCKWELL, Anne F. 1934-

Personal

Born February 8, 1934, in Memphis, TN; daughter of Emerson (an advertising executive) and Sabina (maiden name, Fromhold) Foote; married Harlow Rockwell (a writer and artist), March 16, 1955 (died 1988); children: Hannah, Elizabeth (Lizzy), Oliver Penn. *Education:* Attended Sculpture Center and Pratt Graphic Arts Center. *Politics:* "Liberal Democrat." *Religion:* Episcopalian.

Addresses

Home—4 Raymond St., Old Greenwich, CT 06870.

Career

Author and illustrator. Silver Burdett Publishers, Morristown, NJ, member of production department, 1952; Young and Rubicam (advertising agency), art-buying secretary, 1953; Goldwater Memorial Hospital, New York City, assistant recreation leader, 1954-56. *Member:* Authors Guild, Authors League of America.

Awards, Honors

Boys Club Junior Book Award certificate, 1968, for *The Minstrel and the Mountain: A Tale of Peace;* American Institute of Graphic Arts selection for children's book show, 1971-72, for *The Toolbox,* 1973-74, for *Head to Toe, Games (and How to Play Them), The Awful Mess,* and *Paul and Arthur and the Little Explorer;* Children's Book Showcase selection, 1973, for *Toad,* and 1975, for *Befana: A Christmas Story; No More Work* and *Poor Goose: A French Folktale* were selected as children's books of the year by the Child Study Association, 1976; *In Our House* was named a *Redbook* top ten children's picture book of 1985.

Writings

SELF-ILLUSTRATED CHILDREN'S BOOKS, EXCEPT WHERE INDICATED

Paul and Arthur Search for the Egg, Doubleday, 1964.
Gypsy Girl's Best Shoes, Parents Magazine Press, 1966.
Sally's Caterpillar, illustrated by husband, Harlow Rockwell, Parents Magazine Press, 1966.
Filippo's Dome: Brunelleschi and the Cathedral of Florence, Atheneum, 1967.
The Stolen Necklace: A Picture Story from India, World, 1968.
Glass, Stones and Crown: The Abbe Suger and the Building of St. Denis, Atheneum, 1968.
The Good Llama: A Picture Story from Peru, World, 1968.
Temple on a Hill: The Building of the Parthenon, Atheneum, 1969.
The Wonderful Eggs of Furicchia: A Picture Story from Italy, World, 1969.
(Compiler) *Savez-vous planter les choux? and Other French Songs,* World, 1969.
When the Drum Sang: An African Folktale, Parents Magazine Press, 1970.
(Adapter) *The Monkey's Whiskers: A Brazilian Folktale,* Parents Magazine Press, 1971.
El toro pinto and Other Songs in Spanish, Macmillan, 1971.
Paintbrush and Peacepipe: The Story of George Catlin, Atheneum, 1971.
Tuhurahura and the Whale, Parents Magazine Press, 1971.
What Bobolino Knew, McCall Publishing, 1971.
The Dancing Stars: An Iroquois Legend, Crowell, 1972.
Paul and Arthur and the Little Explorer, Parents Magazine Press, 1972.
The Awful Mess, Parents Magazine Press, 1973.
The Boy Who Drew Sheep, Atheneum, 1973.
Games (and How to Play Them), Crowell, 1973.
(Reteller) *The Wolf Who Had a Wonderful Dream: A French Folktale,* Crowell, 1973.

Befana: A Christmas Story, Atheneum, 1974.
Gift for a Gift, Parents Magazine Press, 1974.
The Gollywhopper Egg, Macmillan, 1974.
The Story Snail, Macmillan, 1974.
(Reteller) *The Three Bears and Fifteen Other Stories,* Crowell, 1975.
Big Boss, Macmillan, 1975.
(Reteller) *Poor Goose: A French Folktale,* Crowell, 1976.
No More Work, Greenwillow, 1976.
I Like the Library, Dutton, 1977.
A Bear, a Bobcat, and Three Ghosts, Macmillan, 1977.
Albert B. Cub and Zebra: An Alphabet Storybook, Crowell, 1977.
Willy Runs Away, Dutton, 1978.
Timothy Todd's Good Things Are Gone, Macmillan, 1978.
Gogo's Pay Day, Doubleday, 1978.
Gogo's Car Breaks Down, illustrated by H. Rockwell, Doubleday, 1978.
Buster and the Bogeyman, Four Winds, 1978.
(Reteller) *The Old Woman and Her Pig and Ten Other Stories,* Crowell, 1979.
The Girl with a Donkey Tail, Dutton, 1979.
The Bump in the Night, Greenwillow, 1979.
Walking Shoes, Doubleday, 1980.
Honk Honk!, Dutton, 1980.
Henry the Cat and the Big Sneeze, Greenwillow, 1980.
Gray Goose and Gander and Other Mother Goose Rhymes, Crowell, 1980.
When We Grow Up, Dutton, 1981.
Up a Tall Tree, illustrated by Jim Arnosky, Doubleday, 1981.
Thump Thump Thump!, Dutton, 1981.
Boats, Dutton, 1982.
(Reteller) Hans Christian Andersen, *The Emperor's New Clothes,* Crowell, 1982.
Big Bad Goat, Dutton, 1982.
The Mother Goose Cookie-Candy Book, Random House, 1983.
Cars, Dutton, 1984.
Trucks, Dutton, 1984.
In Our House, Crowell, 1985.
Planes, Dutton, 1985.
First Comes Spring, Crowell, 1985.
The Three Sillies and Ten Other Stories to Read Aloud, Harper, 1986.
Big Wheels, Dutton, 1986.
Fire Engines, Dutton, 1986.
Things That Go, Dutton, 1986.
At Night, Crowell, 1986.
At the Playground, Crowell, 1986.
In the Morning, Crowell, 1986.
In the Rain, Crowell, 1986.
Come to Town, Crowell, 1987.
Bear Child's Book of Hours, Crowell, 1987.
Bikes, Dutton, 1987.
Handy Hank Will Fix It, Holt Rinehart, 1988.
Hugo at the Window, Macmillan, 1988.
Things to Play With, Macmillan, 1988.
Puss in Boots and Other Stories, Macmillan, 1988.
Trains, Dutton, 1988.
My Spring Robin, illustrated by H. Rockwell and daughter Lizzy Rockwell, Macmillan, 1989.
On Our Vacation, Dutton, 1989.

Apples and Pumpkins, illustrated by L. Rockwell, Macmillan, 1989.

Bear Child's Book of Special Days, Dutton, 1989.

Willy Can Count, Arcade Publishing, 1989.

Hugo at the Park, Macmillan, 1990.

When Hugo Went to School, Macmillan, 1990.

Root-a-Toot-Toot, Macmillan, 1991.

Our Yard Is Full of Birds, illustrated by L. Rockwell, Macmillan, 1992.

What We Like, Macmillan, 1992.

Mr. Panda's Painting, Macmillan, 1993.

Pots and Pans, illustrated by L. Rockwell, Macmillan, 1993.

The Robber Baby: Stories from the Greek Myths, Greenwillow, 1994.

The Way to Captain Yankee's, Macmillan, 1994.

Ducklings and Pollywogs, Macmillan, 1994.

(With David Brion) *Space Vehicles,* Dutton, 1994.

The Storm, illustrated by Robert Sauber, Hyperion, 1994.

No! No! No!, Macmillan, 1995.

(Reteller) *The Acorn Tree and Other Folktales,* Greenwillow, 1995.

Sweet Potato Pie, illustrated by Carolyn Croll, Random House, 1996.

The One-Eyed Giant and Other Monsters from the Greek Myths, Greenwillow, 1996.

I Fly, illustrated by Annette Cable, Crown, 1997.

Show and Tell Day, illustrated by L. Rockwell, HarperCollins, 1997.

Once Upon a Time This Morning, illustrated by Sucie Stevenson, Greenwillow, 1997.

Romulus and Remus, Simon & Schuster, 1997.

Halloween Day, illustrated by L. Rockwell, HarperCollins, 1997.

Our Earth, Harcourt Brace, 1998.

One Bean, illustrated by Megan Halsey, Walker, 1998.

Thanksgiving Day, illustrated by L. Rockwell, HarperCollins, 1999.

Valentine's Day, illustrated by L. Rockwell, HarperCollins, 1999.

Our Stars, Harcourt Brace, 1999.

Ferryboat Ride!, illustrated by Maggie Smith, Crown, 1999.

Bumblebee, Bumblebee, Do You Know Me?: A Garden Guessing Game, HarperCollins, 1999.

Long Ago Yesterday, Greenwillow, 1999.

Pumpkin Day, Pumpkin Night, illustrated by M. Halsey, Walker, 1999.

Career Day, illustrated by L. Rockwell, HarperCollins, 2000.

The Boy Who Wouldn't Obey: A Mayan Legend, Greenwillow, 2000.

Morgan Plays Soccer, illustrated by Paul Meisel, HarperCollins, 2000.

What Good Are Alligators?, illustrated by L. Rockwell, HarperCollins, in press.

Katie Swims, illustrated by P. Meisel, HarperCollins, in press.

Our Seas, Harcourt, in press.

WITH HUSBAND, HARLOW ROCKWELL; SELF-ILLUSTRATED

Olly's Polliwogs, Doubleday, 1970.

Molly's Woodland Garden, Doubleday, 1971.

The Toolbox, Macmillan, 1971.

Machines, Macmillan, 1972.

Thruway, Macmillan, 1972.

Toad, Doubleday, 1972.

Head to Toe, Doubleday, 1973.

Blackout, Macmillan, 1979.

The Supermarket, Macmillan, 1979.

Out to Sea, Macmillan, 1980.

My Barber, Macmillan, 1981.

Happy Birthday to Me, Macmillan, 1981.

I Play in My Room, Macmillan, 1981.

Can I Help?, Macmillan, 1982.

How My Garden Grew, Macmillan, 1982.

I Love My Pets, Macmillan, 1982.

Sick in Bed, Macmillan, 1982.

The Night We Slept Outside, Macmillan, 1983.

My Back Yard, Macmillan, 1984.

Our Garage Sale, Greenwillow, 1984.

When I Go Visiting, Macmillan, 1984.

Nice and Clean, Macmillan, 1984.

My Baby-Sitter, Collier Books, 1985.

The Emergency Room, Collier Books, 1985, published in England as *Going to Casualty,* Hamish Hamilton, 1987.

At the Beach, Macmillan, 1987.

The First Snowfall, Macmillan, 1987.

ILLUSTRATOR

Marjorie Hopkins, *The Three Visitors,* Parents Magazine Press, 1967.

Jane Yolen, *The Minstrel and the Mountain: A Tale of Peace,* World, 1967.

Lillian Bason, *Eric and the Little Canal Boat,* Parents Magazine Press, 1967.

Marjorie Hopkins, *The Glass Valentine,* Parents Magazine Press, 1968.

Paul Showers, *What Happens to a Hamburger,* Crowell, 1970.

Kathryn Hitte, *Mexacali Soup,* Parents Magazine Press, 1970.

Joseph Jacobs, *Munacher and Manacher: An Irish Story,* Crowell, 1970.

Anne Petry, *Legends of the Saints,* Crowell, 1970.

Joseph Jacobs, *Master of All Masters,* Grosset, 1972.

Marjorie Hopkins, *A Gift for Tolum,* Parents Magazine Press, 1972.

Walter Dean Myers, *The Dancers,* Parents Magazine Press, 1972.

Barbara Brenner, *Cunningham's Rooster,* Parents Magazine Press, 1975.

Barbara Williams, *Never Hit a Porcupine,* Dutton, 1977.

Gerda Mantinband, *Bing Bong Band and Fiddle Dee Dee,* Doubleday, 1979.

Clyde Robert Bulla, *The Stubborn Old Woman,* Crowell, 1980.

Patricia Plante and David Bergman, retellers, *The Turtle and the Two Ducks and Ten Other Animal Fables Freely Retold from La Fontaine,* Methuen, 1980.

Steven Kroll, *Toot! Toot!,* Holiday House, 1983.

Anne F. Rockwell expresses the joys of the fall season in **Apples and Pumpkins,** *illustrated by Lizzy Rockwell.*

Adaptations

The Stolen Necklace: A Picture Story from India, was adapted as a film by Paramount/Oxford, 1971; *The Toolbox* and *Machines* were adapted as filmstrips, Threshold Filmstrips, 1974.

Sidelights

In a career spanning more than three decades, prolific author-illustrator Anne F. Rockwell has created over one hundred titles of her own, over thirty collaborative efforts with her husband, Harlow Rockwell, and her daughter, Lizzy Rockwell, and artwork credits for nearly twenty works by other authors. Over the course of her career, Rockwell has gradually decreased the age of her target audience. Initially producing works for middle-graders, she has turned to picture books and board books for preschool and beginning readers, writing in genres from myths and folktales to simple science to feel-good animal picture books. All of Rockwell's works maintain

"a simplicity within diversity ... which both satisfies and stimulates young readers," according to Christine Doyle Stott in the *St. James Guide to Children's Writers.*

Rockwell was born in Memphis, Tennessee, but also spent time in the Midwest and Southwest while growing up. Although she attended both the Sculpture Center and Pratt Graphic Arts Center, the artist relied mainly on self-teaching to learn her trade. She worked at an advertising agency before marrying another artist, Harlow Rockwell. After the couple had their first child, Rockwell realized that she wanted to produce children's books to share the joy of reading she had first experienced as a youngster.

Early publications from Rockwell were aimed at the middle-grade audience and include biographical and historical works such as *Filippo's Dome, Glass, Stones and Crown: The Abbe Suger and the Building of St. Denis, Temple on a Hill: The Building of the Parthenon,* and *Paintbrush and Peacepipe: The Story of George*

Catlin. In the first of these, "a simple, pleasing account," according to Ruth P. Bull in *Booklist,* Rockwell tells the story of Filippo Brunelleschi and the building of the Cathedral of Florence. She does the same for the Gothic gem of St. Denis in Paris with *Glass, Stones and Crown,* mingling the biography of the church's founder with the story of its architecture. "This is a book as interesting for its historical material as for its architectural focus," declared a reviewer for the *Bulletin of the Center for Children's Books.* The Parthenon was put into historical context with *Temple on a Hill,* and the famous painter of Native Americans, George Catlin, went under the biographical lens in *Paintbrush and Peacepipe,* a "superior and pertinent biography," according to a *Publishers Weekly* critic.

Other early self-illustrated publications from Rockwell include *The Dancing Stars: An Iroquois Legend, The Good Llama: A Picture Story from Peru,* and *The Stolen Necklace: A Picture Story from India,* which introduce readers to folktales from different cultures. In the late 1970s, however, Rockwell changed her focus to informative works for children just learning to read. With works such as *I Like the Library, Walking Shoes,* and *When We Grow Up,* Rockwell provides simple text and detailed, attention-grabbing pictures.

Books such as these earned praise as straightforward presentations of everyday objects and occurrences. Kimberly Olson Fakih, writing in *Publishers Weekly,* highlighted editor Ann Durrell's comment that Rockwell shows genius in her nonfiction works. "In [Rockwell's]

books, kids can see what's meaningful to them and what's around them," Durrell stated. An example of her nonfiction work is Rockwell's series of picture books explaining various types of transportation. These books, including *Boats, Cars, Planes, Trucks, Trains,* and *Bikes,* feature lively watercolor illustrations—with animals operating the machinery—and easy-to-understand prose. Reviewing her *Boats,* a *Publishers Weekly* contributor commented that "'Neatness counts' is the maxim Rockwell seems to have taken to heart, but her fastidious standards don't inhibit the artist from infusing the pictures in her many books with animation, appealing creatures and lovely colors." *Horn Book* writer Ann A. Flowers called *Boats* "an outstanding example of an informational picture book."

Rockwell has continued her string of successful, eye-pleasing, and educational works. In her 1989 book *Willy Can Count,* the author presents a counting game played by mother and son during a walk. In her illustrations, Rockwell provides plenty of objects to count, prompting Joanna G. Jones of *School Library Journal* to remark that *Willy Can Count* is "bound to become a favorite." Later additions to her line of informational books are the 1999 *Our Stars,* a book that deals with stars, planets, meteors, comets, and moons, and *Ferryboat Ride!,* which introduces more nautical concepts such as "bow" and "stern" in the context of a young girl and her family being transported to a summer vacation spot. A *Publishers Weekly* critic concluded that readers "will want to set sail themselves after experiencing this ferryboat ride."

In addition to her informational titles, Rockwell's solo picture book efforts for young readers fall into three main categories: easy readers, stories about animals, and folktales and legends. In the first category, by far the largest, Rockwell employs simple, often repetitive language with bright, bold pictures to capture the attention of preschoolers and beginning readers. Typical of such easy readers are *The Gollywhopper Egg, The Story Snail, No! No! No!, Bumblebee, Bumblebee, Do You Know Me?,* and *Pumpkin Day, Pumpkin Night.* Reviewing the first title about a clever peddler who trades his wares—including a "gollywhopper egg"—for farmers' produce, a *Publishers Weekly* reviewer declared that the "noted author-illustrator is at her bright best." The tale of a magical snail who gives young John a hundred stories with which to amaze his friends, *The Story Snail* is "[f]un for the beginning reader," according to *Horn Book*'s Virginia Haviland. Another little boy is at the center of *No! No! No!,* but this one is cantankerous and out of sorts and having a very bad day. Only a soothing bedtime story can begin to put him to rights. *Booklist*'s Hazel Rochman concluded that "Kids will laugh at the common misfortune; they'll sympathize with the irritation and draw comfort from the ending when things begin to change." With *Bumblebee, Bumblebee, Do You Know Me?,* Rockwell "created a graceful primer on the inhabitants of the backyard garden," according to a *Publishers Weekly* writer, while the search for a perfect pumpkin informs *Pumpkin Day, Pumpkin Night.*

My soup was too hot
and my pudding wasn't chocolate.

Everything goes wrong until Mom takes charge in Rockwell's self-illustrated No! No! No!

Spider, spider, do you know us?

Written and illustrated by Rockwell, Bumblebee, Bumblebee, Do You Know Me? *reveals the names of flowers in the answers to simple riddles.*

Animals prove to be a favorite Rockwell motif in many picture books. A Bear Child is featured in *First Comes Spring,* "a good choice for sharing with groups and a popular choice for story hours," according to *Horn Book* contributor Elizabeth S. Watson. An entire bear family heads off to a busy day in *Come to Town,* a book that Nancy A. Gifford, writing in *School Library Journal,* felt "should be extremely popular with preschool children and should be useful for nursery schools." Another sort of bear altogether is at the center of *Mr. Panda's Painting.* When the panda in question, a painter, runs out of paint, he heads off to the art store to buy some more, purchasing an entire rainbow of color. Stephanie Zvirin noted in *Booklist* that "Rockwell's crisp, simple shades, outlined in thick black lines, have much child appeal."

Myths and folktales are another constant motif for Rockwell, and she has collected them from around the world. *The Wolf Who Had a Wonderful Dream* is a French folktale, set in Normandy, while *What Bobolino*

Knew is a Sicilian legend, and *Befana* is a European Christmas tale. More recent additions to the list are Greek myths collected in the 1994 *The Robber Baby* and the 1996 *The One-Eyed Giant and Other Monsters from the Greek Myths.* Reviewing the former title in *Booklist,* Carolyn Phelan noted that "Rockwell has written a dependable source of Greek myths in a format suitable for the early elementary grades." *The Acorn Tree and Other Folktales* is another popular Rockwell title, featuring retellings from Aesop, among others.

Rockwell also wrote and illustrated numerous books with her husband, Harlow Rockwell, until his death in 1988. *Toad* presents "a congenial and informative look at the life cycle" of that animal, according to a *Publishers Weekly* contributor, while *Out to Sea* tells of an unintended maritime adventure involving a brother and sister. Another work, *The Emergency Room,* describes a protagonist's trip to the hospital after spraining his ankle. P. Susan Gerrity, writing in the *New York*

A boy buys just the right pumpkin and makes the perfect jack-o-lantern. *(Cover illustration by Megan Halsey.)*

Times Book Review, remarked that the book "provides excellent background information" and will reassure children afraid of visiting the emergency room. The same demystification process is done for hair-cutting in *My Barber,* in which "[c]lean lines, spacious composition, solid blocks of color, and plenty of white space" are all combined, according to a *Bulletin of the Center for Children's Books* contributor, to present a trip to the barber. The husband and wife team continued their "My World" series with *How My Garden Grew* and *Sick in Bed,* both of which "are alive with realism and color," as noted by Peggy Forehand in *School Library Journal.*

Rockwell has continued the tradition of family collaboration, working with her illustrator daughter, Lizzy Rockwell, on several titles. Their *Apples and Pumpkins* was a "charming seasonal picture book with an easy-to-read text," according to Roseanne Cerny in *School Library Journal,* while *Our Yard Is Full of Birds* is "an appealing backyard bird book" appropriate for "the very young," according to Phelan. Mother and daughter have

also teamed up for a series on holidays of the year. A *Kirkus Reviews* critic noted that *Halloween Day* contains a "simple" text and "sweet watercolor illustrations," making the book age-appropriate for the very young.

Reviewing another Rockwell title, a *Kirkus Reviews* writer called her "a well-loved author known for her simple books for the very young." Rockwell herself concurs with at least the second part of this description. As she wrote in the *St. James Guide to Children's Writers,* "My books are for the youngest of children. I loved, and still love, young children's picture books. I feel fortunate to have retained a sense of how young children see the world which enables me to do books for them . . . . I see that they are visually very alert and that illustrations can communicate where words are still difficult. In pictures they *see* everything."

Works Cited

Review of *Boats, Publishers Weekly,* October 15, 1982, p. 65.

Bull, Ruth P., review of *Filippo's Dome, Booklist,* June 1, 1967, p. 1148.

Review of *Bumblebee, Bumblebee, Do You Know Me?, Publishers Weekly,* January 11, 1999, p. 70.

Cerny, Roseanne, review of *Apples and Pumpkins, School Library Journal,* November, 1989, pp. 91-92.

Fakih, Kimberly Olson, "The News Is Nonfiction," *Publishers Weekly,* February 26, 1988, pp. 108-11.

Review of *Ferryboat Ride!, Publishers Weekly,* May 17, 1999, p. 79.

Flowers, Ann A., review of *Boats, Horn Book,* October, 1982, pp. 512-13.

Forehand, Peggy, review of *How My Garden Grew* and *Sick in Bed,* School Library Journal, May, 1982, p. 56.

Gerrity, P. Susan, review of *The Emergency Room, New York Times Book Review,* April 21, 1985, p. 18.

Gifford, Nancy A., review of *Come to Town, School Library Journal,* November, 1987, p. 96.

Review of *Glass, Stones and Crown, Bulletin of the Center for Children's Books,* March, 1969, p. 117.

Review of *The Gollywhopper Egg, Publishers Weekly,* January 14, 1974, pp. 94-95.

Review of *Halloween Day, Kirkus Reviews,* June 15, 1997, p. 956.

Haviland, Virginia, review of *The Story Snail, Horn Book,* October, 1979, pp. 133-34.

Jones, Joanna G., review of *Willy Can Count, School Library Journal,* January, 1990, p. 89.

Review of *My Barber, Bulletin of the Center for Children's Books,* May, 1981, p. 179.

Review of *Paintbrush and Peacepipe, Publishers Weekly,* November 15, 1971, p. 72.

Phelan, Carolyn, review of *Our Yard Is Full of Birds, Booklist,* January 15, 1992, p. 946.

Phelan, Carolyn, review of *The Robber Baby, Booklist,* June 1 and 15, 1994, p. 1832.

Review of *The Robber Baby, Kirkus Reviews,* June 1, 1994, p. 781.

Rochman, Hazel, review of *No! No! No!, Booklist,* May, 1995, p. 1580.

Stott, Christine Doyle, "Rockwell, Anne," *St. James Guide to Children's Writers,* 5th edition, edited by Sara Pendergast and Tom Pendergast, St. James, 1999, pp. 917-19.

Review of *Toad, Publishers Weekly,* June 26, 1972, p. 63.

Watson, Elizabeth S., review of *First Comes Spring, Horn Book,* July-August, 1985, p. 442.

Zvirin, Stephanie, review of *Mr. Panda's Painting, Booklist,* November 1, 1993, p. 532.

For More Information See

BOOKS

Authors of Books for Young People, 3rd edition, Scarecrow, 1990.

Silvey, Anita, editor, *Children's Books and Their Creators,* Houghton, 1995.

Something about the Author Autobiography Series, Volume 19, Gale, 1995.

PERIODICALS

Booklist, September 15, 1989, p. 189; October 15, 1992, p. 436; December 15, 1994, p. 760; October 1, 1995, pp. 324-25; April 22, 1996, p. 73.

Books for Keeps, May 1990, p. 12.

Bulletin of the Center for Children's Books, March, 1992, p. 191; March, 1993, p. 224; April, 1996, p. 278.

Horn Book, November, 1987, p. 731; November, 1989, p. 764.

Kirkus Reviews, March 15, 1993, p. 378; July 1, 1999, p. 1057.

School Library Journal, August, 1989, p. 131; January, 1991, p. 37; February, 1993, p. 78; January, 1995, p. 92; July, 1995, p. 68; October, 1995, pp. 128-29; February, 1999, p. 88; May, 1999, p. 112; June, 1999, p. 106.*

—Sketch by J. Sydney Jones

S

SHAIK, Fatima

Personal

Education: Attended Xavier University, 1972; Boston University, B.S., 1974; New York University, M.A., 1978.

Addresses

Home—315 Seventh Ave., No. 9A, New York, NY 10001. *E-mail*—Shaik_F@spcvxa.spc.edu.

Career

New Orleans Times-Picayune, New Orleans, LA, summer intern reporter, 1973; *Miami News,* Miami, FL, summer intern reporter, 1974; Gulf South Publishing, assistant editor of *Newsleader,* 1974; *New Orleans Times-Picayune,* city desk reporter, 1974-75; McGraw-Hill Book Co., New York City, assistant editor in World News Division, 1976-81, foreign digests editor, 1981-86, copy editor in Standard & Poor's Division, 1987-88; Southern University at New Orleans, instructor in print journalism, 1990-91; St. Peter's College, Jersey City, NJ, lecturer in English, 1991—, director of communications major program, 1998—. Writers Room, member of board of directors, 1990-98; gives readings from her works.

Awards, Honors

Fellow, National Endowment for the Humanities, 1981; grant, Kittredge Fund, 1997; "Pick of the lists" citation, American Booksellers Association, for *Melitte.*

Writings

(Contributor) Carl Sienna, editor, *Parachute Shop Blues,* Xavier University Press, 1972.

The Mayor of New Orleans: Just Talking Jazz (three novellas), Creative Arts Book Co. (Berkeley, CA), 1987.

(Contributor) Terry McMillan, editor, *Breaking Ice: Anthology of Contemporary African-American Fiction,* Penguin-Viking (New York City), 1990.

(Contributor) Dorothy H. Brown and Barbara C. Ewell, editors, *Louisiana Women Writers: Selected Essays and Bibliography,* Louisiana State University Press (Baton Rouge, LA), 1992.

(Contributor) Doris Jean Austin and Martin Simmons, editors, *Streetlights: Illuminating Tales of the Urban Black Experience,* Penguin, 1996.

(Contributor) Al Young, editor, *African-American Literature,* HarperCollins (New York City), 1996.

Melitte (novel), illustrated by Bill Dodge, Dial Books for Young Readers (New York City), 1997.

(Contributor) Brooke Stephens, editor, *Men We Cherish: African-American Women Praise the Men in Their Lives,* Doubleday (New York City), 1997.

The Jazz of Our Street, illustrated by E. B. Lewis, Dial Books for Young Readers, 1998.

On Mardi Gras Day, illustrated by Floyd Cooper, Dial Books for Young Readers, 1999.

Columnist, Media Alliance, 1983. Contributor of articles and stories to periodicals, including *Working Woman, Black Enterprise, Essence, Southern Review, Review of Contemporary Fiction, Callaloo, Tribes: Multicultural,* and *Xavier Review.*

For More Information See

PERIODICALS

Booklist, December 15, 1987, p. 676; October 15, 1997, p. 398; May 1, 1998, p. 1523; February 15, 1999, p. 1068; March 1, 1999, p. 1223.

Bulletin of the Center for Children's Books, January, 1998, p. 176.

Essence, February, 1988, p. 28.

Horn Book, November, 1997, p. 685.

Kirkus Reviews, October 15, 1997, p. 1588; April 15, 1998, p. 586.

Publishers Weekly, October 30, 1987, p. 52; October 27, 1997, p. 76; February 8, 1999, p. 214.

School Library Journal, October, 1997, p. 138; September, 1998, p. 181.
Stone Soup, July-August, 1998, p. 18.
Voice of Youth Advocates, February, 1998, p. 390-91.

*   *   *

SHOWERS, Paul C. 1910-1999

OBITUARY NOTICE—See index for *SATA* sketch: Born April 12, 1910, in Sunnyside, WA; died July 17, 1999, in Orange, MA. Journalist and children's book author. Showers' youth was spent moving between several states and he graduated from the University of Michigan in 1931 and hoped to make a living as an actor and playwright. When he realized that he was not going to succeed in the theater, Showers devoted himself to writing, a skill that had helped him pay the rent during lean acting days. He was hired by *Life* magazine to design its crossword puzzle and kept that job until 1936, then he took a job on the copy desk of the *Detroit Free Press.* From there he worked at a number of newspapers, including the *New York Herald Tribune* in New York City. His journalism career was interrupted by World War II and Showers served from 1942 to 1945 in the Army. He was editor of the Okinawa edition of the Army weekly *Yank* and after his discharge he was hired at the *New York Times.* At the *Times* Showers filled a variety of positions, working in the Sunday department, travel section and Sunday magazine. While doing his daily duties at the paper he tried writing his first children's book, *Find Out by Touching,* in 1961. The book was scientific in nature and evolved into a series of science-minded books that included *The Listening Walk, Follow Your Nose, How You Talk* and *Use Your Brain,* among others. Showers' books were written in simple, clear terms so children could understand and learn from them. The books have been translated into at least five languages. Showers said books for beginners should be easy to read but not dull, which could be a challenging task for the writer. Most of Showers' books were non-fiction and many have been made into filmstrips or educational videos. Other titles not part of Showers' "Let's Read and Find Out" series include *Indian Festivals, The Moon Walker* and *A Book of Scary Things.* He completed more than twenty-five books and contributed articles to numerous periodicals such as *Judge* and *Ballyhoo.* He retired from the *New York Times* in 1976 but continued freelancing. Showers' last book, *Ears Are for Hearing,* was published in 1990.

OBITUARIES AND OTHER SOURCES:

BOOKS

De Montreville, Doris, and Elizabeth D. Crawford, editors, *Fourth Book of Junior Authors & Illustrators,* H. W. Wilson Co., 1978.

PERIODICALS

New York Times, September 2, 1999, p. C20.

SIEGELSON, Kim L. 1962-

Personal

Born November 16, 1962, in Atlanta, GA; daughter of F. Elmo (a home builder) and Carole (a nurse; maiden name, Blair) Fortenberry; married Henry J. Siegelson (a physician), May 2, 1987; children: Aron Edward, Zachary Dean. *Education:* Agnes Scott College, B.A., 1984; Georgia State University, M.S., 1990. *Politics:* Democrat. *Religion:* Jewish.

Addresses

Home—1942 Grist Stone Ct., Atlanta, GA 30307. *Agent*—Liza Voges, Kirchoff/Wohlberg, 866 United Nations Plaza, New York, NY 10017.

Career

Writer. Community volunteer. *Member:* Society of Children's Book Writers and Illustrators.

Awards, Honors

Grant from Society of Children's Book Writers and Illustrators, 1993; Children's Book Award, Center for Multicultural Children's Books, 1994; Sunshine State Young Readers Award, 1998; Top 100 Children's

Kim L. Siegelson

Books, New York Public Library, 1999, for *In the Time of the Drums.*

Writings

The Terrible, Wonderful Tellin' at Hog Hammock, illustrated by Eric Velasquez, HarperCollins (New York City), 1996.
In the Time of the Drums, illustrated by Brian Pinkney, Jump at the Sun (New York City), 1999.
Dancing the Ring Shout, Disney Press, in press.
Escape South, Golden Books, in press.

Work in Progress

A novel, *Trembling Earth;* a picture book, *The Tanner's Tale;* research on African-American history and on daily life in the Old South.

Sidelights

Kim L. Siegelson told *SATA:* "I am a child of the South, and as such have grown up absorbing the stories and history and language of this place. I find it endlessly fascinating and rich with ideas, characters, and settings. So much has been written about southerners and our home, but there is much more to learn and hear and see and make peace with.

"I always begin my writing with a strong sense of place and let the story unfold from there. I try to include the lyrical quality of southern speech and the rhythm of its language in my prose. I listen for the voices of the old storytellers who held me spellbound as a child.

"I write so that others will hear the stories of the South and, maybe, understand why I love it here with all the faults and goodness and history and beauty of any place called 'home.'"

For More Information See

PERIODICALS

Booklist, June 1, 1996, p. 1724; April 1, 1999, p. 1428.
Bulletin of the Center for Children's Books, September, 1996, p. 29.
Horn Book, July, 1996, p. 465.
Horn Book Guide, fall, 1996, p. 297.
Kirkus Reviews, May 15, 1996, p. 750.
New York Times Book Review, August 15, 1999, p. 24.
Publishers Weekly, April 26, 1999, p. 82.
School Library Journal, August, 1996, p. 144; May, 1999, p. 96.

STAUB, Wendy Corsi 1964-
(Wendy Brody; Wendy Morgan)

Personal

Born October 29, 1964, in Dunkirk, NY; daughter of Reginald S. (a banker) and Francella (a teacher; maiden name, Ricotta) Corsi; married Mark J. Staub (in advertising sales), October 26, 1991; children: Morgan James, Brody Alexander. *Ethnicity:* "White/American." *Education:* State University of New York at Fredonia, B.A., 1986.

Addresses

Agent—Laura Blake Peterson, Curtis Brown, Ltd., 10 Astor Pl., New York, NY 10003. *E-mail*—wnstr@aol.com.

Career

Worked in book stores during college; Macmillan, New York City, textbook marketing division administrator, c. 1986; worked as a temporary in other publishing houses, c. 1987-88; Backer Spielvogel Bates (advertising), New York, account coordinator, 1988-90; Silhouette Books, New York, editor, 1990-92; freelance writer, 1993—. Writing instructor at the Long Ridge Writer's Institute in Redding, CT, 1993-95; runs Cupid Literary Services, a literary consulting business. *Member:* Romance Writers of America, Mystery Writers of America, Young Adult Network.

Awards, Honors

Rita Award for Best Young Adult Novel, Romance Writers of America, 1994.

Writings

NOVELS

Getting It Together (romance), Silhouette (New York City), 1994.
Getting Attached (romance), Silhouette, 1994.
Getting Hitched (romance), Silhouette, 1995.
(Under pseudonym Wendy Morgan) *Obsession* (horror), Zebra (New York City), 1996.
Dearly Beloved (horror), Zebra, 1996.
(With Ed Koch) *Murder on Broadway* (mystery), Kensington (New York City), 1996.
(With Fabio) *Dangerous* (romance), Pinnacle (New York City), 1996.
(With Fabio) *Wild* (romance), Pinnacle, 1997.
(With Koch) *Murder on 34th Street* (mystery), Kensington, 1997.
(With Fabio) *Mysterious* (romance), Pinnacle, 1998.
(With Koch) *The Senator Must Die* (mystery), Kensington, 1998.
Fade to Black (suspense), Kensington, 1998.
Party of Five Scrapbook, Berkley (New York City), 1998.
All the Way Home (suspense), Kensington, 1999.

Wendy Corsi Staub explores a teen's struggle with depression in this fictional account. (Cover photo by Franco Accornero.)

(Under pseudonym Wendy Morgan) *Loving Max* (romance), Zebra, 1999.
The Long Way Home (historical romance), Berkley Jove (New York City), 1999.

YOUNG ADULT NOVELS

Summer Lightning, Harper (New York City), 1993.
Halloween Party, Zebra (New York City), 1994.
Witch Hunt, Zebra, 1995.
Help Me, Pocket (New York City), 1995.
Mitzi Malloy and the Anything-But-Heavenly-Summer, Zebra, 1995.
Brittany Butterfield and the Back-to-School Blues, Zebra, 1995.
Henry Hopkins and the Horrible Halloween Happening, Zebra, 1995.
College Life 101/Cameron: The Sorority, Berkley (New York City), 1997.
College Life 101/Zara: The Roommate, Berkley, 1997.
College Life 101/Kim: The Party, Berkley, 1997.
College Life 101/Bridget: The Fling, Berkley, 1997.

College Life 101/Allison: The Townie, Berkley, 1997.
College Life 101/Christmas Break: The Reunion, Berkley, 1998.

Also contributor of articles to periodicals, including *Writer's Digest* and *The Writer;* contributor of poetry to *Seventeen.*

Work in Progress

A suspense novel; a romance novel under the pseudonym Wendy Morgan; a biography under the pseudonym Wendy Brody to be titled *Wild About Harry.*

Sidelights

Since serving as an editor for Silhouette, Wendy Corsi Staub has gone on to become the author of several books, sometimes using the pseudonyms Wendy Morgan and Wendy Brody. Her literary output is predominantly in the novel form, though she is at work on a biography. Staub has written for the juvenile and young adult audience as well as for adult readers, in the genres of romance, suspense, and mystery. She has also collaborated with celebrity authors—male model and romance cover boy Fabio, and former mayor of New York Ed Koch.

Staub's first book, *Summer Lightning,* saw print in 1993 and was aimed at young adult readers. The novel features a young female protagonist who must choose between a boyfriend in the flesh and an attractive visitor from the spirit world. Another of Staub's young adult titles is 1995's *Witch Hunt,* in which Abbey Harmon, a teenager from 1963, time-travels back to colonial Salem in order to save two girls accused of witchcraft. Jeanne Triner in *Booklist* pronounced Abbey "intelligent, witty, and believable, without being too good to be true," and went on to praise *Witch Hunt* as "a refreshing step-up" from much young adult horror fiction.

Several of Staub's works for young adults became available for readers in 1995. *Help Me!* deals with an adolescent girl's struggle with depression—a struggle she only acknowledges after her mother's suicide. The author also penned several titles about a group of high school friends who die and become angels, assigned to help troubled young people. These include *Brittany Butterfield and the Back-to-School Blues, Henry Hopkins and the Horrible Halloween Happening,* and *Mitzi Malloy and the Anything-But-Heavenly Summer.*

By 1997, another of Staub's novel sets for young adults hit the book stores. Each *College Life 101* book chronicles the experience of one of a group of friends from the same high school in the state of New York who attends a different college. As the subtitle of *Cameron: The Sorority* suggests, Cameron finds herself matriculating at South Florida State and completely obsessed with getting into the right sorority. Complicating matters is Tad, a handsome Cuban-American who has nothing but contempt for the fraternity-sorority system, and Cameron's own mixed racial heritage, which makes her the target of prejudice on the part of some of her peers. *Zara: The Roommate* deals not only with the difficulties of getting along with one's college roommate, but the trials of attending a tough New England girls' school. Zara has always succeeded in high school, but now finds herself fighting to keep her grades high enough to stay in the pre-medical program. The protagonist of *Kim: The Party* chooses a midwestern party school, and constantly goes to her classes with a hangover. Oddly, though, she finds herself attracted to one of the most studious young men on campus. In *Bridget: The Fling,* Bridget had planned to go off to a university in Seattle with her long-time boyfriend Grant, but the sudden death of his father postpones his education by a semester. While they are apart, Bridget fears his attraction to their mutual friend Allison, but must also contend with her own burgeoning feelings for the single father who hires her to babysit. Allison gets her own volume, however. As the subtitle *Allison: The Townie* indicates, she is the only one of the group who must attend their local state university. While studying, she remains in her parents' home, works as a waitress, and must beg to be allowed to drive the family car. The friends come back together in the sixth book, *College Life 101/Christmas Break: The Reunion.*

While continuing to write novels for young people, Staub also put out books for adults. Her first three romances, published under the auspices of her former employer Silhouette, featured the same protagonist. In 1994's *Getting It Together,* C. J. Clarke starts out feeling like a failure at everything from dieting to her career. Her life gradually improves through *Getting Attached,* and by 1995 she is *Getting Hitched,* if her intended's discovery of something in her past doesn't destroy their love. The following year saw the publication of *Dearly Beloved,* Staub's suspense novel in which three women are drawn together by a sinister man who wants revenge on all of them.

Though Staub did not collaborate on the first of former New York mayor Ed Koch's mystery novels, she joined him for his second, 1996's *Murder on Broadway.* Koch writes about himself as a fictional character, still the mayor of New York, and in *Murder on Broadway* Koch is attending a play in which one of the characters is killed. For this performance, however, the bullets are real, and the actor dies. Suspects include the role's former actor, whose attempt at Hollywood has been none too successful; the actress who pulled the trigger, who was bethrothed to the victim; and the actress's lover, possibly jealous of the dead man. The mayor, however, manages to find the killer before the police do. Emily Melton in *Booklist* proclaimed *Murder on Broadway* to be "flamboyant" and "over the top" but "also clever and entertaining." A *Publishers Weekly* reviewer found it better than Koch's previous effort, and predicted that "readers will still wish for more."

Staub also teamed with Koch for *Murder on 34th Street* and *The Senator Must Die.* In the former, department store Santas are being shot and killed, but the mayor manages to solve the crime despite a nasty cold caught at the Thanksgiving Day Parade. In the latter, Koch is on hand for an assassination attempt on his fictional friend Senator Anson Hubbard. In another *Booklist* review, Melton affirmed that *The Senator Must Die* is "mildly entertaining" and "should delight Koch's many fans."

With Fabio, Staub has penned three contemporary romance novels—1996's *Dangerous,* 1997's *Wild,* and 1998's *Mysterious. Wild* features female protagonist A. J. Sutton, who must go into hiding after witnessing a murder at a drug lord's palatial home. A. J. feels she must also fight her attraction to Marco Esteves—who bears a strong resemblance to the male half of *Wild*'s writing team—because she thinks he works for the drug lord. Fortunately, Marco is really working for the United States' Drug Enforcement Agency. A critic for *Publishers Weekly* applauded Staub's second collaboration with Fabio as "a finely plotted story filled with nonstop action and well-developed characters."

One of Staub's later novels aimed at adults is the suspense story *Fade to Black.* This concerns Mallory Eden, a rising young actress who fakes her own death after being shot and robbed of her childbearing capability by a stalker. She assumes the identity of Elizabeth Baxter, a woman who *is* dead, and lives as a freelance writer in a quiet Rhode Island town until she begins receiving threatening letters which indicate her stalker has figured out her ruse. Toni Hyde in *Booklist* reported that "plenty of flashbacks and not-too-subtle innuendos cause the reader to peg the stalker, mistakenly, again and again." She summed up *Fade to Black* as "entertaining." A *Publishers Weekly* critic, however, felt the novel was not sufficiently suspenseful, though the reviewer conceded that "it's easy to sympathize with scared, lonely Elizabeth, and the plotting is competent." A critic for *Kirkus Reviews* concluded that "a hissy catfight during the cliff-hanging finale is a hoot."

Staub comments: "As a third-grader with a voracious appetite for books, I declared to anyone who would listen that I would one day become an author. I would spend the remainder of my childhood and young adulthood in single-minded pursuit of that goal, following a precisely laid plan that now seems, as an adult looking back on my precocious younger self, to be highly calculated and ambitious. I read everything I could get my hands on (from Judy Blume books to the *World Almanac* to my mother's Jacqueline Susann novels), published poetry in *Seventeen* magazine, and held editorial posts on school newspapers and yearbooks. I sought jobs that would provide experience helpful to my future career. In college, I worked part time as a clerk in two different book stores, where I observed first hand the tangible elements that influence browsing buyers to select books by whim—title, cover design, art, copy.

"At twenty-one, I moved—alone and penniless—five hundred miles away from my small hometown, to New York City. My goal in landing an entry-level job in publishing was not to launch an editorial career; rather, it was to establish contacts with agents and editors who might assist me in launching my writing career. I began with an administrative position in the textbook marketing division of Macmillan; then—after temping in various publishing houses before finding it necessary to take a full-time advertising agency job with benefits—I landed an editorial post at Harlequin Enterprises. There, as an acquiring editor of Silhouette romance novels, I found myself in a unique and rewarding situation for an aspiring writer. Establishing contacts with editors and agents through daily contact and at conferences was only part of the process that led to the launch of my career. I also learned how to approach publishers with the utmost level of professionalism, and grasped what elements cause an unpublished author's manuscript to stand out in the slush pile, both favorably and unfavorably. In addition, I participated in various behind-the-scenes publishing processes, from contract negotiation to manuscript preparation to cover design to marketing strategy.

"I sold my own first novel two years after becoming an editor, and have virtually been a full-time author ever since. I'm aware that I might have eventually realized my dream without following the precise career-oriented stepping stones I laid in place according to that arduous childhood plan. I doubt, however, that a more laid-back approach would have allowed me to achieve my goals as quickly and completely as I have, or to, along the way, continually indulge my love of reading and writing as well as my fascination with the book business."

Works Cited

Review of *Fade to Black, Kirkus Reviews,* February 15, 1998, p. 220.
Review of *Fade to Black, Publishers Weekly,* March 16, 1998, p. 54.
Hyde, Toni, review of *Fade to Black, Booklist,* April 15, 1998, p. 1394.
Melton, Emily, review of *Murder on Broadway, Booklist,* July, 1996, p. 1808.
Melton, Emily, review of *The Senator Must Die, Booklist,* September 1, 1998, pp. 70-71.
Review of *Murder on Broadway, Publishers Weekly,* June 3, 1996, p. 65.
Triner, Jeanne, review of *Witch Hunt, Booklist,* May 1, 1995, p. 1563.
Review of *Wild, Publishers Weekly,* May 12, 1997, pp. 73-74.

PERIODICALS

Publishers Weekly, November 17, 1997, p. 63.

*   *   *

STEWART, Paul 1955-

Personal

Born June 4, 1955, in London, England; married Julie Stewart (a primary school teacher); children: Joseph, Anna. *Education:* Lancaster University, B.A. (English), 1977; University of East Anglia, M.A. (creative writing), 1979; studied German literature at Heidelberg University, 1980-82.

Addresses

Home—116 Hythe Rd., Brighton, East Sussex BN1 6JS, England. *Agent*—Pat White, Rogers, Coleridge and White, 20 Powis Mews, London W11 1JN, England.

Career

Author, 1989—. Teacher of English as a Foreign Language in Germany, 1979-82, in Sri Lanka, 1982-83, and in Brighton, England, 1983-90.

Writings

JUVENILE NOVELS

The Thought Domain, illustrated by Jon Riley, Viking, 1988, Puffin, 1989.
The Weather Witch, illustrated by Jon Riley, Viking, 1989, Puffin, 1990.
Adam's Ark, illustrated by Kevin Jones, Viking, 1990, Puffin, 1992.
Giant Gutso and the Wacky Gang, Orchard Books, 1991.
Rory McCrory's Nightmare Machine, Viking, 1992, Puffin, 1993.
The Snowman Who Couldn't Melt, illustrated by Annabel Large, Viking, 1993, Puffin, 1994.

Paul Stewart

Bubble and Shriek, illustrated by Annabel Large, Viking, 1993, Puffin, 1995.
Castle of Intrigue, illustrated by Jane Gedye, Usborne Books, 1994.
Neighborhood Witch, Viking, 1994, Puffin, 1995.
Stage Fright, Usborne Books, 1995.
The Clock of Doom, Usborne Books, 1996.
The Wakening, Transworld Books, 1996.
Football Mad, Hippo, 1997.
The Midnight Hand, Transworld Books, 1997.
Dogbird, illustrated by Tony Ross, Corgi, 1998.
The Hanging Tree, Scholastic, 1998.
(With Chris Riddell) *Beyond the Deepwoods* (volume one of "The Edge Chronicles"), illustrated by Chris Riddell, Doubleday, 1998.
Football Mad II: Off-Side, Hippo, 1998.
Football Mad III: Hat-trick!, Hippo, 1999.
(With Chris Riddell) *Stormchaser* (volume two of "The Edge Chronicles"), illustrated by Chris Riddell, Doubleday, 1999.
(With Chris Riddell) *Midnight Over Sanctaphrax* (volume three of "The Edge Chronicles"), illustrated by Chris Riddell, Doubleday, in press.

OTHER

Trek (adult novel), Jonathan Cape, 1991.
Lucky Luke and Other Very Short Stories (stories for learners of English as a Second Language), Penguin (London), 1997.
(With Chris Riddell) *A Little Bit of Winter* (picture book), illustrated by Chris Riddell, Andersen Press, 1998, HarperCollins, 1999.
Millie's Party (picture novel for beginning readers), illustrated by Bernard Lodge, Blue Bananas, 1999.
(With Chris Riddell) *The Birthday Presents* (picture book), illustrated by Chris Riddell, Andersen Press, 1999, HarperCollins, 2000.

Also the author of numerous short stories published in magazines, including *Me* and *Mayfair,* anthologized in collections from Doubleday, and broadcast on the BBC. Additionally, Stewart has penned *The Australian Connection,* a graded reader for teens, and two graded readers for learners of English as a Second Language, *Blue Eyes* and *The Diary.* Several of Stewart's works have been translated into twelve different languages.

Work in Progress

A series of humorous sci-fi novels for middle readers, "The Blobheads," for Macmillan.

Sidelights

Paul Stewart is a British author of fantasy, time-travel and palpably realistic novels (all with a speculative edge), books which are targeted at an audience of middle-grade readers. Though they find their main audience in Great Britain, many of Stewart's books, such as *Adam's Ark, Bubble and Shriek,* and *The Wakening,* have been distributed with success in North America, as well.

"Most of my books for children originate from a 'what if' question," Stewart told *Something about the Author* (*SATA*). "'What if there was a machine that could record our nightmares?' 'What if there was a snowman that couldn't melt?' 'What if someone didn't know what winter felt like?' Then I play with the idea—researching the background and working on the plot—and decide the genre with which best to explore the story. Only when I am completely certain where the story is heading do I start writing."

Stewart, who was born in 1955 and grew up in southwest London, talks with technical assuredness about his craft, and he should, for he earned a master's degree in the prestigious creative writing course at the University of East Anglia with such British luminaries as Malcolm Bradbury and Angela Carter. "I learnt a lot from [the course]," Stewart told the on-line magazine *Achuka* in an interview. "You learnt to become extremely thick-skinned, because you were surrounded by this little group of people who were ripping to shreds something you'd just written and . . . [it] was very good at pinpointing what was wrong with a piece."

Upon graduation, however, Stewart had no intention of writing for children. He produced short stories for adults, as well as some unpublished novels, while further studying and working as an English teacher in Germany and then Sri Lanka. Returning to England in 1983, he began casting about for a new project and went back to an early idea he had regarding a sister book to *The Phantom Tollbooth* by American writer Norton Juster; it was one of the books that informed his youth. This led to Stewart's first publication, *The Thought Domain,* 1988, a children's novel aimed at ten-to-thirteen year olds.

This initial title was followed the next year by *The Weather Witch,* a time-travel story about a village hidden under a lake for four hundred years. Two children from the present, Kerry and Joe, discover the hidden village when they are sent for the summer to their Great Aunt Eleanor. A dull summer is suddenly filled with danger and excitement when the two are sucked into a time vortex while rowing on the lake. They end up in the ancient village of Cleedale, replete with villagers and resident weather witch Megwyn, an ancestor of Great Aunt Eleanor and the one who imprisoned the villagers four centuries earlier when ostensibly saving them from an invading Protestant army. Kerry and Joe are the long-prophesied duo who will save the villagers. "How they return to Great Aunt Eleanor, and bring into the present a girl and a boy from 400 years back makes exciting reading," a reviewer for *Junior Bookshelf* noted. The rescued Elizabethan village turns into a tourist attraction in the twentieth century. "The whole story is fantastic in more ways than one," the same reviewer added, "but the author's skill renders it quite believable."

Stewart's next title, *Adam's Ark,* has been one of his most popular. "It's about a boy who's been diagnosed as autistic," Stewart explained to *Achuka,* "but he isn't, he's just been born able to communicate with animals rather than humans. It's his cat who teaches him to speak and to act in a way in which he should act, in an appropriate way, so that people don't think he's round the bend." As he grows older, Adam begins to learn that he can communicate with animals of all sorts because he is a holdover from prehistoric times when mammals of all kinds could communicate in a language called Mammalogue. Working at the zoo, Adam can communicate with many animals. From a dolphin Adam learns it is to be his mission to protect animals from human aggression of the sort which his own father carries out in his research laboratory.

"This is an interesting book," commented Jo Goodman in *Magpies,* "imperfect but, it its own way, compelling." Jane Inglish, writing in *School Librarian,* dubbed Stewart's story a "passionate teenage novel," while Linda Newbery commented in *Books for Keeps* that this "moving story will find an appreciative audience in the growing numbers of young people concerned about animal welfare and environmental issues." A reviewer for *Junior Bookshelf* concluded that Stewart "has tackled this theme of some considerable grandeur in a down to earth, matter of fact style which renders easy the

Sam's nightmares bring him a message from the dead in Stewart's horror story for middle-grade readers. (Cover illustration by David Wyatt.)

suspension of disbelief in so unusual a thesis. . . . Young readers will enjoy this cleverly constructed story."

Several more books followed, all published by Viking and edited by Morris Lyon. Next in line was *Rory McCrory's Nightmare Machine,* about a scheme for recording nightmares that goes horribly awry. *The Snowman Who Couldn't Melt,* published in 1993, is a "strange mix of a story," according to Adrian Jackson in *Books for Keeps,* "part fairy tale, which eventually becomes a moving account of . . . attempts to rescue the snowman." Cruel Balthazar Grot has constructed the snowman in question, and has given him ice for a heart; thus, he is unable to melt. Young Amy arranges for the snowman to come to a summertime beach in hopes of helping the snowman by showing him the better side of humans. Unfortunately, they encounter some of the worst examples of the species, and finally it is Amy's own goodness that melts the snowman's heart and sets him free. Jocelyn Hanson noted in *School Librarian* that this "is a cheerful and fast-moving story . . . with a lively and determined girl as the main character."

An amazing bottle of bubbles that, when blown, contain those things most feared, proves the catalyst for *Bubble and Shriek,* a "readable and clever story for smart readers," according to David Bennett, writing in *Books for Keeps.* Young Charlie does not like the continual limelight of being a star in advertisements, while Vinny despises the pressure his father puts on him to succeed. These two apparent enemies at school encounter one another at a fair, and with a little help from the mysterious Madame Tatania and her magic bubbles, Charlie is able to both neutralize the animosity from Vinny and reclaim his childhood from a TV career. "Paul Stewart has some wise things to say about the inner fears of childhood and the consequences of obsessive parenting," commented a reviewer for *Junior Bookshelf.* "He presents a fable in a style which will capture the interest of the primary school reader and may stimulate healthy discussion as a class experience."

By the mid-1990s Stewart moved on from Viking, which had published all his early titles, and began publishing with various other houses in a variety of genres. *The Wakening* was published with Transworld Books, and is still targeted at his usual audience, readers between ten and thirteen. Tom Tiddler's tragic story is known by a child's rhyme, but for Sam it is all too real, visiting his nightmares on a regular basis. Slowly, Sam comes to understand that the real Tom Tiddler, wrongfully accused of a ghastly crime, is trying to clear his reputation through these dreams. Sam is aided in his dream time and at school by the stalwart Jody. In the end, the two are led to Tom Tiddler's fortune and become wealthy, while Tom finally can rest in peace. Jackson noted in *Books for Keeps* that the "drama is set against some bleakly realistic problems with money that impact on Sam's family," and concluded that the book was "[w]ell worth putting in with horror collections to show readers how the genre can be richly exploited."

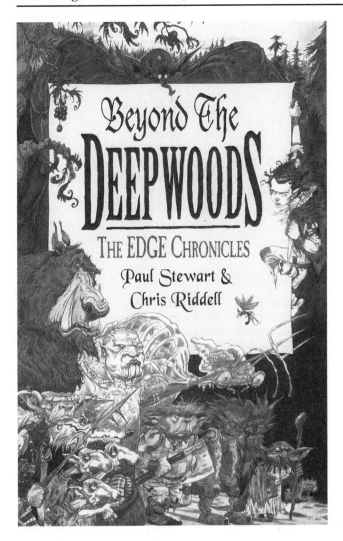

Brought up by a family of woodtrolls, Twig enters a nightmare world in search of his true identity in this elegantly written, marvelously illustrated fantasy. (Cover illustration by Chris Riddell.)

A change of pace for Stewart came in writing for younger audiences in books such as the "Football Mad" series, *Dogbird,* and picture books with Chris Riddell. In the soccer books, Gary, Danny, and Craig have adventures on and off the field; the series is developed for seven-to-nine year olds. Novels for even young readers, such as *Dogbird* and *Millie's Party,* focus on small, generally humorous events to entice beginning readers. In *Dogbird,* for example, a barking parakeet proves to be the perfect pet for young Alice. With Chris Riddell as illustrator, Stewart has also tried his hand at picture books. *A Little Bit of Winter* introduces Rabbit and Hedgehog. When spring reunites the two friends— Hedgehog has hibernated for the season—they share a little bit of the season they just missed together. A reviewer for *Publishers Weekly* commented, "This tale of friendship from a British team gently distills the elements of the winter season." The same reviewer concluded that "the emotional connection between the two [animals] emits warmth and wit."

More ambitious in scope is the collaboration of Riddell and Stewart on the fantasy series, "The Edge Chronicles." As Stewart noted in his *Achuka* interview, Riddell provides line drawings for the series, but also has some editorial input on the story; thus they share the credit for the books. The series is planned as a trilogy, but could go longer. *Beyond the Deepwoods* sets things off when thirteen-year-old Twig is told that the Woodtrolls who brought him up are not his real parents, and that he must venture into the Deepwoods to discover the truth about his parentage and himself. On his journey he stumbles off the path and into a frightening other world, a world full of magic, adventure, and danger. A reviewer for *Interzone* praised the novel and wrote that "Stewart combines the horrific and the absurd to produce an atmosphere of sustained nightmare." The reviewer acknowledged that it is "strong stuff," but claimed "the writing is so full of zest, Stewart's imagination so fertile, his love of language so inventive" that "every child from [age] nine to eleven should be given a copy."

In *Stormchaser,* the second volume of "The Edge Chronicles," Twig is reunited with his sky-pirate father aboard the flying sailship *Stormchaser,* which undertakes a dangerous mission to sail into the heart of a Great Storm. In a review for *Amazon.co.uk,* David Langford wrote that "nothing, absolutely nothing, works out as expected in this madly twisting plot. Twig's companions are beset by spies, traitors, memorable villains and the living dead . . . [and] Stewart's compulsive storytelling, perfectly complimented by Riddell's fine-lined illustrations, makes it all good stuff."

Stewart and Riddell have also teamed up on a series of humorous sci-fi novels, "The Blobheads."

"Some children want to grow up to be a brain surgeon or an astronaut," Stewart told *SATA.* "I always wanted to be an author. It took a long time but, in 1988—and after a lot of other jobs—my first novel for children was published. I am now a full-time author, writing books and short stories for children of all ages, as well as a novel for adults and several readers for foreign learners of English. . . . Writing has always been a compulsion for me, and I count myself so very lucky that I can earn a living from what I enjoy doing best in the world."

Works Cited

Review of *Adam's Ark, Junior Bookshelf,* April, 1991, p. 68.

Bennett, David, review of *Bubble and Shriek, Books for Keeps,* November, 1995, p. 12.

Review of *Beyond the Deepwoods, Interzone,* January, 1999.

Review of *Bubble and Shriek, Junior Bookshelf,* February, 1994, p. 27.

Goodman, Jo, review of *Adam's Ark, Magpies,* July, 1991, pp. 31-32.

Hanson, Jocelyn, review of *The Snowman Who Couldn't Melt, School Librarian,* August, 1993, p. 112.

Inglish, Jane, review of *Adam's Ark, School Librarian,* August, 1991, p. 91.

Jackson, Adrian, review of *The Snowman Who Couldn't Melt, Books for Keeps,* January, 1995, p. 10.

Jackson, Adrian, review of *The Wakening, Books for Keeps,* January, 1997, p. 25.

Langford, David, review of *Stormchaser, Amazon.co.uk,* http://www.amazon.co.uk.

Review of *A Little Bit of Winter, Publishers Weekly,* December 14, 1998, p. 74.

Newbery, Linda, review of *Adam's Ark, Books for Keeps,* July, 1992, p. 13.

Stewart, Paul, interview with *Achuka,* http://www.achuka.co.uk/pssg.htm.

Review of *The Weather Witch, Junior Bookshelf,* December, 1989, p. 303.

For More Information See

PERIODICALS

Booklist, March 1, 1999, p. 1223.
Daily Telegraph, December 12, 1998.
Junior Bookshelf, June, 1992, p. 125; June, 1993, p. 107; December, 1996, p. 261.
Magpies, May, 1992, p. 30; July, 1993, p. 33.
School Librarian, February, 1991, p. 32; May, 1994, p. 62; February, 1997, p. 34.
Sunday Telegraph, November 22, 1998.
Times Educational Supplement, November 3, 1989, p. 32; November 8, 1991, p. 32; August 27, 1999.

—*Sketch by J. Sydney Jones*

*   *   *

STOCK, Catherine 1952-

Personal

Born November 26, 1952, in Stockholm, Sweden; daughter of Vere Guildford (a career diplomat) and Frances B. C. (an artist; maiden name, Coetzee) Stock. *Education:* University of Cape Town, B.F.A., 1974; University of London, postgraduate certificate in education, 1976; Pratt Institute, M.A., 1978. *Hobbies and other interests:* Hiking, swimming, reading, tennis, opera, ballet, chess, skiing, wildlife conservation, crossword puzzles, jazz, chamber music, cooking.

Addresses

Home and office—20 East 88th St., New York, NY 10128.

Career

Hewat Teacher's Training College, Cape Town, South Africa, lecturer in drawing and art history, 1975; Putnam Publishing Group, New York City, art director, 1978-81; University of Cape Town, lecturer in children's book writing, illustration, and design, 1982-83; Macmillan Publishing Co., Inc., New York City, designer, 1984-85;

Houghton Mifflin Co., New York City, art director of Clarion Books, 1985-86; author and illustrator.

Awards, Honors

Award from the American Institute of Graphic Arts, 1981, for design of *A Little Interlude,* written by Robert Maiorano and illustrated by Rachel Isadora; Christopher Award, 1983, for *Posy;* Coretta Scott King Award, 1986, Child Study Association of America's Children's Books of the Year, 1987, both for *Justin and the Best Biscuits in the World;* Book Can Develop Empathy Award, New York State Humane Association and the Fund for Animals, 1991, for *When the Woods Hum.*

Writings

FOR CHILDREN; SELF-ILLUSTRATED

A Christmas Angel Collection, Scribner, 1978.
Emma's Dragon Hunt, Lothrop, Lee and Shepard, 1984.
Sampson, the Christmas Cat, Putnam, 1984.
Sophie's Bucket, Lothrop, Lee and Shepard, 1985.
Sophie's Knapsack, Lothrop, Lee and Shepard, 1988.
Alexander's Midnight Snack: A Little Elephant's ABC, Clarion, 1988.
Armien's Fishing Trip, Morrow, 1990.
Halloween Monster, Bradbury, 1990.
Thanksgiving Treat, Bradbury, 1990.
Christmas Time, Bradbury, 1990.
Secret Valentine, Bradbury, 1991.
Easter Surprise, Bradbury, 1991.
Birthday Present, Bradbury, 1991.
Where Are You Going, Manyoni?, Morrow, 1993.
An Island Summer, Lothrop, Lee and Shepard, 1999.

ILLUSTRATOR

Vernon Pizer, *Shortchanged by History: America's Neglected Innovators,* Putnam, 1979.
Betty Baker, *All-by-Herself,* Greenwillow, 1980.
Maggie Duff, *The Princess and the Pumpkin,* Macmillan, 1980.
Helen Reader Cross, *Isabella Mine,* Lothrop, Lee and Shepard, 1980.
Sally Major, *Eating Out: A Guide to European Dishes,* Grastorf & Lang, 1981.
Lucia Moira Thatcher, *Mr. Tiki Wok,* Tafelberg, 1981.
Marietta Moskin, *A Royal Gift,* Coward, 1981.
Corlia Fourie, *Marianne and the Lion in the Dollhouse,* Human & Rousseau, 1982.
Heinz Winckler, *Tina,* Tafelberg, 1983.
Martin Versfeld, *Food for Thought,* Tafelberg, 1983.
Charlotte Pomerantz, *Posy,* Greenwillow, 1983.
May Joyce Jones, *The Choice of the Herd,* Human & Rousseau, 1984.
De Waal Venter, *Loutjie Helps Find,* Human & Rousseau, 1984.
Liza Fosburgh, *Bella Arabella,* Four Winds, 1985.
Ann Whitford Paul, *Owl at Night,* Putnam, 1985.
Mildred Pitts Walter, *Justin and the Best Biscuits in the World,* Lothrop, Lee and Shepard, 1986.
Alane Ferguson, *That New Pet!,* Lothrop, Lee and Shepard, 1986.

Charlotte Pomerantz, *Timothy Tall Feather,* Greenwillow, 1986.

Ann Warren Turner, *Street Talk* (poems), Houghton Mifflin, 1986.

Carol F. Ra (editor), *Trot, Trot to Boston: Play Rhymes for Baby,* Lothrop, Lee and Shepard, 1987.

Caroline Feller Bauer, *Midnight Snowman,* Atheneum, 1987.

Claudia Mills, *Melanie Magpie,* Bantam, 1987.

Kathryn Lasky, *Sea Swan,* Macmillan, 1988.

Carol Beach York, *Miss Know-It-All and the Three Ring Circus,* Bantam, 1988.

Carol Beach York, *Miss Know-It-All and the Secret House,* Harper and Row, 1988, Bantam, 1988.

Charlotte Zolotow, *Something Is Going to Happen,* Harper and Row, 1988.

Barbara Joosse, *Better with Two,* Harper, 1988.

Charlotte Zolotow, *A Tiger Called Thomas,* Lothrop, Lee and Shepard, 1988.

Molly D'Arcy Thompson, *Willie Stories,* Human & Rousseau, 1988.

Kathleen Hersom and Donald Hersom, *The Copycat,* Atheneum, 1989.

York, *Miss Know-It-All and the Magic House,* Bantam, 1989.

Grace Chetwin, *Mr. Meredith and the Truly Remarkable Stone,* Bradbury, 1989.

Karen Lynn Williams, *Galimoto,* Lothrop, Lee and Shepard, 1990.

Joanne Ryder, *When the Woods Hum,* Morrow, 1991.

C. B. Christiansen, *Mara in the Morning,* Atheneum, 1991.

Barbara Baker, *Oh, Emma,* Dutton, 1991.

Carolyn Haywood, *Eddie's Friend Boodles,* Morrow, 1991.

Bernice Wolman (collector) *Taking Turns: Poetry to Share,* Atheneum, 1992.

Lynn Joseph, *An Island Christmas,* Clarion, 1992.

David LaRochelle, *The Evening King,* Atheneum, 1993.

Christine Barker Widman, *The Willow Umbrella,* Macmillan, 1993.

Barbara Lucas, *Snowed In,* Bradbury, 1993.

Karen Ackerman, *By the Dawn's Early Light,* Atheneum, 1994.

Karen Lynn Williams, *Tap-Tap,* Clarion, 1994.

Leslea Newman, *Too Far Away to Touch,* Clarion, 1995.

Maggie Rugg Herold, *A Very Important Day,* Morrow, 1995.

Jeannine Ouellette-Howitz, *Mama Moon,* Orchard, 1995.

Joan W. Blos, *Nellie Bly's Monkey: His Remarkable Story in His Own Words,* Morrow, 1996.

Nancy Riecken, *Today Is the Day,* Houghton Mifflin, 1996.

Claudia Mills, *Gus and Grandpa,* Farrar, Straus and Giroux, 1997.

Mills, *Gus and Grandpa and the Christmas Cookies,* Farrar, Straus and Giroux, 1997.

Tololwa M. Mollel, *Kele's Secret,* Dutton, 1997.

Claudia Mills, *Gus and Grandpa Ride the Train,* Farrar, Straus and Giroux, 1998.

Mills, *Gus and Grandpa at the Hospital,* Farrar, Straus and Giroux, 1998.

Karen Lynn Williams, *Painted Dreams,* Lothrop, Lee and Shepard, 1998.

Ned Shank, *The Sanyasin's First Day,* Marshall Cavendish, 1998.

Claudia Mills, *Gus and Grandpa and the Two-Wheeled Bike,* Farrar, Straus and Giroux, 1999.

Alice Faye Duncan, *Miss Viola and Uncle Ed Lee,* Atheneum, 1999.

Claudia Mills, *Gus and Grandpa and Show-and-Tell,* Farrar, Straus and Giroux, 2000.

Also contributor of illustrations to magazines and newspapers, including *New Yorker* and *New York Times. By the Dawn's Early Light* by Karen Ackerman has been translated into Spanish.

Sidelights

Award-winning author-illustrator Catherine Stock is known for her tender, fanciful, boldly colored, and factually accurate, watercolors and pastels, as well as for her prolific nature. In addition to the fifteen solo titles she has accumulated since 1978, she has also illustrated numerous books for other well-respected authors such as Charlotte Zolotow, Charlotte Pomerantz, Karen Williams, Joan Blos, and Claudia Mills. In her own titles, including *Emma's Dragon Hunt, Sophie's Knapsack, Armien's Fishing Trip,* and *Where Are You Going, Manyoni?,* Stock takes young English-speaking readers on journeys to places far from home, like China and Africa, introducing them to the diversity and vastness of the world. Stock's own childhood showed her many

The youngest family member helps Grandpa with an important Thanksgiving preparation in Catherine Stock's self-illustrated **Thanksgiving Treat.**

A young boy is eager to be a good birthday-party guest in **Birthday Present,** *written and illustrated by Stock.*

Stock next turned her hand to companion books about a little girl named Sophie. Betsy Hearne, writing in *Bulletin of the Center for Children's Books* called *Sophie's Knapsack* an "enticing picture book" about a family camping trip. In this follow-up to *Sophie's Bucket,* the now kindergarten-age title character enjoys another encounter with nature. The full-page watercolor paintings chronicle the entire trip's events, and "the details of every snack or meal are delicious," proclaimed Hearne. The family drives to the country, they hike in a beautiful setting, and snack on delicious food. The book was replete with "[f]resh writing and art," Hearne concluded, that would inspire young readers. *Booklist*'s Carolyn Phelan appreciated "Stock's lovely, luminous watercolor illustrations." Phelan's positive conclusion about *Sophie's Knapsack:* "would-be and experienced campers will enjoy it again and again."

Two of Stock's books, *Armien's Fishing Trip* and *Where Are You Going, Manyoni?,* are set in Africa. While visiting his old home in Kalk Bay, South Africa, Armien decides to impress his friends by stowing away on Old Sam's fishing boat. During a storm, Old Sam is washed overboard, and quick-thinking Armien gives up his hiding place to save the man. Returning to Kalk Bay, Armien is now a hero, "a victory that will be shared by would-be sailors among the readers," wrote Ann A. Flowers in *Horn Book.* Flowers concluded that the "beautiful illustrations combine impressive watery

different parts of the world, as she grew up in France, England, South Africa, Hong Kong, and the United States.

Stock once told *SATA:* "I'm a rather quiet and shy person, and I've always loved books. I also grew up continually painting pictures—my mother was a painter. Perhaps because we were always moving, our family was very close. Thus, childhood memories are very special to me and a constant source of inspiration."

After studying in Cape Town, South Africa and in London, Stock earned a master's degree from the Pratt Institute and thereafter found work in children's books and publishing. A year spent teaching children's book writing, illustration, and design in Cape Town was succeeded by design positions at both Macmillan and Clarion in New York. Her first self-illustrated title was the 1978 *A Christmas Angel Collection;* much of her work since then has been in illustrating children's books. Her first big success as author-illustrator came in 1984 when her *Emma's Dragon Hunt* was chosen as a "Reading Rainbow" book.

Emma's Dragon Hunt tells the story of young Emma and her grandfather Wong who has just come from China to live with the family. Wong and Emma share a common passion for dragons; he tells her stories of kind dragons and even takes her out to look for the mythical beasts. The reader and Wong clearly see these dragons that cause earthquakes and heat waves, but Emma does not. A reviewer for *Bulletin of the Center for Children's Books* called the book "graceful."

Yese anxiously awaits the return of her father with money to buy new shoes. (From Today Is the Day, *written by Nancy Riecken and illustrated by Stock.)*

Most of all,

Gus loved Grandpa's house

because at Grandpa's house

there was Grandpa.

8

Stock's illustrations depict the loving relationship between Gus and his grandfather in the first of a series of books written by Claudia Mills. (From Gus and Grandpa.)

scenes of the sea with comfortable views of the racially mixed South African town of Kalk Bay."

Zimbabwe is the backdrop for *Where Are You Going, Manyoni?,* the story of a child's long walk to school. Passing a giant baobab tree, a dried river bed, a wild bushpig, and baboons, the little girl experiences the early morning of rural Zimbabwe as she heads toward her village school. Lyn Miller-Lachmann noted in *School Library Journal* that the "expansive double-page spreads provide plenty of opportunities for youngsters to search for Manyoni and to identify a rich array of wildlife." With many unfamiliar terms, the book contains what Miller-Lachmann called a "much-needed glossary." A *Kirkus Reviews* critic called the story "a lovely book that draws the reader right in with Manyoni, among the rocks and trees."

Stocke's series of six books for Bradbury Press detail various North American holidays and celebrations. Late winter and spring holidays are dealt with in *Secret Valentine* and *Easter Surprise,* and birthdays are addressed in *Birthday Present.* Fall and winter are also neatly taken care of with *Halloween Monster, Thanks-*

giving Treat, and *Christmas Time.* These last three holidays are covered in books "that contain simple yet appealing messages," according to *Booklist*'s Ilene Cooper. In *Halloween Monster,* a young African American boy is frightened of Halloween until he climbs into his monster suit and joins in the fun. In *Thanksgiving Treat,* a young boy finds chestnuts to contribute to his family's celebration. Finally, in *Christmas time,* a little girl helps to choose a tree and make cookies. "These books take the time to appreciate the small moments that go into making holidays memorable," concluded Cooper, "and they are also strong on extolling family relationships." Lisa Dennis declared in *School Library Journal* that these titles "fill a definite, even desperate need, for accessible, attractive holiday picture books," while Roger Sutton, writing in *Bulletin of the Center for Children's Books,* asserted that it is "good to see story and concept so smoothly blended; equally good to see a new series so gimmick-free."

In her illustrations for other writers, Stock is equally careful to match the mood of her artwork to that of a particular story. Her illustrations for Leslea Newman's *Too Far Away to Touch,* for example, are gentle and serene, following the tone of the story about a warm and empathetic uncle preparing his niece for his eventual death from AIDS. "Stock's watercolors are sensitive to the tender mood," wrote Roger Sutton in the *New York Times Book Review,* "and they keep sentimentality at bay through a contrast of sunny scenes and nighttime mystery." Maeve Visser Knoth asserted in *Horn Book* that the "effective, understated text is enhanced by Stock's soft watercolor paintings, which express the close relationship between Zoe and her uncle."

Stock teamed up with Newbery Medalist Joan Blos for the 1996 title, *Nellie Bly's Monkey,* a recounting of the reporter's momentous trip around the world told by McGinty, a monkey (with a fetching fez) that Bly bought in Singapore. The monkey tells his story in brief chapters set in Hong Kong, Yokohama, and San Francisco. "Most of the charm here radiates from Stock's illustrations," commented a *Publishers Weekly* critic, "every stroke suggestive of her subjects' personalities." This same reviewer concluded: "Detailed, full-page watercolors evoke the diverse settings of the text, while line art conjures up telling vignettes...." *Booklist*'s Stephanie Zvirin noted that there is "charming humor in Stock's black-and-white sketches and in her attractive watercolor illustrations."

Further adventures around the world come to readers in Nancy Riecken's *Today Is the Day,* set in rural Mexico, and in Tololwa M. Mollel's *Kele's Secret,* set on a Tanzanian coffee farm. In the former title, young Yesenia anxiously awaits the return of her father after a six-month absence, running to meet each bus that arrives. Long after sundown, he finally comes. "Stock's watercolors are exuberant and poignant," observed Denise E. Agosto in *School Library Journal,* "helping readers to understand Yesenia's hopes and fears." *Booklist*'s Susan Dove Lempke also commented on the emotion-filled artwork, writing: "Stock's tender watercolors vividly use facial expression and posture ... to show Yese's feelings."

In *Kele's Secret,* little Yoanes plays detective on his grandmother's coffee plantation. Young Yoanes is an expert at finding the eggs of a chicken named Kele, but finding Kele is another story. Yoanes has to deal with his own fears to find this hen hidden away in a creepy old shed. Stock's "on-site research shows in her fluid, detailed watercolors of contemporary eastern Africa," commented a *Publishers Weekly* contributor. Alicia Eames stated in *School Library Journal* that "Stock's distinguished watercolors successfully capture the action of the story, the lush setting, and Yoanes's changing expressions."

Working with Claudia Mills, Stock has helped create a series of longer picture books for independent readers built around a very imperfect little boy, Gus, and his equally imperfect grandfather. In the first book of the series, *Gus and Grandpa,* the little boy makes three visits to his grandfather's house, trying to train the dog Skippy, and ultimately celebrating their birthdays together. Gentle irony and humor warm the relationship between the two main characters. A *Publishers Weekly* contributor commented that "Stock builds on the breezy mood with dynamic, sketchy art, adding details that amplify the proceedings." "A witty, warm offering," summarized the critic. *Booklist*'s Hazel Rochman concluded that "Stock's line-and-wash illustrations are filled with light and love and commotion."

Further adventures between Gus and his grandfather ensue in *Gus and Grandpa at the Hospital* and *Gus and Grandpa and the Two-Wheeled Bike.* In the former title, Grandpa suffers a heart attack and is admitted to the hospital, but he knows what to do to put his visitor, Gus, at ease. "Soft watercolor wash-and-line drawings complement the well-written text," commented Pamela K. Bomboy in *School Library Journal.* Out of the hospital in *Gus and Grandpa and the Two-Wheeled Bike,* grandfather helps Gus get rid of his training wheels, both literally and figuratively. Maura Bresnahan wrote in *School Library Journal,* "Stock's muted watercolors nicely reflect both the plot's elements and the close bond between grandfather and grandson."

Stock's blend of tenderness and spunk, her ability to fuse words with pictures, and her varied experiences growing up around the world have all contributed to the success of her books. Stock told *SATA:* "Children's literature seems to be the field in which I can contribute something to the world.... Eventually I hope to buy an old house in the French or Italian countryside with artist friends and to divide my time between Europe and New York."

Works Cited

Agosto, Denise E., review of *Today Is the Day, School Library Journal,* August, 1996, p. 128.

Bomboy, Pamela K., review of *Gus and Grandpa at the Hospital, School Library Journal,* September, 1998, p. 177.

Bresnahan, Maura, review of *Gus and Grandpa and the Two-Wheeled Bike, School Library Journal,* April, 1999, p. 105.

Cooper, Ilene, review of *Christmas Time* and others, *Booklist,* October 1, 1990, p. 341.

Dennis, Lisa, review of *Christmas Time* and others, *School Library Journal,* February, 1992, p. 41.

Eames, Alicia, review of *Kele's Secret, School Library Journal,* June, 1997, p. 98.

Review of *Emma's Dragon Hunt, Bulletin of the Center for Children's Books,* January, 1985, p. 95.

Flowers, Ann A., review of *Armien's Fishing Trip, Horn Book,* November-December, 1990, p. 733.

Review of *Gus and Grandpa, Publishers Weekly,* February 3, 1997, p. 107.

Hearne, Betsy, review of *Sophie's Knapsack, Bulletin of the Center for Children's Books,* July-August, 1988, pp. 239-40.

Review of *Kele's Secret, Publishers Weekly,* May 12, 1997, p. 76.

Knoth, Maeve Visser, review of *Too Far Away to Touch, Horn Book,* May-June, 1995, pp. 328-29.

Lempke, Susan Dove, review of *Today Is the Day, Booklist,* September 15, 1996, p. 250.

Miller-Lachmann, Lyn, review of *Where Are You Going, Manyoni?, School Library Journal,* December, 1993, p. 94.

Review of *Nellie Bly's Monkey, Publishers Weekly,* January 15, 1996, p. 462.

Phelan, Carolyn, review of *Sophie's Knapsack, Booklist,* March 1, 1988, p. 1187.

Rochman, Hazel, review of *Gus and Grandpa, Booklist,* February 1, 1997, p. 955.

Sutton, Roger, review of *Christmas Time* and others, *Bulletin of the Center for Children's Books,* November, 1990, p. 72.

Sutton, Roger, review of *Too Far Away to Touch, New York Times Book Review,* August 27, 1995, p. 27.

Review of *Where Are You Going, Manyoni?, Kirkus Reviews,* July 15, 1993, p. 942.

Zvirin, Stephanie, review of *Nellie Bly's Monkey, Booklist,* February 15, 1996, p. 1024.

For More Information See

BOOKS

Contemporary Authors, Volume 119, Gale, 1987.

International Authors and Writers Who's Who, 13th edition, International Biographical Centre, 1993.

PERIODICALS

Booklist, May 1, 1998, p. 1526; September 15, 1998, p. 242; November 1, 1998, p. 508.

Bulletin of the Center for Children's Books, October, 1993, p. 59.

Horn Book, March-April, 1999, pp. 211-12.

School Library Journal, November, 1984, p. 118; October, 1990, pp. 39, 102; November, 1995, p. 74; February, 1999, p. 83.*

—Sketch by J. Sydney Jones

A young Tanzanian girl makes a rock her baby doll in Stephanie Stuve-Bodeen's tender first picture book. (Cover illustration by Christy Hale.)

STUVE-BODEEN, Stephanie 1965-

Personal

Born in 1965. *Education:* Attended University of Wisconsin, River Falls.

Addresses

Home—620 West 7th Ave., Fergus Falls, MN 56537.

Career

Teacher and children's book author. Peace Corps volunteer, Tanzania, East Africa; has taught junior and senior high school.

Writings

FOR CHILDREN

Elizabeti's Doll, illustrated by Christy Hale, Lee & Low (New York City), 1998.
We'll Paint the Octopus Red, illustrated by Pam De Vito, Woodbine House (Bethesda, MD), 1998.

Work in Progress

A young adult novel.

Sidelights

Although Stephanie Stuve-Bodeen has always enjoyed writing, she did not begin to make it a career until after her children were born. Raised on a dairy farm in Wisconsin, Stuve-Bodeen went to Tanzania as a Peace Corps volunteer after graduating from the University of Wisconsin—River Falls. Her experiences in Africa inspired the setting and characters for her first picture book, *Elizabeti's Doll,* the story of a little girl's adjustment to the birth of a new baby brother. Wanting a baby of her own to care for, Elizabeti finds a rock that becomes her doll. She bathes and feeds her doll, and ends up saving it from the cooking fire where her older sister has inadvertently placed it.

Elizabeti's Doll drew warm praise for its unpretentiousness and its sensitivity to Tanzanian culture. A reviewer for *Publishers Weekly* hailed it as an "impressive debut" enhanced by "well-balanced prose" and a fittingly gentle tone. In *School Library Journal,* Martha Topol called the book "a splendid celebration of life and the power of a child's imagination."

Stuve-Bodeen again explores a sensitive topic in *We'll Paint the Octopus Red,* which is about the birth of a baby with Down Syndrome. Again, Stuve-Bodeen approaches the subject through the eyes of a young girl. Emma is at first unhappy that she is about to have a younger sibling, but she warms up to the idea after her father helps her imagine all the fun she will have with the new baby. When Isaac is born with Down Syndrome, Emma must learn that he will be able to do all the things with her that she had hoped, but he will have to do them more slowly. *School Library Journal* reviewer Lisa Gangemi Krapp found the book thoughtful and appropriate for young readers. "The fine text gets right to a child's level of understanding," wrote Ilene Cooper in *Booklist.* Though Cooper pointed out that the book avoided some difficult issues, she recommended the book highly.

Stuve-Bodeen, who lives in Minnesota with her family, is working on a young adult novel. She enjoys visiting schools and speaking with students and readers. In addition to her Peace Corps job, she has worked as a teacher in junior and senior high schools.

Works Cited

Cooper, Ilene, review of *We'll Paint the Octopus Red, Booklist,* September 15, 1998.
Review of *Elizabeti's Doll, Publishers Weekly,* August 24, 1998, p. 56.
Krapp, Lisa Gangemi, review of *We'll Paint the Octopus Red, School Library Journal,* December 1998, p. 92.
Topol, Martha, review of *Elizabeti's Doll, School Library Journal,* September 1998, p. 183-184.

For More Information See

PERIODICALS

Horn Book, November, 1998, p. 720.*

T

TALLIS, Robyn
See MACDONALD, James D.

* * *

TEAL, Val(entine M.) 1902-1997

OBITUARY NOTICE—See index for *SATA* sketch: Born February 14, 1902, in Bottineau, ND; died in her sleep, November 3, 1997, in Rochester, MA. Writer. Val Teal began writing professionally in 1943. Her first children's book was *The Little Woman Wanted Noise* (1943), followed by *Angel Child* (1946), *It Was Not What I Expected* (1948), and approximately two dozen other books and plays, mostly for the children's market. She also contributed numerous short stories to magazines for adults and children, including *Saturday Evening Post, Ladies' Home Journal, Good Housekeeping, American, Woman's Day, Woman's Home Companion, Child Life,* and *Parents' Magazine.*

OBITUARIES AND OTHER SOURCES:

PERIODICALS

Omaha World-Herald, February 19, 1991, p. 27; December 5, 1997, p. 22; February 10, 1998, p. 9sf.

Stephanie Gordon Tessler

1940-

JUST LIKE IN THE MOVIES ...

It is May 11th, 1940, and a star is born. Well, not exactly . . . .

Once upon a time a newborn baby was promised that he would be able to talk to the birds and remember his entire existence before he was born, until he said his first word. I'm sure it must be true, I read it in a book. But in all honesty, I have no recollection of my life, before I was born or after, until I was seventeen days old. And, that is where my life's story most certainly must begin.

You see, there was this phone call . . . .

"Sylvia," said my auntie Ruth, from her office in Children's Central Casting. "How would you like Stephanie to be in the movies?" As gorgeous a baby as my mom thought I was, she was surprised.

"Ruthie," said my mom, "Stephanie is one week old. She can't talk. She can't act. What will she do in a movie?"

Mom was wrong about the acting. I was a born actor.

"A studio needs a newborn baby to play a twin in Lana Turner's new movie. Stephanie would be perfect," said my auntie Ruth.

Mom said, "Yes." The rest is history.

Only seventeen days old and I, Stephanie Anne Gordon, had my first job and my own social security number. Of course, gorgeous baby or not, it's a good thing all newborns look pretty much alike. And, first word or not, I remember a lot of my growing up because most of it became a movie—actually many movies, and was recorded on film. For about fourteen years I worked at all the major motion picture studios, made dozens of movies, and went to school on the studio lots far more than I went to Burnside Avenue, my public school.

But a movie star I was not. I was the backbone and the background of the movie industry—I was a child "extra."

That means in *The Bells of St. Mary's* Ingrid Bergman was the nun, Bing Crosby was the priest, and I was the angel—in the Christmas Nativity play, that is. They were the stars, I was the extra. Every Christmas I watch *Bells* . . . and remember how the director ruined my favorite dress by trying to hang me from wires and attaching wings to me. The wires didn't work, so I ended up standing on a ladder under hot lights for hours. My dress was holey, but I didn't feel very angelic. I think I got the part because of my long blonde curls. A definite case of miscasting.

In *The Boy with the Green Hair,* I was just one of the kids laughing at Dean Stockwell's green hair.

In *Francis the Talking Mule,* I was just one of the kids watching Francis the mule talk—with Chill Will's voice—while Francis chewed a rubber ball.

But once, I was the kid walking in front of the saloon *On Wabash Avenue* at the very moment Victor Mature was running for the swinging doors. I was the kid he grabbed up in his arms and swung around and put down as he ran. I was the kid that got it right the first time, in only one take. I was the kid he carried back on his humongously broad shoulders to my waiting mom to tell her what a great little actress I was. I was the kid he signed his autograph on a dollar bill for and made all the other extra kids jealous. I was the kid who fell in love with Victor Mature that day, and have remained his loyalest fan to this very day.

In *The Greatest Show on Earth,* I was the kid sitting next to my real-life brother and a bunch of my real-life cousins watching Burt Lancaster and Tony Curtis be acrobats. Elephants held tails and marched around the circus ring while we held balloons and ate peanuts and cotton candy—all we wanted. After three days of filming, I was the kid throwing up pink stuff behind the circus tent.

In *Joan of Arc,* I was the kid watching Ingrid Bergman burn at the stake because the bad guys thought she was a witch. I loved that movie and I loved Ms. Bergman, she

Stephanie Gordon Tessler, at nine months.

was so nice. I was glad that when they actually lit the fire to burn her up, instead of Ms. Bergman, they used a dummy with wires to make it move.

I don't remember the name of the movie I was in where I was supposed to be heading west in a covered wagon. But I sure remember the horses getting spooked and taking off across the prairie at a wild gallop. It was great fun. The most exciting thing that had ever happened to me! A stunt cowboy rode after the wagon, jumped on the horses, and reined them in. Yippee-ei-yo! Yippee-ei-yay! It was just like in the movies....

By the time I graduated elementary school I had lived, ever so briefly, the lives of dozens of different people from too many times and places to remember. So, what did I want to be when I grew up....

I do know that when I was born I didn't start out to be a movie actor, but I was. And when I was growing up I didn't think I'd end up being a children's book writer, but I am. I just wanted to be a normal kid, growing up in Los Angeles in the 1940s, going to school and playing with my friends, roller-skating down Meadowbrook Avenue, and getting drippy ice cream bars from the Good Humor Man who jingled his way down my block on sunshiny days. But I have learned that you may think you are just growing up and getting older, and all the while life is busy making up its own exciting plots for the story of your life. It's the stuff that books are made from....

I loved working in the movies. I credit my writer's imagination and love of wonder and my ability to truly believe to those days spent in prairie sod gingham cheering on runaway horses; or escaping the total destruction of New York City from *It Came from Outer Space*; or waiting with my mama, a woman I'd never met until that day on

the movie set, for *A Streetcar Named Desire*. I didn't know how much I loved it, because it was my life. Making movies was something I did. Something I loved. Something that kept me out of regular school a lot. Something that kept me from making friends. Something I finally, desperately, wanted to stop doing. In spite of all the exciting places working in the movies took me, all the famous movie stars I met and spoke to and got autographs from, all the talking mules and Lassies I worked with, I was a lonely little girl.

Because I spent more time in studio school than I did in regular school, my principal at Burnside Avenue didn't like me. I was sure of it. She was tall (I was five years old—everyone was tall) and thin and had silver gray hair. I remember how she was always looking down at me through skinny eyes. That's how I knew she didn't like me—skinny eyes are a dead giveaway. The school nurse wasn't too crazy about me either. I was always constipated as a child, and I was constantly in her office with another stomachache. That nervous stomach of my childhood has haunted me into my adult life as well. The nurse would call my mom, who would come to school, take me home, give me Phillips' milk of magnesia, and send me back to school the next day, so I could have another stomachache and annoy the nurse. Truth is, grammar school was a bust for me. I had no real friends. No one ever wanted me on their team (I stunk at every game but four square). No one told me secrets, or shared their lunch ... well, sometimes Brenda did so she could have my peanut butter and jelly sandwich. She always brought tuna salad, my favorite—I always brought peanut butter and something, my brother, Stevie's, favorite. In third grade, Brenda didn't come to school because she'd had a horrible allergy rash from eating peanut butter (where she got peanut butter from, her mom couldn't imagine—me either) and we stopped trading sandwiches forever.

As sure as I was that my principal hated me, that's how sure I was, Mrs. Powers, my fifth grade teacher, loved me. In fact, I was sure that Mrs. Powers loved us all; the good, the bad, the ugly, even the kid who worked in the studios. She treated us all like there was something special about us, even Leonard, the goofiest kid in our class since kindergarten. It seems to me that we were all nicer to each other that year because of Mrs. Powers.

In the fifth grade we did the best projects. That was when we built a compact car-sized chuck wagon in our classroom and had real cowboy cookouts. That was when we did the ultimate Thanksgiving play and made our own Pilgrim and Indian costumes. And that was when I forever sealed my fate with the principal. It happened over my Indian dress.

Since every girl wanted to be an Indian maiden, those of us who got picked felt very special, indeed. When I was chosen, I was elated. I carried home the pattern for my costume so carefully there wasn't a single wrinkle in it. Pretty good for me, the kid who left for school every morning bathed and braided and came home every afternoon mangled and matted. Even in high school, the backs of my socks were always slipping away into my shoes by the end of the day. I've solved the problem as an adult by wearing the sock heels up where my calves are. My socks are still too big for my feet because my feet are still too small for my size. Size five feet are not the boon ladies with size nine feet think they are.

My mom was terrific. She dyed an old white sheet brown, cut out the Indian dress, and sewed it up on her White sewing machine. Then I meticulously cut fringes into the sleeve ends and around the bottom. I have always loved arts and crafts projects and I was in heaven making my fringes. Then came the best part, sewing on by hand, bead by bead, the "authentic" Indian decorations. We were allowed to design our own trim and pick out our own beads from the pharaoh's treasure chest Mrs. Powers had on her desk. As many beads as we wanted! I actually combed our encyclopedia for the style of dress and decoration every American Indian tribe wore. It never occurred to me to find out what the Indians that befriended the Pilgrims wore, I was looking for elaborate not accurate. My design was indeed elaborate, and I worked on it every chance I got.

Most days I ate lunch from my lunch box even though I loved eating in the cafeteria. The quarter for a hot lunch was hard to come by, and I loved it when my dad got paid (only once a month—he was a fireman) because that meant lunch in the cafeteria, icy cold milk, maybe even a hot dog, and no peanut butter. When I brought my lunch from home, I had to drink warm, nickel-a-carton milk. Even though I had a lunch box, I wasn't allowed to have a thermos after the second grade. I'd broken so many glass liners by that time, a thermos was off-limits to me forever. On one particularly hot day, after the lunch period bell announced we could toss out our trash and go play in our assigned areas, I opted to remain at the lunch benches under the shade of the pergola and sew my beads. To me it seemed

Stephanie, with her parents, Sylvia and Jack Gordon, 1940.

far better than being chosen last for the kickball team, running around after a ball I couldn't possibly catch, getting sweaty making all the outs, and being yelled at by my teammates for being so amazingly unathletic. So, I was beading away when the lunch duty teacher arrived to block my light and ruin my life. Our exchange went something like this . . . .

"Go out to your play area now," she said.

"I want to work on my beads now," I said.

"Growing children need to play," she said.

"I don't need to grow anymore," I said.

"Go!" she said.

"No!" I said.

"We will see about that, missy" she said.

I said nothing as she grabbed me around the waist and tried to pry me from my seat.

The lunch benches under the pergola were attached to the lunch tables, one on each side. I proceeded to wrap my legs around the bar that held the table and bench together, and the yard duty teacher proceeded to drag me (still beading), the bench, and the table across the yard toward the doors to the school—and the principal's office. I only relinquished my ankle hold when we reached the steps, and I knew the bench and table were too much for me to hang on to. You can bet the principal wasn't too happy to see me.

Mrs. Powers fixed it up by promising she would be responsible for my playing in my assigned lunch area every day, and see to it that my Indian dress never saw the (lunchtime or recess) light of day. She made me promise, too. For Mrs. Powers I did what I promised. Even at that age, I knew it was unusual for an adult to stand up for a kid and take a chance on me. I could never have let her down.

As I've grown, and hopefully matured, I've come to understand my principal better. I was a disruption in her schedule. I came and went from her school, and, to her, my life seemed to be wasting away on some studio backlot when I should have been in school like every other normal child. But I was never normal, she was absolutely right. How could I be? I grew up on movie sets with fake turn-of-the-century facades and futuristic time-warp scenery. In the commissary, I ate lunch next to an alien named Tom, chatting over his corned beef sandwich with a cowboy named Dick and a centurion named Harry. I reveled in it. I believed it all. Burnside Avenue School was normal and boring and an unhappy place for me. Life on a movie set was exciting and creative. Anything was possible, and life was mostly happily ever after. I loved happy endings and I loved telling things the way I wanted them to be, not always the way they were. I wanted make-believe to be real, and for me it was. To my principal that was telling lies. Now, that's my writer's creative license.

I even understand the kids I went to school with and why they never seemed to like me much. I think they thought that since I worked in the movies, I must be stuck-up. There was no way to explain that my mom needed to work and taking me to the studio was her job. That never once was I told I was a star, or even a star's stand-in . . . . For years I thought every kid worked in the movies, most of the kids in my family did. Funny thing is, I quit working in the studios forever around fourteen to have a regular life and have more friends. And I found that the kids that were already my friends didn't like me any better, and the kids that weren't my friends still didn't like me much at all. Life is full of hard lessons.

I hope it doesn't sound like I'm being critical of the kids in my grammar school and questioning their ability for compassion. In all truth, I could have used a bit more of that compassion myself. No matter how hard I try to put what happened to us all in the fourth grade behind me, it will never go away. My daddy, Jack, once said to me, "Nothing is forever, Stephie, this too will pass." But it's those things I want most to pass away from my mind that I am most destined to remember.

Doreen and I were the same age when we met while working on a movie. She was nice for a kid that had the only bit part in the film. In most movies there were the extra parts and there were the walk-on parts and there were bit player parts and then there were the stand-ins and the stars. I was basically an extra who got bit parts now and again. I would be the face in the milling crowd, the saved-in-the-nick-of-time baby in the World War II dingy, the kid in the foreground or the kid in the background, the one of many. Doreen was usually a bit player. She had lines. She made more money! We went to studio school together and played on the set and were friends for the duration of the movie, but as soon as the film was done shooting, we went our separate ways. Then one day, in my fourth grade class, there she stood. Doreen! She had moved into my neighborhood, she would be going to Burnside Avenue, she would be in my class.

The other girls hated her immediately. Doreen told them she, too, worked in the movies and that she had speaking parts and that she knew a lot of movie stars. In another more perfect world that would have gotten her the friendship of every girl in her new school, but not in the world I already went to school in. She was a bigger "star" than I was, and, therefore, Doreen was more worthy of their dislike than I was. Suddenly, I found myself off the "we don't like you" list.

I'd like to think I did what any kid who so desperately wanted to belong would have done—I joined the enemy. I didn't do anything mean to Doreen, I just didn't do anything nice. I was finally in because she was out. I sold out, didn't try to stop it, didn't stay her friend. I knew how much she was hurting from being snubbed and on those few occasions when no one could see me, and I did try to talk to her, she turned her back on me. We even made a few more movies together but we never really spoke again.

Then one morning, right after we'd settled into our reading groups, the principal came into our room to tell us that Doreen had been killed on her way to school while crossing Venice Boulevard, a big double street with trolley car tracks down the middle. Her mother had been standing on the far curb watching Doreen, who was holding her little sister's hand. They were too far away to hear when their mother yelled for them to stop. They stepped into the street and they were struck by a car. Doreen was dead. I don't remember if her little sister was hurt or not. It didn't matter. Doreen was dead, and I knew it was my fault as much as if I'd pushed her.

If only I had been her friend. I would have met her every day and walked with her. I would have been waiting on the curb and I would have yelled at her not to cross yet. I would have been there to save her life. I would have if I had been her friend, but I wasn't there and she was dead.

Daddy Jack at his first fire station, Number 29, Los Angeles, 1939.

I got so sick to my stomach that I spent the rest of the day in the nurse's office. She kept asking me what was wrong, but I couldn't tell her because the truth was too terrible. How could she not know that Doreen was dead and it was all my fault?

That night there was an article in the newspaper about the accident, and after my dad threw the paper out, I got it from the trash and cut out the picture of Doreen and the words underneath the picture. Then I hid it in my underwear drawer, in the deepest recess, in the darkest corner, in the only place I could think of to hide such a terrible secret. For weeks I couldn't eat. I cried myself to sleep. I made myself sick. And I told no one what I had done. It was unforgivable, and I could not forgive myself. And then my mom found the picture.

My mom held me in her arms as the whole story came pouring out. Finally I was cried out and I gave her my picture of Doreen. Then holding hands, we walked to the incinerator in the backyard. We had a ceremony, lighting fire to the picture and saying good-bye. I must have promised not to blame myself for what happened and to eat and to get on with my life. And I did, of course. But I remember all this as if it were yesterday, and writing about Doreen has been one of the hardest things I have ever done.

As a writer, I have always known that everything important to me must be turned into words and set down on paper to be preserved. But this is the first time I have come to realize that everything that is important to me must also be put into words and set down on paper so that I can let go of it and move on. Perhaps now, Doreen and I are friends again.

I expect that one day Doreen's story will find its way into one of my books. It will have to be, like this autobiography, my own story, too. Writers know that writing about what they know is what makes their stories come alive and gives the reader a reason to delve on page after page, digging deep to find the story's truth. That is the most painful kind of story to write, and I know I am not ready to write it yet. Still, I have included elements of my childhood and my growing up into every work I've ever created. Even my friends and family have not been spared examination under my writer's microscope.

Growing up in the forties, especially after the end of World War II, was like living in a black-and-white movie with actors who were often chosen for their ability rather than their looks. It was a time of whole family entertainment with a few funny skits along the way, and more often than not, a happy ending you could count on. It was a safe time. It was, I realize now, a time of innocence, not only for me, but for America. We were all the good guys—everybody said so. And the good guys always won.

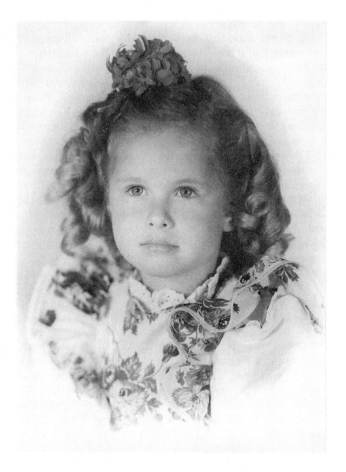

Stephanie at about six years of age.

So many wonderful things are imprinted on my memory and in my heart about being a kid during those amazing growing years, especially the memories of my daddy. To me he was better looking than any movie star, even Hopalong Cassidy whom I intended to marry when I grew up. But just like Hoppy, my daddy was definitely one of the good guys.

Other kids had ordinary dads with ordinary jobs. Their dads didn't drive by their school to say "hi" in his fire truck. My daddy did, he was a fireman. Every other day he went to work at Palms Fire Station #43 in his midnight blue uniform and cap and silver badge. I grew up knowing my daddy could do anything. He was so handsome and the smartest man in the whole world. I could sit and read encyclopedias and do crossword puzzles with him for hours on end. No matter what question I'd ask, he knew the answer, but he'd always make me look it up. I knew he'd make me do it, but I didn't care. Like him, I loved gathering knowledge, and still do. Daddy taught me to love learning for learning's sake, and I still read dictionaries and encyclopedias and take classes for fun.

I thought my fireman daddy had the best job in the whole world. I thought going to the fire station was like going to camp. I'd never been to camp, but I was sure of it. The fire station even had red velour movie seats for the firemen to sit on when they watched TV. They made old-fashioned hand-cranked ice cream in the middle of the day. They all got to sleep in the same room and use one big bathroom together. They all ate together and, just like at my house, my daddy did the cooking. They were having so much fun that it couldn't have been work. I loved going to the station house. I loved climbing on the back of the pumper truck and seeing the hoses hanging down two stories long in the hose tower. I loved playing handball in back of the station house and eating hot dogs at the long mess table that held twenty men at a time. But I loved it most of all when the siren went off and my mom pulled me out of the way as the firemen jumped into their fire gear and climbed on their rig and sped away to fight a fire. Very exciting to a kid!

It wasn't until I was a teenager that I realized how dangerous being a fireman was, and how much it scared my mom. She rarely called my dad at the station, getting my little brother Stevie or me to call because she didn't want to know Daddy was out fighting a fire. As an adult I have only the most overwhelming respect for people who do the kind of life-threatening work my daddy did.

I am very proud of the commendations given to my daddy, Jack Gordon, especially those for his actions during the Baldwin Hills Dam disaster. Television cameras rolled as, tethered by a rope, my daddy was lowered into the huge flooded sinkhole to pull bodies from the cars that had fallen in. He always seemed to be doing wonderful brave things like that, and not because the job made him do it, but because being a human being made him do it. Daddy didn't get a commendation for it, but he was in the newspaper once for risking his life to save a puppy from a burning building. I have always felt that was one of his finest moments. So did Daddy's best buddy, Pepper Pritzy Gordon Jr. the Second, our dog.

As I got older, one of my aunts began taking me to the studios, because my mom got a job at Thrifty Drugs Store in Westchester. As I recall, she was the only woman

With cousin Davey Glassman (right) and little brother Stevie, 1946.

manager the chain had at the time. My mom worked her whole life and she was some saleslady. She could sell you anything and have you thank her for it. It didn't take her long to work her way up to Thrifty's corporate offices in Baldwin Hills. That's where Mom was the day the dam broke. I was at my mother-in-law's house with my friend Dee and my husband watching the disaster news on the TV. Mom was watching the TV, too, even though it was all taking place right in front of her office. We watched the fireman in the air mask and dangling from the rope being lowered into the hole. Then there was a close-up. Mom and I were on the phone. "That was Daddy!" I never thought being a fireman was a fun job again.

But in the 1940s I was still innocent and thought everything—being a fireman and fighting fires, being a soldier and fighting in World War II, being Superman and fighting crime—was all so exciting. Life was like one long, wonderful radio program.

I can still taste the excitement of waiting until my parents went out for the evening and then sitting on the floor with Grams, our backs pressed to the wall so nothing could sneak up behind us, while we scared ourselves to death listening to *Inner Sanctum* and *The Creeping Hand* on our big console radio in the living room. Every evening we had special radio programs we would never miss: *The Lone Ranger, Sky King, Red Rider and Little Beaver, Sergeant Preston* (and his dog, King), and *Buster Brown* (and his dog, Tige). All were welcome regular visitors in my home.

Even on my very own street I met some exceptional people: the man who sharpened knives on his portable whetstone; the pony man; the ice man; and the fruit man.

The Helm's bakery man's whistle only had to toot and my mouth began to water. The Good Humor man's twinkling music and his creamy ice cream bars saved me from many a sweltery summer day. But I did not like the Edgemar Milk man. I remember how I'd beg Grams or Mom or Stevie to smell the milk he left on the front steps every other morning because, "I'm not drinking any if it's even a teeny tiny bit sour." And there was the daily cod-liver oil. Disgusting, foul-tasting cod-liver oil. Boy, do I remember that stuff.

I loved Sunday mornings, eating a bagel with cream cheese and corned beef (my own recipe), and stretching out on the living room carpet to read the funny papers. And I still miss the bike rides across the city with my little brother, feeling as safe as if we were riding on our own street. And our first TV. The first on our block with the bubble magnifier on the front so the screen would look bigger. There are still nights that I think about the Venice Boulevard streetcar lights that raced across my bedroom wall, a magical clickity-clackity night light, clattering me to sleep. And big cardboard boxes! The kind a refrigerator or a washing machine came in. The store around the corner gave them to us kids after they'd unpack the new all-electric, soak-rinse-and-spin-without-ever-touching-the-wet-clothes model washing machines that were rapidly replacing the eat-your-arm-wringers like we had. We even had an old ice box, the kind that used real blocks of ice and had a drip pan to carry and spill all over the kitchen floor. We didn't put ice in ours anymore but it was handy for spices and stuff. We kept our electric Sears and Roebuck Hotpoint on the back porch. Did you ever wonder if the light really does go out when you shut the door?

I always wondered about stuff like that. So I emptied everything out of ours one day when my mom had left me to baby-sit my little brother, Stevie. I talked him into getting in, then I shut the door. Wouldn't you know it? My mom came home, saw the food all over the back porch, and the first thing she said was, "Stephanie Anne (when Mom used my middle name, it meant I was in big trouble)! Where is your brother?"

When Mom opened the door, Stevie was just fine, but she wouldn't listen to my important scientific experiment explanation. I was grounded for a week, which meant I had to miss seeing *A Kiss In The Dark* for nine cents at the Delmar show that Saturday. I was in that movie and had a real close-up with David Niven, whom I thought was so dashing, and I was dying to see it. I cried my eyes out, but grounded at my house meant grounded. Scientifically speaking, the light goes out. Oh! And so will little brothers if you shut them in a refrigerator.

My brother, Stephen Michael Gordon, came into my life on December 11, 1943. He took my mom, my spotlight as my whole family's only little kid, and my name away from me. I had to hate him on sight. Until *he* was born, everyone in my family called me "Stevie," which I loved. Suddenly he was "Stevie" and I was ... his big sister, which I hated. My mom says I took one look at him as she carried him through the front door for the first time and announced, "I'd rather have a puppy." Hey! What normal kid wouldn't?

Over the years my mom always told my brother and me that someday we would only have each other. That she and dad and my grandma Kepniss (who lived with us on and off) and my auntie Ruth and my auntie Rose and everyone I loved in my family would get old and pass on and there would only be Stevie and me. So no matter what, we had to love each other and be there for each other. Over the years, as my beloved Grams, Anna Kepniss, and my daddy Jack, and my auntie Rose left me, I began to see the wisdom in what Mom had been trying to tell us. But she didn't have to worry. I love my brother and I know he loves me. We will always be there for each other, no matter what, just like Mom said. Still, Stevie is darn lucky, with me as his older sister, that he got to grow up at all.

One of our favorite stories (Stevie uses it to tease me and prove how rotten I was to him—and I was, but being an older sister has to have some perks) happened on his fifth birthday. He got a new red wagon I wanted to play with, but he said, "No! Mine!" Standing in it like King of the Hill and shaking his head was a challenge that could not go ignored. I pulled the wagon out from under him. Stevie landed on his arm and broke his green bone.

Before I took him to Mom, I warned him how much trouble *he'd* be in if Mom found out what had happened. What had happened, I explained, was that he had been selfish and wouldn't share his wagon and so he made me have to take it away from him. He wouldn't share! A major crime! But I promised to keep his secret and cover for him. I told my mom how he "just fell out" of his wagon—for no reason, and Stevie didn't say it wasn't so. Then Mom and I drove him to Georgia Street Emergency Hospital and had his arm set.

I am only telling you this next part, because Steve (my now grown-up brother—he may even be older than I am by now) will if I don't. The day the cast came off his arm, the whole thing happened again, and he went back into the cast for another four weeks. Stevie never ratted on me. Not ever! We didn't tell Mom the truth about it until we were both parents ourselves.

So are you beginning to wonder why Steve and I are so close? Probably because no matter what I did to him, no one else was allowed to lay a hand on him—not ever. Stevie was my little brother, and heaven help anyone who touched him or even spoke badly to him. I fought some pretty mean battles to protect him. I guess that counted with Stevie and he knows I'm glad he grew up in spite of me. I am so glad he is my little brother. No one could ask for a better one—not ever! You got that?

W e moved from Meadowbrook Avenue when I was eleven. For years I had wanted to move. Not that I didn't like our duplex. I loved living downstairs from Mr. and Mrs. Hollingsworth and their daughter Phyllis. The Hollingsworths were old and Mr. Hollingsworth was retired. Every day he sat at his workbench tooling leather. He made me the best cowboy belt and wallet in the whole world.

And I really liked Judy Anderson who lived across the street in the big white house with the porch that ran around two sides. The porch had a glider, and there was a hammock in her backyard, and a huge Saint John's Bread tree to climb. Judy was, what I called in those days, a lucky pup. She was an only child, that meant she had her own room and more dolls and games than anybody I knew—and her games had all their pieces. Judy and I were good

enough friends to even share a few secrets. Like my dog that no one else could see but me—and sometimes Judy. His name was Lassie and he looked just like the real Lassie, too. I'd worked in a Lassie movie and I knew that all the Lassies were actually Laddies, and that's why my dog was a boy. And there was the secret about picking (as in stealing) roses for our moms from Mrs. Freeze's house, the lady down the street who guarded her garden like the flowers were gold. And the scary secret about the lady next door to Judy who burned up cats every day in her incinerator. We cut through her yard to the alley on the way to school, and we could smell the cats burning. Burning cats smelled just like garbage. And one of our most daring secrets, looking at her dad's highball glasses when no one was home. These amazing glasses had Vargas Girl decals on them that we found very interesting. On the outside of each glass, the girls were barely clad, and on the inside they were naked. We were ten; it was pretty racy stuff.

Cowboy wallets, a friend to keep secrets with, compared to moving? Nothing stood a chance. I had lived in the same house for eleven years. How boring. I wanted to see other places. Meet other people. Go to a school where the kids didn't already know me, didn't know about my working in the movies, and would like me.

We moved to our first house ever in Westchester, a new suburb near LAX. The Los Angeles Airport in 1951 was nothing like it is today; it was much smaller with only propeller-driven airplanes. I flew home from Oakland on my first plane flight in 1951. I hated it then and I hate flying now. I'm the worst kind of white-knuckle flyer.

Sixth grade was half over when I entered Westport Elementary. I actually felt bad about leaving my old sixth grade class; I was getting good grades, the teacher liked me, and I was finally feeling a little better about the kids, too. Still, life in Westchester promised a new beginning and I could hardly wait for it to start.

Any good writer knows that's a great hook to end a first chapter on . . . . My first day at my new school began after lunch on a Friday—story time.

"We read the best books," the kid next to me whispered.

"Sometimes, even books for grown-ups."

They had just begun *Kon-Tiki,* by Thor Heyerdahl, and I could tell everyone was excited to get to the story. I loved hearing stories. To this day I love being read to and listening to books on tape.

I was introduced and given a desk in the middle of the room. Then we stood by our desks and waited while the principal spoke to the teacher. I already liked the nice principal and the look of the new school. The kids in my new class smiled at me, and things were finally looking up.

"Hands up," said the teacher (whose name I have repressed).

Following the other kids, I held my arms out, palms up. The teacher walked down the rows looking, first at the palms and then at the backs of each kid's hands. She'd nod her head and make little approving sounds as she went past. Each kid sat down after inspection. I knew this teacher was strict because no one spoke and everyone sat with their hands folded on their desk.

I looked at my hands. Clean. Very clean. I hadn't even eaten lunch at home because I was so nervous about my first day. I didn't even have my usual lunch spots on my dress. No problem here I thought.

Hook and end of chapter two....

The teacher stopped in front of me. She looked at my palms and nodded. I turned my hands over.

"No story today," she announced in a loud voice. "Thanks to Stephanie."

Everyone looked at me. The silence took on a deafening roar.

"Bitten. Disgusting." She held my hands over my head to display my chewed-to-the-quick fingernails. "No story until this young lady stops biting her fingernails. Sit down, everyone; take out your spelling books. You!" she looked at me with those all-too-familiar "skinny eyes." "Back there."

My seat was moved to a desk in the back corner of the room. The boy sitting at it was staring at the desk top as I was plunked down beside him. I could see that he had fingernails, but they were dirty. Dirt was probably a crime that required ostracizing too, if not banishment.

And, just like that, I had no friends at my new school either.

The next week the class got their chapter, even though my nails weren't completely grown out. But I guess I didn't count now that I was at the desk in the back of the class. I don't remember another thing about that school or that class except *Kon-Tiki*. It was a great adventure. And when Thor Heyerdahl became the head of the United Nations, I felt like I had a friend in high places. Then, sixth grade was

Fourteen-year-old Stephanie in junior high school.

over and I went on to junior high school and a great adventure of my own.

What an experience it was to be a seventh grader at Westchester Junior High and High School. Not just the going to seven different classes with seven different teachers, or wearing lipstick and real hep bunny shoes, or even sock hops and BOYS! We were the seventh graders in a school that went all the way to the twelfth grade. I had gone to bed a big sixth grade graduate and awoke a nameless newt lost in a twelfth grade twilight zone. We still had the half semester system, so only the B-sevens were dumb enough to get caught by the seniors. The A-sevens were experience tested and fast as fleas. Us poor little B-sevens were fair game, the "gofers" of any big kid that could corner us. We stood in lines, bought lunches, carried books, and hid behind teachers, garbage cans, other kids, anything—not to be noticed. It was really awful ... and it was really fun. And just knowing that every other B-seven was in the same spot, bound us together as a class with a purpose, a common goal ... survival! We helped each other out, became a team, and got to know each other pretty well. For the first time I felt like I had school friends.

I was the only Jewish kid in my crowd and I don't remember meeting many Jewish kids in Westchester, at all. And even though I wasn't brought up going regularly to synagogue and we were not very religious in my home, I had always lived in a neighborhood where almost everyone was Jewish. Now suddenly, no one was. It didn't bother me, and it didn't seem to bother my friends who were for the most part Mormons. I just joined the Mormon church youth group, and went to all their social stuff, and had a ball. My first taffy pull, my first luau, my first hayride, my first real speech, my first boyfriend, and my first kiss all took place in the Mormon church that I helped to build in Westchester. I wasn't the most popular girl in my group, but I wasn't the least popular either. I was happy, as happy as any junior high school girl could be who loved the boy who lived over her back fence, who didn't know she was even alive. My best friend, Deedee, and I spent hours circling the block, hoping Curt would come outside so I could accidently run into him. We always ran into Durwood, instead. Durwood had a crush on Deedee, but we thought he was soooo yucky. And besides, Deedee had a crush on Max. But Max had a crush on the Bishop's daughter.... Oh, you know how that is.

I think those were good years for me. The worst thing that I can remember happening was Adlai Stevenson's losing the election for the presidency to Dwight David Eisenhower. My family were dyed-in-the-wool Democrats and we did not "like Ike." The best thing I remember was my dreamy B-nine English teacher, Mr. Stevens. He was very tall and very handsome, and he read to us! Wonderful books! Magical books! Lyrical books! And he encouraged us to read to ourselves. Every day was special because we discussed what we were reading in class. And then suddenly I knew ... Everything important and exciting, everything wonderful and magical and lyrical was in a book—somewhere.

In the A-nine I moved back to Los Angeles, began Palms Junior High, and became popular. It could have been the hot pink lipstick or my bleached blonde hair or my daring ducktail hair cut or my way too hep bunny shoes. It could have been. But I don't think it was any of that. I think it was my anatomy and the fact that I was new. Most of the kids in ninth grade had been going to school together since kindergarten. The kids I'd gone to Burnside Avenue with, the kids who might have remembered me, had gone on to Louis Pasteur Junior High. No one at Palms knew me. I was a new, unknown quantity, and so the boys liked me, and so the girls liked me, too. That semester was great, I had a boyfriend and boy friends and girl friends and good grades, and I was looking forward to high school.

There were only a few senior high schools in LA worth mentioning in 1956—the one I went to and the ones we wanted most to beat in football. There was LA High, Fairfax High, Venice High, and my school, Alexander Hamilton High School—Hamilton High—Hami High. It was a good school, filled with nice average kids, and nice (for the most part) teachers. The kids were mostly Jewish again, but that never was a problem. We had social clubs that tended to have kids in them that were of the same religion, but, as I recall, the non-Jewish kids were just as well liked, held offices, and made the senior class poll as often as the Jewish kids. I remember very few people of color at Hami. The Mexican kids I knew all had the edge in Spanish class and were well liked anyway. The three black kids that I remember from high school were very popular and two held school offices. The school clubs and service clubs were mixed without consideration to race or religion. Sure, there were bad kids and good kids. Nice kids and tough kids. There were even girls that smoked and boys that carried their cigarette packs rolled up in their T-shirt sleeves. And kids that cut school and kids that failed. But mostly we were just kids going to school and doing our best and trying to graduate and get into a college or find a job. We watched *American Bandstand* on TV. We bought 45 records of Elvis and Doris Day. We hung out on Tuesday club night at DL's, the local drive-in, and scarfed down Jumbo Jims, Susie Q's, and chocolate cokes. We just went to school, had fun, and liked almost everybody. We didn't spend a lot of time concentrating on differences, we were too busy being teenagers and building friendships.

When I look back, I see more good about those years than I see bad. I wasn't the most popular girl in high school, either. I didn't even hang out with her. But I was lucky enough to have friends in all the different cliques and my friends were basically good kids that didn't get into too much trouble. I was considered a nice girl.

Like everyone else in the '50s, I had my share of teenage heartbreaks and successes. But what I remember most about my years in high school happened when I was a senior. In the B-twelve I was elected treasurer for my social club, the Adorians, then I lost the election to be senior class treasurer. I have wondered if the deficit I left in my club treasury had anything to do with that. In the B-twelve I got to see the class name I proposed, "The Shanachies" (which, by the way, means storytellers) chosen our senior class name, and the emerald green and black I promoted become our class colors. Even though I can't carry a tune or sing a note above middle C, I wrote our senior class song with my friend, Sandy Feiger, to the tune of an old Irish standard. It was picked over six other entries.

Flushed with success, Sandy wanted us to try out for the senior class cheerleaders and she spent hours trying to teach me a routine. The only thing I am worse at than singing is being a cheerleader! Poor Sandy was so disappointed, but she has a forgiving heart; we are still good friends to this day.

I was thrilled to be chosen by my classmates to be one of six girls to represent the B-twelves at the A-twelve awards ceremony. And when my name was announced during our senior class poll assembly, I cried all the way up to the stage to claim the five-inch felt leprechaun holding the ribbon for "Best Personality" that was pinned on my shoulder. I'd come a long way from grammar school, and I'd made the trip with many of the same people, and I not only survived, but I triumphed in my own small way.

I went to parties and dances and "sweet sixteen" birthdays for my girlfriends. I fell in love and out of love and back in love. I worried about going to college. I worried about not going to college. I worried about getting married. I worried about not getting married. I had a few serious boyfriends, but none as steady and as serious as Joe.

From the tenth grade on, Joseph David Mayesh had been a very important part of my life. He was my first real love and the boy I thought I would marry. Then, at the beginning of my second year in college, Joe was killed in a car accident. For months my life was too painful to bear and the future impossible to contemplate. Days at school seemed to pass unnoticed. And dating anyone else was a nightmare.

During the summer of my second year of college, I was crossing the UCLA campus when a familiar voice called my name. It was an old friend from high school where we had gone out now and again as buddies. We had started Hami High the same day and knew all the same people. My friend liked Joe. So I stopped to talk, and he asked me out to see Harry Belafonte at the Greek Theater—third row—center!

"Will you take me to see 'Darby O'Gill and the Little People' first?" I'd asked every boy who had asked me out in the last month and they had all said, "NO!"

He said, "Yes."

So I said, "Yes."

And he said, "Yes!"

We went to the movie that weekend, and to see Harry Belafonte the next weekend, and someplace else every weekend after that. Eighteen months later, my old high school friend asked me to marry him … I said, "Yes!"

In order to go to college together, we both transferred to California State University at Los Angeles for our last year of college, me from UCLA and my fiance from USC. On August the sixth, 1961, one term before we both graduated, we were married. We were only twenty-one years old.

In my last term of college, I did my student teaching. I worked at Grant Avenue School, in Hollywood, until 3 P.M. and then went to the Culver School afterschool playground where the kids called me the "coachess." Culver School was only a few blocks from MGM Studios where I'd made a lot of the movies at $14.56 a day. But as a playground coach, I made $1.18 an hour, a lot less than I made working in those old movies.

My husband had already been accepted by the accounting firm of Price Waterhouse, but that job didn't start until he graduated, so he worked after school at a small accounting office, making $50.00 a week. Every day

Pondering a problem with writing partner, Judith Ross Enderle (left), 1980.

he got a ride to and from Cal State and was dropped off at work. I took the car and went to Hollywood to do my student teaching. Then I went home, changed my clothes, made soup for the thermos (of which I took great care not to drop) and went to the playground. After work, it was back to Cal State for our night classes, dinner on the freeway in a little yellow and white Hillman Minx—soup and two tacos each at 25 cents apiece as I drove. It was a grind, but I had planned to graduate in four years, and I did.

Life was going my way. I had interviewed and was hired by Norwood Street School in downtown Los Angeles to teach the first grade. School was almost over, it was just a matter of time now before we'd both be working and earning real salaries.

Each day we went to the mailbox to check for our grades and get ready to celebrate our graduations. My grades came—I was done! My husband's grades came along with an envelope from the Selective Service. Without taking the envelope out of the box, he drove straight to the National Guard and enlisted. I had only been married seven months when the next letter came—report for active duty. It was time for my very new husband to go to Fort Ord, California, for basic training. I had never lived alone! Never paid a bill! *Never lived alone!*

A vivid memory of that era of my life was the "steal from Peter to pay Paul" chart pinned to the back of my apartment door with every bill I needed to pay and the date it was due. Pay this one when it comes in ... pay this one

one week late ... pay this one three days before it's due, and so on.... I lived by the chart!

The second thing was the Cuban Missile Crisis. It happened during my husband's basic training when the army sent me, without explanation, a letter saying I would no longer be hearing from him. He was on red alert! I had no idea what that meant, but I knew it was bad. I tried to get answers but all I got was run arounds.

During that same week, I was put on civil defense duty at my school. I had no one at home who needed me! I ended up having a breakdown under my desk during a "fifteen minute warning" bomb drill. My first graders were being especially uncooperative that day. Oblivious to the seriousness of the Cuban Crisis, they were poking each other under their tables, taking off their name tags, and crawling around like ants. They didn't understand; my barely-used husband was probably on his way to Cuba, the army wouldn't return my calls, the principal put me on civil defense because I had no husband and no children to go home to, and I was scared. When the principal found me crying in the drop position under my desk, she sent me to the nurse's office to rest. It felt familiar! Well, at least my principal still liked me—and I wasn't constipated!

The third thing was the roommates I took in to help me pay the rent. One was a friend and one was a friend of a friend. Both were so messy, they drove me out of my mind. So the chart was redone. I tightened my purse strings and I went to work at a drugstore during the summer in order to have enough money to kick the roommates out. What a relief to be finally living alone—again!

My first real house in was in Canoga Park, California (now known as West Hills). Our oldest son, Jon Adam (now known as Jonathan Adam), was born one month after we moved in, on June 19, 1964. The flooring wasn't even down in his room when I went into labor. But it was when we came home three days later. It must have been that slightly hysterical chat with the contractors.

Our second son, Todd Allyn, was born in that first house, too. We were a family of personalities right from the start. My husband was a Taurus, May 8, 1940. I am a Taurus, May 11, 1940. Todd is a Taurus, May 10, 1967. And Jonathan is a Gemini, June 19, 1964, and I've always felt that was why he needed two first names.

My daughter, Jacklyn Paige, was born on January 3, 1970, two years after my daddy, Jack, died. She is named for him. We adopted Jackee when she was one month old because we wanted a daughter and because I am RH negative and her father is RH positive. The '70s were still the dark ages where negative and positive blood factors doing battle could kill babies and moms. It took thirteen months to get Jackee, the longest pregnancy of my life. I spent hours in her bedroom in the repainted rocking chair hugging her little pink dresses. We adopted Jackee through Los Angeles County and it was a family affair. Jonny was already going on five, he needed to know what was about to happen to us all. He decided it was his job to pick Jackee out. Toddy, at two and a half, wasn't all that interested in getting a new baby sister. But Jonny had it all figured out. He'd thumb through all the babies at the bank (the county's adoption agency was on the fifth floor of a bank) until he found the one he wanted and he'd take her home. Panic! No amount of talking could convince him we weren't going to a baby store. I knew we would get to see one baby and that was it. What if Jonny didn't like her but I was sure she was right for our family? What to do?

I packed up half a dozen adorable little baby girl outfits, put the boys in the car, and off we went. My plan was for the grown-ups to see the baby first and make our decision. If it was yes, then the social worker would bring in the boys. If Jonny gave the baby a thumbs down, the social worker would take her out, redress her, and bring her back for another try. We had six outfits to change his mind and convince him he loved her. We didn't know it yet, but not one of them would have fit our new daughter.

Jackee was a big surprise. A very BIG surprise. She'd weighed 10 pounds 1 ounce at birth, and I had no concept of what that would be in baby terms. Now at one month, she weighed 11 pounds 1 ounce. They brought us a baby girl who was as big as our boys had been at five months, except she couldn't do anything but cry. And cry she did, loud and long, until she was soggy and red. My husband looked at me. I looked at him. I didn't know what he was thinking, but I remembered the skinny little babies they brought me in the hospital each time I gave birth to one of our sons. There never was a decision to be made then. There was no decision to be made now. This was our daughter, Jacklyn Paige. Time to bring in Jonny and Toddy.

Jonny marched into the room dragging Toddy by the hand. Toddy inspected the room while Jonny climbed up into the chair next to me and held out his arms for the baby. I put her, crying and red, into his arms and waited. Jonny patted the baby and said something I couldn't hear.

The baby stopped crying, smiled, and curled her hand around Jonny's finger and sucked on it.

"This one is Jackee," Jonny announced, kissing her.

Now I was crying. That was a moment I have never forgotten. Toddy came over to see which baby Jonny had picked. She must have been okay with him because he hurried away to pull more magazines off of the coffee table.

There she was. Our girl. Our Jackee. Our Jacklyn Paige. We had a daughter. We were a family, whole and complete.

Like every family, things were wonderful and things were rocky. Children have a way of making every day that much more real and alive. They bring a clarity and an insight into your life that you could never know without them. Once during an especially difficult growing period for my oldest son, Jonathan, he was seventeen and I was under contract to write several young adult novels, we seemed to be at each other every time our paths crossed. For many months, his angst and my own seemed to be the only common ground we shared. When my latest book was delivered, I gave him his copy (I have always given all my kids my books—whether they want them or not). When he'd read it, Jonathan came into my converted bedroom office, book in hand.

"It's good. I liked it," he said. "The words sound like you talking. Maybe some day, Mom, I'll get to be the hero."

That was the day I realized how much of myself I put into my writing. How much of my family and friends went into giving each book life. I had made Jonathan the book's antagonist. Given his speech and looks and mannerisms to the boy in the story who had it all, but didn't end up the winner and didn't get the girl. It was my way of striking out at a situation that I didn't like, but had no control over. My oldest child was growing up and I felt helpless to stop it or change what was happening between us—we were becoming equals—adults. That day, I started to stop trying. I made an effort to see him as he deserved to be seen, an individual unto himself, not here to always make me happy or satisfy my mother's wishes for him, even though, over the years, he has. His ready wit and charm are enviable attributes that have brought him to a good place in his life. And his good looks pay homage to his dad and me, but mostly to my daddy, who Jonathan looks so much like it's amazing. My son has become a man. I am proud of his accomplishments, his determination, and his good heart. Jonathan is often my hero and the good guy in my life and my life's story.

Like Jonathan, my middle son Todd has given me reams of material to fill the pages of my books. Todd has always been easy to write about. He does things that amaze and astound me daily—even now. Like me, he loves to debate. Like his father, he has an assured certainty that he is always on the side of right. Like his brother, he feels I need taking care of, and he tries to do that. I think it's sweet that he opens my car door when I drive with him and then buckles me in. He knows I can handle it, it's just the way he is. Todd is a door opener and a flower bringer and a final word giver. He and Jonathan share many good traits, but couldn't be less similar. Where Jonathan is olive-skinned with blue eyes and thick straight brown hair cut short, hazel-eyed Todd is fair with light reddish-brown hair, also cut very short to eliminate the eternal waves. Taller than his brother, Todd is often mistaken for the oldest, and sometimes he acts it, accepting the responsibility for his siblings. Todd is so capable that it can be frightening, even to his lovely new bride, Jane Foster Tessler, or his mom. Todd can fix it or get it fixed, make it or get it made, do it or get it done. I feel safe when he is with me. And we are great fishing buddies. I taught him everything he knows!

My boys, that's how I think of them, my boys, my sons. I had to have them first so there could be Jackee. My youngest child is the daughter that I had to have. A funny thing about my daughter, she likes to be called Jake!

When Jackee was five years old, I began to get antsy. Cooking, feeding the dogs, belonging to the sisterhood at the Jewish temple, being a Cub Scout leader, Brownie and Girl Scout leader, car pooling to ballet school and to soccer games were not as fulfilling as I'd hoped. I loved being a mom, but motherhood wasn't filling some deep creative need that had begun to overwhelm me. Mentally I was becoming a vegetable along the lines of a huge eggplant. So I took classes. Oil painting. Stained glass. Oil painting. Needlepointing. Oil painting. Quilting. Spanish. French. Spanish. French. Oil painting. And a real estate course. I kept up my real estate license and my elementary teaching credential until just a few years ago. But after selling two pieces of property and buying one house for a friend, I gave up real estate forever. I hated doing it.

When Jackee was nine years old, I called UCLA for a catalogue. My dad had always told me that a day gone by without learning something new was a day wasted. I loved learning new things, didn't I? I'd loved my college classes, hadn't I? I should get my master's degree, shouldn't I? Why not?

The catalogue that arrived was for UCLA's extension. I looked it over. I saw WRITING CLASSES! I loved to write. I'd been on the school newspaper, hadn't I? I'd gotten my best test scores on the essays, didn't I? I was a natural, wasn't I? I could write the great American novel, couldn't I? Why not? But I decided to start with something easy, a beginning course in ... writing for children.

How To Write The Picture Book with Sue Alexander was the best thing and the worst thing I'd ever done. And, up till then, it was just about the hardest. I was sure I was doing it all wrong. I wrote stories and the class commented on them. Not too bad, I thought. Then Sue commented on them. Toss it out, I thought. My stories were hopeless. I was hopeless. How would I ever write an adult book of three-hundred pages, if I couldn't even get a kid's book of thirty-two pages right? I was afraid to talk to any of the other students. I didn't want them to ask me why I thought I had any writing ability. I didn't want to know that they didn't think I did have any. I was afraid to ask any questions and let Sue know how dumb I really was. I was close to tears every class. I didn't think Sue knew. She knew, and to this day wonders why I kept at it. I know I had to look like the most unlikely candidate for a business that was and is constant critiquing and rejection. I'd like to

think it's because I'm no quitter? Maybe. But more likely, it's because I'm a glutton for punishment! It was a struggle and I felt unworthy to go on. But I was committed. In Sue's class I began a predestined journey of monumental challenges. And because of Sue, go on I did.

Next came Writing The Middle Grade Novel with Eve Bunting. (I know Sue *and* Eve—I was so lucky, but I didn't know it then!) I started the great American middle grade novel in Eve's class. I wrote and rewrote my first chapter. I listened. I took notes. I listened. I critiqued my fellow students. I listened. I learned. I listened. I got panicky. Eve told us everything she knew, and Eve knew everything. And still, I knew zip! Was I ever going to catch on? What was an SASE? What did AKA mean? What was I doing here?

Then the best thing happened. The big flood hit Malibu, where I now lived, the bottom floor of my house filled up with water, the giant rock fell down on PCH and blocked the whole road, and I met Judith Ross Enderle.

Judy and I both lived in Malibu and could make the hour or more detoured ride to UCLA through the San Fernando Valley together. We talked ... and talked ... and talked. So that was what SASE meant. Oh? You're published? You know what a *Publishers Weekly* is. Want to do lunch? We became friends in no time.

Judy invited me to join her critique group in Malibu. Whatever that was, I said, "sure." Then we formed a critique group from Eve's class. There were ten of us, and all ten of us are published writers now. During one Malibu critique meeting, held in my van at the grammar school one summer so we could watch our kids play, Judy and I introduced our daughters to each other. Jackee and Monica have been best friends ever since. Monica is like a niece to me and, while Jackee was a bridesmaid in Monica's wedding, I was her Matron of Honor. An honor, indeed.

Judy decided to try writing a young adult novel. She sent it out, sold it, and got a three book contract!

Then Judy decided we should try and write an outline for a YA series together.

Then I wrote a YA novel and sent it out, didn't sell it, and got rejected.

Then Judy got an agent and sold more books and got three more book contracts.

Then she introduced me to her agent.

Then the agent sold our YA series and my YA novel. Then I panicked! Then the agent told me the publisher wanted me to cut one-hundred pages out of the YA novel. Then I really panicked! Then the agent told Judy and me the publisher wanted the first two books of the YA series in three months. Then Judy and I really panicked! Then we bought new computers to write the series books on, and we brought them home, and read the manual, and it said *boot up the computer.* You think you've seen panic? You've never seen panic like the panic Judy and I had that day. Thank goodness the computer salesman knew that *boot it up* meant turn the computer on, or we would still be sitting in front of those 64K marvels of modern science wondering what to do, and our first books together would be really really late!

Judy and I met on April 4, 1979. And thanks to Judy and Sue and Eve, I was published in the magazine *Highlights for Children* in 1981. I sold my first YA novel, *Winning Heart,* to Dutton Books in 1982. And Judy and I

Celebrating Mother's Day with her mother, Sylvia; sons, Jon and Todd; and daughter, Jake, 1997.

sold our first books together in the "Bayshore Medical Center" series: *Andrea Whitman, Pediatrics* and *Monica Ross, Maternity* to Walker Books in 1982. I had begun my new career in earnest. I was a children's book writer.

Throughout the years my career has taken many different roads. I have found myself hanging on by my writer's fingertips as I sped around a few of the hairier hairpin turns, and bouncing back again and again after taking a nose dive into some of the more holey potholes of publishing.

But I didn't do it alone. My children's friends tell me that they are always bragging about their mom, the great children's book writer. My mom's lady friends tell me how she was always bragging about her daughter, the great children's book writer. And my writer friends say, Judy is always bragging about her partner, the great children's book writer. That's a lot of pressure to succeed. I have had no choice but to try to become a great children's book writer. My family and friends have always been there for me and put up with a lot of bumps, ditches, and detours in

my writing road. So for them and for myself, I am still trying.

I have to admit, the best reason to keep at it is Judy. We write together, we travel together, we work together, we speak together, we have fun together. Anyone who knows us, knows we are the real *Two Badd Babies,* the tear-around-town-toddlers from the picture book we wrote as Jeffie Ross Gordon (if you put Judy and Stephie together and add our maiden names, we become Jeffie). Together we are Nell from *Nell Nugget and the Cow Caper,* afraid of nothing, gutsy, and always ready to get to getting when things need to get done. We are Littlest Pig from *A Pile of Pigs,* taking chances, giving each other a boost while heading ever upward, and sometimes too curious for our own good. We are Kelly from *What's the Matter Now, Kelly Beans?,* loving words and writing and books and always striving to be wonderful. We are a little bit of every hero and every heroine from every book we've ever written together and every book we have yet to write. Judith Ross Enderle and I are more than writing partners, we are best friends, she is the sister I never had.

One big step forward in my career came through learning about the Society of Children's Book Writers from Sue Alexander. When we, her students, asked about other ways to learn about writing for children, Sue told us about the SCBW. I knew a good deal when I heard one and I joined immediately. Judy was also a member, so we went to the SCBW National Conference together. After four days of lectures and meeting and talking to "real" writers and seeing "live" editors, we were hooked.

Judy and I became the Southern California (SOCA) Co-Regional Advisors for the Society of Children's Book Writers in 1983 and didn't retire until December 31, 1996. And for ten years I have been a member of the National Board of SCBWI as the Regional Advisor Chairperson, the liaison between National and the many Regional Advisors that oversee all the SCBWI chapters, national and international, throughout the world. It has been a rewarding part of my career as a writer to be a part of the SCBWI's (the "I" was added to include our illustrators) growth from a handful of Regional Advisors and a few thousand members to fifty-seven regions with sixty-three Regional Advisors and more than eleven thousand members worldwide. And best of all, SCBWI has brought me priceless friendships that I will treasure all the years of my life.

Over the years I've gone from a baby "extra" to a full grown woman. I've matured from a girl to a woman and then to a mother. I went from avid reader to having written and co-written picture books, middle grade and young adult novels, magazine stories and articles, a children's television series, and an animated children's TV show. I went from student to teacher to editor of a major broadcasting company's children's magazine and freelance editor for a major children's book publisher. I grew from a friend into a writing partner into a business partner in Writers Ink, a critiquing service for up and coming children's book writers. It took me fifty-six years to do it, to become Stephanie, but it seems like only a few minutes have passed since my show began. I've laughed a little and I've cried a little, but I've really enjoyed the movie.

And all of this because in 1940, Sylvia Kepniss Gordon and Jack Gordon produced a daughter they named Stephanie Anne Gordon. Hey! Just like in the movies … there have to be credits . . . .

Writings

FOR CHILDREN; WRITTEN WITH JUDITH ROSS ENDERLE

(Under joint pseudonym Jeffie Ross Gordon) *Rutabaga Ruby* (poetry), Curriculum Associates, 1989.

(Under joint pseudonym Jeffie Ross Gordon) *Hide and Shriek* (riddle book), Lerner (Minneapolis, MN), 1991.

(Under joint pseudonym Jeffie Ross Gordon) *Six Sleepy Sheep,* illustrated by John O'Brien, Boyds Mills Press (Honesdale, PA), 1991.

Six Creepy Sheep, illustrated by John O'Brien, Boyds Mills Press, 1992.

(Under joint pseudonym Jeffie Ross Gordon) *Two Badd Babies,* illustrated by Chris L. Demarest, Boyds Mills Press, 1992.

(Under joint pseudonym Jeffie Ross Gordon) *Muriel and Ruth,* Boyds Mills Press, 1992.

A Pile of Pigs, illustrated by Charles Jordan, Boyds Mills Press, 1993.

The Good-for-Something Dragon, illustrated by Les Gray, Boyds Mills Press, 1993.

(Under joint pseudonym Jeffie Ross Gordon) *Rebus Treasury II,* Boyds Mills Press, 1993.

Six Snowy Sheep, illustrated by John O'Brien, Boyds Mills Press, 1994.

What Would Mama Do?, illustrated by Chris L. Demarest, Boyds Mills Press, 1995.

Francis, the Earthquake Dog, illustrated by Brooke Scudder, Chronicle Books (San Francisco), 1996.

What's the Matter Now, Kelly Beans? Candlewick Press, 1996.

Nell Nugget and the Cow Caper, illustrated by Paul Yalowitz, Simon & Schuster, 1996.

Here's Bobby's World: How a TV Cartoon is Made, Celebration Press (Don Mills, ON, Canada), 1996.

Dear Timothy Tibbitts, illustrated by Carolyn Ewing, Marshall Cavendish (New York City), 1997.

Six Sandy Sheep, illustrated by John O'Brien, Boyds Mill Press, 1997.

Where Are You Little Zack?, illustrated by Brien Floca, Houghton Mifflin, 1997.

Upstairs, illustrated by Kate Salley Palmer, Boyds Mill Press, 1998.

(As Stephanie Jacob Gordon, with Enderle) *Something's Happening on Calabash Street,* illustrated by Donna Ingemanson, Chronicle Books, 2000.

FOR YOUNG ADULTS

Wanted: A Little Love, Tempo/Berkley, 1984.

Crazy Crush, Silhouette, 1984.

I Double Love You, Tempo Books, 1985.

Winning Heart, Dutton, 1993.

"BAYSHORE MEDICAL CENTER" SERIES; WRITTEN WITH JUDITH ROSS ENDERLE

Andrea Whitman: Pediatrics, Walker & Co., 1983.

Monica Ross: Maternity, Walker & Co., 1983.

Elizabeth Jones: Emergency, Walker & Co., 1984.

Gabriella Ortiz: Hot Line/Crisis Center, Walker & Co., 1984.

WRITTEN WITH JUDITH ROSS ENDERLE UNDER PSEUDONYM JEFFIE ROSS GORDON

Jacquelyn, Scholastic, Inc., 1985.

A Touch of Genius, Silhouette, 1986.

The Journal of Emily Ross, Silhouette, 1986.

A Touch of Magic, Silhouette, 1987.

Nobody Knows Me, Silhouette, 1987.

Nora, Scholastic, Inc., 1987.

Gimme a Z, Silhouette, 1988.

Also author (with Enderle) of the "Read-a-Picture" series, Modern Publishing, 1989. Contributor of stories to *Baby Bug, Humpty Dumpty, Lady Bug,* and *Spider.* Story writer and editor (with Enderle) for the first season of FOX TV's *Rimba's Island* series, and writer (with Enderle) for Viacom's *Corduroy* Animation Specials. Tessler's books have been translated into French, Italian, Spanish, German, Danish, and Finnish.

TOUPONCE, William F. 1948-

Personal

Born August 7, 1948, in Pittsfield, MA; son of Mary Louise (Fague) Touponce; married Julie Chang (divorced January 1, 1999); children: Dorothy, Nathan. *Education:* Hampshire College, B.A., 1974; University of Massachusetts at Amherst, M.A., 1977, Ph.D., 1981. *Politics:* Independent. *Religion:* Orthodox Christian.

Addresses

Home—4617 Cavendish Rd., Indianapolis, IN 46220. *Office*—Department of English, Indiana University-Purdue University at Indianapolis, 427 University Blvd., Indianapolis, IN 46202. *E-mail*—wtouponc@iupui.edu.

Career

Tamkang University, Tamsui, Taiwan, assistant professor of comparative literature, 1981-84; Indiana University-Purdue University at Indianapolis, assistant professor, 1985-90, associate professor, 1990-97, professor of English, 1998—. Public speaker; guest on television programs. *Military service:* U.S. Army, 1967-70; served in Vietnam; received Air Medal and Army Commendation Medal. *Member:* Modern Language Association of America, Children's Literature Association, Science Fiction Research Association, Popular Culture Association.

Awards, Honors

Fellow, National Endowment for the Humanities at University of Connecticut, 1985.

Writings

(Contributor) John Teunissen, editor, *Other Worlds: Fantasy and Science Fiction since 1939,* MOSAIC (Winnipeg, Manitoba), 1980.

Ray Bradbury and the Poetics of Reverie: Fantasy, Science Fiction, and the Reader, UMI Research Press (Ann Arbor, MI), 1984, revised edition, Borgo (San Bernardino, CA), 1998.

(Contributor) Walton Becham, editor, *Popular American Fiction,* Research Publishing (Washington, DC), 1987.

Frank Herbert, G. K. Hall (Boston, MA), 1988.

Ray Bradbury, Starmont House (Mercer Island, WA), 1989.

Isaac Asimov, G. K. Hall, 1991.

(Contributor) James W. Hipp, editor, *Dictionary of Literary Biography, Yearbook 1992,* Gale (Detroit, MI), 1993.

Contributor of articles and reviews to periodicals, including *Children's Literature Association Quarterly, Extrapolation,* and *Fantasy Review.* Associate editor, *Tamkang Review,* 1981-84.

Work in Progress

A study of religious themes in modern science fiction.

V

VITALE, Stefano 1958-

Personal

Born August 27, 1958, in Padua, Italy; son of Guido Morassutti-Vitale (a landowner) and Carla Vitale (a homemaker; maiden name, Emanuel); married Pamela Berry (an art director), May 28, 1988; children: Gianmarco, Anna. *Education:* Attended Bell School of Languages, Norwich, England, 1978, University of Venice, 1979, University of Verona, 1980-82, and University of California, Los Angeles, 1982-83; University of Southern California, B.S. (economics), 1984; Art Center College of Design, Pasadena, CA, B.F.A., 1987.

Addresses

Home and office—49 Sandy Hill Rd., Oyster Bay, NY 11771. *Agent*—Lindgren & Smith, 250 West 57th St., New York, NY 10107. *E-mail*—svitale.ix@netcom.com.

Career

Freelance illustrator. Advertising clients have included Absolut Vodka, Mercedes-Benz, Xerox, Marriott Hotels, and New York University. *Exhibitions:* Work has been exhibited at Ursitti, MacGuiness Gallery, Washington, DC, 1988; Art Director's Club, New York City, 1993; Chrysler Museum of Art, Norfolk, VA, 1996; New York Public Library, 1997; Delaware Museum of Art, Wilmington, 1997; Schloss Maretsch, Bolzano, Italy, 1998; Cedar Rapids Museum of Art, Cedar Rapids, IA, 1998; Galleria Civica, Padova, Italy, 1999; and other galleries and museums.

Awards, Honors

Three-dimensional Illustration Award, 1992; Society of Publication Designers Spot Competition awards, 1993, 1994, 1998; Children's Book of Distinction designation, *Hungry Mind Review*, 1993, for *The World in 1492;* certificate of merit, Society of Illustrators, 1993; Society of Newspaper Design award, 1994, for *New York Times Magazine;* Notable Book designations, American Library Association, 1995, 1997; Picture Book Silver Honor, Parents Choice, 1996; Aesop Prize, American Folklore Society/Library of Congress, 1996; Storytelling World Award honor book, 1998; gold award, National Parenting Publications, 1998; Reading Magic Award, *Parenting* magazine, 1999; seven American Illustration awards.

Illustrator

FOR CHILDREN

Jim Aylesworth, *The Folks in the Valley: A Pennsylvania Dutch ABC,* HarperCollins, 1992.

Jean Fritz, Patricia McKissack, and others, *The World in 1492,* Holt, 1992.

Nancy Jewell, *Christmas Lullaby,* Clarion, 1994.

Angela Shelf Medearis, *Too Much Talk,* Candlewick Press, 1995.

Charlotte Zolotow, *When the Wind Stops,* HarperCollins, 1995.

Judy Sierra, *Nursery Tales around the World,* Clarion, 1996.

Valiska Gregory, *When Stories Fell like Shooting Stars,* Simon & Schuster, 1996.

Aileen Fisher, *The Story of Easter,* HarperCollins, 1997.

David Kherdian, *The Rose's Smile: Farizad of the Arabian Nights,* Holt, 1997.

Edward Field, *Magic Words* (poetry), Harcourt, 1998.

N. Jewell, *Sailor's Song,* Clarion, 1999.

C. Zolotow, *If You Listen,* Running Press, 2000.

OTHER

Illustrator of *The Creation* (video), music by Bela Fleck, narrated by Amy Grant, Rabbit Ears. Vitale's artwork has also appeared in periodicals, including *Time, Newsweek, Business Week, Town and Country, Reader's Digest, Glamour,* and *Metropolitan Home.*

Sidelights

Born in Italy, Stefano Vitale made a shift from his career as a painter of large canvases to become a highly praised and successful illustrator of children's books. Vitale developed a unique style suggestive of "primitive" painting or folk-art, incorporating wood-grain texture and saturated colors into many of his illustration projects. Some of these include Jim Aylesworth's *The Folks in the Valley: A Pennsylvania Dutch ABC,* Charlotte Zolotow's *When the Wind Stops,* and David Kherdian's adaptation of *The Thousand and One Nights* titled *The Rose's Smile.* Praising his use of color as "showing great sensitivity" to the medium of oil paint, *Booklist* reviewer Carolyn Phelan noted of Vitale's illustrations for Nancy Jewell's *Christmas Lullaby* that the illustrator "uses line, color, and composition to achieve many different effects." Also admiring the illustrator's work, Cynthia Zarin commented in her appraisal of *Christmas Lullaby* for the *New York Times Book Review:* "Vitale's clear, enchanting illustrations are reproductions of his oil paintings [rendered] gracefully, without a trace of heavy-handedness."

Born in 1958, Vitale began his college education by studying the social sciences, and graduated from the University of Southern California with a bachelor's degree in economics in 1984. Within the next three years he had refocused his interest, however, and received his B.F.A. from Pasadena, California's Art Center College of Design in 1987. Married the following year, Vitale marketed his artistic talents to advertisers who used his designs in selling a host of products, from hotels to motorcars. In his free time, Vitale worked on the large-scale paintings that commanded what was left of his time, creative energy, and resources.

By the early 1990s, Vitale hit upon a way to fund the work he most enjoyed. As he explained to *SATA:* "I began my illustrating career to finance my large-scale paintings." His first published illustrations were included in Jim Aylesworth's ABC book *Folks in the Valley.* Appearing on bookstore shelves in 1992, *Folks in the Valley* is a rhyming book that features "satisfying verses illustrated . . . with wit and naive charm," according to *Booklist* contributor Carolyn Phelan.

Other book illustration assignments have followed for Vitale, including 1994's *Christmas Lullaby,* a revised edition of Charlotte Zolotow's 1962 picture book *When the Wind Stops* in 1995, and *Nursery Tales around the World,* a story collection edited by Judy Sierra that was published in 1996. Focusing on the never-ending, cyclical characteristics of the natural world, *When the Wind Stops* features "exquisite" full-color illustrations that "gloriously depict heaven and earth and give concrete meaning to abstract concepts," according to *Booklist* contributor Lauren Peterson. Commenting on Vitale's artistic references to Old Masters such as painters Vincent van Gogh and Marc Chagall, *School Library Journal* contributor Virginia Golodetz added that the artist adds "interesting detail" to his representation of the elements of nature presented to young readers in Zolotow's award-winning book. And Mary M. Burns noted of Vitale's artistic contribution to Judy Sierra's *Nursery Tales around the World:* "The[ir] folk-art style . . . done in oil paint on wood panels, illuminates the collection's multicultural roots; intricately designed

Stefano Vitale illustrated this lullaby about animals who took gifts to the Baby Jesus. (From Christmas Lullaby, *written by Nancy Jewell.)*

Vitale's distinctive oil-on-wood paintings illustrate **Too Much Talk,** *a retelling of a traditional West African tale by Angela Shelf Medearis.*

borders incorporate motifs" from the many cultures represented by Sierra's eighteen selections.

Vitale's painted illustrations have found a welcome place in books featuring folk tales and legends from many lands. In Angela Shelf Medearis's *Too Much Talk,* his paintings bring to life the West African tale about a group of local neighbors who suddenly find that all manner of animals and vegetables around them have suddenly been given the gift of gab. Praising the book's illustrations, *Booklist* contributor Julie Corsaro noted: "the subtly colored spreads have stylized figures that evoke the region and flowing lines that echo the cadence of [Medearis's] text." And a *Publishers Weekly* reviewer was even more enthusiastic, writing that "Even with lively, kid-pleasing narration, Vitale's . . . glowing, oil-on-wood paintings steal the show in this animated tale."

Citing his illustrations as "enchanting," *School Library Journal* critic Judith Constantinides also praised Vitale's contribution to *The Rose's Smile: Farizad of the Arabian Nights,* a reworking of the classic *Arabian Nights* saga for young people. Vitale's imitation of Persian miniatures and his use of "lush colors" received Constantinides' approval; the reviewer added: "Each page is elaborately framed and, as with medieval and Eastern art, sometimes depicts more than one scene from the story—a nice touch." "The story moves quickly," agreed Karen Morgan in her *Booklist* appraisal, "its appeal magnified by Vitale's rich illustrations, which are lushly

imbued with details of street and palace life and splendid gardens."

"Through the books I illustrate, I try to convey the images that the text suggests to me," Vitale explained to *SATA.* "My working habits are like a nine-to-five job, interrupted by an occasional walk in the woods where I feel at peace." When asked what advice he would give to aspiring young illustrators, Vitale added: "Write your own stories and try to ignore this obsessive desire to be recognized."

Works Cited

Burns, Mary M., review of *Nursery Tales around the World, Horn Book,* May-June, 1996, pp. 343-44.
Constantinides, Judith, review of *The Rose's Smile: Farizad of the Arabian Nights, School Library Journal,* November, 1997, p. 109.
Corsaro, Julie, review of *Too Much Talk, Booklist,* January 1-15, 1996, pp. 840-41.
Golodetz, Virginia, review of *When the Wind Stops, School Library Journal,* August, 1995, p. 131.
Morgan, Karen, review of *The Rose's Smile: Farizad of the Arabian Nights, Booklist,* September 1, 1997, p. 114.
Peterson, Lauren, review of *When the Wind Stops, Booklist,* July, 1995, p. 1879.
Phelan, Carolyn, review of *Christmas Lullaby, Booklist,* October 1, 1994, p. 333.
Phelan, Carolyn, review of *The Folks in the Valley: A Pennsylvania Dutch ABC, Booklist,* May 1, 1992, p. 1598.
Review of *Too Much Talk, Publishers Weekly,* October 23, 1995, p. 67.
Zarin, Cynthia, review of *Christmas Lullaby, New York Times Book Review,* December 18, 1994.

For More Information See

PERIODICALS

Booklist, December 15, 1996, p. 729; January 1-15, 1997, p. 860; October 15, 1998, p. 414.
Horn Book, March/April, 1993, p. 226.
Publishers Weekly, January 27, 1997, p. 97; September 7, 1998, p. 95; March 1, 1999, p. 67.
School Library Journal, May, 1992, p. 96; April, 1996, p. 130; October, 1996, p. 94; December, 1998, p. 135; May, 1999, p. 91.

*   *   *

VOAKE, Charlotte

Personal

Born in England; children: Chloe, William. *Education:* Degree in art history.

Addresses

Agent—c/o Candlewick Press, 2067 Massachusetts Ave., Cambridge, MA 02140.

Career

Children's book author and illustrator. Also worked in an art gallery.

Awards, Honors

Reading Magic Awards Certificate of Excellence, *Parenting* magazine, 1988, for *First Things First: A Baby's Companion;* "best books of 1990" citation, *School Library Journal,* 1990, for *The Best of Aesop's Fables;* Gold Award Smarties Prize, 1997, Reading Magic Awards Certificate of Excellence, *Parenting* magazine, and Sheffield Customers Book Award Commendation, both 1998, all for *Ginger.*

Writings

AUTHOR AND ILLUSTRATOR

Tom's Cat, Lippincott (New York City), 1986.
First Things First: A Baby's Companion, Walker Books (London, England), 1988.
Mrs. Goose's Baby, Joy Street Books (Boston, MA), 1989.
Mr. Davies and the Baby, Candlewick Press (Cambridge, MA), 1996.
Ginger, Candlewick Press, 1997.
Alphabet Adventure, Jonathan Cape Children's Books (London, England), 1998.
Here Comes the Train, Candlewick Press, 1998.

ILLUSTRATOR

Simon Watson, *The New Red Bike, and Other Stories for the Very Young,* Heinemann (London, England), 1978.
Philippa Pearce, *The Way to Sattin Shore,* Greenwillow Books (New York City), 1983.
Emma Tennant, *The Ghost Child,* Egmont Children's Books (London, England), 1984.

Over the Moon: A Book of Nursery Rhymes, introduction by David Lloyd, Clarkson N. Potter (New York City), 1985.
Jan Mark, *Fur,* Walker Books, 1986.
Sarah Hayes, *Bad Egg: The True Story of Humpty Dumpty,* Joy Street Books, 1987.
David Lloyd (adaptor), *The Ridiculous Story of Gammer Gurton's Needle,* Clarkson N. Potter, 1987.
David Lloyd, *Duck,* Lippincott, 1988.
Allan Ahlberg, *The Mighty Slide: Stories in Verse,* Viking Kestrel (Harmondsworth, Middlesex, England), 1988.
Martin Waddell, *Amy Said,* Little, Brown (Boston, MA), 1990.
Margaret Clark (adaptor), *The Best of Aesop's Fables,* Joy Street Books, 1990.
The Three Little Pigs, and Other Favourite Nursery Stories, Candlewick Press, 1992.
Vivian French, *Caterpillar, Caterpillar,* Candlewick Press, 1995.
Eleanor Farjeon, *Elsie Piddock Skips in Her Sleep,* Candlewick Press, 1997.
Joy Richardson, *Looking at Pictures: An Introduction to Art for Young People,* Harry N. Abrams (New York City), 1997.

Sidelights

A prolific illustrator of children's books, Charlotte Voake is also the author and illustrator of her own books. She wrote and illustrated *Tom's Cat,* a 1986 book aimed at preschoolers to second graders. Its main character, Tom, listens to the unidentified noises his cat makes and imagines what the cat could be doing to make those sounds. He discovers that each noise actually accompanies a more mundane activity than he had imagined. Reviewing *Tom's Cat* in the *School Library Journal,* Kathleen Odean stated that "despite delightful pictures, this doesn't add up to much of a story."

A new kitten disturbs an older cat's pampered life in **Ginger,** *written and illustrated by Voake.*

Mrs. Goose is puzzled by her baby's different behavior in Charlotte Voake's self-illustrated **Mrs. Goose's Baby.**

In 1988 Voake wrote and illustrated *First Things First: A Baby's Companion.* Voake includes nursery rhymes, the alphabet, numbers, and information about the days of the week, plants, and animals in a book for very young children in various developmental stages. *Publishers Weekly* contributors Kimberly Olson Fakih and Diane Roback called *First Things First* "perfectly geared to babies and toddlers." Reviewing the book in *Booklist,* Denise M. Wilms observed that it is "a fresh, appealing choice to share with babies and toddlers." *School Library Journal* contributor Ka-ren Litton applauded the book's organization, noting how Voake's "fresh and unconventional" book organization is similar to the unique associations "made by small children discovering the world." A *Horn Book* contributor praised Voake's "tranquil and quiet" illustrations and called *First Things First* "an absolute winner for the very youngest child."

Mrs. Goose's Baby (1989) is another Voake storybook for children. A tale of unconditional maternal love, it describes the tale of a goose who finds an egg, cares for

it, and later raises the hatchling, even though the youngster is a chicken instead of a goose. *Publishers Weekly* contributors Kimberly Olson Fakih and Diane Roback wrote that although it has an obvious ending, *Mrs. Goose's Baby* "is as reassuring as it is dear." Reviewing the book in the *Horn Book Magazine,* Ann A. Flowers praised it as "a fine expression of mother-child affection."

Voake's *Mr. Davies and the Baby* was published in 1996. Mr. Davies is a little dog who accompanies his neighbor and her baby son on a walk. Things start out well, but later, Mr. Davies gets into trouble for chasing ducks, cats, and bicycles. After the neighbor ties Mr. Davies to his doghouse, the dog escapes. The resource-ful neighbor buys her little canine friend a leash, and Mr. Davies is once again able to take walks with his neighbors. "Readers will want to take Mr. D. for a walk anytime," wrote a critic in *Kirkus Reviews. School Library Journal* contributor Marilyn Taniguchi called *Mr. Davies and the Baby* an "appealing story" with an "engaging cast of characters," while *Booklist* contributor Carolyn Phelan admired the work's "piquant charm."

In 1997 Voake's *Ginger* was published. Ginger, the feline protagonist, enjoys his pampered life until his owner unexpectedly brings home a kitten. Instead of welcoming the new arrival, Ginger longs for his old life. A *Kirkus Reviews* critic observed that the book's "parallels to the arrival of a new baby in a household give it a practical dimension." A *Publishers Weekly* contributor praised the book for similar reasons, noting that *Ginger* is "a sound choice for children dealing with not-so-idiosyncratic reactions to the arrival of a newborn."

Works Cited

Review of *First Things First, Publishers Weekly,* September 30, 1988, p. 64.

Flowers, Ann A., review of *Mrs. Goose's Baby, Horn Book Magazine,* May-June, 1989, p. 366.

Review of *Ginger, Kirkus Reviews,* January 1, 1997, p. 66.

Review of *Ginger, Publishers Weekly,* January 13, 1997, p. 74.

Litton, Ka-ren, review of *First Things First, School Library Journal,* December 1988, p. 95.

Review of *Mr. Davies and the Baby, Kirkus Reviews,* January 1, 1996, p. 74.

Review of *Mrs. Goose's Baby, Publishers Weekly,* March 24, 1989, p. 69.

Odean, Kathleen, review of *Tom's Cat, School Library Journal,* May, 1987, p. 94.

Phelan, Carolyn, review of *Mr. Davies and the Baby, Booklist,* March 15, 1996, p. 1269.

Taniguchi, Marilyn, review of *Mr. Davies and the Baby, School Library Journal,* April, 1996, pp. 119-120.

Wilms, Denise M., review of *First Things First, Booklist,* November 15, 1988, p. 588.

For More Information See

PERIODICALS

Booklist, January 15, 1986, p. 759; May 1, 1989, p. 1555; October 15, 1993, p. 446; April, 1996, p. 1269; February 1, 1997, p. 949.

Books for Keeps, November, 1990, p. 2.

Books for Your Children, summer, 1987, p. 21.

Horn Book Magazine, January-February, 1989, p. 62, May-June, 1990, pp. 330-331; November-December, 1990, pp. 757-758.

Kirkus Reviews, July 1, 1992, p. 855.

Publishers Weekly, July 13, 1990, p. 54; March 2, 1992, p. 66; July 6, 1992, p. 54; March 17, 1997, p. 85.

School Library Journal, March, 1986, p. 151; July, 1990, p. 65; December, 1990, p. 20; August, 1992, p. 149; December, 1993, pp. 103-104.*

WELLS, Rosemary 1943-

Personal

Born January 29, 1943, in New York, NY; married Thomas Moore Wells (an architect), 1963; children: Victoria, Marguerite. *Education:* Studied art at the Boston Museum School, Boston, MA; also attended a small private junior college (now defunct) in New York State. *Religion:* "a nominal Episcopalian."

Addresses

Home—732 Sleepy Hollow Rd., Briarcliff Manor, NY 10510.

Career

Allyn and Bacon, Inc., Boston, MA, art editor; Macmillan Publishing Co., Inc., New York City, art designer; freelance author and illustrator, 1968—. Also worked at various jobs, including buyer of women's shoes and accessories for a clothing store. Founder, with Susan Jeffers, of a book design studio, New York City, early 1970s. Speaker for national literacy campaign "Twenty Minutes a Day," 1994—. Founder of "Read to Your Bunny" campaign as part of the "Prescription for Reading" program, 1998. Designed "Read to Me" poster and t-shirt for the Children's Book Council, 1999. *Exhibitions:* The American Institute of Graphic Arts displayed *Morris's Disappearing Bag* in their Bias-Free Illustration Show and included *Noisy Nora, Max's Toys, Two Sisters and Some Hornets,* and *Impossible, Possum* in their Children's Book Shows.

Awards, Honors

Honor Book citation, Book World Spring Children's Book Festival, 1972, for *The Fog Comes on Little Pig Feet;* Children's Book Showcase Award, Children's Book Council, 1974, for *Noisy Nora;* Citation of Merit, Society of Illustrators, 1974, for *Benjamin and Tulip;* Art Book for Children citation, Brooklyn Museum and Brooklyn Public Library, 1975, 1976, 1977, all for *Benjamin and Tulip;* Irma Simonton Black Award, Bank Street College of Education, 1975, for *Morris's Disappearing Bag: A Christmas Story;* Edgar Allan Poe Award runner-up, Mystery Writers of America, 1981, for *When No One Was Looking* and 1988, for *Through the Hidden Door;* New Jersey Institute of Technology Award, 1983, for *A Lion for Lewis* and *Peabody;* Best Illustrated Books designation, *New York Times,* 1985, for *Hazel's Amazing Mother;* Washington Irving Children's Book Choice Award, Westchester Library Association, 1986, for *Peabody,* 1988, for *Max's Christmas,* and 1992, for *Max's Chocolate Chicken;* Golden Sower Award, 1986, for *Peabody;* New Jersey Institute of Technology Award, 1987, for *Max's Christmas;* Virginia Young Readers Award and New York Public Library Books for Teenagers citation, both 1987, for *The Man in the Woods;* Golden Kite Award, Society of Children's Books Writers, 1988, for *Forest of Dreams; Boston Globe-Horn Book* Award and Parents' Choice Award, Parents' Choice Foundation, 1989, for *Shy Charles;* Missouri Building Blocks Picture Book Award nominations, Missouri Library Association, 1998, for *Bunny Cakes* and *McDuff Moves In;* Oppenheim Toy Portfolio Platinum Award, 1999, for *Old MacDonald* and *The Itsy-Bitsy Spider; Riverbank Review* Children's Book of Distinction Award and Notable Children's Book in the Language Arts, National Council of Teachers of English, Children's Literature Assembly, both 1999, for *Mary on Horseback: Three Mountain Stories.* Wells was awarded the David McCord Children's Literature Citation for her body of work, 1991.

School Library Journal named *Noisy Nora, Morris's Disappearing Bag, Leave Well Enough Alone, Stanley and Rhoda, Max's Toys, Max's Breakfast, Max's Bedtime, Max's Bath, When No One Was Looking, Max's Christmas, Shy Charles,* and *Max's Chocolate Chicken* among the Best Books of the Year in their respective years of publication; the American Library Association (ALA) gave Notable Book citations to *Noisy Nora, Benjamin and Tulip, Morris's Disappearing Bag, Max's Breakfast, Max's Christmas, Max's Chocolate Chicken,* and *Max's Dragon Shirt;* an ALA Best Books for Young Adults citation was given to *Through the Hidden Door; Bulletin of the Center for Children's Books* gave a Blue Ribbon to *The Little Lame Prince; American Bookseller* gave Pick of the Lists citations to *Abdul, Stanley and Rhoda, Timothy Goes to School, A Lion for Lewis, Forest of Dreams, Max's Chocolate Chicken* and *Good Night, Fred; Booklist* gave Children's Editor's Choice citations to *Max's Toys, Timothy Goes to School,* and *Through the Hidden Door;* Child Study Association Children's Books of the Year citations were given to *Morris's Disappearing Bag* and *Don't Spill It Again, James; Horn Book* gave a Fanfare citation to *When No One Was Looking,* which also received the West Australian Young Readers' Book Award; a Teacher's Choices List designation was given by the International Reading Association to *Forest of Dreams;* a Children's Choices citation was given by the International Reading Association to *Max's Chocolate Chicken;* Children's Choice citations from the International Reading Association and the Children's Book Council were given to *Timothy Goes to School, A Lion for Lewis,* and *Peabody;* a citation from the Cooperative Children's Book Center was given to *Max's Bedtime.*

Writings

FOR CHILDREN; PICTURE BOOKS, EXCEPT AS NOTED; SELF-ILLUSTRATED, EXCEPT AS NOTED

John and the Rarey, Funk, 1969.
Michael and the Mitten Test, Bradbury, 1969.
The First Child, Hawthorn, 1970.
Martha's Birthday, Bradbury, 1970.
Miranda's Pilgrims, Bradbury, 1970.
Unfortunately Harriet, Dial, 1972.
Benjamin and Tulip, Dial, 1973.
Noisy Nora, Dial, 1973; reissued in a new format with new illustrations, Dial, 1997.
Abdul, Dial, 1975.
Morris's Disappearing Bag: A Christmas Story, Dial, 1975.
Don't Spill It Again, James, Dial, 1977.
Stanley and Rhoda, Dial, 1978.
Good Night, Fred, Dial, 1981.
Timothy Goes to School, Dial, 1981.
A Lion for Lewis, Dial, 1982.
Peabody, Dial, 1983.
Hazel's Amazing Mother, Dial, 1985.
Shy Charles, Dial, 1988.
Forest of Dreams, illustrated by Susan Jeffers, Dial, 1988.
Fritz and the Mess Fairy, Dial, 1991.
Waiting for the Evening Star, illustrated by Susan Jeffers, Dial, 1993.
Night Sounds, Morning Colors, illustrated by David McPhail, Dial, 1994.
Lucy Comes to Stay, illustrated by Mark Graham, Dial, 1994.
The Language of Doves, illustrated by Greg Shed, Dial, 1996.
Mary on Horseback: Three Mountain Stories (middle grade nonfiction), illustrated by Peter McCarty, Dial, 1998.
Yoko, Hyperion, 1998.

(With Maria Tallchief) *Tallchief: America's Prima Ballerina* (nonfiction), illustrated by Gary Kelley, Viking, 1999.
Streets of Gold (nonfiction; based on Mary Antin's memoir *The Promised Land*), illustrated by Dan Andreasen, Dial, 1999.
The House in the Mail, illustrated by Dan Andreasen, Dial, 1999.
Emily's First 100 Days of School, Hyperion, 2000.

"MAX AND RUBY" SERIES; SELF-ILLUSTRATED BOARD AND PICTURE BOOKS; FIRST EIGHT TITLES PUBLISHED AS "VERY FIRST BOOKS"

Max's First Word, Dial, 1979.
Max's New Suit, Dial, 1979.
Max's Ride, Dial, 1979.
Max's Toys: A Counting Book, Dial, 1979.
Max's Bath, Dial, 1985.
Max's Bedtime, Dial, 1985.
Max's Breakfast, Dial, 1985.
Max's Birthday, Dial, 1985.
Max's Christmas, Dial, 1986.
Hooray for Max, Dial, 1986.
Max's Chocolate Chicken, Dial, 1989.
Max's Dragon Shirt, Dial, 1991.
Max and Ruby's First Greek Myth: Pandora's Box, Dial, 1993.
Max and Ruby's Midas: Another Greek Myth, Dial, 1995.
Bunny Cakes, Dial, 1997.
Bunny Money, Dial, 1997.
Max's Ride, Dial, 1998.

RETELLINGS; PICTURE BOOKS

The Little Lame Prince (based on the book by Dinah Mulock Craik), Dial, 1990.
Lassie Come-Home (based on the book by Eric Knight), illustrated by Susan Jeffers, Holt, 1995.
(With Alan Garner) *Jack and the Beanstalk,* illustrated by Norman Messenger, Dorling Kindersley, 1997.
The Fisherman and His Wife: A Brand-New Version, illustrated by Eleanor Hubbard, Dial, 1998.
Rachel Field's Hitty: Her First Hundred Years, with New Adventures (based on the book by Rachel Field), illustrated by Susan Jeffers, Simon & Schuster, 1999.
(With Alan Garner) *Little Red Riding Hood,* illustrated by Norman Messenger, Dorling Kindersley, 1999.

"VOYAGE TO THE BUNNY PLANET" SERIES; SELF-ILLUSTRATED PICTURE BOOKS

Voyage to the Bunny Planet, Dial, 1992.
First Tomato, Dial, 1992.
The Island Light, Dial, 1992.
Moss Pillows, Dial, 1992.

"EDWARD THE UNREADY" SERIES; PICTURE BOOKS

Edward Unready for School, Dial, 1995.
Edward's Overwhelming Overnight, Dial, 1995.
Edward in Deep Water, Dial, 1995.

"McDUFF" SERIES; PICTURE BOOKS; ILLUSTRATED BY SUSAN JEFFERS

McDuff Moves In, Hyperion, 1997.
McDuff Comes Home, Hyperion, 1997.

McDuff and the Baby, Hyperion, 1997.
McDuff's New Friend, Hyperion, 1998.
McDuff, Hyperion, 1998.
McDuff's Birthday, Hyperion, 2000.

"BUNNY READS BACK" SERIES; PICTURE BOOKS

Read to Your Bunny, Scholastic, 1998.
Old MacDonald, Scholastic, 1998.
The Bear Went Over the Mountain, Scholastic, 1998.
Bingo, Scholastic, 1998.
The Itsy-Bitsy Spider, Scholastic, 1998.

"MY VERY FIRST MOTHER GOOSE BOARD BOOKS";
 EDITED BY IONA OPIE

Humpty Dumpty and Other Rhymes, Candlewick, 1997.
Little Boy Blue and Other Rhymes, Candlewick, 1997.
Pussycat, Pussycat and Other Rhymes, Candlewick, 1997.
Wee Willie Winkie and Other Rhymes, Candlewick, 1997.

FOR YOUNG ADULTS; FICTION

(Self-illustrated) *The Fog Comes on Little Pig Feet,* Dial,
 1972.
None of the Above, Dial, 1974.
Leave Well Enough Alone, Dial, 1977.
When No One Was Looking, Dial, 1980.
The Man in the Woods, Dial, 1984.
(Self-illustrated) *Through the Hidden Door,* Dial, 1987.

ILLUSTRATOR

William Schwenck Gilbert and Arthur Sullivan, *A Song to
 Sing, O!* (from *The Yeoman of the Guard*), Macmillan,
 1968.
Gilbert and Sullivan, *W. S. Gilbert's "The Duke of Plaza
 Toro"* (from *The Gondoliers*), Macmillan, 1969.
Paula Fox, *Hungry Fred,* Bradbury, 1969.
(With Susan Jeffers) Charlotte Pomerantz, *Why You Look
 Like You Whereas I Tend to Look Like Me,* Young
 Scott Books, 1969.
Robert W. Service, *The Shooting of Dan McGrew [and]
 The Cremation of Sam McGhee,* Young Scott Books,
 1969.
Rudyard Kipling, *The Cat That Walked by Himself,*
 Hawthorn, 1970.
Winifred Rosen, *Marvin's Manhole,* Dial, 1970.
Marjorie Weinman Sharmat, *A Hot Thirsty Day,* Macmil-
 lan, 1971.
Ellen Conford, *Impossible, Possum,* Little, Brown, 1971.
Beryl Epstein and Dorrit Davis, *Two Sisters and Some
 Hornets,* Holiday House, 1972.
Virginia A. Tashjian, editor, *With a Deep-Sea Smile: Story
 Hour Stretches for Large or Small Groups,* Little,
 Brown, 1974.
Lore G. Segal, *Tell Me a Trudy,* Farrar, Straus, 1977.
Jostein Gaarder, *The Christmas Mystery,* translated by
 Elizabeth Rokkan, Farrar, Straus, 1996.
Iona Opie, editor, *My Very First Mother Goose,* Candlew-
 ick, 1996.
(Watercolorist) E. B. White, *Charlotte's Web: Collector's
 Edition,* HarperCollins, 1999.
(Watercolorist) White, *Stuart Little: Collector's Edition,*
 HarperCollins, 1999.
Iona Opie, editor, *Here Comes Mother Goose,* Candlewick,
 1999.

OTHER

Author, with Joanna Hurley, of the adult nonfiction book
Cooking for Nitwits, photographs by Barbara Olcott,
Dutton, 1989. Contributor to the adult nonfiction book
*Worlds of Childhood: The Art and Craft of Writing for
Children,* edited by William Zinsser, Houghton Mifflin,
1990, and the children's books *So I Shall Tell You a
Story: The Magic World of Beatrix Potter,* edited by
Judy Taylor, Warne, 1993, and *Stories & Fun for the
Very Young,* Candlewick, 1998. Some of Wells's books
have been translated into Spanish.

Adaptations

Morris's Disappearing Bag and *Max's Christmas* were
adapted as short films by Weston Woods in 1982 and
1988, respectively. *Timothy Goes to School* was released
as a filmstrip by Weston Woods in 1982; *Max's
Christmas* was released as a filmstrip and on video by
Weston Woods in 1987. *A Visit with Rosemary Wells*
was released on video by Penguin USA in 1994.
Morris's Disappearing Bag was read on *Kino's Storytime,* a television program produced by KCET (Los
Angeles, CA). *PBS Kids,* six animated programs produced by Nelvana for public television and aimed at the
under-five audience, will air an adaptation of *Timothy
Goes to School* in 2000.

Sidelights

Described as "a master of the delicate art of story" by
School Library Journal reviewer Christy Norris and as
"one of the most gifted picture-book illustrators in the
United States today" by Jennifer Farley Smith in the
Christian Science Monitor, Wells is an American author
and illustrator who is lauded for creating delightful
picture and board books; candid, incisive young adult
novels; and well-received adaptations of classic tales in
picture book form. Wells addresses such genres as
realistic fiction, fantasy, and a blend of the two as well
as historical fiction, biography, the mystery story, the
school story, and the psychological novel. A prolific,
popular writer and artist, Wells is acclaimed for her
originality, versatility, sensitivity, wry sense of humor,
artistic talent, and understanding of both children and the
human condition. She is also praised for her characterizations and is well known as the creator of many
popular characters, several of whom appear in series.
Perhaps the most prominent of the author's creations are
Max and Ruby, sibling bunnies that are featured in a
series of innovative board and picture books. As an
illustrator, Wells has provided the pictures for works by
such authors as W. S. Gilbert and Arthur Sullivan, Paula
Fox, Rudyard Kipling, Beryl Epstein, Robert W. Service, and Ellen Conford. She has also illustrated several
volumes of Mother Goose rhymes and has added
watercolor to the black and white illustrations by Garth
Williams for E. B. White's *Charlotte's Web* and *Stuart
Little.*

In her picture books, Wells characteristically takes a
lighthearted but empathic approach to universal childhood experiences. Many of her books feature engaging

anthropomorphic animals—such as bears, bunnies, foxes, mice, raccoons, and badgers—who are caught up in childhood dilemmas or comic predicaments such as sibling rivalry, bedtime fears, inattentive parents, being embarrassed in class, and dealing with bullies or a new baby-sitter. Wells is credited with evoking the painful aspects of these experiences while providing satisfying, often surprising endings. Noted for accurately reflecting the feelings of children while emphasizing the child as an individual, her works are also acknowledged for giving young readers and listeners the chance to laugh at themselves. In addition, Wells has written atmospheric picture books that address the theme of change, spoofs of evolution and natural history, picture books set in mid-century America that feature the charming West Highland White terrier McDuff, retellings of stories such as Eric Knight's *Lassie Come-Home* and Rachel Field's *Hitty: Her First Hundred Years* that are revised for younger children, and board books based on popular children's songs that foster early reading. Wells's young adult novels characteristically address the ethical dilemmas of adolescence: her male and female protagonists deal with such issues as betrayal, stealing, the pressures of competition, the difficulties of relationships, and the search for truth. Wells, who refuses to provide easy answers, allows her characters to find their inner strength while trying to establish their identities and independence in a confusing world. As a writer, Wells provides texts that range from spare to richly lyrical. She frequently uses the story-within-a-story format and often concludes her books—some of which are written in verse—with unconventional endings. As an artist, Wells favors line and watercolor; she is often praised for her rich use of color and for creating deceptively simple drawings that are filled with nuance and expression.

Wells is often celebrated for capturing the essence of child behavior in books that are eloquent, witty, and affirming. Although some of her picture books are considered slight or overly sentimental and her young adult novels are occasionally criticized for ambiguity, Wells is generally regarded as a gifted author/artist who seamlessly combines humor and panache in books that appeal to, and have a devoted following among, both children and adults. "In a few lines and pale colors," noted Jennifer Farley Smith in *Christian Science Monitor,* "Wells can speak volumes to her young audience." Hazel Rochman of *Booklist* stated that Wells "has that rare ability to tell a funny story for very young children with domestic scenes of rising excitement and heartfelt emotion, and with not one word too many." A critic in *Publishers Weekly* said that Wells has "contributed incomparable picture books, to the joy of the tinies," while another stated that the author "demonstrates a remarkable feel for children's small but important difficulties." In another issue of the same magazine, a reviewer concluded, "The astringent wit of Rosemary Wells, in words and illustrations, is as welcome as a very dry martini after a series of Pink Ladys."

Born in New York City, Wells grew up in a home that was, as she recalled in her essay in *Something about the Author Autobiography Series (SAAS),* "always filled

with books, dogs, nineteenth-century music, and other things my parents held in great esteem." She added, "The love of animals, books, good food, music and languages, theatre, were gifts to me in an extraordinarily close family." Most of her childhood was spent on the New Jersey Shore; her parents moved from Gramercy Park to a home near Red Bank a few years after her birth, and her maternal grandmother lived five miles away, right on the ocean. Wells wrote in *SAAS:* "I spent so much time in her enormous stucco house with its own beach that most of my sentimental and favorite memories, good and bad, come from that place and time on the New Jersey shore." The author's parents and grandmother encouraged her early artistic endeavors. Her father was a playwright until the age of fifty when Rosemary was born. In 1939, he had a play produced on Broadway and later saw it broadcast live on television. Of English-Australian descent, Wells's father—described by his daughter in *SAAS* as "an extraordinary raconteur and amateur historian"—left home at fourteen to work as a rancher in the Australian outback. Two years later, he became a soldier in World War I and later worked as an actor and stunt rider in Hollywood. Wells's mother, whom her daughter called "Pan-European [with] an extraordinary ear for languages" in *SAAS,* also left home at fourteen, traveling to Paris to become a ballet dancer, and later dancing with the Russian ballerina Pavlova before becoming a member of the American Ballet and the Ballet Russe de Monte Carlo. Wells's grandmother, whom she considers the third of her parents, had been a great beauty in New York society and possessed, according to her granddaughter in her essay in *Fourth Book of Junior Authors and Illustrators (FBJAI),* "a steel-trap mind," often reading to Rosemary from works by authors such as Longfellow, Kipling, and Poe. Wells wrote in her website "Meet Rosemary Wells," "Both my parents flooded me with books and stories. My grand-

In Rosemary Wells's self-illustrated picture book, Ruby reads her brother, Max, an altered version of the story of Pandora's Box. (From Max and Ruby's First Greek Myth: Pandora's Box.*)*

mother took me on special trips to the theater and museums in New York." She added in *FBJAI,* "I owe a great deal to my parents, I think as professionals, they treated me as a professional, without ever pushing or condescending, either."

From the age of two, Wells drew constantly. She told Jean F. Mercier in *Publishers Weekly,* "As far back as I can remember, I did nothing but draw. I parlayed this into the sham of a school career. I discovered very early that making a picture of anything meant people saying 'Look at that!' and how else could I get that kind of attention?" She recalled in her essay in *FBJAI,* "I drew pictures all day long in school (when I wasn't supposed to be doing it) and every night after supper for at least a couple of hours before bed, when the lights went out but I could still listen to the Dodgers turned very, very low." Wells wrote in *SAAS,* "I drew curious subjects, at least they were considered curious by others." The fledgling artist sketched policemen, cowboys, baseball players, medieval soldiers, and lots of bloody fights. When Wells was in first grade, the eighth-grade teacher at her school told her that she drew better than anyone in her class. "This, of course," Wells noted in *SAAS,* "gave me a lot of confidence." When asked what she wanted to be when she grew up, Wells could answer "artist" rather than the usual careers for women at that time, such as nurse, teacher, or mother. She wrote in *SAAS,* "Because I could say artist, I had a reprieve from what, even then, I considered to be a life-sentence of drudgery. When I became a teenager, the idea of being an artist was the only thing that stood between me and despair—I was gangly, underdeveloped, a social retard whose mother didn't like her watching 'American Bandstand.'" Writing was also important to Wells as she was growing up. When she wasn't drawing, playing baseball, or roaming the woods, she read books and wrote stories. In grade school, Wells wrote poetry when she should have been doing math. The author wrote in *SAAS,* "I 'learned to write' in school. There was nothing wrong with that. However, there was as much chance of my really writing what was in my spirit as there is of a prisoner, whose mail is opened and inspected, writing that he was dug an escape tunnel." Wells mused, "Whatever was behind those piles of drawings, the drawings themselves were behind the writing; and now that I am over forty, I can say the writing is the better part of my skills. I try mightily to improve my illustrations but my heart is probably more in writing."

At thirteen, Wells was sent to an upscale boarding school for girls; her parents wanted her to get, as she described it in *SAAS,* "a real education." She recalled, "I reacted badly . . . . The school was a jail to me although the other girls seemed to be having a grand time." Wells found the regimentation, scrutiny, and constant supervision to be oppressive; in addition, she wrote, "There was no privacy, no time to draw." She went on a hunger strike and cried all the time. Finally, her parents took their daughter out of the school. Wells remembered, "My grandmother told me, on my return home, that I had lost my first great battle with life. She was stuck with the tuition bill for the rest of the year." Back at

home, Wells entered Red Bank High School. She told Mercier that she was a "very poor student." Wells wrote in *SAAS,* "I'd done badly in high school due to my own laziness and inability to take things like chemistry seriously. This was abetted by my parent's inability to take things like chemistry seriously." She spent her junior year "larking around England with my mother and father." When Wells was accepted at a small private junior college in upstate New York, she was determined, as she wrote in *SAAS,* to shed "the high school stigma of 'not being popular.'" The college turned out to be a sort of finishing school for the daughters of the rich. Wells turned into a top student and made two lifelong friends. However, after a year she left for Boston to be with Tom Wells, a Dartmouth student whom she had met on a blind date. Wells wrote in *SAAS* that after her date, "I was determined to marry Tom Wells."

When she was nineteen, Wells entered the Boston Museum School to study art. She was taught anatomy, perspective, life drawing, and printing by, as she wrote in *FBJAI,* "a battalion of strict, old-school Germans." In 1963, Rosemary and Tom Wells married, and Rosemary dropped out of art school to enter the job market. On the strength of her portfolio, she landed a job as art editor with the publishers Allyn and Bacon. She wrote in *SAAS,* "all the laziness and reluctance to concentrate disappeared. I was assigned an American history book for Catholic high school seniors. It was thirteen hundred pages long and I had to send away for all the prints and photos that would illustrate it. The book was wonderful. The Sisters of the Sacred Heart, who were involved in the editorial end, were splendid women. There was a party when it was published and I felt like a success at something for the first time in my life." Two years later, Tom Wells applied to the Columbia University School of Architecture and he and Rosemary moved to New York City. While working as an art designer for Macmillan, she presented a small illustrated dummy of a Gilbert and Sullivan song, taken from their operetta *The Yeomen of the Guard,* to the editor-in-chief. This became her first published book, *A Song to Sing, O!* A year after the publication of *A Song to Sing, O!,* Wells produced *The Duke of Plaza Toro,* a picture book based on another Gilbert and Sullivan song, this one from *The Gondoliers.*

After illustrating well-received volumes by Paula Fox and Robert W. Service, Wells created her first original work, *John and the Rarey.* A picture book published in 1969, the story features a little boy who does not want to be an airplane pilot like his father. What John does want is a pet: he finds a fantastic, blue-eyed creature that takes him into the sky on its back. A reviewer in *Publishers Weekly* stated, "It took no perception to spot Rosemary Wells as a fresh new talent in children's books . . . . Now she has written her own lyrics and illustrated them in this witty story . . . ." Writing in the *Horn Book,* Sidney D. Long added that the fantasy-nonsense "will appeal to all children who have been faced with a frustrating family situation." Wells continued to write and illustrate her own picture books while providing the art for the works of other authors. She produced her first novel for young adults, *The Fog Comes on Little Pig Feet,* in 1972. In this book, which the author based on her boarding-school experience, thirteen-year-old Rachel Sakasian tells her story in diary form. A Brooklyn girl who wants to become a concert pianist, Rachel longs to attend Music and Art High, a public school in New York City. However, her parents insist that she attend North Place, an elite boarding school. Rachel dislikes the school, which allows her no time to practice the piano or to be alone. Rachel becomes friends with upper-class-man Carlisle Duggett, who is rumored to be mentally unbalanced. Rachel finds herself covering for Carlisle when she leaves the school to go and live in Greenwich Village. When she confronts Carlisle and finds that she has tried to commit suicide, Rachel is torn between protecting her friend and telling the truth. Finally, she opts for the latter. At the end of the novel, Rachel discovers that her parents have decided to let her go to public high school. In a *School Library Journal* review, Alice Miller Bregman predicted, "Young teens will devour this fast-paced, adequately written entertainment," while Jane Langton stated in *Book World— Chicago Tribune,* "The book says something true about life: Evil is not diabolical and nasty, but bland and blind." Mrs. John G. Gray, a contributor to *Best Sellers,* applauded the novel's "priceless vignettes" and conclud-ed that Wells "brilliantly demonstrates her writing abilities are an easy match for her already famous artistic talents."

In 1973, Rosemary and Tom Wells had the first of their two daughters, Victoria; their second daughter, Marguer-ite, nicknamed Beezoo, was born in 1977. A year after Victoria's birth, Wells published what is perhaps her most controversial work, the young adult novel *None of the Above.* The book outlines five years in the life of Marcia, a teenage girl who likes pink angora sweaters, reading movie magazines, and watching television. When her father remarries, Marcia feels out of place with her sophisticated stepmother and ambitious stepsis-ter. Marcia decides to turn herself around: she switches to college prep classes and succeeds, although reluctant-ly, in school. However, Marcia also becomes involved with Raymond, a good-looking though hoodish class-mate. Raymond, who is impotent until he meets Marcia, asks her to marry him. After a grueling English exam, Marcia makes a choice. Although she does not love Raymond and has been accepted by both Sarah Law-rence and the University of Massachusetts, she runs to Raymond's car. Marcia hopes that Raymond will see her engagement ring flashing in the moonlight; however, he is absorbed in *Car and Driver.* Calling Marcia an "unusual and oddly affecting heroine," *School Library Journal* critic Joni Brodart claimed that Wells "captures the girl's confusion in this timely, realistic, and moving novel which should reach a large audience." Writing in *Bulletin of the Center for Children's Books,* Zena Sutherland noted, "The characterization is strong and consistent, and the complexities of relationships within the family are beautifully developed. Wells is particular-ly adept at dialogue . . . ." Although she praised Wells for her "uncompromising honesty," Jean F. Mercier, writing in *Publishers Weekly,* claimed that the "trouble

with the story is that all its people are so unsavoury. That goes double for the 'heroine,' a dolt who is more irritating than sympathetic." Writing in the *New York Times Book Review,* Dale Carlson said that *None of the Above* was "well-written and the characters well-con-ceived. I'm not sure about the ending—sentimentally, but I don't think realistically, conceived." Roger Sutton of *Horn Book* assessed critical reaction to the ending of the novel: "The conclusion caused some confusion for reviewers, who could not decide if the ending was happy, pessimistic, or ambiguous." Wells feels that these responses showed that the critics cared about Marcia. "And later, when the angry ones thought about it," she told Jean F. Mercier, "they did understand the point I was trying to put across. No matter what the girl had decided, it was her own choice, her first choice, the beginning of independence."

In 1979, Wells produced the first four books in her popular "Max" series: *Max's First Word, Max's New Suit, Max's Ride,* and *Max's Toys: A Counting Book.* Concept books that *Children's Books and Their Crea-tors (CBATC)* contributor Maeve Visser Knoth called "the first funny board books for very young children," the titles use story, information, and humor to introduce preschoolers to such concepts as prepositions, getting dressed, and the importance of individuality. The books feature Max, a white toddler bunny, and his older sister Ruby, who thinks that she knows what is best for Max and tries to control him. Although Max is easygoing, he remains undaunted, innocently outsmarting his sister and always getting the last word. Wells uses minimal but lively language and a bright palette for these books; her pictures are done in vivid primary colors on uncluttered but detailed pages. Writing in *Booklist,* Judith Goldber-ger stated, "Someone no less than Rosemary Wells has done it; she has developed a set of durable cardboard books that drive a real wedge into the existing block of unnotable, overcute, didactic baby-toddler tomes." In 1985, Wells produced four more board books in the series—*Max's Bath, Max's Bedtime, Max's Birthday,* and *Max's Breakfast*—that continue the adventures of the brother-and-sister duo. "Each story," wrote Trev Jones in *School Library Journal,* "portrays a typical preschool trauma resolved with humor and understand-ing." In a *Bulletin of the Center for Children's Books* review, Zena Sutherland stated that this set of books are "equally delectable, and they should be as useful for very young children as they are appealing."

Max's Christmas, a title published in 1986, is the first of Wells's full-length picture books about Max and Ruby. The story takes place on Christmas Eve: Max has lots of questions about Santa Claus, which Ruby answers simply with "Because!" Unsatisfied, Max sneaks down-stairs to wait for Santa, who patiently answers Max's questions until he finally has to resort to "Because!" Ruby comes down to find Max on the couch with a lap full of presents, a situation that prompts questions of her own; Max, of course, answers with "Because!" Calling Max "that epitome of the small child in rabbit guise," Judith Glover, writing in *School Library Journal,* claimed that Wells "has an extraordinary talent for capturing a welter of thoughts and emotions with the placement of an eye or a turn of a smile . . . ." *Horn Book* critic Karen Jameyson dubbed Max "that Shirley Temple of rabbits" before concluding that despite the book's longer format "an uncanny perceptive simplicity, both in line and in word, is still Wells's most effective tool."

Subsequent books about Max and Ruby adhere to the picture book, rather than to the board book, format. In two of the titles, *Max and Ruby's First Greek Myth: Pandora's Box* and *Max and Ruby's Midas: Another Greek Myth,* Wells uses the frame of the story-within-a-story to introduce young readers and listeners to Greek mythology. For example, in *Pandora's Box,* Ruby finds Max investigating her jewelry box, which is off limits; she tells him a bunny-centric version of the classic legend. Max, true to form, turns the tables on Ruby: he knows that the sign on her box says "No," but when Ruby asks him who it means, Max says "You!" Writing in *Bulletin of the Center for Children's Books,* Betsy Hearne noted, "More than a tale within a tale, this is a spoof within a spoof, so kids will need a grounding in the myth's straightforward rendition to deconstruct this one." A critic in *Kirkus Reviews* concluded, "A novel, entertaining introduction to the myth; better yet, another delightful episode in the saga of this irrepressible bunny." Wells has also written two stories, *Bunny Cakes* and *Bunny Money,* about how Max and Ruby prepare for their grandmother's birthday. In *Bunny Cakes,* the siblings have separate ideas for cakes: Ruby wants to make an angel surprise cake while Max wants to present his grandmother with an earthworm cake decorated with red-hot marshmallow squirters. At the end of the story, Max—who is too young to read and write—thinks of a way to communicate his shopping list to the grocer, and Grandma is thrilled when she receives two cakes. Pat Mathews, a reviewer for *Bulletin of the Center for Children's Books,* claimed, "In this take on written communication kidstyle, pudgy Max is at his winsome best . . . ." In *Bunny Money,* Ruby takes Max shopping to buy a birthday present for Grandma. The siblings' money goes fast—most of it is spent on Max—but a compromise is reached: Grandma drives the pair home wearing musical earrings from Ruby and plastic vampire teeth from Max. In her illustrations, Wells shows the gradual reduction of the contents of Ruby's wallet at the bottom of each page. A critic in *Kirkus Reviews* called the book "a great adjunct to primary-grade math lessons," while in a *Bulletin of the Center for Children's Books* review, Pat Mathews concluded, "The combination of gentle comedy, shrinking assets, and those expressive bunny eyes commends this story to old and new Max and Ruby fans."

In an essay that she wrote for *CBATC,* Wells commented on the genesis of the "Max and Ruby" books: "Many of the stories in my books come from our two children, Victoria and Beezoo. Ruby and Max are Victoria and Beezoo." In 1977, when Victoria was five and Beezoo nine months, Victoria, according to her mother, "had taken it upon herself to teach her baby sister about the world and dragged her, like a sack of flour, because she

was too heavy to really carry, from object to object, shouting, 'Table, Beezoo, say table, TA-BLE!' Beezoo did not cooperate at all and was always off in a world of her own." Victoria also tried to teach Beezoo how to get dressed—"another complete failure," according to Wells, "as Beezoo preferred to get undressed at all times." The author concluded, "What is funny is not the events, but Victoria's dogged insistence on leading Beezoo in the paths of righteousness and Beezoo's complete insouciance in the face of slightly skewed authority. In part I wrote the board books because there were no funny books around for very young children. But mostly I wrote them because the characters materialized on paper in front of me, under my hand, so to speak. The characters were alive; the stories were going on all around me."

In addition to "Max and Ruby," Wells is also the creator of several other popular series. Among them are the "Voyage to the Bunny Planet" books, in which little bunnies have bad days and imagine themselves transported to the Bunny Planet, where their idylls restore their equilibrium. The "Edward the Unready" series follows a little bear who is not ready to go to school or to stay overnight at a friend's house and prefers to be at home among familiar surroundings. In the "McDuff" series, a West Highland white terrier—based on Wells's own pet—escapes from a dogcatcher's truck and is adopted by a young couple. The author's "Bunny Reads Back" series features board books for youngsters and parents to share that are based on favorite children's songs. Several of Wells's characters—such as Max and Ruby, Edward the Unready, and McDuff—have been turned into stuffed toys. A reteller and adapter, Wells is the creator of picture book adaptations of the classic children's stories *The Little Lame Prince* and *Hitty: Her First Hundred Years* as well as Eric Knight's beloved tale *Lassie Come-Home.* In addition, Wells retold the Grimm Brothers's folktale *The Fisherman and His Wife* with cats as protagonists and collaborated with English author Alan Garner on picture book versions of *Jack and the Beanstalk* and *Little Red Riding Hood.*

As an author, Wells has written several biographies of historical and contemporary women. One of her most acclaimed books in this genre is *Mary on Horseback: Three Mountain Stories,* a book for middle graders published in 1998 that profiles Mary Breckinridge, founder of the Frontier Nursing Service in the Appalachian Mountains. After losing two husbands and two children, Mary became a nurse in Europe before arriving in Kentucky in 1923. Wells shows both the hardships and the triumphs experienced by the valiant nurse from the perspectives of three young people whom Mary helped. Noting the "historical accuracy and elegance" of the volume, a reviewer in *Publishers Weekly* stated, "Three well-honed first-person narratives add up to an outstanding biography . . . ." *Booklist* reviewer Helen Rosenberg added, "These beautifully written stories will remain with the reader long after the book is closed; Wells has given much deserved honor to a true heroine," while Peggy Morgan, writing in *School Library Journal,* concluded, "This one's a gem." In 1999, Wells published *Streets of Gold,* a picture book biography of Mary Antin, a Jewish girl who came to the United States from Russia in the early 20th century. *Streets of Gold* describes Mary's life in Czarist Russia as well as her experiences in America. A year after her arrival, Antin wrote an epic poem about George Washington that was published in a Boston newspaper. A reviewer in *Publishers Weekly* claimed, "Among a profusion of books about turn-of-the-century Russian-Jewish emigrants, Wells's and [illustrator Dan] Andreasen's story about Mary Antin stands out for its exceptional economy and tenderness." Wells also produced a well-received biography of American ballet dancer Maria Tallchief with whom she collaborated on the project.

In addition to her success as an author and illustrator, Wells has become a well known advocate for literacy. She has often spoken on behalf of the "Twenty Minutes a Day" campaign, which proposes that parents should spend twenty minutes each day reading to their children. In 1998, she published the picture book *Read to Your Bunny,* a work that the author was invited to read at the White House to signify the opening of the Prescription for Reading Partnership program, a component of the "America Reads" challenge. Later that year, First Lady Hillary Rodham Clinton joined Wells for a reading of the book at a Maryland bookstore. In evaluating her literary career, which has spanned more than thirty years and has produced approximately sixty books, Wells wrote in *SAAS,* "The job I have now, writing and illustrating children's books, writing novels for teenagers—is pure delight. There are hard parts but no bad or boring parts, and that is more than can be said for any other line of work I know." Writing in *FBJAI,* she stated, "It is for the child in myself that I do picture books, and for the adolescent still lurking there that I do novels." Wells wrote in *CBATC,* "All my stories are written with deeply felt emotional content." In an entry that she wrote for *Worlds of Childhood,* Wells concluded, "I believe that all stories and plays and paintings and songs and dances come from a palpable but unseen space in the cosmos .... According to how gifted we are, we are all given a large or small key to this treasury of wonders. I have been blessed with a small key to the world of the young."

Works Cited

Bregman, Alice Miller, review of *The Fog Comes on Little Pig Feet, School Library Journal,* May, 1972, p. 89.

Brodart, Joni, review of *None of the Above, School Library Journal,* November, 1974, p. 69.

Review of *Bunny Money, Kirkus Reviews,* July 15, 1997, p. 1119.

Carlson, Dale, review of *None of the Above, New York Times Book Review,* November 24, 1974, p. 8.

Glover, Judith, review of *Max's Christmas, School Library Journal,* October, 1986, p. 112.

Goldberger, Judith, review of *Max's First Word, Max's New Suit, Max's Ride,* and *Max's Toys: A Counting Book, Booklist,* October 15, 1978, p. 359.

Gray, Mrs. John G., review of *The Fog Comes on Little Pig Feet, Best Sellers,* July 15, 1972, p. 200.

Hearne, Betsy, review of *Max and Ruby's First Greek Myth: Pandora's Box, Bulletin of the Center for Children's Books,* November, 1993, p. 106.

Jameyson, Karen, "Christmas Books," *Horn Book,* November-December, 1985, pp. 725-28.

Review of *John and the Rarey, Publishers Weekly,* April 21, 1969, p. 64.

Jones, Trev, review of *Max's Bath* and others, *School Library Journal,* March, 1985, pp. 159-60.

Knoth, Maeve Visser, entry in *Children's Books and Their Creators,* edited by Anita Silvey, Houghton Mifflin, 1995, pp. 673, 675.

Langton, Jane, review of *The Fog Comes on Little Pig Feet, Book World—Chicago Tribune,* May 7, 1972, p. 5.

Long, Sidney D., review of *John and the Rarey, Horn Book,* August, 1969, pp. 399-400.

Review of *Mary on Horseback: Three Mountain Stories, Publishers Weekly,* September 14, 1998, p. 70.

Mathews, Pat, review of *Bunny Cakes, Bulletin of the Center for Children's Books,* March, 1997, p. 261.

Mathews, review of *Bunny Money, Bulletin of the Center for Children's Books,* October, 1997, p. 71.

Review of *Max and Ruby's First Greek Myth: Pandora's Box, Kirkus Reviews,* September 1, 1993, p. 1154.

Mercier, Jean F., review of *None of the Above, Publishers Weekly,* August 5, 1974, p. 58.

Review of *Miranda's Pilgrims, Publishers Weekly,* November 15, 1970, p. 1245.

Morgan, Peggy, review of *Mary on Horseback: Three Mountain Stories, School Library Journal,* October, 1998, p. 130.

Norris, Christy, review of *McDuff Comes Home, School Library Journal,* July, 1997, p. 78.

Rochman, Hazel, review of *Bunny Cakes, Booklist,* January 1, 1997, p. 857.

Rosenberg, Helen, review of *Mary on Horseback: Three Mountain Stories, Booklist,* September 1, 1998, p. 113.

Smith, Jennifer Farley, "Animals Are Enduring Heroes," *Christian Science Monitor,* March 6, 1974, p. F2.

Review of *Stanley and Rhoda, Publishers Weekly,* October 9, 1978, p. 76.

Review of *Streets of Gold, Publishers Weekly,* April 19, 1999, p. 73.

Sutherland, review of *None of the Above, Bulletin of the Center for Children's Books,* April, 1975, p. 139.

Sutherland, Zena, review of *Max's Bath, Bulletin of the Center for Children's Books,* April, 1985, p. 157.

Sutton, Roger, "A Second Look: 'None of the Above,'" *Horn Book,* June, 1987, pp. 368-71.

Review of *Yoko, Publishers Weekly,* October 19, 1998, p. 78.

Wells, Rosemary, essay in *Fourth Book of Junior Authors and Illustrators,* edited by Doris De Montreville and Elizabeth D. Crawford, Wilson, 1978, pp. 343-45.

Wells, Rosemary, interview with Jean F. Mercier, *Publishers Weekly,* February 29, 1980, pp. 72-73.

Wells, Rosemary, essay in *Something about the Author Autobiography Series,* Volume 1, Gale, 1986, pp. 279-291.

Wells, Rosemary, "The Well-Tempered Children's Book," *Worlds of Childhood: The Art and Craft of Writing for*

Children, edited by William Zinsser, Houghton Mifflin, 1990, pp. 121-43.

Wells, Rosemary, essay in *Children's Books and Their Creators,* edited by Anita Silvey, Houghton Mifflin, 1995, p. 374.

For More Information See

BOOKS

Authors & Artists for Young Adults, Volume 13, Gale, 1994, pp. 227-236.

Children's Literature Review, Volume 16, Gale, 1989.

Contemporary Literary Criticism, Volume 12, Gale, 1980.

Pendergast, Tom and Sara Pendergast, editors, *St. James Guide to Children's Writers,* Gale, 1999.

Pendergast, Tom and Sara Pendergast, editors, *St. James Guide to Young Adult Writers,* Gale, 1999.

Sadker, Myra Pollack and David Miller Sadker, *Now Upon a Time: A Contemporary View of Children's Literature,* Harper, 1977, pp. 66-67.

PERIODICALS

Horn Book, March-April 1987, pp. 163-170.

Junior Literary Guild, September, 1977; March, 1981.

Publishers Weekly, February 27, 1987, p. 146.

Riverbank Review, spring, 1999, pp. 17-20.

Washington Post Book World, May 1, 1977, p. E4.*

—*Sketch by Gerard J. Senick*

* * *

WIKLER, Madeline 1943-

Personal

Born August 30, 1943, in New York, NY; daughter of Alfred (a health inspector) and Fay (a secretary; maiden name, Dwoskin) Meyers; married Joseph Wikler (an investment advisor), June 21, 1964; children: Judith Wikler Sensibar, Karen. *Education:* Received degree from Pembroke College (now Brown University), 1965. *Religion:* Jewish. *Hobbies and other interests:* Painting, tennis.

Addresses

Home—Silver Spring, MD. *E-mail*—Karben@aol.com.

Career

Artist. Community Progress, Inc., New Haven, CT, writer, 1965-66; National Association for Community Development, Washington, DC, editor and writer, 1966-72; Kirshner Associates (consulting firm), Washington, staff writer, 1972-75; founder and principal, Kar-Ben Copies, Inc. (a publishing company), 1975—. *Member:* Society of Children's Book Writers and Illustrators, Association of Booksellers for Children, Association of Jewish Libraries, Jewish Book Council, Baltimore Watercolor Society, Laurel Art Guild, Western Maine Art Group, Potomac Valley Watercolorists.

Writings

CHILDREN'S BOOKS

Let's Have a Seder!, illustrated by Miriam Sagasti, Kar-Ben (Rockville, MD), 1996.

CHILDREN'S BOOKS WITH JUDYTH R. SAYPOL GRONER

My Very Own Chanukah Book, Kar-Ben (Rockville, MD), 1977.

My Very Own Megillah, Kar-Ben (Rockville, MD), 1977.

My Very Own Rosh Hashanah Book, Kar-Ben (Rockville, MD), 1978.

My Very Own Yom Kippur Book, Kar-Ben (Rockville, MD), 1978.

My Very Own Sukkot Book, Kar-Ben (Rockville, MD), 1980.

My Very Own Simchat Torah, Kar-Ben (Rockville, MD), 1981.

(With Ruth E. Brinn) *Let's Have a Party: 100 Mix and Match Party Ideas for the Jewish Holidays,* Kar-Ben (Rockville, MD), 1981.

My Very Own Shavuot, Kar-Ben (Rockville, MD), 1982.

Where Is the Afikomen?, with pictures by Chari R. McLean, Kar-Ben (Rockville, MD), 1985.

(With Katherine Kahn), *My First Seder,* with pictures by Kahn, Kar-Ben (Rockville, MD), 1986.

The Purim Parade, Kar-Ben (Rockville, MD), 1986.

Let's Build a Sukkah, Kar-Ben (Rockville, MD), 1986.

Madeline Wikler

Miracle Meals: Eight Nights of Food 'n Fun for Chanukah,
  illustrated by Chari Radin, Kar-Ben (Rockville, MD),
  1987.
(With Radin) *I Have Four Questions,* Kar-Ben (Rockville,
  MD), 1988.
All About Hanukah, illustrated by Rosalyn Schanzer, Kar-
  Ben (Rockville, MD), 1988, revised edition, illustrated
  by Kinny Kreiswirth, 1999.
Shabbat Shalom, illustrated by Yaffa, Kar-Ben (Rockville,
  MD), 1989.
(With Sally Springer) *Let's Make Latkes,* Kar-Ben (Rock-
  ville, MD), 1991.
In the Synagogue, illustrated by Schanzer, Kar-Ben (Rock-
  ville, MD), 1991.
(With Kahn) *The Shofar Calls to Us,* Kar-Ben (Rockville,
  MD), 1991.
Hanukah Fun, Kar-Ben (Rockville, MD), 1992.
(With Brinn) *Jewish Holiday Crafts for Little Hands,* Kar-
  Ben (Rockville, MD), 1993.
Thank You, God! A Jewish Child's Book of Prayers,
  illustrated by Shelly O. Haas, Kar-Ben (Rockville,
  MD), 1993.
All About Rosh Hashanah, illustrated by Bonnie Gordon-
  Lucas, Kar-Ben (Rockville, MD), 1997.
All About Yom Kippur, illustrated by Gordon-Lucas, Kar-
  Ben (Rockville, MD), 1997.
Come, Let Us Welcome Shabbat, Kar-Ben (Rockville,
  MD), 1997, revised edition, 1999.
My Very Own Haggadah, illustrated by Chaya Burstein,
  Kar-Ben (Rockville, MD), 1998.
All About Sukkot, illustrated by Kinney Kreiswirth, Kar-
  Ben (Rockville, MD), 1998.
Let's Celebrate Shabbat, Kar-Ben (Rockville, MD), 1999.
Make Your Own Megillah, Kar-Ben (Rockville, MD),
  2000.

AUTHOR AND PHOTOGRAPHER

(With Judyth Saypol Groner) *My Very Own Jewish
  Community,* Kar-Ben (Rockville, MD), 1984.

ILLUSTRATOR

Rachelle Heller and Dianne Martin, *Alef BASIC: A Guide
  to the BASIC Computer Programming with Facts, Fun,
  and Games from Jewish History and Tradition,* Kar-
  Ben (Rockville, MD), 1983.
Marji Gold-Vukson, *The Colors of My Jewish New Year,*
  Kar-Ben (Rockville, MD), 1998.

PHOTOGRAPHER

Andrew Goldstein, *My Very Own Jewish Home,* Kar-Ben
  (Rockville, MD), 1979.

Sidelights

Madeline Wikler told *SATA:* "I co-founded Kar-Ben
Copies, Inc. with Judye Groner in 1975 and built this
niche publisher of Jewish books for kids into a successful business which now includes about 100 titles with a
very strong backlist and about six to eight new books
annually.

"Although we began by writing many of the books
ourselves, we now have worked with over 80 authors

*Wikler illustrated the seven Jewish holidays in Marji
Gold-Vukson's book for young readers. (Cover illustration by Wikler.)*

and illustrators and are proud to have developed a highly
regarded, successful small publishing house with a
distinct focus and loyal following."

Nearly all of these books published by Wikler's company revolve around the calendar of Jewish holidays, and
explain various rites for readers of pre-school or early
elementary age. Some of these early titles that Wikler
wrote with Groner were *My Very Own Rosh Hashanah
Book,* published in 1978, and *Where Is the Afikomen?,*
illustrated by Chari R. McLean. This 1985 picture book
shows a little girl searching her house for the special
piece of matzoh that plays an important part of the
Passover meal known as seder. In 1986, Wikler and her
company published a trio of books—*My First Seder,*
with Katherine Kahn, and *The Purim Parade* and *Let's
Build a Sukkah,* all of which were collaborations with
Groner. Conceived as board books with very little text,
they depict children celebrating the Jewish holy days in
various ways, such as staging a masquerade parade for
Purim, or constructing a sukkah—the thatched-roof
awning for the dinner table that has symbolic meaning
on the Sukkoth, or Feast of Tabernacles, holiday. "These
books can show preschoolers the fun and enjoyment that
these holidays bring," asserted Ruth Shire in her review
of these three works for *School Library Journal.*

Wikler has also co-authored *Miracle Meals: Eight
Nights of Food 'n Fun for Chanukah,* illustrated by
Chari Radin and published in 1987. It features a variety
of games and recipes, the latter categorized according to
their degree of difficulty and labeled for various Jewish
dietary observances. One example of *Miracle Meals's*
Chanukah ideas is a recipe for sheet cake that also shows
how to cut and arrange it into the shape of either a

menorah or dreidel. Micki S. Nevett, reviewing it for *School Library Journal,* called it "a lively, entertaining book." Continuing this theme was Wikler's 1988 title, *All About Hanukah.* Revised and reprinted in 1999 with new illustrations by Kinny Kreiswirth, the colorful book explains the history of the religious holiday, and how contemporary Jews observe it. It includes recipes for special Hanukah dishes, such as donuts called sufganiyot and potato pancakes. A *School Library Journal* reviewer noted that though it was written for Jewish children, *All About Hanukah*'s explanations would be clear to children of other faiths.

Wikler, Groner, and Kar-Ben's subsequent books in the late 1980s included *I Have Four Questions,* illustrated by Radin, which depicts a little girl fulfilling her religious duty on Passover, and *Shabbat Shalom,* which appeared in 1989. This latter work is devoid of text, and contains images by the artist Yaffa showing how a family goes about the weekly observance.

As Wikler's business neared its tenth anniversary, she continued to work with Groner and various artists in creating books for young readers that explored Jewish faith and history. In 1993 she published *Thank You, God! A Jewish Child's Book of Prayers,* featuring watercolor illustrations by Shelly O. Haas. Again, the work is aimed at preschool children, and shows two such youngsters being awakened on the Jewish holiday of Shabbat by their parents. Its pages describe easy Hebrew prayers, transliterated into English phonetics, along with an explanation of their meaning. Prayers for giving thanks daily, for remembering the dead, for peace, and to commemorate certain holidays are among the topics. The images depict children celebrating Jewish holidays in various ways. Reviewing it for *School Library Journal,* Bonnie Siegel called *Thank You, God!* "an excellent choice for family sharing."

Wikler's 1996 title *Let's Have a Seder!,* illustrated by Miriam Sagasti, is a how-to book explaining the celebratory seder for Passover. Through a ruse of a little boy and girl holding a meal with their "friends"—a passel of animals, including household pets, a panda and even some sheep—the book explains the story behind each particular dish.

Wikler has also illustrated books herself, including Marji Gold-Vukson's 1998 book *The Colors of My Jewish New Year.* This board book for young readers explains the seven Jewish holidays. Most recently she indulged her love of watercolors by illustrating the 1999 re-issue of *Come, Let Us Welcome Shabbat.*

Works Cited

Review of *All About Hanukkah, School Library Journal,* October, 1988, p. 34.

Nevett, Micki S., review of *Miracle Meals, School Library Journal,* March, 1988, pp. 184-186.

Shire, Ruth, review of *Let's Build a Sukkah, My First Seder,* and *The Purim Parade, School Library Journal,* February, 1987, pp. 74-75.

Siegel, Bonnie, review of *Thank You, God!, School Library Journal,* April, 1994, p. 119.

For More Information See

PERIODICALS

Booklist, March 15, 1994, p. 1367.

Publishers Weekly, April 28, 1989, p. 75.